WHO | RULES

THE | NET?

INTERNET GOVERNANCE AND JURISDICTION

WHO | RULES
THE | NET?

INTERNET GOVERNANCE AND JURISDICTION

Foreword by Vinton G. Cerf

edited by
Adam Thierer and Clyde Wayne Crews Jr.

CATO
INSTITUTE
Washington, D.C.

Library of Congress Cataloging-in-Publication Data

Who rules the net? : Internet governance and jurisdiction / edited by Adam Thierer and
    Clyde Wayne Crews, Jr.
       p. cm.
    Includes bibliographical references and index.
    ISBN 1-930865-43-0 (cloth : alk. paper)
      1. Internet—Law and legislation. 2. Computer networks—Law and legislation.
    3. Freedom of speech. 4. Electronic commerce. 1. Thierer, Adam D. II.
    Crews, Clyde Wayne.

K564.C6W48 2003
343.09'944–dc21

                           2003055299

Cover design by Amanda Elliott.
Cover Photo: © Bill Frymire/masterfile.

Printed in the United States of America.

CATO INSTITUTE
1000 Massachusetts Ave., N.W.
Washington, D.C. 20001

Contents

Foreword: Who Rules the Net?

Vinton G. Cerf

The title of the book poses an interesting question, but makes the assumption that the Internet is "ruled" in the classical sense of the word. Contributors to this volume provide a range of viewpoints in response, some of which I find compelling and others with which I might disagree. Thus my writing reflects not necessarily endorsement or disagreement with anyone in particular but rather an abiding interest in and commitment to the health and continued growth of the Internet.

There *are* rules. Some of them are mechanical in the sense that the architecture of the Internet and the protocols that define its function determine the way in which it operates and the way in which applications like e-mail are or can be supported. Others are a consequence of policies set in a variety of venues and jurisdictions and informed or motivated by a variety of constituencies. Some rules may even be said to be set by the personal preferences and behaviors of Internet users, almost independent of outside forces. The ensemble of rule sets does not form a consistent or even coherent whole and there are notable conflicts, especially as local jurisdictions seek to enforce local rules on a system that is patently global (and soon, interplanetary!) in scope.

There are several aspects of Internet technology that strongly influence the kinds of policy issues that the system seems to engender. For example, the Internet Protocol (IP) essentially decouples applications from underlying transmission support. This has a profound impact on the nature of telecommunication regulation and bears further exploration here. The IP is largely insensitive to the underlying transport mechanisms and is agnostic with regard to an alphabet soup of transmission and switching services over which it is capable of operating: ATM, Frame Relay, SONET, DWDM, DSL, T1, OC3-OC192, X.25, Ethernet, 802.11a/b/g, 3G/4G, GPRS, satellite links, HF, VHF, UHF, EHF, and so on. This decoupling effect extends to the applications that run above the IP layer. IP is relatively insensitive to the payload it carries (e.g., e-mail, digital files, documents, streaming audio and video, interactive games, voice telephony, instant messages, Web pages).

A consequence of this separation of transport from application is that conventional regulatory regimes may no longer be suited to an environment in which most or all applications are transported as undifferentiated IP packets. Traditional regulatory policies have been bound to service and transport media. We regulate television over the air differently from television over cable. Telephony over copper twisted pair is regulated differently from over-the-air radio. Once all applications are carried over all media through the magical mediation of the Internet, there does not appear to be as much rationale for regulating the operation of these applications.

In the history of the commercial Internet, individual residential users typically gained access to the net by modems through the public switched telephone network (PSTN). Any Internet service provider (ISP) could be reached essentially by any subscriber, provided that the ISP had modem banks that would accept incoming calls vectored to the ISP's routers. In the broadband business and residential world this is less true, either because a choice of dedicated services may not be readily available to the residential or business subscribers or because the providers of broadband service offer little or no choice of ISP.

The Internet is designed to be *layered* in its implementation so that different groups can create software at different layers, take responsibility for operating different parts of the network, and build and operate a variety of applications more or less autonomously, while following the technical standards that permit widespread interworking of independently implemented software.

With regard to standardizing the technology of the Internet, the clearest constituency comprises the Internet Engineering Task Force. The work of this group is guided by the Internet Engineering Steering Group and the Internet Architecture Board. All of these entities function under the auspices of the Internet Society (ISOC) that provides an institutional home for them. ISOC also sponsors the Internet Research Task Force, which pursues topics deemed not yet ripe for standardization.

There are many other groups, formal and informal, that have technical interest in the Internet, and as the system continues to expand in physical scope and functional capability, it seems likely that such interest will also expand. The International Telecommunications Union (ITU) has interest in technologies that support the transport of IP packets and also in the interface between the Internet and the PSTN. This interest is largely expressed through the ITU technical standards organization, ITU-T. In Europe, the European Telecommunications Standards Institute has similar interests. The Institute of Electrical and Electronic Engineers is particularly interested in standards for wired and wireless local area networking. There are innumerable industry forums with interest in Internet technologies such as the World Wide Web Consortium, the ENUM Forum, the ATM (Asynchronous Transfer Mode) Forum, and the merged Frame Relay Forum and MPLS (Multi-protocol Label Switching) Forum. Even the space research agencies have a forum that is interested in this area. The Consultative Committee on Space Data Systems is made up of most of the world's national space research agencies. The military has interest by way of its research agencies such as the U.S. Defense Advanced Research Projects Agency, the Canadian Ministry of Defense, the North Atlantic Treaty Organization's Advanced Studies Institute, and operational agencies such as the U.S. Defense Information Systems Agency. The list is almost endless. (Apologies if your favorite organization was not mentioned.)

What is perhaps of more immediate interest is the range of organizations with policy interests in the Internet. These range from the Australian Parliament and the newly formed Ministry of Communication in Afghanistan, to private sector civil and industry advocacy groups, and everything beyond and in between. One of the more visible organizations is the Internet Corporation for Assigned Names and Numbers (ICANN). Created in September 1998 after a lengthy and fractious international debate that ultimately drew in the White House, the European Commission, and countless interested organizations and individuals, ICANN has a limited but critical mandate to manage policy development for the Internet's domain name system (DNS), the allocation and assignment of IP addresses, and the recordation of protocol parameters critical to the operation of the scores of protocols associated with the Internet's technical standards.

ICANN's constituencies constitute a microcosm of global interest in the Internet, including its Government Advisory Committee,

Generic Names Supporting Organization, Country Code Names Supporting Organization, Address Supporting Organization, Technical Liaison Group, At Large Advisory Committee, DNS Root Server Advisory Committee, Security and Stability Advisory Committee, and Internationalized Domain Names and Internationalized Domain Names Implementation Committees, among others.

Two things about the Internet should be abundantly clear. First, that it is a vast collaboration of many components and, second, that it cannot and will not function without the cooperation and collaboration of the entire range of entities with interest in its operation. There are literally hundreds of thousands of networks that make up the global Internet. They range from modest, local networks in residences and small businesses to campus facilities and globe-girdling backbones operated by for-profit and sometimes nonprofit or governmental organizations. The root server system, a critical component of the DNS, is operated by a collection of *volunteer* organizations that have assumed the responsibility for operation of the root servers for many years. The root server operators cooperate with each other and ICANN to assure stability of the root server system.

ICANN's Internet Assigned Numbers Authority (IANA) has the responsibility for managing the contents of the so-called *root zone* of the DNS. Changes to the *root zone file* are recommended by IANA to the National Telecommunications and Information Agency of the U.S. Department of Commerce, where updates are authorized. Close coordination of root zone file updates and continuous surveillance of the servers by the root server operators contribute to the stable operation of the Internet.

ICANN establishes new generic top-level domains and through a contractual process authorizes organizations to operate the registries and associated registration services (*registrars*). There are hundreds of top-level domain operators, most of them the so-called country code registries (such as .fr, .de, .uk, .za, .cn, etc.) and the generic top-level domain registries (such as .com, .org, .aero, .coop, .gov, etc.). The country code registries are operated either through agreements with ICANN and sometimes the associated government or on the basis of historical assignment by IANA to volunteers. As the Internet continues to evolve, it is common for governments to become more interested than heretofore in the operation of their associated country code top-level domains. Within the ICANN purview, this interest is commonly expressed through the Governmental

Advisory Committee although direct interactions with IANA may occur when operation of a country code TLD registry is redelegated to a new party.

In addition, the management of the Internet address space and autonomous system numbers among ISPs and users falls to the Regional Internet Registries, who work together and with ICANN to develop and execute address space management policies.

It should be evident from these observations that the coordination, collaboration, and cooperation of many distinct entities are vital to the Internet's successful operation and that this characteristic has been a part of the Internet's history from its earliest conception.

Beyond the DNS there are many other elements that must work cooperatively to ensure the Internet's functioning. For example, the thousands of ISPs, worldwide, must interconnect, exchange routing information, and seek to achieve stable operation of each component network. Even in the presence of vigorous competition among service providers, there must be ground-level cooperation and collaboration to ensure that an Internet packet emitted from any source on the Internet can reach its intended destination.

As one moves from the basic operation of the Internet transport systems to applications such as electronic mail, instant messaging, Web services, interactive games, voice over Internet and so on, new players with an interest in policy enter into the picture. For example, with regard to content with intellectual property aspects such as music, films, books, and imagery, the holders of these properties may wish to be compensated for providing access to or instances of these works. The Internet is a vast storehouse of electronic information and much of it is provided without compensation. In the academic tradition, for example, the creators of this information share it freely in exchange for similar information from colleagues. The Internet's technical structure permits it to support free and for-pay models, but the latter suffer from the ease with which electronic copying and distribution can be accomplished.

Organizations concerned with such matters include the Recording Industry Association of America, the American Society of Composers, Authors and Publishers, the Software and Information Industries Association, the Entertainment and Leisure Software Publishers Association, the Motion Pictures Association of America, the World Intellectual Property Organization (WIPO), and many more. Many of these organizations have introduced efforts to detect illegal copying and to pursue offenders in the courts. Among the more famous cases was a service called *Napster* in which a central index was maintained of popular music that could be downloaded from contributors whose computers were online and whose file systems contained the copies of interest. While the ensuing court cases effectively shut Napster down, other alternatives were developed, including Kazaa, that have apparently achieved sustainability owing to the absence of a centralized directory of network-accessible content.

Disputes over property rights extend to disputes over registration of domain names, and ICANN has worked through the WIPO to develop a Uniform Dispute Resolution Policy. While the debate continues over the question of rights inhering in domain names, it is fair to say that they are being treated as if they are inherently valuable while still registered to a particular entity. Bankruptcy court laws, so often exercised in the United States in the wake of the bursting "dot.com" bubble ("dot.bomb"?), have occasionally treated both domain name registrations and IP address allocations as if they are transferable and valuable properties.

It should be obvious that the enforcement of national laws is made difficult by the global nature of the Internet and the difficulty of binding transactions conducted on the Internet to any specific locations. Recent court cases in France, Germany, Australia, and the United States have sought to control access to content on the network deemed inappropriate in each national or provincial jurisdiction. The side effect of these various court cases is to establish a kind of extraterritoriality for the jurisdiction attempting to apply its laws to entities outside its putative territory.

Individual users exercise their own rules when they choose to use the Internet for one application or another. Downloading and copying of Internet content is a popular, controversial, and sometimes illegal pastime on the Internet. On the other hand, in the best academic tradition, many people share information freely on the Internet and do so in a kind of information barter system.

Taxation of transactions on the Internet has been something of a cause célèbre in policy circles. Many legislators believe that transactions undertaken on the Internet should bear no tax. Others see these transactions as the analog of their counterparts in the real world and that they should be taxed in a similar fashion. One of the problems, of course, is localizing the transaction in such a way that one can determine in which tax jurisdiction the transaction has taken place. What is needed is an unambiguous answer to the question: "In which jurisdiction should this transaction be taxed?" The answer may prove to be somewhat arbitrary. For example, the billling address of the credit card used to pay for the transaction might be used arbitrarily, but unambiguously, to define the locus of the transaction.

One finds any number of law enforcement agencies with an interest in the Internet, either because of fradulent or illegal transactions that are conducted using the Internet or because there is content that is considered to be in violation of the law. Courts, legislatures, free speech advocates, industry leaders, politicians, scam artists, spammers, students, parents, and just about every one of the more than 600 million users of the Internet seem to have abiding interests in the Internet and the policy framework in which it operates. While no one "rules" the Internet, the aggregate interest of millions seeks to influence what these rules are or will be. Out of a seething cauldron of conflicting interests and opinions, the Internet is emerging as a key element of our 21st century information and communications environment.

Who rules the Net? You and I and 600 million others, in some measure.

Introduction: Who Rules the Net?

Clyde Wayne Crews Jr. and Adam Thierer

> *No one knows where you are. How near or how far.*
> —Pink Floyd, "Shine on You Crazy Diamond"

It may seem strange to kick off a serious collection of essays with a quote from a psychedelic 1970s rock band, but at times the debate over Internet jurisdiction and governance can seem as bizarre and complicated as some of Pink Floyd's music. Moreover, that quote nicely sums up why Internet and cyberspace activities pose such a quandary for traditional understandings of jurisdiction and governance.

The Internet's challenge to traditional concepts of jurisdiction and governance is multifaceted, but really boils down to two factors. First, when you're online, you're both everywhere and nowhere at once. Ubiquity is perhaps the defining characteristic of this remarkable new "borderless" medium. There are no passports on the Internet; you travel freely from one destination to another at the click of a button. And geography is a remarkably meaningless concept for Internet denizens. Two people could be communicating from the opposite poles of the Earth or from two blocks away and not know the difference. Typically, no one really does know where you are, how near or how far. Indeed, no one really knows "where" the Internet itself is, in the sense of how near or how far it is from traditional notions of property and contract; thus, the governing of cyberspace has jurisdictional and legal problems.

Second, no single entity or country owns or controls the Internet. Portions of this so-called "network of networks" are owned by private companies, organizations, or even governments, but it is impossible to point to any specific "owner" of the Net writ large. Most assuredly, this scattered control has been one of the Net's greatest blessings, but it also has proven to be a curse of sorts.

On the positive side, diffuse sources of ownership and control have resulted in a stunning explosion of human creativity in terms of new global communication channels, new business opportunities, and new consumer options and opportunities. But, on the downside, the diffusion of ownership and control has made it more difficult to assign responsibility or blame when things go wrong or when disagreements arise.

This situation in which a culpable party is unidentified manifests itself in many everyday ways, some sinister, some routine: Net congestion, system crashes, network viruses, e-mail "spam," online identify theft, and so on. Complicating matters is the fact that some jurisdictions and countries also look for someone to blame when their societal norms or legal standards are challenged. Gambling, pornography, intellectual property, libel law, and tax policy are good examples in which tolerances and approaches vary, creating conflict. In each of those areas, policymakers have for years enacted myriad laws and regulations for "real space" that are now being directly challenged by the rise of this parallel electronic universe known as cyberspace.

Who is responsible? What standards should govern such cyber-disputes? Are different standards needed for cyberspace and real space? These nagging questions are being posed with increasing frequency in the emerging field of cyberlaw and constitute the guiding theme of this book's collection of essays.

A Conflict of Visions

When it comes to matters of Internet governance, clashes of values exist just as in any other area of politics and law. At root are the following questions: Is it most appropriate to think of the Internet as a public resource and vast information commons, collectively owned or at least controlled by collective decisionmaking? Or, to look at the opposite choice, is it best to remain open to proprietary avenues, private ownership and control models, and self-selection? We face a choice about which is the best way to treat the Internet. It is not a given that the "public resource" model is the best alternative. As might be expected, governments are moving toward hybrids of the two in dealing with the range of policy issues confronting the online world.

The tilt toward government intervention can be excessive. In an earlier time the unruly Internet was thought to be a virtual Wild West, an unregulated province of libertarians and cyber-anarchists. However, it appears now to be well on the way to becoming a heavily regulated network increasingly encumbered by conflicting demands from federal, state, and international governments, along with assorted special interests.

Not so long ago, that desire to keep the Internet free of regulatory meddling yielded important prominent victories against government activism and calls for "hands off" of cyberspace. The Communications Decency Act to regulate online pornography was widely denounced and declared unconstitutional by the Supreme Court in June 1997, for example. Perhaps most memorable was the widely circulated 1996 "Declaration of the Independence of Cyberspace," penned by John Perry Barlow, former lyricist for the Grateful Dead and cofounder of the Electronic Frontier Foundation. In the preface to his manifesto of cyber-freedom, Barlow questioned and ridiculed the feasibility and legitimacy of the aims of those who would rule and regulate the Internet and famously declared of such individuals, "Well, f**k them."[1] He went on to elaborate, somewhat more elegantly:

> Governments derive their just powers from the consent of the governed. You have neither solicited nor received ours. We did not invite you. You do not know us, nor do you know our world. Cyberspace does not lie within your borders. Do not think that you can build it, as though it were a public construction project. You cannot. It is an act of nature and it grows itself through our collective actions.

But as yet another rock-'n'-roller, Bob Dylan, once famously sang, "The Times They Are A'Changin'." In contrast to the early Wild West reputation and Barlow-esque calls for cyber-independence, the Internet and its still-growing infrastructure is today already subject to substantial regulation, or attempts at regulation, on numerous fronts from even more numerous governmental units.[2] As Michael Totty of the *Wall Street Journal* noted, "If the early cyberspace was a separate frontier, outside the reach of governments and laws, it's now beginning to look more like a later version of the Old West—the one where settlers, marshals, and lawyers come in and impose law and order."[3]

Characteristic of this new view that the Internet must be brought into the fold is the opinion of Zoe Baird of the Markle Foundation, who noted: "The rapid growth of the Internet has led to a worldwide crisis of governance. In the early years of Internet development, the prevailing view was that government should stay out of Internet governance; market forces and self-regulation would suffice to create order and enforce standards of behavior. But this view has proven inadequate as the Internet has become mainstream."[4]

Hundreds of bills have been introduced in recent sessions of the U.S. Congress and at the state level addressing privacy, spam, cyber-security, the alleged "digital divide," Internet taxation, business method patents, various digital copyright issues, children's privacy, a safe children's domain, domain names, broadband subsidies, mandatory telephone and cable network access, and online gambling, just to name some of the more prominent policy battles.[5]

The Internet and the policy issues it raises present a formidable challenge for traditional conceptions of jurisdiction nationally and internationally. In this emerging cyber-policy environment, everybody seems to have "a plan" for the Internet, some more expansive than others. The Progressive Policy Institute talks up the "failure of cyber-libertarianism" and calls for a "national e-commerce strategy" to correct perceived market failures.[6] The New America Foundation calls for "saving the information commons" via "a new public interest agenda in digital media."[7] The Computer and Communications Industry Association of America has its guide to "The Role of Government in the Digital Age."[8] Ralph Nader has called for the creation of a "World Consumer Protection Organization" modeled after the United Nations World Intellectual Property Organization.[9] And open source advocate and computer technology book publisher Tim O'Reilly has proposed a "Sierra Club for the Net" as a way of keeping it under "Netizen" rather than corporate control.[10]

Interests ranging from the American Bar Association, to French courts, to the International Telecommunications Union, and to the United Nations are contemplating new Internet governance models. European officials and organizations seem particularly keen on crafting new governance models. The European Union's Electronic Commerce Directive and the Hague Convention on International Jurisdiction and Foreign Judgments in Civil and Commercial Matters have laid out frameworks to resolve cyber-disputes, for example.

Of course, there is a reasonable question of why the Internet should be treated any differently than the offline world. When you're online in cyberspace, your physical body is still sitting somewhere in real space typing away. Some say that matters a lot, and we ought not make bright-line distinctions between cyberspace and real space. Why treat cyberspace differently from the way we treat "meatspace," goes the refrain. "The Internet creates a veil of separation between you and other people," said Gregory Alan Rutchik, managing partner at the Arts and Technology Group, a San Francisco firm specializing in copyright and publishing law. He warns, "Don't be misled by the fact that you're sitting in a room, behind a locked door, at your computer. There's ways to find out who you are."[11] As *CNET News* described the dilemma, "[S]ome remain puzzled at what they see as artificial distinctions between cyberspace and the physical world. Like other Internet academics and professionals, University of Miami law professor Michael Froomkin dismisses the notion of an unregulated medium as 'cyberpunk dreams that rules are bad. . . . Just because you're using a computer doesn't mean you don't have to follow the law.' "[12]

Perhaps. But ill-conceived regulations are often applied to meatspace too, and a unique opportunity exists to avoid making similar costly errors in cyberspace, or transferring them there, even if that means occasionally treating cyberspace "differently" in practice. Should we regulate cyberspace merely because real space is regulated—or is rethinking of real space regulation itself in order? The question should at least be asked. In any event, conflicting legislative visions that are applied to the Internet commons make for an increasingly unstable mix. In a cyberspace populated by exhibitionists at one extreme and would-be inhabitants of gated communities on the other, what is sound policy for some is reprehensible to others. Moreover, the Internet sports a widening rift between those who see dollar signs and those who long for the days of the Internet as a noncommercial information-sharing tool for researchers and techno-geeks.

Thinking About Borders, Public and Private

That the "libertarian" vision, so to speak, of Internet uniqueness has subsided is not altogether surprising. The Internet, taken as a whole as distinct from the privately owned networks that make it up, is anything but "private." Many regulatory and legislative disputes arise because of the common property status of the Internet, largely owing to its legacy as a government-sponsored network. Despite private involvement at the outset and an explosion in privately owned infrastructure and hardware over the past years, the Internet gained its footing as a public network. While ownership of hardware like routers, servers, and fiber is almost totally private, the setting of network policy is subject to highly politicized, public battles; governance of the public Net emerges from the Internet Corporation for Assigned Names and Numbers (ICANN), the U.S. Commerce Department, Congress, and numerous other governments and treaties rather than those individual system owners and operators. Unlike typical private or proprietary management of assets, a common property model can lead to a "tragedy of the commons," in which conflicting interests seek to impose mutually exclusive regulatory preferences. Visions of what an Internet experience should entail are increasingly in conflict.

That conflict inevitably spawns calls by many for more effective Internet "democracy."[13] Paradoxically, "democracy" applied to private property or infrastructure can harm cyber-freedom and can limit future options that could be more satisfactory than government dictates. Democracy isn't applicable with regard to normal, nonharmful uses of one's private property; rather, property owners set the terms and rules for access to and behavior on their property. The dilemma in the case of cyberlaw lies in the Internet's status as a public/private hybrid. Currently, governance approaches can tilt in either direction, toward public or private management, each with considerable implications for the Internet's future. We ought not shut the door on private approaches to governance for cyberspace. Unfortunately, universally applying the "commons" mindset toward all things Internet would seem enough of an impetus to do precisely that—indeed, to almost guarantee movement away from private resolution.

Plainly, the "common property," nonowned status of the Internet as it exists today has implications for governance of the still-new medium. As is becoming clearer, with common property, there are only two options: regulate it or privatize it. That choice, effectively, is the fundamental one facing the Internet. And how it is decided will have weighty ramifications for governance and jurisdictional issues such as those raised in this book.

In governing the Internet, or whatever communications networks may emerge in the future, the issue isn't really one of whether "borders" will be erected on a heretofore borderless medium: borders—of a sort—will emerge regardless. Indeed, they already have. Rather, the question is *which kind* of border—public or private—is advantageous to commerce, connectivity, and information flows, and which kind increases options rather than hampers them. Even an Internet "commons" will surely have government-created "borders," such as a "dot-kids" domain, "Communications Decency Act"–style speech restraints, mandatory library filters, tax jurisdictions, and perhaps unanticipated liability rules. Private approaches, however, would also develop "borders" in order to help tailor services to consumers. Although government borders would represent unavoidable mandates on users or providers, private "borders" will emerge naturally as a matter of self-regulation or for purely business reasons, out of competitive necessity. Thus, like voluntary agreements, private borders and self-selection can help enhance and foster political liberty or bolster rights and opportunities online.

With the recognition that private actors can deliver tailored borders (such as privacy standards) while governments will impose one-size-fits-all solutions, it becomes increasingly worthwhile to allow those private alternatives to flourish. (EKids Internet,[14] for example, is an alternative to the government-mandated and regulated "dot-kids" domain.) Although private decisions, like overinclusive porn filters or e-mail spam blacklists, can affect the online multitudes, these decisions emerge from voluntary actions of market players trying to solve problems, and mistakes are likely to be easier to correct than repealing ill-considered, one-size-fits-all legislation. As networks and business models adapt to serve customers better, there can be less call for national or transnational authorities to step in.

Private "borders" facilitate personal customization as well, which has itself proven to be controversial among those who decry "balkanization," prefer "openness," and worry over the undermining of "shared experiences" online.[15] Private "filtering," which in some sense can substitute for top-down regulation, will likely grow more pronounced; but that guardedness is itself an exercise of democratic choice. Let's be clear: universal connectivity has been a magnificent breakthrough and isn't going away. But sometimes we don't *want* to be in touch with the entire planet and prefer more isolated communities. As *CNET.com* editorial director Steve Fox put it, "On the Internet, the urge to unmerge isn't borne out of hostility; rather, it comes from a basic human need to find small, defined spaces where everybody knows your URL."[16] And of course, as the Net grows, the portion of the whole accessed by the typical user grows smaller; private filtering is a natural and inevitable response to ensure that one gets the information one wants.

For example, peer-to-peer (P2P) file-sharing technologies "shrink" the universe, so to speak, while at the same time adding to the options on the Internet. Invoking proprietary or alternative architectures like Web TV, Gnutella, and America Online, Fox further noted:

> Instead of one vast network, we're starting to see a collection of interconnected, often closed, networks: communities whose membership will be determined by the kinds of devices people use, the service providers they choose, and the content they find most compelling. . . .These Net city-states aren't always out of the mainstream. Take America Online, the biggest Balkan state of all. Though AOL offers full Web access to its users, millions of them never leave the confines of AOL. In fact, plenty of users think AOL is the Internet.[17]

> Effectively, AOL users have formed their own community built around AOL's exclusive content and features. Outsiders can't peer in, can't access AOL's content, can't even share AOL users' tools. . . .These strategies of content-based communities coexisting within and alongside the Web proper will thrive because they recognize basic human needs. People like to be among their own, to feel like they're part of a neighborhood where they're comfortable.[18]

Balkanization? Sure. But also private self-governance. If an online superhighway is to remain most advantageous for both the exhibitionists and the would-be gated community inhabitants, or for both the Amazon.coms and the commerce-free Internet advocates, then fences, or "borders," very well may multiply. In one sense, there are, or could be, many "cyberspaces," from the early bulletin boards of the 1980s to the peer-to-peer networks of today (Napster, Internet phones, AOL Instant Messenger, and any of numerous peer-to-peer networks with their own rules of participation are examples). It may be increasingly unproductive to insist that all the uses to which the Internet is put—gaming, streaming video, secure commerce, nonprofit reference services, porn, children's content—should necessarily coexist under one set of top-down rules. The point, again, is that borders needn't necessarily be legislative ones. To the extent sorting occurs among vendors and customers on privately administered networks, "democracy" is an inappropriate method of governing them. But to the extent that borders are legislative, competition among jurisdictions, as advocated by Larry Ribstein and Bruce Kobayashi in this volume, is preferable.

Indeed, the best outcome for online governance might be to ensure that the common Internet retains private borders beyond which users can escape damaging political resolutions of regulatory disputes, such as those over privacy, free speech, filtering, and cybersecurity. At the very least, that means we ought not extend regulations imposed on today's capital "I" Internet to whatever other hypothetical networks might emerge in the future. For example, privacy legislation imposed on the existing Internet should not be written to encompass any future, private, non-Internet (or post-Internet) online network that might emerge. Recent privacy legislation would appear to violate this principle by applying to *all* future online networks, not just the capital "I" Internet. There should remain an escape valve, in other words, such that potentially superior private governance of some future online "cyberspace" has an opportunity to emerge if market participants of the future choose to create and sustain it. Ironically, a hodgepodge of laws applied to tame the Net and make it "good enough" could prevent better networks from replacing it. A future network not burdened with ineffective, constraining political privacy legislation could offer superior privacy as a selling feature; but if legislation rules out the advantages of "secession," a superior, better adapted network can't get created. Whether or not a private solution is the answer in any particular case, such as privacy standards, rules of the game that eliminate opportunities for a superior private solution to emerge ought not be the path chosen.

New Technology, Old Borders

Debates will continue to rage over whether the Net should be viewed as a collection of private resources or as a public commons.

Adherents to both camps of thinking have often shared concerns about how old world borders, legal policies, and social norms are applied to this new universe of cyber-technologies. As governments increasingly intervene and look to apply their standards to the global World Wide Web, the specter of overregulation on a massive scale becomes clear. And this threat comes at a time when the vast majority of the world is still not connected; recent data show that 655 million are online worldwide.[19] But even though we've yet to break a billion online Netizens, as more humans join the online realm, efforts by myriad jurisdictions to control Net activity and intervene in ways that spill across borders will pose troubling governance and sovereignty issues.

American politicians have made a point of critiquing regulatory overreach by foreign nations, especially in the case of France's attempt to censor offensive material on the Yahoo! Web portal.[20] Pointing fingers is often appropriate; however, the United States also can be ambitious in seeking to extend the reach of its laws beyond the borders. For example, the U.S. Congress has sought to enact measures that would restrict pornography on the Internet, and it hopes to regulate offshore gambling indirectly by prohibiting the processing of gambling transactions by credit card companies. On one front in the raging digital copyright wars, the United States forced the Canadian company iCraveTV to halt the retransmitting of previously broadcast television shows over the Internet,[21] and in another prominent case prosecuted a foreign programmer under the 1998 Digital Millennium Copyright Act for supposed "anti-circumvention" copyright violations.[22]

Numerous cases of such mischief abound overseas. For example, it's not just the French engaged in extraterritorial Web censorship. A *Wall Street Journal* editorial last summer noted that the government of Zimbabwe had threatened to deport journalists for publishing unflattering stories on the Net even though they were not printed in any paper in that country.[23] Also, the *Journal's* parent company, Dow Jones, has been involved in an important Australian court case regarding libel and the Net that raised the question: does libel take place where the potentially libelous information was uploaded (in New Jersey in this case) or downloaded (in Melbourne, Australia)? In December 2002, Australia's highest court unanimously ruled that the latter should be the rule: libel occurs where the content is downloaded.[24] Given the radically different libel laws on the books in the

United States versus the rest of the world, some fear this precedent could have a chilling effect on speech and expression. A final example: the Vatican last year called for a crackdown on the Internet's "radical libertarianism"[25] and the Rome police force responded in kind by recently shutting down five Web sites that contained blasphemous material about Catholicism and the Madonna.[26]

And the list goes on. These examples mostly focus on speech or expression-related regulation. Many other forms of jurisdictional meddling exist, as was comprehensively documented in the report by the law firm Covington & Burling in February 2003 on *Significant Developments in Global Internet Law in 2002.* The report highlighted 35 pages worth of key cases and laws from countries around the globe but noted, "There are . . . thousands of cases, laws and regulations that touch on aspects of the Internet that we could not mention [in the report]."[27]

What concerns many Net watchers about these laws and cases is that (a) they are growing in number, and (b) they raise the threat of "lowest common denominator" regulation being imposed on the Internet. That is, companies and individuals may be forced to conform their Internet conduct to the standards of those countries with the most repressive regulatory regime for commerce and speech in order to remain compliant globally.

In turn, as the sheer number of cases grows and the specter of such legal and regulatory activism grows more substantial, it raises a host of thorny legal issues. For example, in gauging how to determine appropriate jurisdictional authority in a cyber-setting, how will we decide what "purposeful availment" by a company and "minimum contacts" by sellers or buyers means in the context of electronic speech and communication? These are the traditional standards or legal tests that American courts have used to determine whether a given jurisdiction has the right to exert authority over an individual or entity. Simply stated, U.S. courts have asked: Did the individual or entities in question purposefully interact in some capacity with the citizens of the jurisdiction in question? Did they attain a sufficient threshold of contact with the jurisdiction to make themselves liable to those authorities? What constitutes a sufficient "nexus" of contact between parties to trigger jurisdiction? Variations on this purposeful availment/minimum contacts/nexus framework have been used by other countries when looking at jurisdictional matters. But in the Internet context, everyone is arguably "purpose-fully availing" themselves to the whole world all the time! Companies, consumers, and citizens all place materials online with the hope of communicating with the entire planet. So some skeptics question whether such a standard can have any real meaning in the context of the fluid, borderless world of cyberspace.

More important, while any country can claim jurisdiction over a company or a given issue, how they go about *enforcing* that claim is a different matter entirely. Enforcement is a tall order for a ubiquitous medium like the Net that exists everywhere and nowhere at the same time. Do we really want dozens of countries and jurisdictions policing the Net for violations of their parochial laws or standards? The costs could be enormous in both economic and human terms.

Although dozens or hundreds of cyber-cops patrolling the Net would be bad, it might be equally misguided to invite a single, centralized Super Cyber-Cop to start patrolling cyberspace. Who would be in charge? The United Nations? The World Trade Organization? The International Telecommunications Union (ITU)? And what body of law would they apply? In January of 2003, ITU General Secretary Yoshio Utsumi called on fellow delegates to the upcoming World Summit on the Information Society to devise a global regulatory framework for cyberspace issues such as taxation, intellectual property protection, privacy policy, and others.[28] U.S. officials were quick to denounce Utsumi's call for global Net rule by the ITU but failed to provide a coherent alternative vision.

Such inaction or resistance by U.S. officials may be the best outcome for many issues. Some matters of principle should remain "above the fray," and the United States should remain steadfast and buck international trends to conform to repressive policies. Free speech may be the best example, in which we politely refuse to assist other nations with regulation of what our history and heritage regard as an inalienable right for all humans. Libel law may be another area in which more lax defamation standards globally should not be allowed to trump speech rights in this or other countries. As Rep. Chris Cox (R-Calif.) points out in the first chapter of this collection, the United States should be unashamed about promoting free-speech values worldwide and should stress the importance of the Web as a liberating tool of social interaction and individual empowerment. Governments that oppose First Amendment–style free-speech protections are violating basic human rights and do not have legitimate gripes that we necessarily need to acknowledge. Long live civil disobedience online in this regard.

Perhaps the most important role American policymakers can play in this debate is to maintain emphasis on the importance of human liberty, individual rights, basic due process/legal protections, the rule of law, and property rights. What is perhaps most troubling about the current debate over Internet jurisdiction and governance is that little discussion has occurred about the principles of *legitimacy* and *universality*. That is, there remain the questions of (a) the legitimacy of governments who seek to act on behalf of a group of people, and, (b) whether the laws in question are being equally and fairly applied to the people.

This lack of a discussion recalls John Perry Barlow's concern about governments deriving their just powers from the "consent of the governed," yet having received no such consent from the "Netizenry." Of course, those Netizens have physical bodies that reside within the confines of some government somewhere and can be assumed (in democratic regimes) to have consented to being a part of that polity and being governed by its laws. Nonetheless, if one subscribes to the theory that cyberspace is a unique "place"—or at least should be considered a unique new legal sphere or territory—then the question of legitimacy and universality becomes more important. There is commonality of purpose within constitutional republics such as the United States that may not be present when transnational disputes develop. That is, a universal set of values and standards exists that citizens have agreed to be governed by within a constitutional republic and that Third World dictatorships might scoff at. At a minimum, policymakers both here and abroad who profess to believe in the importance of a classical liberal tradition of individual rights must ensure that certain rights are acknowledged and protected as the growth of the Internet continues to blur the jurisdictional boundaries between meatspace and cyberspace.

Breakdown of the Book

This collection of essays on Internet jurisdiction and governance is divided into two major sections. Part I of the book discusses general frameworks for dealing with these conflicts. Part II explores case studies in Internet governance that are already playing out worldwide.

General Governance Frameworks

The most sweeping revolution brought about by the Internet has been its ability to unite individuals in the cause of freedom and to expose and reject despotic governments. Starting off the volume, Rep. Cox, in "Tear Down This Firewall," describes one vision for global Internet freedom by taking on the efforts of despotic governments to erect "firewalls" between their often oppressed citizens and their connections to the outside world via the Internet.

Jonathan Zittrain, an assistant professor at the Harvard Law School, next provides an excellent overview of the many contentious legal concepts and principles at play in this debate. He warns governments seeking to impose their will on the global Internet to "be careful what you ask for" before rushing headlong into regulating the World Wide Web. "What we might gain in easing jurisdictional tensions we could stand to lose in revolutionary capacity," notes Zittrain. "The point of inflection at which the World Wide Web sits asks us to choose which we value more—international harmony and diversity that includes censorship smacking of repression, or an unavoidable baseline of freedom of expression that permits harmful speech along with constructive speech."

But in a dissent to the general thrust of many of the other essays in this collection, Jack Goldsmith, associate professor of law at the University of Chicago, argues that "Cyberspace transactions are no different from real-space transnational transactions" and that there is "no general normative argument that supports the immunization of cyberspace activities from territorial regulation." Although resolutions of jurisdictional problems will prove a challenge, he sees them as no more remarkable than problems confronted in other transnational venues.

While Goldsmith takes on the regulation skeptics and rejects the idea of cyberspace being particularly "special," David Post, professor of law at Temple University, remains an "unrepentant Exceptionalist." To Post, it "does matter that Digitalbook.com is 'in cyberspace,'" and he believes that "the questions raised by its conduct are indeed different, and more difficult, than the analogous questions raised by its real-space counterpart. To Post, "traditional legal tools" developed for similar problems in real space can't resolve jurisdictional problems."

Taking a more nuanced and legalistic approach to the issue of assessing jurisdictional responsibility, Michael Geist, professor of law at the University of Ottawa, points out the shortcomings of early attempts to base jurisdiction on a crude assessment of whether a website is "passive" or "active." He develops a more rigorous legal approach that involves a three-factor targeting test that includes analysis of contracts, technology, and vendor knowledge. Geist hopes that by employing such a targeting test, "it will provide all parties with greater legal certainty and a more effective means of conducting legal risk assessments. The move toward using contract and technology to erect virtual borders may not solve all Internet jurisdiction issues, but it will provide an upgrade to [previous doctrines] by creating greater clarity and certainty on the issue," Geist concludes.

Pointing out that "Internet users cannot 'vote with their feet' if their feet are in essence planted everywhere," University of Minnesota law professor Dan Burk notes that, "the prospect of states applying haphazard and uncoordinated multijurisdictional regulation to the Internet's seamless electronic web raises profound questions regarding the relationship between the several states and the future of federalism in cyberspace." Burk goes on to conclude that, "In the face of . . . new technology, rote application of established doctrines may produce anomalous or undesirable results, and in such cases, adaptation of those doctrines to the new technological situation may be required. But in accommodating past doctrine to present reality, the role of the relevant constitutional provisions as buffers for competitive federalism must be kept firmly in mind if they are to continue serving their proper function in an online environment."

In a different vein, University of Illinois law professor Larry Ribstein and coauthor Bruce Kobayashi of George Mason University School of Law argue for the efficiency and advantages of decentralized "choice of law" solutions where circumstances permit. If regulation is to occur, competition among jurisdictions for setting ground rules can be superior to relying upon centralized regulation. Ribstein and Kobayashi also note how governments can unintentionally interfere with private solutions, to the detriment of all: "The problem with these private solutions is that whether they are allowed to work depends ultimately on the level of government regulation. Thus, *permitting* private regulation should be viewed as a regulatory option." But at least with state as opposed to federal regulation, "the social costs of legislation are constrained by individuals' opportunities to exit undesirable regimes." At the very least, "To the extent that a variety of regulatory approaches is desirable, relying on state law may provide significant advantages over a federal regime that broadly preempts state law."

Case Studies

Robert Corn-Revere, a partner at the law firm Davis Wright Tremaine, kicks off the case study section of the book with a discussion of perhaps the most notable Internet jurisdiction case to date: the effort by a French court to block French citizens from accessing Nazi memorabilia on the Yahoo.com Web portal. Yahoo! is an American company that is hosted on servers located within the United States, but its Web page remains accessible worldwide. The effort by the French court to censor this global site raised serious First Amendment concerns in the United States and raised the specter of "lowest common denominator" speech controls online in general. For these reasons, Corn-Revere concludes that "While nothing requires the French to embrace the First Amendment's philosophy that society is better protected by more speech rather than by enforced silence, our constitutional traditions should prevent France from exporting its parochial restrictions here."

On issues of defamation and libel online, similar fears of lowest common denominator regulation led Kurt Wimmer, a managing partner of the London office of international law firm Covington & Burling, to conclude that the "strongest argument favoring U.S. court nonenforcement of foreign Internet libel judgments is that such enforcement would contravene the public policy embodied in the First Amendment." To Wimmer, a key policy priority in the future is to refrain from embracing international treaties that would undermine this core principle and eliminate nonenforcement as a policy option available to U.S. authorities. "The 'lowest common denominator' approach naturally flowing from expansive findings of jurisdiction will result in a clear chilling of such companies' Internet speech, and it will deprive U.S. audiences of the level of discourse meant to be guaranteed by the First Amendment," argues Wimmer.

Switching gears to commercial issues, the tax treatment of electronic commerce has increasingly become a heated topic of debate both domestically and internationally. Michael Greve, resident scholar and director of the Federalism Project at the American Enterprise Institute, points out that the destination-based sourcing methodology that underlies most current tax systems, which imposes tax collection responsibilities on the basis of the destination of a transaction, poses particularly serious practical problems in an e-commerce context. "Instead of extending an already unworkable destination principle to e-commerce, we should move to origin-based taxation for *all* sales, through all channels, here and abroad," argues Greve. "An origin-based regime is simple, neutral among industries, and easily administered: each sale would be taxed once, at the same rate, by the single authority—the seller's home state or country."

Online privacy is another significant point of contention surrounding online commerce. Fred Cate, professor of law at the Indiana University School of Law, compares "command"- and "choice"-based privacy standards in an online environment. While European governments tend to impose comprehensive legal requirements on websites for privacy protection, that command approach doesn't necessarily improve upon alternative, private approaches to information security. For example, Cate explains, "Under more recent control-based models that condition information flows on opt-in consent, in the absence of a consumer response, the information cannot be collected or used. As a result, recent privacy mandates that forbid the collection and use of the information without express consumer consent frequently act as an effective ban on using information at all." He continues, "Assuming the information was necessary to provide the service or that the website chose to condition service on the consumer opting in, then the failure to opt in would mean no service. Privacy would be protected, to be sure, but at the price of not using the Internet. Consumers can obtain this type of privacy protection today—just by walking away from websites with whose privacy policies they disagree—without the intervention of the government." Possible unintended consequences of ill-considered command-and-control approaches to privacy abound and range from constrained services to high-enforcement and compliance costs.

Harold Feld, associate director of the Media Access Project, examines ongoing domain name disputes and the controversy over the role of ICANN in Internet oversight. Although privatization and stability were the justifications for the creation of ICANN, Feld argues it has instead led to increased government regulation of the domain name system and become an intrusive bureaucracy and regulator of root server operators, country code top-level domains, and regional Internet registries. The "road not taken"—that of genuine privatization—would eliminate ICANN and protect a dynamic yet stable Internet. Feld proposes a new governance model that reduces ICANN to a ministerial role and affords private domain name asset managers the autonomy to manage the domain name system under the cooperative system that worked before ICANN.

Finally, George Mason University economists Eric P. Crampton and Donald J. Boudreaux address whether antitrust law and its attendant bureaucracies and impacts are appropriate and needed in cyberspace. They argue that "Given antitrust's long history of abuse, along with an even longer history of markets proving to be remarkably adept and creative at protecting consumers from private monopolies, any proposed antitrust treatment of cyberspace should be examined skeptically." In particular, they point out the folly in harmonization of antitrust policy, which "by its nature, eliminates jurisdictional competition—which would be especially ironic for antitrust."

Conclusion

Whether or not one regards the Internet as fundamentally "special" or "exceptional," or merely a variant of ordinary jurisdictional disputes, the collection of thoughtful essays contained herein reflects a variety of reasoned approaches to generally keeping bureaucracy and overgrown government out of cyberspace. The authors explain the pros and cons of the application of traditional legal norms and processes to this new realm of cyberspace.

Nonetheless, each acknowledges—some more reluctantly than others—that some degree of jurisdictional responsibility will probably need to be worked out as the Net grows, especially in a commercial way. For better or for worse, traditional meatspace legal concepts and standards will likely be applied to cyberspace; the challenge is minimizing the negative externalities associated with applying parochial standards to a global medium. The approaches suggested by the contributors for accomplishing this task are varied.

More refined targeting tests provide one possible model. But fights still will occur over who will adjudicate disputes even if those more refined targeting principles do become more commonly accepted jurisprudential guidelines. Multinational treaties and accords may be another model, possibly using the existing General Agreement on Tariffs and Trade (GATT)/World Trade Organization (WTO) mechanisms to help resolve thorny jurisdictional squabbles. But the use of such mechanisms assumes the WTO has the authority or "consent of the governed" to adjudicate disputes under a set of commonly held values or principles. Not only is it unclear what those commonly held values or principles should be in this case, but also such an expansion of GATT/WTO authority would raise serious sovereignty issues.

"Country of origin" standards may provide the best default methodology when jurisdiction in doubt. A great deal of logic is in the notion that a given unit of government may only exert authority over those actors who physically reside within the confines of their traditional geographic borders. In this sense, an origin-based methodology protects the sovereignty of traditional governments while simultaneously giving meaning to the notion of "consent of the governed" in an online setting. Moreover, origin-based standards can foster healthy jurisdictional regulatory and tax competition— perhaps *too much* competition in the minds of some legislators and regulators—by allowing companies and consumers to have a "release valve" or escape mechanism to avoid oppressive jurisdictions who seek to stifle online commerce or expression. To the extent multinational treaties and accords embrace such origin-based rules, it may prove to be the most convenient and consistent principle for resolving current and emerging jurisdictional disputes.[29] As Michael Greve concludes in his entry in this volume: "Origin-based regulation, in other words, is a kind of contractual default rule—an eminently plausible option, and the only plausible alternative, to an international information economy designed by political diktat. The case for the origin principle is strong in the tax area; it is still more powerful in regulatory contexts. Principled insistence on the origin rule in every applicable context would help to advance it in each, or at least some."

But perhaps there will also be times when the issue in play is simply too important to allow the risk of "lowest common denominator" jurisdictional regulation to enter into the picture at all. Free speech is the most prominent example of this so far; many endorse a "thumb-our-nose-at-the-rest-of-the-world" approach to the question of speech standards, and given America's strong and noble tradition of protecting freedom of expression, perhaps that is the sensible approach in this particular case.

The question of "Who Rules the Net?" will only grow in importance in coming years as more and more governments attempt to stake a claim to cyberspace. "It was naive to imagine that the global reach of the Internet would make geography irrelevant," noted a recent report in *The Economist*. "Geography is far from dead."[30] This collection of essays will offer policymakers and the general public a better understanding of the complications and controversies that await us as battles over Internet jurisdiction and governance unfold.

PART I

GENERAL FRAMEWORKS FOR
GLOBAL INTERNET GOVERNANCE

1. Establishing Global Internet Freedom: Tear Down This Firewall

Christopher Cox

Introduction

With nearly 10 percent of the world's population online, and more gaining access each day, the Internet stands to become the most powerful engine for democratization and the free exchange of ideas ever invented. But this great advance in individual liberty is itself the target of authoritarian governments that are aggressively blocking and censoring the Internet. Those who resist these government controls face torture and imprisonment for accessing such "subversive" material as news from the *Washington Post*, the BBC, CNN, and the Voice of America.

The success of U.S. policy in support of the universal human rights of freedom of speech, press, and association requires new initiatives to defeat totalitarian controls over the Internet. If the benefits of the Internet can reach more and more people around the globe, then repressive governments will reform or fall as the citizenry gain the means to exchange views, to obtain information, and to let their voices be heard. To defend and promote freedom, the United States must speak forcefully in support of its expression on the Internet, work internationally to protect people's Internet access, and direct international broadcasting resources to combat Internet jamming technologies.

Patterns of Global Abuse

Increasingly, nondemocratic regimes around the world are denying their peoples unrestricted access to the Internet. Cuba, Laos, North Korea, the People's Republic of China, Saudi Arabia, Syria, Tunisia, and Vietnam are the most notorious violators of Internet freedom. These governments, according to the U.S. State Department and such organizations as Human Rights Watch and Reporters without Borders, are using methods of control that include denying their

3

citizens access to the Internet, censoring content, banning private ownership of computers, and even making e-mail accounts so expensive that ordinary people cannot use them. These countries use firewalls, filters, and other devices to block and censor the Internet.

Monitoring of individual activity on the Internet is common. Repressive governments screen and read e-mail messages and message boards, searching for the use of particular words. Often, government censors simply block individuals from visiting unapproved Web sites. The development of blacklists of users who visit Web sites for political, economic, financial, and religious news and information serves as a first step toward arrest and prosecution.

These are the most common ways in which authoritarian governments interfere with their citizens' access to the Internet:

Denying ISP Access

Many governments in the Middle East and Asia retain monopoly control of Internet service providers (ISPs). This regulation occurs most often in nations that maintain state control of telecommunications systems. This monopoly power enables governments to enforce restrictive policies over the people's access to the Internet.

The Syrian government, for example, attempts to block access to servers that provide free e-mail services. According to the U.S. State Department, even foreign diplomats have had their telephone service disrupted because the lines were being used to access Internet providers outside the country.

In Cuba, the Castro government controls all access to the Internet, and all e-mail messages are censored. Because access to computers is limited, the Internet can only be accessed through government-approved institutions.

In Burma, the Ministry of Defense operates the country's only Internet server. Not surprisingly, according to the State Department, Internet services are being offered "selectively" to a "small number of customers."

Censoring Internet Content

Among the strictest enforcers of Internet censorship are Bahrain, China, Iran, Kuwait, Saudi Arabia, Vietnam, and Yemen, each of which actively blocks Web sites for government purposes. Although these governments often claim that their censorship is necessary for reasons such as protecting public morality, in each case the

4

government controls clearly extend to stifling political dissent and opposition.

Censorship is typically conducted by using proxy servers. By interposing the proxy server between the end user and the Internet—a task easily accomplished when the ISP is the government—the government can filter and block content. In countries where individual access to the Internet is rare, government agents are assigned to monitor activity at Internet cafes, literally watching which sites customers visit. When unapproved Internet use becomes frequent, cafes can be closed, ostensibly for allowing Internet users to access "immoral" materials. In Saudi Arabia, where the government has closed a number of Internet cafes, those established for women have been specifically targeted as being used for "immoral purposes."

Cost Prohibitive Pricing of E-Mail Accounts

In Cuba, where only 60,000 of the country's 11 million people have Internet access, the low number of users is directly related to the Castro government's prohibitively high taxes on e-mail accounts. The e-mail registration tax is $240—in a country with a per capita income of $1,700. In Cuba and elsewhere, such prohibitively high taxes and fees are an effective means of ensuring that only a small minority will have the opportunity to use the Internet.

Banning Personal Computer Ownership

The most dramatic Internet censorship is accomplished by outright government bans on personal computer ownership. In North Korea, dictator Kim Jong Il has forbidden all servers or Internet connections to the outside world, thus making it the only country on earth where the Internet does not exist. The few government Web sites that exist to distribute propaganda in foreign countries are hosted externally.

In March 2002, Castro's government banned the sale of personal computers to the general public. Government decree 383/2001 bans the sale of "computers, offset printer equipment, mimeographs, photocopiers, and any other mass printing medium" to "associations, foundations, civic and nonprofit organizations, and Cuban private individuals."

The Violators

Burma

Reporters without Borders reports that Internet use in Burma is available only to a select few. This limited Internet access is available

5

only through the country's one ISP, which is owned and operated by the Ministry of Defense. Internet use is constantly monitored by the Burmese defense ministry and intelligence services. Dissidents who are active on the Web receive virus-infected messages from these government organizations. In December 1999, Burmese military personnel were arrested for "violating state secrets" by logging onto Burmanet, a Burmese opposition site.

All e-mails are screened by Myanmar Post and Telecommunications (MPT), Burma's national telecom operator. In January 2000, MPT banned all political texts and shared Internet accounts. Later in 2000, the Ministry of Communications barred all foreigners from using private e-mails and required authorization before Web pages could be created or modems and fax machines brought into Burma. Violation of these laws regarding Internet usage can result in up to 15 years in prison.

Cuba

All of Cuba's Internet traffic is processed by one computer, where it is censored and access to most sites is blocked. Cuban citizens believe that the Cuban intelligence services monitor their e-mail, because messages from outside of the country are received hours after being sent or not at all. Although there is now a black market for e-mail addresses, they are only useful if the person has a computer—which must be reported to the government—thus rendering these illegal e-mail addresses useless.

Laos

According to the 2001 Reporters without Borders "Enemies of the Internet" report, Internet use in Laos is extremely restricted: the government prohibits its citizens from publishing any information that could "damage the country's unity and integrity." Citizens and residents are denied access to sites in other countries that may include sources of "subversive information." All Laotians who send and receive e-mails must first provide the government with their password, giving it the ability to intercept and read all e-mails.

The People's Republic of China

In sheer volume, the People's Republic of China (PRC) commits the most Internet abuses. The government seeks to retain control over the large and growing number of Internet users (33.7 million), mainland Web sites (250,000), and Internet cafes (200,000). PRC authorities legally restrict and penalize access to any information on the Internet considered "subversive" or "critical" of the state. China's Ministry of Information Industry regulates access to the Internet, while the Ministries of Public and State Security monitor its use.

On June 17, 2002, 20 Internet users burned to death in an Internet cafe. The owner reportedly locked the doors so that police could not arrest them for illegally using the Internet. The locked doors also trapped the people inside. After the fire, PRC authorities ordered all illegal Internet cafes closed. All nongovernment approved Internet cafes remain banned.

In recent years, the PRC government has stepped up its efforts to restrict Internet access. According to State Department's Human Rights Report:

> Despite the continued expansion of the Internet in the country, the Chinese government maintained its efforts to monitor and control content on the Internet. . . . The authorities block access to Web sites they find offensive. Authorities have at times blocked politically sensitive Web sites, including those of dissident groups and some major foreign news organizations, such as the Voice of America, the *Washington Post*, the *New York Times*, and the BBC.

Dozens of Chinese citizens have been jailed for using the Internet for politics. The State Department reported that one such individual, Huang Qi, was "bound hand and foot and beaten by police while they tried to force him to confess to subversion." Huang, the operator of an Internet site, posted information about missing persons, including students who disappeared in June 1989 in Tiananmen Square.

The Ministry for Information and Technology requires private ISPs to monitor information on the Internet. These new rules include recording information about users (such as their Internet access IDs, their postal addresses, and their telephone numbers) who visit "strategic and sensitive" Web sites including the *Washington Post*, the *New York Times*, CNN, the BBC, Human Rights Watch, and Amnesty International.

The Ministry also requires that ISPs install software to monitor and copy the contents of "sensitive" e-mail messages. Under this directive, ISPs must interrupt the transfer of e-mails containing "subversive" content that pose a threat to "national security and unity." Authors of such e-mail messages must be reported to the Ministry of Information and Technology, the Ministry of Law and Order, and the State Secrets Bureau. The State Department notes that "Internet entrepreneurs have complained that Government regulations controlling the Internet were so broadly written that MSS (Ministry of State Security) officials could find any Web page operator or e-commerce merchant guilty of violating regulations."

The State Department found that, although e-mail is difficult to block, the PRC "attempts to do so by, at times, blocking all e-mail from overseas Internet service providers used by dissident groups, and by filtering and tracking individual e-mail accounts." It also found that Chinese citizens who supply large numbers of e-mail addresses to organizations abroad have been prosecuted. Forwarding dissident e-mail messages to others is illegal.

Reporters without Borders has reported that "about 20 provinces now have special police brigades trained in pursuing 'subversive' Internet users." Currently, 22 cyber-dissidents are in prison for trying to break through this Internet repression and censorship. According to the State Department, in April 2001, Guo Qinghai was given a four-year sentence for posting pro-democracy material on the Internet. That same month, Wang Sen was detained in Dachuan, Sichuan Province, for posting articles alleging the resale of Red Cross–donated tuberculosis medicine. And, in June 2001, police detained Li Hongmin in Hunan province for distributing copies of the Tiananmen Papers over the Internet.

On May 16, 2002, the PRC Arts Ministry announced that students and other persons under the age of 16 will only be allowed into Internet cafes during school holidays, for a maximum of three hours—and only if they are accompanied by a teacher. On the same day, the PRC announced that it had "unblocked" access to a select number of international sites, but access to other sites including VOA, the BBC, and *Time* magazine was still blocked.

Syria

The sole ISP in Syria is the Syrian Telecommunications Establishment, a government-run source that blocks access to "offensive" content and all pro-Israeli sites. The government is able to copy and monitor e-mails because of its control of the service provider. In December 2000, for example, the Syrian government detained an individual without charge for forwarding a political cartoon via e-mail. In order for Syrians to connect to the Internet, a government technician must come to their home, install the software, and assign the user's password—information that the government retains.

Tunisia

Every one of the five Internet service providers in Tunisia is under government control. The Tunisian Internet Agency, created in 1996, regularly provides the names of subscribers to the government. Web sites and online publications in Tunisia that contain information critical of the government are frequently blocked, according to the State Department. Among the Web sites blacklisted by the Tunisian government is, not surprisingly, a report on Internet use in Tunisia by Human Rights Watch.

Vietnam

The one Internet access provider in Vietnam is owned and operated by the Communist government. In August 2001, the Prime Minister of Vietnam issued a decree prohibiting use of the Internet "for the purpose of hostile actions against the country or to destabilize security, violate morality, or violate other laws and regulations."

Although the Internet is nominally available to anyone who wants to use it, the exceptionally high prices severely restrict usage. The Vietnamese government monitors the sites visited, and uses firewalls to block "politically [and] culturally inappropriate" Web sites.

The government is seeking additional authority to monitor Internet cafes and hold the owners of these cafes responsible for customer use of the Internet. This legislation would affect all of the nearly 4,000 Internet cafes in Vietnam.

Yemen

Internet access in Yemen is severely limited by prohibitively high prices of equipment and Internet subscriptions. Although officials say the Yemeni government does not block political sites, mowj.com, the Yemeni national Opposition Front's Web site, was blocked by the government and has now ceased operation completely.

Defeating the Censors

The private sector, including for-profit corporations and nongovernmental organizations, is developing and employing various techniques and technologies such as proxy servers, intermediaries, "mirrors," and encryption to overcome state efforts to deny freedom of the Internet. But the U.S. government has thus far commenced only modest steps to fund and deploy these technologies to defeat Internet censorship. To date, the Voice of America (VOA) and Radio Free Asia (RFA) have budgeted a total of only $1 million for technology to counter PRC Internet jamming, using technology including "Triangle Boy" produced by SafeWeb. Although this technology has been successful in allowing Chinese citizens to freely access the Internet—receiving 100,000 electronic hits per day from users in China—its funding has expired. SafeWeb has also provided a free service to the people of Iran and Saudi Arabia. Due to the $50,000 per month cost of bandwidth to serve each country, however, the firm has discontinued service to both countries. At the time that SafeWeb discontinued service, it was receiving millions of hits per month from these two countries. Yet VOA and RFA must rely on such technologies to ensure access to their programming. Other technologies and products, including Peek-a-Booty, DynaWeb, and Freenet-China (the latter a peer-to-peer network), are also currently in use to help keep information flowing in and out of areas in which Internet censorship and jamming are prevalent.

A Policy for Global Internet Freedom

Congress and the Bush Administration must adopt an effective and robust global Internet freedom policy. The federal government should enlist the help of the private sector in this effort so that the many current technologies used commercially for securing business transactions and providing virtual meeting space can be used to promote democracy and freedom.

To bring to bear the pressure of the free world on repressive governments guilty of Internet censorship, the United States should—

- Direct substantial international broadcasting resources to a global effort to defeat Internet jamming and censorship.

- Establish an Office of Global Internet Freedom within the International Broadcasting Bureau to develop and implement a strategy for defeating Internet jamming.
- Formally declare that all people have the right to communicate freely with others on the Internet.
- Formally declare that all people have the right to unrestricted access to news and information on the Internet.
- Publicly and prominently denounce state-directed practices of restricting, censoring, banning, and blocking access to information on the Internet.
- Submit a resolution at next year's U.N. Human Rights Commission annual meeting in Geneva condemning all nations practicing Internet censorship and denying freedom to access information.
- Compile and publish an annual report on countries that pursue policies of Internet censorship, blocking, and other abuses.

Conclusion

The Internet, originally a U.S. technology, is creating economic prosperity around the world. The value of the Internet, however, must not be limited to money. The Internet has the potential to expand political dialogue and global communication beyond anything that could have been dreamed of throughout history. To ensure that this invaluable advancement in human freedom and knowledge is not subverted by authoritarian governments, the United States must aggressively defend global Internet freedom. This policy must include far more aggressive measures to deploy technologies to defeat Internet censors, and to organize international support for the right of the peoples of the world to have unrestricted access to information and communication on the Internet. The future of human rights, democracy, and freedom throughout the world depends on it.

2. Be Careful What You Ask For: Reconciling a Global Internet and Local Law

Jonathan Zittrain

We used to speak accurately of *the* Internet, a single logical network of entities only a click away from each other, no matter how distant in physical space. That was certainly the ambitious intention of those who designed it; they sought to integrate lots of existing little networks, running on a variety of physical media, into a coherent whole.

They succeeded, and the resulting network and corresponding protocols absorbed almost every other more localized or proprietized network design effort. A globalized Internet running on open protocols meant that users could disregard both their own physical location and that of anyone they traded bits with; an occasional slow-to-respond (even while lightly trafficked) Web site might be the only betrayal of physical distance online for the average user. Web site operators, in turn, embraced the idea that setting up a single site would expose its contents to the entire Internet-connected populace, wherever it might be geographically found.

This cherished fact of Internet life promptly spawned a complementary set of problems loosely categorized as "jurisdictional." At their core lay the fact that perceived serious harm—to one's reputation, digital property, peace of mind, or computer network—could now easily originate at a distance and follow a path in between accuser and accused that traversed the physical territories of any number of sovereigns. As Internet usage has gone mainstream, the problems arising from harm-at-a-distance have intensified in tandem with the ranks of those feeling injury. Individuals complaining of libel or fraud are joined by corporations worried about stock manipulation and domain name cybersquatting, as well as governments anxious about citizens purchasing faraway goods effectively exempt

13

from sales tax, and encountering illegal speech that is not nearly as easily controlled as that issuing from print or broadcast media. The second section of this book features essays that touch on each of these problems, some from the perspectives of those threatened by the Internet's global character, others from the perspectives of those threatened by actions to redress it, such as surfers subjected to Web-site filtering by governments.

In this chapter I will explain two tectonic shifts in Internet architecture that are changing the ways in which these problems are addressed and that together are likely to make them largely evaporate. These shifts will help ease the tension between the certitudes that the Internet is global while the imposition of regulation is almost always local. These cures for the long-standing dilemmas of Internet jurisdiction and governance eliminate the originally cherished aspects of a global Internet as well—urging us to consider the iatrogenic effects of bulldozing online activity to conform more to the boundaries of the physical world that preceded it, and explaining why, in the United States and elsewhere, there are contradictory policies emerging about the Internet's future.

As the kaleidoscopic sweep of topics within this book shows, the governance of behavior on the Internet is a broad topic with meanings that vary by context. All are linked by the global Internet/local law dichotomy. To understand evolving solutions to these issues, it helps to break down the topic along lines that have represented the most persistent problems: determining the proper scope of a well-meaning sovereign's reach over a physically absent accused wrongdoer; reconciling multiple jurisdictions' laws that could be said to touch on a single Internet act; and enforcing whatever judgments are thought proper to make.

Personal Jurisdiction: How Far Should a Government Want Its Legal Reach to Extend?

The early puzzles of Internet jurisdiction invariably began with a chestnut focusing on the location of data rather than people. Thinkers were naturally intrigued by the prospect of Internet data bouncing all over the place from one point to another, such as—

> *A, in Austria, sends a threat by e-mail to C, who retrieves the e-mail from America Online's computers in Virginia and reads it on her screen in California. The packets making up the e-mail*

traveled by way of Great Britain before reaching the United States.
Where has the threat "happened"? Can California prosecute A?
Can Virginia? Where can C sue? Does Great Britain care?

Analysts thinking of this problem as new and distinctly Internet-related were not much deterred by the fact that such hypotheticals could be constructed without any reference to the Internet—one need only imagine the threat being carried by international post or telephone—and that a world comprising hundreds of distinct (and at times contradictory) legal systems had managed not to lapse into legal crisis because of them. Perhaps those analysts thought that the Internet made formerly rare scenarios routine and reasoned that a difference in degree can become a difference in kind. Whatever the explanation, the first jurisdictional puzzles were often based on the remarkable fact that Internet technology contemplated the movement of data to any number of physical locations at any moment, a technicality that Internet users might not bear in mind when sending an e-mail to a next door neighbor.

Of course, the practical answer in the international arena has been clear long before the Internet: C can sue (and A can be prosecuted) wherever a jurisdiction decides it cares to exercise its power—*and* can realistically make the defendant's life worse for failing to show up to contest the case, or for showing up and losing. Many jurisdictions choose to limit its decisions on exercising power on yet further factors: they may require some contact by the absent defendant (perhaps other than the very behavior complained of) before agreeing that "personal jurisdiction" exists, or they may decide that the dispute itself must touch on that physical jurisdiction in a way that makes it especially competent to locate a tribunal there (a form of "subject matter" jurisdiction).

These limits are useful for a sovereign to self-impose, lest it find itself enmeshed in disputes and prosecutions due to the mere fact that data relating to the dispute—at base, electrical impulses—transited that sovereign state's geographic territory. This explanation may clarify why, over time, analyses regarding which countries and governmental subdivisions ought to become involved in a dispute have relied less on the facts about where data might be located or found in transit, and more on the *behavior* itself complained of, and the physical location of the parties engaging in it.

Exceptions still exist where the movement or location of bits alone has been found to matter, generally where a sovereign assigns an ideologically high priority on becoming involved, or where cross-jurisdictional situations are themselves a substantive enhancement to a local crime or tort. In one U.S. case, for example, a Worthington, Ohio, man was prosecuted for illegally importing obscenity into the state because he used America Online to send an e-mail to a minor also in Worthington, Ohio. The Ohio Supreme Court found the movement of bits from the man's computer in Ohio to America Online's computer in Virginia and back to the minor's computer in Ohio to be an importation.[1]

When passing the Anticybersquatting Consumer Protection Act,[2] allowing trademark holders to sue domain name registrants whose domain names are claimed to infringe the holders' marks, the U.S. Congress provided that in those instances in which the defendant was overseas or unknown, an *in rem* action could be brought against the name itself—which, if it has any location at all, reposes as data on certain computers that index domain names.[3] As a result, the *in rem* provisions allow suit wherever the registrar or registry for the name is located. In the case of .com names, that provision means that a federal court in Virginia is available to would-be plaintiffs under the Act because the company running the .com registry is located there.[4] Thus an Austrian registering a name like goodvacations.com for use in Austria might have to answer to an American court if a claim of trademark infringement arises, with theories of jurisdiction resting on the thin reed of the fact that the data management behind the domain name takes place in the United States.

Again, these examples are the exceptions. Jurisdiction based on the movement of bits alone has typically proven too expansive for sovereigns to routinely recognize it. As demonstrated by the use of the *in rem* provisions only as a backstop should the defendant be otherwise unreachable, usually other paths exist to asserting both personal power over a defendant and a subject-matter interest in a case. When those paths are lacking, chances are good that the transit of bits will not and should not interest a sovereign—except in cases in which a sovereign already has practical enforcement power over a defendant and is satisfied with the slimmest of procedural pretexts to claim the right to intervene. The long-term *storage* of bits in a particular physical location might trigger interest by a government

16

with power over that location, but so long as the storage is not inadvertent or uncontrollable by whatever entity is the source of the data in question, would-be defendants can choose to store data in the most hospitable physical legal environment while still having it available worldwide through the Internet.

The existence of the so-called Principality of Sealand brings this possibility into perfect relief. A cyberlaw textbook author's dream, Sealand is an abandoned World War II anti-aircraft platform just off the coast of Great Britain. A man named Roy Bates claimed it for his own in the mid-1960s, and cites the ambiguous outcome of some U.K. court battles over its ownership—and a failed invasion attempt by German nationals in the 1970s—as evidence that it is indeed a sovereign nation.

The most recent use to which Sealand has been put is as the home of a company called Havenco, which touts itself as providing "the world's most secure managed servers in the world's only true free market environment."[6] If the storage of data alone were the anchor for the assertion of jurisdiction, data could simply be stored somewhere, such as on Sealand, that would be out of reach of the sovereigns that might have an interest in exercising jurisdiction. Interestingly, Sealand and Havenco themselves ban the use of their servers to host child pornography—as defined by U.S. law—or to mount hacking or spamming activities.[7] This could simply reflect Prince Roy's sense of right and wrong, but no doubt also results from the fact that Sealand itself must get its network connectivity somewhere—and could be at risk of losing it should its own Internet service providers reject its activities, or be pressured by nearby governments to do so. Further, the benefits to a would-be defendant of safeguarding data there for jurisdictionally evasive purposes are limited by the defendant's location. Unless a person is willing to move to Sealand, he or she would still be within another sovereign's physical and therefore legal reach and would thus risk being personally penalized should undesired activities taking place on Sealand under the defendant's direction not cease or should sought-after data secured there not be produced.

Although intriguing from an academic standpoint, the existence of Sealand doesn't much change the nature of the jurisdiction and governance debates. The debates are less about where the bits themselves are, and more about where the people authoring them—and allegedly causing harm by them—are.

As a government reflects on the proper limits of its reach against a faraway defendant whose Internet activities are causing local grief, it runs into a dilemma. On the one hand, a plaintiff might claim it unfair that the sovereign would decline to intervene simply because a defendant is wholly absent, since the effects of the defendant's Internet behavior are still felt locally. On the other hand, going on an "effects" test alone suggests that anyone posting information on the Internet is unduly open to nearly any sovereign's jurisdiction, since that information could have an effect around the world. Michael Geist's essay in this volume suggests a middle path, that of "targeting," by which something more than effects, but less than physical presence, could trigger jurisdiction. That path tries to peel away many, if not all, extraneous governments from a scrum that could pile up around a single defendant's objectionable behavior while preserving the prospect that jurisdictions other than the defendant's home could stake a legitimate claim to intervene. As with many middle paths, the devil lies in the details. But especially in the midst of a sea change in the fundamental global Internet/local law dilemma—one where a more localized Internet is possible due to geolocation technologies—such a path seems the best compromise in an inherently difficult situation.

The High Court of Australia's decision in *Dow Jones v. Gutnick*[8] vindicates this kind of reasoning in a case that blends personal jurisdiction with choice of law. There, an Australian businessman named Joseph Gutnick sued Dow Jones for an unflattering portrait of him published online in *Barron's*. Dow Jones asked the Australian legal system to decline to intervene, arguing that Dow Jones's U.S. home was the fairest place to hear the dispute. The Australian court was unpersuaded by the pile-on argument that Gutnick could next sue the company in Zimbabwe, or Great Britain, or China. It pointed out that Gutnick himself lived in Australia, and Dow Jones quite explicitly sold subscriptions to the online *Barron's* to Australians. These facts helped Australia escape the dilemma of justifying almost any country's intervention if it was to justify its own. Without its special, if not unique, relationship to one party in the case, Australia may well have declined to intervene in the dispute.

Even as the pure issue of "personal jurisdiction" finds a messy lawyer's compromise, when people or companies are far away from a sovereign's physical territory—or anonymous, and therefore of unknown location—the sovereign's quandaries more typically involve reconciling its laws with those of other governments that might similarly find a right to intervene, or bare-knuckle enforcement of any decrees it enacts against a faraway party once it has assured itself of its right to intervene.

Choice of Law: The Slowest Ship in the Convoy Problem

In the spring of 2003, the *New Yorker's* Seymour Hersh wrote an article about U.S. Pentagon adviser Richard Perle.[9] Perle was quoted in the *New York Sun* as saying that he planned to sue over the article, and in Great Britain at that, since the British libel laws were more generous to plaintiffs than those of the United States.[10] Suppose Perle spent a lot of time in Great Britain and had reputational interests there that were threatened by Hersh's piece, and suppose further that the *New Yorker* sold online subscriptions to British readers. A targeted effects test for personal jurisdiction might be met, but the defendant's objections need not be grounded in a lack of authority of British courts to call it to account. Rather, the *New Yorker* could claim that to have to hew to British law on the Internet would be an inappropriately all-or-nothing choice by the publisher. For the

19

online *New Yorker* to conform to British law would mean that Americans would be deprived of content otherwise protected by the First Amendment. In essence, the global convoy of Internet publishers operating under respective countries' motley laws would harmonize with those of the most restrictive major jurisdiction—the "slowest ship."[11]

This problem is distinct from the legal nuances of personal jurisdiction and has been raised in several other high-profile disputes. For example, the Canadian firm iCraveTV sought to rebroadcast television signals over the Internet, a practice that was arguably legal in Canada at the time though illegal in the United States. Broadcasters and others brought suit in the United States.[12] Personal jurisdiction was not at issue, since at least one relevant iCraveTV executive was an American citizen in residence in Pittsburgh, Pennsylvania, and the firm had an office there.[13] What made the case interesting was the prospect that the Canadian firm could be asked to cease transmitting entirely, so long as any Americans could view their online webcast feeds. The case didn't make it past the temporary restraining order phase—iCraveTV folded not long after it lost the first skirmish[14]— but it was clear from the transcripts of oral argument that the judge was not much impressed by the prospect that iCraveTV's activities were legal in Canada, so long as there could be any American viewers of the site.[15] (The United States has long had an expansive view of its jurisdiction; just ask former Panamanian strongman Manuel Noriega.)

At the state level within the United States, the "dormant commerce clause" of the Constitution is said to proscribe state laws whose effects reach beyond state borders, even if the target of regulation is legitimate within the state. It was by way of this reasoning that a district court struck down a New York law asking Web site operators to ensure that indecent content could not be viewed by minors.[16] The court's view was that every Web site operator in the country would be affected by such requirements since there was no easy way to know when a New York minor might stumble onto a given site and thereby bring its operator under the sway of New York's law.[17] States are thus compelled to limit their lawmaking when an intervention affects parties outside the state who are otherwise operating under other ground rules, even as the federal government is not held to a comparable standard vis-à-vis the international community. This view may be doctrinally inconsistent, but it is perfectly understandable in the obvious absence of a unifying global legal structure.

Enforcement

Even if a country finds itself competent to hear a case and apply its law, enforcement of a resulting judgment against a faraway party can be difficult if the party has no significant in-country assets or interests. Dow Jones's claimed worries about answering for defamation in Zimbabwe[18] might ring hollow here; the practical dynamics of global jurisdiction suggest that a core group of powerful countries can call outsiders to account far more readily than smaller, obscure ones can. Some push exists to allow for more ready enforcement of judgments across international boundaries—converging slowly toward the idea of full faith and credit among nations that already exists among the American states—but where a given country's public policy can be shown to conflict with a fellow sovereign's judgment, the deal might not be honored. When Yahoo! faced an order from a French court threatening damages unless Yahoo! took measures to preclude French citizens from viewing online auctions of Nazi memorabilia, it obtained a declaratory judgment from an American court indicating that any finding of damages there would not be enforced in the United States.[19]

The difficulties of extraterritorial enforcement can be particularly acute for countries like China. The Chinese government has great sensitivity to Internet speech that is perceived to undermine state control, but cannot readily get countries playing host to the speech— and the speakers—to enforce adverse judgments or force a stop to the speech. However, for those looking to do business in China, and thus with something to lose there, power can be brought to bear. A number of overseas content and Internet service providers targeting Chinese audiences have joined hundreds of domestic companies in signing a "Public Pledge on Self-Discipline for China Internet Industry," by which they agree, among other things, to refrain "from producing, posting, or disseminating pernicious information that may jeopardize state security and disrupt social stability, contravene laws and regulations, and spread superstition and obscenity."[20]

Global Internet, Global Law

Each of the major problems of jurisdiction—personal jurisdiction, choice of law, and enforcement—is grounded in dilemmas arising

21

from a global Internet cabined only by local laws. Some attempts to eliminate the dilemmas have sought to simply make for global, rather than local, law. This might be done in two general ways: making a sui generis, noncountry-specific body of law or best practices applicable to Internet activities, or striving toward substantive harmonization among existing sovereigns' laws, along with a common set of practices for personal jurisdiction and mutual enforcement of judgments.

Creating Internet-specific law has been embraced, naturally, by Internet exceptionalists who want to see a cyberspace separate and apart from real space, and generally less regulated. This was colorfully expressed in John Perry Barlow's 1996 "Declaration of Independence of Cyberspace," which demanded that the industrialized nations of the world leave cyberspace alone, since it and its denizens were so unlike any physical world counterparts.[21] "We are forming our own Social Contract," Barlow wrote. "This governance will arise according to the conditions of our world, not yours. Our world is different."

Others refined Barlow's account by imagining not one social contract but many, a series of cyberspaces in which likeminded people could respectively gather.[22] All of these accounts are now thoroughly dated, premised on a digital divide between offline and online that less and less exists. Instead of boasting an elite, libertarian demographic at variance with the mainstream populations of the industrialized world, the Internet is less a conceptually separate space with few direct links to non-Internet life and institutions and more a ubiquitous tool. So long as, say, someone can post messages to thousands of America Online subscribers claiming to be a person named Ken Zeran selling offensive T-shirts—providing the real, offline Ken Zeran's telephone number as a lightning rod for irate calls—it is hard to call cyberspace separate, and its idiosyncrasies something with which "real" governments should not concern themselves. Indeed, in the *Zeran* case,[23] an American law provided for immunities from liability for Internet publishers of others' content without parallel immunities for their physical media counterparts. This resulted in the strange situation of Zeran's suit against America Online being categorically halted, while a suit against KRXO radio— whose disc jockeys had seen the message advertising the offensive T-shirts and conveyed it on air to equally irate radio listeners— could go forward.[24]

22

Internet separatism lives on today primarily in debates about the application of state sales tax to out-of-state purchases made easy by the Internet. Unless pitched as infant industry subsidization, reasons are hard to imagine why Internet-based purchases should effectively avoid tax while purchases consummated in physical space do not.[25] The most direct motive to explain the perspective of those who seek continuing moratoria on taxing Internet purchases is simply a hostility to government regulation in general and taxes specifically. That position is not incoherent; one might seek to prevent the "pristine" territory of the Internet from being ruined by an encroachment of what one sees as irreversible overregulation in real space. But from the point of view of the dilemmas of jurisdiction and governance, one set of fault lines—those between countries and other legal jurisdictions—is traded for a new set, separating the physical and virtual worlds.

The most effective, if not beloved, global law scheme has so far proven to be conveniently centered on cyberspace-specific disputes, namely, those over domain names. As part of its designation by the U.S. Department of Commerce to manage global domain name policy, the Internet Corporation for Assigned Names and Numbers (ICANN), devised a Uniform Dispute Resolution Policy (UDRP) for the adjudication of claims of improper registration of names in .com, .net, and .org.[26] Operating wholly independently from any one nation's trademark laws, the UDRP neatly sidesteps many of the classic jurisdictional conundrums. A faraway or unknown domain name registrant had better step forward to defend against a claim that his or her domain name infringes someone else's rights lest he or she lose the proceeding—and the name. Enforcement is made easy because no money or behavioral change is asked of the losing respondent: the registry is simply notified of the panel's decision and transfers control over the name to the complainant without requiring any acquiescence of the respondent. The substantive principles under which UDRP cases are decided are vague, requiring an assessment of the "rights" and "interests" of both parties to the dispute without specifying just how those rights should be recognized or under what sovereign's system. But that has not stopped thousands of UDRP cases from going forward, or the adoption of the UDRP system by a number of additional registries operating other generic and country-specific top-level domains.

To be sure, use of the UDRP does not necessarily end legal wrangling. As mentioned, the U.S. Anticybersquatting Consumer Protection Act provides its own mechanisms for seeking to complain about another's domain name registration,[27] and any number of trademark actions launched in countries willing to hear them could trump the UDRP's result, whether for complainant or respondent.[28] Harold Feld's chapter in this volume speaks to many shortcomings of ICANN and its UDRP, and highlights that a "universal" law orchestrated by a handful of staffers at a nonprofit corporation may be far worse than the sometimes inconsistent regulation produced by more familiar territorial sovereigns, many of whom are run according to political principles that value and integrate individual voices and votes.

Attempts to bind sovereigns' laws substantively more closely together in a world with burgeoning transborder activity continue, and, to the extent they succeed, some of the structural jurisdictional tensions recede. International treaties and agreements have begun to cluster, if not fully unify, countries' practices on consumer protection, intellectual property, taxation, and, to some extent, privacy. But these shifts are incremental, and often the inking of a treaty— or even, within the European Union, the promulgation of a directive left for individual countries to implement—is only a starting point that tests individual countries' and cultures' mettle to actually enforce what has been abstractly agreed to.

Local Internet, Local Law

The most intriguing developments in the running jurisdictional and governance debates have been those that point toward a reassertion of effective local government control over Internet use by people within each government's territorial boundaries.

Local Control Enabled by the Source of Content: The "Check a Box" Solution

The French courts have indicated an awareness of the convoy problem in the suit brought against Yahoo! for permitting online auctions featuring the display of Nazi memorabilia in claimed contravention of local law. The outcome of that case so far has France asserting its right to demand that Yahoo! cease offering certain kinds of auctions, but only after the court chartered a three-expert panel to assess the extent to which Yahoo! could implement such a ban without having to apply it to non-French residents.[29] The panel concluded that Yahoo! was in a position to more or less determine who was accessing its auctions from France and who was not, and therefore could apply the strictures of French law to French customers without depriving, say, Americans of the opportunity to browse auctions of Nazi material. Firms have sprung up to offer just such geographic determinations, and, while they are far from perfect, they can sort many users into territories and require those who wish to evade the categorization to undertake some burden and inconvenience to mask their geo-identities.[30]

Search engine Google, which offers country- and language-specific variants, apparently obeys the informal requests of officials from Germany to eliminate potentially illegal sites from its google.com counterpart at google.de.[31] So far, Germany does not appear to have asked Google to eliminate such sites from those presented to German-based visitors to google.com, but the notion of geographic-specific information tailoring has lodged.

Geolocation by online service providers is likely to become easier and more accurate over time. Global positioning system chips are decreasing in price and finding their way into laptops, and commercial opportunities exist to offer services on the basis of geography: one might soon be able to step off a plane, open a laptop or handheld personal digital assistant, and find an ad for local restaurants with automatic delivery displayed on the first sponsored Web site one visits. To the extent geolocation is possible, the convoy problem described earlier in this chapter begins to melt away. Purveyors of information may object to the administrative burden of having to tailor information for multiple jurisdictions—just as opponents of nationwide collection of local state sales taxes in the United States point to the difficulties of mastering each state's sales tax collection and remittance rules—but that complaint is much less searing and separate from the objection that one jurisdiction's residents will be de facto subject to another's laws because of a Web site's all-or-nothing exposure to the Net's masses.

Many old-school "Netizens," eager to maintain a global Internet unsusceptible to government control, were furious at their technologically savvy brethren for adverting to the possibility of geolocation in the Yahoo! France case. This led to some perhaps chastened repudiation of the court's decision by at least two members of the panel that enabled it, Internet pioneers Ben Laurie and Vint Cerf. Laurie outright apologized, and Cerf was quoted after the decision as making the observation "that if every jurisdiction in the world insisted on some form of filtering for its particular geographic territory, the World Wide Web would stop functioning."[32] That is an overstatement in the sense that sources of content on the Internet are perfectly able to tailor their information delivery on the basis of whatever demographic they can solicit or discern from those who surf their Web sites. But it is completely accurate if one believes in "World Wide" as an affirmative ideological value for the Internet rather than a technical description of its historically undifferentiated reach.

One can imagine a framework for Internet content providers—whether large Web site operators, individual home page designers, or message board posters—in which, before information going public, a set of checkboxes is presented that the publisher can use to indicate just where in the world the information is to be exposed. One could check or uncheck "United States" as a whole, or select specific states. One could check or uncheck "Zimbabwe," or "Australia," or "European Union." Such technological flexibility, combined with varied demands by countries for providers to filter content to hew to local laws, might induce risk-averse Internet content providers to adopt a very narrow band of publishing for their work, generally asking to limit distribution to those areas in which legal risk is deemed low, or at least to areas in which potential profit from the work's consumption there is thought to exceed such risk.[33] Users eager for information will then be effectively denied access to it by faraway content providers anticipating the actions of zealous local governments that seek to expand their local regulation of more traditional media into the formerly unregulatable Internet space. Worse, overcautious or simply indifferent Internet content providers will omit "unimportant" countries from the list of places able to view their offerings, enhancing a digital divide even though such countries are not explicitly seeking strong control over Internet content. Indeed, the gleam of the World Wide Web would be dulled as it became simply another window into traditional content for many surfers rather than a raucous digital free-for-all.

Such a scenario is not inevitable, however. Countries worried about being left off information providers' checkbox lists could pass safe-harbor legislation providing for immunity as an enticement to content providers to allow them to remain on the list of digital destinations. Or they might index their laws to those of countries that will rarely be omitted from checkbox lists—just as Sealand's ban on the hosting of child pornography is a one-sentence pointer to whatever the United States has legislated on the issue. The search for "global law" might be given a strong push as countries seek to be clumped together in the minds of content providers.

Local Control Enabled Near Content's Destination: The Pennsylvania Solution

Even with the rise of technical abilities to filter the information one places on the Internet according to viewers' locations, overseas sites may still balk at abiding by local governments' demands for change. Rather than writing off, say, Saudi Arabia as an Internet destination for fear of legal liability, an online newspaper might continue to make itself available there anyway, figuring that without in-country assets or other countries willing to enforce its judgments, there is little Saudi Arabia can do to call the newspaper to account. The same reasoning may apply to individual message posters or bloggers wanting to protest China's actions in Tibet, or fly-by-night pornographers and spammers who maintain no obvious central office or corporate staffs sensitive to international legal compliance.

This reasoning may explain why some governments are focusing not on pressuring the sources of content around the world but rather on controlling Internet service providers across which data transits closer to home in an attempt to localize an Internet surfer's online experience. Indeed, Saudi Arabia and China both have comprehensive nationwide schemes by which Internet destinations deemed to run afoul of local law or convention are made unavailable to resident surfers.

In Saudi Arabia, all Internet traffic in the country is routed through a proxy server at the country's Internet Services Unit, the staff of which maintains a list of sites to be filtered, acting both to apply filtering criteria promulgated by the state and on specific filtering requests from individual state agencies.[34] The fact of filtering and some general descriptions of the criteria are available on the Internet Services Unit's Web site,[35] and thousands of sites—including anonymizers and translators that might themselves be easy launching pads to otherwise-blocked sites—are blocked.[36]

In China, thousands of routers around the country are apparently configured to simply drop packets going to or from Internet points of presence that have earned a bad reputation with the authorities, and increasingly subtle forms of filtering—such as temporarily denying access to Google to those who run searches using sensitive keywords, like the name of President Jiang Zemin—can also be found.[37] Private companies offering Internet access in China have long done so on condition that they apply whatever filtering measures are asked of them by the state.

Such filtering is far from perfect, but it can drastically increase the difficulty of getting to desired information, especially when the absence of information may be subtle, as in a missing entry on a list of search results. Peer-to-peer networks can seek to frustrate such attempts by implementing technologies such as "Publius" (the Public Censorship Resistant Publishing System),[38] but particularly when the act of using such technologies can itself be monitored and Internet users can be punished in a distinctly nonvirtual way, a level of resources exists that a state can put into Internet filtering that tips the cat-and-mouse game in favor of the cat much, if not most, of the time.

It is no surprise that comparatively judicially isolated countries with censorship agendas unpopular on the international stage would turn to solutions applied close to home to create an Internet in keeping with local custom. But such practices are starting to take root in other settings as well. In the United States, the state of Pennsylvania passed a law allowing the state attorney general to call a Web page to the attention of a local judge. If the judge finds probable cause that child pornography exists on that page, the attorney general can demand that any Internet service provider with Pennsylvania customers make sure that the page is not visible to those customers. Only one documented instance exists of the Pennsylvania attorney general actually invoking the formal process to demand action by a local Internet service provider.[39] The apparent threat of legal action alone is enough to make a system of informal notifications—and corresponding blocks—take place.

Such a law reflects a clear tension in American thinking about localizing the Internet. Christopher Cox (R-Calif.) has introduced to the U.S. Congress the Global Internet Freedom Act, which is described in Chapter 1 of this volume. It is a clarion call to make it the unabashed policy of America to maintain the Internet as a conveyor of information that repressive governments don't want their subjects to see. He sees the Internet as a precious conduit for the worldwide export of democratic ideas, and contemplates subsidizing technologies to route around local attempts at Internet censorship such as those described in this section. Such attempts, of course, are the very ones that Pennsylvania—and now other Western states and countries—are beginning to undertake to bring the Internet in line with their respective laws.

Straightforwardly argued from the accepted imposition of territorial regulation in physical space, attempts to localize the global Internet seem perfectly reasonable. That is why Jack Goldsmith's chapter in this volume is so compelling: he struggles to understand why the existence of the Internet poses any really new problems for jurisdiction and governance, and largely concludes that it doesn't, or, but for enforcement difficulties, shouldn't.

Yet Post's answer to Goldsmith resonates, too. He recognizes that information is an atomic unit of a free society, and a medium that permits such extraordinary information access and manipulation by individuals so effortlessly across distances—as speakers, browsers, searchers, and consumers—is one that can be more than a new way of shopping, checking the weather, or watching traditional television at user-selected times.

As the Internet becomes part of daily living rather than a place to visit, its rough edges are smoothed and its extremes tamed by sovereigns wanting to protect consumers, prevent network resource abuse, and eliminate speech deemed harmful. The tools are now within reach to permit sovereigns with competing sets of rules to play down their differences—whether by countenancing global privatization of some Internet governance issues through organizations like ICANN, coming to new international agreements on substance and procedure to reduce the friction caused by transborder data flows, or by a "live and let live" set of localization technologies to shape the Internet to suit the respective societies it touches.

What we might gain in easing jurisdictional tensions we could stand to lose in revolutionary capacity. The point of inflection at which the World Wide Web sits asks us to choose which we value more—international harmony and diversity that include censorship smacking of repression, or an unavoidable baseline of freedom of expression that permits harmful speech along with constructive speech. Can those who wish for civil liberty without child pornography and rampant copyright infringement have it both ways?

Barlow wrote: "We cannot separate the air that chokes from the air upon which wings beat."[40] But governments are likely to try. The battles to watch, then, are not abstruse jurisdictional ones that Goldsmith rightly points out as more or less settled or stale whether on or off the Internet, but rather the dueling trajectories by which we embrace the Internet's freedom and curse its anarchy, love its instantaneous, global scope and regret the refuge it offers to those who lie, cheat, and steal at a distance.

3. Against Cyberanarchy

Jack L. Goldsmith

The Supreme Court's partial invalidation of the Communications Decency Act on First Amendment grounds[1] raises the more fundamental question of whether the state can regulate cyberspace at all.[2] Several commentators, whom I shall call "regulation skeptics," have argued that it cannot.[3] Some courts have also expressed skepticism.[4] The popular and technical press are full of similar claims.[5]

The regulation skeptics make both descriptive and normative claims. On the descriptive side, they claim that the application of geographically based conceptions of legal regulation and choice of law to a-geographical cyberspace activity either makes no sense or leads to hopeless confusion. On the normative side, they argue that because cyberspace transactions occur "simultaneously and equally" in all national jurisdictions, regulation of the flow of this information by any particular national jurisdiction illegitimately produces significant negative spillover effects in other jurisdictions. They also claim that the architecture of cyberspace precludes notice of governing law that is crucial to the law's legitimacy. In contrast, they argue, cyberspace participants are much better positioned than national regulators to design comprehensive legal rules that would both internalize the costs of cyberspace activity and give proper notice to cyberspace participants. The regulation skeptics conclude from these arguments that national regulators should "defer to the self-regulatory efforts of Cyberspace participants."[6]

This chapter challenges the skeptics' arguments and their conclusion. The skeptics make three basic errors. First, they overstate the differences between cyberspace transactions and other transnational transactions. Both involve people in real space in one territorial jurisdiction transacting with people in real space in another territorial jurisdiction in a way that sometimes causes real-world harms. In both contexts, the state in which the harms are suffered has a legitimate interest in regulating the activity that produces the harms.

31

Second, the skeptics do not attend to the distinction between default laws and mandatory laws. Their ultimate normative claim that cyberspace should be self-regulated makes sense with respect to default laws that, by definition, private parties can modify to fit their needs. It makes much less sense with respect to mandatory or regulatory laws that, for paternalistic reasons or in order to protect third parties, place limits on private legal ordering. Third, the skeptics underestimate the potential of traditional legal tools and technology to resolve the multijurisdictional regulatory problems implicated by cyberspace. Cyberspace transactions do not inherently warrant any more deference by national regulators, and are not significantly less resistant to the tools of conflict of laws, than other transnational transactions.

Some caveats are in order up front. This chapter argues only that regulation of cyberspace is feasible and legitimate from the perspective of jurisdiction and choice of law. It does not argue that cyberspace regulation is a good idea, and it does not take a position on the merits of particular regulations beyond their jurisdictional legitimacy. For example, it does not examine whether particular national regulations of the Internet promote democracy, or are efficient, or are good or bad for humanity. Similarly, this chapter does not consider substantive limitations on cyberspace regulation such as may be found in the Bill of Rights or international human rights law. Resolution of these substantive regulatory issues turns in part on contested normative judgments and difficult context-specific, cost-benefit analyses that are far beyond this chapter's scope. But resolution of these issues also turns on how we understand the jurisdictional confusions that arise when national regulation, which has traditionally been understood primarily in geographical terms, applies to a phenomenon that appears to resist geographical orientation. This jurisdictional puzzle is the focus of this article.

In addition, this chapter does not deny that the new communication technologies known as cyberspace will lead to changes in governmental regulation. Such changes are to be expected when the speed of communication dramatically increases and the cost of communication dramatically decreases. The invention of the telegraph, the telephone, the radio, the television, and the satellite, among many other communication advances, all possessed these characteristics. And they all gave rise to societal and regulatory changes.[7] So too will cyberspace. But the skeptics claim much more than that cyberspace necessitates changes in governmental regulation. They claim that cyberspace is so different from other communication media that it will, or should, resist all governmental regulation. My aim here is to show why this claim is flawed, and to explain in general terms how traditional tools of jurisdiction and choice of law apply to cyberspace transactions.

Section I of this chapter summarizes the regulation skeptics' claims. Section II provides a richer account than that provided by the skeptics of the realities of real-space multijurisdictional conflicts, and of the tools available to manage such conflicts. Section III analyzes the skeptics' descriptive claim that national regulation of cyberspace is infeasible. Section IV analyzes their normative claim that such regulation is illegitimate. Section V sketches a model for grounding cyberspace transactions in real-space law.

The Regulation Skeptics' Claims

People transacting in cyberspace do things that would be regulated by state, national, or international law if the transactions occurred in person or by telephone or mail. They defame, invade privacy, harass, and commit business torts.[8] They make and breach contracts.[9] They distribute pornography and swap bombmaking tips.[10] They infringe on trademarks, violate copyrights, and steal data.[11] They issue fraudulent securities and restrict competition.[12] And so on.

Are these and other cyberspace activities governed by the same laws that govern similar transnational activities mediated in person, or by phone, or by mail? If so, which jurisdiction's law governs? If not, what governs instead?

The regulation skeptics' analysis of these questions makes two sets of assumptions. The first concerns the nature of legal regulation of noncyberspace events.[13] The skeptics tend to conceptualize a nation's legal authority as extending to its territorial borders and not beyond. This conception makes them skeptical about the legitimacy of one nation regulating activities that take place in another. And it leads them to believe that transnational disputes must be resolved by choice-of-law rules that select a unique governing law on the basis of *where* an event occurs or *where* transacting parties are located. On this view, tort liability is governed by the law of the place where the tort occurred and the validity of a contract is governed by the law of the place where the contract was made. Such choice-of-law rules are thought to promote rule-of-law values like uniformity (that is, every forum will apply the same law in a given case), predictability, and certainty. And they are supposed to give the parties to transnational transactions reasonable notice of governing law.

The skeptics' second set of assumptions concerns the architecture of cyberspace. They view cyberspace as a unique "boundary-destroying" means of communication. Internet protocol addresses do not necessarily correlate with a physical location. As a result, the skeptics assert, persons transacting in cyberspace often do not, and cannot, know each other's physical location.[14] In addition, information mediated by certain cyberspace services appears "simultaneously and equally in all jurisdictions" around the world.[15] A Web page in Illinois can be accessed from and thus appear in any geographical jurisdiction that is plugged in to the World Wide Web. When I participate in an online discussion group, my messages can appear simultaneously in every geographical jurisdiction in which persons participate in the group. In neither case can I control, or even know about, the geographical flow of the information that I upload or transmit.

It is against this background that the skeptics make their descriptive and normative claims. Descriptively, they claim that cyberspace is a borderless medium that resists regulation conceived in geographical terms.[16] One reason is that information transmitted by cyberspace can easily flow across national borders without detection.[17] Another reason is that it is senseless to apply geographically configured choice-of-law rules to a-geographical cyberspace activities.[18] A third reason is that regulation of the local effects of cyberspace information flows permits all nations simultaneously to regulate all Web-based transactions.[19] The result is multiple and inconsistent regulation of the same activity. A final reason is that the architecture of cyberspace enables its users to route around or otherwise evade territorial regulation.[20]

The skeptics' normative arguments build on these assumptions. Their essential normative claim is that it is illegitimate for any particular nation to regulate the local effects of multijurisdictional cyberspace activity. This is so for three reasons. First, such regulation will often apply to acts abroad, and will thus be impermissibly extraterritorial.[21] Second, because cyberspace information flows appear in every jurisdiction simultaneously, unilateral regulation of these flows will illegitimately affect the regulatory efforts of other nations and the cyberspace activities of parties in other jurisdictions.[22] Third is the problem of notice. The skeptics argue that because a person transacting in cyberspace does not know when or whether his or her activity produces effects in a particular jurisdiction, he or she lacks notice about governing law and therefore cannot conform his or her behavior to it.[23] They claim that under these conditions, it is unfair to apply law to his or her cyberspace activities. The skeptics believe that all three of these problems can be avoided by cyberspace self-regulation.

To make these claims more concrete, consider the predicament of one of the scores of companies that offer, sell, and deliver products on the World Wide Web. Assume that the Web page of a fictional Seattle-based company, Digitalbook.com, offers digital books for sale and delivery over the Web. One book it offers for sale is *Lady Chatterley's Lover*. This offer extends to, and can be accepted by, computer users in every country with access to the Web. Assume that in Singapore the sale of pornography is criminal, and that Singapore deems *Lady Chatterley's Lover* to be pornographic. Assume further that Digitalbook.com's terms of sale contain a term that violates English consumer protection laws, and that the publication of Digitalbook.com's *Lady Chatterley's Lover* in England would infringe upon the rights of the novel's English copyright owner. Digitalbook.com sells and sends copies of *Lady Chatterley's Lover* to two people whose addresses (say, anonymous@aol.com and anonymous@msn.com) do not reveal their physical location but who, unbeknownst to Digitalbook.com, live and receive the book in Singapore and London, respectively.

The skeptics claim that it is difficult for courts in Singapore or England to regulate disputes involving these transactions in accordance with geographical choice-of-law rules. In addition, they argue that English and Singaporean regulations will expose Digitalbook.com to potentially inconsistent obligations. Finally, the skeptics claim that Digitalbook.com can easily evade the Singaporean and English regulations by sending unstoppable digital information into these countries from a locale beyond their enforcement jurisdiction.

On the normative side, the skeptics are concerned that the application of English and Singaporean law to regulate Digitalbook.com's transactions constitutes an impermissible extraterritorial regulation of a U.S. corporation. Because Digitalbook.com might bow to the English and Singaporean regulations, and because the company cannot limit its cyberspace information flows by geography, the English and Singaporean regulations might cause it to withdraw *Lady Chatterley's Lover* everywhere or to raise its price. The English and Singaporean regulations would thus affect Digitalbook.com's behavior in the United States and adversely affect the purchasing opportunities of parties in other countries. The skeptics believe these negative spillover effects of the national regulations are illegitimate. They also think it is unfair for England and Singapore to apply their laws in this situation because Digitalbook.com had no way of knowing that it sold and delivered a book to consumers in these countries.

Real-Space Jurisdiction Conflict Management

The skeptics are in the grip of a 19th century territorialist conception of how real space is regulated and how real-space conflicts of law are resolved.[24] This conception was repudiated in the middle of this century.[25] The skeptics' first mistake, therefore, is to measure the feasibility and legitimacy of national regulation of cyberspace against a repudiated yardstick. This section offers a more accurate picture of real-space jurisdictional conflict management as a prelude to analysis of the skeptics' claims.

Three factors led to the overthrow of the traditional approach to choice of law.[26] The first was significant changes in the world. Changes in transportation, communication, and in the scope of corporate activity led to an unprecedented increase in multijurisdictional activity. These changes put pressure on the rigid territorialist conception that purported to identify a single legitimate governing law for transborder activity on the basis of discrete territorial contacts. So too did the rise of the regulatory state, which led to more caustic public policy differences among jurisdictions, and which pressured the interested forum to apply local regulations whenever possible.[27]

A second factor, legal realism, contributed to the demise of hermetic territorialism. All conflict-of-laws problems by definition have connections to two or more territorial jurisdictions. The legal realists showed that nothing in the logic of territorialism justified legal regulation by any one of these territories rather than another.[28] They also argued that a forum's decision to apply foreign law was always determined by local domestic policies.[29] This established the theoretical foundation for the *lex fori* orientation that has dominated choice of law ever since.

A third factor, legal positivism, exacerbated the problem of finding a unique governing law in transactional cases. Courts avoided many choice-of-law problems in such cases by applying universal customary laws tied to no particular sovereign authority, such as the law merchant, the law maritime, and the law of nations.[30] But positivism's insistence on a sovereign source for every rule of decision undermined judicial reliance on these laws.[31] It also contributed to the waning of universal choice-of-law rules that courts applied in circumstances in which transnational customary laws did not govern. In the United States, for example, the general uniformity of choice-of-law approaches that characterized the 19th century gave way in the 20th century to a plethora of choice-of-law regimes.[32] As different jurisdictions adopted different choice-of-law regimes, the goal of a single governing law for transjurisdictional transactions was further frustrated.[33]

These factors did not completely undermine traditional views about territorial regulation. But they did lead to an expansion of the permissible bases for territorial jurisdiction. Today, the Constitution permits a state to apply its law if it has a "significant contact or significant aggregation of contacts, creating state interests, such that choice of its law is neither arbitrary nor fundamentally unfair."[34] In practice, this standard is notoriously easy to satisfy.[35] It prohibits the application of local law only when the forum state has no interest in the case because the substance of the lawsuit has no relationship to the state. Customary international law limits on a nation's regulation of extraterritorial events are less clear because few international decisions are on point, and because state practice does not reveal a settled custom. Nonetheless, it seems clear that customary international law, like the United States Constitution, permits a nation to apply its law to extraterritorial behavior with substantial local effects.[36] In addition, both the Constitution and international law permit a nation or state to regulate the extraterritorial conduct of a citizen or domiciliary.[37] In short, in modern times a transaction can legitimately be regulated by the jurisdiction where the transaction occurs, the jurisdictions where significant effects of the transaction are felt, and the jurisdictions where the parties burdened by the regulation are from.

This expansion of the permissible bases for the application of local law has revolutionized conflict of laws in the second half of this century. Any number of choice-of-law regimes are now consistent with constitutional and international law. The earlier belief in a unique governing law for all transnational activities has given way to the view that more than one jurisdiction can legitimately apply its law to the same transnational activity.[38] The uniformity promised by the traditional approach has thus been replaced by the reality of overlapping jurisdictional authority. This means that the application of one jurisdiction's law often comes at the expense of the nonapplication of the conflicting laws of other interested jurisdictions. Because choice-of-law rules often differ from jurisdiction to jurisdiction, and because a forum applies its own choice-of-law rules, the choice of forum is now often critical to the selection of governing law. In this milieu, *ex ante* notice of a specific governing law is no longer a realistic goal in many transnational situations. Not surprisingly, the Constitution and international law impose very weak notice requirements on the application of local law to extraterritorial activity.

This modern world of jurisdictional conflict poses obvious difficulties for participants in transnational transactions. To understand these problems and their resolution, it is important to distinguish between default laws and mandatory laws. For present purposes, a default law can be understood as one that presumptively governs a particular relationship or transaction, but that can be modified or circumvented by the parties in the relationship or transaction. The default laws of different countries can create a conflict of laws. For example, the estate of a U.S. national who dies intestate in England, which is his domicile, could potentially be subject to the succession rules of either country. Similarly, a contract made in one country for delivery of products in another could be subject to the remedies regime of either country.

Parties in such transnational relationships can alleviate choice-of-law uncertainty with respect to default rules by contracting for specific terms, by selecting a governing law, or both.[39] Most contractual choice-of-law clauses govern the contracts within which they are embedded. But the scope of this private legal control is not limited to traditional contractual issues. In many circumstances, parties can agree to a governing law for torts and related actions that arise from their contractual relations.[40] They can also specify the governing law for matters ranging from intellectual property to trusts and estates to internal corporate affairs.[41]

The possibilities for private legal ordering are not limitless. Every nation has mandatory laws that govern particular transactions or relationships regardless of the wishes of the parties. The primary justifications for such laws are paternalism and protection of third parties.[42] Mandatory laws range from limits on contractual capacity to criminal law to securities and antitrust law. Like default laws, mandatory laws differ in content and scope from jurisdiction to jurisdiction. Unlike conflicts of default laws, conflicts of mandatory laws cannot be resolved easily by private contract.[43] They can, in theory, be resolved by *public* contract—international agreements that embrace uniform international rules[44] or uniform choice-of-law rules.[45] Such solutions are increasingly prominent but still relatively rare. Moreover, these attempts at international uniformity are often limited to default rules, and are littered with mandatory law exceptions.[46]

This discussion shows that conflicts of law can arise when parties to a transnational transaction do not specify the governing default law, or when the transaction implicates a mandatory law that conflicts with the otherwise-applicable law. Absent a governing international law, transnational activity in these contexts will usually be governed by the law of a single jurisdiction.[47] And absent international choice-of-law rules, the forum's choice-of-law rules will determine the governing law. In regulatory contexts, the forum will invariably apply local law.[48] But regardless of which substantive law the forum applies, the application of that law will frequently create spillover effects on activities in other countries and on the ability of other interested nations to apply their own law. In our increasingly integrated world, these spillover effects are likely to extend to many countries.[49]

Consider, for example, the Supreme Court's decision in *Hartford Fire Insurance Co. v. California*.[50] The Court held that the concerted refusal by London reinsurers to sell certain types of reinsurance to insurers in the United States violated the Sherman Act. The rein-surers' acts in England were legal under English law. But the Court determined that the reinsurers were nonetheless subject to U.S. regu-lation because their actions "produced substantial effect[s]" in the United States.[51] U.S. law thus regulated the activities of English companies in England at the expense of the nonapplication of English law. Similarly, had an English court applied English law to adjudge the reinsurers' acts to be legal, it would have produced spillover effects on consumers in the United States, and would have come at the expense of the nonapplication of U.S. law. No matter which law governed the reinsurers' acts, the application of that law would have produced spillover effects on the English reinsurers' activities in other jurisdictions, and on the activities of persons in other jurisdic-tions adversely affected by the reinsurers' acts.

A similar phenomenon occurs in many domestic and international conflicts contexts. For example, the European Commission recently imposed strict conditions on a merger (already approved by the Federal Trade Commission) between two American companies with no manufacturing facilities in Europe.[52] Minnesota applied its pro-plaintiff stacking rules for automobile insurance coverage to an acci-dent in Wisconsin among Wisconsin residents.[53] A United States federal grand jury ordered the local branch of a foreign bank, a nonparty, to disclose bank records in the Bahamas in possible viola-tion of Bahamian law.[54] California applied its workmen's compensa-tion law to benefit an employee of a California corporation who suffered a tort while working in Alaska—even though Alaska pur-ported to make its worker's compensation scheme exclusive, and even though the employment contract specified that Alaska law governed.[55] New York applied its tort law to a car accident in Can-ada.[56] California taxed a British corporation on the basis of the Cali-fornia portion of its world profits.[57]

In these situations and countless others, one jurisdiction regulates extraterritorial conduct in a way that invariably affects individual behavior and regulatory efforts in other jurisdictions. These spillover effects constitute the central problem of modern conflict of laws. The problem is pervasive. It is also inevitable, because the price of eliminating these spillovers—abolishing national or subnational lawmaking entities, or eliminating transnational activity—is prohibi-tively high. Most of the dizzying array of modern choice-of-law methodologies are devoted to minimizing these spillovers while at the same time preserving the sovereign prerogative to regulate effects within national borders.[58] International harmonization efforts seek to achieve similar aims, often at the expense of national prerogatives.[59]

There is widespread debate about which approach, or combination of approaches, is preferable. Resolution of this debate is less important for present purposes than two uncontested assumptions that underlie it. The first assumption is that in the absence of consensual international solutions, prevailing concepts of territorial sovereignty permit a nation to regulate the local effects of extraterritorial conduct even if this regulation produces spillover effects in other jurisdictions. The second assumption is that such spillover effects are a commonplace consequence of the unilateral application of any particular law to transnational activity in our increasingly interconnected world. It is against this background that the skeptics' descriptive and normative claims must be assessed.

Is Cyberspace Regulation Feasible?

This section argues that the skeptics' claims about the infeasibility of national regulation of cyberspace rest on an underappreciation of the realities of modern conflict of laws, and of the legal and technological tools available to resolve multijurisdictional cyberspace conflicts. From the perspective of jurisdiction and choice of law, regulation of cyberspace transactions is no less feasible than regulation of other transnational transactions.

Default Laws and Private Ordering in Cyberspace

Cyberspace transactions that implicate default laws, like other transnational transactions that implicate such laws, are subject to private legal ordering. The architecture of cyberspace facilitates this private ordering and thus enables cyberspace participants to avoid many transnational conflicts of law.

At the most basic level, private ordering is facilitated by the technical standards that define and limit cyberspace.[60] To participate in the Internet function known as the World Wide Web, users must consent to the Transmission Control Protocol/Internet Protocol (TCP/IP) standards that define the Internet as well as to the Hypertext Markup Language (HTML) standards that more particularly define the Web. Similarly, sending e-mail over the Internet requires the sender to use TCP/IP standards and particular e-mail protocols. One's experience of cyberspace is further defined and limited by the more particular communication standards embedded in software.[61] For example, within the range of what TCP/IP and HTML permit, an individual's communication by the World Wide Web will be shaped and limited by (among many other things) one's choice of browsers and search engines. These and countless other technical standard choices order behavior in cyberspace. In this sense, access to different cyberspace networks and communities is always conditioned on the accessors' consent to the array of technical standards that define these networks and communities.

Technical standards cannot comprehensively specify acceptable behavior in cyberspace. Within the range of what these standards permit, information flows might violate network norms or territorial laws. Many network norms are promulgated and enforced informally. A more formal method to establish private legal orders in cyberspace is to condition access to particular networks on consent to a particular legal regime.

This regime could take several forms. It could be a local, national, or international law. When you buy a Dell computer through the company's Web page from anywhere in the world, you agree that "[a]ny claim relating to, and the use of, this Site and the materials contained herein is governed by the laws of the state of Texas."[62] Alternatively, the chosen law could be a free-standing model law attached to no particular sovereign but available to be incorporated by contract. For example, parties to a commercial transaction over the Internet could agree that their transaction is governed by UNIDROIT Principles or the Uniform Customs and Practice for Documentary Credits.[63] Or the governing law could be the contractual terms themselves.[64] Waivers and exclusions operate as private law in this way. So too do chat rooms, discussion lists, and local area networks that condition participation on the user's consent to community norms specified in a contract.

Cyberspace architecture can also help to establish other aspects of a private legal order. Through conditioned access, cyberspace users can consent to have subsequent disputes resolved by courts, arbitrators, systems operators, or even "virtual magistrates."[65] They can also establish private enforcement regimes. Technical standards operate as an enforcer of sorts by defining and limiting cyberspace activity. For example, software filters can block or condition access to certain information, and various technologies perform compliance monitoring functions.[66] In addition, the gatekeeper of each cyberspace community can cut off entry for noncompliance with the community rules, or punish a user for bad acts by drawing on a bond (perhaps simply a credit card) put up as a condition on the user's entry.[67]

Many have proposed a structure for private legal ordering of cyberspace along the lines just sketched.[68] There is nothing remarkable about this structure. It differs little from the legal structure of other private groups, such as churches, merchants, families, clubs, and corporations, which have analogous consent-based governing laws, dispute resolution mechanisms, and private enforcement regimes.[69] But just as private ordering is often not a comprehensive solution to the regulation of real-space private groups, private ordering will not be a comprehensive solution to the regulation of cyberspace either.

In part this is because how to generate consent across cyberspace networks remains an open question. Conditioning access on consent to a governing legal regime is relatively easy at the entry point of a cyberspace network. In theory, it is just as easy to generate such consent at the interface between networks. It is commonplace to click on a hypertext link and be greeted by a message that conditions further access on presentation of an identification code, or credit card number, or personal information such as age and address. A similar demand for consent to a particular legal regime could be added as a condition for access. However, this process might become confusing; the technological and conceptual details of consenting to and coordinating different legal regimes as one works one's way through dozens of cyberspace networks remain to be worked out.[70] In addition, the generation of legal consent across networks will impose time and other costs that are anathema to many cyberspace users.

An important additional difficulty is that many cyberspace activities affect noncyberspace participants with whom *ex ante* consent to a private legal regime will not be possible. Cyberspace is not, as the skeptics often assume, a self-enclosed regime. A communication in cyberspace often has consequences for persons outside the computer network in which the communication took place. For example, a book uploaded on the Net can violate an author's copyright; a chat room participant can defame someone outside the chat room; terrorists can promulgate bomb-making or kidnapping tips; merchants can conspire to fix prices by e-mail; a corporation can issue a fraudulent security; a pornographer can sell kiddie porn; Internet gambling can decrease in-state gambling revenues and cause family strife; and so on. In these and many other ways, communications by cyberspace produce harmful, real-world effects on those who have not consented to the private ordering of the cyberspace community.

Finally, even if the hurdles to consent can be surmounted, consent-based legal orders are limited by a variety of national mandatory law restrictions.[71] These mandatory laws define who may consent to these private regimes. For example, the laws prevent persons of certain ages from entering into certain types of contracts. They also limit the form and scope of such consent. The consideration requirement and limitations on liquidated damages clauses fall into this category, as do requirements that the law chosen by the parties have a reasonable relationship to the subject matter of the contract. Some mandatory laws also limit the internal and external activities of the group's activities. Criminal law, for example, falls in this category.

Private legal ordering thus has the potential to resolve many, but not all, of the challenges posed by multijurisdictional cyberspace activity. Cyberspace activities for which *ex ante* consent to a governing legal regime is either infeasible or unenforceable are not amenable to private ordering. Such activities remain subject to the skeptics' concerns about multiple or extraterritorial national regulation.

The Limits of Enforcement Jurisdiction

The skeptics' concerns are further attenuated, however, by limitations on every nation's ability to enforce its laws. A nation can purport to regulate activity that takes place anywhere. The Island of Tobago can *enact* a law that purports to bind the rights of the whole world.[72] But the effective scope of this law depends on Tobago's ability to *enforce* it. And in general a nation can only enforce its laws against (a) persons with a presence or assets in the nation's territory, (b) persons over whom the nation can obtain personal jurisdiction and enforce a default judgment against abroad, or (c) persons whom the nation can successfully extradite.[73]

A defendant's physical presence or assets within the territory remain the primary basis for a nation or state to enforce its laws.

The large majority of persons who transact in cyberspace have no presence or assets in the jurisdictions that wish to regulate their information flows in cyberspace. Such regulations are thus likely to apply primarily to Internet service providers and Internet users with a physical presence in the regulating jurisdiction. Cyberspace users in other territorial jurisdictions will indirectly feel the effect of the regulations to the extent that they are dependent on service or content providers with a presence in the regulating jurisdiction.[74] But for almost all users, there will be no threat of extraterritorial legal liability because of a lack of presence in the regulating jurisdictions.

A nation or state can also enforce its laws over an entity with no local presence or assets if it can obtain personal jurisdiction over the entity and enforce a local default judgment against that entity abroad. The domestic interstate context presents a much greater threat in this regard than does the international context. This is because the Full Faith and Credit Clause requires a state to enforce the default judgment of a sister state that had personal jurisdiction over the defendant.[75] This threat is attenuated, however, by constitutional limits on a state's assertion of personal jurisdiction. The Due Process Clauses prohibit a state from asserting personal jurisdiction over an entity with no local presence unless the entity has purposefully directed its activities to the forum state and the assertion of jurisdiction is reasonable.[76]

Application of this standard to cyberspace activities presents special difficulties. Under standard assumptions about cyberspace architecture, persons can upload or transmit information knowing that it could reach any and all jurisdictions, but not knowing which particular jurisdiction it might reach. Can every state where these transmissions appear assert specific personal jurisdiction over the agent of the information under the purposeful availment and reasonableness tests?

Full consideration of this issue is far beyond this chapter's scope.[77] I simply wish to point out why there is relatively little reason at present, and even less reason in the near future, to believe that the mere introduction of information into cyberspace will *by itself* suffice for personal jurisdiction over the agent of the transmission in every state where the information appears. Most courts have required something more than mere placement of information on a Web page in one state as a basis for personal jurisdiction in another state where

45

the Web page is accessed.[78] For a variety of reasons, these decisions have limited specific personal jurisdiction to cases in which there are independent indicia that the out-of-state defendant knowingly and purposefully directed the effects of out-of-state conduct to a particular state where the acts were deemed illegal.

Given the skeptics' assumptions about cyberspace architecture, this conclusion appears appropriate. It seems unfair to expose a content provider to personal jurisdiction in all 50 states for the mere act of uploading information on a computer if the provider cannot take affordable precautions to avoid simultaneous multijurisdictional effects. But we shall see below that the skeptics' architectual assumptions are inaccurate. It is already possible for content providers to take measures to achieve significant control over information flows. And filtering and identification technology promise greater control at less cost. In cyberspace as in real space, the ultimate meaning of "purposeful availment" and "reasonableness" will depend on the cost and feasibility of information flow control.[79] As such control becomes more feasible and less costly, personal jurisdiction over cyberspace activities will become functionally identical to personal jurisdiction over real-space activities.

This detour into the technicalities of personal jurisdiction was necessitated by a worry about the extraterritorial enforcement of local default judgments against nonlocal cyberspace users within the American federal system. Such concerns are less pronounced in the international context. In contrast to the domestic interstate context, customary international law imposes few enforceable controls on a country's assertion of personal jurisdiction, and there are few treaties on the subject.[80] However, also in contrast to domestic law, there is no full faith and credit obligation to enforce foreign judgments in the international sphere.[81] If one country exercises personal jurisdiction on an exorbitant basis, the resulting judgment is unlikely to be enforced in another country.[82] In addition, local public policy exceptions to the enforcement of foreign judgments are relatively commonplace in the international sphere, especially when the foreign judgment flies in the face of the enforcing state's regulatory regime.[83] For these reasons, there is little concern that a foreign default judgment will be enforceable against cyberspace users who live outside of the regulating jurisdiction.

The final way that a nation can enforce its regulations against persons outside of its jurisdiction is by seeking extradition. In the

United States, extradition among the several states is regulated by Article IV of the Constitution and the federal extradition law.[84] As a general matter, State A must accede to the proper demand of State B for the surrender of a fugitive who committed an act in State B that State B considers a crime. Nonetheless, a person who in State A transmits information flows that appear in and constitute a crime in State B will not likely be subject to extradition to State B under these provisions. The reason is the extradition obligation only extends to fugitives who have fled State B, and these terms have long been limited to persons who were *physically present* in the demanding state at the time of the crime's commission.[85] A different, but equally forceful, limitation applies to international extradition. International extradition is governed largely by treaty.[86] A pervasive feature of modern extradition treaties is the principle of double criminality. This principle requires that the charged offense be criminal in both the requesting and the requested jurisdictions.[87] This principle, and its animating rationale, make it unlikely that there will be international cooperation in the enforcement of exorbitant unilateral criminal regulations of cyberspace events.

This review of transnational enforcement jurisdiction makes clear that the skeptics exaggerate the threat of multiple regulation of cyberspace information flows. This threat must be measured by a regulation's enforceable scope, not by its putative scope. And the enforceable scope is relatively narrow. It extends only to individual users or system operators with presence or assets in the enforcement jurisdiction, or (in the United States) to entities that take extra steps to target cyberspace information flows to states where such information flows are illegal. Such regulatory exposure is a significant concern for cyberspace participants. But it is precisely how regulatory exposure operates in real space. And it is far less significant than the skeptics' hyperbolic claim that *all* users of the Web will be simultaneously subject to *all* national regulations.[88]

Even with these limitations, the skeptics worry that an individual cyberspace content provider in one jurisdiction faces *potential* liability in another jurisdiction when that provider places information on the Internet. This potential liability can become an unforeseen reality when the provider travels to the regulating jurisdiction, or moves assets there. Such potential liability in turn affects the provider's activities at home and thus can be viewed as a weak form of extraterritorial regulation. This form of regulation is a theoretical possibility, but it should not be exaggerated. No nation has as yet imposed liability on a content provider for unforeseen effects in an unknown jurisdiction. The threat of such liability will lessen as content providers continue to gain means to control information flows. It is also conceivable that weak normative limitations might exist or develop to prevent a jurisdiction from regulating local effects that were truly unforeseeable or uncontrollable. The point for now is that even in the absence of such limits, this potential threat of liability is relatively insignificant and does not come close to the skeptics' broad descriptive claims about massive multiple regulation of individual users.

Indirect Regulation of Extraterritorial Activity

Indeed, if the limits on enforcement jurisdiction support any of the skeptics' descriptive claims, it is their somewhat different claim that because of the potential for regulation evasion, cyberspace transactions are beyond the regulatory powers of territorial governments.[89] Cyberspace content providers can, at some cost, shift the source of their information flows to jurisdictions beyond the enforceable scope of national regulation and thus continue information transmissions into the regulating jurisdiction.[90] For example, they can relocate in geographical space, or employ telnet or anonymous remailers to make the geographical source of their content difficult to discern.[91] These and related regulatory evasion techniques can make it difficult for a nation to regulate the extraterritorial supply side of harmful cyberspace activity.

Regulation evasion of this sort is not limited to cyberspace. For example, corporations reincorporate to avoid mandatory laws and criminals launder money offshore. Closer to point, offshore regulation evasion has been a prominent characteristic of other communications media. For example, Radio Free Europe broadcasted from western Europe into the former Soviet Union but lacked a regulatable presence there.[92] Similarly, television signals are sometimes broadcasted from abroad by an entity with no local presence. The extraterritorial source of these and many other noncyberspace activities is beyond the enforceable scope of local regulation. But this does not mean that local regulation is inefficacious. In cyberspace as in real space, offshore regulation evasion does not prevent a nation from regulating the extraterritorial activity.

This is so because a nation can regulate people and equipment in its territory to control the local effects of the extraterritorial activity.

Such indirect regulation is how nations have, with varying degrees of success, regulated local harms caused by other communications media with offshore sources and no local presence.[93] And it is how nations have begun to regulate local harms caused by offshore Internet content providers. For example, nations penalize in-state end-users who obtain and use illegal content or who otherwise participate in an illegal cyberspace transaction.[94] They also regulate the local means through which foreign content is transmitted. For example, they impose screening obligations on in-state Internet service providers and other entities that supply or transmit information.[95] Or they regulate in-state hardware and software through which such transmissions are received. Or they regulate the local financial intermediaries that make commercial transactions on the Internet possible.[96]

These and related regulations of domestic persons and property make it more costly, and thus, more difficult for in-state users to obtain content from, or transact with, regulation evaders abroad. In this fashion a nation can indirectly regulate the extraterritorial supply of prohibited content even though the source of the content is beyond its enforcement jurisdiction and even though it cannot easily stop transmission at the border. These various forms of indirect regulation will not be perfect in the sense of eliminating regulation evasion. But few regulations are perfect in this sense, and regulation need not be perfect in this sense to be effective.[97] The question is always whether the regulation will heighten the costs of the activity sufficiently to achieve its acceptable control from whatever normative perspective is appropriate.

In the cyberspace regulation context, the answer to this question depends on empirical and technological issues that are unresolved and that will vary from context to context. The prodigious criticism of and lobbying efforts against proposed regulation of (among other things) digital goods, Internet gambling, and encryption technology suggest that governments can raise the costs of many cyberspace transactions to a significant degree. And of course unilateral national regulation is one of many regulation strategies at a nation's disposal. The point for now is simply that offshore regulation evasion does not, as the skeptics think, undermine a nation's ability to regulate cyberspace transactions. Although a nation will sometimes have difficulty in imposing liability on extraterritorial content providers, it can still significantly regulate the local effects of these providers' activities through laws aimed at local persons and entities.

Filtering

We have seen that the skeptics' worries about multiple or extraterritorial regulation of cyberspace activity do not extend to matters for which it is feasible and legal for cyberspace communities to establish private legal regimes, or to matters beyond a nation's enforcement jurisdiction.

But the possibility of extraterritorial and multiple regulations remains. Consider the Bavarian Justice Ministry's threat in December of 1995 to prosecute CompuServe for carrying online discussion groups containing material that violated German anti-pornography laws.[98] CompuServe responded by blocking access to these discussion groups in Germany. Because of the state of then-available technology, this action had the effect of blocking access to these discussion groups for all CompuServe users worldwide.[99] This effect is precisely what the skeptics fear from unilateral regulation of cyberspace. Germany enforced a mandatory law against an international access provider with a presence (office, staff, servers, etc.) in Germany. Faced with multiple regulatory regimes in the many places in which it did business, CompuServe bowed to the most restrictive. The consequence was massive extraterritorial regulation because the German regulation interrupted the flow and availability of the discussion groups for CompuServe clients everywhere in the world.

The skeptics frequently recount this story to show how unilateral national regulation of cyberspace can have multijurisdictional consequences.[100] But the rest of the story suggests a somewhat different lesson. After closing down transmission of the offending discussions, CompuServe offered its German users software that enabled them to block access to the offending discussion groups.[101] The company then began to search for a more centralized way to filter the illegal newsgroups in Germany alone. German prosecutors subsequently indicted a CompuServe executive, alleging that the company failed to implement such national-level filtering technology to prevent dissemination of other illegal information in Germany.[102] At about the same time, the German parliament enacted a law clarifying that cyberspace access providers are liable "if they are aware of the content" and fail to use *"technically possible and reasonable"* means to block it.[103]

The subsequent events of the CompuServe controversy, like the response to the Supreme Court's invalidation of the Communications Decency Act in *Reno*,[104] make clear the growing importance of information discrimination technology to the cyberspace regulation debate. Many jurisdictional challenges presented by cyberspace result from the purported inability of content providers to prevent information flows from appearing simultaneously in every jurisdiction. Thus far I have assumed, with the skeptics, that this is a necessary (and accurate) feature of cyberspace architecture. But it is not.[105] Cyberspace information can only appear in a geographical jurisdiction by virtue of hardware and software physically present in the jurisdiction. Available technology already permits governments and private entities to regulate the design and function of hardware and software to facilitate discrimination of cyberspace information flows along a variety of dimensions, including geography, network, and content.[106] This technology is relatively new and still relatively crude, but it is growing very quickly in both sophistication and effectiveness. This technology facilitates discrimination and control of information flows at any of several junctures along the cyberspace information stream.

At the most basic level, the content provider can take steps to control the flow of the information. This happens, for example, whenever a Web-page operator conditions access to the page on the users' presentation of information. Consider the many precautions taken by adult Web pages. Some pages simply warn minors or persons from certain geographical locations not to view or enter, and disclaim legal liability if they do.[107] Others condition access on proof of age or on membership in one of dozens of private age-verification services.[108] Others require potential end-users to send by fax or telephone information specifying age and geographical location.[109] Still others label or rate their pages to accommodate end-use filtering software, as described below. Finally, digital identification technology developed for Internet commerce provides a way to authenticate the identity of a party in a cyberspace transaction.[110] Although digital identification is usually used to verify who someone is, it can also be used to verify other facts about cyberspace users, such as their nationality, domicile, or permanent address.

At the other end of the distribution chain, end-users can employ software filters to block out or discriminate among information flows.[111] Parental control software is the most prominent example of an end-user filter, but many businesses and other local area networks also employ these technologies. Content filters also can be imposed at junctures along the cyberspace information stream between content providers and end-users. They can be imposed, for example, at the network level or at the level of the Internet service provider. They can also assist governments in filtering information at the national level.[112] A government can choose to have no Internet links whatsoever and to regulate telephone and other communication lines to access providers in other countries.[113] China, Singapore, and the United Arab Emirates have taken the somewhat less severe steps of (a) regulating access to the Internet through centralized filtered servers and (b) requiring filters for in-state Internet service providers and end-users.[114] We have seen that Germany has chosen to hold liable Internet access providers who have knowledge of illegal content and fail to use "technically possible and reasonable" means to filter it.[115] The Federal Communications Commission recently required V-chip blocking technology to be placed in computers capable of receiving video broadcasting,[116] and pending anti-spam legislation would impose identification requirements on commercial e-mail senders and filtering requirements on Internet service providers.[117] There are numerous other possibilities.[118]

Although technological predictions are precarious, it seems likely that the techniques and technologies for controlling cyberspace information flows will continue to develop in scope and sophistication and will play an important role in resolving the jurisdictional quandaries presented by the "borderless" medium. Information is not particularly useful unless people can organize, select, and block it.[119] This is one reason why information filtering is an essential component of all communications media.[120] Filtering is especially important for cyberspace because the costs of information production and dissemination are extremely low, and thus information overload is a serious concern. Indeed, the explosive growth of the World Wide Web is directly attributable to the invention of identification and filtering technologies that made it possible to organize and select from the morass of available information.[121]

An additional reason that techniques for controlling cyberspace information flows are likely to be at least moderately successful is that so many participants in the cyberspace regulation debate—parents, businesses, content suppliers, service providers, governments, and even some anti-censorship civil libertarians[122]—desire such control. As Paul Resnick has pointed out, "meta-data systems . . . are going to be an important part of the Web, because they enable more sophisticated commerce, . . . communication, indexing, and searching services."[123] Many jurisdictions have already mandated the use of filtering and identification mechanisms.[124] Even in the absence of government mandates, content filtering and digital identification technologies have flourished for commercial reasons and in response to the threat of regulation, and have become de facto standards in many cyberspace contexts.

Many commentators are skeptical about these filtering and identification technologies.[125] They argue that content filters invariably both over- and underfilter, that identification technologies sometimes misidentify, and that some hackers will access prohibited information. These worries are to some degree well-founded. What is not well-founded, however, is the belief that imperfect regulation means ineffective regulation.[126] Real space is filled with similarly imperfect filtering and identification techniques: criminals crack safes and escape from jail, 15-year-olds visit bars with fake IDs, secret information is leaked to the press, and so on. In cyberspace as in real space, imperfections in filtering and identification regimes do not render the regimes ineffective.[127] Although the ultimate accuracy of cyberspace filtering and identification technologies remains an open question, there is little doubt that such technologies will contribute significantly to cyberspace regulation by enabling governments, content providers, end-users, and service providers to raise significantly the cost of accessing certain information. Indeed, this has already happened throughout cyberspace, where content filtering, conditioned access, and identification codes are pervasive.

The ability to control information flows alleviates the many cyberspace regulation problems that are premised on the assumption that information in cyberspace appears simultaneously in every jurisdiction. To see why, consider one set of differences between a newspaper publisher and a cyberspace content provider. It is relatively uncontroversial that a newspaper publisher is liable for harms caused wherever the newspaper is published or distributed. This seems appropriate because, among other reasons, we think the publisher can control the geographical locus of publication and distribution. Requiring such control imposes modest costs on the publisher; the publisher must, for example, keep abreast of regulatory developments in different jurisdictions and take steps to exclude publication and distribution in places where the publisher wants to avoid liability.

Now consider the cyberspace content provider. Many have an intuition that such content providers should not be liable for harms caused wherever the content appears.[128] The primary basis for this intuition is that the content provider cannot control the geographical and network distribution of his or her information flows. But this latter point is groundless. Content providers already have several means to control information flows.[129] As the cost of such control continues to drop, and the accuracy and ease of this control increase, cyberspace content providers will come to occupy the same position as the newspaper publisher. It will thus be appropriate in cyberspace, as in real space, for the law to impose small costs on both types of publishers to ensure that content does not appear in jurisdictions and networks where it is illegal.

International Harmonization

Private legal ordering, the limitations on enforcement jurisdiction, indirect regulation, and effective information flow control, taken together, go a long way toward redressing the skeptics' descriptive claims about the infeasibility of cyberspace regulation. These techniques will not resolve all conflict of laws in cyberspace any more than they do in real space. Nor will they definitively resolve the problem of the relative ease by which information suppliers can "relocate" into a safe haven outside of the regulating jurisdiction, a problem that also has many real-space analogies. When similar spillover and evasion problems have occurred with respect to non-cyberspace transactions, nations have responded with a variety of international harmonization strategies.

The same harmonization strategies are being used today to address the challenges presented by cyberspace transactions. A few examples will suffice. Several recent treaties and related multinational edicts have strengthened digital content owners' right to control the distribution and presentation of their property online.[130]

These harmonization efforts grow out of an international copyright regime that is more than one hundred years old.[131] The G8 economic powers have recently begun to coordinate regulatory efforts concerning cyberspace-related crimes in five areas: pedophilia and sexual exploitation, drug-trafficking, money-laundering, electronic fraud, and industrial and state espionage.[132] These initiatives mirror similar efforts to redress similar regulatory leakage problems in real-space contexts such as environmental policy, banking and insurance supervision, and antitrust regulation.[133] Several international organizations have drafted model laws and guidelines to facilitate Internet commerce and related digital certification issues.[134] There are scores of other international efforts in a variety of cyberspace-related contexts.

International harmonization is not always (or even usually) the best response to the spillovers and evasions that result from unilateral regulation.[135] And harmonization is often not easy to achieve. However, the proliferation of international organizations, combined with modern means of communication and transportation, has helped to facilitate international harmonization. Harmonization is especially likely in those contexts—like many aspects of criminal law enforcement—where nations' interests converge and the gains from cooperation are high. But nations sometimes lack the incentive to participate in international regimes, and there are often international and domestic political economy obstacles to harmonization.[136] It is too early to tell how successful international efforts will be in addressing the challenges of cyberspace. It is clear, however, that international harmonization will play an important role in nations' overall cyberspace-regulation strategy.

Residual Choice-of-Law Tools

The skeptics' implicit goal of eliminating all conflicts of laws that arise from cyberspace transactions is unrealistic. Private legal ordering, the limits of enforcement jurisdiction, indirect regulation of extraterritorial activity, filtering and identification technology, and international cooperation facilitate and rationalize legal regulation of cyberspace. These tools, however, will not eliminate all conflicts of laws in cyberspace any more than they do in real space. Transnational activity is too complex. As mentioned previously, the elimination of conflict of laws would require the elimination of decentralized lawmaking or of transnational activity.[137] In this light, the enormous increases in the pervasiveness and complexity of conflict of laws in this century can be viewed as an acceptable cost to a world that wishes to expand transnational activity while retaining decentralized lawmaking. As persistent conflicts become prohibitively costly to private parties and regulating nations, public or private international coordination or technological innovation becomes more attractive and thus more likely.

Short of these developments, transnational transactions in cyberspace, like transnational transactions mediated by telephone and mail, will continue to give rise to disputes that present challenging choice-of-law issues. For example, "Whose substantive legal rules apply to a defamatory message that is written by someone in Mexico, read by someone in Israel by means of an Internet server located in the United States, injuring the reputation of a Norwegian?"[138] Similarly,

> which of the many plausibly applicable bodies of copyright law do we consult to determine whether a hyperlink on a World Wide Web page located on a server in France and constructed by a Filipino citizen, which points to a server in Brazil that contains materials protected by German and French (but not Brazilian) copyright law, which is downloaded to a server in the United States and reposted to a Usenet newsgroup, constitutes a remediable infringement of copyright?[139]

It would be silly to try to formulate a general theory of how such issues should be resolved. One lesson of this century's many failures in top-down choice-of-law theorizing is that choice-of-law rules are most effective when they are grounded in and sensitive to the concrete details of particular legal contexts. This does not mean that standards are better than rules in this context. It simply means that in designing choice-of-law rules or standards, it is better to begin at the micro rather than macro level, and to examine recurrent fact patterns and implicated interests in discrete legal contexts rather than devise a general context-transcendent theory of conflicts.[140]

With these caveats in mind, I want to explain in very general terms why the residual choice-of-law problems implicated by cyberspace are not significantly different from those that are non-cyberspace conflicts. Cyberspace presents two related choice-of-law problems. The first is the problem of *complexity*. This problem concerns how to choose a single governing law for cyberspace activity that has multijurisdictional contacts. The second is the problem of *situs*. This problem concerns how to choose a governing law when the locus of activity cannot easily be pinpointed in geographical space. Both problems raise similar concerns. The choice of any dispositive geographical contact or any particular law in these cases will often seem arbitrary because several jurisdictions have a legitimate claim to apply their laws. Whatever law is chosen, seemingly genuine regulatory interests of the nations whose laws are not applied may be impaired.

The problems of complexity and situs are genuine. They are not, however, unique to cyberspace. Identical problems arise all the time in real space. In fact, they inhere in every true conflict of laws. Consider the problem of complexity. The hypotheticals concerning copyright infringements and multistate libels in cyberspace are no more complex than the same issues in real space.[141] They also are no more complex or challenging than similar issues presented by increasingly prevalent real-space events such as airplane crashes, mass torts, multistate insurance coverage, or multinational commercial transactions, all of which form the bread and butter of modern conflict of laws.[142] Indeed, they are no more complex than a simple products liability suit arising from a two-car accident among residents of the same state, which can implicate the laws of several states, including the place of the accident, the states where the car and tire manufacturers are headquartered, the states where the car and tires were manufactured, and the state where the car was purchased.[143]

Resolution of choice-of-law problems in these contexts is challenging. But the skeptics overstate the challenge. Not every geographical contact is of equal significance. For example, in the copyright hypothetical mentioned, the laws of the source country and the end-use countries have a much greater claim to governing the copyright action than the laws of the country of the person who built the server and the country of the server whose hyperlink pointed to the server that contained the infringing material.[144] The limits on enforcement jurisdiction may further minimize the scope of the conflict. In addition, even in extraordinarily complex cases in which numerous laws potentially apply, these laws will often involve similar legal standards, thus limiting the actual choice of law to two or perhaps three options.[145] Finally, these complex transactions need not be governed by a single law. Applying different laws to different aspects of a complex transaction is a perfectly legitimate choice-of-law technique.[146]

The application of a single law to complex multijurisdictional conflicts will sometimes seem arbitrary and will invariably produce spillover effects. But, as explained, the arbitrariness of the chosen law, and the spillovers produced by application of this law, inhere in all conflict situations in which two or more nations, on the basis of territorial or domiciliary contacts, have a legitimate claim to apply their law. When in particular contexts the arbitrariness and spillovers become too severe, a uniform international solution remains possible. Short of such harmonization, the choice-of-law issues implicated by cyberspace transactions are no more complex than the issues raised by functionally identical multijurisdictional transactions that occur in real space all the time.

Like the problem of complexity, the situs problem is a pervasive and familiar feature of real-space jurisdictional conflicts. A classic difficulty is the situs of intangibles like a debt or a bank deposit.[147] More generally, the situs problem arises whenever legally significant activity touches on two or more states. For example, when adultery committed in one state alienates the affections of a spouse in another, the situs of the tort is not self-evident. It depends on what contact the forum's choice-of-law rule deems dispositive. Similar locus difficulties arise when the tort takes place over many states, such as when poison is administered in one state, takes effect in another, and kills in a third. The situs problem even arises when a bodily injury occurs in one state based on negligence committed in another, for there is no logical reason why the place of injury should be viewed as *the place* of the tort any more than should the place of negligence.[148] In all of these situations, the importance of any particular geographical contact is never self-evident; it is a *legal* rather than a *factual* consideration that is built into the forum's choice-of-law rules. As the geographical contacts of a transaction proliferate, the choice of any one contact as dispositive runs the risk of appearing arbitrary. But again, this problem pervades real-space conflicts of law and is not unique to cyberspace conflicts.

So the complexity and situs problems inhere to some degree in all transnational conflicts, and are exacerbated in real space and cyberspace alike as jurisdictional contacts proliferate. No choice-of-law rule will prove wholly satisfactory in these situations. However, several factors diminish the skeptics' concerns about the infeasibility of applying traditional choice-of-law tools to cyberspace. For example, the skeptics are wrong to the extent that they believe that cyberspace transactions must be resolved on the basis of geographical choice-of-law criteria that are sometimes difficult to apply to cyberspace, such as where events occur or where people are located at the time of the transaction. But these are not the only choice-of-law criteria, and certainly not the best in contexts in which the geographical locus of events is so unclear. Domicile (and its cognates, such as citizenship, principal place of business, habitual residence, and so on) are also valid choice-of-law criteria that have particular relevance to problems, like those in cyberspace, that involve the regulation of intangibles or of multinational transactions.

The skeptics are further mistaken to the extent that their arguments assume that all choice-of-law problems must be resolved by *multilateral* choice-of-law methodologies. A multilateral methodology asks which of several possible laws governs a transaction, and selects one of these laws on the basis of specified criteria. Multilateral methods accentuate the complexity and situs problems. But the regulatory issues that are most relevant to the cyberspace governance debate almost always involve *unilateral* choice-of-law methods that alleviate these problems.[149] A unilateral method considers only whether the dispute at issue has close enough connections to the forum to justify the application of local law.[150] If so, local law applies; if not, the case is dismissed and the potential applicability of foreign law is not considered. For example, a jurisdiction typically does not apply foreign criminal law. If a Tennessee court has personal jurisdiction over someone from across the Virginia border who shot and killed an in-stater, the court does not consider whether Tennessee or Virginia law applies. It considers only whether Tennessee law applies. If so, the case proceeds; if not, it is dismissed.[151]

Unilateral choice-of-law methods make the complexity and situs problems less significant. They do not require a determination of which of a number of possible laws apply. Nor do they require a court to identify where certain events occurred. What matters is simply whether the activity has local effects that are significant enough to implicate local law. By failing to recognize that courts can and will use unilateral rather than multilateral choice-of-law methods to resolve cyberspace conflicts, the skeptics again exaggerate the challenge of cyberspace regulation.

Number and Velocity of Transactions

The skeptics' final descriptive claim is that even if cyberspace transactions appear like real-space transnational transactions in other respects, they differ significantly with respect to the velocity and number of transactions.[152] Cyberspace dramatically lowers the costs of multinational communication. With only a computer and Internet access, anyone in the world can communicate with anyone, and potentially everyone, in the world. The skeptics believe communications by cyberspace will be so prevalent that governments will not find it cost-effective to regulate them.[153]

A dramatic increase in the number and speed of transactions might well multiply the aggregate harms from such transactions. But this increases rather than decreases a nation's incentives to regulate. Consider Internet gambling. In pre-Internet days, individuals in the United States could gamble from home or work by telephone with domestic and offshore bookies. Although this form of gambling was regulated by a variety of state and federal statutes, the statutes were filled with loopholes and rarely enforced because transactions were relatively infrequent.[154] Internet gambling makes it significantly easier to gamble from home or work. This has led to a dramatic increase in gambling and a related rise in the costs of gambling that governments worry about: fraud, diminution in local gambling and other entertainment expenditures, loss of tax revenues, decreased productivity, gambling by children, and so on. Not surprisingly, federal and state governments are beginning to regulate gambling much more extensively, and seriously, than ever.[155]

Even with governments' heightened incentives to regulate Internet transactions, some believe that the sheer number of transactions will overwhelm governments' ability to regulate. A related argument is that because *individuals* can so easily engage in transnational communications by the Internet, governmental regulation will be less effective because individuals operating on the Internet are hard to identify, isolate, and thus sanction. Once again, the conclusion that regulation is infeasible simply does not follow from these premises. The mistake here is the belief that governments regulate only through direct sanctioning of individuals. But of course this is not the only way, or even the usual way, that regulation works. Governments regulate an activity by raising the activity's costs in a manner that achieves desired ends. This regulation can be accomplished through several means other than individual sanctions. Governments can, for example, try to alter the social meaning of the activity, regulate the hardware and software through which the activity takes place, make individual penalties severe and notorious, or impose liability on intermediaries like Internet service providers or credit card companies.

In short, a dramatic increase in the number and velocity of transactions by itself says very little about the feasibility of governmental regulation. Numerous communication advances, beginning with the telegraph, dramatically increased the velocity and number of communications, and lowered their costs. The skeptics have provided no reason to think that the differences between cyberspace and prior communication technology are so much greater than the differences between pre- and post-telegraph technology (which reduced communication time from weeks and months to hours and minutes), or between pre- and post-telephone technology (which also dramatically reduced the cost and enhanced the frequency and privacy of transjurisdictional communication) to justify the conclusion that governmental regulation will be nonefficacious.

Is Cyberspace Regulation Legitimate?

Section III explored some of the many ways that nations might regulate cyberspace transactions. This section considers the skeptics' normative claim that such regulation is illegitimate. This claim is directed primarily to the application of mandatory laws. The skeptics argue that cyberspace should be self-regulated, and that national mandatory laws should not limit these private legal orders. This argument subsumes three closely related claims: (a) unilateral regulation of cyberspace is extraterritorial; (b) unilateral regulation of cyberspace produces significant spillover effects; and (c) the structure of cyberspace makes effective notice of territorial regulation impossible. I address each claim in turn.

Extraterritoriality

In the Digitalbook.com example, Singapore and England regulated the local effects of Digitalbook.com's activities in the United States.[156]

In the CompuServe example, Germany regulated transmission flows from other countries.[157] These types of extraterritorial regulation are the ones that worry the skeptics. But such extraterritorial regulation is commonplace in the modern world. As we saw earlier, it is settled, with respect to real-space activity, that a nation's right to control events within its territory and to protect its citizens permits it to regulate the local effects of extraterritorial acts.[158]

The same rationale applies to cyberspace because cyberspace is for these purposes no different than real space. Transactions in cyberspace involve real people in one territorial jurisdiction either (a) transacting with real people in other territorial jurisdictions or (b) engaging in activity in one jurisdiction that causes real-world effects in another territorial jurisdiction. To this extent, activity in cyberspace is functionally identical to transnational activity mediated by other means, such as mail or telephone or smoke signal. The new medium of communication is richer, more complex, and much more efficient. But in terms of real-space acts in one jurisdiction that produce real-space effects in another, it is no different from other forms of transnational transaction and communication. And the justification for and legitimacy of regulating local effects are no different. Under current conceptions of territorial sovereignty, a jurisdiction is allowed to regulate extraterritorial acts that cause harmful local effects unless and until it has consented to a higher law (for example, international law or constitutional law) that specifies otherwise.

Spillover Effects

The skeptics argue that unilateral extraterritorial regulation of cyberspace differs from similar regulation of real-space activities because of the regulation's spillover effects in other jurisdictions. These effects are inevitable, they think, because information flows in cyberspace appear simultaneously in all territorial jurisdictions. As a result, unilateral territorial regulation of the local effects of cyberspace transmission flows will sometimes affect the flow and regulation of Web information in other countries. This is especially true when the regulation is directed at a multijurisdictional access provider, as was the case with Germany's regulation of CompuServe.

Section III described how technology and international cooperation can diminish these spillover effects. But even without these mitigating factors, there is nothing extraordinary or illegitimate about unilateral regulation of transnational activity that affects activity and regulation in other countries. Germany's regulation of CompuServe is no less legitimate than the United States' regulation of the competitiveness of the English reinsurance market, which has worldwide effects on the availability and price of reinsurance.[159] Nor is it any different in this regard from national regulation of transborder pollution, or from national consumer protection regulation of transnational contracts, or from national criminal prohibitions on transnational drug activities, all of which produce spillovers. In many contexts, there are powerful reasons for nations to surrender their regulatory prerogatives to reduce spillover and other costs. But at least under our current conceptions of territorial sovereignty, such reforms must proceed by national consent. The need for such consent begins from the premise that in its absence, national regulation of local effects is a legitimate incident of sovereignty, even if such regulation produces spillover effects.

Germany's regulation of CompuServe is not just a legitimate incident of territorial sovereignty. It is also fair to CompuServe under a straightforward reciprocal benefits rationale. CompuServe reaps financial and other benefits from its presence in Germany.[160] Without this presence, German enforcement threats would be largely empty. CompuServe need not remain in Germany; it could close its shop there. Its decision to stay in Germany and comply with German regulations might increase the price of its services in Germany and elsewhere. For CompuServe, this is a cost of doing business by a new communication medium. The desire to reduce this and related costs is driving the development of technology that permits geographical and other forms of discrimination on the Internet. But even in the absence of such technologies, Germany's local regulation of CompuServe remains within traditional reciprocity-based justifications for regulating local effects.

What about CompuServe users in other countries who are affected by the German regulation? It is hard to see how the German regulation unfairly burdens them. They remain free to choose among dozens of Internet access services that are not affected by the German regulation. Consider further the German perspective. Germany bans certain forms of pornography within its borders. If the medium of this pornography were paper, there would be no fairness-based jurisdictional objection to a German prohibition on the pornography's entry at the border or to German punishment of those who are later discovered to have smuggled it in.[161] From Germany's perspective, it makes no difference whether the pornography enters the nation by cyberspace or the postal service. The rationale for the regulation is the same in both cases: something is happening within Germany that implicates the government's paternalistic concerns or that harms third parties within its borders. The fact that the local regulation might affect the cost or availability of pornography in other countries is, from this perspective, irrelevant. Fairness does not require Germany to yield local control over its territory to accommodate the users of a new communication technology in other countries. Nor does it require Germany to absorb the local costs of foreign activity because of the costs that the German regulation might impose on such activity.

This latter point sheds light on one of the major fallacies of the skeptics' normative project. The skeptics argue that the spillover effects caused by territorial regulation of cyberspace justify cyberspace self-regulation. Spillover-minimization is not the criterion of legitimacy for national regulation of harmful local effects. But even if it were, the skeptics' conclusions would not follow because the skeptics completely ignore the spillover effects of cyberspace activity itself. They do not consider these effects because they take it as an article of faith that cyberspace participants form a self-contained group that can internalize the costs of its activity.[162] But this assumption is false. Cyberspace participants are no more self-contained than telephone users, members of the Catholic Church, corporations, and other private groups with activities that transcend jurisdictional borders. They are real people in real space transacting in a fashion that produces real-world effects on cyberspace participants and nonparticipants alike. Cyberspace users solicit and deliver kiddie porn, launder money, sexually harass, defraud, and so on. It is these and many other real-space costs—costs that cyberspace communities cannot effectively internalize—that national regulatory regimes worry about and aim to regulate.

So the spillover argument runs in both directions. Cyberspace activity outside of Germany produces spillovers in Germany, and German regulation produces spillovers on cyberspace activity beyond its borders. The legitimacy and fairness of Germany's territorial regulation do not depend on minimization of these costs. But even if it did, the skeptics' desired normative conclusion that cyberspace should be self-regulated would only follow if the costs of cyberspace self-regulation were less significant than the costs of territorial regulation. The skeptics have not begun to try to demonstrate that this is true. And any such attempt is very unlikely to succeed at the level of generality at which their arguments are invariably pitched.

Notice

The skeptics' final normative argument against mandatory law regulation of cyberspace concerns notice. In real space, parties can direct the flow of their transnational transactions and can in most cases avoid jurisdictions that prohibit the transactions. The skeptics claim that this cannot be done in cyberspace. They worry that cyberspace participants therefore lack notice about governing mandatory law and hence cannot conform their behavior to it. The skeptics claim this lack of notice violates basic norms of fairness.

This argument rests on a number of empirical assumptions that have been questioned in Section III. The assumption that cyberspace involves uncontrollable universal information flows is inaccurate today and will become even less accurate with time. Information flows can be directed and controlled in a variety of ways, with varying costs that will almost certainly decrease in the future. Concerns about notice are further attenuated by the many limitations on enforcement jurisdiction that effectively limit the application of mandatory laws to entities with a local presence. In none of the many cases in which regulations have been enforced against cyberspace transactions has an out-of-state defendant had a basis to claim unfair surprise.

It is nonetheless worth considering how the notice issue will play out in cyberspace. The Constitution and international law impose weak notice requirements on the application of local law to extraterritorial conduct. The Constitution permits a state with significant contacts to the case to apply its law if the defendant could have reasonably foreseen its application.[163] International law might impose a similar restraint on legislative jurisdiction.

This requirement of reasonable foreseeability does not mean that harmful local effects of extraterritorial activity are automatically immune from local regulation just because they were accidental, or because the agent of the activity did not know the precise locus of the effects. "Reasonable foreseeability" is a dynamic concept. A

65

manufacturer that pollutes in one state is not immune from the anti-pollution laws of other states where the pollution causes harm just because it cannot predict which way the wind blows. Similarly, a cyberspace content provider cannot necessarily claim ignorance about the geographical flow of information as a defense to the application of the law of the place where the information appears. At first glance it appears unfair to expose Digitalbook.com to the anti-pornography laws of Singapore. But it would not seem unfair if Digitalbook.com could at a small cost prevent its information from entering Singapore. Nor would it seem unfair to expose Digital-book.com to liability for the damage caused in Singapore by a virus that it released into cyberspace that destroyed every Apple computer hard drive connected to the Internet.

These intuitions show that, like the related personal jurisdiction question,[164] the standard of foreseeability depends on a complex mixture of what the content provider knows or reasonably should have known about the geographical consequences of its acts, the significance of the extrajursidictional harms caused by the acts, and the costs of precautions.[165] Content providers can already achieve pretty reliable information flow control by conditioning access to content on telephone or facsimile proof of geographical location. To many this is an unacceptable burden on Internet communication. But there is nothing sacrosanct about Internet speed and ease, and dimunitions in speed and ease might be warranted by the social costs imposed by uncontrolled information flows. And, in any event, as filtering and identification technologies continue to raise the feasibility and lower the costs of information flow control, the problem of notice in cyberspace will look much like the problem of notice in real space.

Grounding Cyberspace in Real-Space Law

I have argued that national and international regulations of cyberspace transactions are legitimate and feasible. I have not argued for any particular regulation, or that such regulation should be pervasive. I have tried to show only that the skeptics' global arguments against national and international regulation of cyberspace are unfounded. Cyberspace self-regulation will often be difficult to achieve. And like noncyberspace transactions, cyberspace transactions will in any event be limited by national mandatory rules.

The challenging issue from a jurisdictional perspective is to develop a legal structure that both facilitates private legal ordering of cyberspace transactions and accommodates national mandatory law limitations. Consider the predicament of a person in England who wants to buy a security from a Web page on a server in Japan. The parties want the sale to circumvent U.S. securities regulations, and, more broadly, the interference of national courts. The parties thus agree that the sale will be governed by Japanese law and that any disputes will be resolved by private arbitration in Japan. Will this contract be enforceable? This example involves a commercial transaction. But the problem is generic, for, as we saw previously, parties can by contract create governing legal structures for a variety of noncommercial activities. Thus, for example, the same basic problem arises when chat room participants from different countries agree that the tort law principles of the state of Illinois govern chat room activities, and that all disputes will be resolved privately. Will the parties' *ex ante* consent be respected when a chat room participant from France claims in his national court that he suffered a tort in the chat room in violation of French law?

To avoid national court litigation and minimize national regulation, the parties to these transactions need to satisfy the following conditions. They must consent *ex ante* to a governing law, a private method of dispute resolution, and a private enforcement regime. The consent must be consistent with the mandatory law applied by any national court where a defector from the contract might seek to have any part of the contract declared invalid.[166] To ensure the sanctity of the private order and to discourage such defection, the national court must be willing to (a) treat the consent to the private order as valid, (b) enjoin litigation in derogation of the contract, and, sometimes, (c) specifically enforce the defector's agreement to abide by the private order. Moreover, it is not enough that the courts of a single country will enforce the contract. There must be coordinated enforcement among national courts in every country in which the recalcitrant party might go to seek to avoid the obligation. Finally, national courts must subsequently recognize the validity of the private dispute resolution process. They must enjoin subsequent litigation in derogation of the results of the private dispute resolution, and enforce any judgments that cannot be done so privately.

Such a structure might appear hopelessly complicated and thus fanciful. But this appearance is deceiving. The essentials for such a regime already exist in the system that governs international commercial arbitration.[167] This system works through the interplay of three layers of law. The first layer is the private law of the parties' contract. In the contract, the parties specify the law governing the transaction (in the examples given, the laws of Japan and Illinois), agree to use private arbitration to resolve certain disputes that arise out of or relate to the transaction, and choose the place for the arbitration and the procedures that govern it.[168] The second layer is the national arbitration law.[169] A national arbitration law defines the scope of permissible arbitration within the country, renders arbitration agreements within this scope valid, and provides various forms of judicial assistance for, and judicial review of, arbitration. Most nations have generally similar national arbitration laws that ensure harmonization of enforcement across jurisdictions. This harmonization is substantially bolstered by the third layer of legal regulation: the international enforcement treaty. By far the most important such treaty is the New York Convention on the Recognition and Enforcement of Arbitral Awards, which almost every nation has signed.[170] The Convention obligates the national courts of signatory states to recognize and enforce arbitration agreements and awards, subject to limited exceptions.[171]

The basic structure of international commercial arbitration could easily be modified to cyberspace. As explained earlier, the law of the contract—both the substantive law and the dispute resolution mechanism—could be agreed to as an incident of the securities transaction or as a condition of access to the chat room. National arbitration laws could be modified to include dispute resolution in cyberspace. For example, the Federal Arbitration Act (FAA) would require modification in only two important respects. First, the FAA's requirement that the arbitration agreement be made in writing might need to be amended to accommodate cyberspace realities.[172] Second, FAA rules that turn on the place of the arbitration[173] require modification for virtual arbitrations that lack a geographical locus.[174] The New York Convention would likely require a similar amendment.

The accommodation of mandatory laws presents special challenges. In the securities example, assume that the English purchaser is unhappy with the security, and defects from the contractual agreement to arbitrate by bringing a private securities action in a U.S. court that alleges that the sale was fraudulent and in violation of

U.S. securities law. This raises two basic mandatory law issues. The first is whether the U.S. court will enforce the agreement to arbitrate, or will instead adjudicate the mandatory law (and perhaps other) claims. Assuming the court enforces the arbitration agreement, the second question is whether the arbitrator can apply the U.S. mandatory law consistent with the jurisdictional limits imposed by the parties' contractual choice of Japanese law.

Both difficulties frequently arise with respect to noncyberspace transnational transactions, and can be addressed within the framework of international commercial arbitration. As for the first problem, national courts increasingly permit private arbitrators to resolve claims involving economic regulation and quasi-criminal laws subject to subsequent, deferential judicial review.[175] The deferential nature of such review, combined with the costs of seeking it, mean that private arbitrators will often have the final say. As for the second problem, arbitrators have established a number of devices grounded in (often fictional) party consent that permit them to apply a mandatory law of a country other than the one specifically chosen by the parties' contract.[176]

To many it will seem ironic and damning that my description of a legal regime that supposedly promotes private ordering focuses so much on the role of national courts and national laws. This focus is misleading. Much of the regulation of these private matters is, and will continue to be, governed by a variety of privately enforceable rules, norms, and enforcement mechanisms. Yet the overarching national and international legal regimes remain necessary for two reasons. First, they provide a ready-made coordination and enforcement regime that transnational parties can invoke in the many situations in which information-gathering and related costs of purely private enforcement are prohibitively high. Second, they give private parties enormous flexibility in creating a private regime in a fashion that can accommodate and minimize the intrusion of oft-conflicting mandatory laws. In this connection, it should be emphasized that the international commercial arbitration model is not as litigious, and would not be as intrusive on private cyberspace orders, as it might at first glance appear. If real-space commercial arbitrations are any guide, recourse to national courts will be relatively infrequent as the background public enforcement patterns become relatively clear.

I do not mean to suggest that international commercial arbitration is a comprehensive panacea for the jurisdictional challenges of cyberspace. It is not. Many, probably most, cyberspace transactions will have such a low value that affected parties will not bother to enter into contractual relations, much less contract for governing law and private enforcement. In addition, cyberspace transactions that adversely affect third parties are beyond the ken of international commercial arbitration, which depends upon *ex ante* consent for its effectiveness and legitimacy. Relatedly, although the international arbitration regime has taken steps to privatize the enforcement of mandatory laws, many mandatory laws—most prominently traditional criminal laws and certain limits on contractual capacity—are not subject to enforceable international arbitration. Indeed, some might object that cyberspace-related choice-of-law and private arbitration agreements that are not dickered should be viewed as unenforceable contracts of adhesion.[177]

These limitations on the international commercial law regime are not, of course, unique to cyberspace transactions. These same limitations characterize real-space transnational transactions. Such limitations are inevitable when it is difficult for parties of transnational transactions to craft private legal regimes *ex ante*, or when these transactions harm third parties or implicate the paternalistic interests of affected nations. The important point is that these limitations are difficult to overcome in real space and cyberspace alike. My modest aim has been to show that the governing law challenges presented by cyberspace are not significantly different from the ones presented by other transnational transactions.

Conclusion

Cyberspace transactions are no different from real-space transnational transactions. They involve people in real space in one jurisdiction communicating with people in real space in other jurisdictions in a way that often does good but sometimes causes harm. There is no general normative argument that supports the immunization of cyberspace activities from territorial regulation. And there is every reason to believe that nations can exercise territorial authority to achieve significant regulatory control over cyberspace transactions. Resolution of the choice-of-law problems presented by cyberspace transactions will be challenging, but no more challenging than similar problems raised in other transnational contexts.

4. Against "Against Cyberanarchy"

David G. Post

It makes me indignant when I hear a work
Blamed not because it's crude or graceless but
Only because it's new . . .
Had the Greeks hated the new the way we do,
Whatever would have been able to grow to be old?

Horace, *The Epistles*, II, I
(David Ferry, Trans.)

Professor Jack Goldsmith's "Against Cyberanarchy" [1] has become one of the most influential articles in the cyberspace law canon. The position he sets forth—what I call "Unexceptionalism"—rests on two main premises. The first is that activity in cyberspace is "functionally identical to transnational activity mediated by other means" (e.g., "mail or telephone or smoke signal"). The second is that, as a consequence of this functional identity, the "settled principles" and "traditional legal tools" of the international lawyer are fully capable of handling all jurisdictional and choice-of-law problems in cyberspace—that the "choice-of-law problems implicated by cyberspace are not significantly different from those [of] noncyberspace conflicts," and that we therefore need make no special provision for these problems when they arise in *cyberspace.*

I beg, in what follows, to differ. I remain an unrepentant Exceptionalist. Communication in cyberspace is not "functionally identical" to communication in real space—at least, not in ways relevant to the application of the choice-of-law and jurisdictional principles under discussion, nor can the jurisdictional and choice-of-law dilemmas posed by cyberspace activity be adequately resolved by applying the "settled principles" and "traditional legal tools" developed for analogous problems in real space.

Unexceptionalism in Cyberspace

Border-crossing transactions have always presented the international legal system with difficult and challenging jurisdictional questions: Whose law applies to such transactions? Which sovereign(s) have "jurisdiction to prescribe" law for transactions that "originate" in one country and "terminate" elsewhere? When and to what extent is "extraterritorial regulation" permissible? In "Against Cyberanarchy," Goldsmith asked us to consider—

> the predicament of one of the scores of companies that offer, sell, and deliver products on the World Wide Web. Assume that the Web page of a fictional Seattle-based company, Digitalbook.com, offers digital books for sale and delivery over the Web. One book it offers for sale is *Lady Chatterley's Lover*. This offer extends to, and can be accepted by, computer users in every country with access to the Web. Assume that in Singapore the sale and distribution of pornography is criminal, and that Singapore deems *Lady Chatterley's Lover* to be pornographic. Assume further that Digitalbook.com's terms of sale contain a term that violates English consumer protection laws, and that the publication of Digitalbook.com's *Lady Chatterley's Lover* in England would infringe upon the rights of the novel's English copyright owner. Digitalbook.com sells and sends copies of *Lady Chatterley's Lover* to two people whose addresses (say, anonymous@aol.com and anonymous@msn.com) do not reveal their physical location but who, unbeknownst to Digitalbook.com, live and receive the book in Singapore and London, respectively.[2]

This scenario, Goldsmith acknowledged, raises some difficult problems: Does English law, or Singaporean law, or both, apply to Digitalbook.com's conduct? Would application of either of these bodies of law constitute "impermissible extraterritorial regulation of a U.S. corporation"?[3] If Digitalbook.com "cannot limit its cyberspace information flows by geography,"[4] would application of English, or Singaporean, law cause Digitalbook.com to "withdraw *Lady Chatterley's Lover*"[5] from circulation (or, at the very least, to "raise its price"[6]), thereby "adversely affecting the purchasing opportunities of parties in other countries"?[7] And if so, are these "negative spillover effects" of national regulation "illegitimate [and] unfair"[8]—especially given that "Digitalbook.com had no way of knowing that it sold and delivered a book to consumers in these countries"?[9]

Goldsmith's position—what I term "Unexceptionalism"—is straightforward: however difficult and complicated Digitalbook. com's problems may be, they are no *more* difficult or complicated because the underlying transactions take place "in cyberspace."

> Transactions in cyberspace involve real people in one territorial jurisdiction either (a) transacting with real people in other territorial jurisdictions or (b) engaging in activity in one jurisdiction that causes real-world effects in another territorial jurisdiction. *To this extent, activity in cyberspace is functionally identical to transnational activity mediated by other means, such as mail or telephone or smoke signal.*[10]

To the Unexceptionalist, whether a transaction occurs in cyberspace or real space does not matter. The questions of jurisdiction and choice of law posed by Digitalbook.com's conduct are not "unique to cyberspace"[11] and "identical problems arise all the time in real space."[12] After all, people have been communicating and transacting with other people in other territorial jurisdictions for a long time, well before the Internet raised its head. Thus, the questions raised by Digitalbook.com's conduct may be complex and challenging, but they are "no more complex or challenging than similar issues presented by increasingly prevalent real-space events such as airplane crashes, mass torts, multistate insurance coverage, or multinational commercial transactions, all of which form the bread and butter of modern conflict of laws."[13]

Over the past century or so, a number of important principles of law and analytical tools have evolved to resolve the jurisdictional problems posed by border-crossing transactions. These traditional principles and tools, though developed to deal with real-space phenomena, do not spontaneously disintegrate or misfire when we apply them to phenomena on the global electronic network, according to Goldsmith. Cyberspace transactions "are not significantly less resistant to the tools of conflict of laws, than other transnational transactions;"[14] it would be a mistake to "underestimate the potential of [these] traditional legal tools and technology to resolve the multijurisdictional regulatory problems implicated by cyberspace."[15]

Those who think otherwise—Goldsmith calls them "regulation skeptics,"[16] though I prefer the less loaded and more symmetrical term "Exceptionalists"—believe that cyberspace *is* somehow different, that it matters, for purposes of understanding these jurisdictional questions, that Digitalbook.com is operating on the World Wide Web and not in a bricks-and-mortar real-space storefront. Exceptionalists, in Goldsmith's view, are skeptical of the "potential of traditional legal tools and technology to resolve the multijurisdictional regulatory problems implicated by cyberspace."[17] They believe that "the application of geographically based conceptions of legal regulation and choice of law to a-geographical cyberspace activity either makes no sense or leads to hopeless confusion,"[18] and that because "cyberspace transactions occur 'simultaneously and equally' in all national jurisdictions, . . . regulation of the flow of this information by any particular national jurisdiction illegitimately produces significant negative spillover effects in other jurisdictions."[19]

Exceptionalists, Goldsmith tells us, are "in the grip of a 19th century territorialist conception of how 'real space' is regulated and how 'real-space' conflicts of law are resolved."[20] This outdated and discredited territorialist conception—"hermetic territorialism," [21] he calls it—involves a belief that there must be a "*unique* governing law for all transnational activities,"[22] a "*single* legitimate governing law for transborder activity based on discrete territorial contacts."[23] Hermetic territorialism directs us to identify one body of law applicable to Digitalbook.com's behavior, and to define the "discrete territorial contact" that is a necessary prerequisite to the application of local law to its conduct.

Hermetic territorialism, though it held sway for several hundred years, was "repudiated" as part of a "revolution [in] conflict of laws in the second half of [the 20th] century."[24] Many factors—including "changes in transportation, communication, and in the scope of corporate activity [leading] to an unprecedented increase in multi-jurisdictional activity"[25]—led directly to an "expansion of the permissible bases for territorial jurisdiction."[26] The result is that in "modern times," a transaction "can legitimately be regulated" not only "by the jurisdiction where the transaction occurs [and] the jurisdictions where the parties burdened by the regulation are from,"[27] but also by "the jurisdictions *where significant effects of the transaction are felt.*"[28] Under "current conceptions of territorial sovereignty," a sovereign "is allowed to regulate extraterritorial acts that cause harmful local effects unless and until it has consented to a higher law (for example, international law or constitutional law) that specifies otherwise."[29] If that means, as it often does, that "more than one jurisdiction can legitimately apply its law to the same transnational activity,"[30] so be it; under the "modern view," there is no need to find the single discrete territorial event on which to base the application of any single body of law.

As a result of this change in viewpoint and the repudiation of hermetic territorialism, extraterritorial regulation is "commonplace in the modern world." Both "customary international law" and the U.S. Constitution "permit a nation to apply its law to extraterritorial behavior with substantial local effects."[31] It is, for instance, "relatively uncontroversial"[32] that a newspaper publisher "is liable for harms caused wherever the newspaper is published or distributed."[33] There is "nothing extraordinary or illegitimate" about this "unilateral regulation of transnational activity that affects activity and regulation in other countries."[34] Singapore's, or England's, regulation of Digitalbook.com is "no less legitimate than the United States' regulation of the competitiveness of the English reinsurance market, which has worldwide effects on the availability and price of reinsurance."[35]

The bottom line: It is settled with respect to real-space activity[36]— elsewhere Goldsmith refers to this as an "uncontested assumption"[37]—"that a nation's right to control events within its territory and to protect its citizens permits it to regulate the local effects of extraterritorial acts."[38] Thus,

> prevailing concepts of territorial sovereignty permit a nation to regulate the local effects of extraterritorial conduct even if this regulation produces spillover effects in other jurisdictions, [and that] such spillover effects are a commonplace consequence of the unilateral application of any particular law to transnational activity in our increasingly interconnected world.[39]

And if all that is "settled with respect to real-space activity," why would we think that cyberspace is any different?

Settled Principles

The core of the Unexceptionalists' argument thus contains a simple, but very powerful, syllogism:

75

- Transnational activities of an ordinary bricks-and-mortar bookstore—"Analogbooks, Inc."—are subject to "settled principles" of "customary international law."
- These settled principles hold that if Analogbooks' real-space activities produce "substantial local effects" in Singapore, or in England, those activities can "legitimately be regulated" by those governments.
- Digitalbooks' activities are "functionally identical" to Analogbooks' activities.
- Therefore, if Digitalbook's cyberspace activities produce "substantial local effects" in Singapore, or in England, those activities can "legitimately be regulated" by those governments.

The logic is unassailable: If X is true in environment 1, and if environment 2 is "functionally identical" to environment 1, then X is true in environment 2. The argument, however, is not quite as persuasive as it might appear at first glance.

Take, for instance, the Unexceptionalists' reliance upon "settled principles [of] customary international law." I have no reason to question Goldsmith's assertion that these principles—in particular, the "uncontested assumption(s)"[40] that, at least in "modern times," transactions "can legitimately be regulated [by] the jurisdictions where significant effects of the transaction are felt,"[41] and that "a nation's right to control events within its territory and to protect its citizens permits it to regulate the local effects of extraterritorial acts"[42]—are "settled."

But this "modern view" of international jurisdiction, as Goldsmith himself points out,[43] is *itself* the product of profound changes in the world over the past century or so; these now-settled principles were once, themselves, in conflict with then-settled principles. It was once "settled" law that a state *cannot* regulate extraterritorial acts, the "substantial local effects" of those acts notwithstanding, *and* that therefore Analogbooks' activities could not "legitimately be regulated" in either Singapore or England. The Unexceptionalists of 100, or even 50, years ago might have made an argument very much like Goldsmith's, pointing to this "settled" principle to argue that rail transport, the telephone, or radio broadcasting would (and should) have *no* effect on our analysis of jurisdictional problems. We can imagine the following colloquy:

Scene: A New York street corner, circa 1900. Two law professors—Professor E and Professor U—meet.

Professor E: "Have you noticed? This telegraph thing changes everything! I can step inside a Western Union office in New York and execute a contract in San Francisco *instantaneously*! Incredible, eh?"

Professor U: "Well, I suppose it is. But what of it?"

E: "What of it? Surely you jest. The world as we know it will never be the same. We're going to need new principles of law to deal with this phenomenon. Our jurisdictional principles—especially the one that requires *physical presence* for the exercise of "jurisdiction to prescribe"—must yield to this new context, no?"

U: "Not at all. Transactions completed by telegraph are functionally identical to those completed by mail or by smoke signal; they all involve real people in one territorial jurisdiction either (a) transacting with real people in other territorial jurisdictions or (b) engaging in activity in one jurisdiction that causes real-world effects in another territorial jurisdiction. It is settled law that the people of California *cannot* reach people and transactions occurring outside of its borders. Why would we need to adjust those principles now?"

Life, Kierkegaard said, must be lived forward, but it can only be understood backward.[44] Looking backward, of course, we know that events proved *those* Unexceptionalists wrong. Though it was surely difficult to see at the time, the world was changing, and changing profoundly; settled understandings were becoming unsettled because of that change. How would Professors U and E have known that this unsettling was occurring before their very eyes? How would *we* know if the world were again changing, unsettling *our* settled understandings? In retrospect, it may be easy to identify such seismic shifts in the legal landscape, phase transitions between different ordered states of an entire domain of legal thought and practice. But in prospect, that may not be so easy.

The world, sometimes, does that—changes profoundly. When it does, settled understandings sometimes change with it. Unless we think that for some reason this cannot happen again, questions about the *legitimate* scope of a nation's jurisdictional reach cannot rest on

77

the notion that those questions are somehow already, and forever, "settled."

Functional Identity

That the world *can* change so as to unsettle settled principles does not, of course, mean that it has done so, or that it has done so in ways that are relevant to the questions at hand. The Unexceptionalists say that it has not; activity in cyberspace is *"functionally identical to transnational activity mediated by other means, such as mail or telephone or smoke signal."*[45]

What could that possibly mean? It doesn't take a great deal of insight or deep thinking—in fact, it is trivially easy—to come up with ways in which activity in cyberspace is functionally *not* identical to activity in real space. Here are a few, off the top of my head: In cyberspace, I can communicate an offer to sell some product

- instantaneously (or nearly so)
- at zero marginal cost (or nearly so)
- to several million people (including hundreds of thousands in Singapore and the United Kingdom)
- with near-zero probability of error in the reproduction or distribution of that offer
- which can be stored, and retrieved, and translated into another language, by each of the recipients (instantaneously, and at zero marginal cost)—each of whom has the capability to respond to my offer (instantaneously, and at zero marginal cost).

I surely cannot do all that—I cannot engage in a transaction having *all* of those features—using mail, telephones, or smoke signals.

The Unexceptionalists are intelligent and sophisticated thinkers; how could they possibly think that activity in communication in cyberspace is "functionally identical"—not, mind you, merely "functionally similar," or even "roughly equivalent," but *identical*—to real-space communication? What are they talking about?

Asking whether real-space and cyberspace transactions are "identical to" or "different from" one another is like asking whether life on land is "identical to" or "different from" life in the ocean. The answer is that it is, and it must be, simultaneously, both; it depends entirely on the questions you're asking.[46] The second law of thermodynamics, gravity, and the principle of natural selection work identically in the two environments; the mechanics of sound propagation, buoyancy, and chemical diffusion do not. For the purpose of answering some questions (e.g., about the mechanics of genetic recombination in mammals, or energy transmission within food webs, or the relative advantages of sexual and asexual reproduction), we ignore the differences between the two environments and lump terrestrial and oceanic organisms together. For the purpose of answering other questions (e.g., about social communication within animal populations, or the mechanics of oxygen transport, or the design of the mammalian forelimb), we must distinguish between terrestrial and oceanic organisms, because for these purposes the two environments are very different indeed.

It is true that events and transactions in real space and cyberspace are identical in many ways and can be treated identically for many purposes. Transactions between human beings are still transactions between human beings, whether they take place by e-mail, postcard, telegraph, or smoke signal, and whatever it is that motivates human beings to engage in one transaction or another—love, hate, greed, curiosity, fear, and the rest—remains the same, on or off the Internet. A dollar is still a dollar, whether it is earned by a seller of goods from a showroom transaction or a transaction at www.i'vegotstuff-forsale.com. Digitalbook.com and Analogbooks will thus have many identical characteristics. Digitalbook.com, like Analogbooks, provides a forum in which buyers and sellers can exchange consideration for goods; a system for making sure that those goods get shipped from seller to buyer after a transaction is consummated; rules for identifying the winners and losers of individual auctions; and means for obtaining payment for its services, accounting for those payments, and transferring money to its suppliers.

Questions, too, therefore, about how Digitalbook.com and Analogbooks spend the money they earn—questions, say, about the investment strategies of book dealers, and the laws regulating those investment strategies—can surely lump cyberspace and real-space earnings together.

However, it is also true that events and transactions in real space and cyberspace are *not* identical in many other ways. Transactions in cyberspace, for example, can take place at much greater physical remove; they are consummated by means of the movement of bits rather than atoms; they are digitally encoded; they are unaffected by the participants' senses of smell; they are embedded in and mediated by computer software; they travel at the speed of light, . . .

> Transactions in cyberspace involve real people in one territorial jurisdiction either (a) transacting with real people in other territorial jurisdictions or (b) engaging in activity in one jurisdiction that causes real-world effects in another territorial jurisdiction. *To this extent, activity in cyberspace is functionally identical to transnational activity mediated by other means, such as mail or telephone or smoke signal.*[47]

Now I get it: *to that extent, but only to that extent*, cyberspace and real-space transactions are identical. To the extent that our question requires us to ask whether "real people [are] transacting with [other] real people in other territorial jurisdictions," we can ignore the distinctions between cyberspace and real-space transactions. And to the extent that our question requires us to ask something else—whether, say, they involve bits and software, and instantaneous communication with enormous numbers of people across the global network, and so forth—they're not.

The question we need to be addressing, then, is this one: are Digitalbook.com's and Analogbooks' transactions identical—or, at least, sufficiently similar—to one another *with respect to the relevant principles of international choice of law and prescriptive jurisdiction*? If so, it is reasonable to ignore the many differences between them; if not, it is not.

Scale

To the Unexceptionalist, Digitalbook.com's and Analogbooks' transactions *are* identical with respect to these principles. The issues raised by application of the relevant principles of international law and prescriptive jurisdiction to Digitalbook.com's cyberspace transactions, they say,

> are *no more complex than the same issues in real space.* They also are *no more complex or challenging than similar issues presented by increasingly prevalent real-space events such as airplane crashes, mass torts, multistate insurance coverage, or multinational commercial transactions,* all of which form the bread and butter of modern conflict of laws. Indeed, they are no more complex than a simple products liability suit arising from a two-car accident among residents of the same state, which can implicate the laws of several states, including the place of the accident, the states where the car and tire manufacturers

are headquartered, the states where the car and tires were manufactured, and the state where the car was purchased.[48]

This may well be true; Digitalbook.com's sale of an individual book to a customer in Singapore, in isolation, is no more "complex or challenging" as a matter of international law than Analogbooks' sale of the same book to the same customer.

To stop the analysis there, however, is to miss the forest for the trees. A rose is a rose is a rose; 3 roses, or 300 roses—a garden—is a different, a more "complex and challenging," phenomenon. Scale matters; the engineers and the biologists know this. Network protocols that can manage a thousand transactions may not be able to handle a million, or a billion. The tree is one thing; the forest, though it is nothing more than a large number of trees, is another, more "complex and challenging," thing. The movement of a single clump of dirt down a slope is one thing; an avalanche, though it is nothing more than the movement of lots of individual pieces of dirt down a slope, is another, more "complex and challenging," event.[49] The motion of a single pendulum—which has been understood with great precision since Galileo's day—is one thing; connect a number of pendulums together—connect their shafts together with small springs, for example, or with bits of string—and you have a much more "complex and challenging" phenomenon.[50]

You get the idea: the anthill is more "complex and challenging" than the ant. Ignoring the anthill when making rules for the ant— ignoring the ways in which the individual ant's behavior is embedded within a complex system of large numbers of other individuals—would be odd indeed.[51]

Therefore, although Digitalbook.com and Analogbooks each may be doing the "same" things, the *systems* within which they operate are not necessarily the same as a consequence of that identity. *Scale matters*. Differences in degree sometimes become differences in kind; quantitative changes can become qualitative changes.[52] Rules and principles that may be quite reasonable at one scale may become incoherent and unreasonable at another.

To take an example of the ways in which the scale of activities in cyberspace can unsettle settled legal principles, consider the following. In 1995, Dennis Erlich, a former-minister-turned-critic of the Church of Scientology, took the texts of a number of works authored by Scientology founder L. Ron Hubbard and, using the services of Netcom Online Communication Services, Inc., distributed them to the Usenet newsgroup alt.religion.scientology. Netcom, for its part, reproduced each of those documents dozens, perhaps hundreds or thousands, of times in the course of transmitting Erlich's messages (and the files he included in those messages) to other Usenet sites. Hubbard's works are protected by U.S. copyright law, and the owner of the copyright in Hubbard's works—Religious Technology Center—appeared in Judge Ronald Whyte's courtroom in the Northern District of California to enjoin Netcom's violation of its statutory rights.[53]

Judge Whyte, I think it fair to say, found this case somewhat unsettling. On the one hand, one would be hard-pressed to find a case in the federal reporters in which the law, and the application of the law to particular facts, were more straightforward than in this one. There was a nice, "settled" principle of law to work with: it is an infringement of copyright to "reproduce" a copyrighted work of authorship "in copies" without the copyright holder's authorization.[54] Netcom, it was hard to deny, had done just that. It was true, of course, that Netcom didn't *know* that it was making copies of the copyrighted works;[55] that the "copies" it made were merely transient arrangements of bits on its disk drives;[56] that it had not taken any "affirmative action" other than "installing and maintaining a system whereby software automatically forwards messages received from subscribers onto the Usenet, and temporarily stores copies on its system" to carry out its copying activities;[57] and that it was only doing exactly what thousands of other Usenet servers around the globe were doing with the documents that Erlich had posted.[58]

All true, and all, under the settled law of 1995, irrelevant. The Copyright Act is a "strict liability statute;"[59] because infringement "does not require intent or any particular state of mind,"[60] whether Netcom knew of the infringing nature of the messages it was transmitting didn't matter. There was, similarly, "no question,"[61] given a recent Ninth Circuit decision squarely on point,[62] that the transient collections of bits on Netcom's disk drives constituted "copies" within the meaning of the Copyright Act;[63] that while the infringing messages remained on Netcom's system "for at most eleven days," they were "sufficiently 'fixed' to constitute copies under the Copyright Act;"[64] that while one could argue that "there *should* still be some element of volition or causation"[65] in a copyright claim, there was no such element; and that, finally, there was no "lots of other people are doing what I'm doing, so you should not hold me liable" defense established in copyright law.

On the other hand, imposing liability on Netcom for these activities somehow "does not make sense,"[66] in Judge Whyte's words. The individual acts on the basis of which Netcom was charged with infringement were "functionally identical" to any number of things we had seen before; after all, whether you're operating a photocopying machine, or a CD-burner, or a Usenet server, you're just "making a copy of a document," hardly an unfamiliar activity. But the system within which those acts were embedded had changed, and application of the settled law to the *aggregate* of those individual actions somehow needed to change along with it. The file storage and reproduction activities in which Netcom was engaged were "necessary to having a working system for transmitting Usenet postings to and from the Internet."[67] If Netcom were deemed liable for copyright infringement, "*any* storage of a copy that occurs in the process of sending a message to the Usenet [would be] an infringement,"[68] and "every single Usenet server in the worldwide link of computers transmitting Erlich's message to every other computer"[69] would be liable. Carried to its "natural extreme"[70]—scaled up, we might say—application of settled law in this case "would lead to *unreasonable liability.*"[71] It "does not make sense," Judge Whyte wrote, to "adopt a rule that could lead to the liability of countless parties whose role in the infringement is nothing more than setting up and operating a system that is necessary for the functioning of the Internet."[72] A theory of infringement that would hold *every Internet server worldwide* liable for activities that each of them was undertaking thousands of times a second was not "*workable.*"[73] Because there was no "meaningful distinction . . . between what Netcom did and what every other Usenet server does,"[74] Judge Whyte found that Netcom "cannot be held liable for direct infringement."[75]

Settled law, in other words, didn't *scale.* So Judge Whyte unsettled it.

Effects

> A nation's right to control events within its territory and to protect its citizens permits it to regulate the local effects of extraterritorial act. . . .[76]

Figure 1

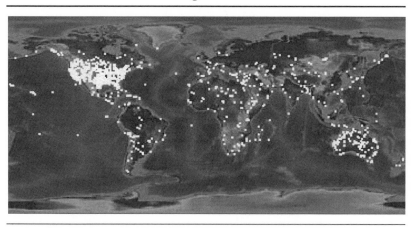

> Prevailing concepts of territorial sovereignty *permit a nation to regulate the local effects of extraterritorial conduct* even if this regulation produces spillover effects in other jurisdictions, [and] such spillover effects are a commonplace consequence of the unilateral application of any particular law to transnational activity in our increasingly interconnected world.[77]

We live in a world of interconnected and geographically complex causes and effects; a butterfly flapping its wings in Beijing can change weather patterns in New York; the presence of poisons in the soil in Central Asia can affect the abundance of fish in the Gulf of Mexico; a local currency trader, or bolt manufacturer, in Hong Kong can cause the crash of markets, or automobiles, in Frankfurt.

Imagine for the moment something we might call an "effects map." To construct such a map, we mark the location of every event taking place at any specific moment the "effects" of which will be felt in, say, Singapore. An "effects map" would look something like the familiar nighttime satellite images of "The Earth from Space" (see Figure 1); each point of light on the effects map, however, would represent not an actual source of illumination but rather the location of an event or transaction whose effects were felt by some person, or institution, in Singapore.

Consider an effects map depicting a moment in, say, 1450. Inasmuch as the effects of most activity taking place in 1450 declined

rapidly with increasing geographical distance, most events or transactions having an effect in Singapore would themselves take place
in, or around, Singapore. Our effects map would therefore show the
territory around Singapore as a dense concentration of points, a
small patch of intense light, with the remainder of the globe in
almost total darkness.

An effects map for 1950 would undoubtedly show greater relative
"brightness" *outside* of Singapore's borders, reflecting changes in
communication and transportation technologies over the past several centuries and increased numbers of border-crossing events and
transactions with widely dispersed geographical effects—"airplane
crashes, mass torts, multistate insurance coverage, or multinational
commercial transactions."[78]

But the 1950 map would, I submit, retain its geographical coherence because the effects of most human activity in 1950, notwithstanding "mail, the telephone, and smoke signals," remained geographically constrained. There would still be a bright cluster of
points down on the southern tip of the Malaysian peninsula. Even
if Singapore's actual political boundaries were omitted from our
effects map, we would probably be able to reconstruct those boundaries with reasonable accuracy without too much trouble, on the
basis of this patch of relative brightness alone.

However, an effects map plotting events and transactions taking
place today in cyberspace would look very different from this. A
plot of the location of all events and transactions taking place in
cyberspace that have an effect on persons and property in Singapore
will have virtually no geographical structure at all; points of light
will be wildly scattered about the map, seemingly at random. It's a
cliché, but it's true nonetheless: On the global network all points
are (virtually) equidistant from one another, irrespective of their
location in real space, and the effects of the butterfly on the Web
site in Beijing can be felt as strongly in Philadelphia as in Shanghai.
All transactions in cyberspace are potentially border-crossing, *all*
have geographically indeterminate effects, *all* resemble the "airplane
crashes, mass torts, multistate insurance coverage, and multinational
commercial transactions" of real space. We would have much, much
more trouble reconstructing Singapore's actual boundaries from a
map limited to cyberspace events and transactions in 2002 than from
any of our previous maps.

With respect to the "Effects Principle" at the heart of the Unexceptionalist argument—the principle that "a nation's right to control events within its territory and to protect its citizens permits it to regulate the local effects of extraterritorial acts"[79]—the world *has* changed, rather dramatically. Border-crossing events and transactions, previously at the margins of the legal system and of sufficient rarity to be cabined off into a small corner of the legal universe—"airplane crashes, mass torts, multistate insurance coverage, or multinational commercial transactions"—have migrated, in cyberspace, to the core of that system.

A world in which virtually *all* events and transactions have border-crossing effects is surely not "functionally identical" to a world in which most do not, at least not with respect to the application of a principle that necessarily requires consideration of the distribution of those effects. A world in which the Effects Principle returns the result "No Substantial Effects Outside the Borders" when applied to the vast majority of events and transactions is not "functionally identical" to a world in which application of the same principle to the vast majority of events and transactions returns the opposite result. A world in which, on occasion, bullets are fired from one jurisdiction into another[80] is not "functionally identical" to a world in which all jurisdictions are constantly subjected to shrapnel from a thousand different directions.

To paraphrase Judge Whyte: carried to its "natural extreme,"[81] application of the (settled) Effects Principle is not "workable."[82] Like Judge Whyte, I "cannot see any meaningful distinction . . . between what [Digitalbook.com does] and what every other [Web site does],"[83] and I think that subjecting *all* Web sites to dozens, or perhaps hundreds, of different and possibly conflicting legal regimes "does not make sense."[84] Like Judge Whyte, I "do not find workable"[85] a theory of prescriptive jurisdiction that would hold Digitalbook.com (and all Web site operators) responsible for complying, simultaneously, with the laws of all jurisdictions worldwide. Like Judge Whyte, I think that, "carried to its natural extreme,"[86] the Effects Principle leads to "unreasonable liability."[87]

Consent

If governments "deriv[e] their just powers from the consent of the governed,"[88] how can Singapore, or England, legitimately exercise lawmaking power over Digitalbook.com?

The Unexceptionalists are not unduly troubled by this question, because settled principles of international law have already resolved it. While consent may be a prerequisite for the legitimate exercise of *private* power, it is, apparently, no longer a prerequisite for the legitimate exercise of *governmental* power.[89] Thus, Goldsmith writes, it is an "uncontested assumption" of the international legal order that the need to demonstrate consent to assertions of sovereign power "begins from the premise that *in its absence, national regulation of local effects is a legitimate incident of sovereignty,*"[90] that "in the *absence* of consensual international solutions, *prevailing concepts of territorial sovereignty permit a nation to regulate the local effects of extraterritorial conduct.*"[91]

The Effects Principle itself, in other words, is, as a normative matter, a source of sovereign authority, independent of the consent of the governed; transactions "can *legitimately* be regulated [by] the jurisdictions where significant effects of the transaction are felt"[92] whether or not the parties engaged in or affected by those transactions have consented to the application of the laws of those jurisdictions.

Though I find this view of the relationship between the Consent Principle and the Effects Principle normatively unappealing, this is not the place to engage in *that* argument. Though I happen to believe, contra Goldsmith et al., that the former principle should take precedence over the latter in the event of a conflict between them, I raise the issue here merely to suggest that scale may matter here as well, that the way we resolve this conflict at one scale, in the conditions of real space, does not necessarily dictate how we should resolve it at a different scale, in cyberspace. I suggest, in other words, that cyberspace is, for these purposes and with respect to this question, different.

Consider an expanding balloon. Molecules at the surface of the balloon are giving off prodigious amounts of heat (per molecule) as the energy from the inrushing air causes some of the bonds between the balloon's atoms to shear apart (releasing small quanta of energy in the form of heat). The expanding surface rubs up against outside air molecules, causing the production and release of more heat through friction. Fortunately for whoever is holding the balloon, not all molecules are exploding in this way, or the balloon would quickly become too hot to handle.

The legal system is the balloon. There has been friction at the surface, border-crossing events and transactions—"airplane crashes, mass torts, multistate insurance coverage, or multinational commercial transactions"—where the Consent Principle and the Effects Principle collide, setting off small explosions. As long as these remain on the surface—at the margin—the system as a whole is stable. If, however, these collisions start to occur throughout the entire volume of the balloon, no longer confined to a narrow band at the surface, the heat generated becomes overwhelming and the balloon explodes.

All conduct in cyberspace has geographically far-flung effects on people and institutions around the world; on this Unexceptionalists and Exceptionalists agree. In cyberspace, there will continually be conflicts between a principle that permits sovereigns to regulate on the basis of those effects, and a principle that sovereigns can only regulate where they have the consent of the regulated. The "prevailing concepts of territorial sovereignty" evolved in a world in which these explosions between the Effects Principle and the Principle of Consent only presented themselves at the margins of the legal system, impacting a relatively small number of transactions. A world in which *all* actors, and *all* transactions, at *all* times, are subject to rules to which they have not consented, is not "functionally identical" to that world. We have a different problem before us now.

Conclusion

"Against Cyberanarchy" has been one of the most influential and oft-cited pieces in the cyberspace law canon.[93] I remain, however, unpersuaded, an unrepentant Exceptionalist. I think it does matter that Digitalbook.com is "in cyberspace"; I think that the questions raised by its conduct are indeed different, and more difficult, than the analogous questions raised by its real-space counterpart; and I do not believe that we can resolve the jurisdictional dilemmas posed by Digitalbook.com's transactions by applying the "traditional legal tools" developed for similar problems in real space.

The problem of "jurisdiction," as generations of law students can testify, can glaze over even the most attentive eyes. At its core, though, it reaches fundamental questions of order and legitimacy; lest we forget, we fought a revolution over the "jurisdiction to prescribe."[94] Cyberspace should give us pause. I am not quite ready to throw in the towel just yet. Settled law, and received principles, are worthy of respect; but at times they need to be reconsidered. This is one of those times.

5. The Shift Toward "Targeting" for Internet Jurisdiction

Michael Geist

> The Internet has no territorial boundaries. To paraphrase Gertrude Stein, as far as the Internet is concerned, not only is there perhaps 'no there there,' the 'there' is everywhere where there is Internet access.[1]
>
> Judge Nancy Gertner, *Digital Equipment Corp. v. Altavista Technology, Inc.*, 1997

> We order the company YAHOO! Inc. to take all measures to dissuade and make impossible any access via Yahoo.com to the auction service for Nazi objects and to any other site or service that may be construed as constituting an apology for Nazism or contesting the reality of Nazi crimes. . . .[2]
>
> Judge Jean-Jacques Gomez, *UEJF et LICRA v. Yahoo! Inc. et Yahoo France*, May 2000

Introduction

As business gravitated to the Internet in the late 1990s, concern over the legal risks of operating online quickly moved to the fore, as legal issues inherent in selling products, providing customer service, or simply maintaining an information-oriented Web site began to emerge.[3] Certain legal risks, such as selling defective products or inaccurate information disclosure, were already well-known to business, as these risks are encountered and addressed daily in the offline world.[4]

The unique challenge presented by the Internet is that compliance with local laws is rarely sufficient to assure a business that it has limited its exposure to legal risk. Since Web sites are instantly accessible worldwide, the prospect that a Web site owner might be haled

91

into a courtroom in a far-off jurisdiction is much more than a mere academic exercise. It is a very real possibility.[5] Businesses seeking to embrace the promise of a global market at the click of a mouse must factor into their analysis the prospect of additional compliance costs and possible litigation.

The risks are not limited to businesses. Consumers anxious to purchase online must also balance the promise of unlimited choice, greater access to information, and a more competitive global marketplace with the fact that they may not benefit from the security normally afforded by local consumer protection laws. Although such laws exist online, just as they do offline, their effectiveness is severely undermined if consumers do not have recourse within their local court system or if enforcing a judgment requires further proceedings in another jurisdiction.[6]

Moreover, concerns over the legal risks created by the Internet extend beyond commercial activities. Public interest information-based Web sites on controversial topics may face the prospect of prosecution in far-away jurisdictions despite their legality within the home jurisdiction.[7] Meanwhile, anonymous posters on Internet chat sites face the possibility that the target of their comments will launch a legal action aimed at uncovering their anonymous guise.[8]

In *International Shoe Co. v. Washington,* the Supreme Court outlined the contemporary basis for jurisdiction.[9] Under *International Shoe,* a court can exercise personal jurisdiction over a nonresident defendant if that defendant has "certain minimum contacts with [the forum] such that the maintenance of the suit does not offend 'traditional notions of fair play and substantial justice.'"[10] The minimum contacts standard serves two purposes: protecting defendants from burdensome litigation and ensuring that states do not reach too far beyond their jurisdictional limits.[11]

"Minimum contacts" have been defined as "conduct and connection with the forum . . . such that [the defendant] should reasonably anticipate being haled into court there."[12] A defendant's contacts are sufficient to satisfy the minimum contacts standard where they are "substantial" or "continuous and systematic," such that the defendant "purposefully avail[ed] itself of the privilege of conducting activities within the forum State, thus invoking the benefits and protections of its laws."[13] The plaintiff has the burden of showing that the defendant took action "purposefully directed" at the forum and that the cause of action arises from this action.[14] A defendant "purposefully avails" himself of jurisdiction when "the contacts proximately result from actions by the defendant himself that create a 'substantial connection' with the forum State."[15]

In determining whether the exercise of jurisdiction comports with notions of fair play and substantial justice, a court must balance several factors: (a) the extent of a defendant's purposeful interjection, (b) the inconvenience to the defendant of defending in that forum, (c) the extent of conflict with the sovereignty of the defendant's state, (d) the forum state's interest in adjudicating the dispute, (e) the interstate judicial system's interest in the efficient resolution of conflicts, (f) the plaintiff's interest in obtaining convenient and effective relief, and (g) the existence of an alternative forum.[16]

As courts struggled to adapt this jurisdictional framework to the Internet, a Pennsylvania district court case, *Zippo Manufacturing v. Zippo Dot Com, Inc.* emerged as the leading Internet jurisdiction case.[17] In the *Zippo* framework, commonly referred to as the passive-vs.-active test, courts gauge the relative interactivity of a Web site to determine whether assertion of jurisdiction is appropriate. At one end of the spectrum lie "passive" Web sites—minimally interactive information-based Web sites.[18] At the other end of the spectrum lie "active" Web sites, which feature greater interactivity and end-user contacts.[19] The *Zippo* test suggests that jurisdictions of Web site users should refrain from asserting authority over passive sites based in a distant locality, while jurisdiction over active sites is appropriate.

In light of the various standards being applied by courts in establishing jurisdictional rights in the online environment, this chapter examines the effectiveness of the current approaches and recommends possible reforms. I argue that the passive-vs.-active test established in *Zippo* has, with time, become increasingly outdated and irrelevant. I argue instead for the adoption of a three-factor targeting test that includes analysis and knowledge of contract, technology, and jurisdictional effects as the standard for assessing Internet jurisdiction claims.

The next section contains a review of recent Internet jurisdiction jurisprudence in both the United States and Canada, beginning with the development of and subsequent approval of the *Zippo* passive-vs.-active test. It identifies the subtle changes that have been occurring since late 1999 as courts have begun to find the *Zippo* test

93

too constraining and have shifted their analysis toward an effects-based paradigm.

Having argued that the *Zippo* test should be replaced, the concluding section presents an alternative. It proposes a targeting-based test for Internet jurisdiction that is supported by the growing acceptance of targeting in both case law and international policy levels. The section then advocates the adoption of a three-factor approach to targeting that includes assessments of any contractual provisions that address choice-of-forum or choice-of-law concerns, the technological measures employed to identify the targeted jurisdiction, and the actual or implied knowledge of the Web site operator with respect to targeted jurisdictions.

The Rise and Fall of the *Zippo* Test

Since 1996, United States courts have regularly faced litigation that includes an Internet jurisdiction component. As courts grapple with the issue, the jurisprudence has shifted first toward the *Zippo* passive-vs.-active test, then more recently toward an effects-based test with elements of targeting analysis.

The Emergence of the Zippo Passive-vs.-Active Test

The first North American application of jurisdictional principles to the Internet traces back to 1996 and *Inset Systems, Inc. v. Instruction Set, Inc.*, a Connecticut district court case.[20] In this instance, Inset Systems, a Connecticut company, brought a trademark infringement action against Instruction Set, a Massachusetts company, arising out of its use of the domain name "Inset.com."[21] Instruction Set used the domain name to advertise its goods and services on the Internet, a practice to which Inset objected since it was the owner of the federal trademark "Inset."[22] The legal question before the court was one of jurisdiction. Did Inset's conduct meet the minimum contacts standard outlined by the United States Supreme Court in *World-Wide Volkswagen*?[23] Did Instruction Set's activity, the establishment of a Web site, properly bring it within the jurisdiction of Connecticut under that state's long-arm statute?

The *Inset* court concluded that it could properly assert jurisdiction, basing its decision on Instruction Set's use of the Internet.[24] Likening the Internet to a continuous advertisement, the court reasoned that Instruction Set had purposefully directed its advertising activities toward Connecticut on a continuous basis and therefore could reasonably have anticipated being sued there.[25]

The court's decision was problematic for several reasons. First, its conclusion that creating a Web site amounts to a purposeful availment of every jurisdiction distorts the fundamental principle of jurisdiction.[26] Second, the court did not analyze the Internet itself but merely drew an analogy between the Internet and a more traditional media form, in this case a continuous advertisement.[27] If the court was correct, every court, everywhere, could assert jurisdiction where a Web site was directed toward its forum. This decision would stifle future Internet growth, as would-be Internet participants would be forced to weigh the advantages of a presence on the Internet with the potential of being subject to legal jurisdiction throughout the world. Third, the court did not assess Instruction Set's actual activity on the Internet.[28] The mere *use* of the Internet was sufficient for the *Inset* court to establish jurisdiction.[29] In fact, the court acknowledged that Instruction Set did not maintain an office in Connecticut nor did it have a sales force or employees in the state.[30]

A more complete analysis of the underlying facts would have included an assessment of precisely what was happening on the Internet. Was Instruction Set selling products directly to people in Connecticut through its Web site? Was it providing a service directly through its Web site? Was it actively soliciting the participation of potential users by encouraging correspondence? What was the approximate number of Connecticut users who actually accessed the Web site? Asking these and similar questions would have provided the court with a much stronger basis for holding that Instruction Set had purposefully directed its activity toward Connecticut.

Although several U.S. cases followed the *Inset* approach,[31] a New York district court case stands out as an important exception.[32] The Blue Note was a small Columbia, Missouri, club operated by Richard King. King promoted his club by establishing a Web site that included information about the club, a calendar of events, and ticketing information.[33] New York City was also home to a club named the Blue Note, this one operated by the Bensusan Restaurant Corporation, which owned the federal trademark to the name.[34] King was familiar with the New York Blue Note as he included a disclaimer on his Web site that stated: "The Blue Note's Cyberspot should not be confused with one of the world's finest jazz club[s], [the] Blue

Note, located in the heart of New York's Greenwich Village. If you should find yourself in the Big Apple give them a visit."[35]

Within months of the establishment of King's Blue Note Web site, Bensusan brought a trademark infringement and dilution action in New York federal court.[36] Once again, the court faced the question of personal jurisdiction in a trademark action arising out of activity on the Internet. Unlike the court in the *Inset* line of cases, however, the *Bensusan* court considered the specific uses of the Web site in question. It noted that King's Web site was passive rather than active in nature—several affirmative steps by a New York resident would be necessary to bring any potentially infringing product into the state.[37] Specifically, tickets could not be ordered online, so that anyone wishing to make a purchase would have to telephone the box office in Missouri, only to find that the Missouri club did not mail tickets.[38] The purchaser would have to travel to Missouri to obtain the tickets.[39] Given the level of passivity, the court ruled that the Web site did not infringe Bensusan's trademark in New York.[40] The court argued "the mere fact that a person can gain information on the allegedly infringing product is not the equivalent of a person advertising, promoting, selling or otherwise making an effort to target its product in New York."[41]

The *Bensusan* decision, which the Court of Appeals for the Second Circuit affirmed in September 1997,[42] provided an important step toward the development of deeper legal analysis of Internet activity. Although the decision did not attempt to reconcile *Inset* and its progeny, it provided the groundwork for a new line of cases.[43] Notwithstanding the *Bensusan* decision, by the end of 1996 the majority of Internet-related decisions evidenced little genuine understanding of activity on the Internet. Rather, most courts were unconcerned with the jurisdictional implications of their rulings and instead favored an analogy-based approach in which the Internet was categorized en masse.[44]

In early 1997, a new approach emerged, led by a Pennsylvania district court decision, *Zippo Manufacturing Co. v. Zippo Dot Com, Inc.*[45] It was with this decision that courts gradually began to appreciate that activity on the Internet was as varied as that in real space, and that all-encompassing analogies could not be appropriately applied to this new medium. Zippo Manufacturing was a Pennsylvania-based manufacturer of the well-known "Zippo" brand of tobacco lighters.[46] Zippo Dot Com was a California-based Internet news service that used the domain name "Zippo.com" to provide access to Internet newsgroups.[47] Zippo Dot Com offered three levels of subscriber service—free, original, and super.[48] Those subscribers desiring the original or super level of service were required to fill out an online application form and submit a credit card number through the Internet or by telephone.[49] Zippo Dot Com's contacts with Pennsylvania occurred almost exclusively on the Internet because the company maintained no offices, employees, or agents in the state.[50] Zippo Dot Com had some success in attracting Pennsylvania subscribers; at the time of the action, approximately 3,000, or 2 percent of its subscribers, resided in that state.[51] Once again, the issue before the court was one of personal jurisdiction arising out of a claim of trademark infringement and dilution.[52]

Rather than using analogies as the basis for its analysis, the court focused on the prior, somewhat limited Internet case law.[53] The court, which clearly used the *Bensusan* decision for inspiration, determined that, although few cases had been decided, the likelihood that personal jurisdiction can be constitutionally exercised is *directly proportionate to the nature and quality of commercial activity that an entity conducts over the Internet.*[54]

The court proceeded to identify a sliding scale based on Internet commercial activity:

> At one end of the spectrum are situations where a defendant clearly does business over the Internet. If the defendant enters into contracts with residents of a foreign jurisdiction that involve the knowing and repeated transmission of computer files over the Internet, personal jurisdiction is proper. At the opposite end are situations where a defendant has simply posted information on an Internet Web site, which is accessible to users in foreign jurisdictions. A passive Web site that does little more than make information available to those who are interested in it is not grounds for the exercise of personal jurisdiction. The middle ground is occupied by interactive Web sites where a user can exchange information with the host computer. In these cases, the exercise of jurisdiction is determined by examining the level of interactivity and commercial nature of the exchange of information that occurs on the Web site.[55]

Although the court may have conveniently interpreted some earlier cases to obtain its desired result, its critical finding was that the jurisdictional analysis in Internet cases should be based on the nature and quality of the commercial activity conducted on the Internet. There is a strong argument that before *Zippo*, jurisdictional analysis was based on the mere use of the Internet. Courts relying solely on the inappropriate analogy between the Internet and advertisements developed a legal doctrine poorly suited to the complexity of Internet activity. In the aftermath of the *Zippo* decision, Internet legal analysis underwent a significant shift in perspective.

Post-*Zippo* *Case Law*

In the years following *Zippo*, the passive-vs.-active approach has been cited with approval in numerous cases.[56] For example, in *Cybersell, Inc. v. Cybersell, Inc.*, the Ninth Circuit considered whether it could exercise jurisdiction over a Web site containing an allegedly infringing service mark.[57] Both Cybersell Arizona, the owner of the "Cybersell" federal service mark, and Cybersell Florida provided Internet marketing and consulting services.[58] Cybersell Florida's presence in Arizona was limited to a Web site advertising its services and inviting interested parties to contact it for additional information.[59] The court, in determining the appropriateness of exercising jurisdiction, noted:

> No court has ever held that an Internet advertisement alone is sufficient to subject the advertiser to jurisdiction in the plaintiff's home state. Rather, in each, there has been "something more" to indicate that the defendant purposefully (albeit electronically) directed his activity in a substantial way to the forum state.[60]

The court followed the *Zippo* approach by attempting to ascertain the nature and quality of Cybersell Florida's Web-based activity.[61] The court considered the passive nature of the site, the fact that no Arizonian other than Cybersell Florida Arizona visited the site, and the lack of evidence that any Arizonians had entered into a contractual relationship with Cybersell.[62] On these facts, the court concluded that it could not properly assert jurisdiction in the matter.[63]

The widespread approval for the *Zippo* test should come as little surprise. The uncertainty created by the Internet jurisdiction issue led to a strong desire for a workable solution that provided a fair balance between the fear of a lawless Internet and one burdened by overregulation. The *Zippo* test seemed the best available alternative.

This is particularly true in light of the *Inset* line of cases, which illustrated that the alternative might well be the application of jurisdiction by any court, anywhere. The court in *Neato v. Stomp L.L.C.*, a 1999 federal court case in California, aptly summarized the potentially competing policy positions of consumers and businesses: protecting consumers and encouraging the development of Internet commerce, respectively.[64] The court chose to side squarely with consumers, noting that businesses can choose to sell their goods only to consumers in a particular geographic location:

> When a merchant seeks the benefit of engaging in unlimited interstate commerce over the Internet, it runs the risk of being subject to the process of the courts of those states.[65]

The *Zippo* passive-vs.-active test is grounded in traditional jurisdictional principles. The analysis conducted as part of the test draws heavily from a foreseeability perspective, which suggests that it is not foreseeable for the owner of a passive Web site to face the prospect of being sued in multiple jurisdictions worldwide. Conversely, as the court in *Neato* recognized, the active e-commerce Web site owner must surely foresee the possibility of disputes arising in other jurisdictions and recognize that those courts are entitled to protect local residents by applying local law and asserting jurisdiction.

Most important, however, in an emphatic repudiation of the "Internet as a separate jurisdiction[al]" approach, the *Zippo* case made it explicit that local law still applies to the Internet. Although it is at times difficult to discern precisely whose law applies, there is little doubt that at least one jurisdiction, if not more, can credibly claim jurisdiction over any given Internet dispute. With this principle in hand, the *Zippo* court sent a clear signal to the Internet community: courts were willing to establish a balanced approach to Internet jurisdiction.

The Shift Away from Zippo

Despite the widespread acceptance of the *Zippo* doctrine (and indeed the export of the test to foreign countries, including Canada), limitations of the test began to appear late in 1999. In fact, closer examination of the case law indicates that by 2002 many courts were no longer strictly applying the *Zippo* standard, but were using other criteria to determine when assertion of jurisdiction was appropriate.[66]

A number of judgments reflect that courts in the United States have moved toward a broader, effects-based approach when deciding whether or not to assert jurisdiction in the Internet context. Under this new approach, rather than examining the specific characteristics of a Web site and its potential impact, courts focused their analysis on the actual effects that the Web site had in the jurisdiction regardless of whether the site might be characterized as passive or active. Indeed, courts are now relying increasingly on the effects doctrine established by the Supreme Court in *Calder v. Jones*.[67]

The effects doctrine holds that personal jurisdiction over a defendant is proper when the defendant's intentional tortious actions, expressly aimed at the forum state, cause harm to the plaintiff in the forum state, harm that the defendant knows is likely to be suffered.[68] In *Calder*, a California entertainer sued a Florida offline publisher for libel in a California district court.[69] In ruling that personal jurisdiction was properly asserted, the Court focused on the effects of the defendant's actions.[70] Reasoning that the plaintiff lived and worked in California, spent most of her career in California, suffered injury to her professional reputation in California, and suffered emotional distress in California, the Court concluded that the defendant had intentionally targeted a California resident and thus it was proper to sue the publisher in that state.[71]

The application of the *Calder* test can be seen in the Internet context in *Blakey v. Continental Airlines, Inc.*,[72] an online defamation case involving an airline employee. The employee filed suit in New Jersey against her coemployees, alleging that they published defamatory statements on the employer's electronic bulletin board, and against her employer, a New Jersey-based corporation, alleging that it was liable for the hostile work environment arising from the statements.[73] The lower court granted the coemployees' motion to dismiss the case for lack of personal jurisdiction and entered summary judgment for the employer on the hostile work environment claim.[74]

In reversing the ruling, the New Jersey Supreme Court found that defendants who published defamatory electronic messages with the knowledge that the messages would be published in New Jersey could properly be held subject to the state's jurisdiction.[75] The court applied the effects doctrine and held that while the actions causing the effects in New Jersey were performed outside the state, that did not prevent the court from asserting jurisdiction over a cause of action arising out of those effects.[76]

The broader effects-based analysis has moved beyond the defamatory tort action at issue in *Calder* and *Blakey* to a range of disputes including intellectual property and commercial activities. On the intellectual property front, *Nissan Motor Co. Ltd. v. Nissan Computer Corp.*[77] typifies the approach. The plaintiff, an automobile manufacturer, filed a complaint in a California district court against a Massachusetts-based computer seller. Prompting the complaint was an allegation that the defendant altered the content of its "nissan.com" Web site to include a logo that was similar to the plaintiff's logo and links to automobile merchandisers and auto-related portions of search engines.[78] In October 1999, the parties met to discuss the possibility of transferring the "nissan.com" domain name.[79] These negotiations proved unsuccessful.[80] The defendant brought a motion to dismiss for lack of personal jurisdiction and improper venue, and the plaintiff brought a motion for a preliminary injunction in March 2000.[81]

In considering the defendant's motion, the court relied on the effects doctrine, ruling that the defendant had intentionally changed the content of its Web site to exploit the plaintiff's goodwill and to profit from consumer confusion.[82] Moreover, since the plaintiff was based in California, most of the harm was suffered in the forum state.[83] The court rejected the defendant's argument that it was not subject to personal jurisdiction because it merely operated a passive Web site.[84] Although the defendant did not sell anything over the Internet, it derived advertising revenue through the intentional exploitation of consumer confusion.[85] That fact, according to the court, satisfied the *Cybersell* requirement of "something more," in that it established that the defendant's conduct was deliberately and substantially directed toward the forum state.[86]

Courts have also refused to assert jurisdiction in a number of cases in which insufficient commercial effects were found. For example, in *People Solutions, Inc. v. People Solutions, Inc.*,[87] the defendant, a California-based corporation, moved to dismiss a trademark infringement suit brought against it by a Texas-based corporation of the same name. The plaintiff argued that the suit was properly brought in Texas because the defendant owned a Web site that could be accessed and viewed by Texas residents.[88] The site featured several interactive pages that allowed customers to take and score performance tests, download product demonstrations, and order products online.[89]

The court characterized the site as interactive but refused to assert jurisdiction over the matter.[90] Relying on evidence that no Texans had actually purchased anything from the Web site, the court held that "personal jurisdiction should not be premised on the mere possibility, with nothing more, that defendant may be able to do business with Texans over its Web site."[91] Instead, the plaintiff had to show that the defendant had "purposefully availed itself of the benefits of the forum state and its laws."[92]

Similarly, in *Robbins v. Yutopian Enterprises, Inc.*,[93] the Maryland district court acknowledged that the site in question would be characterized as active under a Zippo analysis, yet reasoned that without a connection between the claim and a specific transaction within the state, the conclusion that the site in question was active was of "limited significance."

In fact, even courts that cite *Zippo* with approval increasingly tend to adapt the passive-vs.-active test to account for alternative factors. For example, in *ALS Scan, Inc. v. Digital Service Consultants, Inc.*,[94] the Fourth Circuit Court of Appeals addressed an Internet jurisdiction issue by expressly adopting *Zippo*, yet it applied a jurisdictional analysis that required (a) direct electronic activity into the state, (b) with the manifested intent of engaging in business or other interactions within the state, and (c) that the activity creates, in a person within the state, a potential cause of action cognizable in the state's courts.[95] Although the *ALS* court indicated that it was adopting the *Zippo* test, it actually adopted a test that bears far greater resemblance to an effects- and targeting-based analysis.

Although the case law illustrates that there is no single reason for the courts to shift away from the *Zippo* test, a number of themes do emerge. First, the test simply does not work particularly well in every instance. For example, with courts characterizing chat room postings as passive in nature,[96] many might be inclined to dismiss cases involving allegedly defamatory or harassing speech on jurisdictional grounds. Such speech may often be targeted toward a particular individual or entity located in a jurisdiction different from the poster or the chat site itself. Characterizing the act as passive does not result in a desirable outcome because the poster knows or ought to know that the effect of his or her posting will be felt most acutely in the home jurisdiction of the target. If the target is unable to sue locally due to a strict adherence to the passive-vs.-active test, the law might be seen as encouraging online defamatory speech by creating a jurisdictional hurdle to launching a legal claim.

The *Zippo* test also falls short when active sites are at issue, as the courts in *People Solutions* and *Yutopian* recognized.[98] The *People Solutions* court's request for evidence of actual sales within the jurisdiction illustrates that the mere potential to sell within a jurisdiction does not necessarily make a Web site active.[98] Although the owner of an active Web site may want to sell within every jurisdiction, the foreseeability of a legal action is confined primarily to those places in which actual sales occur. The *Zippo* test does not distinguish between actual and potential sales, however, but rather provides that the mere existence of an active site, a criterion viewed as an effective proxy for commercial activity, is sufficient to assert jurisdiction.

The problems with the *Zippo* test are not limited to inconsistent and often undesirable outcomes. The test also encourages a perverse behavior that runs contrary to public policy related to the Internet and e-commerce. Most countries have embraced the potential of e-commerce and have adopted policies designed to encourage the use of the Internet for commercial purposes.[99] The *Zippo* test, however, potentially inhibits e-commerce by effectively discouraging the adoption of interactive Web sites. Prospective Web site owners who are concerned about their exposure to legal liability will rationally shy away from developing active Web sites because such sites increase the likelihood of facing lawsuits in far-off jurisdictions. Instead, the test encourages passive Web sites that feature limited legal exposure and therefore present limited risk. Since public policy aims to increase interactivity and the adoption of e-commerce (and, in doing so, enhance consumer choice and open new markets for small and medium-sized businesses), the *Zippo* test acts as a barrier to that policy approach.

One of the primary reasons for the early widespread support for the *Zippo* test was the desire for increased legal certainty for Internet jurisdiction issues. Although the test may not have been perfect, supporters thought it offered a clear standard that would allow businesses to conduct effective legal risk analysis and make rational choices with regard to their approach to the Internet.[100]

In the final analysis, however, the *Zippo* test simply does not deliver the desired effect. First, the majority of Web sites are neither entirely passive nor completely active. Accordingly, they fall into the "middle zone," which requires courts to gauge all relevant evidence and determine whether the site is "primarily passive" or "primarily active." With many sites falling into this middle zone, legal advisers are frequently unable to provide a firm opinion on how any given court might judge the interactivity of the Web site.

Second, distinguishing between passive and active sites is complicated by the fact that some sites may not be quite what they seem. For example, sites that feature content best characterized as passive may actually be using "cookies" or other data collection technologies behind the scenes unbeknown to the individual user.[101] Given the value of personal data,[102] its collection is properly characterized as active, regardless of whether it occurs transparently or surreptitiously.[103] Similarly, sites such as online chatrooms may appear to be active, yet courts have consistently characterized such sites as passive.[104]

Third, it is important to note that the standards for what constitutes an active or passive Web site are constantly shifting. When the test was developed in 1997, an active Web site might have featured little more than an e-mail link and some basic correspondence functionality. Today, sites with that level of interactivity would likely be viewed as passive, since the entire spectrum of passive-vs.-active has shifted upward with improved technology. In fact, it can be credibly argued that owners of Web sites must constantly reevaluate their positions on the passive-vs.-active spectrum as Internet technology changes.

Fourth, the *Zippo* test is ineffective even if the standards for passive and active sites remain constant. With the expense of creating a sophisticated Web site now easily in excess of $100,000,[105] few organizations will invest in a Web site without anticipating some earning potential. Since revenue is typically the hallmark of active Web sites, most new sites are likely to feature interactivity and therefore be categorized as active sites. From a jurisdictional perspective, this produces an effect similar to that found in the *Inset* line of cases— any court anywhere can assert jurisdiction over a Web site because virtually all sites will meet the *Zippo* active benchmark.

In light of the ever-changing technological environment and the shift toward predominantly active Web sites, the effectiveness of the *Zippo* doctrine is severely undermined no matter how it develops. If the test evolves with the changing technological environment, it fails to provide much-needed legal certainty. On the other hand, if the test remains static to provide increased legal certainty, it risks becoming irrelevant as the majority of Web sites meet the active standard. In the next section, this chapter will offer an alternative test.

Toward a Trio of Targets

Given the inadequacies of the *Zippo* passive-vs.-active test and the primarily offline approach of the effects test, a new standard is needed to determine jurisdiction over Internet contacts. This section sketches the components of a targeting test by focusing on three factors: assessments of any contractual provisions that address choice-of-forum or choice-of-law concerns, the technological measures employed to identify the targeted jurisdiction, and the actual or implied knowledge of the Web site operator with respect to targeted jurisdictions.

Advantages of a Targeting Approach

The *Zippo* experience suggests that the new test should remain technology neutral so as to (a) remain relevant despite ever-changing Internet technologies, (b) create incentives that, at a minimum, do not discourage online interactivity, and (c) provide sufficient certainty so that the legal risk of operating online can be effectively assessed in advance.

The solution submitted here is to move toward a targeting-based analysis that could be used by courts to gauge the appropriateness of asserting jurisdiction and by Internet companies and users to assess potential jurisdictional risks. Unlike the *Zippo* approach, a targeting analysis would seek to identify the intentions of the parties and to assess the steps taken to either enter or avoid a particular jurisdiction. Targeting would also lessen the reliance on effects-based analyses, which may generate some uncertainty because Internet-based activity can ordinarily be said to cause effects in most jurisdictions.

A targeting approach is not a novel idea. Several U.S. courts have factored targeting considerations into their jurisdictional analysis of Internet-based activities. One of the strongest indications of a move toward a targeting test for Internet jurisdiction came in April 2001 in *American Information Corp. v. American Infometrics, Inc.*, a Maryland district court case.[106] Targeting was an important consideration in the court's jurisdictional analysis:

> In the case at bar, non-customers cannot interact with the Web site except to submit their contract information to inquire about available services or jobs, according to Goreff, and no one from Maryland has ever inquired, or been a customer of American Infometrics. On a company's Web site, neither the "mere existence of an e-mail link, without more," nor "receiving . . . an indication of interest," without more, subjects the company to jurisdiction. The ability of viewers to ask about the company's services, particularly in the absence of any showing that anyone in Maryland has ever done so, does not subject the company to jurisdiction here.[107]

Fourth Circuit cases on minimum contacts supported the view that the American Infometrics Web site did not create jurisdiction in Maryland. A company's sales activities focusing "generally on customers located throughout the United States and Canada without focusing on and targeting" the forum state did not yield personal jurisdiction.[108] An Internet presence that permits no more than basic inquiries from Maryland customers, that has never yielded an actual inquiry from a Maryland customer, and that does not target Maryland in any way should not yield personal jurisdiction.[109]

The importance of targeting also arose in *Bell v. Imperial Palace Hotel/Casino, Inc.*,[110] as a Missouri district court ruled that it would not assert jurisdiction over an out-of-state entity with an active Web site in the jurisdiction after noting that the "defendant's business is not targeted to Missouri residents."[111]

Targeting-based analysis has also become increasingly prevalent among international organizations seeking to develop global minimum legal standards for e-commerce. The Consumer Protection Guidelines of the Organisation for Economic Co-operation and Development refer to the concept of targeting, stating that "business should take into account the global nature of electronic commerce and, wherever possible, should consider various regulatory characteristics of the markets they target."[112]

The American Bar Association (ABA) Global Cyberspace Jurisdiction Project, a global study on Internet jurisdiction released in 2000, also recommended targeting as one method of addressing the Internet jurisdiction issue.[113] The report noted—

> Entities seeking a relationship with residents of a foreign forum need not themselves maintain a physical presence in the forum. A forum can be "targeted" by those outside it and desirous of benefiting from a connection with it via the Internet. . . . Such a chosen relationship will subject the foreign actor to both personal and prescriptive jurisdiction, so a clear understanding of what constitutes targeting is critical.[114]

It is the ABA's last point—that a clear understanding of what constitutes targeting is critical—that requires careful examination and discussion. Without universally applicable standards for assessment of targeting in the online environment, a targeting test is likely to leave further uncertainty in its wake. For example, the ABA's report refers to language as a potentially important determinant for targeting purposes with the presumption that a site in Greek would be targeting Greece. That criterion overlooks the fact that the development of new language translation capabilities may soon enable Web site owners to display their sites in the language of their choice, safe in the knowledge that visitors around the world will read the content in their own language through the aid of translation technologies.[115]

The Targeting Test

Targeting as the litmus test for Internet jurisdiction is only the first step in the development of a consistent test that provides increased legal certainty. The second, more challenging step is to identify the criteria to be used in assessing whether a Web site has indeed targeted a particular jurisdiction. This article cites three factors: contracts, technology, and actual or implied knowledge. Forum selection clauses found in Web site terms of use agreements or transactional clickwrap agreements allow parties to mutually determine an appropriate jurisdiction in advance of a dispute. They therefore provide important evidence as to the foreseeability of being haled into the courts of a particular jurisdiction. Newly emerging technologies that identify geographic location constitute the second factor. These technologies, which challenge widely held perceptions about the Internet's architecture, may allow Web site owners to target their content by engaging in "jurisdictional avoidance." The third factor, actual or implied knowledge, is a catch-all that incorporates targeting knowledge gained through the geographic location of tort victims, offline order fulfillment, financial intermediary records, and Internet traffic.

Although all three factors are important, no single factor should be determinative. Rather, each must be analyzed to make an adequate assessment of whether the parties have fairly negotiated a governing jurisdiction clause at a private contract level, whether the parties employed any technological solutions to target their activities, and whether the parties knew, or ought to have known, where their online activities were occurring. Although all three factors should be considered as part of a targeting analysis, the relative importance of each varies. Moreover, in certain instances, some factors may not matter at all. For example, a defamation action is unlikely to involve a contractual element, though evidence from the knowledge factor is likely to prove sufficient to identify the targeted jurisdiction.

It is also important to note that the targeting analysis will not determine exclusive jurisdiction but rather identify whether a particular jurisdiction can be appropriately described as having been targeted. The test does not address which venue is the *most* appropriate of the jurisdictions that meet the targeting threshold.

Contracts. The first of the three factors for the recommended targeting test considers whether either party has used a contractual arrangement to specify which law should govern. Providing parties with the opportunity to limit their legal risk by addressing jurisdictional concerns in advance can be the most efficient and cost-effective approach to dealing with the Internet jurisdiction issue. The mere existence of a jurisdictional clause within a contract, however, should not, in and of itself, be determinative of the issue, particularly when consumer contracts are involved. In addition to considering the two other targeting factors, the weight accorded to an online contract should depend on the method used to obtain assent and the reasonableness of the terms contained in the contract.

Courts in the United States have upheld the per se enforceability of an online contract,[116] commonly referred to as a clickwrap agreement. In *Kilgallen v. Network Solutions, Inc.,*[117] the court faced a dispute over the reregistration of a domain name. The plaintiff claimed that Network Solutions, the defendant, was in breach of contract when it transferred its domain name to a third party.[118] Network Solutions defended its actions by countering that the plaintiff had failed to make the annual payment necessary to maintain the domain.[119] Moreover, it sought to dismiss the action on the grounds that the registration agreement specified that all disputes were to be resolved in the Eastern District of Virginia.[120] The federal court in Massachusetts agreed, ruling that forum selection clauses are enforceable unless proven unreasonable under the circumstances.[121]

Notwithstanding the apparent support for enforcing forum selection clauses within clickwrap agreements, the presence of such a clause should only serve as the starting point for analysis. A court must first consider how assent to the contract was obtained. If the agreement is a standard clickwrap agreement in which users were required to positively indicate their agreement by clicking on an "I agree" or similar icon, the court will likely deem this to be valid assent. Many jurisdictional clauses are not found in a clickwrap agreement, however, but are contained in the terms-of-use agreement on the Web site. The terms typically provide that users of the Web site agree to all terms contained therein by virtue of their use of the site.

The validity of this form of contract, in which no positive assent is obtained and the Web site visitor is unlikely to have read the terms, stands on shakier ground. Three recent U.S. cases have considered this form of contract, and the consensus is moving toward nonenforcement. In *Ticketmaster v. Tickets.com*,[122] a dispute over links between rival event ticket sites, the court considered the enforceability of the terms and conditions page found on the Ticketmaster site and concluded that the forum selection clause was not enforceable.[123] The terms and conditions set forth on the Ticketmaster home page provided that users going beyond the home page were prevented from making commercial use of the information and were prohibited from deep linking.[124] Ticketmaster defended on the grounds that courts enforce "shrink-wrap licenses" where "packing on the outside of the CD stated that opening the package constitutes adherence to the license agreement . . . contained therein."[125]

The court found that Ticketmaster's system of notification did not create a binding contract on the user.[126] Unlike the agreement on the Ticketmaster site, "the 'shrink-wrap license agreement' is open and obvious and in fact hard to miss."[127] Ticketmaster's terms and conditions did not require the user to "click on 'agree' to the terms and conditions before going on" as many Web sites do.[128] The court further noted that customers were required "to scroll down the home page to find and read" the terms and conditions.[129] Given this system, "many customers . . . are likely to proceed to the event page of interest rather than reading the 'small print.' *It cannot be said that merely putting the terms and conditions in this fashion necessarily creates a contract with any one using the Web site.*"[130] This case suggests that mere inclusion of a forum selection or other jurisdictional clause, within the terms and conditions, may not be enforceable because the term is not brought sufficiently to the attention of the user.

Several months after the Ticketmaster decision, another federal court adopted a different approach in *Register.com, Inc. v. Verio, Inc.*[131] This case involved a dispute over Verio's use of automated software to access and collect the domain name registrant's contact information contained in the Register.com WHOIS database. Verio collected the data to use for marketing purposes.[132] Register.com provided the following terms and conditions for those wishing to access its WHOIS database:

> By submitting a WHOIS query, you agree that you will use this data only for lawful purposes and that, under no circumstances will you use this data to: (1) allow, enable, or otherwise support the transmission of mass unsolicited, commercial advertising or solicitations via direct mail, electronic mail, or by telephone; or (2) enable high volume, automated, electronic processes that apply to Register.com (or its systems). The compilation, repackaging, dissemination or other use of this data is expressly prohibited without the prior written consent of Register.com. Register.com reserves the right to modify these terms at any time. By submitting this query, you agree to abide by these terms.[133]

Unlike the court in the *Ticketmaster* case, the court in *Register.com* ruled that these terms were binding on users, despite the absence of a clear manifestation of assent.[134] The court relied on the users' willingness to engage with the Web site, by using the WHOIS database, as evidence that the user could by implication be considered to have agreed to the terms of the contract.

In *Specht v. Netscape Communications Corp.*,[135] the *Register.com* court distinguished between clickwrap contracts, which it argued feature positive assent in the form of clicking "I agree," and browsewrap contracts, in which the user is merely alerted to the existence of a contract through a disclaimer or other notice. The court, whose decision was upheld on appeal in October 2002 by the Second Circuit Court of Appeals,[136] ruled that the latter form of contract, employed in this case by Netscape Communications, was not binding against the user since Netscape had failed to obtain the user's positive assent. Netscape argued "the mere act of downloading indicates assent."[137] As the court noted, however, "downloading is hardly an unambiguous indication of assent" because "the primary purpose of downloading is to obtain a product, not to assent to an agreement."[138] The court criticized Netscape for not drawing the user's attention to the contract, for not requiring an affirmative manifestation of assent, and for only making a "mild request" that the user review the terms of the licensing agreement.[139]

While the form of assent may call into question the validity of an online contract, the actual terms of the contract itself are of even greater consequence. Courts are required to consider the reasonableness of the terms of a contract as part of their analysis. Within the context of a jurisdictional inquiry, several different scenarios may lead the court to discount the importance of the contract as part of a targeting analysis. A court may simply rule that the forum selection clause is unenforceable in light of the overall nature of the contract.

This ruling occurred in *Mendoza v. AOL*,[140] a 2000 California case involving a disputed Internet service provider bill. After Mendoza sued America Online in California state court, AOL responded by seeking to have the case dismissed on the grounds that the AOL service contract contains a forum selection clause that requires all disputes arising from the contract to be brought in Virginia.[141] The court surprised AOL by refusing to enforce the company's terms-of-service agreement on the grounds that "it would be unfair and unreasonable because the clause in question was not negotiated at arm's length, was contained in a standard form contract, and was not readily identifiable by the plaintiff due to the small type and the placement of the clause at the conclusion of the agreement."[142] Though cases such as *Mendoza* are the exception rather than the rule, they do point to the fact that a forum selection clause will not always be enforced, particularly in consumer disputes where the provision may be viewed by a court as too onerous because of the small amount at issue.[143]

Courts may also be unwilling to enforce such clauses when the court perceives the clause to be an attempt to contract out of the jurisdiction with the closest tie to the parties. Courts must be vigilant to ensure that forum selection clauses are not used to create a "race to the bottom" effect whereby parties select jurisdictions with lax regulations in an attempt to avoid more onerous regulations in the home jurisdictions of either the seller or the purchaser.[144]

Contracts must clearly play a central role in any determination of jurisdiction targeting since providing parties with the opportunity to set their own rules enhances legal certainty. As the foregoing review of recent Internet jurisdiction case law reveals, however, contracts do not provide the parties with absolute assurance that their choice will be enforced, particularly in a consumer context. Rather, courts must engage in a detailed analysis of how consent was obtained as well as consider the reasonableness of the terms. The results of that analysis should determine what weight to grant the contractual terms when they are balanced against the remaining two factors of the proposed targeting analysis.

Technology. The second targeting factor focuses on the use of technology to either target or avoid specific jurisdictions. Just as technology originally shaped the Internet, it is now reshaping its boundaries by quickly making geographic identification on the Internet a reality. The rapid emergence of these new technologies challenges what has been treated as a truism in cyberlaw—that the Internet is borderless and thus impervious to attempts to impose on it real-space laws that mirror traditional geographic boundaries.[145]

The fact that courts have largely accepted the notion that the Internet is borderless is reflected in their reluctance to even consider the possibility that geographic mapping might be possible online. In *American Libraries Ass'n v. Pataki,*[146] a Commerce Clause challenge to a New York State law targeting Internet content classified as obscene, the court characterized geography on the Internet in the following manner:

> The Internet is wholly insensitive to geographic distinctions. In almost every case, users of the Internet neither know nor care about the physical location of the Internet resources they access. Internet protocols were designed to ignore rather than document geographic location; while computers on the network do have "addresses," they are logical addresses on

the network rather than geographic addresses in real space. The majority of Internet addresses contain no geographic clues and, even where an Internet address provides such a clue, it may be misleading.[147]

Although the New York district court's view of the Internet may have been accurate in 1997, the Internet has not remained static. Providers of Internet content increasingly care about the physical location of Internet resources and the users that access them, as do legislators and courts who may want real-space limitations imposed on the online environment.[148] A range of companies have responded to those needs by developing technologies that provide businesses with the ability to reduce their legal risks by targeting their online presence to particular geographic constituencies. Those technologies also serve the interests of governments and regulators who may now be better positioned to apply their offline regulations to the online environment, since the "insensitivity to geographic distinctions" that many attribute to the Internet is removed.[149]

Because both business and government share a vested interest in bringing geographic borders to the online environment (albeit for different reasons), it should come as little surprise that technologies facilitating geographic identification have so quickly entered onto the marketplace. Although critics often point to the inaccuracy of these technologies,[150] few users actually require perfection.[151] Business wants either to target its message to consumers in a specific jurisdiction or to engage in "jurisdictional avoidance."[152] Government, on the other hand, may often want to engage in geographic identification so that it can more easily identify when its laws are triggered. For example, the state of Nevada recently enacted legislation that paves the way for the Nevada State Gaming Commission to legalize online gambling.[153] Jurisdictional identification is central to the new legislation, as provided in Section 3(2):

> The commission may not adopt regulations governing the licensing and operation of interactive gaming until the commission first determines that:
> (a) Interactive gaming can be operated in compliance with all applicable laws;
> (b) Interactive gaming systems are secure and reliable, and provide reasonable assurance that players will be of

lawful age and communicating only from jurisdictions where
it is lawful to make such communications;[154]

Geographic identification has actually been used on the Internet
on a relatively primitive scale for some time. For example, Internet
Protocol lookups, which determine users locations by cross-checking
their IP addresses against databases that list Internet service provider
locations, have been used by Microsoft to comply with U.S. regulations prohibiting the export of strong-encryption Internet browser
software for many years.[155] Although imperfect, the process was
viewed as sufficiently effective to meet the standards imposed by
the regulations.

Recently, several companies have begun offering more sophisticated versions of these technologies. Akamai, a network caching
service, provides a geographic identification service called Edge-
Scape, which maps user IP addresses to their geographic and network points of origin.[156] This information is assembled into a database and made available to EdgeScape customers. Each time a user
accesses a client's Web site, EdgeScape provides data detailing the
country from which the user is accessing site, the geographic region
within that country (i.e., state or province), and the name of the user's
origin network. Similarly, Quova,[157] a California-based company,
has developed GeoPoint, which boasts 98 percent and 85 percent
accuracy, respectively, at determining Internet surfers' countries of
origin and cities.[158]

Businesses are implementing these technologies with increasing
frequency as they seek to replicate offline business models online by
targeting their online presence to certain jurisdictions. For example,
CinemaNow Inc., a California-based online distributor of feature-
length films, uses the technology to limit distribution of its films to
ensure it is compliant with distribution-license agreements that vary
by country.[159] Similarly, until recently, Internet users from outside
of the United States who tried to access the Web site of Showtime
Online, a national pay cable channel, were identified as coming from
outside of the United States and advised that the site was solely
available to users from within the country.[160] In fact, Google, the
world's most popular search engine, has acknowledged using these
technologies to meet variations in local laws by delivering different
search results to users in different countries.[161]

Because of the development of new technologies that allow for geographic identification with a reasonable degree of accuracy, a targeting test must include a technology component that places the onus on the party contesting or asserting jurisdiction to demonstrate what technical measures, including offline identifiers, it employed to either target or avoid a particular jurisdiction. The suitability of such an onus lies in the core consideration of jurisdiction law— that is, whether jurisdiction is foreseeable under the circumstances. Geographic identifying technologies provide the party that deploys the technology with a credible answer to the jurisdictional foresee-ability question at a cost far less than comparable litigation expenses. Since parties can identify who is accessing their sites, they can use technical measures to stop people from legally risky jurisdictions— including those jurisdictions where a site owner is reluctant to con-test potential litigation or face regulatory scrutiny—from doing so. A fair and balanced targeting jurisdiction test demands that they do just that.

It is important to note that parties are not typically required to use geographic identification technologies.[162] In many instances, they do not care who accesses their sites and thus will be unwilling and may not have the incentive to incur the expense of installing such systems. In other instances, the party may be acutely aware of the need to identify users from a jurisdiction that bans access to certain content or certain activities. In such instances, the party may wish to limit access to those users it can positively identify from a safe jurisdiction.

The inclusion of technology in the targeting test does not, there-fore, obligate parties to use the technology. Rather, it forces parties to acknowledge that such technologies are available and that prudence may dictate using them in some capacity. Moreover, the test does not prescribe any specific technology—it only requires that consider-ation be given to the technologies used and available at a particular moment in time. This technology-neutral prong of the targeting test, which does not prescribe a particular type of technology but rather the outcome, also provides an effective counterbalance to the con-tract and knowledge factors. It removes the ability to be willfully blind to users who enter into a clickwrap contract stating that they are from one jurisdiction while the technological evidence suggests something else entirely.

Actual or Implied Knowledge. The third targeting factor assesses the knowledge the parties had or ought to have had about the geographic location of the online activity. Although some authors have suggested that intent and knowledge are rendered obsolete by virtue of the Internet's architecture,[163] the geographic identification technologies described do not support such a view. That factor ensures that parties cannot hide behind contracting technology by claiming a lack of targeting knowledge when the evidence suggests otherwise.

The implied knowledge factor is most apparent in the defamation tort cases that follow from the *Calder* decision. In those cases, courts have accepted that the defaming parties are or should be aware that the injury inflicted by their speech would be felt in the jurisdiction of their target. Accordingly, in such cases a party would be unable to rely on a contract that specifies an alternative jurisdiction as the choice-of-forum.

The court's desire to dismiss any hint of willful blindness is evident in the *People v. World Interactive Gaming* case referred to earlier.[164] In that case, the online casino argued that it had limited access to only those users that had entered an address of a jurisdiction where gambling was permitted. The court saw through this ruse, however, firmly stating the following:

> This Court rejects respondents' argument that it unknowingly accepted bets from New York residents. New York users can easily circumvent the casino software in order to play by the simple expedient of entering an out-of-state address. Respondents' violation of the Penal Law is that they persisted in continuous illegal conduct directed toward the creation, establishment, and advancement of unauthorized gambling.[165]

The relevance of a knowledge-based factor extends beyond reliance on contracts that the parties know to be false. In an e-commerce context, the knowledge that comes from order fulfillment is just as important. For example, sales of physical goods, such as computer equipment or books, provide online sellers with data such as a real-space delivery address, making it relatively easy to exclude jurisdictions that the seller does not wish to target. Courts have also begun to use a knowledge-based analysis when considering jurisdiction over intellectual property disputes. In *Starmedia Network v. Star Media, Inc.,*[166] an April 2001 federal case from New York, the

116

court asserted jurisdiction over an alleged out-of state trademark infringer, noting—

> The defendant knew of plaintiff's domain name before it registered "starmediausa.com" as its domain name. Therefore, the defendant knew or should have known of plaintiff's place of business, and should have anticipated being haled into New York's courts to answer for the harm to a New York plaintiff caused by using a similar mark.[167]

Although the application of the knowledge principle is more complex when the sale involves digital goods for which there is no offline delivery, the seller is still customarily furnished with potentially relevant information. As discussed previously, most telling may be credit card data that the purchaser typically provides to the seller. In addition to the credit card number and expiration date, the purchaser is often also required to supply billing address information so that the validity of the card can be verified before authorization. Since the seller is supplied with a real-space billing address for digital transactions, there remains the opportunity to forego the sale if a jurisdictional concern exists. For example, the Washington Capitals hockey team recently rejected attempts by rival fans from Pittsburgh to purchase tickets on the team's Web site. The site was set to reject purchase attempts from customers entering a Pittsburgh-area code.[168] Although some sellers may be loathe to use consumer payment information in this fashion, the approach reflects a more general trend toward recognizing the important role that payment intermediaries such as credit card companies play in the consumer e-commerce process.[169]

Conclusion

With courts increasingly resisting the *Zippo* passive-vs.-active approach to Internet jurisdiction, the time for adopting a new targeting-based test has arrived. Unlike the *Zippo* test, which suffers from a series of drawbacks, including inconsistent and undesirable outcomes as well as the limitations of a technology-specific approach, a targeting-based analysis provides all interested parties—including courts, e-commerce companies, and consumers—with the tools needed to conduct more effective legal risk analysis.

Under the three-factor targeting test, it is important to note that no single factor is determinative. Analysis will depend on a combined assessment of all three factors to determine whether the party knowingly targeted the particular jurisdiction and could reasonably foresee being haled into court there. In an e-commerce context, the targeting test ultimately establishes a trade-off that should benefit both companies and consumers. Companies benefit from the assurance that operating an e-commerce site will not necessarily result in jurisdictional claims from any jurisdiction worldwide. They can more confidently limit their legal risk exposure by targeting only those countries in which they are compliant with local law.

Consumers also benefit from this approach since they receive the reassurance that online companies that target them will be answerable to their local laws. The test is sufficiently flexible to allow companies to deploy as many or as few precautions as needed. For example, if the company is involved in a highly regulated or controversial field, it will likely want to confine its activities to a limited number of jurisdictions, avoiding locations with which it is unfamiliar. Under the targeting test, the company could adopt a strategy of implementing technological measures to identify its geographic reach while simultaneously incorporating the desired limitations into its contract package. Conversely, companies with fewer legal concerns and a desire to sell worldwide can still accomplish that goal under the targeting test analysis. Such companies would sell without the technological support, incurring both the benefits and responsibilities of a global e-commerce enterprise.

Notwithstanding the advantages of a targeting test, some potential drawbacks still exist. First, the test accelerates the creation of a bordered Internet. Although a bordered Internet has certain advantages, it is also subject to abuse because countries can use bordering technologies to keep foreign influences out and suppress free speech locally.[170] Second, the targeting test may also result in less consumer choice because many sellers may stop selling to consumers in certain jurisdictions in which risk analysis suggests that the benefits are not worth the potential legal risks.

Although the targeting test will not alter every jurisdictional outcome, it will provide all parties with greater legal certainty and a more effective means of conducting legal risk assessments. The move toward using contract and technology to erect virtual borders may not solve all Internet jurisdiction issues, but it will provide an upgrade to *Zippo* by creating greater clarity and certainty on the issue.

6. Federalism in Cyberspace Revisited

Dan L. Burk

Introduction

Public availability and use of the Internet have proliferated rapidly in the United States over the past decade, opening new avenues of communication and of commerce. With this growth of Internet usage has come a surge of regulation at the international, national, and state levels. State regulation of Internet activity has included both application of existing law and enactment of new law and has been aimed at a wide range of real or perceived online evils: pornography, libelous statements, unsolicited bulk e-mail, fraudulent advertisements and sales, unauthorized use of publicly posted data, unwanted hypertext linking, electronic trespass to computers, and myriad other activities.

The potential negative effects of such state regulation on the growth and productivity of the Internet are at the very least alarming. The Internet extends beyond the boundaries of any of the states, and the effects of any particular state regulation will likewise spill over that state's borders. Such regulatory leakage implicates constitutional doctrines designed to preserve both the sovereignty of the individual states and the coherence of the United States as a whole. Thus, the prospect of states applying haphazard and uncoordinated multijurisdictional regulation to the Internet's seamless electronic Web raises profound questions regarding the relationship between the several states and the future of federalism in cyberspace.

Some commentators have dismissed this prospect as implicating only the most routine application of existing legal doctrine.[1] Such commentary adopts the position that new technology, particularly this technology, poses no unusual or fundamentally novel challenge to the current legal regime, only the "unexceptional problem" of Internet jurisdiction.[2] Yet, curiously, this exceptional "unexceptional" problem has been the subject of hundreds of legal disputes, scores of scholarly papers, and countless news stories. To read the unexceptionalist commentary, one would conclude that either global computer networks require a monumental change in the jurisdictional paradigm—or, well, they don't.

The truth, as I hope to show, likely lies somewhere in between the poles of apocalypse and convention. In this chapter, I shall argue first that technology matters; just as past technological revolutions, such as widespread adoption of the automobile, have required adjustments in jurisdictional standards, so the widespread adoption of Internet technology will require new adjustments. Because the Internet presents the current jurisdictional structure with a new factual profile, rote application of current jurisdictional rules to the particular technology of the Internet would lead to anomalous and undesirable results. Thus, in approaching this new technology, legal "business as usual" will not do; rather, the application of legal rules must be adjusted to provide the socially optimal outcome.

Second, I shall argue that where application of state law is concerned, such outcomes must be calibrated with the purposes of federalism firmly in mind; in particular, jurisdictional doctrines should be applied so as to maximize opportunities for state regulatory innovation while minimizing the interstate regulatory interference, spillovers, and jurisdictional opportunism that are the inevitable products of new information technology. In such an environment, maximizing opportunities for state regulatory innovation cannot be done by simplistically favoring state regulation in every instance; it may instead require curtailment of certain types of state regulation, and substitution of federal regulation where necessary.

Competitive Federalism

In the United States, the federal constitutional structure allocates regulatory power "vertically" between the states and the federal government, and "horizontally" among the several states. The latter division of power is what we are primarily concerned with here, although the allocation of certain functions to the federal government may serve to modulate certain interstate regulatory interactions. At first blush, the social value of horizontal federalism may seem elusive or nonexistent; a plurality of possible fora, each with a different legal structure, might seem to foster only chaos and confusion in allocating interstate legal obligations. At a minimum, the reality of operating under a variety of legal regimes introduces an element of complexity and additional cost into both individual and business planning. If the existence—indeed, the promotion—of such a jurisdictional patchwork is to be at all defensible, then the benefits of such a system must somehow outweigh the costs of multiple compliance and uncertainty imposed by fostering multiple jurisdictions.

However, the benefit of jurisdictional diversity has long been celebrated at least anecdotally in the legal literature: diversity forestalls legal and political stagnation. Within the so-called "laboratories of the states,"[3] various legal regimes may be composed and field tested in an attempt to evolve optimal systems. As between the states, deficiencies or virtues in their respective systems are expected to become manifest, leading to a "weeding out" of undesirable rules and promotion of superior approaches. The implication of the "laboratory" metaphor has been that regulatory schemes that prove successful on a small scale may be adopted on a larger scale, either by other states or by the federal government.

Governmental Competition

More formal public choice models have built upon this somewhat intuitive recognition of the benefits of federalism.[4] Modern public choice theory predicts that representative government will frequently be subject to capture by special interest groups.[5] This arises in part from the low marginal value of voting as compared with the higher marginal value of activities such as lobbying. Voters may tend to be "rationally ignorant" or "rationally indifferent"—because a given vote is so unlikely to affect the outcome of an election that it is frequently not worth individual voters' time and effort to bother learning enough about the issues to cast an informed vote, or even to engage in voting itself. By contrast, special interest groups may see substantial payoffs from activities that may be characterized as "rent-seeking," that is, expending time and money to use governmental mechanisms to secure competitive advantages.[6]

As a consequence, jurisdictions may potentially become encrusted with special-interest legislation that not only fails to reflect the interests of the majority of voters but also burdens a wide variety of business and personal activity.[7] However, one of the virtues of a federal system is that individuals and businesses may express their preferences in a different manner: where voting at the ballot box fails, they may opt to "vote with their feet."[8] Local governments that are captured by special interests, or that fail to reflect voter preferences, may find themselves losing constituents to more responsive regimes. Conversely, jurisdictions that are responsive to constituent preferences may tend to attract new constituents.

The production of local public goods and services might thus resemble the production of private goods in a competitive market: competitive pressure from other jurisdictions will prevent any given jurisdiction from offering too much or too little in the way of public services. Jurisdictions that offer too much will experience an influx of immigrants from less generous jurisdictions; jurisdictions that offer too little will experience an exodus to more generous jurisdictions. Migration in or out of the jurisdiction will continue until parity with competing jurisdictions is reached. These forces will tend to act as a check on overproduction or underproduction of local public goods. By "voting with their feet," or exiting, citizens force local politicians toward efficiency in allocation of resources to such goods.[9] Indeed, just as in classic cartel theory the threat of entry deters monopoly profits, so in public choice theory the threat of "exit" may deter special interest regulation from accumulating.[10]

The seminal analysis in this field is Tiebout's classic model, which describes local provision of public services on a theory of interjurisdictional competition that closely resembles market competition for provision of private goods.[11] Tiebout theorized that if citizens were free to migrate between jurisdictions, competition for desirable citizen immigrants would arise. Local communities will offer to potential immigrants the most attractive packages of goods and services at the lowest tax rate possible. Similarly, migrants will relocate to jurisdictions offering the maximum package of public goods at the tax rate that the migrant is willing to pay. Local communities may even tailor their offerings to appeal to particular types of immigrants, and immigrants would be expected to sort themselves out into groups of similar means and tastes by jurisdiction.

Although business firms were not part of Tiebout's original model, his insight was quickly expanded to encompass strategic preferences of local governments regarding such firms. Just as in the consumer/citizen model, businesses too may "vote with their feet," locating their operations in jurisdictions that offer the most attractive set of local public goods. This in turn implies that jurisdictions may tailor their offerings to attract businesses, or to attract certain kinds of desirable businesses, or even to repel undesirable businesses.

This type of competition in fact appears to occur, giving rise to the so-called "Delaware phenomenon."[12] It is fairly widely recognized that in the United States surprisingly large numbers of corporations choose to incorporate or reincorporate under the laws of the state of Delaware. The proper explanation for this phenomenon is less well settled than is the observation itself. Analyses of the phenomenon tend to fall into two broad schools of thought. The first of these schools, originally set out by law professor William Carey, suggests that competition for incorporation represents a "race to the bottom," that is, a race to liberalize incorporation law for the benefit of officers and directors.[13] By enacting laws to appeal to the interests of officers and directors, states may attract incorporation, but at the expense of shareholders' rights. As states vie with one another for incorporation franchises, they successively liberalize their laws, until the rights of shareholders are entirely subordinated. Carey recommended federal intervention to halt what he perceived as a downward spiral of ruinous interstate competition.

The second school, which coalesced in response to Carey's claims, questioned whether shareholders would in fact be stupid enough, or oblivious enough to their own interests, to leave their investment dollars with firms incorporated under laws detrimental to the shareholders' interests.[14] If in fact jurisdictions such as Delaware were subordinating shareholder rights, one might expect to see shareholders "vote with their feet" by abandoning Delaware corporations for firms incorporating under laws more favorable to investors.[15] Such a loss of investment dollars to Delaware corporations might in turn provide an incentive for firms not to incorporate there. The fact that there appeared to be no such migration of investors from Delaware firms, or of firms from Delaware itself, led commentators of the second school to interpret Delaware's success in attracting franchisees as indicating that such incorporation is attractive to investors, probably due to the superior returns on investment received from such firms.

This latter analysis suggested that Delaware, far from winning a "race to the bottom" for inefficient incorporation laws, had won a "race to the top" for efficient incorporation laws that permitted maximum returns to investors. A subset of the "race to the top" school, exemplified by Roberta Romano, particularly emphasized the Delaware phenomenon as a competition between jurisdictions

123

for "law as a product."[16] Delaware may not necessarily have attracted the lion's share of incorporation because of the absolute superiority of its governing rules but because the Delaware legal system has specialized in corporate law, offering additional certainty to firms seeking incorporation. Thus, Delaware offers not merely a highly developed statutory system, but also a court system with a high degree of expertise in resolving corporate conflicts, and a considerable body of case precedent governing such conflicts. Thus, these scholars argue, the total package of Delaware's law succeeds in the incorporation marketplace as a superior product.

Competition and Cooperation

The Tiebout model, like most pure economic theories, rests upon a number of simplifying assumptions. The model assumes that voters have full knowledge of the package of local services offered in various jurisdictions, that there are a large number of jurisdictions from which to choose, that individual mobility is relatively unconstrained, and that communities have an optimal size that will be dictated by the balance between resource constraints and economies of scale. Most important for this discussion, the Tiebout model assumes that jurisdictions are tightly compartmentalized so that no external costs or benefits accrue from the local provision of public services. If jurisdictions are "leaky," then individuals could perhaps enjoy the positive benefits of a neighboring jurisdiction's policy without actually incurring the cost of migrating there.[17] More significantly, in a world of "leaky" borders, jurisdictions could lower the costs of regulation to local firms by imposing all or part of those costs on neighboring jurisdictions; this would serve to attract firms, but not necessarily by generating a net gain in efficiency. As one commentator observes—

> Each state has an incentive to impose taxes the burden of which will, as much as possible, fall on resident of other states. Such taxation not only deflects the state from the search for taxing methods that maximize efficiency and distributive values for the nation as a whole, it also leads to socially excessive government expenditures, by enabling the state to externalize the costs of its public services.[18]

The states may attempt to avoid such a race by entering a cooperative agreement that forbids such a "race to externalize."[19] However, as in the case of classic economic cartels, such a governmental cartel is likely to be highly unstable.[20] Theories of cooperation predict that, much as in the famous "Prisoner's Dilemma" game theory model,[21] a sovereign state will remain party to a cooperative agreement only to the extent that the agreement is "self-enforcing," that is, only so long as it has more to gain from cooperation than from defection.[22]

If in fact cooperative strategies prove impossible or unworkable, rational competitors may have yet another option. If "horizontal" cooperation between jurisdictions proves unstable, the creation of a "third party" standing in a vertical relationship to the competitors may be necessary.[23] Tiebout recognized this in his original model by noting that where externalities exist, centralized decisionmaking, rather than interjurisdictional competition, may be required to achieve an efficient outcome. Stated in game theoretic terms, knowing that their own rational short-term competitive preferences will inevitably lead to their own detriment in the long term, states may choose to voluntarily surrender all or part of their decisionmaking power to a third party.

This strategy is in essence the one adopted by the individual states of the United States in acquiescing to the constitutional compact that created a centralized federal government; similar benefits may be found in the federal compacts of Canada, Australia, and to some extent the European Community. As the colonial parties to the Articles of Confederation quickly found, certain activities are poor subjects for a cooperative agreement, because it is too attractive to "defect" from the agreement. The solution was to shift regulation of such activities to a central government under the federal constitution.[24] However, under the federal constitution, even when some types of interstate regulation have been centralized, the benefits of interstate competition have also been preserved to the extent deemed practical.[25] Because competitive benefits will be lost in whichever markets are centralized, centralization must be considered a drastic measure taken only where no such efficiencies are to be had; that is, where externalities prevent the development of competition in the first instance.

However, for competitive benefits to be maintained, jurisdictional compartmentalization is essential. Thus, the federal compact not only "vertically" transfers certain powers to the federal government, it also defines the "horizontal" relationships between the states that

125

are party to the compact. Significant portions of the constitution are given over to defining "horizontal" federalism, and, as I shall argue, are particularly given over to preserving the jurisdictional conditions necessary for competition of "law as a product." Chief among these provisions are the Due Process Clause of the Fourteenth Amendment and the Commerce Clause in its dormant aspect. But the jurisdictional functions of these provisions face a new challenge in the unprecedented interconnectivity created by the Internet.

Virtual Exit

The Internet presents new challenges for the "spillover" problem among the states, as this burgeoning technology increases the leakiness of the federal system. The potential for new jurisdictional spillover is reflected in the technical features of the network. The Internet is primarily defined by a set of computer protocols that enable machines to exchange information.[26] The machines comprising the network may be connected by a variety of media, including fiber-optic cable, twisted pair copper wire, microwave transmission, or other wireless connections.[27] The physical connections may be carrying other types of signals, such as television signals. Internet communications, however, are broken up into information "packets" that can be routed along the connections to make the most efficient use of the connections' carrying capacity.[28] Instead of dedicating an open channel to a communication in real time, Internet computers route packets from many different communications over the channel.

Access to Internet resources is typically provided through a system of request and reply; when an online user attempts to access information or services on the network, his or her local computer requests such access from the remote server computer where the desired material is housed.[29] The remote machine may grant or deny the request, based on its programmed criteria; only if the request is granted does the server tender the information to the user's machine. Machines connected to the Internet are assigned a logical address on the system, and each information packet transmitted over the network carries the address of the machine for which the packet is intended. Special computers called routers maintain databases of the addresses assigned to certain machines and compare packet addresses with the database to route packets toward the machine

126

designated by the packets' address.[30] The packets are reassembled when they reach their destination machine, according to an encoding system that is part of the communication protocol.

The governing design principle of this system has been dubbed the "end-to-end" principle, which holds that network operation will be most efficient if specific applications for computing or data processing are located at the end of the network, not in its communications protocols.[31] The network thus remains as simple or "stupid" as possible, doing essentially one thing well: moving packets toward their intended destination. The network does not differentiate between packets, or the contents of packets, but simply treats them all the same, performing its one function of routing them to their destination.

As a consequence, the Internet enables many types of machines to interoperate with one another, since information in otherwise incompatible formats is treated as fungible by the network. Specific and possibly incompatible functions are pushed to the end-user machines at the ends of the network, and the standard protocols connecting the machines at the edge of the Internet act as a kind of translator between them. Indeed, few Internet users actually use computers that are directly connected to the Internet. Users typically gain access to the network through an intermediary, such as an Internet service provider (ISP) that maintains computers with an actual network connection.[32] The user may use a telephone dial-up connection, cable broadband connection, or other conduit to access the ISP gateway machine.

The result of this design is a system that is relatively insensitive to geography in several different aspects. Within the system, it is logical location that counts, and not geographic location: the network is designed to route packets according to their Internet addresses, without regard to geographic origin or destination. The machine to which an Internet address is assigned has, of course, a physical location, but that is not reflected in the logical address of the machine. This fact is well demonstrated by the very common technique of dynamic Internet Protocol (IP) address assignment, used as a strategy for managing user connectivity.[33] Rather than managing a single IP address, ISPs will frequently manage a block of addresses, assigning them to users temporarily as needed for a particular network session. Thus, the connection used by a given subscriber will likely resolve to different IP addresses on a daily, perhaps hourly, basis.

The network also renders geography less important in several other dimensions. The marginal cost of moving bits of information as electrical signals is relatively low compared with moving a physical instantiation of the information. Because the network is delivering bits of information rather than solid media, physical distance between sender and recipient becomes relatively unimportant. The simple packet-switching protocols of the network can also be layered over a variety of media, from twisted pair copper telephone wire to satellite transmission. Thus, unlike any single medium, such as broadcast, that might be confined to a particular geographic foot-print, Internet services can be delivered wherever connections may be found.

As a consequence, the availability of Internet communication makes relocation of businesses much more practical, particularly for those businesses that offer information goods or services to customers. There is no reason for such businesses to be tied to a particular geographic location when their products can be offered to consumers online from remote locations.[34] Information-based production can thus be located on the basis of local production factors, including regulation, without the constraint of proximity to market. In essence, the Internet increases the ability of information industries to literally exit a jurisdiction. As we have seen, this will tend to increase the incentive of jurisdictions to compete in the market for regulation of desirable business activity.

But by the same token, the network enables consumers to access the informational goods and services of remote businesses that have been attracted to or fostered by the regulatory regime of distant jurisdictions. This access essentially lets consumers engage in virtual exit from their jurisdiction, "voting with their feet" without physi-cally moving.[35] Yet the structure of the regulatory market is still essentially geographic, which creates a discontinuity between the costs of local regulation to which consumers are subject and the costs of the environment producing goods and services that the same consumers are able to access remotely. The network makes the tight compartmentalization required for Tiebout competition increasingly leaky, and, as we have seen, states may take advantage of such leakiness to export the cost of their local regulatory system to other jurisdictions.

If provisions of the constitutional compact are intended to curtail such abuses of the system, realigning the incentives and costs of jurisdictions competing in the regulatory market, then we would expect increased leakiness and spillover effects to place some strain on those provisions. That is to say, we would expect the increased use of the Internet to place a strain on constitutional doctrines intended to preserve competitive federalism. In the face of such a new technology, rote application of established doctrines may produce anomalous or undesirable results and, in such cases, adaptation of those doctrines to the new technological situation may be required. But in accommodating past doctrine to present reality, the role of the relevant constitutional provisions as buffers for competitive federalism must be kept firmly in mind if they are to continue serving their proper function in an online environment.

Due Process Limits

The potential impact of the Internet on the interjurisdictional mediation of the Constitution is perhaps most evident with regard to the jurisdictional aspects of the Due Process Clause of the Fourteenth Amendment. This provision plays a key role in determining the jurisdiction in which disputes may be adjudicated, and most particularly in which a person may be required to defend a lawsuit. Unlike criminal trials, which require some actual appearance by the defendant, civil trials can be conducted and even decided in the absence of the defendant.[36] Consequently, a good deal of constitutional jurisprudence has been devoted to explaining the circumstances under which it is constitutionally permissible to conduct a proceeding in the defendant's absence or, in other words, under which the defendant may be put to the choice of either traveling to a distant forum or suffering a default judgment.

The personal jurisdiction problems posed by virtual commerce and Internet telepresence are in many ways the culmination of a long evolution of legal doctrine occasioned by changing technology.[37] Traditionally, jurisdiction over the person was premised on the physical presence of the individual in the forum;[38] this continues to be a viable jurisdictional basis.[39] However, increased physical mobility due to automobiles and other modern transportation placed this jurisdictional basis under severe strain,[40] as did disputes over "virtual" entities such as corporations that have no physical situs,[41] and over "virtual" properties such as stocks[42] and debts[43] that similarly lack physical form.

As a response to the imminent collapse of jurisdiction based on physical presence, the Supreme Court configured new rules based on a kind of "virtual" presence. Beginning with the notorious *International Shoe* opinion, the Supreme Court began developing a set of criteria for requiring nonresidents of a state to defend lawsuits in that state.[44] According to *International Shoe* and its progeny, the Due Process Clause of the Fourteenth Amendment constrains state courts from exercising personal jurisdiction over defendants who lack sufficient contacts with the forum state.[45] Unless the defendant has sufficient contact with the forum state, that state's exercise of jurisdiction over the defendant would offend "traditional notions of fair play and substantial justice."[46]

Minimum Contacts Analysis

In analyzing the defendant's contacts, two broad classes of jurisdictional situation have been recognized. The first, known as "general jurisdiction," involves an attempt to assert jurisdiction over a defendant when the defendant's contacts are unrelated to the dispute.[47] An assertion of general jurisdiction over the individual is permissible if the defendant's contacts with the forum are systematic and continuous enough that the defendant might anticipate defending any type of claim there.[48] A second jurisdictional situation arises when the defendant's contacts arise out of the facts of the dispute. A court may exercise jurisdiction over the defendant if the defendant has "minimum contacts" with the forum such that he might anticipate defending that particular type of claim there.[49] The contacts relied on may be isolated or occasional, so long as they are purposefully directed toward the forum.[50]

The specific jurisdiction situation is rather more problematic than that of general jurisdiction, as the nature and extent of the contacts, as well as their relationship to the claims asserted, must be carefully examined. The general requirement that must be satisfied for due process purposes is a sort of "foreseeability" that the defendant is on notice of fora where he or she may be called on to defend a suit.[51] This "foreseeability" requirement allows the defendant to structure his or her activities so as to prepare for potential liability, or avoid states in which he or she does not wish to assume liability.[52]

In certain cases, the foreseeability analysis is relatively straightforward—for example, when a contract indicates the parties' purposeful intent to place jurisdiction in a particular state. Assuming that the contract in fact reflects the parties' intention to avail themselves of a particular jurisdiction's law product, the issue becomes more complicated where one of the parties is in a manifestly superior bargaining position, or where the jurisdictional "contract" is one of the mass-market licenses proliferating in the form of "clickwrap" or "webwrap" licenses. Courts have rightly regarded with suspicion choice-of-law provisions for Internet services when there is no reason to believe that the provision in fact indicated any "choice" on the part of the consumer.[53]

The Supreme Court has also indicated that in some cases in which an intentional tort is directed toward an individual or entity within a particular jurisdiction, the tortfeasor should anticipate defending a suit in that forum. The Supreme Court decision in *Calder v. Jones*[54] held that California jurisdiction over a Florida defendant was proper because the allegedly libelous statements directed at the defendant injured her in her home state of California. Some intermediate courts of appeal have seized on this doctrine to formulate a so-called "effects test." Under this test, jurisdiction would be proper when some effect of a defendant's actions is felt within the forum state.[55] Other circuits have flatly rejected this test, observing that it flies in the face of much of the Supreme Court's due process jurisprudence.[56] These courts recognize that the standard cannot simply be that whenever an intentional tort is alleged, jurisdiction is proper in the plaintiff's home state because the harm will be felt there.

The opinion in *Calder* repeatedly emphasizes that the defendants knew that the plaintiff resided in California and that their newspaper's largest circulation was in that state.[57] Moreover, the definition of the intentional tort in *Calder* required actual malice or reckless disregard of the truth—the standard set out by the Supreme Court in *New York Times v. Sullivan* for libel actions against newspaper publishers.[58] The Court in *Calder* refused to take the "chilling effect" of liability into account in the jurisdictional analysis, stating that to recognize such a new jurisdictional factor would be "double counting." The standard to prove the tort, they said, already takes First Amendment concerns into account.[59] This reasoning seems sound if we consider that the facts necessary to allege actual malice or reckless disregard themselves indicate activity purposefully directed toward the defendant's place of residence. Thus, the libel standard encompasses the jurisdictional standard, but not every intentional tort will do so.

Where a more extensive contacts analysis is called for, the Supreme Court has also offered a list of five jurisdictional "fairness factors" that may require a separate assessment, especially when the defendant's contacts with the forum are attenuated.[60] The factors to be weighed before subjecting the defendant to jurisdiction include the inconvenience to the defendant of defending in that forum, the forum state's interest in adjudicating the dispute, the plaintiff's interest in obtaining convenient and effective relief, the interstate judicial system's interest in efficient resolution of interstate conflicts, and the shared interest of the states in furthering substantive social policies.[61]

These oft-repeated jurisdictional criteria, though familiar, have not necessarily produced recognizably coherent results when applied to real-space activity. A comprehensive theory of personal jurisdiction has largely eluded commentators. Indeed, although we may discern the broad outlines of the legacy of *International Shoe*, predicting the outcome of the "minimum contacts" test under a given set of transactions is something of a black art. However, no matter how perplexing the application of the test has been in real space, its application to Internet activity may prove to be even more arcane. Anomalous results may be expected because the network's structural indifference to geographic position is incongruous with the fundamental assumptions underlying the *International Shoe* test.

Virtual Contacts

Much of the Supreme Court jurisprudence on due process jurisdiction appears ill-suited to the practicalities of the Internet. Where jurisdiction from Internet contacts is at issue, physical presence of the defendant within the forum state will likely be the exception rather than the rule: Internet users do physically reside somewhere in real space, and, if the defendant user physically resides within the forum, the law seems well settled that its courts can exercise jurisdiction over that user. However, given the far-flung nature of the Internet, far more defendants will reside outside any given plaintiff's preferred jurisdiction than will reside within it. A significant number of online disputes will therefore require an *International Shoe* analysis. Thus, personal jurisdiction over an Internet user will most frequently be premised on the user's contacts with the forum.

In many cases, Internet contacts will comprise only a subset of an individual's interactions with a particular jurisdiction and so will be analyzed together with telephonic, postal, and other communicative contacts. But given the nature of online transactions, many cases may be premised solely on Internet-based contacts, and such cases are likely to be problematic. The business activity conducted online will not for the most part be directed toward a particular physical jurisdiction, as traditional contacts analysis assumes. Businesses will frequently be ignorant of a customer's physical location, and customers equally ignorant of the business's. If the transaction results in shipment of physical goods, then the veil of ignorance may be rent; the goods must end up somewhere and the shipping address will give actual or constructive notice of the physical jurisdiction targeted. But the unique aspect of Internet commerce is that the Internet provides not only negotiation and payment online but also delivery of goods if the goods are digitized information products: software, pictures, movies, music, novels, data, and the like. Information-based services such as systems monitoring, education, data processing, or consulting can also be offered wholly online.

The geographic indeterminacy of such transactions calls into question the ostensible criterion of purposeful availment. In some very broad sense one might argue that an Internet user who accesses remote resources is "purposefully availing" himself of the benefits of the forum in which the resource is located; the laws and public services of that jurisdiction likely help to maintain the physical infrastructure of that resource, protect it from theft and vandalism, and facilitate its continued operation. But the remote user is entirely indifferent, and frequently ignorant, as to which jurisdiction is providing these benefits. The resource could just as well be in one jurisdiction as another. Thus it is difficult to assert with a straight face that the remote user has purposefully or knowingly availed himself of *that* particular jurisdiction's benefits.

It is similarly difficult to seriously assert that an Internet business should "reasonably anticipate" being haled into court in a geographical location concerning which it was ignorant, or at least indifferent, with regard to contact. At least in theory, Internet businesses could use IP address locations to screen access to their Internet resources, denying those requests originating in jurisdictions with which the host machine's operator did not wish to have contact. One French court, for example, has ordered an Internet business to block French users from accessing auctions of Nazi paraphernalia, which is illegal under French law.[62] Using a combination of IP address screening, language screening, and other techniques, the court found that a fairly high percentage of French Internet users could be prevented from accessing the objectionable auctions.[63] Some Internet businesses have in fact begun offering geographic screening services based on IP address identification; such services are useful for targeting advertisements to users in certain languages, or to potential customers of geographically based businesses. Some commentators have concluded that such services can and should form the basis for enforcing geographically based regulation on Internet-based businesses.[64]

But, as described earlier, Internet protocols were not designed to facilitate geographic documentation; in general, they ignore it. Geographic screening, functioning at the ends of the network, will be imprecise and error-prone, offering only coarse approximate guesses as to a user's location. Even if in some instances an Internet address tells one something about the location of a given machine, it tells nothing about the location of the user of that machine. Users of nongeographically-designated networks, such as aol.com, will tend to slip past a geographic filter. So will users telnetting from locations unrelated to the physical location of the machine. So will users employing similar kinds of dial-up access, as well as common Internet features allowing remote access and anonymous login that obscure meaningful clues by which one might screen users by geographic region. So will users using "anonymizer" systems to preserve their privacy, as well as users whose systems employ certain types of proxy servers. None of these users need be actively trying to avoid geographic filters; these are simply normal functions employed in the routine operation of the network.

This is not to say that information from the ends of the network can never be assembled to yield geographic information. Suppose that the user of a dynamically assigned IP address is to be located. The different addresses of the user's Internet sessions may of course be traced to the block of addresses held by the ISP, and the ISP's records, if the ISP keeps such records, may show which user was assigned to a given address at a particular time. If the user is a paying customer, the ISP may be able to connect a password or identifier used in the session with billing information that may include a physical address. Thus, the location of a user can in many instances eventually be determined, and law enforcement or other investigators often do so, using legal process to elicit the various records needed to piece together the location of a given user. However, the process involves assembling clues from a variety of sources, which are frequently in the hands of many different entities, and is in no way speeded or accommodated by the design of the network.

These examples should make clear that a user need not actively cloak his or her activities on the Internet for his or her physical location to be obscured; geographic indeterminacy is simply part of the network's normal operation. Certain commentators, noting the features of the network that obscure geographic identification, have compared the use of such network features with other activity, such as lock-picking, that circumvents legal restrictions.[65] But it is unhelpful to argue that some Internet users will be able to evade geographic identification much as some burglars will be able to pick locks. Lock-picking is an extraordinary activity; locks are of course designed to deter the activity in which burglars are engaged. But the Internet is not designed to facilitate geographic discrimination, and no extraordinary activity is required for geographic screening to fail.

In addition, if one is to look beyond the most routine uses of the Internet's capabilities, there is plenty of exotic—but readily available—technology, such as public key cryptography or anonymous remailers, that could be used to *actively* conceal a user's location.[66] Neither do the examples cited contemplate illegal activity, such as unauthorized hacking into another's computer account to mask a user's physical location. The enormous difficulty of preventing "spam," or unsolicited bulk e-mail messages, where spammers actively evade screening measures by changing IP addresses and sending their messages through open relays in various Internet computers unrelated to the spammers' activity, should amply demonstrate the difficulty of screening users who are attempting to avoid detection.[67]

Certainly a sovereign can, in those instances where coercion can be exercised against an extraterritorial entity, impose limitations upon the entity's use of the technology.[68] This was perhaps most famously demonstrated by a U.S. court enforcing a decades-old prohibitory injunction against an Italian magazine publisher in *Chuckleberry v. Playboy.*[69] Distribution of the Italian magazine had been prohibited within the United States but adjudicated to be legal in Italy. The publisher years later developed an Italian-based Web site accessible to the United States, which the U.S. court held to be a violation of the previous injunction. The court ordered the publisher to somehow prohibit U.S. access. When presented with evidence that such screening would be difficult or impossible online, the court required the defendant to issue passwords for the site by postal mail, using the postal address to screen out American applicants. The case rather starkly demonstrates that geographic discrimination can be imposed on Internet users, but only by imposing extremely significant costs on the use of the network: in *Chuckleberry*, this meant discarding the technology itself.

Competitive Contacts

The Internet therefore poses a difficult conundrum for due process jurisprudence: to the extent that personal jurisdiction rests upon ascertaining a defendant's geographic predilections, the network will tend to obscure or nullify such a determination. But much of the difficulty in articulating a sensible standard of jurisdictional due process for Internet activity, or any other kind of activity, stems from the misleading terminology employed in personal jurisdiction analysis. Consider the Supreme Court's core criterion of "foreseeability" or "reasonable anticipation." This standard is in a very real way circular. A defendant should anticipate being haled into fora with which he has minimum contacts. But what constitutes minimum contacts? On the Internet, in particular, one could very easily anticipate having contacts with every jurisdiction in the nation. The Supreme Court has indicated that only certain kinds or levels of contacts will render a defendant amenable to suit. What contacts are those? Why, the kind of contacts that one might reasonably anticipate would render one amenable to suit. But this brings us precisely back to where we started—in other words, defendants should reasonably anticipate being haled into any court into which they should reasonably anticipate being haled.[70] This kind of tautology is, to say the least, not helpful in structuring one's primary conduct.

Foreseeability. There is a way out of the tautology, however. Previous personal jurisdiction analyses have already recognized that this problem may be illuminated by reference to relevant substantive law.[71] A similar tautology appears to occur, for example, when the term "reasonably foreseeable" is employed in tort law: the law of negligent torts requires that an actor be held liable for the reasonably foreseeable consequences of his acts. This rule does not contemplate a standard of actual foreseeability. On the one hand, tortfeasors may clearly be held liable for consequences that they should have foreseen but in fact did not. On the other hand, given sufficient time and contemplation, any consequence in theory is foreseeable. An actor thus should expect to be held liable for those consequences that the law considers reasonably foreseeable—but this standard is supposedly based on what the ordinary prudent person would foresee— an apparent tautology.

In tort law, courts and commentators have avoided chasing their tails by recognizing that "reasonable foreseeability" in fact comprises a social value judgment. The parameters of this policy are embodied in the famous "Learned Hand inequality," which would impose liability where the cost of taking additional preventive measures would be less than the expected cost of additional accidents.[72] Under this calculus, actors would be required to take precautions up to the point at which the marginal cost of an additional unit of prevention equaled the marginal cost of the next unit of accidental harm; taking more precautions would be socially wasteful.[73] In the causation context, this means that cost-effective precautions would be taken only against the most likely consequences of an act; precautions against remote or unlikely accidents would cost more than they are worth.[74]

This reasoning suggests that to avoid chasing our tails in the law of personal jurisdiction, we must similarly recognize that "reasonable anticipation" comprises a social value judgment regarding costs and benefits, allowing us to articulate a procedural analogue for the Learned Hand negligence calculus. Stated simply, societal interests are best served when we require defendants to defend suits in a particular forum only when the societal benefits accruing from the defendant's activity there exceed the aggregate social costs of forcing him to defend in that forum.[75] Understood in this fashion, the "reasonable anticipation" test no longer requires circular guessing about how prescient defendants must be; the standard rather recognizes that a societal value judgment is being made, and should be made on the basis of at least roughly quantifiable costs and benefits.

This approach helps to solve certain vexing puzzles of the Supreme Court's jurisdictional jurisprudence. For example, some previous commentators have noted that in many cases the amount of the cost of defending in a distant forum appears irrelevant; minimum contacts may be lacking even when the cost to the defendant appears relatively modest.[76] This result can be explained in part on the aggregate social welfare model: because the absolute magnitude of the cost is not the issue; it is rather the comparative magnitude of the cost of defending in that jurisdiction against the benefit conferred by the jurisdiction.

However, the court's calculus is not finished with the determination of "minimum contacts." In performing the contacts calculus, the court risks the costs of both type I and type II error; that is, finding jurisdiction in which it should have found none, or failing to find jurisdiction in which it should have been found. Either mistake is eminently possible, as the question of jurisdiction will be decided at the initial stages of the proceeding, before discovery or any other significant development of the facts of the case, and thus likely on incomplete information about relevant costs and benefits. Error of the first kind is likely to be unnecessarily costly to the defendant, whereas error of the second kind will likely be unnecessarily costly to the plaintiff: one party or the other will be forced by the decision to defend in a distant forum.[77] Consequently, as it is making its decision under uncertainty, the court is required to balance the five "fairness factors" to determine the probability of harm given one type of error against the probability of harm given the other type of error. It is critical to note that the court is balancing the possible harm under one set of assumptions against the possible harm under a different set of assumptions—that is, the social harm if jurisdiction is erroneously asserted against the social harm if jurisdiction is erroneously declined.

Sovereignty and Contacts. This general framework takes us a considerable way toward articulating a coherent standard for personal jurisdiction. One important puzzle remains, however, which is the problem of sovereignty. The Supreme Court has repeatedly stated that state sovereignty forms an integral part of the personal jurisdiction calculus. In particular, the Court has stated that its personal jurisdiction jurisprudence incorporates the limits imposed on state sovereignty by the sovereignty interests of sister states.[78] On its own terms, this is somewhat puzzling since the Due Process Clause is generally understood to guarantee a personal freedom for individuals—in other words, it defines a relationship between an individual and the state, not between sovereign states. Neither is it immediately clear where the matters of horizontal federalism fit into a personal jurisdiction cost/benefit calculus such as that just described.

In resolving this puzzle, the precepts of competitive federalism prove exceptionally helpful. As noted, competition between jurisdictions may function to promote personal liberty, and the ability to "vote with one's feet" is integral to such competition. Of course, as in the case of Delaware incorporation, such "exit" may or may not be physical exit; consumers of law products may simply select from among jurisdictions the "law product" best suited to their individual needs or business transaction. But to preserve this ability to choose, a theory of personal jurisdiction must respect the individual's choice. If I write a contract anticipating that it will be enforced in California courts but it is instead haled into court in Texas, my choice of law products is nullified. Similarly, if I move to Arizona to take advantage of that state's community property law but my estate is instead divided under the law of Illinois, my revealed preference for Arizona law is frustrated. Neither can such preferences be properly implemented under choice-of-law rules alone.[79] Recall that in the Delaware phenomenon, the attractiveness of Delaware incorporation arises not simply from the substantive law of the state but from the expertise of Delaware courts in corporate law. Even if the Illinois court decides to apply Arizona community property rules to the division of my estate, my true preference may have been to have an Arizona court with expertise in community property perform the division.

Stated differently, due process requires a jurisdictional rule that encourages interstate entrepreneurs to take advantage of the benefits offered by a particular state, but does so only up to the point where the costs of doing so exceed the aggregate social benefits of doing so; when that point is reached, we want to leave the entrepreneur free to shift his activities to any more cost-efficient venue. The federal system accomplishes this end by allowing entrepreneurs to "vote with their feet" among the 50 states, selecting the law "products" of the jurisdiction that best suits the particular transaction or set of transactions in which the entrepreneur wishes to engage.

Problems may arise, however, because the application of a jurisdiction's rules occurs only after something has gone wrong with a transaction. On the basis of their own cost-benefit analysis, entrepreneurs may select one set of law "products" *ex ante*, but prefer a different set after a mishap in fact occurs. Such strategic behavior may be particularly prevalent where contracts are silent as to choice of forum, or in situations of negligence where the parties had no opportunity to negotiate forum at all. And, if the defendant will frequently have reason to engage in *ex post* forum selection, so too will the forum itself; as described previously, states are under competitive pressure to lower the cost of domestic regulation, and if they can do so by forcing those costs onto extraterritorial actors, it is to their advantage to engage in such a "race to externalize."[80]

In such situations, the arbiter of a dispute will be called on to infer from the defendant's course of conduct which set of law "products" the defendant would have selected had he explicitly done so. The determination must be done both with an eye to prevent windfalls to defendants attempting to free-ride on the benefits of a jurisdiction's regulatory offerings, and also to prevent states from imposing their regulatory costs on out-of-state actors who did not and would not have chosen to assume those costs. In some instances, this determination will be relatively straightforward, as where a forum selection clause has been included in a contract. Strong inferences as to jurisdictional preference may also be drawn from the residence or business domicile that a defendant has chosen. In the majority of cases, however, the arbiter will be required to draw inferences on the basis of the defendant's course of conduct; only when the course of conduct reaches the level of minimum contacts is a revealed preference for the forum inferred.[81]

And here the calculus of costs and benefits described previously comes fully into play. If defendants must take the bitter with the sweet—if amenability to suit in a jurisdiction is the price interstate actors pay for the benefits of that forum's law "products"—then we may infer that a rational defendant would cheerfully choose to defend a suit in a jurisdiction so long as the marginal benefits associated with doing so at least equal the marginal costs.[82] In addition, this approach suggests that the costs to be balanced are not merely the costs of traveling to a distant forum; they also include the external costs of allowing the jurisdiction to export its substantive law. Thus, all the important considerations of such a "competitive federalism" analysis are found embedded within the fairness factors that have been articulated by the Supreme Court.

Finally, as in any adjudicatory system, an additional factor may be the cost of administering the rule chosen. It may be possible to identify situations in which jurisdiction is nearly always justified and apply a rule automatically granting jurisdiction in every such situation. The rule becomes in essence a presumed outcome for balancing the factors in the competitive jurisdictional analysis. Application of such a rule may on occasion improperly find jurisdiction where more nuanced analysis would have denied jurisdiction. However, if such occasions are rare, the cost of such mistakes may be outweighed by the savings from avoiding costly case-by-case inquiries within the situations governed by the rule.

This consideration may explain the "effects test" of *Calder v. Jones,* which has become almost a per se rule of jurisdiction for the forum in which a libel defendant dwells. When a tort requires intentionality toward the plaintiff, purposeful direction of activity toward the forum will be likely in the majority of cases. Thus, the *Calder* rule may entail a procedural "shortcut" designed to truncate expensive inquiries into the nature of contacts in a given set of circumstances when the cost of detailed inquiry will typically be greater than the savings from applying a consistent rule.

This perspective on jurisdiction clearly shows that online contacts or transactions by themselves will frequently, if not routinely, fail to support an assertion of jurisdiction over the person engaging in the activity. The argument that an Internet user exposes himself to lawsuits in any and every jurisdiction that his packets may reach is an argument unsupported by either doctrine or policy. From a purely doctrinal standpoint, this standard affords Internet users no meaningful opportunity to "structure their primary conduct" so as to accept or avoid the risk of litigation in a given forum: Internet users cannot "vote with their feet" if their feet are in essence planted everywhere. As a matter of policy, the standard would similarly afford states enormous opportunities for overreaching by imposing their domestic regulatory costs on out-of-state Internet users.

In the context of general jurisdiction analysis, courts have tended to comprehend and apply this principle. For example, in *McDonough v. Fallon McElligott, Inc.,*[83] the district court rejected the assertion that

Internet access could form the sole basis for general jurisdiction. The suit involved misappropriation of a photographer's work; the defendant moved to dismiss the case for lack of personal jurisdiction. In response to the plaintiff's allegation that accessibility to the defendant's Web site within the forum established general jurisdiction, the court noted:

> Because the Web enables easy worldwide access, allowing computer interaction via the Web to supply sufficient contacts to establish jurisdiction would eviscerate the personal jurisdiction requirement as it currently exists; the Court is not willing to take this step. Thus, the fact that Fallon has a Web site used by Californians cannot establish jurisdiction by itself.[84]

Unfortunately, courts have had more difficulty grasping this principle when specific jurisdiction is involved. Several early cases found specific jurisdiction based merely on the availability of the Web site in the forum.[85] Subsequently, courts realized the error of such a position and moved toward an "interactivity" analysis, by which the degree of interaction between a user and a Web site was held to determine the purposeful availment of the Web site owner.[86] Such a rule is fine, so long as the interactivity analyzed is jurisdictionally relevant interactivity: that is, the interactions must be such that they would meaningfully indicate to the potential defendant the location of the users, or otherwise show purposeful direction of activity toward the forum. Recent cases suggest that courts are now moving past formalistic inquiries into "interactivity," recognizing the need to base jurisdiction on real indicia of purposeful availment.[87]

Dormant Commerce Limits

The extensive discussion of due process and competitive federalism set forth here should facilitate similar discussion of a second and equally significant constitutional barrier against state jurisdictional overreaching. Separate constitutional grounds for limiting state Internet regulation may be found in dormant commerce analysis. The standard formulation of this analysis is well known. In its negative or "dormant" aspect, the Commerce Clause limits the ability of states to impede the flow of interstate commerce. Most especially, the dormant Commerce Clause enjoins the states from the problem that prompted its adoption and that was endemic under the Articles of Confederation: economic protectionism.[88] A state may not discriminate solely on the basis of geographic origin against articles of commerce from outside the state.[89] Neither may a state sacrifice the unity of the national market to reap purely local benefits.[90] Tariffs and taxes against out-of-state commerce are almost per se prohibited,[91] but more subtle nontariff barriers may be prohibited as well.[92]

If the statute treats domestic and out-of state commerce equally to achieve some legitimate local purpose, incidental effects on interstate commerce will be tolerated unless those effects exceed the putative local benefits.[93] This test requires courts to balance local benefits against systemic detriments, looking particularly to the effect on the interstate economic compact should many states adopt measures similar to the one in question.[94] In addition, the court balancing the costs and benefits should look to whether the same benefit could be achieved by some other means with a lesser degree of burden on interstate commerce.[95]

Commerce Holdouts

Many of the state laws now being enacted or enforced with regard to online activity lie within the "traditional police powers" of the states and so may be given special deference in this balancing test. For example, states have inherent power to safeguard the health and safety of their citizens and to protect them from fraud and deceptive trade practices.[96] The state interest component for such regulation will weigh heavily in the balance.[97] At the same time, the courts must be wary when a health and safety rationale is the purported basis of an enactment that tends to burden interstate commerce. The degree of deference accorded states in this area naturally makes consumer protection rationales particularly attractive to state legislatures, and, where possible, they will likely articulate such a rationale to avoid dormant commerce nullification of a given statute.[98] The courts are not blind to such subterfuge, and so-called health and safety measures cannot be simply "convenient apologies"[99] for constructive trade barriers between the states.

These rules constitute in part an adjunct to the federal system for situations in which the right of exit alone may not preserve the benefits of interjurisdictional competition.[100] For example, the dormant commerce requirements modulate the multistate coordination problem inherent in building interstate facilities such as a railroad, or in operating interstate business ventures such as those of a major insurer.[101] If each state can impose restrictions on the portions of the venture within its territory, then each state can act as a "holdout," seeking to extract from the interstate enterprise the profits from the entire venture.[102] Alternatively, the aggregate cost of inconsistent state demands may well exceed the total value of the interstate enterprise. However, the dormant Commerce Clause forestalls such dissipating regulation by its nearly per se rule prohibiting open discrimination against out-of-state commerce, and by prohibiting even facially nondiscriminatory regulation that is overly burdensome to interstate commerce. Thus, courts have been quick to strike down overly burdensome state regulation of "instruments of commerce" such as railroads or trucking; interstate disparities in the requirement of train length or mudflap size may constitute a counterproductive burden on national systems of transportation and communication.

The similarity of the Internet to previous interstate "instruments of commerce" such as railroads or trucks is striking. Given that the Internet is not simply a means of communication but a conduit for transporting digitized information goods such as software, data, music, graphics, and videos, there may be a variety of instances in which state regulation of network traffic constitutes an impermissible burden on commerce similar to burdensome regulation of tractor-trailer mudflaps, or of the length of railway trains. For example, several states have enacted burdensome provisions designed to prohibit access to online pornography; some such provisions would make the ISP liable if such images were transmitted on the provider's system. Several courts have recognized, as discussed at some length earlier, that it is unrealistic to believe that ISPs can reliably screen or block such images, and, more important, that the aggregate cost of attempting to do so may be significant.[103] ISPs facing the choice between liability and cost may simply choose to shut down or to significantly curtail their services, a result that suggests that such regulation is properly challenged as an impermissible burden on interstate commerce.

Thus, there are already examples of state Internet regulation that raise the same kind of "holdout" or coordination problems previously addressed by the dormant Commerce Clause cases. However, in the case of the Internet, such state regulatory peccadilloes will strike far closer to core liberties than those previously experienced. One of the Internet's great benefits is that the average citizen can participate for a relatively small investment. In the past, communicating or catering to a national constituency required heavy capital outlays; the Internet makes nationwide communication and commerce accessible to citizens for as little as a few hundred dollars. Similarly, smaller or entrepreneurial businesses may be able to reach customers that could previously only be reached by large established businesses with extensive marketing and distribution channels. The dramatically lowered costs of Internet communication promise to increase interstate commerce and communication.

But the prospect of multijurisdictional liability, or the imposition of multijurisdictional regulatory costs, may very well raise the price of participation beyond the reach of the average citizen or the small entrepreneur. Much of the network's democratizing influence may be lost if costs deter all but the most heavily capitalized entrepreneurs from pursuing all but the most highly profitable ventures—essentially re-creating the marketplace without the benefit of the network. The average user simply cannot afford the cost of defending multiple suits in multiple jurisdictions, or of complying with the regulatory requirements of every jurisdiction the user might electronically touch. Thus, the need for dormant commerce nullification of state overreaching is greater on the Internet than it has been for any previous scenario.

Exporting Law

The impact of dormant commerce analysis on problems of state Internet "holdouts" is intriguing and deserves further exploration. However, consistent with my competitive federalism analysis of due process limitations on the states, I wish to focus here on a different set of dormant commerce cases which indicate that the dormant Commerce Clause operates to prohibit states from exporting their law "products" into the local markets of sister states. In particular, I wish to focus on the line of cases beginning with *Edgar v. MITE Corp.*,[104] which explicitly analyzes dormant commerce not in terms of the "vertical" relationship between the states and the federal government but as a significant regulation on the "horizontal" relationship between sister states. The language of these cases implicitly recognizes a competitive federalism role for the dormant commerce clause, and hence for modulating horizontal federal relationships with regard to the Internet.

Extraterritoriality. The seminal case of *Edgar v. MITE Corp.* dealt with an Illinois securities law requiring a tender offerer in a takeover to register with the Illinois secretary of state in order for the secretary to oversee the fairness of the takeover and full disclosure to the offerees.[105] In the particular case decided, the shareholders of the takeover target were scattered throughout the country; 27 percent of the shareholders lived in Illinois. In addition, on its face the statute could have allowed the Illinois secretary to block takeovers in which not a single Illinois shareholder was affected. In a plurality opinion, Justice White suggested that a statute allowing one state to interdict a tender offer to not only its own residents but shareholders in other states offended the dormant Commerce Clause.[106] The opinion suggested that this was not simply because the state had intruded on power reserved to Congress but because of the intrusion upon the sovereignty of sister states.

The extraterritoriality portion of the *Edgar* opinion commanded only a plurality of the court.[107] However, *Edgar* was cited with approval and relied upon in a subsequent majority holding, *Healy v. The Beer Institute.*[108] In *Healy*, the Court struck down a Connecticut statute that required beer merchants to certify that they offered their products for the same price in states neighboring Connecticut as they did in Connecticut itself. The court held that the effect of the statute was to impermissibly regulate beer pricing outside the borders of the state. Citing *Edgar v. MITE*, the majority reaffirmed the principle that state regulation of activity wholly outside the borders of a state offends the commerce clause, whether or not the activity has some effect within the state.[109]

The Court then went on to explain:

> A statute that directly controls commerce wholly outside the boundaries of a State exceeds the inherent limits of the enacting State's authority and is invalid regardless of whether the statute's extraterritorial reach was intended by the legislature. The critical inquiry is whether the practical effect of the regulation is to control conduct beyond the borders of the State. . . . [T]he practical effect of the statute must be evaluated not only by considering the consequences

of the statute itself, but also by considering how the challenged statute may interact with the legitimate regulatory regimes of other States and what effect would arise if not one, but many or every, State adopted similar legislation.[110]

The Court concluded by emphasizing that "the Commerce Clause dictates that no State may force an out-of-state merchant to seek regulatory approval in one State before undertaking a transaction in another."[111]

Most recently, the Supreme Court has invoked the *Edgar/Healy* line of cases in its analysis of federal due process limitations on punitive damage awards. In *BMW of North America v. Gore*,[112] the Supreme Court addressed a punitive damage award assessed against an automobile manufacturer that failed to disclose repainting of new cars damaged in transit from the factory. This nationwide practice by the manufacturer violated the consumer fraud provisions of the state of Alabama. However, the defendant showed that its practice complied with the requirements of at least 25 states. In analyzing BMW's challenge to the constitutionality of the punitive damage award, the Supreme Court laid considerable significance on the impact that punitive damages awards in one state might have on the substantive policies of sister states. The majority cited both *Healy* and *Edgar* for the proposition that "One state's power to impose burdens on the interstate market . . . is not only subordinate to the federal power over interstate commerce, but is also constrained by the need to respect the interests of other states."[113] The opinion particularly stressed that a state cannot impose economic sanctions on violators of its laws in order to induce those entities to alter their lawful conduct in other states.[114]

Regulation and Competition. The function of the *Edgar/Healy* rationale seems clear as a matter of competitive federalism: states may not attempt to externalize the costs of their domestic regulatory schemes on other states, or "export" their domestic regulations into another jurisdiction.[115] The most blatant attempt to do this appears in Healy, where Connecticut's certification program was admittedly designed to deter Connecticut residents from driving to neighboring states to purchase beer at lower prices than those available in Connecticut. In other words, Connecticut hoped to deter its residents from exiting or from voting with their feet against the state's regulatory scheme.

147

Only by inducing beer distributors to artificially inflate their prices in neighboring states could Connecticut hope to stem deter such exit. But by forcing a price increase in neighboring states, Connecticut would effectively export the costs of its domestic regulation to its neighbors, potentially frustrating their own domestic regulatory schemes. *Edgar* and *BMW* arose from similar attempts to export the costs of domestic regulation of, respectively, securities and products disclosures.

Much as in the case of due process, the dormant commerce doctrine articulated in these cases functions as a buffer against such externalization. Yet, although the court in the *Edgar* line of cases analogizes its dormant commerce analysis to due process analysis, it is clear that the two doctrines perform different, though complementary, functions. In each of the dormant commerce cases described, the individual or entity that the state sought to regulate was properly subject to personal jurisdiction in that forum, but the activity the state sought to reach was territorially exempt from that state's regulation. The net result is that even if an entity's activities within the forum may be reached by domestic regulation, its activities within a sister jurisdiction remain insulated from regulatory "leakage."

This difference in doctrines is thrown into sharp relief when examined in light of the Court's ruling in *Quill v. North Dakota*.[116] There, the Supreme Court held that a mail order company was properly subject to North Dakota's jurisdiction for purposes of taxation: shipment of goods into the state provided sufficient contacts.[117] However, in the second half of the same opinion, the Court held that taxation of a business with no physical presence in the state violated the dormant commerce clause.[118] This holding, which fully accords with the *Edgar* line of cases, illustrates that due process analysis is a necessary, but not sufficient, criterion for regulatory jurisdiction in a federal system: states cannot be allowed to impose their domestic policies extraterritorially, even if minimum contacts are present in the particular instance.[119] As the Court explained the distinction:

> Due process centrally concerns the fundamental fairness of governmental activity. Thus, at a most general level, the due process nexus requires that we ask whether an individual's connections with a State are substantial enough to legitimate the State's exercise of power over him. We have, therefore,

148

often identified "notice" or "fair warning" as the analytic touchstone of due process nexus analysis. In contrast, the Commerce Clause, and its nexus requirement, are informed not so much by concerns about fairness for the individual defendant as by structural concerns about the effects of state regulation on the national economy. . . . Thus, the "substantial nexus" requirement is not, like due process' "minimum contacts" requirement, a proxy for notice, but rather a means for limiting state burdens on interstate commerce. Accordingly . . . a corporation may have "minimum contacts" with a taxing State as required by the Due Process Clause, and yet lack the "substantial nexus" with that State as required by the Commerce Clause.[120]

The principle applied in *Quill* and in the *Edgar* line of cases has important ramifications for online commerce. Take for example, Internet enforcement activities of the Securities Bureau in the state of New Jersey. Early in the history of public Internet usage, these state regulators adopted a highly proactive stance toward supervision of investment solicitations offered online, and with good reason: a variety of fraudulent investment schemes have appeared both on the Internet and on proprietary systems such as Prodigy and America Online.[121] However, at least some of these regulators have adopted the rather extreme position that any electronic communication that may be received in New Jersey and that meets the statutory definition of a "security" is subject to New Jersey securities law, including requirements of registration and disclosure.[122] A former chief of the FBI has opined that online offerings by registered brokers in other jurisdictions, even when legitimate and accompanied by full disclosure, violates New Jersey law if the broker is not registered in New Jersey.[123]

This position looks suspiciously similar to that of Illinois in *Edgar v. MITE*: a state demanding that out-of-state businesses comply with its domestic securities law, even if the business has fully complied with the securities law of its own state. Indeed, under the New Jersey rationale, the online activity is subject to New Jersey regulation whether or not it has any effect in the state; to trigger regulation the offer need only be electronically accessible from New Jersey, let alone accessible to anyone actually investing. In effect, under this policy New Jersey is attempting to dictate to the entire nation—if not the world—what the standards for investment offerings shall

149

be. Although a clearer example of a state attempting to export its domestic law can hardly be imagined, any area in which the state attempts to regulate dissemination or receipt of online information, including its sale, will raise similar problems.

Other examples abound. As electronic commerce grows, among the most valuable services available to consumers are automated data retrieval systems that "crawl" commercial sites on the World Wide Web, using automated data retrieval systems to aggregate pricing data for a variety of consumer products, from books and music CDs to airline tickets.[124] The easy availability of such data is an attractive benefit of online markets, as enhanced consumer information spurs competitive pricing. But some Internet vendors, who might prefer that consumers not be able to easily compare prices, have objected to retrieval of information from their sites as constituting state law "trespass" against their computer systems.[125] Application of such trespass law clearly burdens the interstate commerce system, potentially disabling data aggregation services that supply valuable pricing information to consumers and enhance the function of online markets. The local benefits are dubious at best, which suggests that the application of this state law would fail dormant commerce balancing.

But, in addition, such application of trespass law may trigger the extraterritoriality prong of dormant commerce analysis. The components of Internet systems are rarely located in only one state; for example, the Web site for an airline such as American Airlines or Northwest Airlines may be ostensibly located on servers in a particular state, such as, respectively, Texas or Minnesota. But the ticket pricing data for either Web site are in fact drawn from airfare databases such as SABRE, APOLLO, GALILEO, or WORLDSPAN, which are housed in other states entirely. Yet other elements or services of the Web site may be located in yet other states. Application of Texas or Minnesota state trespass law to such conglomerate sites would in fact constitute application of those states' laws to computers residing elsewhere, an impermissible export of one jurisdiction's regulatory scheme to a sister jurisdiction.

As a practical matter, such regulation is counterproductive. As described earlier with regard to due process, Internet businesses and content providers simply cannot tell with any degree of assurance the geographic location from which access to data has been requested, and there is no practical way to screen out contacts from particular jurisdictions, especially particular English-speaking jurisdictions. The end result is that online businesses have no way of knowing whether their communications, advertisements, transactions, and even shipments of digital goods comply with the regulatory regime of wherever the goods or information may end up. If a rule other than that of *Quill* were to be applied to online businesses, and they were subject to the regulation of the recipient jurisdiction, online commerce would face an almost insurmountable burden in attempting to predict which requirements might be imposed on it.

Since there are a finite number of U.S. jurisdictions that might have contact with an online site, and so a finite number of regulations, a business could gather information on the complete universe of potential regulations—a burdensome task but not an impossible one. The question would then be which strategy a business should adopt, knowing the possible rules but being uncertain which might apply. Two strategies might be expected to emerge, depending on the pattern of regulation. Where the regulation of the 50 states was consistent but merely different in magnitude, the "lowest common denominator" would have to prevail. If, for example, various states required increasing levels of disclosure about a product or transaction, an online business could opt to offer the highest level of disclosure required. By complying, as the case might be, with either the most demanding or restrictive regulatory regime, a business might satisfy the lesser requirements of all the other jurisdictions as well.

A different result would be expected where state regulations were inconsistent—if, for example, some jurisdictions required disclosure of certain facts about a product or service but other jurisdictions forbade such disclosure. In such instances, being unable to predict which jurisdiction's regulation might apply, and being unable to comply with all the potential requirements, online businesses might choose to comply with the rule of the majority of jurisdictions and hope that no transactions occurred where compliance was lacking. But unless the possibility of such transactions was very small, or the penalties for noncompliance were substantially outweighed by the profit to be had from taking the risk, it seems more likely that rational businesses would simply cease to transact business online.[126]

One set of commentators has suggested that state regulation should be accommodated via changes in the "architecture" of the

151

network that may facilitate determinations of geographic location.[127] The particular suggestions made in fact are not architectural changes but more application-level retrofits of the type described earlier, overlaying the actual architecture of the network. Actual architectural changes could of course be imagined. For example, U.S. Attorney General Janet Reno once suggested that pressure should be brought to bear on the engineers designing the next generation of Internetworking Protocols, IP version 6, to ensure that the next IP upgrade made law enforcement easier by facilitating packet tracing and end-user location. Another idea that has been circulated is that of requiring global positioning devices to be incorporated into all computing equipment and their geographic coordinates attached to packet routing information. Such fundamental changes in the architecture of the network might indeed make jurisdictional discrimination feasible and even routine.

Sufficient regulatory pressure placed on the network might in fact result in such changes; just as law adapts to new technological challenges, technology may respond to legal challenges. Ironically, though, these kinds of costs seem to be precisely the ones that the dormant commerce cases are intended to deter. It would of course be possible to facilitate the different requirements of state mudflap regulation by redesigning all models of freight-hauling trucks so that the mudflaps could be quickly and efficiently changed, or perhaps by redesigning the interstate highway system itself. Railroad tracks and cars could no doubt be redesigned to simplify the lengthening and shortening of trains to lower the cost of differing regulatory requirements as trains passed from state to state. But the costs associated with such redesign, together with the propensity of states to act opportunistically were such redesign to occur, creates the need for dormant commerce doctrine to deter such regulatory pressure. One would expect the dormant commerce cases to be properly employed in deterring state-induced redesign of the Internet as well.

The Interstate Laboratory

Under the traditional commerce analysis, either of these results is likely to place a serious burden on interstate commerce; depending on the local benefits to be gained from the regulations, the burden may or may not be undue. At least in situations in which the demands of conflicting regulations drive an online business out of the market, the detriment to commerce would appear so severe that it is difficult to imagine what local benefits would be sufficient to compensate. This may not always be true in the lowest common denominator situation. In the example given of product disclosure, excessive disclosure dictated by the most demanding jurisdiction may be costly, but one can imagine that consumers might benefit enough to outweigh the costs.

However, from the perspective of competitive federalism, the situation is far more grave than the traditional balancing test might suggest. If the lowest common denominator prevails among online services, then the "laboratory of the states" is disabled. No state wishing to experiment with a lesser level of regulation will be able to do so. Similarly, it goes almost without saying that the "laboratory" is disabled when online services are driven out of business by conflicting requirements. Either result arises out of the inability in an online environment to geographically circumscribe contacts. In essence, if businesses are subjected to a state's regulation merely on the basis of online contacts, then the businesses cannot "exit" or "vote with their feet" to escape the burdensome regulation of a particular jurisdiction. The regulation follows them wherever they go.

This situation constitutes an enormous problem for horizontal federalism. It is one thing if a particular state wishes to regulate all the businesses within its borders out of existence: the result simply constitutes a terrible failure (or, depending on the state's goal, perhaps a spectacular success) of that state's regulatory experiment within its own laboratory. But it is another matter entirely if a state regulates out of existence businesses that its sister states are attempting to foster within their borders. A particular state cannot be permitted to dictate to the entire country the regulatory standards for any activity. If national uniformity is to be imposed on a regulatory matter—and I have shown that for some types of "law products" it must be—then it is the prerogative of the federal government to do so, and not the prerogative of a particular state.

Consider, for example, Pennsylvania legislation ostensibly intended to block the availability of child pornography on remote servers that may lie beyond the geographic reach of the state authorities.[128] The statute allows the state attorney general to obtain an ex parte order requiring ISPs operating within the state to block access

153

to the IP address of the offending material. For example, the attorney general might obtain an order requiring WorldCom to block a site in the Philippines.[129] WorldCom, however, is a national ISP whose system operates not only in Pennsylvania but in many other states. WorldCom cannot feasibly determine whether users of its system are located in Pennsylvania or elsewhere; consequently, by blocking the offending site in response to Pennsylvania regulation, it will cut off access to the site for subscribers in other states. This, again, constitutes a severe burden on interstate commerce, which may or may not be justified by the local benefit of blocking child pornography. But even if this balance tips in the state's favor, the Pennsylvania rule dictates WorldCom's activity not only within its own borders but also within the borders of other sovereign states. And while it is unlikely that other states will object to having their citizens deprived of access to child pornography, they might well object if this approach were applied to some other online activity, such as advertising, about which regulatory attitudes might differ. Indeed, even in the case of child pornography, the Pennsylvania blunderbuss approach may disrupt another state's experimentation in finding a more innovative and nuanced solution to the problem.

It may be, of course, that in some instances the Internet will facilitate externalization of domestic regulatory costs. A state might decide to attract businesses by permitting lax Internet advertising standards bordering on deception. One would expect that the costs of any deception resulting from the lax regulation would accrue primarily outside the permissive jurisdiction, effectively forcing out-of-state residents to pay for the permissive state's system. Might such a situation justify extraterritorial application of other states' stringent regulation to reach the shady advertisers? Under the dormant commerce analysis, clearly not. To the extent that some Internet activity may facilitate externalization of regulatory costs, then the competitive federal model will function poorly in those areas. But this means that federal regulation, not extraterritorial state regulation, is required—precisely the reason that, under the federal Constitution, regulation of commerce was placed in the hands of a central authority.

State regulators may of course complain that the constitutional constraints I have outlined will prevent them from protecting their citizenry against the very real threats of fraud and vice on the

Internet. The answer to such an objection is that although the state may not regulate the citizenry of other states, it is perfectly free to regulate its own citizenry: Pennsylvania is welcome to penalize Pennsylvanians who peruse online child pornography, and New Jersey is welcome to require its residents to file disclosures certifying that they have thoroughly investigated any online opportunity in which they decide to invest. Demand-side regulation is naturally less convenient for the state regulators, but the federal system considered here was not designed with the convenience of regulators in mind. Rather, if citizens value stringent protection from online fraud and vice, and one state or another offers such protection, then that state may expect an influx of citizens seeking the safety of that regime. If, on the other hand, citizens find such regulation overly burdensome, then that judgment will similarly be manifested by either voice or exit, and the regime should go the way of previous failed experiments in the laboratory of the states.

Conclusion

There should be little doubt that the widespread availability of the Internet has changed the nature of commerce and of communication, and changed them profoundly. The unprecedented speed and reach[130] of communication now available to average citizens have dramatically altered the frequency, transparency, and nature of contacts between jurisdictions in the federal system. At the same time, in another sense, the more things change, the more they stay the same. Dramatic technological change is not unprecedented, nor is the accommodation of legal rules to new technology. There is little question, for example, that the advent of affordably priced automobiles radically changed the jurisprudence of jurisdiction in the federal system as courts were for the first time faced with an exceptionally mobile populace that could exit territorially based jurisdictions at will. The jurisdictional jurisprudence we take for granted today has been shaped by this and similar technological change.

Thus, the difficulty courts have had in formulating a coherent and sensible approach to Internet-based jurisdiction suggests that the "unexceptionalists" are in some sense correct that nothing about the challenge of this technology is new. The rules governing personal jurisdiction are just as predictable and lucid as they ever were— which is of course to say that those rules are decidedly turbid and

155

nearly incomprehensible to the majority of lawyers, let alone to the general populace. Experts on civil procedure are no doubt accustomed to operating under dysfunctional rule sets, but that is cold comfort to consumers and businesses engaged in trying to build new online markets. Indeed, the jurisdictional difficulties posed by this new technology may finally have pushed such incomprehensible analyses to the breaking point, necessitating a fresh look at the familiar rules, much as occurred years ago in the landmark *International Shoe* decision. As Kuhn observed with regard to "normal science," discrepancies in the dominant paradigm accumulate until it must be discarded in favor of a new analytical framework.[131]

Neither is it helpful to argue that we can force technology to conform to previous legal outcomes; this gets the result precisely backwards, much like ranting that the automobile was spoiling the "established principles" of jurisdiction before *International Shoe*. Unexceptionalists at the time might have demanded that automobiles be redesigned to accommodate the pre–*International Shoe* physical presence rule, perhaps by limiting automobile speed or the size of their fuel tanks, so that extraterritorial jaunts would be impractical or infrequent. This strikes us in hindsight as silly, and for good reason. The clear benefits of automotive range and speed required a readjustment of the legal framework, not a readjustment of technology that might have been inconvenient to the prevailing legal regime. The benefit that Internet technology brings to commerce and communication may require similar adjustments to the legal regime that is the legacy of previous technology. Both law and technology are malleable, but it is counterproductive to impose costs upon the technology and the users of the technology to accommodate a "settled principle" of law simply because it is a settled principle, especially when the cost of altering the settled principle is low relative to the benefits of the new technology.

This is not to say that some sovereigns will not try to force technology to fit their preferred legal model, or that such changes cannot be forced to occur if the sovereign is willing to pay the price of diminished speed, reach, and usability.[132] But it is to say that if there is an established legal principle to be regarded, it is that a given sovereign state within the federal system may not impose such idiosyncratic costs on other states, or on the system as a whole. Consequently, in considering state regulation of the Internet, we are

156

required to ask whether application of current jurisdictional law will yield desirable results, to adjust the rule where it does not, and to assess the desirability of the result by its compatibility with the goals of competitive federalism.

7. Multijurisdictional Regulation of the Internet

Bruce H. Kobayashi and Larry E. Ribstein

Introduction

Electronic commerce provides both opportunities and challenges for markets. Reduced transaction costs and more rapid dissemination of information offer the potential for more efficient consumer markets. At the same time, however, new markets and technologies can create perceived regulatory gaps and apparent opportunities for new regulation. One example is venders' use of consumer marketing information that they obtain on the Internet. The Federal Trade Commission has recommended regulating privacy,[1] and Congress has legislated practices for using personal information collected from consumers.[2] Another is the debate concerning regulation of the licensing of software and other computer information, particularly in transactions over the Internet. The National Conference of Commissioners for Uniform State Laws (NCCUSL) has promulgated the Uniform Computer Information Transactions Act (UCITA).[3] The FTC has considered the possibility of federally regulating such transactions.[4]

Some commentators dispute the notion that new legislation is required,[5] and have noted the potential costs of such regulation.[6] This chapter focuses on the more fundamental question of who should make such regulatory decisions. The chapter mainly concerns the issues specifically relating to federal and state regulation within the United States. We also discuss broader questions concerning regulation by nations in the international setting.

In contrast to the substantial disagreement over the substantive provisions of new legislation regulating electronic commerce, there is widespread agreement that such regulatory decisions should be made at the federal level.[7] Those favoring new substantive regulation of electronic commerce argue that states are not the appropriate regulators because new contracting technologies and the global nature of the Internet will allow firms to evade state regulation easily. Moreover, businesses engaging in electronic commerce do not want to be subject to overlapping regulation by many states, and thus support broad federal preemption of state regulation.

This chapter shows, instead, that allowing states to make the decision whether or not to regulate electronic commerce has a significant chance for success relative to having such decisions made at the federal level, and that the criticisms of leaving these decisions to the states are not persuasive. Allowing the states to decide if and how to regulate electronic commerce has the important advantages of being dynamic and decentralized, and so more suitable to the evolving nature of electronic commerce than top-down methods of lawmaking. Moreover, the costs of overlapping state regulation can be minimized by the use and enforcement of parties' contractual choice of jurisdiction and law.

Finding the Right Regulatory Balance

There is significant uncertainty about how to regulate electronic commerce, about whether there is any market failure that requires regulation, and about whether government needs to supply whatever regulation is required. This is important background for the discussion below of state law's advantage over federal law by allowing for a variety of approaches and facilitating legal experimentation with and competition among diverse regimes. Two specific types of transactions have figured prominently in the debate over regulating electronic commerce—consumer marketing information and sales of software and other electronic information. These issues are intended only as illustrations. The chapter's basic analysis of state and federal regulatory approaches can be generalized to deal with other regulatory issues concerning electronic commerce.

Arguments for Regulation of Electronic Commerce

The regulation of electronic commerce is typically invoked as a way of addressing potential harms to consumers in an unregulated market, assuming there are defects in the private contracting process. The benefits are discussed separately regarding consumer marketing information and sales of computer information.

Consumer Marketing Information. The technology of Internet shopping has generated new types of markets for information. Consumers who move through a Web site leave behind two types of data trails they would not generate in a shopping mall: the more conventional track from e-mail addresses or other information needed to enter a Web site, which can be linked with other information through databases and search tools; and clickstream data, which are more significant for present purposes because they are generated silently and therefore raise more significant issues about informed consent. Web sites place unique identifying numbers called "cookies" on the hard drives of surfing consumers who use the popular Netscape and Internet Explorer browsers. Web site operators can use cookies to combine all information generated by visits to the site by a particular computer. Thus, the Web site operator knows which pages the computer visited and how long it spent on each page.

The most important concern about consumer marketing information is not with clickstream data itself, but with the Web site operator's ability to link this information with identifying information the consumer has supplied, including e-mail addresses, passwords, and credit card numbers. Such linkages explain how Amazon.com knows not only that you are "Larry" or "Bruce" when you visit, and what books you have bought in the past, but also your address and credit card information.

Concern over such linkages has led some to advocate regulations that would prohibit the sale or further dissemination of consumer marketing information. The assurance that their information will not be resold can increase consumers' willingness to transact business and disclose information, either explicitly or through visiting a Web site.[8] Moreover, some argue that individuals have fundamental privacy rights and that mandatory rules should enforce the protection of personal information.[9]

Before continuing the analysis, it is important to distinguish the issues concerning cookies from those concerning other types of privacy invasions. First, government intrusions differ qualitatively from those of firms. Private firms that abuse consumer information lose customers. People lack analogous exit opportunities regarding government intrusions. A state's residents must comply with the entire bundle of state rules mandating disclosure of personal information when they engage in state-regulated or state-monitored activities, including birth, driving, working, or dying. Equating governments' and firms' privacy incursions, as some commentators have done,[10] questionably assumes that product markets are so deficient that they

161

leave people as helpless to deal with private companies as they are to deal with state governments.

Second, it may be helpful to further distinguish relatively mundane identifying information from information that consumers clearly expect to be kept private, such as medical records.[11] People turn over such information expecting that it will not be disclosed to others without their consent. The main issues here concern whether firms and governments should be able to use the information notwithstanding this expectation, and how and under what circumstances violators should be punished. Given greater uniformity of preferences and expectations, state law's advantage of offering diverse approaches does not come as strongly into play.[12]

Electronic Information Sales. Electronic information sales (e.g., the sale of databases or e-books over the Internet) involve many of the same problems of fraud and product defects as other products sold over the Internet. This raises questions of whether special rules should apply to contracting for electronic information because of the rapid nature of the Web site contracting process.

There are also questions regarding the seller's ability to restrict use of the information through the license agreement and by design of the product. In general, limiting use of information has external effects on other users by allowing contracting parties to keep private information that would otherwise fall into the public domain. This applies, for example, to license terms that restrict the buyer's right to resell[13] and that let licensors price discriminate among users.

Costs of Regulating Electronic Commerce

The costs of regulating electronic commerce are as uncertain as the benefits. This fact is demonstrated in the following subsections, again focusing on consumer marketing information and electronic information sales.

Consumer Marketing Information. In general, consumer marketing information, like other arguably private information, benefits both merchants and consumers by reducing information and transaction costs, and, in turn, inefficient transactions and fraud.[14] Such disclosures can be part of a mutually beneficial exchange of money and information for goods and services on terms that incorporate the value of the information. Exchange of this information allows Web site merchants to monitor how many and what types of consumers they are reaching, and helps them target particular advertisements to particular consumers. More precise targeting of Web site advertising increases its information value to consumers, thereby helping consumers satisfy their preferences.[15] Consumers also get reduced prices or free benefits for using Web sites that collect data and from an expanded choice of products and services.[16] Thus, prohibiting collection of cookies containing consumer information could impede the development of valuable databases and increase transaction costs.[17]

Privacy regulation of cookies could have other negative consequences. In general, privacy is not always desirable because it cloaks undesirable activity.[18] This is as true of privacy concerning Web site–related conduct as it is outside the Internet context. An important recent example concerns *A&M Records v. Napster*,[19] in which the district court found that the majority of files transferred by persons using the Napster service were unauthorized copies of copyrighted music, and ordered Napster to cease operations for contributing to copyright infringement. The Ninth Circuit affirmed the district court's grant of the plaintiff's motion for a preliminary injunction but remanded for a determination as to whether Napster could differentiate infringing and noninfringing uses so that a remedy would not unduly interfere with legitimate activities, noting that the "mere existence of the Napster system, absent actual notice and Napster's demonstrated failure to remove the material, is insufficient to impose contributory liability."[20] In an attempt to comply with the preliminary injunction subsequently ordered by the district court, Napster employed filtering technologies to block the sharing of copyrighted materials.[21] The district court concluded that these filters were ineffective and ordered Napster to shut down.[22] Napster subsequently sought bankruptcy protection.[23]

Limitations on the ability of Napster users to remain anonymous might have been useful here. Napster or the recording companies could use cookies or Globally Unique Identifier (GUID) technology to allow copyright holders to identify those engaged in licensing or copyright violations without deterring noninfringing uses.[24] Indeed, some type of identifier may be necessary to prevent the sharing of copyrighted works through the newer generation of peer-to-peer (P2P) file sharing software that proliferated after Napster's demise, such as Gnutella, Aimster, Kazaa, and iMesh. These programs do not use a central server to connect users, thereby precluding the use of filtering software.[25]

In short, cookies provide valuable information. Because information generally has some of the qualities of a public good in that it is difficult for suppliers to internalize all of the benefits, there is reason to suspect that a socially suboptimal amount of this information will be produced.[26] It is, therefore, important not to overregulate.

Attempts to determine the appropriate regulatory balance focus on whether an individual should have a privacy right and, if so, what form this right should take.[27] Cookies are not protected as an intellectual property right of the consumer who is the subject of the information.[28] Some privacy protection for consumer data may be sought—for example, when there is concern over such data being collected and used without the consumer's knowledge or agreement. A potential conflict exists between the social benefits of disclosure (such as the creation of new databases), and an individual's desire to control the further dissemination of consumer information (perhaps out of concern over reputation, a general taste for privacy or autonomy, or the possibility of identity theft).[29]

The fundamental issue is whether a default rule of privacy is more efficient than a default rule that allows collection and dissemination of consumer data. Because circumstances vary across transactions, a contract default rule may be more efficient than a mandatory rule.[30] Even if merchants collect and use information for purposes other than completing the transaction, as when they sell transactional and clickstream data to third parties, there is no problem if the consumer is informed and agrees. Informed consumers will give up personal information when its privacy value is less than what someone else is willing to pay for it, which in turn depends on the value of subsequent use of the information. The default rule could be embodied in statutes or tort law,[31] although protection against dissemination of accurate and factual personal information based on the tort of invasion of privacy is limited.[32] There is limited protection of privacy based on the tort doctrine of breach of trust,[33] and it has been suggested that this doctrine should be expanded.[34] However, a separate economic analysis is not required, as the only discernable principle underlying such duties is one of implied contract and efficient default rules.[35]

In the presence of positive transaction costs, an efficient default rule would be the rule that results in the highest social surplus net of the costs incurred by those that choose to contract out of the default rule.[36] This choice of a default rule depends partly on what the parties would have agreed to *ex ante*, in the absence of transaction and information costs.[37] As noted, parties presumably would agree to allow collection and dissemination of consumer data if and only if the expected value of future uses of the information at the time of contracting exceeds the value of privacy. For example, in *Moore v. University of California*,[38] where a valuable and patented cell line was eventually established from tissues obtained from a patient being treated for leukemia, the court recognized a fiduciary duty by the doctor to disclose the reasons for taking the cells, but denied the patient an intellectual property right to his cells because the medical research use of his cells did not require attribution to or identification of him, and because Moore had signed a standard form before surgery consenting to having blood and tissue samples taken after surgery for medical research.[39] In a case like *Moore*, the fiduciary duty is arguably based on the patient's ability to demand payment for his continued cooperation if he knows the medical value of his cells. But this might prevent valuable medical research. More generally, the law encourages production of information by enforcing contracts despite one party's failure to disclose material information about which it knows the other side is mistaken (e.g., Moore's mistaken belief that his blood is only being used for diagnostic purposes).[40] This supports a default rule in the *Moore* situation permitting use of the information even without explicit patient consent.[41]

In contrast to the *Moore* context, a default rule that requires disclosure of the potential uses of consumer data may be efficient because one consumer could not capture the value of a compilation of cookies by threatening to withhold his future cooperation, and because privacy concerns may be greater regarding consumer data that identifies the individual. Thus, in *Dwyer v. American Express*,[42] where American Express (Amex) had collected and analyzed cardholders' spending patterns without obtaining informed consent, the court held, consistent with *Moore*, that there was no tort misappropriation because the defendant created the value "by categorizing and aggregating [cardholders'] names."[43] However, the court held that Amex's failure to inform cardholders that their spending habits would be analyzed and their names sold to advertisers constituted a deceptive practice under the Illinois Consumer Fraud Statute because some consumers might not have used the card if they had known of the practice.[44]

Still another situation is invoked in a case involving medical information that identifies the individual. Here, the individual's need for protection may be stronger than for other private information because of the greater sensitivity of the information. An example is *Weld v. CVS Pharmacy*,[45] where CVS used information collected from customers who filled prescriptions at its stores to maintain, without customers' informed consent, a database that CVS used to conduct a direct mail campaign funded by several pharmaceutical companies. The trial court denied the defendant's motions for summary judgment on customers' privacy-related claims, noting individuals' special expectation of privacy concerning medical information, and distinguishing *Dwyer*.[46] But medical information that identifies the patients may be at least as valuable as the information collected in *Moore*, which suggests a possible collision between the individual's privacy rights and the social costs of privacy.

These cases indicate the difficult trade-offs involved in creating efficient privacy rules, and how these rules should depend on, among other things, the consumer's expectations of privacy and on how regulation will affect incentives to produce valuable information. Thus, a particular rule may be wrong for a significant number of transactions.[47]

In general, given the transaction-specific nature of the appropriate rules and the costs associated with adopting too high a level of privacy protection, contract default rules would appear to be the right approach. But even if that principle is accepted, it may not be clear what the default rules should be or who should provide them. These issues do not lend themselves to a one-size-fits-all, all-at-once federal approach.

Computer Information Transactions. Internet sale of computer information, such as computer software programs, raises several questions about the appropriate level of regulation. First, what does "merchantability" mean with respect to computer software, where consumers expect some "bugs" but not too many? Second, what terms are appropriate to the sorts of licensing transactions that occur in this context as distinguished from outright sales? Third, what levels of detail and clarity should be required in disclosures to consumers? Fourth, how explicitly must consumers waive warranties or other protections? In general, highly detailed disclosures and explicit assent procedures impose additional transaction costs in terms of reducing the speed of electronic commerce that may or may not be outweighed by the benefits in terms of effectuating consumer preferences.

There are additional issues concerning the social costs and benefits of regulation, particularly including those relating to incentives to produce information. Unlike the usual sale of a consumer product, software licenses typically restrict or limit resale of the product by the consumer. By preventing resale by original buyers, these terms allow licensors to price discriminate between low-value and high-value users.[48] Price discrimination, in turn, may enable licensors to extract more profits from the product and thus increase their incentives to produce the information. Although licensors may be able to use self-help even without legal enforcement, this may significantly increase licensors' costs.[49]

Apart from rules regarding resale, contracts may protect property that is not protected by intellectual property laws,[50] such as databases,[51] thereby remedying Congress's failure to foresee the path of technological development. This protection increases the return on a compiler's investment, and therefore the probability that the information will be produced.[52] Any policy that leaves everything to Congress' limited foresight might create a centralized, uninformed, and inflexible system that provides inadequate incentives for the creation of intellectual property, and therefore would not serve the intellectual property laws' goal to "promote the progress of the sciences and useful arts."[53] Indeed, private ordering may produce more efficient results than those under the copyright laws.[54]

Arguments for Market Failure

It is known that regulators face significant questions in balancing the costs and benefits of regulation. This raises the question of whether merchants and consumers are likely to do a better job in formulating and agreeing to mutually beneficial terms and prices. More specifically, is there anything about the contracting process in this context that may be conducive to market failure, and that therefore may justify having regulators making the difficult cost-benefit decisions discussed earlier? These arguments will be discussed generally in this section and then revisited later in the specific context of enforcing contractual choice of law.

The Internet as a "Lemons" Market. Some have argued that consumers will resort to bricks-and-mortar merchants unless online merchants are tightly regulated.[55] This claim implies that consumer marketing information involves a "lemons" market: because consumers cannot distinguish between high- and low-quality promises of data protection and enforcement levels, they will not be willing to pay for higher levels of protection and low-quality merchants will dominate the market.[56] It arguably follows that merchants and consumers both would benefit from strong legal rules that induce consumers to rely on Web site merchants.

The "lemons" argument assumes that companies can survive on the Internet by selling low-quality goods at high prices to dumb consumers. However, this argument seems inconsistent with several important features of Internet markets.

First, the Web site enables consumers to deal in a brief period and at low cost with many different merchants. This opportunity lets consumers compare terms and products offered by many merchants.

Second, because online merchants need to encourage consumer trust in this new market, they have ample incentives to build reputations for and otherwise signal their trustworthiness. Merchants that frustrate consumer expectations devalue their reputations and effectively forfeit their bonds.[57] Consumers, after all, can choose not to deal with merchants that are perceived as untrustworthy or can limit their disclosure of information. Consumers can refuse to make personal disclosures, turn off the cookie feature of their browsers, or use a variety of devices that control the amount of marketing information consumers make available and to whom they give it.[58]

Third, various media, including the Internet itself, spurred by highly vocal privacy advocates, rapidly disseminate information about background facts regarding new uses of consumer information and the behavior of individual merchants. For example, when DoubleClick acquired a direct-mail company and planned to merge its cookie data with the direct-mail database, "a fierce backlash" forced DoubleClick to postpone the database merger plan and hire prominent consumer advocates as privacy monitors.[59] Because consumers can refuse to deal with offending Web sites or deny marketing information to these sites, a consumer backlash can reduce Web site operators' ability to accumulate information and give them an incentive to change their practices. Moreover, it is cheap and easy for individual consumers and competing merchants as well as organizations to post information about defective products and dishonest merchants, and sophisticated search engines enable shoppers to find this information.

It is unnecessary for all consumers to be sophisticated or aware of the problems for markets to protect all consumers. Because of venders' high costs of discriminating between the informed and uninformed in this setting, due partly to their reliance on standard form contracts, competition for the marginally informed consumer protects the uninformed consumer.[60] Marginal Internet consumers, who are likely to be more informed than consumers generally, therefore will set contract terms in this setting.

The Nature of Web Site Contracts. The process of contracting on the Web site might seem to handicap consumers. Consumers typically do not bargain over terms but rather either accept or reject the standard form contracts they are offered on merchants' Web sites. The rushed and casual atmosphere of Web site surfing might be said to be nonconducive to contracting.[61] However, even if consumers cannot bargain with each of their venders, they can easily shop among many alternative venders, as discussed in the previous subsection. Accordingly, the non-bargained-for or "adhesive" nature of a contract does not alone make it inefficient.[62] Moreover, regulation that, in effect, requires bargaining by refusing fully to enforce adhesion contracts would be inefficient if the benefits of bargaining did not outweigh the costs.[63]

A Web site may actually offer more opportunities for viable bargaining than contracting off the Web site, because it makes more feasible mechanisms by which consumers can carefully read contracts before buying or licensing products. This fact particularly applicable to the problem of licensing software. Because it is difficult to design a mechanism for reaching agreement on complex terms of a license before sale, venders commonly use licenses that are included in the product that consumers do not see until they have bought and paid for the product, taken it home, and torn off the product's shrink wrap. Consumers thus are bound by a complex contract with little opportunity to negotiate or read it. On the other hand, if consumers' consent is not deemed to occur until a later period, they might benefit from the product without paying for it. A Web site makes it easy for merchants to give consumers as much time as they want to read the contract before they click on the download button. In addition, a Web site facilitates a kind of automated contracting where consumers can configure Web site agents, or bots, to look for and accept or reject certain types of contract terms.[64]

Finally, the Internet does not necessarily involve the asymmetry of bargaining position that often seems to exist between buyers and sellers. Because the Web site has reduced the costs of selling by eliminating the need for bricks-and-mortar storefronts, it is conducive to smaller venders.

The Internet as a "Lamb's Market." Even if consumers can compare the deals offered by many merchants, they still have to understand what they are buying and (in the case of consumer marketing information) selling. Advocates of privacy regulation argue that consumers may be unable to value their information accurately in monetary terms.[65] Like lambs, they will be shorn unwittingly of their information. Merchants able to obtain consumer marketing information at less than its value to consumers will have little incentive to offer high levels of consumer protection to lure consumers to the Web site. Having obtained the information cheaply, merchants will be better able to price discriminate among consumers, thereby reducing customers' surplus.[66]

As previously discussed, consumers probably are not ignorant of merchants' use of consumer marketing information.[67] The question is whether consumers systematically undervalue their information, or value it correctly but nevertheless derive enough benefit from Web site transactions that they are willing to give up the information for less than its value to merchants. Assuming that consumers know that their marketing information is valuable to merchants, it is not clear why they would systematically undervalue the information, rather than either systematically overvalue it or, more likely, value it accurately on average across consumers and transactions. The fact that merchants, such as Internet service providers, are willing to buy advertising space on consumers' computers by offering free or heavily discounted services suggests that consumers are aware of the value of their data.[68] If consumers accurately value their information but nevertheless choose to sell it for less than it is worth to Web site operators, then there is a further question of whether this division of the surplus is somehow inefficient.[69]

Advocates of regulation argue that markets are inadequate because they do not protect nonmarket values such as dignity and self-expression.[70] Circulating information about individuals constrains their ability to take positions and lead lifestyles that do not conform to social norms, thereby becoming a strong force for conformity. But again, it is not clear why these considerations would not lead people to overvalue their information and therefore make too little of it available from a social welfare standpoint. Moreover, it is not clear why government would make better choices than individuals. Regulators' estimates of values higher than those reflected in market transactions might be wrong. If so, they might reduce rather than increase individual autonomy—for example, by preventing people from effectuating their shopping preferences through cookies. This suggests that government should move carefully in second-guessing market decisions. One way it could do so is by increasing choice of what law would apply to any given transaction through an emphasis on state, rather than federal, regulation.

Externalities. Contracts may lead to inefficient results if they materially affect noncontracting parties. This is arguably the case, for example, with respect to restrictive software licenses that impede the flow of information and therefore inhibit productive efforts that would benefit society as a whole. Some commentators claim that venders' use of consumers' personal information involves social costs that the consumers themselves do not bear—for example, by restricting self-expression and thereby the choices made in a democratic society.[71] However, it is not clear why restricting self-expression by Internet tracking also would affect nontracked decisions like those people make in voting booths. Moreover, as discussed previously, it is just as plausible that restricting consumer marketing information will impede individuals' expression of preferences.

A particular externality that may affect regulation of electronic commerce involves network effects. Network externalities are discussed in more detail below. For present purposes, it is enough to summarize the phenomenon as involving failure by new adopters of a standard or service to consider the benefits that adoption might confer on other users. The result is that people may not buy a new product or adopt a new standard even if it is better than the old one apart from network benefits, and a new product or standard might not emerge even if it might have given rise to a superior network but for externalities. Thus, information "norms" may be unfavorable to consumers,[72] or technical standards may not efficiently reflect consumer preferences. For example, consumers and venders may not want to incur the costs of implementing the privacy standard Platform for Privacy Preferences Project (P3P) until it has become successful, creating a kind of vicious cycle. In other words, P3P will be unable to create a new "network" in which users can connect efficiently with Web sites. But this ignores the fact that if a new standard such as P3P is efficient, venders as well as users will gain and therefore will have incentives to invest in marketing the standard. Conversely, the market's failure to adopt a new standard may be due to its inherent inferiority rather than to network externalities.[73] Thus, if P3P fails, despite all of the attention it has been given and its high-profile backers, that may be because few consumers want the privacy it enables.[74] If so, mandating the device through government regulation obviously will entrench inefficiency rather than cure a market failure.

A final kind of externality concerns wealth distribution. It has been argued that permitting consumers to sell marketing information lets rich consumers reap merchant discounts, while the poor get higher prices because merchants do not value their information.[75] But it is not clear that the advantage the rich get in this context can be distinguished from other problems associated with the allocation of wealth in a capitalist economy. The rich get better schools, housing, health care, information, and so forth, all of which enables them to get richer still. Perhaps this is a social injustice that government should address, but it is not clear why government should start with electronic commerce.

Thus, arguments for government regulation of Internet contracting rest on questionable assumptions concerning consumers' ability to protect themselves and the existence of externalities. All of this is not to say that markets will operate perfectly. For example, even if most firms have market incentives to respect consumer privacy, a failing firm with no further reputation to protect may make an unauthorized one-shot sale of consumer data before going out of business. But it is unlikely any regulation could solve problems like this. More important for present purposes, even if some regulation is appropriate, it should not necessarily be all-encompassing regulation imposed by federal law. As discussed below, state regulation and enforcement of contractual choice facilitates diversity, experimentation, and competition among regulatory approaches.

Alternative Forms of Regulation

Even if some form of regulation is appropriate, it may not be clear which form the regulation should take. The following discussion compares some possible requirements concerning consumer marketing information. Many of these requirements have been proposed in state bills regulating consumer marketing information. This variety of approaches reflects the extent of experimentation that is possible under a state regulatory approach and that would be precluded by full or even partial federal regulation.

Disclosure Mechanisms. Regulation may require, or subject contract enforcement to the condition, that venders disclose certain information to consumers. With respect to any disclosure requirement, the question for regulators is how the disclosure must be made. For example, venders may be required to disclose through an information screen flashed as the individual user logs on, a statement that the information is available at a specified Web site address or a location on the Web site the consumer is already surfing, or by e-mail request, telephone, or letter. The appropriate approach obviously depends on balancing the costs to both the vender and the consumer of more affirmative disclosure methods—including forcing Web site surfers to click through disclosure screens—against the benefits of reducing consumers' search costs.[76] The appropriate approach also may depend over time and across situations on rapidly developing technologies. For example, a form of privacy notice that is appropriate for a 19-inch monitor may not be appropriate for a Personal Digital Assistant (PDA),[77] or its appropriateness for computer displays may depend on developments regarding screen resolution. Thus, prescribing a particular standard may stunt or inefficiently direct the development of technology.

Opting In vs. Opting Out. Regulators might provide for certain types of protection but allow contrary agreements. The main question in this situation is whether the consumer must opt in to the protection or opt out. For example, a Web site operator might be prohibited from collecting any information *unless* it obtains the consumer's affirmative consent to the particular use, or alternatively

173

only *if* the consumer opts out of the practice the operator proposes. In either case, disclosure to the consumer is required. Or, software might be sold with certain types of warranties *unless* consumers waive the protection. Consumer consent in either case might be as simple as clicking on an "I accept" box or even just deciding to use the Web site that gathers the information. On the other hand, the law might require an actual written, or at least electronic, signature. Where use of the product precedes precise disclosure, consent may or may not be predicated on the consumer's general knowledge of the information-gathering activity. An opt-in procedure draws the consumer's attention to his or her right to refuse to consent. By contrast, an opportunity to opt out of a Web site operator's or seller's practice, such as use of consumer marketing information, would give legal significance to consumer inaction, and therefore reduce the directness with which the consumer is presented an explicit choice.

As with disclosure, the appropriate policy depends on balancing the costs to Web site operators and consumers of offering and making choices against the benefits to consumers of making the choices more obvious.[78] Aggressively presenting choices to consumers might give them more leverage over merchants. On the other hand, affirmative disclosures slow down consumers' Internet surfing, increase transaction times, and tie up servers. Although these costs increase directly with the number of disclosures, repetitively reminding consumers of privacy choices may have diminishing benefits.

Minimum Requirements. The foregoing discussion makes the amount of regulation turn on consumer choice. An alternative would be to require Web sites to offer certain minimal protections, such as warranties or restrictions on use of marketing information, to all consumers. This approach could be combined with one of the others by requiring disclosure of additional protections, perhaps coupled with opt-in or opt-out rules. This alternative is generally identified with government regulation and is discussed as such below. But a minimum standards approach also might be applied by private regulatory groups, or incorporated into consumer self-help if consumers configure their computers to accept only certain vender policies. In the latter situation, the standard applies to all Web sites but varies from one consumer to the other.[79]

Again, policymakers must balance costs and benefits. Offering choices may consume valuable resources of both consumers and

Web site operators. On the other hand, adopting minimum standards precludes some choices that might better balance costs and benefits. The efficiency of this approach depends on, among other things, consumers' ability to obtain and process information relevant to bargaining, regulators' ability to anticipate vender and consumer preferences in particular situations, and the degree of variation among transactions. Thus, the efficiency of minimum standards may depend on who imposes the constraints. Particular minimum standards might make sense for individual consumers or industries, but not for across-the-board federal regulation.

Public vs. Private Regulators

Rather than governments supplying default rules or enforcement mechanisms, firms could post their own rules or subscribe to organizations that supply the rules and police violations through fines or expulsion.[80] Johnson and Post discuss the potential for private regulatory structures on the Internet, possibly including consumer protection doctrines,[81] analogizing these organizations to the private regulatory structures that have developed in other areas, including securities exchanges[82] and the law merchant.[83] Third-party control and monitoring is currently provided by organizations such as TRUSTe.[84] Commercial entities might select private providers of legal rules whose judgments are enforced as final in state courts.[85] Another example is the "P3P" protocol, which would permit a kind of automated contracting whereby consumers' computers can block access to personal information by firms whose privacy policies do not meet user-configured standards.[86] This would permit individuals, at low cost, to contract for precisely the level of privacy protection they prefer.[87]

The problem with these private solutions is that whether they are allowed to work depends ultimately on the level of government regulation. Thus, *permitting* private regulation should be viewed as a regulatory option. Regulators might choose to impose liability on Web site venders for violation of rules of self-regulatory organizations, leave these violations to private procedures, or impose wholly separate regulations or remedies. For example, a firm may be liable if it changed its privacy policy after obtaining information without getting customer consent, could not adequately document how they used consumer information, or slipped in giving consumers access to their information. Although the firm could try to contract with the consumer to make private remedies exclusive, that contract might be rendered unenforceable by a judicial rule or regulation because of its "adhesive" nature. This, in turn, would deter firms from relying on such private solutions. Johnson and Post assert that territorial governments will have incentives to grant "comity" to, and not interfere with, these regimes,[88] but these incentives are not self-evident.

The many e-commerce–related policy issues and regulatory options discussed in this section are summarized in Table 1. This discussion is intended to emphasize the difficulty faced by a single set of federal regulators in formulating a regulatory policy in this area. This suggests the appropriateness of offering a multiplicity of approaches through 50 state legislatures.

Advantages of a State Approach

This section discusses three important advantages of resolving Internet policy issues through a multiplicity of state laws, as opposed to a uniform federal law. First, we discuss how market participants' ability to exit states limits the extent to which powerful interest groups can control regulation and secure inefficient rules that transfer wealth from weaker interest groups. Second, we outline how states can offer a variety of laws that suit different sets of preferences, including a preference for no regulation. Third, we discuss how, even in the absence of active competition, variety in state law facilitates experimentation with alternatives and promotes an evolutionary process as individuals and firms choose the laws under which they prefer to operate.

Exit and Political Discipline

Legislation may favor the interest groups that can organize most cheaply and effectively to raise and spend money, or to mobilize votes and other political resources.[89] Since a successful interest group's gains reflect its organization costs, these gains may not outweigh losses to the rest of society. Interest group dynamics at the federal level may lead to stringent regulation of consumer marketing information. Larger and more established Web site operators may favor disclosure and monitoring burdens that would restrict entry into the industry. This meshes with the interests of consumer advocates and trial lawyers who gain from increased remedies. Also, privacy advocates would favor legislation that heightens public

176

Table 1
REGULATORY ALTERNATIVES

Nature of regulated data	• Sensitivity
	   Sensitive (with clear expectation of privacy) vs. nonsensitive personal data
	• Substitutability
	   Idiosyncratic vs. fungible (valuable only when aggregated with data from others)
	• Identity
	   Personally identifiable vs. anonymous
	• Method of collection
	   Passive (clickstream/tracking) vs. active collection

Disclosure requirements	• Information to be disclosed
	   Fact of collection and potential use vs. specific detail, including nature and type of information collected, how information is to be used, identity of any third party that will receive the information
	• Method of disclosure
	   On welcome screen, available on site, or available by request

Consent requirements	• Consent trigger
	   Collection vs. use by third party or use related to collection
	• Type of consent
	   Negative (opt-out) vs. affirmative (opt-in)
	• Manner of consent
	   Assent/clicking vs. in writing/electronic signature
	• Frequency of disclosure/consent
	   At time of initial agreement or visit vs. each time disclosure of data occurs

Exemptions to government regulation	• Industry self-regulation • Consumer self-protection (e.g., P3P)

Preemption of state law	• Scope
	   Broad preemption of state law vs. no preemption
	   Exclusive federal enforcement vs. concurrent state and private enforcement
	• Preemption with Exceptions
	   Fraud and consumer protection
	   Tort, common law, and other state or private civil actions

awareness of the privacy issue and thereby increases the demand for these groups' lobbying activities. Large, established firms such as AOL Time Warner, Inc., may want federal regulatory standards suitable to a closed architecture or at least prefer federal preemption of burdensome state regulation to an open Internet.[90] Mostly lost in this mix are those who would tend to oppose strict regulation, including low-margin operators and potential new entrants who are hurt most by regulatory burdens, and consumers who prefer convenience to disclosure screens and "I accept" boxes.

Although interest groups operate at the state level as well, here the social costs of legislation are constrained by individuals' opportunities to exit undesirable regimes.[91] Charles Tiebout recognized that people decide on their preferred levels of taxes and expenditures by voting with their feet.[92] Any interest group compromise at the state level faces competition with the laws of 50 other jurisdictions operating on the level playing field set by the Constitution, including the dormant Commerce Clause. By contrast, competition between U.S. federal law and that of other countries is constrained by the costs of dealing with different legal systems, languages, and infrastructures and has no constitutional protection. The significant potential for exit in the U.S. federal system means that overregulating state lawmakers may lose "clientele."

Exit is a potentially more effective disciplinary mechanism than the political process because it operates through individual choice rather than the need to coordinate through interest groups. As exit costs fall, such as by letting people contract for the applicable law rather than having to move physically from one jurisdiction to another, so does the effect of inefficient laws. For example, because firms can avoid application of local state corporation laws through their ability to easily choose their states of incorporation, such laws have been described as "trivial."[93]

Parties' ability to exit inefficient laws reduces the effect of those laws and therefore potentially increases efficiency. This is a relatively weak form of the state competition argument because it does not depend on exits having any effect on the substance of the laws themselves but rather only on the laws' effect on regulated parties. A stronger form of the argument is that exit, particularly given parties' ability to contract for the applicable law, disciplines state lawmakers to compete to enact efficient laws. This argument is discussed below.

Variation and Individual Preferences

Legal rules are most likely to vary in two distinct cases. First, legal rules are likely to vary when different rules are likely to have similar effects, so that the choice of a particular rule does not much matter and there is little incentive to unify them. Second, rules are likely to vary when there is substantial disagreement or uncertainty over the effects or wisdom of alternative legal rules.[94] As previously discussed, regulation of electronic commerce may be a prime example of the latter situation, given not only the uncertainty concerning the effects and efficiency of various legal rules, but also varying effects in different situations.

Given these varying effects, state regulation may result in an equilibrium in which different laws appeal to different types of venders rather than the emergence of a single dominant or uniform law across states. For example, some firms might seek the flexibility and lower transaction costs offered by a more permissive regime, while other firms would not take that option because their customers would be wary of such a choice. Firms would seek to cater to these different preferences just as they do regarding preferences along other dimensions.[95]

To the extent that a variety of regulatory approaches is desirable, relying on state law may provide significant advantages over a federal regime that broadly preempts state law. Under such circumstances, while state law would enable the use of different regulatory approaches, federal and other centralized approaches would perversely attempt to achieve a uniform approach.[96] Thus, whether or not state competition effectively disciplines interest groups, relying on state law is more likely to allow firms and individuals to select from among different types of regulatory approaches and to produce efficient variation.[97]

Experimentation and Evolution

Even if a single law ultimately proves desirable, that law should not be imposed at the federal level until state experimentation identifies the best approach.[98] Once federal law is imposed, it is difficult for opponent interest groups to mobilize to change the law. Moreover, Web site architecture and industry practices necessarily would follow the law, which would make change costly.[99] On the other hand, a variety of state laws enables efficient alternatives to emerge

179

and attract adherents, even if state legislators are not knowingly competing or attempting to supply efficient laws.[100] This process operates with the effects of exit discussed previously. Assuming only that market actors have incentives to minimize their transaction and information costs and an ability to choose legal regimes that accomplish this goal, efficient regimes will end up governing more transactions and inefficient regimes fewer transactions.[101]

State Overregulation

This section evaluates an important potential argument against relying on states to regulate electronic commerce: sellers would be exposed to regulation in every state in which their Web sites are accessible. Although complying with multiple rules may be costly for any business, it is arguably particularly so for a Web site vender that presents buyers with a single interface on their Internet pages. Thus, Johnson and Post claim that territorial-based restrictions will lead to each jurisdiction's attempt to regulate the entire Web site, and argue that cyberspace itself should be considered a distinct regulatory jurisdiction to avoid such overlapping regulations.[102]

The real problem with state regulation of the Internet, however, is not that multiple states might regulate a given transaction but rather how the regulating state is selected. As long as state regulation does not require inconsistent acts—such as some states prohibiting disclosures that other states require—venders can protect themselves by complying with the most rigorous state law that a court or regulator might apply. The problem is that, under open-ended default conflict of law and jurisdiction rules, the courts decide which state's law applies *ex post*, after a dispute arises, rather than *ex ante*, at the time of entering into the transaction.[103] This uncertainty over what law will apply *ex post* can negate state law's advantage of offering a variety of regulatory alternatives by impeding parties' ability to choose the law that is most efficient or that best fits their situation.

This section discusses the choice of law and jurisdiction rules that create this problem. This discussion shows that the overregulation problem with state regulation of the Web site is not as serious as might first appear. As discussed below, under U.S. jurisdiction rules a state cannot regulate Web site transactions based solely on the local accessibility of the Web site. Also, in determining the applicable state law, a court needs to sort through only a limited number of options and must evaluate only the sufficiency of the local basis for regulating rather than the claims of all states that can exercise jurisdiction.[104] Moreover, as discussed below, state law becomes an even more viable approach to regulating the Web site when the potential for enforcement of contractual choice of law and forum is taken into account.

Conflict of Laws

The approach contained in the American Law Institute's influential Restatement (Second) of Conflict of Laws is frequently used by courts to determine which state's law applies in conflicts cases. The Restatement's approach depends on weighing a variety of facts in the particular case. If the transaction involves a breach of contract, as is likely the case for either software sales or use of consumer marketing information, the applicable law would depend on place of contracting, negotiation of the contract, performance, subject matter, and domicile, residence, nationality, place of incorporation, and place of business of the parties,[105] weighed in light of such general considerations as the parties' expectations and the policies of the forum and other interested states.[106] Alternatively, under the Uniform Commercial Code (UCC), a court would apply its own law if the transaction bears "an appropriate relation to this state."[107] If the merchants' use of consumer marketing information is considered a tort invasion of privacy, the applicable law may be that of the state where the defendant communicated the information and thereby appropriated the plaintiff's name or likeness, or the plaintiff's domicile if the invasion is deemed to occur in multiple states.[108]

These rules obviously could support application of the buyer's local law in many electronic commerce cases.[109] For example, if the case involves a software sale, or if the court deems the vender's use of cookies to be a breach of its contract with the buyer, it might reason that the consumer's purchase, or the vender's placing a cookie on a consumer's computer, locates the performance, subject matter, one of the parties, and perhaps contracting and negotiation in the consumer's state. If sale of a consumer marketing information database is considered a tort breach of privacy, the applicable law may be that of the plaintiff's domicile, the purchaser's location, or some other place.

181

The Constitution only loosely checks state courts' selection of the applicable law. In *Allstate Insurance Co v. Hague*[110] the Supreme Court held as a matter of due process and full faith and credit that Minnesota, where the decedent worked, the widow resided, and the insurer did business, could apply its rule "stacking" uninsured motorist coverage on the insureds' vehicles. Despite the fact that the policy was issued and the insured resided in Wisconsin, the Court chose to apply the Minnesota rule over the Wisconsin rule that did not allow stacking, reasoning that Allstate would not be unfairly surprised by the application of Minnesota law.[111] An expectations-based test provides little predictability as long as the parties' expectations can be shaped by the choice of law rules the courts happen to apply.[112]

The dormant Commerce Clause might play some role in choice of law.[113] The Supreme Court arguably has endorsed an interpretation of the Commerce Clause that invalidates state regulation that involves significant "spillovers"—that is, where costs fall mostly on interest groups outside the state while benefits accrue to those within it.[114] This theory could be applied to regulation of the Internet. Indeed, courts have invalidated, on Commerce Clause grounds, state statutes regulating Internet conduct based on minimal jurisdictional contacts that significantly burdened multistate Internet operations.[115]

However, state regulation should not be deemed to violate the dormant Commerce Clause merely because it might have out-of-state effects. Rather, courts should, and in effect do, balance any costs imposed on out-of-state parties against the local harms the statute is intended to redress.[116] Courts must analyze costs and benefits of state regulation of electronic commerce in light of the available and potential technology, including Web site operators' ability to block access to their site by users in particular states and users' ability to configure their browsers to avoid intrusive Web sites. Thus, the application of the Commerce Clause to electronic commerce may depend on how easily Web site operators can restrict access to their sites or avoid sales in states where their sites are illegal, on whether application of the law takes such efforts into account, and on whether customers can cheaply avoid dealing with companies whose sales or privacy policies they do not like. In other words, constitutional constraints may not be justified under a balancing test for the same reasons that state law is ultimately likely to produce efficient results, as discussed below.

Jurisdiction

The applicable state law is determined not only by conflict of laws rules but also by where the plaintiff can obtain personal jurisdiction over the defendant. The Due Process Clause generally permits the state to assert jurisdiction over only those parties who have had minimum contacts with the state.[117] The most likely rule to be applied is that the jurisdiction must be based on an action directed toward the forum rather than merely on the defendant's awareness that action might result there.[118] Once a state with jurisdiction enters judgment, the judgment may be enforced in any state where the defendant has assets.[119]

Internet jurisdiction has gone through three phases. A few courts initially held that a state could exercise jurisdiction merely on the basis that a Web site was broadcast into the state.[120] However, courts now generally deny personal jurisdiction based merely on a receiver's downloading.[121] In the second phase of Internet jurisdiction cases, the courts focused on the degree of interactivity of the Web site in the relevant jurisdiction.[122] Several cases have based jurisdiction primarily or exclusively on the maintenance of an interactive Web site that can take orders.[123]

In the third phase, a defendant may be able to escape jurisdiction in a state if it has not "targeted" that jurisdiction or has targeted its conduct elsewhere. The leading case suggesting this approach, *GTE New Media Services, Inc. v. Bellsouth Corp.*,[124] reasoned that due process requires predictability, analogizing Web site access to an out-of-state telephone call that had been held not to trigger long-arm jurisdiction. The Court also distinguished this case from prior cases involving activities directed toward the forum that had held in favor of minimum contacts.[125] It has been said that *GTE* endorses a "strict purposeful availment standard," and that "because defendants can control whether they engage in activities targeted toward a specific forum, it is easier for them to predict whether a court will find that they have done so than to predict whether a court will label their Web sites as sufficiently interactive to warrant jurisdiction."[126] Some other cases also hint at a targeting standard.[127]

The American Bar Association (ABA) Committee on Cyberspace Law has recommended a targeting limitation on jurisdiction based on devices sponsors use to purposefully avail themselves of states' commercial benefits, or that they use to avoid jurisdictions, such as blocking and screening, disclaimers, identification of their home state, listing targeted or nontargeted destinations, and, more generally, controlling how goods are advertised, sold, and shipped.[128] Restrictions on jurisdiction also may take into account the availability of intelligent software agents, or bots, that consumers can program to prevent access to particular sites, aided by sellers' electronic agents and global protocol standards.[129]

In general, although the law is still developing, the trend in jurisdiction law is toward viable limits on state law's reach. Technology and flow control will determine the meaning of minimum contacts in cyberspace and ultimately may erect electronic borders that make personal jurisdiction in cyberspace comparable to that in real space.[130] Based solely on rules regarding choice of law and jurisdiction, it sometimes may be difficult for Web site venders to predict precisely which state's law will be applied at the time of the transaction. However, as discussed next, *ex ante* predictability may be enhanced by contractual choice of law and forum, particularly when these are combined with the limitations on jurisdiction.

Uniform State Laws as a Solution to Overregulation

Uniform state laws theoretically could address the potential problem of overregulation of electronic commerce by multiple state laws.[131] Specifically, a uniform lawmaking body such as the NCCUSL could propose a law that is then adopted by all states. There are, however, reasons to be skeptical about the potential for uniform laws to solve this problem.

The basic problem, of course, is that legislators would have an incentive not to adopt a uniform law that restricted their freedom, so that uniform laws are unlikely to deal effectively with the spillover problem.[132] The NCCUSL has an interest in maximizing the states' adoption of their proposals and therefore is likely to craft its proposals to achieve that result. Thus, in order to minimize controversy, the NCCUSL will pay close attention to groups that can influence enactment in states,[133] and try to broker compromises that lead to unclear rules.[134] The NCCUSL is unlikely to be effective in reforming the law because it will be reluctant to adopt proposals that states will shun.[135] Because the uniform law process depends on states' cooperation, it is unlikely to place significant constraints on states' adoption of legislation that has local benefits but exports costs to other states.[136] Moreover, the uniformity process is particularly susceptible to interest group influence. Because uniform legislators lack even the modest resources that state legislators have for investigating interest group claims,[137] and because (as discussed immediately below) a uniform law proposal may have an impact on state legislators, some interest groups may have an even greater incentive to lobby at the uniform lawmaking level than they would in individual state legislatures.

The Uniform Computer Information Transactions Act, in particular, involves a specialized area about which uniform lawmakers may not be well informed and in which several interest groups—such as software manufacturers, sellers, and users—had strong incentives to lobby.[138] Reformers, who may be no better able than interest groups to speak for the "public" interest, also can have their say in the uniform lawmaking process. UCITA involved a battle between the American Law Institute, which sought strong protections for consumers, and the more practical-minded lawyers and politicians associated with the NCCUSL, who relied on traditional notions of unconscionability and consumers' self-help rights—for example, the consumer's right to obtain a full refund before using the product if the consumer objects to the terms of a shrink-wrap license.[139]

States can disregard uniform law proposals, and indeed tend to do so where uniformity is likely to have greater costs than benefits.[140] Thus, it might be argued that NCCUSL-type proposals can do little harm. Conversely, the NCCUSL might do some good if it leads to uniformity in a situation in which it is efficient, as is arguably the case for sales transactions like those covered by UCITA.[141] Nevertheless, the NCCUSL's influence may cause states to enact inefficient provisions that they would not otherwise adopt by cloaking interest group legislation in the NCCUSL's officially accredited mantle, focusing attention on a particular proposal that helps spur widespread adoption, and lobbying state legislators.[142]

A Contractual Solution

This section discusses an important way of enhancing the viability of state regulation of the Internet—through enforcement of contractual choice of law and forum.[143] We begin by discussing the law on enforcement of these contracts. Next, we discuss how firms can

185

induce increased enforcement through their power to avoid nonenforcing jurisdictions. Then, we respond to arguments that this might lead to underregulation of electronic commerce. Finally, we discuss the emergence of efficient state law from enforcement of contractual choice.

Enforcing Jurisdictional Choice

The courts' applications of the preceding conflicts rules do not necessarily let merchants and consumers jointly determine the applicable rules at the time of their transaction, when the winners and losers from a particular rule have not yet been determined and when knowledge of the law could shape the parties' conduct. Rather, these rules let consumers choose the law unilaterally at the time of injury by picking a forum in which to sue, which often turns out to be local law. Under this *ex post* approach to resolving conflicts of law, states have incentives to respond to consumers' or trial lawyers' interests rather than to maximize the contracting parties' joint wealth.[144]

Web site venders can, however, counteract the effects of application of these conflict rules through their ability to select the applicable forum, adjudicator, and law contractually. Enforcing these forum selection clauses maximizes the welfare of all affected parties rather than just the welfare of the one who happens to sue. Contractual jurisdictional choice addresses the most significant problems inherent in diverse state laws. These contracts are particularly useful in dealing with state regulations that, for example, impose onerous mandatory limitations on software licenses, restrict use of consumer information even with disclosure, require onerous disclosures or consent procedures, significantly impose costly consumer access requirements, or provide for draconian liability.

More specifically, under our proposal, merchants might condition the use of their Web sites on consumers' acceptance of the designated law and forum. Such a clause was enforced in the consumer marketing information context:

> This License Agreement shall be governed by the laws of the State of Washington, without regard to conflicts of law provisions, and you hereby consent to the exclusive jurisdiction of the state and federal courts sitting in the State of Washington. Any and all unresolved disputes arising under

this License Agreement shall be submitted to arbitration in
the State of Washington.[145]

The contract might be entered into by placing the clause in a
general "terms of use" section of the Web site, or by making acceptance of the clause a condition of entering the Web site. Alternatively,
states might offer firms the opportunity to select their laws through
a procedure analogous to incorporation or formation of other types
of business associations. For example, a Virginia bill proposed permitting firms to "domesticate" their Web sites in Virginia by making
a local public filing and thereby effectively to disclaim certain types
of liabilities.[146]

General Rules on Enforcing Contractual Choice of Law and Forum.
Restatement (Second) of Conflicts of Laws, Section 187(1), uses the
law selected by the parties as the starting point for determining
the law applicable to a contract dispute. However, Section 187(2)
qualifies this rule by permitting nonenforcement of this selection as
to the validity of the contract where—

(a) the chosen state has no substantial relationship to the
parties or the transaction and there is no other reasonable
basis for the parties' choice, or

(b) application of the law of the chosen state would be contrary to a fundamental policy of a state which has a materially
greater interest than the chosen state in the determination
of the particular issue and which, under the rule of § 188,
would be the state of the applicable law in the absence of
an effective choice of law by the parties.[147]

The first exception may restrict shopping for the applicable law
in some cases by requiring a connection with the chosen jurisdiction.
The second limitation can operate to prevent evasion of state
regulation.

Courts applying the Restatement rule have quite generally
enforced contractual choice of law, at least in commercial contracts.[148]
Several states, including California, Illinois, Delaware, New York,
Oregon, and Texas, have promulgated statutes that, to varying
degrees, clarify the enforcement of contractual choice of law clauses
in large, commercial-type cases.[149] Also, the UCC provides that
"when a transaction bears a reasonable relation to this state and
also to another state or nation the parties may agree that the law

either of this state or of such other state or nation shall govern their rights and duties."[150] Thus, the UCC does not currently include the Second Restatement "fundamental policy" exception.

The enforceability of contractual choice is most doubtful in consumer cases and in statutory provisions that apply to such cases. The court may refuse to enforce the contract because it may have doubts about consumers' ability to make an informed decision and to have a realistic choice concerning choice of law. The court may first decide that the contractually selected state's law is inapplicable under law concerning contract validity,[151] which may be determined by the Restatement test first discussed, and then decide the applicable law under the open-ended default choice of law rules that apply in the absence of contract.

Perhaps the most important limitation on contractual choice in consumer cases may enter the law through the American Law Institute's revision of the UCC.[152] The draft proposed for adoption would sharply distinguish consumer and nonconsumer transactions. The proposed provision would enforce contractual choice in business-to-business transactions as long as it has a "reasonable relationship" to the transaction,[153] and is not "contrary to a fundamental policy of the State or country whose law would govern in the absence of agreement."[154] For transactions in which one of the parties is a consumer, however, the revision would refuse to enforce the clause where the chosen law would deprive the consumer of the protection of any rule of law, that both is protective of consumers and may not be varied by agreement, of the state or country (a) in which the consumer habitually resides, unless subparagraph (B) applies; or (b) if the transaction is a sale of goods, in which the consumer makes the contract and takes delivery of those goods, if such state or country is not the state or country in which the consumer habitually resides.[155]

As noted, courts have stronger incentives to enforce contractual choice of forum and adjudicator than to enforce contractual choice of law. This is confirmed by the case law. U.S. Supreme Court cases have recognized the enforceability of consent to jurisdiction[156] and forum-selection[157] clauses even in "adhesion" contracts between merchants and consumers.[158] Although the Supreme Court was deciding constitutional issues or admiralty cases rather than applying state law, the cases represent an important general recognition of enforceability.

With respect to arbitration clauses, Section 2 of the U.S. Federal Arbitration Act[159] mandates enforcement of arbitration agreements involving transactions in interstate commerce. Consistent with its approach to choice of forum, the Supreme Court has been very receptive to enforcement of arbitration clauses even in cases involving important federal rights.[160]

The Link between Choices of Law, Forum, and Adjudicator. It is useful to emphasize the importance of contracting not only for the applicable law but also to require disputes to be tried in the state whose law is selected and that the parties consent to the jurisdiction of that court. Because the forum court ultimately decides which law to apply, the parties seeking the application of a particular state law likely will choose the forum that is most likely to apply that law, including a forum that is likely to enforce the parties' contractual choice. Moreover, because a court has a tendency to apply its own law, and a comparative advantage in applying that law, the contractual choice of law and forum likely will be the same.[161]

Although a court in which a plaintiff sues theoretically can decide not to enforce a choice of forum clause, it may be willing to defer to the contractual selection of a different forum even if it would not be willing to apply another state's law.[162] And although a judge may face difficulty and not much reward in making new law when applying another state's law, enforcing a choice of forum clause lets a court both enforce the contract and avoid directly contravening legislative policy or establishing a potentially troublesome precedent on contractual choice of law. Thus, contractual choice of forum helps courts resolve conflicting incentives regarding enforcement of contractual choice of law.

The contract also might adopt a private regulatory regime or provide for arbitration.[163] Again, a court may be willing to permit arbitration even if it would not enforce contractual choice of law.[164] Although state judges have incentives to enforce local law because the local legislature controls their tenure, salary, and perks,[165] arbitrators have less incentive to resist evasion of state regulation because they are paid by the parties rather than by the state. A recent paper confirms this observation by showing that franchisers tend to use arbitration clauses in their agreements when they also contract for the applicable law.[166]

An important relationship exists between contracting over the forum and contracting for private remedies. States may regulate

Internet transactions whether or not the parties want to deal with the problem only in cyberspace. A consumer or regulator therefore may circumvent attempted contractual privatization by suing in a state that is likely to apply its strong regulatory policy. Thus, firms effectively can contract for private rather than government rules and adjudication only by contractually designating a state forum that respects private remedies. Accordingly, our proposal for enforcing contractual choice of state law and forum does not mean that we prefer government to private ordering but rather it provides a way to make private remedies viable. We do not necessarily disagree with Johnson and Post's arguments for private regimes operating and competing in cyberspace.[167]

Enforcing the Clauses in Electronic Commerce Cases. This subsection considers enforcement of contractual choice of law, forum, and adjudicator in the specific context of electronic commerce. Whether consumers' bargaining and information problems may lead to a "race-to-the-bottom" in electronic commerce law is discussed below. For present purposes, it is enough to note that, consistent with the above analysis of so-called "adhesion" contracts, merchants' designation of the applicable law without bargaining does not necessarily make the contract one-sided or unenforceable. A consumer, in effect, votes with his mouse for the applicable law and forum by contracting with the seller or Web site operator, perhaps using an automatic contracting mechanism such as P3P. Moreover, consumers' lack of information concerning various legal systems is not as serious a problem as might first appear, given various market devices and the availability of abundant information.

The law on enforcing contractual choice in electronic commerce cases reflects a division in the courts concerning the nature of the requisite consent in Internet contracting generally. Recent federal and state decisions have enforced arbitration provisions in Gateway, Inc.'s mail-order and telephone computer sales without evidence of the plaintiff's overt consent to or actual awareness of the provision.[168] In a frequently cited case, *Hill v. Gateway 2000, Inc.,*[169] Judge Frank Easterbrook held in favor of enforcement of the clause in a contract included with a Gateway computer based on retention of the computer for the requisite period to indicate consent under the agreement even in the absence of explicit consent.[170] A later federal case, relying on *Hill,* held that the arbitration clause in the license accompanying the computer purchase was broad enough to cover related purchase of software services, although there was no arbitration clause in the agreement specifically relating to those services.[171]

In *Brower v. Gateway 2000, Inc.*,[172] a New York state court, also relying on *Hill*, held that the provision was not unenforceable as an unconscionable "adhesion" contract despite inequality of bargaining position between the seller and the consumer, the consumer's failure to read or understand the agreement, and the fact that the arbitration provision foreclosed a low-cost class action remedy.[173] It was enough that the consumer had 30 days after receiving the computer to return it (although return would have entailed expense and inconvenience), and that the agreement was not unduly lengthy (3 pages and 16 paragraphs, all in the same size print).[174] The court did invalidate the agreement but on the sole ground that it designated arbitration by the International Chamber of Commerce, an organization based in France and little known in the United States.[175]

Judicial recognition of jurisdictional choice has been extended to clickware Internet contracts. An important recent case involving consumer marketing information is *Lieschke v. RealNetworks, Inc.*,[176] in which the court enforced contractual arbitration in the defendant's home state of customers' claims of privacy and trespass to property based on RealNetworks' use of its products to access users' electronic communications and stored information without the users' knowledge or consent.[177] Before installing the software, users were required to accept the RealNetworks license agreement quoted above,[178] which provided that Washington law governed and that users consented to exclusive jurisdiction and arbitration in state and federal courts in Washington. The court interpreted this as applying the law of the Seventh Circuit (the forum) rather than enforcing the agreement to arbitrate, which, as discussed immediately below, is notably favorable to enforcement of computer and software agreements,[179] rather than the less pro-enforcement law of the Ninth Circuit, where the contractually selected forum was located.[180] It also rejected an intervenor's unconscionability arguments based on the location of the agreement, the size of the font, difficulty of use, distance of the designated forum from some users' homes, and the failure to provide for classwide arbitration.[181]

Courts have enforced contractual choice of law and forum in other types of Internet transactions. New Jersey residents injured in a Nevada hotel had to go to Nevada for trial under a clause entered into on the defendant's Web site providing for trial in Nevada state and federal courts.[182] The forum selection clause helped justify holding against jurisdiction in New Jersey, the court reasoning in part that "the forum selection clause in defendant's Web site demonstrates that it could not reasonably anticipate being haled into court in New Jersey." Contractual choice of Ohio law was enforced in a declaratory judgment action on an Internet transaction based on repeated interactions between an Ohio computer network and a customer who agreed to market his product over the defendant's system.[183]

UCITA also strongly supports contractual choice of law and forum in the context of computer information sales, and perhaps in consumer marketing information transactions also under a trade secret licensing approach to those transactions.[184] UCITA would enforce a choice-of-law clause in electronic consumer sales unless it would vary a mandatory rule in the licensor's state.[185] UCITA drops the "reasonable relationship" requirement under the general Restatement rule for enforcing contractual choice of law.[186] The Reporter's Notes state that in a "global information economy, limitations of that type are inappropriate and arbitrary" and cite the costs of complying with the inconsistent laws of many jurisdictions as the reason for mandating application of the law of the licensor's state in electronic transactions.[187] Although the rule upholds mandatory rules in states where licensors are located, licensors can escape application of stringent rules in states that adopt this UCITA provision by establishing the contacts that UCITA finds critical, including place of business and chief executive office,[188] in permissive states. The Reporter's Note to UCITA also adopts a permissive approach to enforcing choice of forum clauses, noting that the choice "is not invalid simply because it has an adverse effect on a party, even if bargaining power is unequal" and that "in an Internet transaction, choice of forum will often be justified on the basis of the international risk that would otherwise exist. Choice of a forum at a party's location is reasonable."[189]

There is, however, authority against enforcing contractual arbitration in an Internet transaction that did not, as in *Lieschke*, require the consumer to assent before downloading the product. In *Specht v. Netscape Communications Corp.*,[190] the Court refused to enforce a

provision for binding arbitration in California in what it characterized as a "browsewrap" license where the consumer could download the product (the SmartDownload feature of Netscape) without
going through an acceptance procedure.[191] The license agreement
triggered by the download was visible only if the user scrolled to
the next screen.[192] Below the screen used for downloading, the user
was invited to view and agree to the license agreement before downloading and using the software but was not told at that point (but
only in the license itself) that he had to agree to the license terms
before downloading and using the software. The court sharply distinguished cases in which the user had to click the "accept" box
before being able to use the product, stating:

> The case law on software licensing has not eroded the impor-
> tance of assent in contract formation. Mutual assent is the
> bedrock of any agreement to which the law will give force.
> Defendants' position, if accepted, would so expand the defi-
> nition of assent as to render it meaningless. Because the user
> Plaintiffs did not assent to the license agreement, they are
> not subject to the arbitration clause contained therein and
> cannot be compelled to arbitrate their claims against the
> Defendants.[193]

The court also noted that:

> From the user's vantage point, SmartDownload could be
> analogized to a free neighborhood newspaper, readily
> obtained from a sidewalk box or supermarket counter with-
> out any exchange with a seller or vender. It is there for
> the taking."[194]

Consistent with this demand for something approaching actual
consent, the ABA's Committee on Cyberspace Law has recommended enforcement of nonbinding arbitration clauses that call for
enforcement of awards pursuant to adequately disclosed choice of
forum and law and jurisdictional choices, where the consumer has
"demonstrably bargained with the seller" or if the contract was
made through a bot programmed to reflect the consumer's choices.[195]

Thus, it is not clear that a plaintiff will be bound to contractual
choice provisions, including those for arbitration, in a Web site-
based transaction (as distinguished from those based on shrink

wrap) unless they are contained in an agreement to which the consumer must explicitly consent before downloading. It is not clear how such a rule can be reconciled with the Gateway cases discussed previously, which upheld enforcement of clauses in the absence of such explicit consent. Ripping off a plastic shrink wrap is more comparable to a license notice somewhere on a Web site than requiring positive assent to downloading. And a requirement of explicit consent before downloading can be costly. Although software sellers easily can comply with the condition that the consumer go through an acceptance procedure as specified in *Specht*—indeed, Netscape itself used an assent procedure similar to the one in *Lieschke* for its main product[196]—the *Specht* procedure may complicate transfer of cookies because the consumer may have to assent explicitly before the vender can place a cookie on the Internet surfer's computer.

The biggest risk for merchants involves actions by state attorneys general, primarily under state consumer fraud statutes.[197] Although such actions would not appear to be constrained by clauses in particular contracts selecting states with less restrictive laws, they do not undercut the case for state rather than federal law. First, unlike private plaintiffs, state attorneys general are subject to political pressures, including those that may arise from merchants avoiding strict regulation as discussed below. Second, and perhaps most important, as discussed in more detail below, federal law not only is unlikely fully to address the problem of state enforcement actions but may even exacerbate it.

Finally, one commentator has raised questions concerning the constitutionality of enforcing contractual choice of law under the Full Faith and Credit Clause to the extent that venders can choose jurisdictions that otherwise have no relationship to the parties or transaction, as under the proposed revised UCC and UCITA provisions discussed previously.[198] However, no case law or policy support exists for the argument that the Full Faith and Credit Clause demands that a state have a relationship with the parties or transaction other than having been selected in the contract. Indeed, a restrictive interpretation of Full Faith and Credit may bring it into conflict with the policies underlying other constitutional provisions. For example, such a restrictive interpretation arguably conflicts with the policy of the dormant Commerce Clause to the extent that it eliminates a contractual device for eliminating spillovers of costs to other jurisdictions. Moreover, enforcement of contractual choice of law may be necessary to preserve privacy regulation from constitutional challenge under the First Amendment.[199] Given these competing considerations, to preserve an efficient balance regarding choice of law, the Constitution should be applied neither to support nor undermine enforcement of contractual choice.

Avoiding Nonenforcing Jurisdictions

Even if contracting parties cannot be sure that courts will enforce their contractual choice of law or forum, they can avoid giving a nonenforcing or excessively regulating state a jurisdictional predicate for imposing its law, or can reward states with reasonable regulation by investing or paying fees in those jurisdictions. Thus, contractual jurisdictional choice can be made more effective by combining it with physical jurisdictional selection and avoidance. We envision a multistage process—involving regulation, contracting, and moving in reaction to inefficient regulation and failure to enforce contracts—that ultimately can discipline inefficient state attempts to regulate. This process has worked before to constrain inefficient laws, most notably relating to corporations and other business associations and franchise contracts.[200] It is particularly likely to work in the Internet context, given the availability of cheap information and the ease and potential mechanization of the contracting process.

First, sellers may be able to block access to their Web sites at some addresses, including in states that do not enforce choice-of-law or choice-of-forum clauses.[201] To the extent that this action is fully successful, states would have no basis for exercising jurisdiction under any jurisdiction rule. Even if sellers cannot block their Web sites from nonenforcing jurisdictions, the targeting tests discussed earlier may let them avoid jurisdiction in a state if they show that they have taken all available precautions to block access and disclaim the making of an offer there. Sellers who successfully avoid nonenforcing states will, of course, have to forego the benefits of transactions in those states. Thus, a Web site operator can avoid jurisdiction in a state with regard to consumer marketing information only by not planting cookies on and taking information from computers in that state. But consumers also incur costs if their state's onerous law cuts them off from many Web sites or forces them to go through extra steps to access the sites. Consumers may respond either by lobbying against the regulation or by refusing to support consumer groups' efforts in favor of the regulation.[202]

Second, firms can minimize the possibility that a state's law will apply by avoiding placing significant assets or headquarters there. Even if states can exercise long-arm jurisdiction over remote sellers, the seller's location is relevant for purposes of general jurisdiction and the enforcement of choice-of-law and choice-of-forum clauses. As previously discussed, the Restatement provides for nonenforcement of contractual choice where the contractually selected state lacks a "substantial relationship" to the parties or the transaction or "other reasonable basis for the parties' choice," or where the chosen law contravenes a "fundamental policy" of a state that has "a materially greater interest than the chosen state" and would be the applicable law under the default choice of law rule. The default rule, in turn, looks to such factors as the parties' place of incorporation and place of business. UCITA looks to similar factors in determining the state whose mandatory rules apply. A seller therefore is better able to secure enforcement of choice-of-law or choice-of-forum clauses over the range of its Internet dealings if it has its home office in the selected state.

These rules may marginally influence some seller location decisions. Analogously, firms have generally avoided locating in states that have the most stringent franchise regulations and that fail to restrict application of their laws to residents.[203] In addition, insurers have shown that they will pull out of states where regulation constrains profits.[204] Because Internet firms can connect their servers to the Internet from any location and their assets consist mostly of highly mobile human capital and intellectual property, states easily can attract Internet companies with favorable regulation, and just as easily lose such companies by increasing regulatory burdens.

Firms' location decisions, in turn, have real economic consequences for states' residents who depend on the firms' business, including local lawyers.[205] These residents could be expected to lobby their legislators for rules that attract, or at least do not repel, firms that might be clients or customers, including moderate levels of regulation, narrow application of the regulation, or enforcement of contractual choice.[206] This may counteract lobbying by pro-regulatory groups.[207]

In general, therefore, contractual and physical jurisdictional selection and avoidance can significantly reduce the need for a federal rule. To be sure, contracts alone may not be enough because of nonselected jurisdictions' incentives to enforce local law, and physical avoidance and selection may not alone be enough because of multistate firms' costs of avoiding large state markets. But the two strategies together can effectively constrain state law. Moreover, even if state competition does not fully constrain inefficient regulation, the relevant question, considered next, is whether it is likely to produce better laws over time than a federal regime.

It is important to emphasize that the analysis so far in this section mainly responds to the perceived problem of inefficient state laws resulting from states' excessive exercise of jurisdiction. The analysis suggests that venders may be able to choose to be governed by laws that are at least not very contrary to their interests. The question of how far states are likely to go in actively competing to provide efficient laws is discussed further below.

Underregulation, Contractual Choice, and Markets

If courts enforce choice of law and forum contracts, the question arises whether electronic commerce, having avoided overregulation by a multiplicity of states, will be subject to underregulation because venders will be able to designate state law that is favorable to them and thereby evade efficient state regulation. In other words, if firms can effectively shop for state law, some critics claim that state legislatures will "race for the bottom" to see who can regulate least.[208]

Choice of law and forum might be said to involve even more serious problems than contracting over other terms because the relevant terms are embedded in the chosen law rather than disclosed directly.[209] It has been argued that sellers, as experts and repeat players, have a strong advantage over consumers in choosing the law.[210] Consumers usually cannot justify the cost of hiring legal help, while sellers enter into similar deals with a number of other parties and therefore can afford to invest in legal expertise about various state laws.[211] Indeed, one commentator ridicules the idea that consumers "shop" for law.[212] Similarly, in the corporate context it has been said that states attract incorporation business by exploiting principal-agent problems resulting from the separation of ownership and control.[213] The contrary argument, that corporate law is a "race to the top" disciplined by efficient capital markets,[214] arguably does not apply to Internet transactions in the absence of the disciplinary force of an informationally efficient market.

197

These arguments might lead nonselected states either to refuse to enforce clickware choice of law or forum clauses, or to condition application of another state's law on disclosure and consent procedures that address this problem. Mandating such procedures might significantly reduce consumers' ability to choose among varying levels of state law protection. These arguments might also be used to justify federalizing Internet rules.

However, contractual choice of law and forum in the context of electronic commerce does not handicap consumers to the extent that the critics have supposed. Although venders rather than consumers may be the ones who "shop" for law, the market is capable of disciplining venders' choices in this regard. Some of these arguments already have been discussed for the general electronic context and now will be applied specifically to contractual choice of law and forum.

First, as already discussed, Internet firms have strong reputational incentives to disclose and not to cheat customers. Lacking bricks-and-mortar storefronts that give assurances to customers, the firms cannot afford to generate suspicion by proposing outlandish legal terms, such as relying on a provision hidden in the contractually chosen law that frustrates buyers' expectations. For example, in the Gateway situation discussed previously, Gateway apparently made a point of explaining to consumers a change in its arbitration provision in the magazine it voluntarily sends to its customers as a way of building customer loyalty and goodwill.[215] While fly-by-night venders may try to get away with legal tricks, they are least likely to be concerned about legal sanctions. In any event, the costs of regulating an entire market solely to catch miscreants may outweigh the benefits.

Second, informed buyers protect the uninformed.[216] Because Web site merchants sell through a single Web site rather than through personalized communications with consumers, they would find it hard to aim different law choices at informed and uninformed consumers. Thus, as long as there are enough knowledgeable consumers in the marketplace, the general price is likely to reflect knowledgeable consumers' awareness of the effect of harmful choice-of-law or choice-of-forum clauses.

Third, it might be argued in response to the last point that there will be few expert consumers to lead the market because they face high costs of learning about the chosen law or forum. However, consumers have cheap access to many sources of buyer-oriented information about sellers, including third-party ratings services, competitors, consumer magazines, and the Internet. For example, a consumer who wants to buy computer or electronic products can view on Cnet.com not only the current prices of various venders but also how the venders' services are rated by a service known as Gomez.com. It may be that such information intermediaries alone cannot be fully relied on to create fully efficient markets—for example, if consumers will not pay for accurate information about specific products, if advertising-supported services skew recommendations, or if the low-marginal-cost nature of the Internet market limits the number of competitors.[217] But their consumers' efforts are supplemented by the general news media that reports on legal developments such as vender misuse of choice-of-law clauses that are of general interest to consumers. In particular, litigated cases can generate publicity and work together with reputational constraints to deter sellers from using oppressive choice-of-law clauses.[218] Because the Internet market circulates so much seemingly obscure data, it has some of the characteristics of efficient capital markets, which commentators have argued discipline corporations' choice of incorporating state.[219] The Internet market does not necessarily have to be fully efficient[220] to provide a suitable alternative to costly and imperfect regulation.

Fourth, contractual choice of law and forum may not be very different from many other highly technical aspects of products such as computers, software, and electronic products. One might argue that important characteristics of a product, such as a computer's clock speed, a television's scanning mechanism, or countless other product characteristics, are beyond the understanding of most consumers. However, no one has suggested special federal regulation to ensure that consumers are adequately informed about such features. Moreover, these details provide further evidence of the information efficiency of Internet markets, since computer and electronics magazines, Web sites, and the like have been effective in broadly disseminating such information.

Finally, even if markets do not adequately protect consumers from oppressive choice-of-law and choice-of-forum clauses, it is important to keep in mind that these clauses are subject to political as well as market discipline, in the sense that political entities rather than private parties design the relevant choices. Thus, even if venders could get away with oppressive clauses in the product market, they may still be unable to find states that provide the low level of regulation they seek. A state legislature that fails adequately to regulate consumer marketing information lets merchants harm users who live in the state. Internet users can use the same information and sophistication that they use in the product market in making political choices, and the pro-regulatory coalition of consumer groups and big firms will have some influence at the state level. These interest groups also influence state attorneys general, elected officials who have ample incentive to bring highly publicized enforcement actions against Internet firms.[221]

Of course, these above arguments may fail to persuade all states to enforce contractual choice.[222] Pro-regulatory interest groups may be able to inhibit enforcement of contractual choice or other forms of exit up to the point that venders' losses provoke them completely to avoid offending jurisdictions or lobby effectively to change the law. This may explain Iowa's "bomb shelter" provision in its Uniform Electronic Transactions Act denying application of another state's law pursuant to a choice-of-law clause if UCITA is the chosen law.[223] This equilibrium may be less efficient than one in which choice-of-law clauses are enforced everywhere. But the potential for state resistance actually supports a state rather than federal approach to regulating the Internet to the extent that it constrains excessive laxity. By contrast, federal legislation may lock in inefficiently lax or excessively rigorous regulation.

The Emergence of Efficient State Law

The discussion so far has shown that state regulation of the Internet coupled with enforcement of contractual choice of law and forum at least enhances efficiency by enabling firms to exit excessive state regulation. This means that the least efficient state laws will govern fewer parties and transactions and the more efficient state laws will govern more parties and transactions. However, without change in the law, contractual choice of law might do no more than help affected parties make the best of a bad lot. If individual states lack adequate incentives to compete to supply efficient law, this strengthens the argument for uniform or federal law. This section discusses whether contractual choice of law has the additional effect of causing the laws themselves to become more efficient. First, it considers whether state legislators and regulators have the political incentives to respond to these competitive pressures by enacting more efficient laws. Second, it discusses whether development of efficient state laws will be inhibited by lock-in of existing standards.

States' Ability and Incentives to Compete. It is not clear what states have to gain from passing innovative laws dealing with electronic commerce. This contrasts with Delaware's incentive to attract substantial incorporations, where franchise fees of large corporations form a significant fraction of the state budget.[224] Moreover, even if it is in a *state's* interest to provide a suitable environment for electronic commerce, it is not clear that individual state *legislators* have incentives, resources, and expertise to compete.[225] Even if the state as an entity would gain by attracting users of its law, public choice theory assumes that state lawmakers act in their own, rather than the state's, interests by maximizing the rents they receive from interest groups. Legislators who can earn support from trial lawyers, pro-consumer groups, and others by brokering changes in mandatory rules may lack incentives to sponsor enabling rules. Even if politicians have some incentive not to provide inefficient laws, they may have little incentive to innovate because other jurisdictions can easily copy their successes while the innovators suffer the embarrassments and loss of rents from their failures.[226]

There are, however, several reasons why states might actively compete to supply efficient laws for electronic commerce. First, lawyers, who are one of the most influential interest groups because they are highly organized and know the law, have incentives to lobby for efficient laws. Because of firms' ability to contract for law and forum, efficient laws would attract both litigation and planning business to enacting states.[227] Indeed, there is significant evidence that lawyers played an active role in spurring state competition to supply limited liability company statutes[228] and that this competition has produced efficient state laws.[229] Second, state legislators can earn political credit, which can generate funds, votes, and other rents, by making their states attractive centers for business and technology generally and electronic commerce in particular. These industries attractively combine high wages and low pollution as well as offer an increasing returns phenomenon whereby the presence of more skilled workers attracts more firms and reduces the costs of skilled labor.[230] Many areas of the country might seek to build on their existing attractions for these industries, such as the presence of prestigious universities, by offering the appropriate "legal infrastructure."[231] For example, Virginia, which has aggressively sought to become a hub of high-tech or Internet activity, was the first state to enact the generally pro-seller UCITA.[232]

This does not necessarily suggest that all or even many states will have an incentive to offer innovative laws on electronic commerce.[233] Even states that seek to attract high-technology companies can do so by, in effect, free-riding on other states' efforts by copying their laws or by enforcing contractual choice of law and forum to permit local firms to take advantage of other states' laws. But as long as a few states have incentives to attract business by innovating, that may be enough to spur development of efficient laws even if other states only copy or enforce these statutes and other states do not compete at all.

Network Externalities and Lock-In. State-by-state lawmaking arguably can be inefficient because of the importance of "networks" of users that can arise from adoption of a national standard. For example, a statutory disclosure rule relating to terms of software licenses might require that the disclosure be where the buyer is likely to see it—for example, "in close proximity to a description of the computer information, or to instructions or steps for acquiring it" or "in a prominent place on the site from which the computer information is offered."[234] Although a legislature cannot practicably go much further in Web site design, the market can provide useful information in the form of venders' actual practices in complying with the rule. More generally, the parties' transaction and information costs in complying with a statutory standard may depend on the size of the network of users of this standard that generates these forms and practices.

The development of a network involves a potential externality. Vendors or consumers who adopt a standard consider only their own benefits from the adoption and not the benefits conferred on others who use the standard. As a result of this externality, although society may gain from a user's move to a new network, the old network may be "locked in."[235] Commentators have argued that there are similar effects in connection with contracts and statutes.[236]

For example, Michael Klausner suggests that the long dominance of Delaware law might be due to lock-in effects rather than to the superiority of the Delaware regime.[237]

"Network externalities" may affect the development of state laws dealing with electronic commerce. Standards may not develop under individual state laws, or if they do develop they may become locked in because they determine the technological architecture of Web site commerce, or because a new standard would forego the benefits of case law that interprets the existing standard. For example, if a first-mover state becomes an early "Delaware" of the Internet and provides for particular default rules, contracting mechanisms, or disclosures, all clarified by interpretive case law, the many firms that select this state's law will design their Web site pages accordingly. Consumers, for their part, may expect venders to use particular standardized procedures. Thus, even if a new standard is more efficient than an existing one, network externalities may prevent the standard from developing a large enough network of users to generate interpretive devices or to induce venders and consumers to change their procedures or configurations. This phenomenon, for example, might prevent widespread adoption of the P3P protocol. In light of these problems, the law regulating electronic commerce arguably should be provided by a centralized, expert body rather than by the first state law that happens to become widely accepted.

The network externalities theory is, however, a questionable basis for abandoning the process of state-by-state lawmaking because of the many uncertainties about how and when the theory operates.[238] First, even if an inefficient standard has developed, lock-in is a problem only if users' costs of moving to a new standard are high enough to outweigh their present discounted benefits under the new standard. It is not clear under what conditions that will be the case. Second, users' failure to move to the new standard is likely to be inefficient only if neither users nor any third party will internalize the benefits of doing so. Again, it is not clear when that will occur. Among other things, venders themselves may benefit from sponsoring a new standard, as in the case of the P3P protocol. Third, even if lock-in of inefficient standards occurs, it does not in itself justify using a centralized lawmaking process because lock-in may occur under that process as well. Thus, the question is whether the centralized process is more likely to lead to an efficient result than a standard arrived at by a decentralized process.

203

Given these theoretical uncertainties, it would be prudent at least to have some data on network externalities in the context of state lawmaking before using this theory to support relying on centralized lawmaking. Data on an analogous issue support the opposite conclusion. Our study of lock-in in the context of state laws regarding statutory business forms showed evidence that lock-in was not a significant factor in explaining choice of form.[239] In contrast, a broad federal solution that preempts state law eliminates competition, in effect ensuring that parties will be locked in to the mandatory parts of the regulation.[240]

The Federal Alternative to State Law

As discussed, an argument in favor of federal regulation of electronic commerce is that states will tend to overregulate because ambiguities in the law of jurisdiction and conflict of laws give states substantial reach. Moreover, although enforcing contractual choice of law and forum addresses this overregulation problem, it does not immediately or completely solve the problem because state courts will retain some ability and incentive to override contractual choice of law and forum. That, however, does not necessarily justify a federal solution because of the Nirvana fallacy: the inadequacies of state law must be compared with those of federal law.

This section shows that federal law is unlikely to eliminate, or even to significantly address, overregulation of electronic commerce. We first discuss problems regarding preemption of state by federal law and then outline inherent problems with any federal law that may be adopted in this area. Next, we show that actual adoption of federal law is not only premature but unnecessary at this time because the *threat* of federal regulation may constrain inefficient state law. Finally, we discuss a limited approach to federal regulation focusing on enforcement of contractual choice of forum.

Incomplete Preemption

The biggest problem is that federal regulation of aspects of electronic commerce may not preempt all state law on the subject. Many of the federal privacy bills that have been introduced do not purport to preempt state law, particularly including state actions based on common law fraud or tort or on general consumer fraud statutes.[241] To the extent that preemption is unclear, plaintiffs' lawyers and state regulators can be expected to exploit the gaps. For example, the

Gramm-Leach-Bliley Financial Services Modernization Act, which does not preempt state law but is subject to the Fair Credit Reporting Act,[242] which does preempt, has not stopped state legislators from passing state privacy laws relating to third-party information firms.[243] Moreover, in the absence of preemption, federal law could even multiply regulatory burdens by imposing stringent disclosure requirements that might give rise to misleading statements that in turn trigger state fraud remedies.

Although federal laws theoretically could purport to preempt all relevant state law, that would be extremely difficult. In the first place, every state has general law that may apply to electronic commerce, including sales law, the common law of tort, privacy regulation, and regulation of deceptive transactions. It may not be clear how this law relates to or conflicts with federal regulation.[244]

Second, even if complete preemption were technically possible, it is politically infeasible because of the interest groups allied against preemption. They include, of course, state regulators—particularly state attorneys general acting through the National Association of Attorneys General—and consumer groups. Even without explicit interest group opposition, Congress would be unlikely to invade traditional areas of state legislation such as regulation of fraud unless there were a strong constituency supporting such invasion.[245]

Inherent Problems with Federal Law

Apart from the preemption problem, federal law dealing with electronic commerce might be even more inefficient than forcing firms to comply with the most rigorous state law in the absence of federal law. First, as discussed, the resulting law might end up favoring influential pro-liability interest groups such as power-seeking consumer groups and trial lawyers at the expense of low-margin operators, potential new entrants, and individual consumers.

Second, even electronic commerce firms might favor a strong federal law if they do substantial business outside the United States and are subject to foreign country law. U.S. firms may be tempted to tailor their policies to foreign laws rather than fight them and then seek federal regulation that conforms to European standards so that they can compete on a level playing field with U.S. firms that do not do business internationally. However, as a matter of general policy it would be better to give the state law approach a chance to take root and demonstrate its merits in preference to a one-size-fits-all federal or global standard. U.S. firms can use their considerable market clout to force non-U.S. regulators to abandon or moderate their protectionist approaches. Moreover, a choice-of-law model, having demonstrated its success in the United States, could be scaled up to provide a model for global regulation. The alternative of U.S. firms complying with European standards would be a global victory for mandatory privacy policies.[246] Thus, what may be good policy for some firms in the short run may be bad policy for the regulation of electronic commerce in the long run.

Third, even if the federal law appears benign, it may be inefficient in the hands of the federal agency that administers it. Bureaucracies can promote expansionist agendas through aggressive interpretation of statutes.[247] One technique is to promote self-regulation as a way of avoiding government regulation and then apply federal remedies based on violation of voluntarily adopted policies, as the FTC has done with respect to consumer marketing information.[248]

Fourth, federal law can have unpredictable effects because of litigators' efforts to apply it to new technologies. For example, litigators have attempted to apply older laws relating to interception of electronic communications and unlawful access to stored communications to cases involving the placing of cookies on consumers' computers.[249]

Fifth, even if federal law does preempt state law and is relatively innocuous, it might still have perverse effects because the existence of broad federal regulation discourages the development of state law. A similar phenomenon has been observed, for example, with regard to the effect of federal bankruptcy law on state debtor-creditor law.[250]

The current set of federal privacy laws provide a preview of what federal regulation of the Internet might entail. For example, the Children's Online Privacy Protection Act adopted in 1998,[251] as interpreted by the FTC's 1999 rules,[252] requires "operators" of Web sites or online services "directed to children under 13," or who have actual knowledge that the person from whom they seek information is a child, to comply with strict notice and parental consent requirements before collecting and disclosing individually identifiable information.[253] The application of the Act's burdensome requirements is potentially quite broad despite the actual knowledge requirement because sites may have to collect age information from users to avoid appearing to evade the rule.[254]

Congress also has regulated privacy of particular types of information. Under Gramm-Leach-Bliley,[255] financial institutions must provide a "clear and conspicuous" disclosure of their privacy policies to consumers "at the time of establishing a customer relationship with a consumer and not less than annually during the continuation of such relationship."[256] Gramm-Leach-Bliley has resulted in the costly mailing of billions of privacy notices, not just once but annually, whether or not firms change their policies or contemplate further disclosure of information.[257] The act applies to "any information" provided to or obtained by a financial institution during a transaction or an attempt by a consumer to obtain a financial product or service, either online or offline.[258] It applies not only to financial institutions but also to "other persons," such as lawyers, who receive protected information from a financial institution.[259]

Another example is the Health Insurance Portability and Accountability Act of 1996,[260] which regulates privacy of health information. The Act's regulations regarding consent are extremely complex and costly.[261] The regulations require notice even where collection of information is obvious, when no further use of information is intended, and when the subject of the information is deceased. More important, these rules' costly disclosure requirements can deter medical research.[262]

Finally, an important federal law affecting electronic commerce generally is the Electronic Signatures in Global and National Commerce Act.[263] Among other things, this Act requires firms that use electronic means to communicate with consumers to follow certain rules in providing the information and obtaining consumers' consent.[264] These requirements may impede firms' use of low-cost means of providing information by raising questions about when consumers have validly consented to electronic communications.[265]

The point of reviewing these laws is not to demonstrate that such federal laws are inefficient but rather to emphasize that the supposed excesses of state law should be compared with a realistic view of the burdens imposed by federal law. The main difference between federal and state law is that federal laws like those discussed immediately above are not easily avoided and do not accommodate experimentation or contextual variation.

When Should Congress Regulate the Internet?

If, contrary to the analysis in this chapter, state law proves inadequate to the challenge of regulating electronic commerce, then federal regulation ultimately may be efficient. The point of this chapter is that federal regulation is inefficient at this early stage in the history of electronic commerce because of the substantial issues that have not been resolved, the rapidly developing technology in the area, and the potential for evolution of state law.

It is important to note in this regard that, even without actual federal regulation, the *threat* of federal preemption may be significant in constraining inadequate or excessive state regulation. The threat of takeover by a broader jurisdictional authority can be viewed as a "vertical" dimension of jurisdictional competition.[266] Indeed, the threat of preemption contributes to a presumption that state regulation is efficient.

A Compromise Approach to Federal Regulation: Contractual Choice of Forum

Congress might eliminate doubt about enforcement of contractual choice by enacting a statute mandating the enforcement of contractual choice of law. Congress could do so by exercising its powers under the Commerce Clause or the Full Faith and Credit Clause.[267] The statute might provide for application either generally or in Internet transactions in which choice of law is a particular concern.

There would, however, be significant problems with a federal statutory approach.[268] Apart from the basic statute implementing the clause,[269] Congress has exercised its Full Faith and Credit power only once in the last 200 years—to empower states *not* to enforce a state law, including one contractually selected in a contract, to the extent that it authorizes same-sex marriage.[270] Enacting neutral procedural rules probably would not earn enough rents for federal legislators to justify the political risks of interfering with the traditionally state-governed area of conflict of laws.[271] This suggests that Congress is unlikely to pass a general choice-of-law statute. It may act specifically regarding Internet transactions, but then probably in response to the pro-regulatory coalition that is likely to influence federal substantive regulation, and therefore subject to significant exceptions. Indeed, the federal statute might serve only to lock into inefficient regulation that which state competition ultimately would have eroded in the absence of federal law.

Federal law might, however, play a limited role as an adjunct to a state regime of contractual choice rather than as the source of substantive regulation. Specifically, federal law might provide a shortcut around the evolutionary process discussed by ensuring immediate enforcement of contractual choice of law and forum. That would be consistent with federal cases favoring enforcement of choice-of-forum clauses and with the Federal Arbitration Act that mandates enforcement of arbitration clauses in some situations. Such a statute would not involve the same problems as a choice-of-law statute, since it would be neutral as to the type of law that is enforced. However, there remains the danger of exceptions to enforceability, which inhibits evolution of efficient law.

Beyond Contracts and States

This chapter has focused on a relatively easy case of multijurisdictional conflict in Internet regulation—that among U.S. states in cases that are potentially amenable to a contractual solution. More difficult issues are raised in cases involving conflict among sovereign nations that have sharply contrasting values and whose disputes are not mediated by a Constitution. In addition, contracting parties would seem to be inherently unable to contract out of regulation that is intended for the protection of others or of society as a whole, such as speech restrictions. These situations might seem to justify moving regulation to a federal or global body rather than permitting states or nations potentially to impose their laws and values on the rest of the country or the world.

Despite the differences between the international and noncontractual contexts and those discussed, this section shows that aspects of the foregoing analysis remain relevant. In particular, firms can use their power to exit to discipline overregulating jurisdictions. In contexts such as privacy, in which contracts between the beneficiaries of regulation and regulated firms are feasible, enforcement of those contracts is a possible outcome even in the international context. Even where contracts are not an answer, the threat of exit can still have a moderating influence on regulation. Accordingly, jurisdictional competition and variation need not give way to regulation by a central governing body.

To concretize the analysis, consider the following specific scenarios. First, a U.S. company may deal with customers outside the

209

United States who are protected by privacy or consumer-protection regulation that gives significantly more rights than that in any U.S. state. For example, privacy advocates are pushing for globalization of privacy norms,[272] and European countries already mandate stringent fair information practices.[273]

Second, a U.S. state may attempt to impose content or other regulation on an interstate entity that affects the firm's national operations and that the firm cannot avoid by contracts with customers. For example, Pennsylvania recently enacted a law that requires an Internet service provider to "remove or disable access to child pornography items residing on or accessible through its service in a manner accessible to persons located within this Commonwealth within five business days of when the Internet Service Provider is notified by the Attorney General . . . that child pornography items reside on or are accessible through its service."[274] The Pennsylvania attorney general obtained an order pursuant to the statute to force WorldCom to remove or deny access to certain offending sites.[275] Although WorldCom did not host any of the sites, it responded by preventing routing through its system to any sites that had not already been removed by the host. Thus, if any of these sites remained on the Internet, they were rendered inaccessible by World-Com users located anywhere in the United States.[276]

Third, U.S. firms are subject to regulation by jurisdictions located outside the United States. This was illustrated graphically when La Ligue contre le Racisme et l'Antisemitisme (LICRA) and L'Union des Etudiants Juifs de France sued Yahoo!, Inc., a Delaware corporation based in California, for offering on its Yahoo.com auction service Nazi-related propaganda and Third Reich memorabilia, *Mein Kampf, The Protocol of the Elders of Zion*, and purported "evidence" of the nonexistence of the Holocaust.[277] Offering access by French citizens to these materials violated French law.[278] A Paris court entered an order on May 20, 2000, that, among other things, required Yahoo! to eliminate French citizens' access on Yahoo.com to Nazi items and Internet pages on Yahoo.com displaying text, extracts, or quotations from *Mein Kampf* and *The Protocol of the Elders of Zion,* upon penalty of 100,000 Euros (approximately $13,300) for each day of noncompliance.[279] The court reaffirmed its order on November 20, 2000, ordering Yahoo! to comply with French law within three months or begin facing the penalty, to be assessed against Yahoo!, Inc, and not collectible from Yahoo! France. Yahoo! was served with this order in California.

In the wake of the French lawsuit, Yahoo! has amended Yahoo.com's auction policies so that they now prohibit auction of

> Any item that promotes, glorifies, or is directly associated with groups or individuals known principally for hateful or violent positions or acts, such as Nazis or the Ku Klux Klan. Official government-issue stamps and coins are not prohibited under this policy. Expressive media, such as books and films, may be subject to more permissive standards as determined by Yahoo! in its sole discretion to prohibit items that promote hate groups, including the Nazis.[280]

However, Yahoo! continues to offer some Nazi memorabilia and materials for sale in apparent violation of the French order.

Along similar lines, Dow Jones was sued for allegedly defaming Harrods, Limited, in a story appearing in the *Wall Street Journal*.[281] Harrods April Fool's Day press release said that it was going to "float" Harrods by building a ship version of the store on the embankment of the Thames River. The *Wall Street Journal* responded a few days later with an article it says was intended to be humorous. Titled "The Enron of Britain," the article suggested that "if Harrods, the British luxury retailer, ever goes public, investors would be wise to question its every disclosure." Harrods promptly sued Dow Jones in England.[282]

These cases illustrate the potential effect of regulation in one corner of the world, whether in Pennsylvania, Paris, or London, on firms doing business on the global Internet, and the clash of values that may result from such regulation. The Pennsylvania case involved special U.S. concerns with obscenity in general and child pornography in particular. The French case illustrates Europeans' special concerns with Nazi material, perhaps understandable in light of Europe's history. The British case may illustrate the consequences of varying senses of humor, even among people who seem to share a common language. Although the suits arose from country-specific values, they imposed their outcomes on firms' worldwide operations.

These cases indicate not only a special need to limit the geographical scope of regulation of the Internet but also the inadequacy in such contexts of the sort of contractual choice-of-law solution this chapter proposes. In none of these cases did the interests protected by the relevant statute—children exploited by child pornographers, victims of anti-Semitism, a defamed firm, and society as a whole— have an actual or potential contractual interface with the regulated parties. This contrasts with cases involving consumer marketing information, where the party whom regulation seeks to protect is a party to the case and therefore at least arguably capable of protecting his or her own interests by contract.[283] Even where there is a contractual interface, contracts may not be a full solution in the international context because of cross-country differences regarding enforcement of contracts. In particular, international law limits enforcement of a choice of forum clause in a consumer contract.[284]

Despite the differences between the contexts described in this section and that which is the focus of this chapter, a significant element of our analysis remains relevant. Regulated parties retain some ability to cause governments to limit their reach by choosing where to maintain contacts and hold assets. Moreover, this ability, especially as it relates to withdrawal of assets, is greater in the foreign than in the domestic U.S. context, which mitigates the greater clash of values in the former context.

With respect to firms' ability to exert discipline by withdrawing assets, it is important to keep in mind that foreign judgments are not entitled to full faith and credit in U.S. courts as are judgments by U.S. state courts. Instead, such judgments are entitled only to "comity."[285] Accordingly, where a foreign judgment does not reflect U.S. values, it may not be enforceable in the United States. That gives U.S.-based firms some incentive to move assets out of countries with offensive laws.[286] In the wake of the Yahoo! judgment, a Web site operator was quoted as saying that "companies are going to ensure that they have no assets in Europe to reduce the chances of being successfully sued."[287]

Firms not only may be able avoid collection of foreign judgments from U.S. assets but also may be able to persuade a U.S. court to enjoin the suit. Thus, Yahoo! sued in California federal court for a declaratory judgment that the French court's orders are not enforceable under U.S. law. Yahoo! claimed that it was not technically able to block French citizens from accessing the Yahoo.com auction site to view prohibited materials and therefore could not comply with

212

the order without banning Nazi-related material, which would infringe its First Amendment rights. After denying a motion to dismiss based on personal jurisdiction,[288] the court granted the declaratory judgment.[289] The court held that the French court's order violated the First Amendment as an impermissible restriction on Yahoo!'s speech right irrespective of its ability to comply with the French order. The court reasoned that the order's intended effect was to deprive a U.S. citizen of its First Amendment rights as to activities in the United States, so that French sovereign interests were outweighed by those of the United States. [290]

A more recent case indicates the limits of the procedure used in *Yahoo!* to protect U.S. firms from actions in the courts of other countries. A New York federal court held that Dow Jones could not block a suit in England for defamation arising out of the *Wall Street Journal* article.[291] The court emphasized the risks of exercising preemptive global jurisdiction, including the possibility of foreign retaliation against U.S.-originated actions,[292] and the unlikelihood that the English court would enforce the U.S. court's order. The court also noted critical differences from *Yahoo!*, including the fact that that case involved consequences of adjudication already reduced to judgment and involved enforcement and modification of corporate actions in the United States rather than in the foreign country.[293] This case indicates that, while U.S. firms may be able to avoid punishment abroad for actions centered in the United States, they are not immune from consequences for actions with effects specifically in the foreign country (i.e., defamation of a British firm).

In general, the spectre of chaotic regulation of global firms by individual nations may not be as serious as it might seem at first glance. Global firms can balance the effect on their business of complying with the regulation and of avoiding contacts with the regulating country. Firms that suffer enough from the regulation and that do not value business in the regulating country can avoid contacts with it. [294] The impact of the regulation depends on a variety of factors, including firms' technical ability to avoid sanctions by blocking access to offending materials while permitting access to non-offending materials, and firms' reputational incentives to self-regulate, as Yahoo! did in the French case. These factors mitigate the feared effects of permitting regulation at every national node.

213

It is important to emphasize the differences and similarities between situations that do, and do not, involve a potential contractual interface. In both situations, firms' ability to exit overregulating countries may cause nations to moderate their regulation. Where contracts are feasible, firms' ability to exit may persuade countries to enforce contractual choice of law and forum. In *Yahoo!*-type cases, on the other hand, moderation may have to take the form of reducing the impact of the regulation on all transactions. For example, the court may be willing to accept a less strict blocking of access to offending materials than it initially indicated.

To be sure, these potential outcomes are not perfect. Firms may find themselves having to comply with offensive regulation as a cost of maintaining valuable local markets. But attempting to cure the problem of overlapping national jurisdiction by giving regulatory authority to a world body may be worse than the disease because it invites heavy-handed and inflexible regulation.

Conclusion

Electronic commerce is best regulated at the state rather than the federal level. It would be counterproductive to straightjacket emerging technologies and business practices with a federal law, at least before a process of state experimentation, competition, and evolution has had an opportunity to discover the right approach or mix of approaches. At this point, there is not even a clear basic model for allocating rights in this area. A state law approach will not lead to over- or underregulation as some have predicted as long as merchants and consumers can contract for the applicable law and forum. Indeed, this approach points the way toward solutions for other aspects of Internet regulation.

First, although this chapter has focused on situations in which there is a contractual interface between suppliers and the most directly affected parties, aspects of the analysis also apply as to conduct, such as child pornography and gambling, where regulation is arguably necessary to protect noncontracting parties. In such situations, states may be justified in refusing to enforce contractual choice of law and forum where the conduct has caused harm within the jurisdiction. Thus, enforcing such contracts is not a viable solution to costly diversity and potential overregulation by multiple state laws. However, firms still have the option of avoiding jurisdictional contacts with states that impose excessive regulation, which may be enough to constrain the most egregious forms of state regulation. Moreover, it is important to keep in mind that any federal law will not necessarily be more reasonable, might be subject to bureaucratic agency creep, and might not preempt all existing state laws related to the conduct. Further, federal regulation may not be a political option. For example, regulation of gambling is a cherished state prerogative, particularly in that state-run gambling provides a large source of state revenue. It is hard to believe that Congress would incur the political costs of stepping on this prerogative.[295]

PART II

CURRENT DISPUTES IN
INTERNET GOVERNANCE

8. Caught in the Seamless Web: Does the Internet's Global Reach Justify Less Freedom of Speech?

Robert Corn-Revere

> An instance of the inexplicable conservatism and arrogance
> of the Turkish customs authorities was recently evidenced
> by the prohibition of the importation of typewriters into the
> country. The reason advanced by the authorities for this step
> is that typewriting affords no clew to the author, and that
> therefore in the event of seditious or opprobrious pamphlets
> or writings executed by the typewriter being circulated it
> would be impossible to obtain any clew by which the opera-
> tor of the machine could be traced. . . . The same decree also
> applies to the mimeograph and other similar duplicating
> machines and mediums.
>
> *Scientific American,* July 6, 1901

Introduction: Technologies of Freedom

The history of censorship is inextricably intertwined with technological progress. From the printing press, through television, and
on to the Internet, innovations in communication inevitably have
prompted official efforts to limit or control new media. The United
States was the first nation to provide formal protection for freedom
of the press. Nevertheless, despite America's foundational commitment to liberty for the technology of print, policymakers and courts
in the United States historically have been slow to extend the same
freedom to newer innovations.

The Internet bucked that trend. In the brief time between 1996
and the present, U.S. courts were presented with a number of significant cases involving attempts to restrict information available on
the Internet and the World Wide Web.[1] That growing body of law

required courts to devote significant attention to the nature of the Internet as a medium of communication and to assess its importance to the American system of free expression. As a result of this review, virtually every federal judge who was asked to rule on direct censorship of protected expression on the Internet held that such restrictions violate either the First Amendment to the U.S. Constitution or the Commerce Clause, or both. The U.S. Supreme Court struck down key portions of the Communications Decency Act, and federal courts have invalidated similar laws in New York, Michigan, Virginia, New Mexico, Arizona, and Vermont.[2] Most recently, the Supreme Court held that restrictions on Internet speech based on community standards did not necessarily invalidate a federal law targeting such speech, but the Court kept in place an injunction blocking the law's enforcement while lower courts grapple with other difficult issues, including whether the law bans too much speech, is unconstitutionally vague, or supplants less restrictive alternatives.[3]

The consensus thus far is that the Internet fulfills the ultimate promise of the First Amendment and should receive the highest level of constitutional protection. The Supreme Court found that the information available on the Internet is as "diverse as human thought" with the capability of providing instant access to information on topics ranging from "the music of Wagner to Balkan politics to AIDS prevention to the Chicago Bulls."[4] Judge Stuart Dalzell of the U.S. District Court for the Eastern District of Pennsylvania characterized the Internet as "a never-ending worldwide conversation" and "the most participatory form of mass speech yet developed."[5] Judge Lowell Reed wrote that in "the medium of cyberspace . . . anyone can build a soap box out of Web pages and speak her mind in the virtual village green to an audience larger and more diverse than any the Framers could have imagined."[6] Another district court judge, noting that "it is probably safe to say that more ideas and information are shared on the Internet than in any other medium," suggested that it may be only a slight overstatement to conclude that "the Internet represents a brave new world of free speech."[7]

One key aspect of this "brave new world" that has played a central role in the decisions to fully protect Internet speech is the global nature of the medium. The Supreme Court described the Internet as a "unique and wholly new medium of worldwide human communication" that makes information available "not just in Philadelphia, but also in Provo and Prague."[8] As it more recently noted, "One can use the Web to read thousands of newspapers published around the globe" and "can access material about topics ranging from aardvarks to Zoroastrianism."[9] Cyberspace has no particular geographical location, has no centralized control point, and is available to anyone, anywhere in the world, with access.[10] It is "ambient—nowhere in particular and everywhere at once."[11] That quality makes geography "a virtually meaningless construct on the Internet."[12] Accordingly, U.S. courts have been strongly influenced by the "unique character of these new electronic media."[13]

Such a reaction is not unexpected where a free and open medium of communication is compatible with a political system predicated on the free exchange of ideas. But that also is the very reason the Internet is seen as a threat in societies that lack the same free speech traditions as the United States. Other nations have responded to the advent of the Internet in various ways, ranging from open hostility to attempts to regulate it in the same way as traditional electronic media. Such divergent national responses to technology and political freedom are nothing new and historically have had little impact on the United States. But when such differences are applied to a global medium of communication, the resulting legal conflict can have significant ramifications for freedom of speech in this country.

The Yahoo! Case

A decision by a county court in France has crystallized questions arising from the application of national standards to an international medium. The case began in April 2000, when La Ligue contre le Racisme et l'Antisemitisme (LICRA) and L'Union des Etudiants Juifs de France (UEJF), two organizations opposed to racism and anti-Semitism, sent a "cease and desist" letter to the California headquarters of the Internet service Yahoo! demanding that "unless you cease presenting Nazi objects [on the U.S. online auction site] within 8 days, we shall size [sic] the competent jurisdiction to force your company to abide by [French] law." The law on which the demand was based, Article R645-1 of the French Criminal Code, prohibits the display of any symbol associated with an organization deemed criminal, such as the Nazis.[14]

Yahoo! is an Internet service provider that operates various Web sites and Internet-based services that are offered through its main

U.S. servers as well as through servers operated by foreign subsidiaries. Yahoo! subsidiary corporations operate regional services in 20 countries (for example, Yahoo! India and Yahoo! Korea) through Web sites that use the local region's primary language, direct their services to the local population, and abide by local laws. Yahoo!'s services include an automated auction site, online shopping, e-mail, a search engine, personal Web page hostings, Internet chat rooms, and club listings. The auction site allows users to post items for sale and to solicit bids from other users from around the world. In short, Yahoo! epitomizes the type of worldwide communication made possible on the Internet. Yahoo!'s home Web site (http://www.yahoo.com) is accessible globally, even though its services are in English, are oriented toward a U.S. audience, and are hosted entirely on servers located in the United States.

That the Yahoo! U.S. site can be reached by French citizens was the basis of the demand by LICRA and UEJF. They did not send a cease and desist letter to Yahoo! France, the regional subsidiary that serves the local population, because that service complies with French law, including Article 645-1. Instead, it was sent to Yahoo!'s U.S. service, which is, like all Internet-based services, available internationally for those who seek it. When Yahoo! declined to alter its U.S.-based service in response to the demand, the French groups filed suit in Paris.

In May 2000 the French court ordered Yahoo! to dissuade and render impossible any access through yahoo.com by Internet users in France to the Yahoo! Internet auction site displaying Nazi artifacts, including objects, relics, insignia, emblems, and flags. It also ordered Yahoo! to block access by French citizens to personal Web pages displaying text, extracts, or quotations from such works as Adolph Hitler's *Mein Kampf* and *The Protocol of the Elders of Zion*, the anti-Semitic report of the czarist secret police. After an interval during which the court heard evidence on the technical feasibility of its order, it reaffirmed its directive for Yahoo! in November 2000 and ordered it to "take all necessary measures to dissuade and make impossible any access via Yahoo.com to the auction service for Nazi merchandise as well as to any other site or service that may be construed as an apology for Nazism or contesting the reality of Nazi crimes."[15] The French court held that "the simple act of displaying [Nazi artifacts] in France violates Article R645-1 of the Penal Code and therefore [is] a threat to *internal* public order."[16] It described the mere availability of such information as "a connecting link with France, which renders our jurisdiction perfectly competent to rule in this matter."[17]

In specific terms, the order of the Paris county court directed Yahoo! to (a) reengineer its content servers in the United States and elsewhere to enable them to recognize French Internet protocol (IP) addresses and block access to Nazi material by end-users assigned such IP addresses, (b) require end-users with "ambiguous" IP addresses to provide Yahoo! with a declaration of nationality when they arrive at Yahoo!'s home page or when they initiate any search using the word "Nazi," and (c) implement these changes within three months or face a penalty of 100,000 francs (approximately $13,300) for each day of noncompliance. The French court order also provided that the penalties assessed against Yahoo! Inc. may not be collected from Yahoo! France. In other words, if the plaintiff groups want to enforce the judgment, they must persuade a U.S. court to recognize it and apply it against Yahoo!'s U.S. service.

The French Yahoo! decision cuts sharply against the grain of the emerging jurisprudence in the United States that strongly protects Internet speech because of its global reach. The French view is not that geography is "a virtually meaningless construct on the Internet" but that geography is all-important and should determine which information should be available online. It envisions a world in which Internet surfers must "show their papers" at the border, even when that border exists in a server located wholly outside the nation whose law would be applied. Accordingly, the French Yahoo! decision represents a direct attempt by a foreign nation to apply its law extraterritorially to restrict the freedom of expression of U.S.-based online speakers who are protected by the First Amendment.

You Say That Like It's a *Bad* Thing

The French Yahoo! decision has its defenders—not just among Europeans who sneer at America's "free speech fetish." Supporters include people who evidently would like to see the Internet get its comeuppance. Sebastian Mallaby of the *Washington Post*'s editorial page staff cited the Yahoo! case to support his conclusion that "the real story on the Net these days is that the cyberanarchists are losing." He noted the existence of technology "that can pinpoint the geographic whereabouts of cybernauts." "Once that is done," he concluded, "French surfers can be blocked from Nazi sites while leaving Americans to enjoy the full freedoms of the First Amendment." Such creative use of law and technology debunks "the old cyberanarchist nostrum that national governments can no longer expect to enforce national laws."[18]

Mallaby's repeated use of the word "cyberanarchist" as an epithet brings to mind the February 2002 Vatican position paper decrying the "radical libertarianism" of the Internet.[19] The paper notes that a consequence of deregulation has been "a shift of power from national states to transnational corporations" and that the Internet has produced "a mindset opposed to anything smacking of legitimate regulation for public responsibility." That has led to an "exaggerated individualism" and a view of cyberspace as a "new realm" where "every sort of expression was allowed and the only law was total individual liberty to do as one pleased."

In the Vatican's view, "The only community whose rights and interests would be truly recognized" would be "the community of radical libertarians." Such thinking "remains influential in some circles," according to the Vatican paper, "supported by familiar libertarian arguments also used to defend pornography and violence in the media generally."[20] Describing the "ideology of radical libertarianism" as both mistaken and harmful to "legitimate free expression in the service of truth," the paper concludes that the Internet "is no more exempt than other media from reasonable laws against hate speech, libel, fraud, child pornography, and pornography in general." Accordingly, it calls for "international cooperation in setting standards and establishing mechanisms to promote and protect the common good."[21]

Coming, as it did, just as stories were breaking about the pedophilia scandals in the Catholic Church and decades of cover-ups, the Vatican paper's theme of "freedom" versus "truth" might seem a bit hypocritical.[22] Nevertheless, the pontifical pronouncement dovetails with Mallaby's conclusions that "government must act as the ultimate enforcer" of norms in cyberspace[23] and that the "real debate will not be whether you can enforce rules on the Net but how the enforcers should adapt to the new medium."[24] In addition to discussing the French Yahoo! case, Mallaby pointed out that the Chinese dictatorship has found new ways to stifle dissent online:

"The regime blocks out much of the content it dislikes, official news agencies get a new way of disseminating the party line and dissidents become the victims of Web-enabled smear tactics."[25] As for regulating pornography, Mallaby notes, "Scary offshore porn sites won't seem so scary anymore. If a government wants to block them, it can tell credit card companies not to process payments to them."[26]

Mallaby has recognized that applying myriad national laws to cyberspace could cause the Net to "lose some of its borderless appeal" and that we risk converting the World Wide Web to "Numerous National Nets."[27] He notes, for example, that an online magazine oriented toward teens could violate the law in countries with severe restrictions on advertising to children. But from the perspective of other countries, Mallaby concludes, there is no reason to abandon local regulation. "If a European country feels strongly about marketing to kids, why should it let American publishers subvert its policies? Countries have varying regulations for the good reason that cultures vary. The Internet won't change that."[28]

Jack Goldsmith, formerly a professor at the University of Chicago School of Law, agreed with this assessment: "When French citizens are on the receiving end of an offshore communication that their government deems harmful," he wrote, "France has every right to take steps within its territory to check and redress the harm."[29] Although Goldsmith assumed incorrectly that "a country can enforce its regulations only against companies with assets in its territory," he described the French Yahoo! decision (which applies primarily to Yahoo! in the United States and not to Yahoo! France) as a "reasonable middle ground." He argued that it is legitimate to force offshore content providers to use filtering technology "to identify recipients of information by geography and screen out content to them."[30] Goldsmith acknowledged that such measures will "marginally raise the cost of doing e-business" but concluded that geographical filtering will "force Yahoo! to take account of the true social cost of its auction activities."[31]

A Little Bit Pregnant

Goldsmith's balancing approach assumes that cross-border regulation of the Internet can be carefully calibrated by using technology to keep information out of restrictive jurisdictions while allowing its free availability everywhere else. Unfortunately, the real world is not so amenable to neat solutions that sound plausible only in academic journals (or in France). The sheer volume of information, much of it posted by third parties, and the fact that it is constantly changing distinguish the type of communication available on the Internet from most traditional communication. Attempting to restrict the availability of information in certain countries on Yahoo!'s auction Web site is not the same thing as declining to publish a book in England because of its plaintiff-friendly libel laws or refusing to mail an adult video to Tennessee for fear of its Bible Belt obscenity standards.

Under the logic of the French Yahoo! decision, an Internet publisher or Web host must create filters to block access to any content that is illegal in the jurisdictions in which its service is available— that is, everywhere. The publisher need not preclude access to all offending content in all jurisdictions but may use geographic filtering to coordinate its blocking decisions with local laws. Even assuming this is technically possible, it presents Web publishers with a daunting task. At least 59 different countries limit freedom of expression online.[32] Theoretically, publishers would have to code each item of information they posted (or otherwise made available) to meet each of the national standards, and set their geographic filters to block access to the content in the relevant jurisdictions. A few examples illustrate the widely varying restrictions that would apply.

China

The People's Republic of China severely restricts communication by the Internet, including all forms of dissent and the free reporting of news. The so-called Measures for Managing Internet Information Services are regulations that prohibit private Web sites from publishing "news" without prior approval from Communist Party officials.[33] Another set of laws, known as the "Seven No's," bars the publication of materials that negate "the guiding role of Marxism, Leninism, Mao Zedong, and Deng Xiaoping's theories," go against "the guiding principles, official line or policies of the Communist Party," or violate "party propaganda discipline." Chinese law also bans "content that guides people in the wrong direction, is vulgar or low."[34] Armed with that authority, Chinese officials are trying to stop online protest messages available on overseas Web sites, particularly those located in the United States, from which so much pro-democracy speech emanates.[35] Such restrictions pose a particular threat to groups like VIP Reference (also known as Dacankao), the leading Chinese pro-democracy electronic newsletter. Although it is based in Washington, D.C., VIP Reference is read by countless individuals in mainland China.[36] If U.S. courts begin enforcing foreign speech standards such as the French law that gave rise to the judgment against Yahoo!, Chinese authorities could pursue similar quasi-civil penalties in the hopes of silencing other pro-democracy speech.

Singapore

The Singapore Broadcasting Authority (SBA) maintains strict control over the free speech activities of that country's Internet users. A U.S. human rights audit explained that the SBA has regulated access to content on the Internet since 1996 by licensing both domestic Web sites and Internet service providers (ISPs). Service providers must install "proxy servers" that filter out content that the government considers objectionable. The SBA directs service providers to block access to Web pages that, in the government's view, undermine public security, national defense, racial and religious harmony, and public morals. In 1997 the SBA announced an Internet Code of Practice to block access to material that contains pornography or excessive violence or that incites racial or religious hatred.[37] In July 2001 the government of Singapore imposed new restrictions on political content, which led at least one organization, Sintercom, to shut down its online activities.[38]

Saudi Arabia

Saudi Arabia bans publishing or even accessing various types of online expression, including "anything contrary to the state or its system," "news damaging to the Saudi Arabian armed forces," "anything damaging to the dignity of heads of states," "any false information ascribed to state officials," "subversive ideas," and "slanderous or libellous [sic] material."[39] All 30 of the country's Internet service providers (ISPs) are linked to a ground-floor room at the Riyadh Internet entranceway, where all of the country's Web activity is stored in massive cache files and screened for offensive or sacrilegious material before it is released to individual users.[40] The central servers are configured to block access to "sensitive" sites that might violate "the social, cultural, political, media, economic, and religious values of the Kingdom."[41] Several key overseas Web sites have received special scrutiny and blocking, including the Movement for Islamic Reform in Arabia—a group based in England. Saudi Arabian authorities have also issued a fatwa against Pokémon, claiming that the popular children's games and cards possess the minds of children while promoting gambling and Zionism.[42]

Syria

Syria bans many types of content on the Internet, such as statements that would endanger "national unity" or otherwise divulge "state secrets"—categories that include pro-Israeli speech.[43] Syrian citizens can be jailed for sending e-mail to people overseas without government authorization. Syrian authorities enforce the bans in several ways, including by intensive surveillance. Online access is severely restricted. There is only one Internet service provider in the country, which is government run and imposes heavy blocking and monitoring schemes.[44]

Australia

The Australian government has issued regulations that bar many forms of expression on the Internet. Amendments to the Broadcasting Services Act require Australian-based content hosts to deny access to sites that lack content-based classifications or are X-rated. In addition, the scheme is designed to deny Australian minors access to any R-rated Web sites. Specifically, access to Internet content hosted outside Australia may be prohibited if the Internet content has been classified RC or X by the Classification Board.[45] The list of subjects that can be banned as unsuitable for minors includes suicide, crime, corruption, marital problems, emotional trauma, drug and alcohol dependency, death and serious illness, racism, and religious issues.[46] Violators may be subject to Web site shutdowns and other criminal penalties.[47]

Italy

Italy restricts both online and offline speech in various ways. The Italian constitution contains broad language that forbids "printed publications, performances, and all other exhibits offensive to public morality."[48] Italy also allows law enforcement agents to seize questionable "periodical publications" under certain conditions.[49] The ability of the state to regulate speech gains added significance in light of a court decision declaring that those standards should be applied globally—not just in Italy. A Roman tribunal held that it has the power to shut down foreign Web sites to the extent they can be viewed in Italy.[50] The court found that "if confronted with a [defamatory statement] initiated abroad and terminated . . . in our Country, the Italian State is entitled to jurisdiction and the meting [out] of punishment."[51] The court added that "the use of the Internet for defamatory statement embodies one of the cases of aggravation described in Article 595 of the penal code" and that in this case "the sender deserves to be meted a more severe form of punishment."[52] The court's decision may well have been influenced by the fact that the speech at issue contained not only statements about a private party but also "extremely negative defamatory opinions" about "the work of the Italian judicial authorities."[53]

Sweden

Swedish laws ban several types of Internet speech, including "illegal description of violence" and "racial agitation."[54] Those strictures require the proprietors of "electronic bulletin boards" to remove or make inaccessible such content.[55] In March 2002 a Swedish court applied those rules to the Web site of the country's biggest newspaper, *Aftonbladet*, and fined the Web site's editor for anonymous statements posted to the newspaper's online comment forum.[56]

France über Alles

Because the French Yahoo! decision applies to Yahoo! U.S., the plaintiffs in that case must seek enforcement of the order by an American court. Normally, courts will enforce such foreign judgments as a matter of international cooperation. But, the Yahoo! case presents special problems: enforcing the judgment here would have practical and legal ramifications that extend far beyond one nation's law or a single court order. It would establish a legal framework wherein *all* Web sites on the global Internet potentially are subject to the laws of *all* other nations, regardless of the extent to which such a requirement conflicts with the law of the place where the speakers are located. Any finding that the French order may be enforced in the United States portends the development of an international law in which any nation would be able to enforce its legal and cultural "local community standards" on speakers in all other nations. In such a regime, Internet service providers and content providers would have no practical choice but to restrict their speech to the lowest common denominator to avoid potentially crushing liability.

The impact of such a lowest common denominator approach is not measured by counting the number of nations that already have sought to apply their laws beyond their borders, although that number is growing. It is determined by assessing the effects on Web site operators, considering how the challenged rule "may interact with the legitimate regulatory regimes of other [nations] and what effect would arise if not one, but many or every, [nation] adopted similar legislation."[57] By that standard, Web publishers could be forced to block access to information that "sabotages national unity" in China; undermines "religious harmony and public morals" in Singapore; offends "the social, cultural, political, media, economic, and religious values" of Saudi Arabia; fosters "pro-Israeli speech" in Syria; facilitates viewing unrated or inappropriately rated Web sites in Australia; or makes available information "offensive to public morality" in Italy—to cite just a few examples.

Many Web publishers and service providers likely would cease offering content that could run afoul of such restrictions. But assuming it is even possible to monitor the various national requirements as they might apply to all of the information available by a particular site, and to calibrate filters accordingly, the effect on Internet communication would be significant. In the international arena, inconsistent regulation of Internet content acts like a "customs dut[y]."[58] A 1997 White House report on electronic commerce called for a minimum of international government regulation and warned that content regulation "could cripple the growth and diversity of the Internet." The report described content regulations as nontariff trade barriers.[59] Similarly, the U.S. Department of Commerce has said, "Full realization of the economic promise of information technology depends on the development of the same safeguards and predictable legal environment that individuals and businesses have come to expect in the offline world."[60]

By contrast, refusing to enforce the French judgment would in no way undermine the rule of law in France. France has full authority to regulate the behavior of its citizenry and to require that citizens limit their Web browsing to conform to local norms, just as other nations do. Countries such as China, Singapore, and Saudi Arabia permit their citizens to see only officially approved Web sites and use technology to try to block access to nonconforming sites. Such policies may offend American notions of free expression and respect for the individual, but if other nations want to treat their citizens like fragile children, that is not the concern of the U.S. government. Such repressive policies present a significant problem here only if the American government is enlisted as a partner in enforcing foreign speech restrictions on U.S.-based speakers.

Yahoo! Take Two

After the French court reaffirmed its initial order, Yahoo! took preemptive action in the United States. It filed a declaratory judgment action in the U.S. District Court for the Northern District of California, seeking a ruling that the French judgment is unenforceable because it is inconsistent with U.S. constitutional law and policy. While the judge in Paris had reasoned that requiring Yahoo! "to extend its ban to symbols of Nazism" would satisfy "an ethical and moral imperative shared by all democratic societies," the question Yahoo! raised in the U.S. forum is whether that "moral imperative" includes censoring disfavored speech.

Judgments of foreign courts are not entitled to automatic recognition or enforcement in American courts. Whether a U.S. court will honor a foreign judgment is determined by principles of international respect and cooperation.[61] Among those is the rule that a court need not enforce a foreign judgment if to do so will offend the public policy of the nation where the court has jurisdiction.[62] A classic example of a foreign judgment that will not be enforced on public policy grounds is a ruling that unconstitutionally impairs individual rights of personal liberty.[63] This includes a judgment based on laws or procedures that do not comport with fundamental First Amendment principles.[64] Similarly, judgments cannot be enforced if they violate an explicit public policy expressed by Congress.

The Yahoo! order highlighted the stark differences in the way nations value freedom of expression. The French law prohibiting the mere viewing of Nazi insignia, including its display on plainly expressive items such as books or flags, flies in the face of fundamental principles of free expression. In the United States, the Supreme Court has held that the most stringent protections of the First Amendment protect marching in Nazi uniforms, displaying the

231

swastika, and even "distributing pamphlets or displaying . . . materials that incite or promote hatred against persons of Jewish faith or ancestry, race, or religion."[65] That is because our constitutional jurisprudence is based on the following understanding:

> Those who won our independence . . . believed that freedom to think as you will and to speak as you think are means indispensable to the discovery and spread of political truth; that without free speech and assembly discussion would be futile; that with them, discussion affords ordinarily adequate protection against the dissemination of noxious doctrine.[66]

As the Supreme Court explained recently, "The history of the law of free expression is one of vindication in cases involving speech that many citizens may find shabby, offensive, or even ugly."[67]

Constitutional law does not stringently protect such "low-value" speech because of a belief that "one idea is as good as any other, and that in art and literature objective standards of style, taste, decorum, beauty, and esthetics are deemed by the Constitution to be inappropriate, indeed unattainable." Rather, the First Amendment protects such speech "precisely so that opinions and judgments, including esthetic and moral judgments about art and literature [and politics], can be formed, tested, and expressed." In our system, "these judgments are for the individual to make, not for the Government to decree, even with the mandate or approval of a majority."[68]

On the basis of those principles, U.S. courts have refused to enforce defamation judgments based on foreign law because of the strict First Amendment limits of American libel law.[69] For example, in *Telnikoff v. Matusevitch*, the Maryland Court of Appeals held that enforcement of an English libel judgment would be contrary to public policy as embodied in the First Amendment even though the allegedly defamatory statements were published only in the *London Daily Telegraph*.[70] Similarly, in *Ellis v. Time, Inc.*, a plaintiff brought suit in the United States under both American and English law and argued that the court should apply the more restrictive English defamation law for articles published in England. The court disagreed, holding that applying English law in the United States would violate the Constitution.[71] The court held that "United States courts must apply rules of law consistent with the Constitution, regardless of where the alleged wrong occurs."[72]

Judicial decisions extending First Amendment protections to the Internet, as well as congressional recognition of the value of free expression online, further distinguish the United States from other nations. For example, it is the statutory law of the United States that "no provider or user of an interactive computer service shall be treated as the publisher or speaker of any information provided by another information content provider."[73] Section 230 of the Communications Act establishes the clear policy that the public interest is best served by "promot[ing] the continued development of the Internet and other interactive computer services" and by "preserv[ing] the vibrant and competitive free market" for these services, "unfettered by Federal or State regulation."[74] Accordingly, Congress has created "a federal immunity to any cause of action that would make service providers liable for information originating with a third-party user of the service."[75] U.S. courts have applied this statutory immunity broadly.[76]

Such immunity from liability for third-party content is not the international norm. In *Godfrey v. Demon Internet, Ltd.*, for example, an English court held that an ISP could be held responsible for defamatory postings by a third party to the extent it made newsgroups containing the postings available. The court considered U.S. authorities, including Section 230, and concluded that British law "did not adopt this approach or have this purpose."[77] It also noted, "The impact of the First Amendment has resulted in a substantial divergence of approach between American and English defamation law."[78] As in the traditional defamation cases, there are significant differences between U.S. policies and those of other nations with respect to third-party liability for Internet service providers.

The U.S. District Court for the Northern District of California considered the significant differences between U.S. and French law regarding free expression and held that the Yahoo! order could not be enforced in the United States. Judge Fogel wrote that "the French order's content and viewpoint-based regulation of the Web pages and auction site of Yahoo.com, while entitled to great deference as an articulation of French law, clearly would be inconsistent with the First Amendment if mandated by a court in the United States."[79] "Although France has a sovereign right to regulate what speech is permissible in France," he reasoned, "this Court may not enforce a foreign order that violates the protections of the United States

Constitution by chilling protected speech that occurs simultaneously within our borders."[80]

Judge Fogel's decision was unaffected by the French court's shaky finding that Yahoo!'s auction site could be "filtered" geographically to block access to forbidden items only to French citizens. Noting that the foreign order would affect Yahoo!'s actions "in the United States" and how it "configures and operates its auction and Yahoo.com sites," he found the question of whether Yahoo! "possesses the technology to comply with the rule" to be "immaterial."[81] Judge Fogel wrote that the French order would require Yahoo! not only to "render it impossible for French citizens to access the proscribed content" but also "to interpret an impermissibly overbroad and vague definition" of what is prohibited. Accordingly, he found that enforcement of the French order against Yahoo! would be inconsistent with the First Amendment because compliance would involve an impermissible restriction on speech.[82]

And the Beat Goes On . . .

The District Court's decision was an important milestone in securing First Amendment protections on the global Internet, but it is by no means the end of the story. The French parties appealed the decision to the U.S. Court of Appeals for the Ninth Circuit and argued that the lower court should not have exerted jurisdiction over them since they were taking actions only in France to vindicate their rights under French law. Seemingly oblivious to the fact that the French court's order seeks to limit speech on Yahoo!'s servers in the United States, they complain, without a trace of irony, that Judge Fogel's decision would "give U.S. courts worldwide jurisdiction over any nonforum conduct that has the potential of offending local sensibilities."[83] The Court of Appeals is expected to decide the case some time this year.

Meanwhile, the civil court findings in France have become the basis for a criminal prosecution of Yahoo!'s former CEO Timothy Koogle, who resides in the United States, under the French Press Law of 1881.[84] In February 2002 the Paris Criminal Court declined to dismiss the charges, based on facts similar to those in the earlier civil case, and held that the case could go forward.[85] The court was unimpressed by Judge Fogel's ruling in the United States and noted, "Following the example of the district judge for the Northern District of California, the French judge is free to adopt his own principles of international criminal jurisdiction to sanction offenses that are completely or partially committed abroad and are likely to threaten national interests" to the extent that "the Web site's message or contents are made accessible, through the Internet, within French territory."

The court held that providing public access to an auction site offering Nazi articles "and which Internet users can access by virtue of the mere existence of a 'search' link inviting them, establishes" the predicate element of "publicity" for the crime of justifying war crimes and that it is not necessary "that the Internet users be specifically solicited by the owner of the Web site."[86] The court deemed irrelevant the fact that Yahoo.com is "based in the United States and intended for the American public." Rather, the court concluded that it is appropriate to apply French criminal law "even if the alleged offense is not prohibited by the criminal laws of the country of origin of the presumed operator of the acts or the country in which the Web site's host is geographically located."[87]

Although Timothy Koogle left his job at Yahoo! in May 2001, the court found that he could be tried under French law for making available offending auction postings, but the court acquitted him of the charges in February 2003. If convicted, he could have faced up to five years in prison and fines of approximately $49,000, The court found that Koogle and Yahoo! did not condone or praise Nazism by selling objects from the Third Reich.

Despite this favorable outcome, such cases may become more widespread under a side agreement to a European treaty on crime in cyberspace. The 43-member Council of Europe (CoE) last November ratified a Convention on Cybercrime, the first international treaty on criminal offenses committed through the use of the Internet and other computer networks. Although the CoE comprises European nations, the United States was one of four nonmember signatories to the convention.

The main aim of the convention, according to its preamble, is to "pursue, as a matter of priority, a common criminal policy aimed at the protection of society against cybercrime" and to take measures such as "adopting appropriate legislation and fostering international co-operation." The convention deals in particular with offenses related to infringements of copyright, computer-related fraud, child pornography, and offenses connected with network security. It also covers a series of procedural powers such as searches for and interception of material on computer networks.

An additional protocol to the convention would oblige signatories to "adopt legislative and other measures as may be necessary" to criminalize "distributing or otherwise making available racist or xenophobic material to the public through a computer system;" "insulting publicly, through a computer system, persons for the reason that they belong" to an ethnic, racial, national, or religious group; and distributing material "which denies, grossly minimizes, approves or justifies . . . genocide or crimes against humanity." It also would require the adoption of laws prohibiting "aiding or abetting the commission of any of the offenses established in accordance with this Protocol, with intent that such offense be committed."[88] A draft explanatory report makes clear that those provisions are intended to apply to, among other things, the exchange of racist and xenophobic material in Internet chat rooms or by postings on newsgroups and discussion fora.[89] The protocol was developed as a side agreement so as not to impede ratification of the main convention by the United States and other nations that might have a conflict with the new provision. Although the United States is not expected to sign it, the protocol will exacerbate the problems presented by the French Yahoo! case.

The adoption of the protocol by CoE members will place added pressure on the United States to go along, but that pressure should be resisted. It is doubtful that the United States could find a way to comply with the protocol that would survive First Amendment scrutiny in any event, but this country should affirm its commitment to constitutional principles by rejecting the protocol categorically. Although such measures are vulnerable under American law, they become less so if we begin to entertain the notion that it is legitimate for governments to dictate matters of individual conscience. As Supreme Court Justice Robert Jackson warned, "The First Amendment to our Constitution was designed to avoid these ends by avoiding these beginnings."[90]

Epilogue

The struggle between government authorities and the technologies of free expression is hardly new. A century ago, Turkish customs officials sought to quell seditious pamphlets by keeping typewriters out of the country. Even now, the North Korean dictatorship of Kim Jong Il directs government officials to "tighten controls over use of typewriters and photocopiers."[91] Jamming of Western radio broadcasts was widely practiced in the Soviet bloc during the Cold War until the practice was terminated officially in November 1988. Such technical measures, while initially effective, were abandoned eventually as futile. Lech Walesa wrote: "When it came to radio waves, the iron curtain was helpless. Nothing could stop the news from coming through—neither sputniks nor mine fields, high walls nor barbed wire. The frontiers could be closed; words could not."[92] Whether jamming was effective or not, the costs were colossal. In 1956 the jamming operation in Poland alone cost $1.4 million and used enough electricity to supply a medium-sized town. In 1981 the BBC estimated that the cost of four days of jamming by the Russians was equal to the annual budget of BBC's Russian radio service.[93]

The Internet has upped the ante on these issues by empowering individuals to communicate instantly with others across the planet. This unprecedented power of the medium to transmit and receive information has increased the sense of urgency on the part of some in authority to limit disfavored speech, whether that speech takes the form of pro-democracy writings, Nazi memorabilia, or sexually explicit imagery. The technology of the Internet makes this extremely difficult, for as Internet pioneer John Gilmore has said, "The Internet treats censorship as system damage and routes around it." Yet, while the nature of the medium makes it inherently difficult to prevent Internet speech, a number of governments have focused on restricting the speakers themselves.

In this regard, the ability to impose "futile" censorship regimes can have a significant effect. With radio jamming at least, the governments that sought to block foreign messages bore their own costs, a factor that contributed to the demise of the practice. But if foreign judgments can be used to impose costs on U.S.-based Internet speakers, either by requiring the use of filtering systems or by levying fines, they may lead to widespread restrictions on speech regardless of the ineffectiveness of the technical "fixes." Professor Goldsmith may characterize this as forcing Yahoo! "to take account of the true social cost of its auction activities,"[94] but the effect would be to change fundamentally the open nature of the medium by allowing foreign governments to "tax" free speech. For that reason, the District Court held correctly that enforcement of the French Yahoo! judgment in the United States would be repugnant to First Amendment values.

One final point about futility is worth mentioning. French laws prohibiting the display of Nazi artifacts and restricting speech did nothing to prevent the burnings of synagogues in France during the past year, nor did they forestall frustrations that led to the rise of right-wing politicians like the National Front's Jean-Marie Le Pen. To the contrary, restrictions on speech may contribute to such phenomena by impairing the social safety valve that free expression provides. Although nothing requires the French to embrace the First Amendment's philosophy that society is better protected by more speech rather than by enforced silence, our constitutional traditions should prevent France from exporting its parochial restrictions here.

9. International Liability for Internet Content: Publish Locally, Defend Globally

Kurt Wimmer

For decades, international treaties have promised freedom of expression "regardless of frontiers."[1] The global Internet finally has provided a means by which this promise may be achieved. Geopolitical frontiers, however, remain crucial to issues of responsibility and risk even on a borderless medium such as the Internet. This is particularly true for U.S. media companies that now find themselves being sued or prosecuted in foreign courts for libel, invasion of privacy, or other causes of action based on content accessed through the Internet outside of the United States.

The prospect of foreign litigation is a constant challenge for publishers because of the complexity, inconvenience, and expense involved in defending an action outside one's home country. But these traditional concerns pale next to the greatly increased risk profile of publishing on the Internet at all because of the growing potential for a foreign court or prosecutor to seize jurisdiction over an Internet content dispute and apply local law that does not protect speech as robustly as does U.S. law governed by the First Amendment. International plaintiffs, governments, and courts have begun using the Internet to manipulate jurisdictional principles to avoid application of the First Amendment to claims against the U.S. media's publication of content through the Internet.

Recent cases from Australia to Zimbabwe highlight the danger of the exercise of international jurisdiction against foreign Internet publishers. A just-commenced consultation by the European Commission, moreover, proposes applying the law of the plaintiff's country to all Internet-related tort disputes, regardless of where the content is published, accessed, or hosted. The problem of foreign Internet content liability is most vexing for U.S. media companies that maintain assets abroad, because such assets may be used to satisfy adverse judgments. These companies may be forced to conform their Internet conduct to the standards of the least-speech-protective countries in which jurisdiction might be found. The "lowest common denominator" approach naturally flowing from expansive findings of jurisdiction will result in a clear chilling of such companies' Internet speech, and it will deprive U.S. audiences of the level of discourse meant to be guaranteed by the First Amendment.

In the future, however, this issue may be more troubling for *all* U.S. Internet publishers—not simply media—because of the potential for agreement on the Hague Convention, which may provide for the enforcement in U.S. courts of international judgments regarding Internet content. This principle is also threatened by recent questioning of this First Amendment doctrine by the American Law Institute in its current efforts to restate the law applicable to international recognition of judgments. These developments threaten to undermine a delicate balance that now exists, under which U.S. courts have steadfastly refused to enforce foreign defamation judgments that are rendered in legal systems that do not provide protections similar to those provided by American constitutional law. If American courts continue to refuse to enforce foreign libel judgments that are not consistent with the First Amendment, there is less chance that American media companies that do not have substantial assets and reporting staffs abroad will be significantly affected by the potential for foreign liability. If, on the other hand, U.S. courts do enforce foreign Internet libel judgments, the speech-restrictive laws of foreign jurisdictions will chill Internet speech across the board, for American audiences as well as the global Internet community.

This chapter considers the likely success of actions by foreign claimants to enforce content-liability judgments rendered by distant courts in the United States, and it offers arguments that can be used by U.S. media attorneys in defending against these actions. First, the chapter offers a brief overview of dangerous recent precedents and then provides a general overview of emerging jurisdictional doctrine in the Internet context in the European Union. Second, the chapter reviews the consistent refusal by U.S. courts to enforce foreign libel judgments, based on statements in non-Internet media, that are inconsistent with the standards of the First Amendment, and the effect that those refusals had on the successful efforts of

Yahoo! Inc. to obtain a declaratory judgment that a recent French decision against Yahoo! violates the U.S. Constitution. Finally, part three of this chapter discusses generally accepted principles of international law and the emerging negotiations surrounding the Hague Convention.

International Principles of Jurisdiction

International Imposition of Liability on Foreign Internet Publishers

In several recent cases, foreign law has been applied to Internet speech originating outside of the country seeking to exercise jurisdiction over the content in question. The most widely publicized cases involve the exercise of jurisdiction over Dow Jones, Inc., by Australian courts in a libel dispute and the exercise of jurisdiction over Yahoo! Inc. by French courts. Other cases, however, can be seen as even more threatening toward free expression on the Internet. Those cases include the imposition of a criminal sentence on an Australian Internet publisher by German courts, the closing of U.S. Web sites by Italian police and an exercise of jurisdiction by Italian courts in a controversial libel decision involving an Israeli defendant, and the criminal prosecution of an American journalist and a British newspaper in Zimbabwe. These cases provide a fitting backdrop for a discussion of how an Internet publisher may protect itself against foreign judgments.

Australia. Australia's High Court has held that the Dow Jones publication *Barron's* is subject to the jurisdiction of Australian courts because it can be accessed over the Internet in Australia. In *Dow Jones & Co. v. Gutnick*,[2] the court held that Dow Jones was subject to suit in Victoria for allegedly defamatory material that appeared in the online version of *Barron's*, despite the fact that the Web site is published and hosted in New Jersey.[3] Interestingly, the court's decision rested, in part, on the subscription nature of the site by which *Barron's* is accessed in Australia. Because the publication at issue was available through a subscription service with a handful of subscribers who paid using Australian credit cards, the court found that Dow Jones had accepted the risk of being sued in Australia and would be required to defend the suit there.

Dow Jones argued against a finding of jurisdiction in Australia, pointing out that the material on which the complaint was based was published in New Jersey and that 99 percent of the circulation

241

of *Barron's* 300,000 subscribers are in the United States. The online version of the magazine had only 500,000 subscribers, and only 1,700 of these were in Victoria. The High Court focused on where "publication" occurs in an Internet publication, and rejected Dow Jones' argument that publication occurs where the material is last edited before being placed online. "Harm to reputation is done when a defamatory publication is comprehended by the reader, the listener, or the observer," the Court said. "This being so, it would be wrong to treat a publication as if it were a unilateral act on the part of the publisher alone. It is not. It is a bilateral act—in which the publisher makes it available and a third party has it available for his or her comprehension."[4] This "comprehension" rule in print or broadcast defamation cases commonly leads to the result that jurisdiction will be found at the place where the damage to reputation occurred, which is most often the country of residence of the claimant. The High Court had no difficulty extending this concept to Internet publication, finding that "the material is not available in comprehensible form until downloaded" and thus that "it is where that person downloads the material that the damage to reputation may be done."[5]

The High Court disposed quickly of Dow Jones' arguments that this rule led to the result that Internet publishers would be required to assume that they could be subject to suit anywhere in the world under this rule:

> The spectre which Dow Jones sought to conjure up in the present appeal, of a publisher forced to consider every article it publishes on the World Wide Web against the defamation laws of every country from Afghanistan to Zimbabwe, is seen to be unreal when it is recalled that in all except the most unusual of cases, identifying the person about whom material is to be published will readily identify the defamation law to which that person may resort.[6]

The High Court also pointed out that other limiting factors would be at play, including the fact that a claimant ordinarily will be able to win damages only in a jurisdiction where the claimant has a reputation and that any judgment rendered in such a jurisdiction would only be of practical concern if it could be enforced in a jurisdiction where the defendant has assets.

France. In *Association Union des Etudiants Juifs de France v. Yahoo! Inc.*,[7] a French court ordered Yahoo!—a U.S. company—to use all means necessary to prevent French users from accessing its auction site, which featured Nazi paraphernalia in violation of French laws. The *Yahoo!* case caused widespread concern in the Internet publishing community over the ability of a foreign court to apply foreign law to a U.S. publisher.[8]

French law generally prohibits the possession, sale, and public display in France of uniforms, insignias, or emblems worn by Nazi organizations, before or during World War II (except in historical performances) and the publication of "revisionist" statements and literature disputing Nazi war crimes or inciting racism or antisemitism. The Union des Etudiants Juifs de France (UEJF) and Ligue Contra la Racism et L'Antisémitisme (LICRA) claimed that Yahoo! Inc. and Yahoo! France had made available to French residents, operating from French territory, auction sites displaying and proposing the sale of approximately 1,000 items of Nazi memorabilia. The UEJF claimed in addition that Yahoo! Inc. and Yahoo! France had made available to French residents, either directly or through hyperlinks, two works of anti-Semitic literature (*Mein Kampf* and *Protocole des Sages de Scion*) as well as photographic depictions purportedly proving that the gas chambers operated by the Nazis never existed.

On May 22, 2000, the Tribunal de Grande Instance de Paris rejected requests that had been made by Yahoo! Inc. and Yahoo! France for summary dismissal of the case on jurisdictional and standing grounds. According to the court, permitting the visualization in France or the sale to French residents of Nazi-related messages and memorabilia constitutes "a wrong on the territory of France . . . regardless of the fact that the activity complained of is marginal in relation to the entire business of the auction sales service offered on the Yahoo.com auction site." The court ordered Yahoo! Inc. "to take any and all measures of such kind as to dissuade and make impossible any consultations by surfers calling from France to its sites and services . . . which infringe on the internal public order in France, especially the selling of Nazi objects." The court gave Yahoo! Inc. two months to formulate compliance proposals.

Shortly after the May 22 order was entered, Yahoo! Inc. discontinued its link to the *Protocole des Sages de Sion*. Yahoo! Inc. resisted the court's May 22 order in other respects by renewing its jurisdictional and standing arguments and arguing that full compliance with the court's order was technically impossible. Yahoo! Inc. also emphasized that the Yahoo.com server was located in the United States, the Yahoo.com auction site was addressed primarily to users based in the United States, and the messages and memorabilia at issue in the case were protected by the First Amendment to the United States Constitution.

Yahoo! France responded to the court's May 22 order by adding a section to the conditions of use section of the Yahoo! France Web site.[9] If a user of Yahoo! France initiated a category search that had a clear relationship to Nazism, the following warning appeared: "Warning: By continuing your search on Yahoo! US you may be led to consult revisionist sites whose content is illegal under French law and whose consultation, if you continue, is punishable."

After having rejected again the jurisdictional and standing arguments lodged by Yahoo! Inc., the Court de Grande Instance de Paris held on November 20, 2002, that Yahoo! Inc. had failed to comply with the core provisions of its earlier order. The court gave Yahoo! Inc. three months to comply with the November 20 order, after which time Yahoo! Inc. was made subject to a penalty of FRF 100,000 (approximately U.S. $13,400) "for each day of delay until perfect accomplishment." The court received evidence that there were technical mechanisms that could be used to block at least some—but certainly not all—access to the content by French nationals. Vinton Cerf, who is widely acknowledged as one of the major developers of the Internet, was part of a panel of experts who testified to the methods that could be employed.[10]

Germany. On December 12, 2000, Germany's highest court, the Bundesgerichthof, held that a Web site based in Australia could be subjected to Germany's laws against denial of the Holocaust and "denigration of the memory of the dead."[11] The case was brought against Frederick Toben, a Holocaust revisionist who was born in Germany but who is now an Australian citizen.[12]

In the *Toben* case, the trial court found that Toben's Australian Web site, as well as paper pamphlets distributed in Germany by Toben, violated the German criminal law provision against the denial of the Holocaust.[13] Toben was arrested while traveling in Germany, tried, and sentenced to 10 months in prison. He appealed his conviction, arguing that German law could not apply to an Australian Web site. An intermediate appellate court agreed with

Toben and held that German speech laws could only be applied against German Web sites. But the highest court in Germany disagreed and reinstated Toben's sentence. Toben reportedly has returned to Australia and has challenged German authorities to attempt his extradition to Germany.

Italy. Two actions in Italy have raised concerns about extraterritorial application of Italian law against Internet content. First, an Italian court has issued a ruling asserting its jurisdiction over an alleged incident of libel carried out online.[14] An Italian father took his minor daughters from Israel where they had been living with their mother and adhering to an "ultra-orthodox" form of Judaism. A Web site, the content of which was created and hosted outside of Italy, invited Jews to "free" the girls from the captivity imposed by their father, criticizing him for preventing his daughters' profession of Judaism. The father complained to the Italian prosecutorial authorities that the Web sites in question defamed him, and the prosecutor initiated a criminal prosecution for defamation. The lower court dismissed the case for lack of jurisdiction because the Web sites were not published in Italy.

An Italian appeals court reversed the lower court's dismissal for lack of jurisdiction, finding that although the Web sites were "published abroad," the offense was within the jurisdiction of the Italian courts. Under the Italian penal code, an offense is considered to have been committed within Italian territory when the act or omission, or even the effects of the act or omission, occurred within Italy. Thus, an Italian court could have jurisdiction over suits about Internet content based on an allegation that the content caused the complainant harm in Italy, regardless of where the content was published.

Second, on July 9, 2002, Italian police closed five Web sites that were critical of the Catholic Church, despite the fact that the sites were hosted in the United States. The Italian authors of the Web sites, which had names that translate to *Pig Madonna* and *Blasphemy*, are being prosecuted under Italian laws criminalizing blasphemy and the publication of sacrilegious material. The sites were closed without the involvement of any court, in Italy or the United States. The police investigating the sites simply accessed the computer by which the defendants uploaded content to the U.S. hosting services that published the sites and replaced the allegedly illegal content with a police crest.[15] Although this action concerned only Italian citizens and thus can be seen as less intrusive into U.S. speech rights, it is worth pointing out that the unilateral actions of Italian law enforcement did alter content hosted within the United States.

Zimbabwe. Andrew Meldrum, an American journalist writing for *The Guardian,* a London newspaper, has become the first foreign journalist to be prosecuted under Zimbabwe's new press law. The law, the Access to Information and Protection of Privacy Bill, came into force in March 2002 and has been widely criticized as violating international norms on freedom of expression. Meldrum is being prosecuted on charges of "abuse of journalistic privileges by publishing falsehoods" on the basis of stories published in *The Guardian* in England and posted on its Web site, which is published and hosted in England.[16] This prosecution is noteworthy not only because of its own significance but also because it may portend a trend: criminal defamation statutes are commonplace in Europe, the Middle East, and Africa, and government officials routinely use such statutes in attempts to silence internal critics. The Internet may provide an opportunity for such regimes to attempt prosecutions of the international media as well.

The subject of the prosecution involves a story, which had been reported in the local *Daily News* and which Meldrum verified with eyewitnesses, who later recanted, of the beheading of a woman in front of her family by forces loyal to Zimbabwe's President Mugabe. Although it is not entirely clear that the story was inaccurate, *The Guardian* nonetheless published a retraction. If convicted, Meldrum and others prosecuted could have been sentenced to two years' imprisonment. (Meldrum has lived in Zimbabwe since 1980 as a permanent resident, but also could be subject to a prison term even if he left Zimbabwe and returned there, or entered countries such as South Africa, which have extradition treaties with Zimbabwe.) Conviction also means that the license to publish, which is required by the act, would be revoked and any future reporting or publication by the defendant prohibited (obviously an important consideration for Zimbabwean journalists, and for foreign journalists who report from Zimbabwe).

The Guardian is unavailable in Zimbabwe. The prosecutors in Meldrum's case have taken the position that Zimbabwe's criminal courts have jurisdiction over any content published on the Internet if that content could be accessed in Zimbabwe, which would essentially allow domestic jurisdiction over Internet speech arising anywhere in the world.[17] The act under which Meldrum was charged creates a strict liability offense under which reporters and editors may be charged for any publication that is false, regardless of fault. Under this approach, all publishers become guarantors of the accuracy of all stories published.[18]

On July 15, 2002, Meldrum was acquitted of the charges against him by the district court in Harare. Immediately upon acquittal, however, Meldrum was served with deportation papers. Importantly, Judge Godfrey Macheyo refused to address the jurisdiction argument, effectively leaving the door open for future prosecutions against foreign journalists on the basis of the Internet distribution of the journalists' stories.[19]

European Union Principles of Jurisdiction and Choice of Law

In almost all cases, the issue of whether a publisher will be subject to the jurisdiction of national courts is a matter of the internal laws of the nation in which the publisher is located. One of the few exceptions to this principle is the European Union (EU), which is one of the few multinational entities that has established principles of jurisdiction and choice of law that apply to multiple countries. This section will present a brief survey of emerging choice-of-law principles in the 15-member EU (which will grow to 25 members in the near future upon the accession of several Eastern European nations).

One exceptionally positive legislative effort within Europe may set the stage for a more enlightened view of Internet jurisdiction. On June 8, 2000, the EU adopted Directive 2000/31/EC on electronic commerce (the E-Commerce Directive), which establishes basic harmonized rules in areas such as electronic contracts, electronic commercial communications, and online provision of professional services.[20] Under Section 4 of the E-Commerce Directive, the member states must adopt uniform limits on most types of liability for service providers that carry illegal content while acting as a "mere conduit" or engaging in caching or Web hosting. Under the E-Commerce Directive, which only applies to electronic commerce activities within the 15 member states of the European Union, companies are subjected only to the jurisdiction and the law of the member state in which they are established. This is a sensible rule that will spur the growth of e-commerce in the European market. European companies setting up online sales will have a relatively high degree of certainty regarding the law that will apply to their activities and the forum in which they can reasonably expect that law to be applied. This "country-of-origin" rule is becoming the dominant rule under both U.S. and European law, and its adoption in other countries (and in disputes between various countries) would both foster the development of online commerce and permit Internet publishers to know which country's law would apply to online publishing.

It can, of course, be argued that the concept of a "country of origin" for information hosted on the Internet is not an entirely obvious concept. Reporters, photojournalists, and editors can upload electronic information to a publication from literally anyplace on the globe, and the location of servers hosting content can be manipulated easily to locate foreign content in a jurisdiction where it may be safely published (in the United States, for example). In an attempt to provide definition to the country-of-origin approach, the E-Commerce Directive speaks in terms of the "Member State" where the publisher is "established":

> Information society services should be supervised at the source of the activity, in order to ensure an effective protection of public interest objectives; to that end, it is necessary to ensure that the competent authority provides such protection not only for the citizens of its own country but for all Community citizens; in order to improve mutual trust between member states, it is essential to state clearly where the services originate; moreover, in order to effectively guarantee freedom to provide services and legal certainty for suppliers and recipients of services, such information society services should in principle be subject to the law of the Member State in which the service provider is established.[21]

This principle is sensible because only the country in which a publisher is "established" can fully regulate its activities; it also is a concept that is sensitive to general principles of international law, discussed below, which recognize that one state should not prescribe its laws in a manner that interferes with a sister state's ability to prescribe its own legal concepts.

Another attempt to make the country-of-origin approach more precise is the advocacy of a "single point of publication" rule to determine which country's law should apply to a particular content claim. Under this framework, claims would be governed by the law of the nation in which the publisher last had an opportunity to exercise editorial control over the publication. This proposal, which members of the U.S. media industry have advanced before the European Commission and the High Court of Australia in an amicus curiae brief in the *Gutnick* litigation, is designed for an Internet publishing context in which content can be viewed instantaneously in many locations but there is only one place from which the publisher controls content as a final matter (that is, the point at which final editorial decisions are made and final technical work is done to upload the material).[22] The advocates of the "single point of publication" rule point out that it complements the country-of-origin rule by ensuring that there is a principal place of publication, and therefore the country of origin, for every article. The proposal also accounts for the widespread phenomenon of inadvertent digital publishing: even publishers who attempt to prevent their publications from being distributed in certain countries may fail to control circulation completely, especially if a publisher releases content online. The content may be forwarded without the publisher's consent to other individuals, or it may be recirculated at a later point in time by others. The single point of publication rule accounts for this fact because "publication" would be deemed to take place at the point at which there is a final opportunity for the publisher to exercise control over content. This rule has not, to date, been adopted.

The country-of-origin approach is not, however, the sole view on jurisdiction and choice of law in the European Union. There are emerging elements in European law that are legitimate areas for concern in the publishing community. Two seminal accords, the Brussels convention,[23] dealing with interstate enforcement of judgments, and the Rome convention,[24] dealing with enforcement of contracts, generally adopt a positive country-of-origin rule. However, both provide that under particular limited circumstances, consumers should be allowed to rely on local consumer protection laws instead of the laws of the country of origin.[25] Although this "local loophole" does not apply to disputes over Internet content, it does demonstrate a potential precedent in favor of permitting individuals to take actions against Internet companies in their own countries.

This consumer-centered approach has, in fact, been extended to proposals to permit claimants to pursue defamation suits in their own countries regardless of the nationality of the publisher of the alleged libel. In June 2002, the Justice and Home Affairs Council of the European Commission commenced a consultation proposing to apply the law of the country in which the plaintiff resides to any tort action based on Internet content.[26] This approach, if adopted, could have broad repercussions for publishers not only in Europe but throughout the world. Proposed Article 7 of the regulation on defamation provides as follows:

> The law applicable to a noncontractual obligation arising from a violation of private or personal rights or from defamation shall be the law of the country where the victim is habitually resident at the time of the tort or delict.

Although this regulation would be binding formally only on EU member states (and it is unclear whether all EU member states, and in particular the United Kingdom, would agree to implement it), the precedential effect of an action by one of the most influential regional political bodies in the world cannot be understated. The process of moving through the steps required to convert a consultation proposal into a binding directive, however, is a slow one. The process may take years, particularly given the controversy attached to this proposal, and initial comments were only received in late 2002.[27]

This regulation would follow the basic approach set in the Brussels Regulation, which was adopted on November 30, 2000, by the Justice and Home Affairs Council of the European Union to govern consumer contract jurisdiction. This regulation provides, in short, that the courts of the country where a consumer resides will have jurisdiction over consumer-protection disputes when the merchant "pursues commercial or professional activities in the Member State of the consumer's domicile or by any means directs such activities to that Member State . . . and the contract falls within the scope of such activities."

Not surprisingly, Internet companies and publishers are deeply involved in advocating the country-of-origin approach taken by the E-Commerce Directive rather than the plaintiff-focused approach taken by the Brussels Regulation and the new proposed regulation for jurisdiction over noncontractual harm. Other arguments may, of course, be raised against the imposition of national law against an

250

international medium such as the Internet, including arguments based on treaties such as the European Convention for Human Rights and other similar documents, as well as public international law principles generally (discussed below).

U.S. Courts' Refusal to Enforce Foreign Libel Judgments That Do Not Comply with the First Amendment

As a practical matter the assertion of jurisdiction over U.S. media companies who do not maintain substantial assets abroad will be limited by the fact that the jurisdictional requirements of U.S. law must be satisfied for those judgments to be enforced, at least insofar as such requirements are grounded in the constitutional guarantee of due process. The Restatement (Third) of the Foreign Relations Law of the United States § 482 explains that "[a] court in the United States may not recognize a judgment of the court of a foreign state if the judgment was rendered under a judicial system that does not provide . . . procedures compatible with due process of Law." The Supreme Court has repeatedly made clear that jurisdictional standards of minimum contacts and purposeful availment are rooted in the Due Process Clause of the Constitution.[28] Accordingly, U.S. courts cannot enforce a foreign judgment rendered without sufficient contacts or purposeful availment to justify jurisdiction.[29]

U.S. courts generally enforce foreign-money judgments under principles of comity—the respect of one country's courts for the courts of another country.[30] However, U.S. courts are not required to enforce foreign judgments when such judgments conflict with U.S. public policy.[31] Cases in which U.S. courts have refused to enforce foreign judgments on policy grounds have been relatively rare outside the First Amendment context.[32] Within the First Amendment context, however, courts have consistently refused to enforce foreign libel judgments on policy grounds.

In *Matusevich v. Telnikoff,*[33] the leading case in the area, the plaintiff brought an action to preclude enforcement of a British libel judgment. The U.S. District Court for the District of Columbia granted the defendant's motion for summary judgment, holding that recognition of the British judgment would violate both Maryland's Uniform Foreign-Money Judgments Act (which tracks, almost exactly, the U.S. act) and the First and Fourteenth Amendments to the U.S. Constitution. In so holding, the court compared the differing libel

251

standards of the English and U.S. jurisdictions. The court then determined that the speech found libelous under English law would have been protected by the First Amendment in a U.S. action. Emphasizing the drastic distinction between the two standards,[34] the court determined that it would not enforce the judgment.[35]

In the most recent and high-profile application of the *Matusevich* principle, Yahoo! Inc. succeeded in its efforts to avoid French jurisdiction over the dispute concerning Nazi speech on its global Internet site. In *Yahoo! Inc. v. La Ligue Contre Le Racisme et L'Antisemitisme*,[36] Yahoo! succeeded in its arguments that the French court's orders "are not recognizable or enforceable because they violate the U.S. and California public policy of protecting free speech" and because they "constitute an unconstitutional prior restraint on speech that is protected by the First Amendment to the U.S. Constitution and by Article I of the Constitution of California."[37] The district court first held, importantly, that it did have jurisdiction over the French defendants against whom Yahoo! initiated its U.S. action (the plaintiffs in the French action) by virtue of the fact that they sought to avail themselves of the benefits of U.S. law by, among other things, serving Yahoo! with their French complaint with the assistance of U.S. marshals.[38] It then granted summary judgment to Yahoo! Inc., preventing enforcement of the French judgment against it. An appeal of this decision currently is pending in the United States Court of Appeals for the Ninth Circuit, and a decision is expected during 2003.

This decision illustrates a new strategic avenue for the defense of foreign actions by U.S. Internet publishers. Although publishers with assets and subsidiaries in foreign countries always will be vulnerable to off-shore litigation and the enforcement of foreign judgments against those assets and subsidiaries, the *Yahoo!* decision makes clear that the *Matusevitch* doctrine applies with full force and effect to Internet publishing in contexts additional to defamation judgments. In *Yahoo!*, the matter at stake was not defamation—as it has been in most cases in which U.S. courts have refused to enforce foreign judgments—but other speech that was protected by the First Amendment. This case thus makes it more feasible for U.S. Internet publishers to extend the *Matusevich* doctrine to cases involving invasion of privacy, the increasingly controversial area of hate speech that is criminalized under the laws of many European countries, prosecutions for newsgathering offenses, and the like.

The *Matusevitch* principle has been applied straightforwardly in a variety of different factual contexts outside of the Internet. In *Abdullah v. Sheridan Square Press*,[39] for example, the U.S. District Court for the Southern District of New York, applying New York choice-of-law doctrine, refused to apply British libel law in an action by a former Jordanian army officer living in Britain against a New York publisher because "establishment of a claim for libel under the British law of defamation would be antithetical to the First Amendment protection accorded the defendants."[40] In *Bachchan v. India Abroad Publications, Inc.*,[41] an Indian national sought to enforce a British libel judgment granted by the High Court of Justice in London against the New York operator of a news service; the court held that the values underlying the First Amendment "would be seriously jeopardized by the entry of foreign libel judgments granted pursuant to standards deemed antithetical to the protections afforded the press by the constitution."[42]

The principle has been applied in suits initiated in U.S. courts as well. In *Desai v. Hersh*,[43] for example, the former Prime Minister of India asked a U.S. court to apply Indian defamation law in a suit against the U.S. author of an allegedly defamatory book published in both the United States and India. Indian law, unlike U.S. law, does not require a public figure to prove actual malice on the part of a libel defendant, and the court thus refused to apply Indian law. Notably, however, the *Desai* court refused to adopt the defendant's broad argument that the First Amendment applies to all American-written documents published abroad. The court used the public figure/actual malice requirement as a constitutional dividing line—it held that where a libel action is brought by a foreign public figure in U.S. court, the public figure must show actual malice on the part of the U.S. defendant.

Finally, some cases have applied foreign law but added First Amendment protections to that law. In *DeRoburt v. Gannett Co.*,[44] for example, the President of Nauru brought a federal action for defamation against a U.S. newspaper publisher under the law of Nauru. Nauru law contains no analog to the First Amendment. The court adopted a choice-of-law analysis, rather than categorically refusing to apply foreign libel law, and viewed the First Amendment as one of the policies that should be considered in the choice-of-law calculus.[45] The court ultimately held that Nauru law could be applied, but only as modified by the imposition of First Amendment safeguards.[46]

In sum, these cases illustrate the reluctance, if not absolute refusal, of U.S. courts to apply foreign libel law in American courts, or to enforce foreign libel judgments on the basis of laws inconsistent with the First Amendment. This is perhaps the single most important protection against the increasing trend toward aggressive assertion of jurisdiction over Internet content claims by courts outside the United States.

One troubling aspect of the recent development in this area of constitutional law has been the questioning of the validity of the *Matusevich* doctrine by the American Law Institute (ALI), a group of judges, lawyers, and professors founded in 1923 that publishes proposed model legislation and influential "restatements" of the law in various areas to provide guidance to courts in interpreting U.S. law. ALI currently is drafting a model act on "International Jurisdiction and Recognition of Judgments," and its reporter's notes on the December 2002 discussion of the *Matusevich* doctrine raise questions about its necessity and proper scope:

> The appropriate scope for the public policy exception has given rise to sharp debate in the context of several recent libel cases in the United States. . . . Several aspects of [the public policy exception] are raised by these cases. The first is whether the differences between American and English libel law—with respect to issues such as the standard for liability in actions brought against the press and differences over where the burden of proof lies—are so fundamental that they are repugnant to basic concepts of justice and decency in the United States. That issue remains subject to intense debate. [Citations omitted.] The second aspect relates to the territorial connection or nexus with American interests necessary to trigger the exception of U.S. public policy. If the reason for enforcement in the United States is simply the presence of assets here, the values represented in differences about the limits of free expression do not appear to be engaged. In contrast, where expression emanates from the United States or is directed or connected to the United States in some way—e.g., an alleged libel in Singapore by the *Asian Wall Street Journal*—consideration of the effect of the differences in approach to freedom of expression is an appropriate consideration in the public policy calculus. . . .

It has been suggested by the ALI reporter in charge of drafting these interpretive notes that they will continue to suggest that not every difference between U.S. law and the content laws of other countries should constitute such a matter of "fundamental public policy" as to preclude enforcement of the judgment as a First Amendment matter.[47]

The public policy exception to enforcement of judgments is becoming increasingly important in a networked world. The questioning of the First Amendment value of that exception, particularly at this important juncture in its development, by an influential group drafting model legislation undoubtedly injects additional uncertainty into Internet publishing by U.S. companies and individuals.

International Law

Threshold Protections

The First Amendment, as well as the precedent that has emerged under it, is unique in the world. Although other countries do not protect free expression to the same degree as the United States, however, one should not assume that speech governed by the laws of other countries does not have a degree of protection.

International law, both conventional and customary, protects free expression as a basic human right. The United Nations 1948 Universal Declaration of Human Rights, the model for a host of succeeding global and regional treaties, recognizes this right. Succeeding accords have defined the contours of the required protections, articulating the extent of permissible restrictions on free expression. The International Covenant for Civil and Political Rights provides that all restrictions on speech must be "necessary for respect of the rights or reputation of others; for the protection of national security or of public order, or of public health or morals."[48] Regional treaties can protect free expression as well. In Europe, for example, the European Convention for the Protection of Human Rights provides that "everyone has the right to freedom of expression. This right shall include freedom to hold opinions and to receive and impart ideas without interference by public authority and regardless of frontiers."[49] Provisions echoing this right are often provided in European constitutions as well. This right is, however, subject to significant exceptions for national security, the prevention of crime, the protection of minors, public health, and other bases. Notably, however,

255

this right can be enforced by the European Court of Human Rights, which has a significant body of precedent protecting freedom of expression.[50]

Despite the breadth and strength of these protections, it is clear that the domestic laws of virtually all countries outside the United States do not protect free speech to the same extent as the First Amendment. For example, foreign law typically does not require libel plaintiffs to meet the "actual malice" standard of *Sullivan* or, indeed, any standard of fault at all. In some key jurisdictions, therefore, libel recovery is far more common than in the United States.

Under English law, for example, the defendant must prove the truth of allegedly defamatory statements, whereas under the U.S. system the plaintiff must prove the falsity of those statements (at least in media cases involving matters of public concern). Also, a libel plaintiff need not prove actual malice on the part of the defendant under English law. "In the tort of defamation [English] law presumes malice in this sense from the mere act of the defendant in publishing the defamatory matter."[51] "Even a bona fide belief that the words are true will afford no defence in the absence of privilege."[52] As one U.S. court has recognized, "in dramatic contrast to American law, English law makes libel a strict liability offense."[53]

Despite its inconsistency with the First Amendment, there is no serious argument that English libel law fails to comport with the threshold protections required by international law. U.S. attorneys representing media clients in defending enforcement suits, therefore, should not limit their arguments to the general failure of English libel law to comport with U.S. constitutional requirements. In addition, they should consider constructing an argument emphasizing that England should not impose liability upon Internet statements specifically. To put it differently, they may be able to argue that because of the uniquely global nature of the Internet, England's assumption of jurisdiction over the libel action was unreasonable under traditional jurisdictional principles of international law.

The dramatically less stringent protection for speech under laws outside of the United States makes it important to determine strategies under which U.S. law may be applied to Internet publishing originating in the United States. To determine how this principle may be relied on, it is useful to review principles of international jurisdiction.

Jurisdiction to Prescribe and Jurisdiction to Adjudicate

Section 402 of the Restatement (Third) of the Foreign Relations Law of the United States articulates the "universally accepted" principle that a state has jurisdiction to prescribe internal law so long as such law does not infringe upon other states' ability themselves to prescribe "internal" law.[54] The United Nations Declaration on the Inadmissibility of Intervention in the Domestic Affairs of States and the Protection of their Independence and Sovereignty provides: "No State has the right to intervene directly or indirectly, for any reason whatever, in the internal or external affairs of any other state."[55] Thus, jurisdiction based on territoriality is limited by interstate respect for sovereignty.

The Internet's structure transcends borders. Accordingly, regulation by one state necessarily involves some degree of interference with the law of another. To put it differently, regulation of the Internet by one state impairs the ability of other states to regulate. Because of the Internet's global character, states must exercise heightened care in regulating it; their jurisdiction to prescribe law for the medium is limited. However, jurisdiction to prescribe and jurisdiction to adjudicate do not necessarily provide nations with the same authority. Section 421 of the Restatement (Third) of the Foreign Relations Law of the United States explains that "the fact that an exercise of jurisdiction to adjudicate in given circumstances is reasonable does not mean that the forum state has jurisdiction to prescribe in respect of the subject matter of the action."[56]

Accordingly, an exercise of jurisdiction to adjudicate in the Internet context may be characterized as unreasonable under international law. The Internet vastly increases the extent and number of a user's contacts with foreign jurisdictions. As noted, this accounts for the increased amenability to potential liability in foreign court. Once a publisher posts information on a Web page, that publisher is without an effective means of limiting access to the information. For that reason, when liability is imposed on Internet conduct by adjudication, such adjudication operates in a manner functionally equivalent to legislation. By way of example, if England were to impose libel liability on a U.S. Internet media company (and any resulting judgment was enforceable under international law in U.S. court), the U.S. company would be forced to conform its conduct to English libel standards since it could not escape liability through other means such as publishing the alleged libel only in other countries. Such adjudication thus would functionally control conduct within the United States and would impair the United States' ability to regulate Internet conduct in accordance with its own policy favoring extensive protection of speech. In turn, this adjudication would violate the noninterference principle of international law, under which one nation is not permitted to use its own powers of prescribing its internal law to limit another nation's ability to prescribe its own domestic law.

In sum, the unique nature of the Internet raises the jurisdictional threshold with respect to states' right to both prescribe law and adjudicate claims. Where a foreign judgment fails to account for the special nature of the Internet by imposing liability under law applicable to non-Internet media, U.S. courts should refuse to enforce the judgment. This principle may be extended to other nations as well, under principles of international law.

The Hague Convention on Jurisdiction and Enforcement of Judgments

A treaty currently being negotiated may have an effect on jurisdiction and enforcement of judgments relating to all international disputes, including those involving digital intellectual property rights. Representatives from 52 countries met during 2001 for the 19th Diplomatic Session of the Hague Conference on Private International Law[57] to negotiate the Proposed Hague Convention on Jurisdiction and the Recognition and Enforcement of Foreign Judgments in Civil and Commercial Matters (the Hague Convention).[58] At present, the United States is not party to any treaty governing the recognition and enforcement of civil and commercial judgments in other countries.[59] Consequently, European courts rarely recognize or enforce U.S. judgments.

The United States initiated these treaty talks in 1992, hoping to obtain more equitable treatment of U.S. civil and commercial judgments abroad. Now, in part because of the subsequent growth of international e-commerce, the United States seeks to prolong the Hague Convention negotiations and opposes certain aspects of the treaty more vehemently than any other Hague member. At this point negotiators have realized the potentially serious implications of the treaty, and have been unable to agree on the final form of any major treaty provisions.[60]

A primary subject of contention in the negotiations is whether U.S.-based Internet providers will be globally liable for information-related torts and other forms of content-related censorship that might be enforced in jurisdictions outside the United States. Because the treaty calls for the enforcement of judgments issued in one member state across all member states, if the U.S. becomes a signatory, U.S. citizens may be held liable for posting online information that is protected by the First Amendment in America but is regarded as defamatory, libelous, or a copyright infringement in another Hague member country. Thus, although the Internet undoubtedly provides an avenue by which speakers can reach a global audience, if ratified, the Hague Convention would ultimately limit freedom of expression by restricting that global expression to only that speech permissible in every Hague member country.[61]

The proposed Hague Convention would (a) create jurisdictional rules governing international lawsuits and (b) provide for the recognition and enforcement of judgments by the courts of member states. Article 10 of the Hague Convention draft articulates the requirements for court actions, including copyright infringement:

> The plaintiff may bring an action in the courts of the Contracting State in which the act or omission that caused injury occurred, or in which the injury arose, unless the defendant establishes that the person claimed to be responsible could not reasonably have foreseen that the act or omission would result in an injury of the same nature to the State. The plaintiff may also bring an action in accordance with paragraph 1 when the act or omission, or the injury is threatened in the Contracting State. If an action is brought in the courts of a Contracting State only on the basis that the injury arose or is threatened there, those courts shall have jurisdiction only in respect of the injury that occurred or may occur in that State, unless the injured party has its habitual residence or seat in that State.[62]

In short, a plaintiff can bring an action in tort in the state where the act or omission that caused the injury occurred or in the state where the resulting injury occurred. The court's jurisdiction would be limited to the injury, unless the injured party also resides in that state, in which case the court may have general jurisdiction.

The determination envisaged by the proposed Hague Convention, however, is not always straightforward. For example, assume that party A in country X perceives material online that a party B placed online in country Y. Assume that B's speech injures A in country X. Under the provisions of the Hague Convention, A could bring suit against B in either country X or country Y. This would not seem particularly problematic but for the fact that even when B's speech is legal in Y and every other country where B intends to direct his speech, that speech may be considered defamatory, libelous, or otherwise illegal in X.[63] If a single reader in any signatory country accesses a Web page containing information considered illegal in that country, the publisher could be sued in the jurisdiction of the one signatory that considers the material illegal. Thus, one Hague member country's restrictions on speech may effectively limit speech in every Hague member country because, where one country would have jurisdiction to enter judgment under the terms of the Hague Convention, the convention would require every signatory country to recognize and enforce the original judgment absent specific exceptions.

The Hague Convention would also apply to the recognition of a judgment rendered by a court in another signatory country. Article 23(a) defines "judgment" as "any decision given by a court ... including a decree or order, as well as the determination of costs or expenses by an officer of the court, provided that it relates to a decision which may be recognized or enforced under the convention."[64] The key principle of the proposed treaty is that all judgments issued in any signatory state shall be recognized in all other signatory states. Judgments would be enforced even in countries that have no link to a particular dispute, as long as the court issuing the judgment had jurisdiction under the terms of the Hague Convention, not jurisdiction pursuant only to national law.

Article 25 establishes three conditions for the recognition or enforcement of a signatory country's judgment. First, the judgment must be based on a ground of jurisdiction provided for in Articles 3 through 13 or be consistent with such a ground.[65] Second, the judgment must have preclusive effect (res judicata) on future judgments in the state where it originates to be enforceable in another state.[66] Third, a state cannot enforce a judgment that is not enforceable in the state initially rendering the judgment.[67] Even when these three conditions are met, however, if the state that originally issued the judgment might still review it, a second state may postpone recognition or enforcement of the judgment.

The Proposed Convention also identifies exceptions to the general rule of honoring judgments. Article 28 articulates the following grounds on which a state may refuse to recognize or enforce judgments:

1. proceedings between the same parties and having the same subject matter are pending before a court of the State addressed and those proceedings were the first to be instituted in accordance with Article 23;
2. the judgment is irreconcilable with a judgment rendered [between the same parties], either in the State addressed, or in another State, provided that in the latter case the judgment is [capable of being] recognised or enforced in the State addressed;
3. the judgment results from proceedings incompatible with fundamental principles of procedure of the State addressed, including the right of each party to be heard by an impartial and independent court;
4. the document which instituted the proceedings or an equivalent document . . . was not notified to the defendant in sufficient time and in such a way as to enable him to arrange for his defence;
5. the judgment was obtained by fraud in connection with a matter of procedure;
6. recognition or enforcement would be manifestly incompatible with the public policy of the State addressed.[68]

As a practical matter, these limitations mean that not all judgments would be enforced under the Hague Convention. But they are nevertheless defined narrowly enough that the exceptions will not swallow the general rule of recognition and enforcement. Although the exceptions will result in a certain small category of judgments being unenforceable, most judgments rendered in any signatory state could be enforced in any other signatory state.

The public policy exception to recognizing and enforcing the judgments of other states, section (f), is among the most important provisions of Article 28. Because the United States is not currently bound by any treaty requiring the reciprocal recognition of judgments, it already relies on national policy to defend against the enforcement of international judgments that would violate the U.S. Constitution. In theory, the Article 28 public policy exception would allow the

United States to continue refusing to enforce judgments that contravene U.S. policy as embodied in the Constitution, but it is not clear how broad the exception would be in practice.

Although the proposed Hague Convention's terms for jurisdiction over tort claims and provisions for the recognition and enforcement of judgments are the most contentious with respect to speech issues, other jurisdictional provisions have proved contentious as well. The proposed articles have very different ramifications for different countries and for different economic interests within a given country as well.[69] As a general matter, U.S. delegates oppose the draft convention. Within the United States, however, copyright holders and consumer groups have expressed support for the proposed language.

Prospects for Ratification of the Convention. Whether the Hague Convention will be adopted remains unclear. The United States initiated the Hague Convention on jurisdiction in 1992 with hopes of gaining increased international recognition of its judgments. U.S. delegates, however, now are among the strongest opponents of the present draft because of the potential for leaving companies open to suits from all over the world and the effect such expanded jurisdiction could have on incentives to expand e-commerce.[70] There are concerns that laws relating to content—copyright infringement, defamation, invasion of privacy, and the like—could be applied against media companies in countries whose legal systems provide less protection than those of the United States.[71] Interestingly, the diverse nature of the interests of modern media companies makes this issue a complex one. This concept would be beneficial to U.S. publishers who are concerned about content liability in foreign jurisdictions, but it equally might work against them in their attempts to protect their intellectual property against infringement and piracy globally.

Although the United States has powerful market influence and is still the dominant force guiding the development of the Internet, it seems to have little clout at the Hague Convention.[72] Thus far, the United States has had little success in modifying the treaty. However, as Rep. William J. "Billy" Tauzin (R-La.) stated, "the U.S. Congress will not sit back and watch e-commerce become hostage to old modes of thinking."[73] The U.S. delegates will likely continue to raise objections to the current draft, advocating provisions more friendly to the growth of Internet commerce and to the First Amendment. Negotiations have already been extended several times beyond the original anticipated date of completion, and it seems likely that the United States will continue to delay final agreement on the provisions of the Hague Convention.

Although the delegates representing the United States at the Hague Convention are arguably leading the opposition to several provisions of the proposed treaty, support for and opposition to the treaty divide between specific interest groups. Even at this stage of treaty negotiations, American business interests have yet to resolve their disagreement over the appropriateness of exposure to liability for tort actions across the globe.

Owners of intellectual property and copyrights generally favor the treaty as presently drafted.[74] The treaty would effectively protect their property interests by essentially applying the copyright law of whichever signatory country provides the strongest protection for these interests. Copyright holders are hopeful that the agreement will enable them to crack down on infringements in new, more stringent ways. This group opposes proposals to exclude intellectual property from the scope of the Hague Convention.

Consumer groups also favor the proposal, arguing that consumers should always be able to seek justice in the courts of their home jurisdiction and that home jurisdiction is particularly important for consumers in the electronic marketplace.[75] Consumers arguably have a considerable disadvantage when they are subject to the jurisdiction of distant courts. Consumer advocates ultimately seek the application of local laws for online customers and further argue that it should be easy to have local judgments against foreign businesses easily recognized and enforced in foreign jurisdictions.

Consumer advocates support the Hague Convention's jurisdictional rules because they would enable them to more easily seek redress for alleged wrongs that occur through the Internet. If consumers know they can obtain redress for problems arising during electronic transactions rapidly and cost-effectively, it will arguably contribute to the growth of Internet business and e-commerce. Thus, although they support the language of the Hague Convention as it stands, ultimately consumer advocates think the convention does not go far enough; in addition to making suits easier for consumers who make electronic purchases for personal reasons, they advocate the inclusion of similar provisions for business-related consumption.[76]

Businesses tend to object to the Hague Convention for financial reasons: commerce on the Internet is less expensive if business can avoid dealing with consumer protection and privacy laws in different countries. Business interest groups thus prefer to adjudicate claims through alternative dispute resolution. The proposed treaty would allow choice of forum clauses in business-to-business agreements, but it would not recognize such clauses in business-to-consumer transactions.[77] Companies ideally want a treaty that allows them to impose one-click agreements on their Web sites, because they can handle lawsuits much more effectively if the suits are decided under local law.[78]

Finally, groups such as the American Civil Liberties Union, the American Library Association, and Internet service providers (ISPs) oppose the proposed treaty on grounds that it would infringe on American civil liberties. In light of the strong protection for speech afforded under the First Amendment, U.S. ISPs have not been responsible for monitoring the content of material placed on the Internet through their servers. Under the Hague Convention, not only could a plaintiff potentially sue a publisher for placing online material considered illegal in the plaintiff's country and have the judgment enforced in the United States, but the plaintiff could also sue an ISP. ISPs that do global business fear that under the proposed Hague Convention, they would be forced to monitor every transmission moving over their network, which would mean constantly scanning for copyright violations, libel, defamation, and other speech infractions. Data communications companies do not want to be forced to police their customers' activities and urge modification or derailment of the treaty.

Thus, although U.S. delegates to the Hague Conference oppose the language of the proposed treaty, the conflicting views of interest groups within the United States demonstrate the breadth of implications that would follow from the Proposed Convention. That being said, these concerns reflect only a small fraction of the debates occurring among delegates to the Hague Diplomatic Conference.

The Impact of Online Media Issues. In spite of the numerous meetings that occurred in preparation for the Hague Diplomatic Conference,[79] the media has not devoted significant attention to the impact that the convention will have on freedom of speech. Those who consider the issue commonly assume that the Article 28(f) public policy exception and the protections of the First Amendment will make global laws restricting freedom of speech irrelevant to American citizens. But that assumption may not be accurate.

264

Several recent international cases that involve speech published on the Internet demonstrate the potential for foreign law to infringe on the free speech protections of the First Amendment. The recent French judgment against Yahoo!, along with similar rulings in Italian and German courts, have "set a dangerous precedent for countries seeking to impose restrictions on speech outside their borders" by demonstrating that it is possible to do so when the speech is online.[80]

Opponents of the treaty argue that if widely adopted, it will "lead to a great reduction in freedom, shrink the public domain, and diminish national sovereignty."[81] One valid concern is that the proposed treaty may force ISPs to become policemen of global content on the Internet. Specifically, telecommunications firms and Internet access providers have complained that under some countries' laws they would be responsible for content-monitoring and filtering. Critics argue that enacting the Hague Convention would make "the most restrictive laws anywhere the effective law of the Internet."[82] If an ISP knows that certain conduct will be prohibited in one Hague country and that the judgment will be enforced in every member country, the ISP is likely to either block users in particular countries from accessing its sites or to stop some online business altogether. Ultimately, this would reduce the Internet to the lowest common denominator and enable one country to unilaterally determine whether a particular activity is legal or illegal.

Supporters of the Hague Convention argue that the Internet will not be reduced to the lowest common denominator and that speech will remain protected in the United States because the public policy exception will mean the United States does not have to recognize and enforce judgments in conflict with the First Amendment. Even so, American delegates to the convention and free speech advocates fear that U.S. citizens may lose their constitutional right to freedom of expression if every Web site has to ensure that it is following the narrowest laws throughout the signatory countries. U.S. laws may not protect the liberties of American citizens under the Hague treaty.

More important, critics of the public policy exception note that these exemptions may not go far enough to prevent forum shopping or protect U.S. law. A primary reason the public policy exception may not be very strong in practice is that a country may have difficulty refusing to enforce a judgment on public policy grounds if it wants its own judgments enforced.[83] The United States initiated

Hague treaty negotiations in 1992 precisely because it wanted other countries to more consistently enforce its judgments. Thus, it would be somewhat ironic for the United States to now sign a treaty originally intended to increase recognition of U.S. judgments when it has evolved into a treaty that requires the United States to risk further nonrecognition of its judgments simply to protect liberties that were guaranteed in America before treaty negotiations began.

Furthermore, the United States will not be able to rely on the public policy exception in many Internet cases. A censorship judgment, for example, can be enforced against an ISP in any country in which that provider has assets. In a country where there is no Bill of Rights, the ISP may be forced to shut down a publisher's site simply to avoid liability.[84] Even where a country does successfully refuse to enforce a judgment on public policy grounds, third-party countries with no policy interests will still be required to cooperate with the judgment.

Whether for the sake of practicality or out of legal necessity, it seems likely that under the Hague Convention the United States would enforce orders like the French Yahoo! order in the majority of situations. It is reasonable to conclude that the convention would at least increase pressure on the United States to enforce the judgments of other signatory countries.

The Future. In light of the concerns discussed, it is unclear how the United States will resolve its concerns about the proposed convention. During the two years before the June conference, the United States and many other countries consulted with the public and with private industry to develop a better understanding of the nuances of the debate. Because many countries sought input, many opinions have been articulated, and the Hague negotiators have to face the extremely difficult task of reconciling the different views. According to Representative Tauzin, the U.S. State Department and other interest groups have demonstrated a willingness to either address the existing flaws in the proposed articles or walk away from the Hague Convention altogether.[85] The United States could always simply refuse to sign the treaty produced by the negotiations it initiated almost a decade ago, and because the United States is home to so many Internet companies, its refusal to participate would weaken the Web portion of the treaty.

The document that will result from the Hague Diplomatic Conference is expected to be significantly more complex than the 1999 draft.[86] It will offer alternative texts for nearly every provision of the proposed convention. In fact, at present there are 111 documents proposing alternatives for the treaty's 40 articles.[87] Negotiations have revealed that it will be extremely difficult to draft specific provisions addressing jurisdiction on which the member countries will be able to agree.

The second part of the 19th Diplomatic Session is still to occur.[88] This will theoretically be the final meeting of the Convention. Opinions differ about how close the treaty is to ratification at this point. The chief U.S. negotiator, Jeffrey Kovar of the U.S. State Department, does not think the treaty is close to being ratifiable.[89] Others believe approval is likely and have even expressed optimism that the negotiations might inspire Congress to enact better domestic jurisdictional law.[90]

Early in 2002, negotiations reached an impasse and were suspended. However, in April 2002 a commission met to determine how to proceed on the remaining issues. This commission set up a drafting committee, which has been tasked to develop a new text for the consideration by mid-2003. Comments are expected to be received throughout 2003, with hopes of reaching consensus by the end of the year.

Conclusion

The strongest argument favoring U.S. court nonenforcement of foreign Internet libel judgments is that such enforcement would contravene the public policy embodied in the First Amendment. The cases cited indicate the U.S. courts' near-unanimous adherence to this view, and the efforts by Yahoo! Inc. to use this line of cases to challenge the French court's imposition of liability on it are an important development. It will be important in coming years to ensure that the availability of this line of argument is not diminished by international treaties such as the Hague Convention. It also will be important for advocates of U.S. media companies to construct new arguments based on international law to attack increasing eager attempts by foreign courts and governments to impose their own laws on Internet publishers, and to argue against jurisdictional and choice-of-law rules in the European Union and elsewhere that would extend the global influence of restrictive speech laws while undermining the influence of the First Amendment. As in all areas of First Amendment adjudication, vigilance is crucial; in this area, however, the area in which advocates must be vigilant is the world stage.

10. If It Ain't Broke, Why Is Everyone Trying to Fix It? Taxing E-Commerce in a Destination-Based World

Michael S. Greve

Introduction

The political debate over the taxation of Internet commerce, both internationally and in the United States, seems strangely shrill. In the United States, state and local governments warn of an impending collapse of sales tax revenues, but the scale of retail e-commerce— a mere 1 percent of all retail sales—lends little credence to those complaints.[1] On the international scene, conflicts have arisen over the taxation of electronically supplied services to individual customers. The volume of such services is very low though, and is likely to remain so for some time. Even allowing for the prospect of rapid e-commerce growth (and attendant government revenue "losses"), it is fair to say that the decibel level exceeds the economic stakes. The debate owes its intensity to larger political and ideological considerations.

The Internet is a driving force behind the pervasive trend toward increased competition among governments. Electronic commerce enhances competition by making citizens and businesses more mobile, by reducing the costs of transborder transactions, and by "disintermediation" (that is, by eliminating middlemen who provide governments with easily regulated "chokepoints"). E-commerce has thus come to provide a focal point for the fundamental debate about the consequences of intensified government competition and the need—if any—to counter that trend through increased government cooperation and cartelization.

In the Internet tax debate, moreover, two issues overlap. The first of these is the general question of tax competition—or, as governments and intergovernmental entities prefer to say, "harmful tax practices." The second controversy revolves around regulation of the Internet and the peculiar problems raised by that still-new medium, from consumer privacy to hate speech to intellectual property questions. Government and business lobbies apprehend that the legal principles applied to Internet taxation might set a precedent both for other tax questions (with larger economic stakes) and for regulating the Internet. That well-warranted perception explains why the e-commerce debate has been so contentious—and why it is important to get the jurisdictional solution right.

The central bone of contention, and the exclusive focus of this chapter, is the imposition of consumption taxes on goods and (in the international context) services sold over the Internet. Cross-border sales—through the Internet or any other channel—can be taxed either on the basis of their *destination* (that is, the buyer's domicile) or their *origin* (that is, the seller's home state or country). The e-commerce debate has unfolded against the background of a con sumption tax system that is largely based on the destination principle. Any such regime poses a central difficulty: since governments typically find it impossible to collect consumption taxes from purchasers, they must use the sellers of goods and services as a choke-point and collection agent. That imperative entails two consequences.

First, since destination-based taxation compels sellers to calculate, report, and remit consumption taxes for each jurisdiction in which sales occur, it generates extravagant compliance costs, especially for small and medium-sized firms.[2] Even with the best intentions (and the best tax software), companies find it inordinately difficult to determine their tax remittance obligations in thousands of jurisdictions with different, and constantly changing, tax rates, definitions, and reporting requirements. Tax authorities, for their part, confront a regime of daunting administrative complexity.

Second, a destination-based system requires a high degree of inter-governmental cooperation. That is because the imposition and enforcement of tax collection obligations on sellers who conduct their business abroad often requires their home government's consent and cooperation. The only equilibrium point under a destination-based regime, moreover, is perfect collusion among *all* governments. A government that withholds its consent effectively places its domestic firms beyond the reach of foreign tax collectors and, in that manner, hands them a competitive advantage. Both in the United States and in the international context, this free rider problem has bedeviled attempts to generate unanimous government consensus on destination-based taxation.

For reasons discussed below, destination-based taxation poses particularly serious practical problems in an e-commerce context. Nonetheless, internationally and in the United States, large majorities of governments—supported by traditional retail industries—have insisted on extending the destination principle to e-commerce taxation. They argue, with some plausibility, that a selective departure from the destination principle would create unjustifiable distortions between e-commerce and sales through conventional channels. Thus, the task is to make destination-based taxation "work" for e-commerce, principally through tax simplification and technological innovation (so as to reduce compliance and administrative costs) and, foremost, through enhanced intergovernmental cooperation.

A minority of governments—predictably, those without a sales tax or with a high concentration of e-commerce firms—have opposed that agenda. Their opposition, however, has been somewhat diffident. It has rested principally on the practical difficulties of subjecting e-commerce merchants to destination-based consumption taxes. That argument has considerable merit, and the first part of this article will demonstrate the futility of applying the destination principle to electronic commerce. Still, the argument has proven insufficient to counter, let alone dislodge, legitimate insistence on equal treatment for e-commerce and conventional industries.

The stronger and more principled argument is that destination-based taxation is highly problematic *even for conventional sales*. Instead of extending an already unworkable destination principle to e-commerce, we should move to origin-based taxation for *all* sales, through all channels, here and abroad. An origin-based regime is simple, neutral among industries, and easily administered: each sale would be taxed once, at the same rate, by the single authority—the seller's home state or country.

Origin-based sales taxation has been proposed in the tax literature,[3] by think tanks (such as the American Enterprise Institute, the Cato Institute, the Competitive Enterprise Institute, the Heritage Foundation, and the Progressive Policy Institute),[4] and in some political venues.[5] The response to those advances has been distinctly hostile. The reasons have little to do with tax theory. They all converge on a single point—a desire to protect and expand governments' tax base.

The modest theoretical case for the destination principle rests on its perceived neutrality: since taxes are identical for all sales in a given jurisdiction, sellers have no incentive to locate in a low-tax jurisdiction. Under an origin-based system, in contrast, jurisdictional variations with respect to both the tax base and the tax rate will at the margin induce sellers to locate in low-tax jurisdictions. For this reason, destination-based taxation is attractive—and origin-based taxation is anathema—to tax theorists who place a high premium on "locational neutrality"—that is, the notion that the tax system should not unduly distort private economic decisions.[6] The argument is plausible—but, as we shall see, only at a very high level of theoretical abstraction. In any event, it has played only a marginal role in the national and international e-tax debate. Tax neutrality requires a single, centrally determined tax rate and base. That is not a serious political option even in the United States, let alone internationally.[7]

The argument that *has* proven politically potent is a variation on the neutrality theme: by rendering sellers indifferent to the local tax rate, destination-based taxation minimizes tax competition. Under an origin-based regime, in contrast, the local sales tax is a component of the sellers' cost structure. Sellers in low-tax jurisdictions enjoy a competitive advantage. As jurisdictions attempt to stem the flight of business firms into low-tax jurisdictions, sales taxes will spiral downward. If sellers are perfectly mobile and transaction costs (such as shipping cost) are negligible, the equilibrium tax rate—all else equal—is zero. For this reason (and this reason alone), governments consistently and vociferously oppose origin-based taxation.

That overwhelming resistance should obviously be taken into account in assessing the political viability of origin-based reform proposals. (I will conclude that the cause may not be entirely hopeless.) It has nothing to do, however, with the substantive merits of origin-based proposals, and on that score, the case for origin-based taxation—and against destination-based taxation—is compelling.

First, as a general rule, tax competition is preferable to an intergovernmental tax cartel. Origin-based taxation, as just noted, enhances the former, whereas destination-based taxation produces the latter. One ought to adhere to a strong presumption in favor of competition unless and until countervailing or independent considerations can be shown to overcome that presumption. As we shall see, however, all those considerations cut against destination-based taxation, and for competitive, origin-based taxation.

Second, origin-based taxation limits the coercive reach of each jurisdiction to its own citizens and businesses. Destination-based taxation, in contrast, systematically reaches across borders and, moreover, requires intergovernmental agreement to facilitate such movement. We should be loath to pay that price—the direct and unavoidable cost of destination-based taxation—even if destination-based taxes could otherwise be shown to be efficient in some technical sense.

Third, even if the origin principle were somehow "wrong" in the context of transaction taxes, it is unquestionably the right principle for many issues of multijurisdictional Internet *regulation*.[8] Precluding a bad precedent for those debates—where the destination principle would let the most restrictive or spiteful jurisdiction dictate the terms of regulation for the entire world—is an added, pragmatic reason for championing origin-based taxation.

The OECD and the Problem of the Remote Haircut

International organizations have devoted considerable attention—and reams of paper—to the problems of taxing electronic commerce. Their emphasis has been on the need for tax harmonization and international cooperation in enforcement. The European Union (EU) has been the leading advocate of that position, although individual member-countries have differed in their degree of enthusiasm. The United States has often—though not consistently—opposed the push for harmonization and cooperation.

The Organisation for Economic Co-operation and Development (OECD) has discussed Internet commerce under the so-called Ottawa principles, agreed upon in 1998. The OECD's averred principles are tax neutrality between electronic and conventional commerce, administrative efficiency, certainty and simplicity, effectiveness and fairness, and flexibility in adjusting tax regimes to novel technologies and market conditions.[9] Crucially, the OECD also insists that consumption taxes should be levied at the place of consumption, as distinct from the place of origin of the good or service.[10] In other words, the OECD officially insists on destination-based taxation.

The application of these principles to electronic commerce poses great difficulties. The most vexing problems arise from the already-mentioned fact that while governments can tax consumption, they are rarely able to *collect* the tax *from consumers*. Thus, collection obligations must be imposed on the seller of a particular product or service. Such collection is possible—typically without extensive intergovernmental cooperation—so long as the taxing jurisdiction has a controllable chokepoint. Tangible goods provide that convenience: they can be intercepted and taxed at the border regardless of whether the good was purchased through the Internet or some other channel. That strategy, though, obviously does not work with respect to intangible goods or services. Such services, as noted, constitute only a tiny fraction of international e-commerce, let alone all commerce. If the international e-tax debate has nonetheless revolved almost exclusively around the taxation of Internet services, that is because governments have found it exceedingly difficult to identify a reliable tax collector in that setting.

A consulting or other such service provided through the Internet (or other means of remote communication) differs from a taxable haircut in two ways. First, the "place of consumption" is not necessarily the place where the customer receives it or derives value from it. The seller, for his part, may have no easy way of verifying the customer's physical location. The OECD has acknowledged that a pure place of consumption test would impose "a significant, and in some instances an impossible, compliance burden" on remote service providers.[11] For the time being, the OECD has recommended a rough proxy: the "place of consumption" should be the country of the recipient's business presence or, for individual consumers, their "usual jurisdiction of residence." Even that determination, of course, becomes problematic when the buyer resides principally in cyberspace. Thus, the OECD has acknowledged that "further work is required on appropriate means of verifying" the customer's residence.[12]

Second, the hairdresser typically lives—or at any rate delivers the service—in the taxing jurisdiction. This enables the government to turn him, or her, into a collection agent. In cross-border transactions, in contrast, the service provider resides and operates in a different country. The attendant difficulties are typically manageable with respect to so-called "B2B" services—that is, services sold by one business to another. Under the value added tax (VAT) systems administered by European countries, a firm's receipt of taxable services is a business expense that reduces reportable income. Since firms have an incentive to report "B2B" services, self-assessment and "reverse charges" will ensure relatively reliable tax reporting and collection.[13] The ultimate consumers, of course, have no such incentive. Thus, with respect to "B2C" commerce (i.e., services sold to consumers), taxation at the "place of consumption" means that collection, reporting, and remittance obligations will fall on parties in foreign jurisdictions. Hence, the question that has driven the entire international e-tax debate: how can tax authorities reach the foreign sellers of Internet consumer services?

Foreign sellers—almost by definition—have *some* linkage to the jurisdiction where their services are consumed, which might in some instances permit an imposition of tax collection obligations. On this train of thought, the European Union at one point considered the option of refusing to enforce intellectual property rights for e-commerce products sold inside the EU by noncomplying, non-EU firms. Such strategies, however, pose serious legal obstacles and diplomatic dangers. (The EU abandoned its design in recognition of the fact that the taxable firm might not actually own the intellectual property rights.)[14]

The only plausible (and permissible) chokepoint is the foreign seller's physical presence—through an office or a subsidiary—in the taxing jurisdiction. Foreign firms presumably attach some economic value to that presence, and they may tolerate an expropriation of that value and submit to tax collection obligations—up to a point. That point, though, is hard to identify. In any event, for sellers *without* any in-country presence, the imposition of collection and remittance obligations requires the cooperation of the service provider's jurisdiction.

The OECD has committed itself to a post-Ottawa agenda of "developing options for ensuring the continued effective administration and collection of consumption taxes."[15] Although that endeavor is to be undertaken in a spirit of cooperation and consultation among governments and affected industries, the actual agenda is the construction of intergovernmental mechanisms for the collection of consumption taxes on international B2C services. The OECD has entrusted that process to its Committee on Fiscal Affairs.

275

Post-Ottawa, the Committee on Fiscal Affairs and its subcommittees have examined several options. In particular, in an effort to reduce industry resistance to destination-based taxation, the OECD committees studied technological options to reduce the compliance costs that sellers would confront under a destination-based system— but found that such technologies are currently unavailable.[16] For the time being, the OECD favors "some form of registration-based mechanism for B2C transactions," meaning that foreign sellers should voluntarily register for tax reporting and payment obligations in the country where their services were purchased. The OECD acknowledges that this system "has its shortcomings"[17]—for the affected industries, inordinate compliance costs; for governments, substantial underreporting and enforcement problems.

Even so, the OECD remains confident of its general direction. Some business sectors have argued for a zero tax rate, observing that B2C commerce—and especially B2C commerce carried on from wholly remote locations—constitutes only a tiny fraction of international commerce and of OECD countries' revenues. OECD bodies have rejected those proposals with uncharacteristic clarity. The no-tax option, the OECD has proclaimed, would generate an intolerable preference for e-commerce, while the alternative of zero taxation for all transborder services (through whatever channel) would produce an "unacceptable erosion of the tax base."[18] The OECD's insistence on tax neutrality between electronic and conventional commerce, coupled with its insistence on protecting each country's local tax base, dictates the organization's agenda—a single-minded search for viable B2C tax collection mechanisms. Those, in turn, will "necessitate a very strong level of administrative cooperation" among member-countries' tax authorities.[19] The OECD is committed to generating that cooperation.

Destination Taxes for Thee: The European Union

The EU's thinking about e-commerce taxation has developed in tandem with the OECD's. More precisely, the OECD has served as a quasi-global stage for the EU and its member-states' e-commerce ambitions. The EU formulated its e-commerce position in anticipation of the Ottawa Conference, where the OECD adopted the EU's principles without major change or qualification. But while the OECD and its various committees have since kept talking, the EU has put its policies into practice—unilaterally, as it were, and in a rather dramatic form.

In May 2002, the European Union's Council of Ministers adopted amendments to the so-called Sixth VAT Directive.[20] The new rules, scheduled to take effect in July 2003, address "electronically supplied services" (not goods) provided by non-EU firms to parties inside the EU. The amendments subject such services to the VAT. At the same time, the new rules exempt from the VAT services supplied by EU businesses to parties outside the EU.

The directive reiterates the EU's long-standing position that things of value provided through the Internet should be considered services rather than goods. It adopts a broad understanding of "services," including (among other things) Web site supply and maintenance; software and upgrades; the supply of images, text, and information; provision of database access; and distance teaching— anything transmitted through the Internet for consideration. (The directive helpfully clarifies that the exchange of e-mails per se does not constitute an "electronically supplied service.") Unlike proposals floated earlier by the EU, the directive contains no *de minimis* exemption for small firms or low-volume sales. *Every* service and firm is subject to the tax scheme.

For business-to-business commerce, the VAT on electronic services is administered through self-assessment by the European business receiving the service (whether from inside or outside the EU). The rules for B2C services—that is, services provided to individual customers inside the EU—are considerably more complicated:

- If the seller has a permanent establishment in an EU country and supplies consumers from outside the EU, it must register and account for the VAT in each EU country where it supplies services. If such a firm supplies services from its European establishment, it will owe VAT in the country where its establishment is located.
- Firms without a fixed European establishment may choose to register with a single country inside the EU for VAT reporting and payment purposes. (The country of registration will distribute the proceeds to each member country.) Registered firms must file VAT returns each quarter. They must report their total sales and VAT due for each EU country where sales have been

made, and they must retain their records for 10 years. Evasion of the tax and reporting obligation may entail deregistration of the business as well as civil and criminal prosecution by the country of registration or the country where the VAT has been or should have been paid.

The EU shouts its commitment to tax neutrality—among electronic and conventional commerce, and among sellers from different countries—from the rooftops. The e-commerce amendments to the VAT Directive are purportedly designed to advance that objective—but conspicuously fail to accomplish it. The point bears emphasis and italics: *internally, with respect to services supplied from EU countries to EU consumers, the EU generally administers an origin-based tax regime.* Each firm must report and pay the VAT only once—in its home country. The applicable rate is that of the *origin* country (except for services rendered to non-EU customers, where the applicable rate is zero). Non-EU firms with a physical presence inside the EU will enjoy the same treatment. Not so, however, with entirely foreign firms: they will be subject to the rules of the *destination* country. Thus, a Luxembourg firm, or a U.S. firm with an office in that country, will pay a 15 percent VAT for services rendered anywhere in the EU, including Sweden. A U.S. firm without a European presence—even one that chooses Luxembourg as its country of registration—will, for the same service to the same Swedish customer, owe Sweden's VAT of 25 percent.

Leading e-commerce firms outside the EU—U.S. firms, to name the devil—have complained vociferously about the EU's directive. They have found an open ear at the U.S. Department of Commerce, which protested the EU policy before its enactment and is at this time weighing formal international complaints against the EU's unilateral measure. The Commerce Department has complained both about the inordinate compliance costs that the EU has chosen to inflict and about the infringement on tax neutrality between EU and non-EU firms.[21] As a matter of economics, the American complaints seem overwrought—because the volume of B2C e-commerce is so small; because the disadvantages suffered by U.S. firms vis-à-vis low-VAT firms in the European market may be compensated by competitive advantages vis-à-vis Swedish firms; because U.S. firms sell electronic services that cannot be obtained from European firms at any price;

and because the establishment of a parity-ensuring European presence—for U.S. firms that do significant business in Europe—is a relatively low-cost proposition. The force of the American objections is that the EU is, in the end, perfectly willing to betray the very principles—tax neutrality and destination-based taxation—that purportedly command the awkward and inefficient tax regime that it has chosen to inflict on non-EU firms.

The U.S. Debate: "Simplification"?

The question of taxing remote *services*, which has preoccupied the OECD and the EU, has played no role in the United States, for the simple reason that intangible goods and services are generally not subject to sales or other consumption taxes in the U.S.[22] The vast majority of states, however, as well as more than 7,500 local jurisdictions, tax the sale of tangible goods; and, unlike actual countries, U.S. jurisdictions cannot intercept and tax those goods at their borders. Thus, the fear that e-commerce might evade local taxation by substituting "remote" Internet purchases for local transactions—a very minor concern in the international arena—has dominated the e-commerce debate in the United States. In all other structural respects, however, the American debate has run parallel to the international debate—and, in drearily predictable ways, to earlier U.S. debates over the taxation of interstate commerce in general and catalogue sales in particular.[23]

In the 1930s, the U.S. Supreme Court permitted states (and local jurisdictions) to levy a "use tax" on out-of-state goods. Although such taxes patently discriminate against out-of-state producers and sellers, the Court justified them as "offsets" for equivalent sales taxes imposed on domestic sellers. Ever since, the problem has been how and from whom state and local jurisdictions may collect use taxes. Consumers, as noted, are unlikely to report their use tax obligations (except for purchases that are subject to independent registration requirements, such as boats and automobiles). Here, as in the international context, the seller emerges as the only plausible collection agent.

In the *Quill* decision of 1992,[24] a case arising over the taxability of interstate catalogue sales, the U.S. Supreme Court ruled that states may impose use tax collection obligations only if the seller has a "nexus" (such as a physical presence) in the taxing jurisdiction.

State tax authorities and courts have interpreted this requirement in widely varying ways, including very expansive ways.[25] It has remained clear, however, that the routine use of the postal service or local roads for service delivery does not constitute a sufficient "nexus" for purposes of taxation. The accessibility of a Web server for customers in a given state does not satisfy that requirement either. Thus, the *Quill* regime creates a de facto taxation difference between local sales and "remote" sales—that is, sales by companies without a nexus to the taxing jurisdiction. A book sale through the local store—and usually even through Barnes&Noble.com—will be taxable at the local sales tax rate and be collected from the seller. The equivalent sale from Amazon.com (outside the company's home state) will be subject to the local *use* tax. But since that tax can be collected neither from the buyer nor from the company—which has no nexus to the taxing jurisdiction—the sale will in effect be "tax free."

State and local governments have implored Congress to lift the *Quill* restriction on taxing remote sales. That proposal enjoys the support of "bricks-and-mortar" firms and industries, which suffer a competitive disadvantage under the extant tax regime. Congress has so far resisted those entreaties. In the (misleadingly named) Internet Tax Freedom Act of 1998,[26] Congress enacted a three-year moratorium on "special and discriminatory" taxes on Internet commerce while leaving the *Quill* regime intact. That arrangement was extended in 2001 for another two years.

Unable to have their way in Congress, states and intergovernmental organizations—the Multistate Tax Commission, the Federation of Tax Administrators, and the National Council of State Legislatures—have initiated the so-called Streamlined Sales Tax Project (SSTP). The SSTP rests on the same formula as the OECD's Ottawa principles: tax sales—including remote sales—at the place of consumption; enhance intergovernmental cooperation and policy coordination; and facilitate tax administration and reduce compliance costs. The SSTP hopes to achieve the latter objectives through a combination of centralization, harmonization, and technological innovation. Sellers, who currently have to calculate, charge, and remit use taxes in every jurisdiction where they have a "nexus" and make a sale, would report sales and the customer's location to a single entity (the SSTP).

States would "simplify" the sales and use the tax regime by harmonizing the tax base (though not necessarily the tax rates) both internally, among local jurisdictions, and across states. Sophisticated computer software, it is hoped, will permit a prompt, accurate, and inexpensive calculation of tax obligations.

For the time being, the SSTP is voluntary both for states and for participating industries. Thirty-four states have worked out a seventy-page compendium containing common definitions for tangible goods. The agreement will take effect when at least ten states agree to bring their sales and use tax regimes in line with the agreement. The SSTP states hope to achieve that goal over the coming year.[27] Despite the protagonists' determined effort to put on a cheerful face, though, the SSTP is facing intractable obstacles on all fronts—technology, simplification, and harmonization.

The SSTP has sponsored experiments with centralized data collection systems to facilitate an accurate, low-cost calculation of sales tax obligations. The first such test run, "involving four states, three technology venders, and one online seller," provided little reason to believe that such projects are technically feasible: only one vender managed to create a working system, and even that "successful" model provides no clues concerning the viability of a vastly larger system involving thousands of firms and millions of customers.[28] More recently, several of the largest retailers in the United States, including Wal-Mart, Target, and Toys "R" Us, have volunteered to collect taxes on their online sales.[29] These behemoths possess the resources to integrate their internal accounting systems with the SSTP. (In any event, they already have to report and remit sales taxes in multiple states.) For the vast majority of online retailers though, existing technology simply cannot cope with the maze of definitions, exemptions, and reporting and remittance requirements.[30] Operability and industry acceptance of a centralized collection system depend on comprehensive sales tax simplification and harmonization.

Those objectives have proven elusive for decades, and not for lack of trying.[31] The SSTP will suffer the same fate, notwithstanding its modest progress to date. Simplification presupposes universal state participation. Several states, however—including New York and California, with thousands of local taxing jurisdictions—have refused to participate in the SSTP, and will likely continue to do so.

Even within the SSTP, moreover, simplification and harmonization will remain very limited. The SSTP agreement, as noted, adopts common definitions, and it commits states to tax all items (except food and medicine) at the same rate. From a tax efficiency standpoint, though, what really needs simplification is not the tax *rate* but the tax *base*.[32] The SSTP leaves states and localities free to decide whether or not they wish to tax any particular item. A common-base agreement is politically impossible: coupled with a single-rate regime, it would effectively wipe out the tax autonomy of local jurisdictions.[33] That is not going to happen.

The SSTP is a transparently political enterprise. By demonstrating a commitment to "simplification," the SSTP states are seeking to forge an alliance with traditional, bricks-and-mortar industries. That coalition, they hope, will prove sufficiently strong to force the desired bargain—an extension of destination-based taxation to remote sales, in exchange for some simplification—through the Congress, over the objections of e-commerce and catalogue sellers and their (low-tax) home states.[34] The pro-tax coalition may at some point succeed in obtaining a congressional override of the *Quill* regime. Simplification and harmonization, however, will remain elusive.

"Principles"?

The OECD and the EU, as noted, profess allegiance to established principles of taxation: taxation at the place of consumption, neutrality, simplicity and fairness, and ease of administration. The SSTP and its academic cheerleaders have pledged allegiance to the same principles. Those proclamations are typically followed by an observation that the principles may conflict and, in the taxation of Internet commerce, often do conflict.[35] Thus, the principles must be harmonized and reconciled, so far as practicable. This thinking, though, is one part confusion and nine parts snake oil. The perceived conflicts are not true conflicts. They derive, one and all, from the ironclad commitment to destination-based taxation, and they would dissolve in a world of origin-based taxation. Among all the principles, moreover, only the destination principle conflicts with every other principle.

Consider the perceived conflict between neutrality and simplicity. All admit that the taxation of remote B2C services, and, in the United

States, of remote sales of goods, poses unique and daunting difficult-ies—for sellers, who must calculate tax collection obligations for thousands of jurisdictions and, moreover, may have no practical way of ascertaining each customer's tax jurisdiction; and for tax authorities, who will have a hard time proving and enforcing tax collection obligations. Exempting e-commerce from such obligations would keep the system (relatively) simple, but that would violate neutrality—since comparable conventional sales *are* subject to taxa-tion. Neutrality vis-à-vis different industries and sales channels, on the other hand, will compromise the proffered commitment to simplicity and ease of administration. Contrast this conflict with an origin-based regime: all sales, through whatever channel, would be taxed by only one jurisdiction, on the same base and at the same rate—that of the seller's home state or country. The system would be both simple and neutral. The two principles conflict only under, and because of, a destination-based regime.

In truth, moreover, destination-based taxes cannot be simple *or* neutral. The simplicity point is simple (as it were): since a destina-tion-based regime involves tax obligations in multiple jurisdictions, it will always be more complicated than an origin-based regime. The marginally more complicated neutrality point emerges from a brief look at the real world.

Tax neutrality, the SSTP states insist, commands an extension of destination-based taxation to remote sales: otherwise, e-commerce and catalogue retailers will possess an unfair advantage over local sellers. The tax regime, however, will not be neutral—regardless of its scope—unless it covers goods *and services*. The SSTP states and their allies have understandably sidestepped that problem: in their uphill struggle to extend sales tax obligations, they do not need the added weight of a proposal that would draw fierce opposition from heretofore uncovered industries. That said, a selective commitment to neutrality seems politically convenient rather than principled.

Professor Charles E. McLure of the Hoover Institution, the most relentless and insistent advocate of neutral and destination-based taxation, has recognized this point and argued for the introduction of a Retail Sales Tax covering all goods and services, from all states and through all channels (while exempting all business purchases).[36] In view of the monumental political obstacles, Professor Walter Hell-erstein, the nation's leading authority on state taxation and a defender of destination-based taxation, has described McLure's proposal as belonging to the "assume a can opener" school of economics, a characterization to which McLure has objected only mildly.[37] Even McLure, however, must ultimately surrender the purity of his theoretical commitments. Insistent on neutrality, he proposes an extension of tax collection obligations to remote sellers—and then acknowledges the need for a *de minimis* exemption "to eliminate the burden of collecting use tax on small amounts of remote sales."[38] That rule may preserve neutrality between electronic and nonelectronic commerce—but only at the price of violating tax neutrality in other respects. If the *de minimis* exemption is based on each firm's total sales volume, it will favor small firms over large firms. If the exemption is based on a firm's sales volume in a given state (as McLure advocates),[39] it will favor large states over small states. (Even small firms may exceed the threshold in New York State, whereas even Land's End or Amazon.com may remain below the threshold in Wyoming.) Neither of these implicit advantages is more rational than an implicit preference for one sales channel over another.

Similarly, McLure admits (as he must) that the "troubling problem" of cross-border shopping introduces an unavoidable element of origin-based taxation.[40] New York consumers will board Delaware-bound buses and avail themselves of that state's zero sales tax in utter disregard of the effect on McLure's elegant blackboard scheme. Their conduct presents a serious problem for all neutrality-minded tax economists: the option of cross-border shopping is a function of income and location. (It is more available to rich people than to the poor—more available to New Yorkers than to residents of Salt Lake City.) Origin-based taxation over remote sales—when the good rather than the buyer crosses the border—would extend and democratize that option. Resistance to that policy choice must be based on rationales outside the theory of neutral and efficient taxation.

Real-world experience provides further evidence that destination-based taxation is ultimately unsustainable. In the United States, local sales taxes are based on the point of sale, not the customer's residence or the place of consumption—a fact that the SSTP and its cheerleaders conveniently ignore.[41] And even the European Union has, as noted, betrayed its purported commitments to neutrality and destination-based taxation: inside the EU, cross-border B2C services are generally taxed at the place of origin. That policy may reflect a

284

grudging concession to reality; more likely, considering the EU's refusal to extend the policy to non-EU vendors, it reflects a discriminatory "Fortress Europe" mindset. Either way, the corruption of purportedly sacrosanct principles is palpable.

Why Not Origin-Based Taxation?

If the SSTP states, the EU, and the OECD were seriously committed to their averred principles *as principles*, they would long have abandoned destination-based taxation. That principle, as just shown, puts all other sensible taxation principles in conflict and conflicts with all other principles. Origin-based taxation, in contrast, eliminates all those conflicts and—excepting locational neutrality, which is unsustainable in any event—conflicts with no other principle. The swift move from destination to origin would solve equity and efficiency problems. Amazon.com's sales would be taxed in the same fashion, at the same rate, by the same entity as would the sales of the local book store—that is, by the state of Washington. No discriminatory tax treatment would occur unless a particular state or local jurisdiction decided, for the sorts of industrial policy reasons that often induce jurisdictions to favor some industries over others, to extend tax advantages (or disadvantages) to some sales channel or other.

Administrative and compliance costs would plummet. To be sure, *local* sales in state or country A would be taxed, as they are now, at the locally applicable rate, even if the seller maintained its principal place of business in state or country B. (An origin-based system is the equivalent of a destination-based system with a very tight "nexus" requirement—that is, a permanent physical sales location.) Thus, a company with stores in all 50 states would continue to collect, report, and remit sales taxes in all states. Those obligations, however, are identical to those imposed on local establishments, and they are in any event easily manageable. The administrative headaches, inequities, and political problems all arise over interstate sales, and origin-based taxation would solve those problems. Regardless of how and where a company's products are sold, each company will be subject to reporting and remittance obligations for *interstate* sales only in its domicile jurisdiction and nowhere else.

Although the "place of origin" for purposes of interstate sales can be defined in a number of ways (for example, the seller's state of incorporation or the physical location of its Web servers), the most natural choice is the seller's principal place of business. Among other advantages (briefly described below), a company's principal place of business is unambiguous and easily identifiable. It is, moreover, already defined for other tax and regulatory purposes—in the United States, by the Uniform Commercial Code; internationally, by the OECD's model treaty and related guidelines.

In an interconnected world and especially in an e-commerce environment, origin-based taxation still presents some technical problems and hard cases (for example, the tax treatment of internet sales initiated at a local store). Such problems, however, will arise under any imaginable tax regime. Origin-based taxation minimizes the difficulties, and even its opponents have conceded its theoretical elegance and practical advantages.[42] Their resistance to such a regime—notwithstanding all its advantages—is based on a single consideration: a concern over "excessive" tax competition. All other proffered objections are transparently pretextual, and mostly nonsensical. [43]

Defenders of destination-based taxation have argued that the principle is essential to the purpose of taxing *consumption*. An origin principle, they say, would "conceptually" transform a consumption tax into a tax on production.[44] That argument, though, will not bear even casual scrutiny. Its proponents think of a destination-based consumption tax as a "complementary" tax: citizen-consumers may impose local costs, or benefit from public services, for which the local government cannot tax them directly. A destination-based consumption tax supposedly serves as a rough offset. McLure has explicitly based the case for a destination-based retail sales tax on the assumption that public services are provided principally to households and, moreover, complementary to private consumption.

It is strange that McLure should not care to defend these assumptions, for they are fundamental to his case—and wildly implausible. They may be plausible with respect to tangible, big-ticket items such as cars or boats (although, it bears mention, those items are often subject to two use taxes: the tax on their sale and a tax or fee for their actual local use). But the assumption seems manifestly absurd with respect to the local consumption of books, intangible products, or "remote" services. True, an Internet book sale depends on a stream of public services (such as roads) that are not easily captured.

But why should one assume that all those transaction-facilitating services are being provided by the *customer's* home state, rather than the seller's? Viewed as a complementary tax, an origin-based sales tax is every bit as sensible as a destination tax, and quite probably more so.[45]

Nor is it true that a shift to origin-based taxation would imply a move from taxing consumption to taxing production. First, and most obvious, the place of *sale* has nothing to do with *production*. The sale of a diamond ring by a Delaware establishment may be taxed at the seller's point or the customer's state (say, Texas); either way, the ring was probably produced in South Africa. Second, and more important, the collection obligation has nothing to do with the economic *incidence* of the tax. One way or the other, it is the *transaction* that is being taxed. Whether the seller or the buyer ends up paying the tax has to do with demand elasticities, not with collection mechanisms.

The question is not what is being taxed: in principle at least, destination- and origin-based taxes will cover the same set of transactions. The question is which government winds up with the proceeds—the seller's or the buyer's. And aye, there's the rub.

Under a perfectly operating destination-based sales tax regime, sellers will be indifferent to the local tax rate. The tax depends on the customer's home state, and it is identical regardless of whether the sale originated in a high-tax or low-tax jurisdiction. Under an origin-based tax regime, in contrast, the local tax rate is part of the seller's cost structure. In economic parlance, it operates like a kind of factor endowment, akin to the local transportation system or the availability of qualified labor. All else equal, sellers in a low-tax jurisdiction enjoy a competitive advantage. States and countries will seek to attract firms by offering a low tax rate. Eventually, one might think, the sales tax rate will eventually be zero in every jurisdiction. This "race to the bottom" argument is the sum and substance of the case for destination-based taxation. It is unpersuasive.

As an initial matter, all else is not in fact equal. The zero-tax equilibrium would probably result if sellers were entirely free to designate their home state, or to designate their place of incorporation as their home state. The principal-place-of-business rule, in contrast, disciplines sellers' choices. As already suggested, sales taxes are one stick in a bundle of services and obligations that are being offered by each jurisdiction. Thus, a jurisdiction that provides an educated labor force, an excellent infrastructure, a favorable regulatory environment, a sensible and efficient judicial system, or "quality-of-life" attractions will be able to exact a sales tax or its economic equivalent (for example, in the form of an income tax). An unattractive jurisdiction that drives up the cost of doing business, meanwhile, will be unable to compensate those self-inflicted disadvantages by becoming a "sales tax haven."

More fundamentally, one cannot assume that the downward pressure attendant to tax competition necessarily translates into a race to the *bottom*. On certain (heroic) assumptions, tax competition may compromise local governments' ability to finance public goods; in that event, the race is to the bottom. On different, more realistic assumptions, though, tax competition reduces the "political residuum" that is available to local politicians for purposes of redistribution—without, at the same time, compromising local governments' ability to levy taxes, akin to user fees, to finance public goods.[46] If that is the case, the perceived bottom is in fact a top.

It is possible to paint a picture of cash-strapped governments that are cracking under the strains of global tax and regulatory competition. On that view, destination-based taxation merits support on account of its tendency to suppress, so far as possible, sell-side tax competition. But one cannot simply *assume* that governments act in the fashion of benevolent despots. It is equally plausible (to my mind, more plausible) to welcome tax competition as a much-needed discipline and countervailing force to local rent-seeking and interest group exploitation. The evidence is messy and inconclusive and, in any event, cannot decide the question: one's answer eventually implicates, and probably depends on, one's normative views about the proper scope of government. Those views have to be defended and argued for. The apostles of destination-based taxation rarely bother.

Sovereignty

An endorsement of destination-based taxation implies normative and empirical assumptions about the desirability—rather, the undesirability—of tax competition. That, to be sure, is also true of the case for origin-based taxation. But, whereas a feared erosion of governments' tax base constitutes the *only* substantive argument for destination-based taxation and its extension to electronic commerce, the case for origin-based taxation need not rest on (although it does, of course, imply) a general preference for tax competition. It can be justified on independent, institutional grounds.

The central question in the e-tax debate, in the United States and internationally, is not whether states or countries may levy sales or use taxes on their own citizens: of course they may. The question is whether governments may impose the obligations to calculate, collect, and remit those taxes *on out-of-state sellers.* An origin-based tax regime permits each state or country to tax and regulate its own businesses and citizens as it sees fit. Each jurisdiction's regulatory autonomy and authority, however, would stop at the border—which is precisely where they ought to stop. A destination-based tax regime, in contrast, imposes tax collection, reporting, and remittance obligations on out-of-state parties. That imposition does not necessarily amount to extraterritorial *taxation.* (Whether or not that is the case depends on the economic incidence of the tax—which, as noted, depends not on the characterization of the tax or its private collection agent but on demand elasticities.) In all events, however, a destination-based regime entails an extraterritorial imposition of a coercive regime that can be enforced, if need be, through civil and criminal sanctions. Such a projection of government authority into another jurisdiction is profoundly troublesome, both in the American and in the international context.

Federalism

The United States Constitution rests on the principle of equal, territorial states. How does one structure the horizontal relations among those entities? One possible solution is to permit mutual discrimination, aggression, and exploitation. That answer is coherent, but it is not an option for a single *country.* The only other available principle is mutual nondiscrimination and nonaggression: one state's rights must end where the next state's rights begin. Those federalist principles are enshrined in the Constitution.[47]

If it has proven difficult to make the constitutional bargain stick, that is because federalism's principles subject the states to brutal competition for their citizens' assets, talents, and business. Citizens choose their state. States, of course, would rather have it the other way around—just as every private company would love to have monopolistic access to its customers. State competition, however, is not some flaw in the system; it is the genius of American federalism.[48]

Constitutional, competitive federalism does not bar all forms of extraterritorial taxation. State taxes on hotels and accommodations, for example, are largely extraterritorial, in the sense that they are paid mostly by visitors from out-of-state. Those effects, however, flow from the citizens' deliberate choice of the state, under conditions of competition. (Tourists who detest Florida's taxes can vacation in Alabama.) One can have a long and difficult debate about the precise point at which a retail business can similarly be said to have "chosen"—or, in the legal language of a bygone era, to have "purposely availed" itself of—a particular state jurisdiction (for example, by soliciting customers in that state). The constitutional line is plainly crossed, however, when state A asserts jurisdiction and coercive authority over a company in state B solely on the grounds that that company has established a Web site accessible to consumers in state A.

Against this backdrop, the U.S. Supreme Court's aforementioned *Quill* decision—the focal point of the e-commerce debate in the United States and the target of the SSTP states' political project—is in fact rather scandalous, though not for the reasons proffered by its critics. The decision, as noted, bars states from imposing tax collection obligations on out-of-state sellers unless the seller has a "nexus" (such as a warehouse) in the taxing jurisdiction. Tax lawyers and economists have harshly criticized *Quill* as a source of economic distortions between local retailers and "remote" (catalogue or Internet) sellers. In McLure's scheme, the decision certainly looks like an artificial obstacle to neutral taxation. The true scandal, though, is constitutional. *Quill* mowed down every constitutional principle that would bar extraterritorial state taxation.[49] The only bar to such taxation, the Supreme Court maintained, is the Commerce Clause: the inordinate complexity of state and local tax rules, in thousands of jurisdictions, would impose an intolerable burden on interstate commerce. In that so-called "dormant" application, the Commerce Clause is not a constitutional bar but merely a judge-made default rule, which Congress—under its authority to regulate interstate commerce—may change at its will and convenience. Such an override, as noted, is the purpose of the SSTP.

Quill is (for now) the latest and most appalling entry in a long line of decisions, beginning in the mid-1930s, in which the Supreme

Court developed increasingly creative doctrines to expand the extra-territorial reach of state tax authority. That same judicial trend characterizes related fields, such as the state taxation of business income, and it partakes of the post–New Deal Court's deliberate refusal to police federalism's constitutional boundaries. The constitutional rules and structure, however, command respect even, and perhaps especially, in the face of judicial abdication.

Global Governance

The power to tax is a quintessential exercise of sovereign state power. While "sovereignty" may sound like a metaphysical abstraction or an obsession among folks who fantasize about black helicopters, it is neither. Rather, it is an essential principle of a liberal order.[50] Taxation is coercion, and liberal, democratic government requires that citizens know where the coercion comes from. It requires, moreover, that citizens suffer coercion only at their own government's hands—not some foreign government's. A government that fails to defend its citizens against foreign impositions has surrendered its sovereignty—and, in so doing, has failed to perform its most elementary obligation.

Destination-based taxation need not compromise national sovereignty. In the case of tangible goods, a destination-based sales tax operates—like a tariff or customs duty—on stuff that crosses a border. The taxation of intangibles and services, however, often requires extraterritorial exertions of authority—the imposition of collection and reporting obligations; independent verification of record-keeping and remittance obligations; and the imposition of penalties for noncompliance. Such practices reach deep into another country's governance. They presuppose consent among governments and, in a multinational context, supranational institutions with the authority to make intergovernmental agreements stick.

Well, then: when some international tax inspector shows up at the offices of an American bank or insurance company, the better to verify the company's tax obligations on services rendered in Bremen or Barcelona—pursuant to the inspector's authority under some OECD protocol and codicil—whose fault is that? Should we blame the OECD or rather the U.S. administration that consented to those agreements? Upon sober reflection, we should do neither. We should refuse our consent to any agreement that entails such intrusion and diffusion of authority.

291

WHO RULES THE NET?

Recall, moreover, that destination-based taxation has only one equilibrium point: perfect government collusion. That aspiration requires an authority to corral potential free-riders and to prohibit defections—in other words, something like a United Nations or OECD with teeth and claws. That project is already on the UN's agenda, and it enjoys a measure of academic support.[51] Insistence on the destination-based taxation of Internet services pushes in the same direction. The policy demand and the institutional agenda go hand in hand.

In fact, the OECD's and the EU's inordinate preoccupation with the marginal B2C service sector raises serious questions about the relation between means and ends. The central institutions of the European Union have deliberately used policy arenas that pose seemingly intractable cross-border problems as vehicles for international integration and centralization. (Antitrust policy is a prominent example.[52]) In that same vein, the OECD's post-Ottawa agenda looks very much like an attempt to instrumentalize a grossly exaggerated economic "problem" for purposes of international institution-building and for establishing a precedent to press American corporations into service as tax collectors for the European welfare states. Among all the arguments for destination-based taxation, that is the absolute worst.

The E-Tax Debate and Beyond: A Few Good States

Proposals for origin-based taxation confront daunting political obstacles—foremost, the opposition of revenue-hungry governments and intergovernmental organizations whose institutional interests lie in harmonization and cartelization rather than competition. Still, the cause may not be entirely hopeless. The governments' massive collective action problems, coupled with sharply divergent interests among the affected industries, leave room for sober second thoughts and principled reform proposals. Insistence on the origin principle, moreover, would bring useful dividends even if origin-based sales taxation itself remained stillborn.

In the international context, the United States should take an unambiguous position in favor of origin-based taxation of B2C services. (Most emphatically, we should never consent to anything resembling the European VAT Directive.) Of course, the OECD has already swatted down industry suggestions to that effect, and it will

292

continue to reject similar advances—both because the organization is dominated by the EU and its member-states and because it has an independent institutional interest in promoting tax harmonization. Adoption of the proposal as the official U.S. position, however, would probably slow down the already-cumbersome OECD process. In the interim, it may be possible to negotiate bilateral treaties for the origin-based taxation of cross-border consumer services with countries that recognize the virtues of that approach.

The greater advantage lies in adopting the principle of origin-based treatment as a general default rule for global Internet governance. On such matters as the protection of consumer information, for example—a question that has caused considerable friction between the United States and Europe—origin-based treatment is the only alternative to regulatory balkanization or, more likely, wholesale centralization. The regulation of Internet privacy by the customer's jurisdiction compels service providers to tailor their products to each jurisdiction's specifications or, if tailoring proves impossible or excessively expensive, to comply with the most restrictive jurisdiction, which will by definition reflect nobody else's preference. Since either result is intolerable to business, customers, and most countries, the destination principle will prompt centralized intervention and regulation. That, too, is unacceptable. Under an origin-based regime, in contrast, buyers and sellers will sort themselves into jurisdictions that match their privacy preferences.[53] (If European consumers are as fearful of data sharing as their governments proclaim, they will refuse to deal with U.S. firms.) Origin-based regulation, in other words, is a kind of contractual default rule—an eminently plausible option, and the only plausible alternative to an international information economy designed by political diktat. The case for the origin principle is strong in the tax area; it is still more powerful in regulatory contexts. Principled insistence on the origin rule in every applicable context would help to advance it in each, or at least some.

The U.S. international position would be strengthened if our domestic arrangements conformed to it. On Internet taxation (as on other questions), we can in some sense afford to suppress tax competition here at home and yet champion it in the international arena—simply by throwing our considerable weight around. We do so, however, at the peril of international resentment and recrimination. It is much better to practice at home the competition that we preach abroad.

The most likely scenario for the future e-tax debate is a series of short-term extensions of the Internet Tax Freedom Act, including an implicit reaffirmation of the *Quill* regime. (The current enactment is set to expire this year.) That scenario is optimal for the Congress, since it forces evenly matched coalitions to lobby—and to pay contributions—on a virtually permanent basis. It is preferable to a congressional endorsement or enactment of the SSTP's agenda. In all other respects, however, a continued standoff is decidedly suboptimal. One can easily envision circumstances—a fiscal "crisis" in the states, continued rapid growth of e-commerce and tax revenue "losses," and some cosmetic progress on the states' simplification efforts—that might prompt Congress to enact the SSTP model. That dismaying prospect aside, the existing sales and use tax regime makes no sense for e-commerce or any other commerce. The absurd status quo needs no defense; it needs an origin-based reform agenda.

Constituencies in support of that agenda should certainly advance it in future debates over federal legislation. They should harbor no illusions, however, about their ability to argue the Congress or their political opponents into accepting the proposal. The e-tax controversy is a mature political debate. All the arguments have been rehearsed ad infinitum (certainly ad nauseam), and the principal players are locked into their respective positions. Foremost, the state and local government lobby's shrill insistence on the establishment of a sales tax cartel ensures the swift rejection of a proposal to institutionalize tax competition. A stale debate accompanying a legislative logjam cannot be broken with an elegant theoretical presentation; it can only be broken with a successful practical experiment.

As it happens, experiments with origin-based taxation already exist. We follow the origin principle in interstate transactions with respect to flowers[54] and, since 2001, mobile telephone calls.[55] It may be possible to learn from and to extend those experiments.

One reason why the origin principle has proven readily acceptable for interstate commerce in flowers and telephone calls is an expected reciprocity of advantage.[56] A few jurisdictions (such as college towns) may experience a net export of flowers, thus reaping a benefit from origin taxation; a few other areas (such as those with lots of retirement communities) may experience sizable net imports. By and large, though, states are content to ignore the question (Where have all the flowers gone?) because the flows will average out. So, for that matter, will telephone calls.[57]

It may prove possible for at least some of the non-SSTP states (such as Colorado, Georgia, and Idaho) to launch an experiment with origin-based taxation of all tangible goods: through mutual reciprocity agreements, the states could agree to refrain from imposing use tax collection obligations on each other's interstate businesses. Colorado would abolish such obligations for sellers in any state that agrees to do the same vis-à-vis Colorado firms.[58] To be sure, the economic benefits for interstate sellers in each state might be fairly small so long as only a few states participate; but then, so would the expected costs to "Main Street" merchants and local governments. Precisely the small scale of the experiment would facilitate its adoption. The demonstration value of the project—call it the "Origin-Based Sales Tax Project"—might prove attractive to politicians in states that are seeking to play a role as high-tech havens. The experiment could be tracked, and its results could be ascertained, through an accompanying econometric study. We may find that the sky will not cave in on state revenues and local merchants. That evidence and argument would add a new dimension to the e-tax debate.

America's ornery states are often viewed as relics and as obstacles to a new world without borders. Contrary to that reputation, the best of them might yet make a contribution to a more modern and competitive world.

11. Privacy Protection and the Quest for Information Control

Fred H. Cate

Concerns about the privacy of personal information and the role of law in protecting it predate the Internet, but the development of digital networks and applications, such as the World Wide Web, and their proliferation throughout the industrialized world have intensified and provided a focal point for a global privacy debate.

There are a variety of reasons for this global concern. Many are the result of Internet technologies. For example, since the Internet requires personally identifiable information to provide even the most basic service, the Internet, out of necessity, shares that information widely. Personal data must pass through the hands of multiple parties for an individual to access the Internet, retrieve a specific Web page, or send and receive e-mail. Fortunately, in institutionalizing that reliance on personal information, digital technologies generate, access, and transfer information routinely, rapidly, and often undetectably. But, unfortunately, that reliance on personal information creates an inherent tension between the many desirable uses of the vast store of personal data that Internet technologies facilitate (such as the "Back" button on browsers, "cookies" that eliminate the need to remember passwords and account numbers, and the availability to resuscitate deleted files and access backed-up data) and the perceived threat of these same technologies to personal privacy.

Because of the Internet's wide availability, the ease of connecting to it, and the comparatively low cost of storing, manipulating, and moving data across it, the Internet has become an ideal medium for individuals connecting and accessing collections of personal data. The many advantages, such as real-time access to account information, personalized service, and instant approval for credit transactions, also pose privacy-related risks. Online databases are used for purposes that many people find intrusive or annoying, such as profiling and sending unsolicited commercial e-mail. Warehouses of personal information have also proved vulnerable to hackers, identity thieves, and other threats to data integrity and security.

As these examples suggest, economic and technical features of the Internet have helped provoke a privacy firestorm. One of the most important of these features is that the Internet has evolved as a largely "free" medium. The cost of access and content is largely subsidized by businesses, employers, government agencies, universities, schools, public libraries, and other institutions, even as the Internet is transformed from its primarily academic origins into an increasingly market-oriented medium. This transformation and the absence of significant direct revenue from the Internet are creating tremendous need and incentives to develop the commercial potential of online personal data, for example, by using these data to provide targeted banner and pop-up ads, and e-mail to generate higher response rates at lower cost than traditional marketing. The unstated assumption is that businesses and other entities provide "free" access to information and services online, in exchange for which they collect and use personal data about the individual users.

Rapid technological change and powerful economic incentives have contributed to extraordinary growth and proliferation of the Internet and the services it provides. The World Wide Web was only developed in the 1980s; since then, it has proved the world's fastest-growing communications medium—not only in terms of number of users but in terms of the number of countries from which it is accessed. The rapid pace of change itself creates concerns for Internet users, many of whom are unfamiliar with the technologies involved. Rapid change has also made it difficult for privacy norms or expectations to emerge either among Internet users or institutional collectors of personal data. The multinational nature of the medium has only exacerbated these issues, given different historical treatments of privacy.

The Internet has helped to focus and intensify the privacy debate in another way as well. Precisely because of the privacy concerns it has raised, and the features of digital networks that give rise to those concerns, the Internet has become a testing ground for demonstrating the potential and limits of modern data protection techniques. The Internet has prompted nations to adopt privacy laws, only to discover that the inherently global nature of the medium turns those laws into little more than local ordinances. The Internet has been the setting in which national approaches to data protection and varying cultural expectations with regard to privacy have come into conflict most directly. Meanwhile, while Internet technologies are cited as invasive of privacy, the Internet has also been heralded for its technological promise for protecting privacy (for example, through anonymous communications and privacy-protecting applications such as P3P, the Platform for Privacy Preferences). And it is an environment in which technology both frustrates and facilitates legal measures for data protection. For example, the current technological structure of the Internet makes authenticating the age, nationality, or location of users difficult, so data protection laws that depend on those factors are frustrated. Yet the same structure makes it possible to create meaningful privacy policies and makes them easily accessible to users and suppliers of personal information.

As a result, the Internet has both fueled the debate over the privacy of personal information and the role of the government in protecting it, and increasingly become a major focal point of that debate. Much of that debate has focused on the question of how personal information about individuals can be used and who should make that decision. Historically, six models have emerged, and the evolutionary trend among these is toward broader laws that impose greater restrictions on the collection and use of personal information. Those who advocate these restrictions are motivated by the desire to invest individual data subjects with the right to control information about them. However, these restrictions often take such a bureaucratic and burdensome form that their real effect is to shift control over personal information to the government or to prohibit outright even innocuous or desirable uses of that information. This trend has significant ramifications for the cost and effectiveness of data protection; the availability of information on which democracies and market economies depend; the respective rights and obligations of the government, information users, and data subjects; and the answer to the question, at least in the context of information flows online, of "who rules the Net."

Models of Privacy Protection

Constitutional Privacy Model

Privacy law has always responded to technological change. Concern about technological innovation prompted the earliest scholarly examination of the subject, "The Right to Privacy," in the 1890 *Harvard Law Review*.[1] Louis Brandeis and Samuel Warren wrote that the press, armed with "instantaneous photographs" and "numerous mechanical devices," "is overstepping in every direction the obvious bounds of propriety and of decency." That article and its authors were the foundation of the two earliest strands of U.S. privacy law: protection against government invasions of citizen privacy and protection against injurious uses of personal information.

The first, and best-developed, privacy protection model emerged from Justice Brandeis's 1928 dissent in *Olmstead v. United States*.[2] Five of the nine justices had found that wiretapping of telephone wires by federal officials did not constitute a search or seizure since there had been no physical trespass and nothing tangible had been taken. Justice Brandeis disagreed: "The makers of our Constitution . . . conferred, as against the Government, the right to be let alone— the most comprehensive of rights and the right most valued by civilized men."[3]

Almost 40 years later, the Court adopted Justice Brandeis's reasoning in *Katz v. United States*.[4] The case addressed the constitutionality of federal authorities' use of an electronic listening device attached to the outside of a telephone booth used by Charles Katz, whom the authorities suspected of violating gambling laws. The Court found that this method of gathering evidence infringed on Katz's Fourth Amendment rights, even though his property had not been invaded. The Court found that the Constitution protects whatever one "seeks to preserve as private, even in an area accessible to the public. . . ."[5]

In his concurrence, Justice Harlan introduced what was later to become the Court's test for what was "private" within the meaning of the Fourth Amendment. Justice Harlan wrote that the protected zone of Fourth Amendment privacy was defined by the individual's "actual," subjective expectation of privacy, and the extent to which that expectation was "one that society was prepared to recognize as 'reasonable.'"[6] The Court adopted that test in 1968 and continues to apply it today.[7]

Protection of privacy from government intrusion soon expanded beyond the Fourth Amendment area to include a more general constitutional right against government-compelled "disclosure of personal matters."[8] Nevertheless, despite having identified this new privacy interest, the Supreme Court has never decided a case in which it found that a government regulation or action violated it.

The focus of this model of privacy protection on government intrusion reflects the reality that only the government exercises the power to compel disclosure of information and to impose civil and criminal penalties for noncompliance. Only the government collects and uses information free from market competition and consumer preferences. The constitutional model therefore has little direct application outside the context of government collection or disclosure of personal information. However, the focus on objectively reasonable expectations of privacy, and the explicit balancing of the severity of the intrusion with the public interest in disclosure, are instructive and have clearly influenced the development of other models of privacy protection.

Tort Model

Warren and Brandeis and the concept of an objective standard of a reasonable expectation of privacy were influential in the development of the second strand of privacy law—protection against harmful disclosures of personal information. By 1960 courts in many states had recognized some form of the common law privacy tort that Warren and Brandeis had advocated.

Three varieties of that tort are relevant to information privacy. The tort of unreasonable intrusion into the seclusion of another requires that the intrusion involve "solitude or seclusion of another or his private affairs or concerns" and that it be "highly offensive to a reasonable person."[9] The tort of "unreasonable publicity given to the other's private life" applies when there is public disclosure of private information that would be "highly offensive to a reasonable person" and is not of "legitimate public concern to the public."[10] The third privacy tort is "publicity that unreasonably places the other in a false light before the public." To be actionable under the false light tort, the publication must be both false and highly offensive to a reasonable person.[11] In 1967, the Supreme Court extended the First Amendment privileges previously recognized in the context of defamation to actions for false light privacy.[12] The Court thus requires plaintiffs to show that the defendant knew the publication was false or recklessly disregarded its truth or falsity.

The privacy torts then apply only when the information is "highly offensive to a reasonable person" and either false or of no "legitimate public concern to the public." Because the torts restrict expression and therefore must withstand First Amendment review, they are rarely successful. To date, only one award to a privacy tort plaintiff has survived the Supreme Court's First Amendment scrutiny.[13]

Statutory Harm/Disclosure Model

A third privacy protection model began to evolve in the United States in the 1970s. This model relied on statutes to restrict certain uses of information that were considered likely to pose a risk of harm to individuals. These restrictions—almost always including disclosure—usually took one of two forms. Most often, the laws created procedural requirements that had to be met before personal information could be used. In some cases, particularly when the statute applied against the government, the new laws created substantive limits on certain uses of personal information.

For example, the federal Privacy Act, adopted in 1974 in the aftermath of the Watergate scandal, obligates government agencies to (a) store only relevant and necessary personal information, (b) collect information to the extent possible for the data subject, (c) maintain records with accuracy and completeness, (d) establish administrative and technical safeguards to protect the security of records, and (e) comply with certain limitations on the disclosure of individual records.[14] The Act explicitly restricts its provisions from prohibiting the release of any material for which disclosure is required under the Freedom of Information Act.[15] In addition, the Privacy Act provides 12 exemptions that permit disclosure of information to other government agencies.[16] For example, the Act does not restrict disclosures to law enforcement agencies and does not apply to data requested by another government agency for "routine use." As with virtually all privacy laws applicable to the government, the Privacy Act reflects the balance between privacy and legitimate uses of personal information.

Congress has also enacted many similar laws addressing the protection of personal information in private industry sectors. Laws applicable to the context of financial transactions were among the earliest and provide a typical example of this model of privacy protection. The Fair Credit Reporting Act (FCRA) of 1970 restricts "consumer reporting agencies" from sharing information "bearing on a consumer's credit worthiness, credit standing, credit capacity, character, general reputation, personal characteristics, or mode of living" with a third party unless the intended use fits within one of the broad "permissible purposes" set forth in the Act.[17] The Act requires that credit reporting agencies follow "reasonable procedures to assure maximum possible accuracy" of the information in their credit reports and implement a dispute resolution process to investigate and correct errors. Agencies also must inform consumers about whom adverse decisions on credit, employment, or insurance are made based on a consumer report of the use and source of the report. The agencies must provide consumers with a copy of their reports upon request.

Following amendment of the Act in 1996, consumers have the right to be notified of, and to object to (opt out of) certain uses of personal information (for example, target marketing or prescreening for credit or insurance purposes). In two instances, affirmative (opt-in) consumer consent is required: providing credit reports for employment purposes and including medical information in a credit report furnished in connection with employment, credit, insurance, or direct marketing.[18]

The FCRA and many other laws adopted in this same period each apply in only one industrial sector. They impose few substantive limits on the collection or use of personal data. Instead, they require that consumers be informed of uses of personal information that could pose a risk of harm. Only when that risk is particularly great (and, in the case of the FCRA, then only after the 1996 amendments) do they require that consumers be given an opportunity to object, or in a very few instances condition the use on obtaining explicit consumer consent. Like the U.S. constitutional and tort models of privacy protection, these laws permit most uses of personal information and virtually all that serve a public interest.

"Voluntary" Control/Disclosure Model

By the mid-1990s a variety of developments prompted new concerns about privacy: the proliferation of the Internet and other new technologies, the spread of privacy law in Europe, public perceptions of increasingly invasive press stories, a new awareness of how much personal information is collected and used, and the growth of identity theft. Although those concerns have not excluded the government, they have focused primarily on information collection and use by the private sector. And the remedy that polls suggest most people favor—and that legislators have sought to provide—is to grant consumers a legal right to control the collection and use of information about them. William Safire summed up this movement in 1999 when he wrote in the *New York Times*: "Your bank account, your health record, your genetic code, your personal and shopping habits, and sexual interests are your own business. That information has value. If anybody wants to pay for an intimate look inside your life, let them make you an offer and you'll think about it." Safire concluded: "Excepting legitimate needs of law enforcement and public interest, control of information must rest with the person himself."[19]

This movement toward investing individuals with the right to control certain uses of information about them, without regard to the potential of the information to cause harm or the public's interest in that information being available, is reflected in two models of privacy protection. The first focuses on "voluntary" disclosures of privacy policies, backed up with strict-liability enforcement for violation of those policies. The second model, discussed in the next section, relies on statutory mandates.

The "voluntary" approach has been prominent in the context of the Internet. Beginning in the mid-1990s, the Federal Trade Commission encouraged U.S. operators of commercial Web sites to adopt and publish online privacy policies. The primary inducement offered by the Federal Trade Commission (FTC) was avoiding statutory regulation of online privacy.

The Commission has pursued this approach both with industry groups that collect or use personal information and with individual Web site operators. For example, in 1997 the majority of companies providing look-up services on individuals agreed to abide by the Individual Reference Services Group (IRSG) Principles, which not only establish data protection standards but also require annual compliance audits by third parties and a commitment not to provide information to entities whose practices are inconsistent with the IRSG Principles. The Commission supported the development of these principles and in 1997 reported them to Congress as a good example of effective self-regulation.[20] Similarly, under pressure from the FTC, the major providers of online advertising formed a coalition, the Network Advertising Initiative, (NAI) that in 2000 promulgated a privacy code and provides a convenient way for consumers to opt out of having personal information used to target banner advertising to them.[21] The FTC was similarly supportive of this effort, although so much of its outlook had changed between 1997 and 2000 that, when the FTC reported the NAI code to Congress, it recommended using the code as a basis for statutory privacy protection.[22]

Efforts by the FTC to encourage voluntary posting of privacy policies by individual Web site operators began in earnest in 1998, when it conducted its first survey of commercial Web sites. The FTC reported that 92 percent collected personal information in some form, but only 14 percent of those had some form of privacy disclosure while 73 percent of the "most popular" sites had a privacy disclosure.[23] Nevertheless, the Commission recommended in 1998 and again in 1999 that Congress delay action to give self-regulation— under growing pressure from the FTC—a chance to work. The FTC did recommend, and Congress adopted, legislation protecting the privacy of children online.[24] (One result of this legislation was that it ironically led to the demand for more information from users.)

The threat of congressional action had its desired effect. By 2000, the Commission found that 88 percent of a random sample of commercial Web sites and 100 percent of the most popular commercial Web sites posted a privacy policy.[25] However, while in its earlier surveys the Commission had counted Web sites that had privacy disclosures irrespective of the content of those disclosures, by 2000 the Commission was "analyz[ing] the nature and substance of these privacy disclosures" to determine if the disclosures provided an adequate substantive level of privacy protection. No longer was it sufficient, in the FTC's view, to provide Internet users with notice of how a Web site collected and used personal information; it was now necessary for Web sites to collect or use personal information only in ways specified by the Commission.

This change in focus reflected a shift in purpose as well. The goal of the FTC's regulatory efforts was no longer limited to informing individuals to empower their individual choice. Now it was to bring commercial Web sites into compliance with the FTC's substantive data protection requirements. Those requirements were as follows:

1. Notice—data collectors must disclose their information practices before collecting personal information from consumers;

2. Choice—consumers must be given a choice as to whether and how personal information collected from them may be used;
3. Access—consumers should be able to view and contest the accuracy and completeness of data collected about them;
4. Security—data collectors must take reasonable steps to ensure that information collected from consumers is accurate and secure from unauthorized use; and
5. Enforcement—there must be a reliable mechanism in place to impose sanctions for noncompliance with these fair information practices.[26]

The Commission's 2000 survey found that only 10 percent of the random sample and 42 percent of the most popular sample met these substantive standards. The Commission therefore recommended that Congress give it explicit authority to require compliance by commercial Web site operators.

The Commission and state attorneys general also stepped up their enforcement efforts against Web site operators that violated their privacy policies. The Commission brought its first Internet privacy case in 1998 against GeoCities for allegedly misrepresenting the purposes for which it was collecting personal identifying information from children and adults through its Web site. The primary legal theory on which the Commission proceeded was that by posting a privacy policy with which it did not comply, GeoCities had engaged in a "deceptive" trade practice. Section 5 of the Federal Trade Commission Act prohibits "unfair and deceptive practices in or affecting commerce" and empowers the FTC to investigate and prosecute them.[27] GeoCities ultimately settled with the FTC, the first in a series of such settlements the Commission has managed to obtain against offending Web site operators.[28] Most of these cases have in common that the only or primary offense alleged was the failure to comply with a voluntarily adopted privacy policy. None involved a finding of harm. In addition, the Commission has enforced compliance with privacy policies on a strict liability basis.

In the absence of congressional action to require that Web sites post privacy policies that comply with FTC standards, FTC officials have speculated as to whether it might already have that authority under Section 5's prohibition against "unfair" trade practices. Collecting personal information without notice that complies with FTC standards, the argument goes, might be unfair and therefore subject the Web site operator to liability under a strict liability standard.

But Congress may beat the FTC to the punch. In 2002 the Senate Commerce Committee reported S. 2201, the Online Personal Privacy Act (a variant of which will be reintroduced in the 108th Congress). The Act would prohibit providers of Internet or online services, including commercial Web sites, from collecting, using, or disclosing personal information online without

- Providing "clear and conspicuous" notice generally; "robust" notice whenever information is collected; and an unspecified level of notice upon any "material change" in privacy policy, any violation of the Act, or in the event the "security, confidentiality, or integrity" of the information is compromised;
- Obtaining "affirmative consent" (opt-in) if the information is "sensitive" or providing an opportunity to "decline consent" (opt-out) for other information;
- Providing access and an opportunity to "suggest a correction or deletion" of collected information; and
- Maintaining "reasonable procedures" necessary to protect the "security, confidentiality, and integrity" of information.[29]

Any violation of the Act would be deemed an "unfair or deceptive" act and subject the perpetrator to investigation and suit by the FTC or other competent federal agency, suits by state governments, and private lawsuits if the information involved were "sensitive."

Whether through interpretation of the FTCA or through passage of S. 2201, the FTC may soon be able to require Web site operators to post privacy notices that comply with government-established standards and to enforce that requirement under a strict liability standard without regard for whether any injury has been caused. This is a significant change from the statutory harm/disclosure and tort models of privacy protection, and even further from the constitutional model with its focus on government collection and use of personal information. In fact, in an ironic twist, the same year that the FTC determined that 88 percent of commercial Web sites voluntarily posted privacy policies and nonetheless recommended that Congress compel them to do so, a Brown University study of 1,700 state and local government Web sites found that only 7 percent posted a privacy policy.[30]

Statutory Control Model

The movement to invest individuals with legal rights to control the use of information about them, and couch those rights in increasingly bureaucratic and burdensome procedural requirements, is also reflected in statutory mandates. This model of privacy protection, like the previous one, reflects a substantial change from prior models, as the discussion of S. 2201 suggests. The laws are broader. They invest consumers with greater rights to control the use of information about them. They do so with less if any regard for the potential of the information to cause harm. They are highly bureaucratic, conditioning any use of information on compliance with notice, consent, and other requirements that burden and may effectively prohibit uses of information.

There are many examples. One that involves fewer substantive limits, but many bureaucratic ones, is Title V of the Gramm-Leach-Bliley Financial Services Modernization Act,[31] passed in 1999. Enacted as part of a law breaking down decades-old barriers between financial services, Title V contains three substantive restrictions on the use of personal information: prohibitions on the providing of account numbers to third parties for marketing purposes, on pretext calling (obtaining information dishonestly), and on transfers of personal information to third parties for marketing purposes if the data subject has opted out.

The real burden of the new law is in its procedural requirements. The law permits a financial institution to transfer any "nonpublic personal information" to nonaffiliated third parties only if the institution "clearly and conspicuously" provides consumers with a notice about its information disclosure policies and an opportunity to opt out of such transfers. That notice must be sent at least annually even if there is no change in its terms. The Act provides certain exceptions to the notice and opt-out requirements when, for example, the use of information is necessary to provide a product or service requested by a customer, protect against fraud or other liability, or comply with applicable laws.

The scope of Gramm-Leach-Bliley is broader than its title might at first suggest. The term "financial services" includes all insurance-related activities, real or personal property leases, investment advisory services, tax planning, management consulting, financial career counseling, the extension of credit to consumers by any institution, and any other activity in which a Financial Holding Company is permitted to engage. The law applies to anyone who is "significantly engaged" in one or more of these activities. Moreover, the law restricts anyone, whether or not they provide a financial service, from redisclosing personal information received from a financial institution.

A second and more onerous example of the statutory control/ disclosure model is found in the rules for protecting the privacy of personal health information adopted in April 2001 by the Department of Health and Human Services, under the Health Insurance Portability and Accountability Act (HIPAA).[32] As amended in August 2002,[33] the rules regulate the use of information that identifies, or reasonably could be used to identify, an individual, and that relates to physical or mental health, the provision of health care to an individual, or payment for health care. The rules apply to "covered entities," namely, anyone who provides or pays for health care in the normal course of business, and, indirectly, to anyone who receives protected health information from a covered entity. A covered entity may use personal health information to provide, or obtain payment for, health care only after first providing the patient with notice and making a good faith effort to obtain an "acknowledgment." Notices must meet detailed requirements set forth in the rules; proof of providing notice and acknowledgments must be retained for six years after the date on which service is last provided.

A covered entity may use personal health information for purposes other than treatment or payment only with an individual's opt-in "authorization." An "authorization" must be an independent document that specifically identifies the information to be used or disclosed, the purposes of the use or disclosure, the person or entity to whom a disclosure may be made, and other information. A covered entity may not require an individual to sign an authorization as a condition of receiving treatment or participating in a health plan. The rules contain a number of exceptions, under which personal health information may be disclosed, usually to government agencies, with neither consent nor authorization.

A covered entity may use or disclose personal health information for directories and to notify and involve other individuals in the care of a patient if the covered entity obtains the "agreement" of the individual. An agreement need not be written, provided that the individual is informed in advance of the use and has the opportunity to opt out of any disclosure. This is the only consent requirement under the amended rules for which opt-out (rather than opt-in) consent is sufficient.

Ironically, HIPAA federal health privacy rules originally developed as a reaction to the Act's push for more uniform electronic data standards to make health care and health insurance cheaper and more efficient (just as the financial privacy provisions in Gramm-Leach-Bliley were enacted in response to that law's effort to make obtaining financial services easier). The legislation's "administrative simplification" provisions were aimed at reducing costs and making health benefits more portable by smoothing and accelerating the flow of health and health insurance information. But political demands for greater individual control of personal health information pushed HIPAA privacy rules in the opposite direction. Indeed, federal rulemakers declined to preempt more restrictive state privacy rules, inviting states to go beyond the federal privacy standards. Texas has taken Congress up on its invitation, by enacting the HIPAA regulations into state law but dramatically expanding the definition of "covered entity" to include anyone who "comes into possession of protected health information," "obtains or stores protected health information," or "maintains an Internet site."[34]

A final example of statutory mandates that impose restrictions on information flows, in an effort to give individuals control over even innocuous uses of data about them, is found in the many laws adopted over the past decade limiting access to public records. For example, in 1994 Congress enacted the Driver's Privacy Protection Act.[35] The law prohibits state departments of motor vehicles (DMVs) and their employees from releasing "personal information" from any person's driving record, unless the request fits within any of 14 exemptions, including use by government agency, insurance company, or licensed private investigator. States are permitted to release information from drivers' records if the DMV has provided drivers with the opportunity to opt out of such disclosures. The DPPA took effect in 1997, by which time a majority of states had enacted laws complying with the Act, including opt-out provisions. Two years later, however, Congress amended it to require that states, as a condition of receiving federal highway funds, obtain explicit opt-in consent from individuals before information about them contained

310

in motor vehicle records is used for "surveys, marketing, or solicitation" purposes.[36]

The 1994 version is a good example of the statutory harm/disclosure model of privacy protection, imposing moderate limits on the use of DMV records but then exempting even from those the uses most likely to serve public interests. The 1999 enactment, by contrast, well illustrates the statutory control/disclosure model, imposing a practically insurmountable barrier to the use of DMV records without regard for the value of the "surveys, marketing, or solicitation" activities.

A majority of states have adopted other laws and executive orders restricting access to traditionally open public records, such as hunting and fishing license registration forms, autopsy reports, driver's license photos, and state employee address information, without first obtaining the opt-in consent of the individuals involved. South Carolina has gone even further to ban outright the use of public records for marketing.[37] This may point to the next generation of U.S. privacy protection: not merely burdening the responsible use of personal information with disclosure and consent requirements but prohibiting those uses altogether—substituting government control for even the illusion of individual control.

Collectively, these enactments reflect a much broader concept of privacy protection than previously recognized by U.S. law. These statutes are focused on information collection and use by the private sector, not the government; in fact, some would make it easier for the government to access personal information. They apply very broadly. And they do not purport to restrict or punish only harmful uses of information; in fact, liability under these statutes in no way depends on causing harm or injury. Except for a few specific exemptions, these laws all condition the collection and use of broad categories of information on consumer consent, but they then put in place burdensome requirements that make obtaining that consent expensive and difficult. The very breadth and bureaucratic nature of these laws—restricting both many private sector uses of personal information and access to that information in the first place—increase the extent to which they conflict with other important values and impose unanticipated costs on consumers and on society at large.

The European Control Model

The high-water mark for protecting privacy by creating legal rights for individuals to control most uses of information about them is the European Union's (EU) data protection directive.[38] Adopted in 1995, the directive requires each of the 15 EU member states to enact laws governing the "processing of personal data," which the directive defines as "any operation or set of operations," whether or not automated, including but not limited to "collection, recording, organization, storage, adaptation or alteration, retrieval, consultation, use, disclosure by transmission, dissemination or otherwise making available, alignment or combination, blocking, erasure or destruction."[39] "Personal data" are defined equally broadly as "any information relating to an identified or identifiable natural person."[40] This would include not only textual information but also photographs, audiovisual images, and sound recordings of an identified or identifiable person, whether dead or alive. As a practical matter, the directive does not apply in only two contexts: activities outside of the scope of community law, such as national security and criminal law, and the processing of personal data that is performed by a "natural person in the course of a purely private and personal activity."[41]

National laws enacted in compliance with the directive must guarantee that processing of personal data is accurate, up-to-date, relevant, and not excessive. Personal data may be used only for the legitimate purposes for which they were collected, and kept in a form that does not permit identification of individuals longer than is necessary for that purpose. Personal data may be processed only with the consent of the data subject, when legally required, or to protect "the public interest" or the "legitimate interests" of a private party, except when those interests are trumped by the "interests of the data subject."[42] The processing of personal data revealing "racial or ethnic origin, political opinions, religious or philosophical beliefs, trade-union membership, and the processing of data concerning health or sex life" are severely restricted and in most cases forbidden without the written permission of the data subject.[43]

The directive requires member states to enact laws guaranteeing individuals access to, and the opportunity to correct, processed information about them. Those laws must also permit data subjects to correct, erase, or block the transfer of "inaccurate or incomplete data," and the opportunity to object at any time "on legitimate grounds" to the processing of personal data. Processors must inform persons from whom they intend to collect data, or from whom they have already collected data without providing this disclosure, of the purposes for the processing; the "obligatory or voluntary" nature of any reply; the consequences of failing to reply; the recipients or "categories of recipients" of the data; and the data subject's right of access to, and opportunity to correct, data concerning him or her.[44]

The directive requires that data processors notify the applicable national "supervisory authority" before beginning any data processing. Each member state must establish such an independent authority to supervise the protection of personal data. Each "supervisory authority" must have, at minimum, the power to investigate data processing activities, including a right of access to the underlying data, as well as the power to intervene to order the erasure of data and the cessation of processing, and to block proposed transfer of data to third parties. The supervisory authority must also be empowered to investigate complaints from data subjects.

The directive requires that member states' laws provide for civil liability against data controllers for unlawful processing activities and provide "dissuasive" penalties for noncompliance with the national laws adopted pursuant to the directive. In addition to requiring the supervisory authority to enforce those laws and to hear complaints by data subjects, the directive mandates creation of a "right of every person to a judicial remedy for any breach of the rights guaranteed by this Directive."[45]

Finally, Article 25 of the directive requires member states to enact laws prohibiting the transfer of personal data to nonmember states that fail to ensure an "adequate level of protection," although member states are forbidden from restricting the flow of personal data among themselves because of data protection or privacy concerns. The directive provides that the adequacy of the protection offered by the transferee country "shall be assessed in the light of all circumstances surrounding a data transfer." The prohibition in Article 25 is subject to five exemptions, for example, when the data subject has consented "unambiguously" to the transfer, or when the transfer is necessary to protect "the vital interests of the data subject."[46] Effective October 1998, these became the minimum levels of protection; individual countries are permitted to adopt more stringent protection.

The EU data protection directive is noteworthy for its breadth, its sweeping requirements, and its singular focus on privacy, often to the exclusion of other values. It not only is unconcerned with harm, it also reverses the presumption present in prior data protection models that personal data generally may be collected and used unless restricted. The directive creates a quasi-property right in personal data. Some lawmakers in Europe and the United States have suggested going even further and creating an explicit legal right of ownership in such data. Under these proposals, individuals would own information about themselves. The use of that information without consent would constitute theft, just like stealing any other form of personal property. As political activist Phyllis Schlafly testified before the Senate Banking Committee in September 2002, "I think the information about what I do and what I buy is my property. I don't think it belongs to somebody else. If there's anything the United States stands for, it's individual property rights."[47]

The Challenge of the Internet and the Control over Personal Information

These six models demonstrate a movement toward creating legal rights for individuals to control the collection and use of information about them. Earlier models had focused on preventing harm, protecting objectively reasonable expectations of privacy, and allowing recovery for outrageous disclosures of information that was false or of no public interest. The control-based models, by contrast, condition the collection or use of broad categories of personal information on individual or government consent, without regard for whether that information might reasonably be considered private or whether it has any potential to cause harm. Privacy protection has largely given way to data protection.

Some of those issues relate to the requirements of specific control-oriented laws and the ways in which they have been implemented. Most of the issues, however, are inherent to the control model itself.

The Problem of Not Opting

The focus on control ignores that fact that most consumers, in practice, do not exercise control—by either consenting or withholding consent—over the information they disclose and generate. Polling data, newspaper editorial pages, and political rhetoric all suggest that individuals are concerned about personal information and how it is accessed and used both by the government and private industry. Lou Harris & Associates found in the 1999 IBM Multi-National

314

Consumer Privacy Survey that 80 percent of U.S. consumers and 79 percent of German consumers surveyed agreed with the statement "consumers have lost all control over how personal information is collected and used by companies." Similarly, 71 percent of the U.S. sample and 70 percent of the German sample agreed that "it is impossible to protect consumer privacy in the computer age." In fact, despite the greater legal protections for privacy available in Europe, Americans (64 percent) were more likely than Germans (55 percent) or Britons (58 percent) to believe that businesses will handle personal information in a "proper and confidential way."[48]

Individuals' concern is not surprising, in light of the amount of press and political attention given privacy issues, and the growing prevalence of privacy policies online and off. What is surprising, in view of professed consumer concerns, is the almost complete absence of consumer response to new privacy protections. Individuals are widely ignoring the many opportunities to control information about themselves that laws are providing. There are practical reasons for this that call into question control-based models of data protection.

Consumers are typically presented with meaningful opportunities to make choices concerning the collection and use of their personal information in two settings. The first occurs when a consumer seeks a service, and the business (or other information user) responds by seeking consent to collect and use the personal information necessary to provide the requested service. The business and the individual are already in contact and focused on the transaction for which the information is necessary.

In this situation, individuals tend to ignore privacy policies and consent requests if they can, or to simply click through or sign them without reading them if they are not permitted to ignore them completely. This is especially evident online, where most consumers click through pop-up screens with terms and conditions as rapidly as possible, almost never reading them, and rarely if ever voluntarily click on privacy notices. In fact, the chief privacy officer of Excite@ Home told an FTC workshop on profiling that the day after *60 Minutes* featured his company in a segment on Internet privacy, only 100 out of 20 million unique visitors accessed that company's privacy pages.[49] The opportunities to exercise choice created by choice-based models of data protection are illusory if the product or service cannot, or will not, be provided without consent. In this setting, data protection laws impose costs without generating benefits.

The second setting in which consent may be sought is when the business wishes to use information about a consumer who is not at that moment seeking a service or product. The need for such consent may arise because the consumer is not a customer of the business, the business wishes to make a new use of information about an existing customer that goes beyond the uses described in the original privacy notice, or the business wishes to use information that it has observed or collected from a third party.

The major problem here is the difficulty of reaching the customer who is not currently in contact with the business. Most requests for consumer consent never reach their intended recipient. The U.S. Postal Service reports that 52 percent of unsolicited mail in this country is discarded without ever being read.[50] Unsolicited e-mail, even when sent by a company with which the recipient has a relationship, is often not even opened.

U.S. West found that obtaining permission to use information about its customer's calling patterns (e.g., volume of calls, time and duration of calls) required an average of 4.8 calls to each customer household before the company even reached an adult who could grant consent. In one-third of households called, U.S. West never reached the customer, despite repeated attempts. Consequently, many U.S. West customers received more calls, and one-third of their customers were denied opportunities to receive information about new products and services that they may have valued.[51] Although online efforts to contact individuals might be less expensive than with telephone or mail, there is no evidence that they are any more effective. The difficulties of reaching consumers are greatly exacerbated where the party wishing to use the information has no (and may not have ever had) direct contact with the consumer.

Even when privacy notices are received, the evidence suggests they are often ignored. To comply with the Gramm-Leach-Bliley financial privacy provisions, by July 1, 2001, the tens of thousands of "financial institutions" to which it applies had mailed approximately 2 billion or more notices. Crafting, printing, and mailing those notices is estimated to have cost $2 billion to $5 billion, and much of that cost will be repeated annually. If ever consumers would respond, this would appear to be the occasion: The notices came in

316

an avalanche, the press carried a wave of stories about the notices, privacy advocates trumpeted the opt-out opportunity and offered online services that would write opt-out requests for consumers, and the information at issue—financial information—is among the most sensitive and personal to most individuals.

By mid-August 2001, fewer than 5 percent of consumers had opted out of having their financial information shared with third parties. For many financial institutions, the response rate was lower than 1 percent. A late September survey revealed that 35 percent of the 1,001 respondents could not recall even receiving a privacy notice, even though the average American had received a dozen or more.[52] This is not atypical. Extensive experience with company-specific and industrywide opt-out lists demonstrates that less than 10 percent of the U.S. population ever opts out of a mailing list—often the figure is less than 3 percent.

Response rates appear to remain low, without regard for whether the consent sought is opt-in or opt-out. A major U.S. company recently tested the response rates to opt-in and opt-out by sending e-mail messages describing the same use of personal information to statistically similar subsets of their customer base. One e-mail said that the information would be used unless the customer opted out. The other said the information would not be used unless the customer opted in. The response rates were the same for both sets of messages: Customers did not respond to either.

Individuals' concerns about privacy are apparently not great enough to prompt them to do much to protect it. This is consistent with polls that show that consumer angst about privacy appears unrelated to actual experience with incursions into privacy. Less than a third of Americans (29 percent) and Germans (28 percent) and less than a quarter of the British (23 percent) reported in 1999 that they personally have been a victim of what they felt was an improper invasion of privacy by a business.[53] Data protection models that rely on individual choice are problematic if consumers ignore those opportunities, never learn of them, or are unwilling to respond in any event.

The Problem of the Default

The apparent inability or unwillingness of individuals to read privacy notices and make thoughtful choices about information uses heightens the importance of the default: What happens in the absence of consumer choice? Under prior harm-based models, in the absence of consumer objection, data could be collected and used in any way that did not cause significant harm or conflict with community norms about what constitutes a reasonable expectation of privacy or outrageous conduct. Under more recent control-based models that condition information flows on opt-in consent, in the absence of a consumer response the information cannot be collected or used. As a result, recent privacy mandates that forbid the collection and use of the information without express consumer consent frequently act as an effective ban on using information at all. By setting the default rule to no use of information, these laws act as a de facto prohibition on the collection and use of personal information—no matter how little the risk of harm or great the benefit that would result from that use.

The issues raised by the default in the choice-based models are especially acute in the context of the Internet. Internet technologies cannot function without collecting Internet Protocol (IP) addresses and other information that these laws regard as personally identifiable. Under opt-in, Web sites could no longer provide their privacy notices as they currently do or as they would under mandated opt-out, but instead would have to force every consumer to see the notice in an effort to obtain his or her consent to collect and use personal information. Privacy notices would become like the intellectual property license that computer users today universally click through without reading to install software or obtain access to protected sites.

Assuming the information was necessary to provide the service (for example, an IP address) or that the Web site chose to condition service on the consumer opting in, then the failure to opt in would mean no service. Privacy would be protected, to be sure, but at the price of not using the Internet. Consumers can obtain this type of privacy protection today—just by walking away from Web sites with whose privacy policies they disagree—without the intervention of the government.

Moreover, the repeated interruption of being asked to consent, and being compelled to respond, would have even the most patient Internet user asking how to opt out of opt-in. As new uses for the information were developed, the operator would have to contact every consumer individually to ask him or her to opt in to the proposed use of the information. When users failed to respond, as experience suggests most would, the Web site operator would face two choices: give up, thereby eliminating the proposed service, or try again and again to gain consent, thus increasingly burdening the consumer with more unsolicited e-mail, telephone calls, and/or mail, and increasing the cost of providing the new service or product for which consent was being sought.

The Problem of Financial Cost

The breadth of increasingly bureaucratic tools employed by choice-based data protection models imposes considerable costs on the public. A major component of that cost results from the interference of privacy laws with open information flows. The greater the practical interference, the higher those costs will be. As the Federal Reserve Board reported to Congress in the context of personal financial information, "it is the freedom to speak, supported by the availability of information and the free-flow of data, that is the cornerstone of a democratic society and market economy."[54] Data protection laws also impose considerable compliance costs. In some cases, those costs are so great as to make the collection or use of personal information, or the provision of products or services that depend on information, untenable. In either case, it is individuals, in the words of Alabama Attorney General Bill Pryor, who "pay the price in terms of either higher prices for what they buy, or in terms of a restricted set of choices offered them in the marketplace."[55]

For example, crafting, printing, and mailing the 2 billion disclosure notices required by Gramm-Leach-Bliley is estimated to have cost $2 billion to $5 billion. That cost will be repeated annually. In the context of health privacy, the cost of disclosure, acknowledgment, authorization, and agreement forms, together with the other requirements of the HIPAA rules, in purely economic terms, is estimated to be between $25 billion and $43 billion (or three to five times more than the industry spent on Y2K) for the first five years for compliance alone, not including impact on medical research and care or liability payments.[56] During its opt-in test, U.S. West found that to obtain permission to use information about its customer's calling patterns to market services to them cost almost $30 per customer contacted.[57]

A 2000 Ernst & Young study of financial institutions representing 30 percent of financial services industry revenues found that financial services companies would send out three to six times more direct marketing material if they could not use shared personal information to target their mailings, at an additional cost of about $1 billion per year.[58] The study concluded that the total annual cost to consumers of opt-in's restriction on existing information flows—precisely because of the difficulty of reaching customers—was $17 billion for the companies studied, or $56 billion if extrapolated to include the customers of all financial institutions. And those figures do not include the costs resulting from the reduced availability of personal information to reduce fraud, increase the availability and lower the cost of credit, provide cobranded credit cards and nationwide automated teller machine networks, or develop future innovative services and products.

Other types of privacy protections may cost even more. According to a 2001 study by Robert Hahn, director of the AEI-Brookings Joint Center on Regulation, the initial cost of complying with even a modest access requirement in online privacy legislation would be $9 billion to $36 billion.[59] And these costs are not limited to business users of information. A 2002 study by Michael Turner calculates that the annual cost to charities of complying with opt-in privacy laws when fund-raising would be $16.5 billion—21 percent of the total amount raised by U.S. charities in 2000.[60]

Another recent study sought to calculate the cost of specific forms of opt-in restrictions. The study examined the operations of MBNA Corporation, a diversified, multinational financial institution that services 15 percent of all Visa/MasterCard credit card balances outstanding in the United States.[61] The company, which has no retail offices, makes extensive use of direct marketing to attract customers. It relies heavily on personal information to identify, out of the one billion prospect names the company receives annually from its more than 4,700 affinity groups for which MBNA issues credit cards, the 400 million names of people who are likely to be both qualified for and interested in a credit card solicitation.

Considering the low response rates to opt-in requests made other than at time of service or in response to a communication initiated by the customer, the case study concludes that even the least restrictive opt-in regime—for third-party information sharing—would result in MBNA's marketing materials being 27 percent less well targeted. As a result, 109 million people would receive solicitations who should not have. This translates into an 18 percent lower response rate and a 22 percent increase in direct mail costs per account booked. There would also be an additional 8 percent reduction in the company's net income because of increased defaults and reduced account activity, resulting from less qualified people receiving and acting on credit card solicitations.

Opt-in for sharing personal information with affiliates and opt-in for any use (other than statutorily excluded uses) of personal information would result in more significant losses to MBNA and its customers. MBNA's affiliates would be unable to cross-sell services to existing customers or provide one-stop customer service, because of the restriction of sharing information across affiliates. MBNA's corporate structure, which currently includes affiliates for tax and regulatory reasons, would be less efficient and more expensive because centralized service units would no longer be able to provide services for all of the affiliates. And opt-in would interfere with fraud detection and prevention efforts that depend on information sharing across affiliates and among companies.

These costs would be incurred despite the fact that as of the end of 2000 only 130,000 customers (.25 percent of MBNA's customer base) had exercised their legal right to opt out of having their credit report information transferred across MBNA affiliates, and approximately a million customers (less than 2 percent) had taken advantage of MBNA's voluntary opt-out from receiving any type of direct mail marketing offers. In sum, any of the three opt-in regimes would threaten MBNA's viability and the services the company provides to 51 million customers, to protect the interests of the fewer than 2 percent who already achieve the identical level of protection by opting out.

The Problem of Other Costs

As noted, the greatest cost of onerous data protection laws is their interference with the beneficial uses of information. According to Federal Reserve Board Governor Edward Gramlich: "Information about individuals' needs and preferences is the cornerstone of any system that allocates goods and services within an economy." The more such information is available, "the more accurately and efficiently will the economy meet those needs and preferences."[62] There are many examples of the significant noneconomic costs that control-based privacy laws may impose. In the case of health privacy rules, those costs will include the annoyance and time required to read and complete the additional forms necessary to receive service; more follow-up contacts from covered entities seeking to get them to read and acknowledge privacy notices and sign authorization forms that were sent after service; the confusion of facing entirely different sets of forms for notice, acknowledgment, authorization, and agreement; and the greater consequences of not acting that is the case today under opt-out rules.

Those costs will also include the impact on medical research. Researchers rely on personal information to conduct "chart reviews" and perform other research critical to evaluating medical treatments, detecting harmful drug interactions, uncovering dangerous side effects of medical treatments and products, and developing new therapies. Such research cannot be undertaken with wholly anonymous information because the detailed data that researchers require will always include information that could be used to identify a specific person. The costs of interfering with that research will be borne not just by patients and covered entities but by everyone who benefits from medical research and innovation. Helena Gail Rubinstein has written that "As individuals rely on their right to be let alone, they shift the burden for providing the data needed to advance medical and health policy information. Their individualist vision threatens the entire community. . . ."[63]

Control-based privacy laws often fail to serve the interests even of the individuals who claim to desire them. The most obvious example is what happens when, for the variety of reasons already discussed, individuals never learn of the opportunity to consent or learn of it only in a manner that is inconvenient or annoying. Recall that in the U.S. West opt-in trial, the company never reached one-third of its customers. Those customers were therefore denied the opportunity to consent. Of those reached by telephone, 28 percent indicated that they desired the service. Between 6 and 11 percent of U.S. West customers responded to a variety of written opt-in requests. However, 72 percent opted-in when the opportunity to consent was presented to the customer at the conclusion of a call that the customer initiated.[64] This suggests that the greatest impediment to securing opt-in consent wasn't that customers did not want their information used but rather that they never learned of the opportunity or didn't like the intrusive contacts that the opt-in system necessitated.

The control-based model of data protection can also harm individuals by forcing them to make decisions about information collection long before they can anticipate how it might benefit them, or by making the information useless precisely because it was collected subject to individual consent. Both are true in the context of credit information: Its value derives from the fact that the information is obtained routinely, over time, from sources other than the consumer. Allowing the consumer to block use of information would mean that the complete historical data necessary to make a credit report reliable would not be available when the consumer needed it to obtain a mortgage or auto loan. Even if complete, the credit report would be useless if the consumer *could* have selectively blocked data. In the words of FTC Chairman Timothy Muris, the credit reporting system "works because, without anybody's consent, very sensitive information about a person's credit history is given to the credit reporting agencies. If consent were required, and consumers could decide—on a creditor-by-creditor basis—whether they wanted their information reported, the system would collapse."[65]

Many of the beneficial uses of information that individuals now enjoy and to which they have the opportunity to consent depend on spreading the cost of collecting and maintaining the information over a variety of uses. If the law restricted too many of those uses or made them prohibitively expensive, then the data and systems to access them would not be in place for any purpose. Information sharing allows new businesses to break into markets and smaller businesses to compete more effectively with larger businesses. Laws that restrict the use of that information can stall the development of new products and services and the emergence of new competitors in the market. According to Robert E. Litan, director of economic studies at the Brookings Institution and a former deputy assistant attorney general of the United States, strict choice-based laws "raise barriers to entry by smaller, and often more innovative, firms and organizations."[66] Moreover, many of the legal mechanisms in recent privacy laws for vindicating consumer choice are so bureaucratic and burdensome that they increase the cost of using personal information and, in the case of choice-based tools such as opt-in, may effectively prevent the use outright.

The opportunity for consent is unjustified, as well as undesirable, if the service or product cannot or will not be provided without personal information. Consider the experience of every Internet user who has tried to download or install software. The first window that opens during the installation process is a notice of terms and conditions, usually relating to intellectual property rights but increasingly including privacy-related disclosures. The user is given two options: "I Accept" or "I Decline." Research shows that these notices are universally ignored, and that the reason for this is perfectly clear: Clicking on the "I Decline" button will terminate the installation process. The only option is to choose "I Accept," because consent is a condition of service.

Other requirements of the most recent choice-based privacy laws can impose even greater costs. For example, virtually all of those laws require that individuals be given some degree of access to personal information collected about them as well as an opportunity to dispute or correct data. These mandates create enormous risks for data subjects, especially online. Many of these risks were highlighted by the FTC's Advisory Committee on Online Access and Security. One of the most important, as the Advisory Committee noted, is the "very real tension between access and security":

> Unlike the other Fair Information Practice principles, the access principle sometimes pits privacy against privacy. . . . Privacy is lost if a security failure results in access being granted to the wrong person—an investigator making a pretext call, a con man engaged in identity theft, or, in some instances, one family member in conflict with another.[67]

The problem is how to provide access without "running the risk that others will also gain access to that data." To date, this has proved very difficult, especially online. If a user provides a Web site with his or her name and address to enter a contest or request a brochure, and later wishes to access that information, how does the Web site know that the person requesting access is the same person who provided the information? Yet the risk of providing access to, and an opportunity to correct, one individual's personal information to another individual is significant; access would then become the perfect tool for identity theft, and the government that mandates access the unwitting accomplice of identity thieves. "Giving access to the wrong person could turn a privacy policy into an anti-privacy policy."[68]

To date, virtually all of the measures currently available for authenticating identity require that the individual provide more information about himself or herself. To maintain the necessary authentication tools, providers will likely have to seek and store more personal information, such as Social Security number or mother's maiden name, or require the user to create an account. Moreover, many access requirements would obligate information users to centralize disparate pieces of information collected from users. So, for example, under the EU data protection directive or legislation like the Online Personal Privacy Act, information users would have to access usage logs and backup tapes, which usually contain information about individual users. Although these sources are normally used only in the event of a system failure, a dispute regarding a transaction, or, in the aggregate, to monitor and enhance system performance, these laws require processors to bring together all of this information—together with all of the other information collected about an individual—to engage in the very data aggregation against which privacy principles have traditionally argued.

In fact, these laws often require access to information that may not be within the control of the information user, such as cookies (which are stored on individual Internet users' computers), or may not otherwise have been stored. For example, laws that require processors to provide updated notice to individuals of changes in and breaches of their privacy policy presuppose that processors collect contact information. This is often not the case online. The ironic result is that processors may be required to collect and store more information or to provide users with access to files that the users—not the providers—possess. After studying these "complicated" and "controversial" issues in detail for months, the FTC Advisory Committee could not reach any consensus on whether or how access should be provided. But this did not deter the FTC from recommending such requirements, the Senate Commerce Committee from passing them, or the European Union from adopting them.

The Promise of Technology

Internet technologies offer great promise for effective privacy protection, by making it easy and cheap to engage in anonymous or pseudonymous communications and to determine which Web sites comply with predetermined personalized privacy preferences. For example, privacy settings in Internet browsers such as Netscape Navigator and Microsoft Explorer, stand-alone programs such as encryption and firewall software, and other technologies offer individual users a high degree of customized control over their own personal information. The P3P initiative allows consumers to set their preferences in sharing personally identifiable information with Web sites and then to interrogate Web sites electronically to see which comply.

The Internet has also given rise to a number of privacy services (not all successful financially), including online privacy certifications like BBBOnline and TRUSTe, anonymization services like Zero Knowledge and anonymizer.com, and a wide range of identity-protecting intermediaries. FTC Commissioner Orson Swindle has noted the variety and potential of these services. "AllAdvantage.com acts as an agent on behalf of consumers to create a market for the use of their information without consumers' losing control over their information. Digital Me from Novell stores a consumer's personal information and uses it to automatically fill out forms at Web sites, allowing the consumer to review what is being submitted. Persona by PrivaSeek allows a consumer to surf anonymously and sell his or her specified, personally identifiable information in exchange for discounts."[69] A more comprehensive service, iPrivacy, makes it possible for an individual to browse, make purchases online, and even ship goods to his or her home or a drop-off location without ever disclosing her real identity, address, e-mail address, or credit card number to anyone.

These services take advantage of Internet technologies to offer demonstrated privacy protection. Moreover, they offer far better protection than even the most restrictive legal regime because they protect users from information processors that operate outside of the law or the jurisdiction. However, if the control-based model makes the Internet an inhospitable place for businesses to offer commercially viable services, these opportunities for technological privacy protection will no longer exist. To date, few of these services have met with market success, which suggests that Internet users are less interested in protecting privacy than polling data might indicate.

Technology presents other issues for protecting privacy online, some of which have already been noted, for example, the dependence of Internet technologies on personal data. Another critical technology issue is the impediment the structure of the Internet creates to verifying identity, age, or relationships online. This was illustrated by the experience with Internet-specific privacy legislation applicable to processing data concerning children under 13. The Children's Online Privacy Protection Act was widely supported because it seemingly represented a moderate, sensible approach to protecting children's privacy online. Subject to very limited exceptions, the law prohibits Web sites from collecting data about children without first obtaining "verifiable parental consent." In practice, however, the law has had the effect of causing most Web sites to eliminate the personalized services they offer to children because of the inherent, and so far insoluble, difficulties of determining how to obtain "verified parental consent" with any confidence that the consent comes from an adult, much less a parent.

Internet technologies present an especially great challenge to centralized, choice-based laws, like the EU data protection directive. Ambassador David Aaron has noted that the directive was conceived "when there was no World Wide Web and information technology was dominated by mainframe computers, not distributed information networks, laptops, and digital assistants. As a result the directive is often rigid or silent in dealing with privacy issues growing out of new technology and new business models."[70] The directive's centralized data protection regime is ill-suited to a far-flung, multinational medium such as the Internet, as EU data protection officials have acknowledged. Its focus on data "controllers" and its centralized system of data protection authorities, registration, investigation, and enforcement are inapplicable to the Web, where anyone with a computer and a modem can collect, process, and transfer personal data. Moreover, legal controls are particularly easy to circumvent in the Internet environment.

The Problem of Constitutionality

Individual control, much less ownership, of information raises serious constitutional issues. The unanimous U.S. Supreme Court has written in the context of copyright law: "The most fundamental axiom of copyright law is that 'no author may copyright his ideas or the facts he narrates. . . .' Copyright assures authors the right to their original expression, but encourages others to build freely upon

327

the ideas and information conveyed by a work."[71] Although it may seem unfair that the law does not allow a creator or discoverer of data to own them, "this is not 'some unforeseen byproduct of a statutory scheme,'" the Court has written. "It is, rather, 'the essence of copyright,' and a constitutional requirement."[72]

The same constitutional principle is reflected with even greater force in the First Amendment. When information is true and obtained lawfully, the Supreme Court has repeatedly held that the government may not restrict its disclosure without meeting "strict scrutiny"—the highest level of constitutional scrutiny. Punishing the publication of true expression, the Court has written, is "antithetical to the First Amendment's protection. . . ."[73] As a result, the Court has struck down laws that sought to protect privacy by restricting the publication of confidential government reports,[74] the names of judges under investigation,[75] juvenile suspects,[76] and rape victims.[77]

The Supreme Court has struck down many ordinances that would require affirmative (opt-in) consent before receiving door-to-door solicitations,[78] before receiving Communist literature,[79] even before receiving "patently offensive" cable programming.[80] The only federal court to review modern opt-in data protection rules concluded that they violated the First Amendment.[81] In 2001, the Supreme Court reiterated the remarkable nature of the First Amendment's protection for expression when it held that even the broadcast of an illegally intercepted cellular telephone conversation was protected by the First Amendment. The Court wrote, "Exposure of the self to others in varying degrees is a concomitant of life in a civilized community. The risk of this exposure is an essential incident of life in a society which places a primary value on freedom of speech and of press." The Court concluded, "our decisions establish that absent exceptional circumstances, reputational interests alone cannot justify the proscription of truthful speech."[82]

The Problem of National Laws in a Global Medium

Perhaps the most difficult issue presented by the choice-based model of privacy protection, and the one most acute on the Internet, is the problem of conflicting national data protection laws. Information has always challenged traditional notions of jurisdiction because of the ease with which it crosses borders. In fact, precisely because of its inherently transnational character, information has been the subject of some of the earliest multinational agreements, treaties, and organizations. Binational postal treaties were concluded as early as 1601 between France and Spain and 1670 between France and England. The Postal Congress of Berne in 1874 established a multinational postal regime—administered today by the Universal Postal Union—74 years before the General Agreement on Tariffs and Trade was opened for signature.

In the case of the Internet, the digital technologies involved make the borderless nature of information even more pronounced. The Internet is accessed in 205 countries, and online data move invisibly and effortlessly among them. But nations have not responded with broad multinational agreements addressing privacy online. Instead, national (or, in some instances, state or provincial) law is being applied to an inherently global medium. Even an apparently multinational regime, such as the EU data protection directive, permits nations to adopt more stringent data protection laws. In fact, national implementation has proved so idiosyncratic that a 2001 study by London law firm D. J. Freeman found that almost every member state "was operating its own regime in terms of data laws" with "wide latitude in the interpretation of the 1995 directive."[83] In the United States, even comprehensive national enactments, such as Gramm-Leach-Bliley and the HIPAA regulations, explicitly permit states to adopt more restrictive privacy laws.

The choice-based model of data protection greatly exacerbates the problem of inconsistent laws, because of the breadth of information covered, the reliance on bureaucratic requirements, and the restrictiveness of their terms. Under prior models, while national laws could and very often did intersect, conflict could be avoided because it was comparatively easy to determine whether a harm had resulted from a disputed use of personal information. More recent choice-based laws, however, can be violated just by not using the right form of notice, failing to register, or some other administrative shortcoming. These laws are more likely to come into conflict because they are so broad, and they are less amenable to multinational application because they depend so heavily on national compliance and enforcement mechanisms, such as registration with a national authority, or providing individuals with access to data about them in the country where those individuals reside. This is especially true when choice-based laws are so broad that they apply extraterritorially (for example, Article 25 of the EU data protection directive expressly applies outside of the European Union). The end result of applying national choice-based data protection laws in the context of a global medium like the Internet has been called "a maze of conflicting provisions that create a complex, perilous, and potentially non-navigable environment" for consumers and businesses.[84]

The Future

The future of privacy protection on the Internet is far from clear. In Europe, which has the longest experience with the control-based model of data protection, pressure is mounting to move to a less bureaucratic, less burdensome system. There is no likelihood that Europe will abandon individual control as the focus of data protection; rather, it may require less costly means for individuals to exercise control. The pressure is prompted by the growing recognition that broad-based privacy regimes like that embodied in the data protection directive do little to calm consumer angst and provide no greater level of actual privacy protection than less costly and burdensome systems. In fact, a January 2001 study by Consumers International found that while U.S. and European Web sites collect personal information at nearly comparable rates (66 percent in the United States, 63 percent in Europe), U.S. sites provide better privacy protection, despite having no specific legal obligation to do so, than European sites, which are subject to comprehensive legal requirements: "Despite tight EU legislation in this area, researchers did not find that sites based in the EU gave better information or a higher degree of choice to their users than sites based in the United States. Indeed, U.S.-based sites tended to set the standard for decent privacy policies."[85] One reason for this may be that the European system is so burdensome that it cannot be effectively enforced, especially in the context of media like the Internet.

The governments of Austria, Finland, Sweden, and the United Kingdom, recently joined by the Netherlands,[86] have proposed amending the directive to reflect a more reasonable balance between data protection and the responsible use of personal information. "The purpose of data protection rules is not to prevent the processing of personal data. Rather, it is to ensure the proportionate regulation of such processing. The rules must give effective protection to individuals' personal data without unnecessarily restricting the processing needed to deliver the services which our increasingly technologically sophisticated society demands."[87] The directive, in the view of the five governments, at present fails to achieve the proper balance between those two requirements.

To do this, the governments have proposed eliminating the directive's "unnecessary, and in some cases costly, bureaucratic requirements" on the flow of personal information.[88] In addition, the governments propose refocusing the directive, at least to a small degree, on the concept of harm. This, they stress, requires less attention to data and more attention to the types of process that can cause injury to individuals. "Data themselves are neutral. It is their processing which can give rise to risk."[89] Under the governments' proposal, the directive would still retain many of its administrative requirements and its extraterritorial application, but those requirements would be reduced and streamlined to interfere less with the benefits that result from accessible personal information.

It is not clear whether Europe will actually enact these moderating amendments, or what course the United States and other countries will take. The change in leadership at the FTC occasioned by the election of President George W. Bush, and the reestablishment of Republican control in the Senate following the November 2002 elections, may cause a slowing of the movement toward increasingly bureaucratic, control-based privacy laws in the United States. In any event, there is no suggestion anywhere of returning privacy protection to a focus on preventing harmful uses of personal information, and little, if any, discussion of how to deal with conflicts among national data protection laws on the Internet.

The answer to the question "Who rules the Net?" in the context of privacy is mixed. Individual users have gained substantial legal rights throughout most of the industrialized world, but there is little indication that those rights have much value for most people. What is clear is that those rights have been secured at considerable cost, not only in financial terms but in an increased array of notices, the blocking of potentially beneficial uses of information, increased hacking risks, and interference with alternative sources of revenue for Internet content. Moreover, it seems clear that those rights, perhaps because they are based in national law and are often so difficult to enforce meaningfully, are doing little to deter the misuse of personal information by spammers, hackers, and other out-of-the-mainstream entities.

Businesses and other entities face few substantive limits on the use of personal information, but very significant and changing procedural burdens on their use of personal information. The likely long-term impact of the control model of data protection has been less on large, established businesses, which already have a large user base and warehouses of consumer information, than on small and start-up enterprises, which lack those resources. But the business community as a whole has expended considerable resources in complying with overlapping or even conflicting laws and fighting off worse ones. Ironically, legitimate businesses that have attempted to comply with applicable laws may have paid a higher price, especially through hair-trigger, strict-liability enforcement of privacy policies, than entities that ignored the laws altogether.

National governments seem to have fared better than any other Internet constituency, due in part to the fact that many of the choice-based laws actually make it easier for governments to obtain access to personal information and also due to the fact that governments almost universally exempt all or part of their operations and those of their political parties from the administrative requirements applicable to businesses and charities. Finally, data protection has proved a useful political issue for some elected and appointed officials, allowing them to command attention and resources previously beyond their reach. None of this, of course, translates into real "control" of the Internet. The penchant of many national governments to enact increasingly broad, bureaucratic, and restrictive national data protection laws, without considering how these laws will in fact operate or interact in the context of this unprecedentedly global medium, bodes ill for individuals and responsible data users online.

12. Structured to Fail: ICANN and the "Privatization" Experiment

Harold Feld

Introduction

In July 1997, as part of its "Framework for Global Electronic Commerce," the Clinton administration issued a directive to the Department of Commerce requiring it to "support efforts to make the governance of the domain name system private."[1] This command should have seemed odd, since the governance of the domain name system had been private (albeit supported by federal money) for years. Further reading, however, revealed that the Clinton administration did not intend to cut the domain name system loose from regulation and permit private markets to operate. It didn't simply wait for the government contracts to expire and allow the private actors to operate in a free market. Instead, the Clinton administration further instructed the Department of Commerce to "create a contractually based self-regulatory regime" with the specific policy objective of addressing potential conflicts between domain name usage and trademark laws on a global basis."[2]

More than a year later, the Department of Commerce entered into a memorandum of understanding with the Internet Corporation for Assigned Names and Numbers, or ICANN—a nonprofit corporation ostensibly formed independently by the "Internet community" but in fact a result of a compromise mediated between opposed factions by the Department of Commerce. Hailed by its supporters as an experiment in privatization and industry self-regulation, it was, in fact, none of those things. As described by Milton Mueller and others,[3] ICANN represented a compromise between the Department of Commerce and various interest groups. Its primary purpose was not to privatize the management of the domain name system, but to centralize its control under the rubric of "stability." While this proposal met resistance, and failed to satisfy many significant players, the lack of any alternative plan supported by a significant party or coalition permitted ICANN to move forward despite opposition and dissatisfaction from a broad base of stakeholders.[4]

Bringing control of the Internet naming system under one roof, however, proved far more difficult than simply creating ICANN. In part, this has proved difficult because the Internet naming system consists of more than the single central naming file, the so-called root zone file.[5] Even after ICANN received effective authority to make changes to the root zone file through its contracts with the Department of Commerce and Verisign, Inc., the custodian of the root zone file and the holder of the .com, .org, and .net generic top-level domains (gTLDs),[6] it needed to assume authority over the other centers of the Internet naming system: the root server operators,[7] the country code top-level domain (ccTLD)[8] registries, and the regional Internet registries (RIRs) that allocate Internet Protocol (IP) address blocks.[9]

After four years, ICANN had still not achieved its goal of signing binding agreements with the RIRs, the majority of ccTLD registries, and the root server operators (collectively "DNS asset managers"), which would require them to follow ICANN policy directives or contribute financially to ICANN.[10] Declaring the process "stalled," ICANN President Stuart Lynn announced that ICANN would reorganize itself to become more efficient and able to accomplish its goals.[11] Lynn expressly invoked the need to involve governments to a greater degree. In October 2002, ICANN adopted a new set of bylaws designed to achieve this end by centralizing authority in the ICANN Board of Directors and staff and thus, in the words of Lynn, eliminating ICANN's "too much process" and making the organization more "lightweight."[12] Although unspoken, it appears that ICANN's hope was that involving governments to a greater degree in the process would either add coercive weight to ICANN's authority or would be seen as further insulating private parties from government regulation by "cabining" them within ICANN.

Whatever ICANN's theory, the reform failed to mollify the DNS asset managers. To the contrary, the DNS asset managers have proposed alternate reform plans;[13] or even proposed alternatives to ICANN.[14] Their primary complaint is that ICANN seeks to make inappropriate policy decisions for the DNS using a bureaucratic, top-heavy "command and control" process that impinges on the independence of the relevant asset holders. At the same time, as

334

discussed below, governments have insisted on greater oversight in ICANN affairs, and have sought to use ICANN to expand government regulation of the DNS.

Finally, the ICANN Board and staff have shown a general predilection for expanding the scope of ICANN's authority and for establishing intrusive regulatory regimes at the behest of governments or other special interests. This trend has made many DNS asset managers nervous. Since the reform eliminated constraints on direct Board action (or staff action in the name of the Board), thus making it more "lightweight" in terms of formulating policy but even more "weighty" in its ability to regulate, the reform has only served to increase those that fear ICANN's authority.

This chapter examines the ICANN domain name governance "experiment" in the wake of this reorganization. The first section discusses the domain name system (DNS), providing technical description as to how it works and a guide to the distinct assets that, taken together, encompass the DNS. Notably, before the formation of ICANN, the DNS assets were in private hands and operating under a system of voluntary coordination and loose federal supervision.

The next section describes the formation of ICANN and how ICANN represented a step not toward privatization but toward increased regulation. At the same time, the compromises that made the formation of ICANN possible also contained an inherent tension. While government and special interests sought to regulate the DNS, holders of DNS resources sought to maintain their independence. The compromise left the gTLD space subject to regulation, but failed to bring the IP address space or ccTLD address space under ICANN's control.[15]

The following section examines the growing tension between ICANN and the DNS asset managers that led ICANN to its reorganization in 2002. It argues that ICANN's failure to persuade or coerce the DNS asset managers to enter into voluntary agreements forced ICANN to embrace a greater role for sovereign governments and to more closely resemble a regulatory agency. The more ICANN embraces governments, however, the more it antagonizes the DNS asset managers. As a result, it appears likely that ICANN will either continue its transformation into a regulatory agency dependent on the coercive power of governments to bring the DNS asset managers into agreement, or the DNS asset managers will attempt to place themselves beyond ICANN's control with potentially disastrous results for the stability of the Internet as a whole.

The closing section proposes a possible solution. ICANN should be reduced to a ministerial role and private DNS asset managers should have the autonomy to manage the DNS assets under the cooperative system that worked before ICANN. The only necessary change from the 1997 regime is a clear, nonsubjective, nondiscriminatory system for introducing new gTLDs on a predictable basis and in sufficient quantity to avoid monopoly or oligopoly control of the gTLD name space. Given the incentives to cooperate, and absent an artificial scarcity of gTLDs, market mechanism will provide a stable, robust DNS free from intrusive regulation. While political pressures require that certain intrusive regulatory regimes remain in place—notably the artificial distinction between "registries" providing wholesale name registration and "registrars" selling names at retail to the public and the Uniform Dispute Resolution Procedure for addressing trademark disputes—these schemes are based on existing contracts and do not require ICANN for maintenance.

The Domain Name System

The domain name system,[16] or the DNS, has been poetically described as "the spark that breathes life and the very existence on the Internet. The loss of a name on the Internet is death without a trace. In fact, when reassigned, the name breathes life into another being."[17] Somewhat more technically, computers that use the Internet Protocol rely on lengthy—and unique—strings of numbers called "IP addresses" to find the intended destination of information packets. The computer at the receiving end then uses an appropriate software package to assemble these packets into the intended form, such as a Web page, or e-mail, or streaming video.

The Root

Because human beings do not remember long strings of numbers very well, early Internet engineers developed a system for associating a string of standard keyboard characters with an IP address. This string is a domain name. For the Internet to work properly, each domain name and each IP address must be unique (although more than one name can resolve to the same IP number). If the name "example.com" had two possible IP addresses, packets would flow to the two separate addresses, producing gibberish at both receivers.

To ensure this uniqueness, a central master table keeps a list of the "name servers" that match up (or, as DNS folks like to say, "resolve") the addresses and names. Internet cognoscenti refer to this database table as the root zone file.[18] The ability to enter or delete names in the root zone file, therefore, confers the ability to control who will or will not speak on the Internet either directly (by refusing to give someone a name or IP address) or indirectly (by prohibiting those with names and addresses from doing business with those excluded).

When a computer needs to resolve a name typed by a user into an IP address, it sends a query up to the central table. The central data table then directs the question to the relevant name server. If the central table answered all queries directly, it would cause tremendous congestion. So the table is distributed through 13 "root servers" that maintain copies of the root zone file. One root server, the "A Root," is considered the authoritative copy of the root zone file. It is maintained by Verisign, Inc., pursuant to Verisign's memorandum of understanding with the Department of Commerce. Two of the root server operators are U.S. military agencies and one is the National Aeronautics and Space Administration. One is also maintained by ICANN.

The remaining root server operators are private entities, three of which are located outside of the United States. Maintenance of the root servers was arrived at over time by voluntary agreements among the members of the Internet networking community with the blessings of the modest federal oversight that characterized the management of the Internet until the formation of ICANN. At the time of ICANN's formation, none of the root server operators had any formal contract or requirement to operate the root servers (other than Verisign, which operated the A Root server pursuant to its contract with the Department of Commerce) and did so on a voluntary basis.

For both engineering and esthetic reasons, the designers of the DNS created a hierarchical naming system. They divided the name system into domains. The holder of a top-level domain can register a second name or second-level domain under the top-level domain.

337

The holder of the second-level domain can further register or "delegate" a third-level domain, and so forth. Addresses read from right to left, with the top level at the furthest right.

Thus, for my.example.com, .com is the top-level domain. The holder of .com (i.e., Verisign) can allow the registration of second-level domains, like "example" and the holder of "example.com" can allow registration of the third-level "my." The holder of the top-level domain can impose any conditions it wishes on the would-be registree, provided the would-be registree agrees. Holders of top-level domains have generally required registrants to agree to future revisions of the registry agreement, and have required renewal on a regular basis rather than a grant of an absolute right in a name.

Top-Level Domains: Generic and Country Code TLDs

Since formalization of the system in the mid-1980s, top-level domains have been divided between generic top-level domains, or gTLDs, and country code top-level domains or ccTLDs. The ccTLDs were not intended to be "official" to any particular country.[19] Indeed, at the time of formulation, the International Telecommunications Union had developed an "official" packet switched network addressing system and the IP-based Internet remained an "unofficial" network for academic researchers and anyone else who wished to join. What distinguished gTLDs from ccTLDs was that gTLDs were not associated with particular geographies but were meant as catch-alls for particular sorts of users. The ccTLDs, however, were associated with geographic regions based on a list of two-letter country abbreviations promulgated by the United Nations' International Standards Organization, the ISO 3166-1 list.[20]

By the time of the formation of ICANN, the registries for nearly all top-level domains had been assigned to private parties.[21] The most important gTLDs—.com, .org, and .net—were operated by Network Solutions, Inc.,[22] a private company. Network Solutions assumed control of the gTLD registries in 1993 when the National Science Foundation (NSF) issued a request for proposals for private companies to support the naming function of the DNS. NSF paid Network Solutions for the service until the dramatic increase in registrations prompted the parties to renegotiate in 1995. Under the new agreement, NSF permitted Network Solutions to charge name registrants a fixed fee per year for each registered name. The agreement under which Network Solutions operated the gTLDs was set to expire in 1998, after which subsequent operation of the gTLDs remained unclear.[23]

The ccTLDs were in most cases operated by private individuals or entities. Increasingly, as the Internet assumed importance, national governments began to assert an interest in the assignment of ccTLD registries, if not outright authority over the ccTLD registry. Nevertheless, at the time of ICANN's formation, the vast majority of ccTLD registries remained in private hands.[24]

The Regional Internet Registries

The remaining element of the DNS, assignment of IP address blocks, was also firmly in private hands by the time of the formation of ICANN. By 1997 three regional Internet registries, or RIRs, had evolved to handle the allocation of IP addresses.[25] Because the underlying protocols of the Internet both limit the number of IP addresses available and requires that these IP addresses be unique, IP numbers represent a critical resource and assignment of them represents another potential source of regulatory authority over the Internet. IP addresses are even more critical than names for communicating on the Internet. An address without a name still functions, although it is difficult for a human being to use. But a name without a corresponding address does not resolve, because the computer lacks the information it needs to transmit the information.[26]

In the early 1990s, as part of the effort of the Internet technical community to facilitate global use of the Internet protocols and network compatibility, two Internet address registries were created outside of the United States and given blocks of IP addresses to allocate to non-U.S. networks: RIPE-NCC (based in Europe) and APNIC (covering the Asia-Pacific region).[27] In 1997, just as the Department of Commerce became active in DNS policy, the NSF and Network Solutions facilitated the creation of a third RIR, ARIN, to administer IP address allocation for North, South, and Central America, and Africa.[28]

The RIRs are private organizations. They have generally sought to avoid controversy or the limelight, focusing on technical coordination and charging fees designed to cover the costs of administering the IP address system.

The "Internet Community" and Its Institutions

All of these institutions grew out of the loose association of early Internet engineers, often referred to as the "Internet community" or, after the emergence of a large number of nonengineers claiming membership in the Internet community, "the Internet technical community." This older Internet community revolved around the Internet Assigned Numbers Authority (IANA), a private organization with a formal role in setting DNS policy; the Internet Engineering Task Force (IETF), a loose association open to anyone who cared to participate in setting voluntary standards for the Internet; the Internet Architecture Board (IAB), a collection of DNS "village elders;" and the Internet Society (ISOC), a membership organization designed in part as a corporate entity to house the various DNS policy institutions in some kind of legal framework.[29]

The IANA was the personal vehicle of Jon Postel, one of the early developers of the DNS and its dominant figure.[30] At the beginning of the development of the DNS, Jon Postel, with the help of his colleague Joyce Reynolds, assumed the mantle of "number czar" with the consent of the rest of the Internet community. This function of maintaining the original root zone file earned Postel the respect and trust of the Internet community as a whole, which continued to operate in a voluntary and informal basis under the very loose supervision of federal funders. As the DNS evolved, Postel and those around him acted as the central coordinators of this evolution and, to the extent policy decisions were made, they were made by Postel on the basis of consensus within the still small and relatively homogenous Internet community.[31]

This coordinating function became known as the IANA or the IANA function. Although members of the Internet community exhibited a high degree of loyalty to Postel and the IANA—some even expressing a willingness to risk arrest by defying U.S. policy for root management at Postel's request[32]—no formal contracts existed between the root server operators and the IANA, the ccTLDs and the IANA, or the RIRs and the IANA.[33] With the exception of the formal cooperative agreement between Network Solutions and the NSF, the DNS immediately before the formation of ICANN functioned as a cooperative and voluntary association of private managers of resources.

The mechanisms for distilling this consensus were a number of Internet mailing lists and the Internet Engineering Task Force. The IETF was, and still is, a voluntary organization established in the late 1980s and early 1990s as the Internet technical community grew from a population of a few researchers well known to each other and to a community of unrelated researchers, engineers, and private-sector entrepreneurs. The IETF proposed a process for establishing standards by consensus to facilitate the interoperability of networks. Its slogan "rough consensus and running code" embodied its non-compulsory and practical nature. Anyone was free to implement anything. If use of it in the real world, "running code," proved the validity of an approach and enough people adopted it, then the IETF ratified it as a standard.[34]

These informal processes became somewhat more formalized in the IAB and the ISOC.[35] This represented a step by Postel and his friends and allies to retain their influence in the growing Internet engineering community. In 1992, the IAB—fearful that the growing DNS community would dilute their ability to control the development of the DNS—attempted to formalize their leadership role and impose a more rigid, hierarchal arrangement. This effort met with fierce resistance from the IETF. As a result, before the formation of ICANN, coordination around the Internet naming system remained voluntary and informal.[36] At the same time, it created a faction within the DNS community clustered around the IANA/IAB/ISOC that sought to retain its own authority against subsequent challenges from both within and without the traditional DNS community.

The Lone Outsider—Network Solutions

Significantly, Network Solutions alone stood outside of this community consensus building process. NSF initially awarded Network Solutions a contract to manage the naming databases in 1993. Although other contractors were also initially involved, Network Solutions ultimately became the only contractor other than IANA. Network Solutions administered the various name databases, notably the gTLD name servers and the A Root.[37]

As a private company working under an explicit contracting arrangement with the federal government, Network Solutions made policy based on its perception of its own best interest and negotiations with the other party to the contract, the National Science Foundation.[38]

By the time of ICANN's formation, Network Solutions' status as a for-profit entity that did not work within the framework of the Internet community had created considerable friction with the rest of the Internet community.[39] Postel and other Internet stalwarts gradually began to regard Network Solutions as a monopoly provider of gTLD registration services that sought to exploit the naming system for personal profit rather than regarding itself as steward of a public resource for the benefit of the Internet community as a whole.[40] This hostility would translate itself into various policy initiatives designed to break or regulate the perceived monopoly.

The Emergence and Structure of ICANN

The first proposal to break the Network Solutions gTLD monopoly came from Postel and involved a straightforward solution: direct competition by rival gTLDs. Postel initially sought to open the gTLD name space to competition directly by allowing the immediate introduction of 150 new gTLDs at a cost of a one-time $10,000 fee to the IANA for processing the application. The plan failed to achieve consensus, however, and Postel ultimately withdrew it.[41]

This unfortunate failure of private competition and the failure to provide a mechanism for the allocation of new TLDs proved the rock on which voluntary cooperation in the management of the DNS would founder. The Internet continued to expand at a heady rate, and DNS registrations skyrocketed. The mechanisms in place continued to function smoothly and private actors continued to address and cooperatively overcome problems of stability. But the IANA found itself paralyzed on the key issue of expanding the number of gTLDs in the root.

Surprisingly, antagonism to Postel's plan to expand the DNS did not come from Network Solutions, the gTLD monopolist. Apparently comfortable with a dominant position in DNS and eager to avoid regulation or antitrust litigation, Network Solutions took the position that it would enter any new TLDs into the root zone file the U.S. government directed.

Rather, antagonism came from a number of different sources reflecting the diversity of interests that by 1997 had become the Internet community. A community of would-be gTLD registries objected to paying any fee at all, and challenged Postel's authority to impose an entry fee that bore no clear relationship to any cost of processing the new TLD application. This community began to express considerable opposition to the IANA, IAB, and ISOC. At the same time, another clique in the Internet technical community (heavily associated with the IAB and the ISOC) resented the rise of the commercial Internet generally and disliked any exploitation of the naming system for profit. Finally, some members of the community simply feared that the increasing controversy over DNS invited regulatory intervention or some other change in the status quo that would dilute their traditional authority to develop the DNS. For them, the motivating factor was fear that "their" Internet was rapidly escaping into other hands.

The Expansion of the "Internet Community"[42]

This fear that the Internet's expansion jeopardized the traditional freedom of the Internet technical community had considerable merit. The explosive growth of the Internet brought numerous new actors into the Internet community. Most did not care how the DNS worked as long as it continued to do so in a stable and predictable manner. Many businesses, however, came to the Internet to discover that "their" name was already taken by someone else. In some cases, the name registrants sought to extort payments from trademark holders, or direct traffic to Web sites by confusing consumers. Others sought to use the names of others for purposes of humor or political satire. In other cases, speculators had bought hundreds of "genericword.com" names at the NSF regulated rate and then sought to resell them to entrepreneurs seeking to establish businesses on the basis of perceived consumer use of the DNS. Some of these generic words corresponded with the trademarks of others.

Attorneys representing trademark holders and organizations devoted to intellectual property rights, such as the International Trademark Association, and multinational treaty organizations devoted to intellectual property, such as the World Intellectual Property Organization, reviled these "cybersquatters." Furthermore, while generally successful in using existing trademark law to pry away infringing names in federal court, they sought a less expensive means than litigation. The intellectual property interests saw in the DNS a means by which they could regulate the domain name space and effect a transfer of names. After all, if the holder of the root zone file altered the registration information to assign example.com to a new party, the previous holder would have no recourse beyond its registration agreement. If the registration agreement contained a clause permitting the registry to reassign the name under certain conditions—say after a swift online arbitration process invoked by a trademark holder—then the registrant would have no recourse at all.

Regarding the introduction of new gTLDs, intellectual property organizations expressed unbridled horror. Because those organizations viewed any use of "their" name in any TLD as infringing, an increase in the number of TLDs would only result in an increase in the cost of policing the domain space for infringers.

In addition to these industry players, sovereign governments, notably the European Union and Australia, resented U.S. dominance of the Internet and control of the DNS in particular. But objecting to American dominance did not mean favoring privatization to American private organizations such as Network Solutions or the IANA. Some foreign governments were also unhappy with the delegation of "their" country code to a private party by the IANA without any consultation. These governments did not want deregulation, but a new system that would allow them to exercise control over the ccTLD registry.

In addition, the International Telecommunications Union viewed the dispute over DNS as a means of making itself relevant in the Internet world. In the 1980s and early 1990s, the ITU had supported an alternative form of packet-switched technology with a highly regulated namespace analogous to the telephone network. That technology failed to gain popularity in the market, in no small part because the private-sector actors found it much easier and cheaper to use the open Internet architecture. While some regarded the ITU as the ultimate antithesis of the free-wheeling Internet, others viewed it as a means of countering American dominance or conferring legitimacy in traditional regulatory circles. In addition, the fear that the ITU would, in some undefined and unspecified way, "take over," proved an effective bogeyman for rallying the rest of the Internet technical community to support alternative approaches.

None of these new entrants, therefore, had any incentive to favor genuine privatization. To the contrary, intellectual property interests, governments interested in the DNS, and multinational treaty organizations with relevant interests, such as the World Intellectual Property Organization and the ITU, all wanted a system that would allow them to achieve their regulatory ends.

Against this backdrop, the IAB/IANA/ISOC clique again attempted to reassert their authority over the DNS. From the death of Postel's plan in mid-1996 until the formation of ICANN in 1998, a section of the Internet technical community centered on Postel and the IANA sought to create a new regulatory scheme with themselves at the top by providing these new stakeholders with a mechanism for internationalizing DNS policy (by subjecting the American gTLD registry Network Solutions to a regulatory scheme and moving the DNS policy organizations to Europe) and providing the intellectual property interests with a controlling voice in name policy. At the same time, Postel and the rest of the IAB/ISOC group sought to insulate what they considered the purely technical decisions outside of domain name politics (i.e., issues surrounding the RIRs and root server operators) from political regulation and to retain these within the technical community (albeit subordinate to the IANA).

The Federal Government Opposes Privatization in Favor of Regulation

The rise of the Internet's popularity as a medium of communications and commerce that attracted this host of new stakeholders also attracted the active regulatory attention of the U.S. government. The government increasingly regarded the Internet as a key economic driver in the "new economy."[43] While extolling the virtues of its unregulated state, and attributing the Internet's vitality to this lack of regulation, the federal government did not appear ready to let go completely. Indeed, rather than terminate the existing government contracts, the Clinton administration convened a multiagency task force to explore its options and formulate a position.

That the U.S. government had no desire to genuinely privatize the DNS became quickly apparent. In the spring of 1997, NSF and Network Solutions agreed to terminate the cooperative agreement under which Network Solutions operated by the end of 1997. NSF had previously privatized the Internet transport market by turning pieces of the publicly built and regulated network infrastructure over to private actors under conditions that encouraged competition.[44] NSF apparently proposed to do the same thing in DNS, turning over the existing commercial gTLD registries to Network Solutions and expecting the private actors to resolve the policy issues without further government oversight.[45]

At the same time, a would-be gTLD operator, Name.Space, filed an antitrust suit against Network Solutions, demanding that Network Solutions add Name.Space's TLDs to the root zone file. After the

IANA disclaimed any legal responsibility for root policy, Network Solutions forwarded the request to NSF. In addition, Network Solutions appended a request that Network Solutions and NSF create an orderly process for taking applications for new TLDs to the root zone file.[46]

NSF's strategy of simple withdrawal and reliance on genuine privatization—that is, turning the DNS over completely to private actors—appeared justified. Network Solutions indicated its willingness to allow competitors into the root zone file (albeit under threat of litigation) in a neutral manner, resolving the one conflict that had paralyzed the DNS. The rest of the DNS continued to function smoothly. No technical barriers remained to a purely private DNS regime.

The U.S. government task force, however, preempted NSF. It asserted control of DNS policy and ordered the NSF contract manager to instruct Network Solutions to introduce no new TLDs to the root zone file or make any other substantive changes until the governmental task force had settled on a policy. NSF complied with the task force's order and issued a directive to Network Solutions prohibiting any independent action by Network Solutions. Soon after, authority over the Network Solutions contract was transferred by NSF to the National Telecommunications and Information Administration (NTIA) at the Department of Commerce, which assumed the lead role in the policy formation in the U.S. government.[47] The hope for a genuine privatization of the root ended with this assertion of NTIA's authority.

The ICANN Compromise

As Mueller and others have described,[48] the combination of the old Internet community, non-U.S. governments, and intellectual property interests combined to form a "dominant coalition" in negotiating with the U.S. government (through the Department of Commerce, which displaced NSF and the multiagency task force as the lead U.S. agency on domain name management) and Network Solutions on a final governance structure for the DNS. Although the United States did consult others, the ability of those outside of the dominant coalition, the U.S. government and Network Solutions, was profoundly limited.[49]

As a result, and in the absence of any better alternative, the Department of Commerce announced in June 1998 that it intended to "privatize" the domain name system by giving a new nonprofit corporation control over the root zone file.[50] The Department of Commerce selected ICANN, the compromise vehicle of the dominant coalition, in October. For a combination of reasons, primarily Network Solution's reluctance to accept ICANN as its new overseer and doubts as to how the new entity would ultimately evolve, the Department of Commerce did not immediately transfer control of the root zone file (and, by extension, the DNS) to ICANN. Instead, the Department of Commerce agreed to a two-year transition, which allowed it to retain ultimate control over the root zone file.[51]

ICANN's regulatory power derives from its ability to designate the name servers in the root zone file. A top-level registry only exists if it exists in the root zone file. Only the Department of Commerce has the authority to make changes in the root zone file. It generally rubber-stamps changes recommended by ICANN, although it retains the right to review and approve such changes. As a practical matter, however, the Department of Commerce does not initiate any changes to the root zone file and has never blocked a change recommended by ICANN.[52]

The ICANN "privatization" carried within it a host of internal contradictions reflecting its compromise nature. In keeping with the fiction that this transition represented a privatization of the DNS from U.S. government or other government control, the ICANN bylaws prohibited any government representative from sitting on the Board.[53] At the same time, however, acknowledging the desire of governments to have a role in ICANN, the bylaws created the Government Advisory Committee that would "provide advice on the activities of the Corporation as they relate to concerns of governments."[54]

Similarly, the U.S. policy statement on which ICANN was predicated eschewed any notion that ICANN should act as a regulatory body or Internet "world government."[55] ICANN, the U.S. government, and ICANN's supporters insisted that ICANN was simply a technical coordinating body. At the same time, ICANN had an explicit mandate to address the trademark problem by imposing uniform rules on gTLDs to govern conflicts among rival claimants to names—a policy issue having nothing whatsoever to do with technical coordination.[56] Similarly, while ICANN was to address the question of the introduction of new gTLDs, nothing in ICANN's mandate or bylaws limited it to mere technical issues attendant upon such introduction.[57] ICANN also had a mandate to introduce competition to the business of registering gTLDs, another issue that hinged upon traditional policy concerns of politics and economics rather than on technical coordination.[58]

Finally, ICANN's mandate and bylaws required it to be a "consensus" body making decisions through "bottom-up" processes. The mandate and supporters of ICANN explicitly and repeatedly invoked the IETF standards process as the model ICANN would follow.

Such comparisons overlooked the critical differences between ICANN and the IETF. The IETF relied on voluntary coordination and comparison among alternatives implemented in the real world— "rough consensus and running code." By contrast, ICANN existed to impose *mandatory* compliance. Nor did ICANN have any meaningful objective mechanism for determining "rough consensus." This allowed the ICANN Board to simply announce consensus and impose it on the community.[59]

These internal contradictions made ICANN a compromise acceptable to the dominant coalition, but also ensured that ICANN would remain controversial, contentious, and prone to failure.

The structure of ICANN gave the majority of Board seats to the Internet technical community. In addition, Jon Postel was to assume control of the organization as chief technical officer. To the Internet technical community—most important, to the root server operators, RIRs, and ccTLD registries—ICANN appeared to be a more formal version of IANA that walled off outside influences by confining business interests and the politics around domain names to a separate "domain name supporting organization" and government interests to the Government Advisory Committee.[60]

But to the business interests, government interests, and others not part of the old Internet technical community, ICANN represented an opportunity to centralize management of the DNS. Its formal structure and the potential to control DNS resource providers through a contractual regime that avoided the usual constraints on federal agencies or multinational treaty organizations provided a mechanism for regulating a variety of behaviors on the Internet rather than relying on market mechanisms or existing legal fora.

What prevented ICANN from immediately becoming a regulatory body was the lack of any formal contracts with the ccTLD registries, the root server operators, and the RIRs.[61] ICANN also initially lacked a formal contract with Network Solutions, but Network Solutions, the U.S. government, and ICANN ultimately concluded an agreement in July 1999. The 1999 agreement placed ICANN firmly in control as regulator of the gTLD space, subject to final approval of any ICANN decisions by the Department of Commerce.[62] Its next priority, after a spate of industry regulation in the gTLD space, was to seek to impose binding contracts on RIRs, ccTLDs, and root server operators. Getting agreement from the RIRs and ccTLDs, however, proved much more difficult than ICANN or its supporters predicted.

The Breakup of the Dominant Coalition and ICANN's Current Crisis

Almost immediately after the formation of ICANN, Jon Postel died of heart failure. This one event removed from ICANN its single greatest claim to legitimacy among the Internet technical community.[63] Although other Internet luminaries—notably Vinton Cerf, an engineer heavily involved in the Internet from the beginning and often referred to as one of the "fathers" of the Internet—served on the ICANN Board or publicly supported ICANN, none had the same level of trust and legitimacy for management of Internet coordination as Postel.

From 1998 through the ICANN restructuring of 2002, ICANN unsuccessfully sought to bring the remaining DNS asset managers into the fold. The RIRs, the root server operators, and the majority of ccTLD registries refused to sign binding contracts with ICANN. Indeed, the ccTLD operators have threatened to pull out of ICANN entirely,[64] while the RIRs have offered "suggestions" for altering ICANN's governance structure that would radically reduce the authority of the ICANN Board.

The Roots of Discontent: ICANN's Expansion of Authority and Control

Significantly, although ICANN has unilaterally assessed "fees" from the RIRs and ccTLDs for maintaining their entries in the root zone file,[65] the core dispute does not revolve around money.[66] Indeed, while declining to sign binding contracts with ICANN, the ccTLDs and RIRs have made "voluntary" payments to ICANN. Nor is the principal objection the dispute about the existence of ICANN itself or any of the issues that have concerned civil liberties groups, such as user representation on the Board. As the RIRs recently emphasized, "we are not 'anti-ICANN.' "

Rather the RIRs and the ccTLDs object to two critical structural issues. First, despite the commitment of ICANN and its supporters that ICANN remain a "narrow technical coordinating body" governed by "bottoms-up consensus" and not a "government of the Internet," ICANN has increasingly expanded its authority beyond technical coordination to industry regulation. Since its inception, ICANN has laid claim to trademark policy as an area for its regulation. At the behest of its Government Advisory Committee, ICANN placed a freeze on registering country codes in the new .info TLD.[67] After the terrorist attacks of September 11, 2001, ICANN extended its authority to the realm of Internet security. None of these actions pertains to technical coordination. All speak to an alarming tendency toward mission creep.

Second, ICANN has no apparent meaningful limits on its authority. Despite a requirement in its agreement with the Department of Commerce to create an "independent review board" to ensure that ICANN did not exceed its authority or stray from its mission, ICANN declined to do so. The fact that failure to meet with this contractual requirement has had no negative consequences for ICANN renders ICANN's subsequent assurances that it is, in fact, both unambitious and restrained less than reassuring.[68]

This assignment is particularly true after the redelegation of the Australian country code, .au. In September 2001, at the behest of the Australian government, ICANN transferred control of the .au ccTLD (or, in ICANN-speak, "redelegated") from Robert Elz to a nonprofit entity formed by the Australian government. Elz had been a friend of Jon Postel who had administered .au since its creation.[69] It is noteworthy that ICANN did not justify this on the grounds of "Internet stability." Indeed, in a nod to the technical community, the Board thanked Elz for his "profound contributions to the evolution and stable performance of the global Internet."[70] Rather, ICANN exercised its authority at the behest of, and with the cooperation of, a sovereign government. No more clear alarm bell could ring for the Internet technical community—particularly those in possession of Internet assets.

As a result, the RIRs and the ccTLDs have sought to protect themselves by stripping ICANN of the authority to make binding policy that impacts either number delegation or the ccTLDs. They have steadfastly refused to be tempted by lesser reforms offered by ICANN. Indeed, the ccTLDs in particular have increasingly threatened to look "outside the ICANN structure" for "management of the IANA function."[71]

ICANN's Failure to Coerce an Agreement without the Support of Governments

Unfortunately for ICANN, its coercive powers are limited. It achieved the .au redelegation with the cooperation of a sovereign government and at a time before the ccTLDs understood that ICANN would exercise its power to administer the root zone file for political purposes. A move against any other ccTLDs could trigger a mass exodus by ccTLDs to a new "alternate" root. In this scenario, two entities each claiming to be authoritative would enter names. When those names conflicted, individual network operators would need to make individual determinations on how to resolve names, and packets could be directed to conflicting destinations.[72]

The scenario in which ICANN's root zone file competes with an alternate, potentially authoritative database is frequently referred to as "splitting the root." While a minority of proponents believe that splitting the root would have positive consequences because it would decentralize control of the DNS and encourage competition, the vast majority of the technical and policy community view splitting the root as the ultimate collapse of Internet stability and a potential doomsday scenario for the globally accessible Internet. So far, even proponents of the "alternate root" community—those who advocate using a master list other than the root zone file that includes gTLDS not found in the root zone file—avoid conflicting with existing registries where possible.[73]

Accordingly, neither ccTLDs nor ICANN are particularly interested in bringing about such a doomsday scenario. As a result, ICANN has attempted to pressure ccTLDs in other ways.

As custodian of the "IANA function" of maintaining the root zone file, ICANN enters any changes in the ccTLD administrative records in the root zone file. These records, among other things, inform computers seeking to resolve ccTLD addresses of the IP address of the relevant machine, or "name server," for the ccTLD. ICANN has, at times, refused to enter changes requested by ccTLDs, intimating that it would facilitate requests for changes enormously if the ccTLD registries agreed to sign a binding contract with ICANN.

This tactic backfired in the summer of 2002. KPNQwest, a major European telecommunications company that provided critical name services, went bankrupt. As a result, many European ccTLDs needed to change their name server information. ICANN refused to make the necessary changes until the European ccTLDs acceded to certain demands. Ultimately, the threat to the stability of the name space reached a critical juncture and ICANN made the necessary changes.[74]

This exercise, however, demonstrated to the Internet technical community that ICANN would risk the stability of the Internet—its entire reason for existence from the technical community's perspective—to achieve its policy objectives. Thus, not only did the refusal to make changes fail to gain the necessary concessions, it solidified opposition in the ccTLD registries and the technical community generally. As a result, the ccTLDs have moved from veiled hints that they might use an alternative to ICANN's root zone file to open discussion as to whether ICANN is necessary to the "IANA function" and how to achieve stability in the face of ICANN's misconduct.[75]

ICANN has an even weaker hold over the RIRs than over the ccTLDs. Parties receive delegations of IP address space directly from the RIRs. The RIRs do not enter their assignments into the root zone file. Indeed, it is name registrants who must get IP addresses, then report back to the name registrar to what IP address a name will resolve. Nor does the registrant receive the IP address from the RIR. RIRs are wholesalers of IP addresses, providing large blocks to major telecommunications carriers who sell smaller blocks "downstream" to smaller Internet service providers or hosting services.[76] By the same token, however, RIRs cannot split the root by threatening to move their services elsewhere.

ICANN has, since its inception, claimed a responsibility for coordinating IP address policy.[77] The RIRs, as part of the dominant coalition, acceded to this claim on the understanding that ICANN would respect the RIRs' autonomy and would remain primarily in the hands of the technical community. ICANN's actions toward the ccTLD community, its expanding bureaucracy, and its increasing deference to world governments (described below) have dissipated that trust.

A similar situation applies to the root server operators. The root servers work because the individual private name servers that resolve domain names to IP numbers for the numerous interconnected networks that make up the Internet look to the root servers for this information. ICANN cannot prevent them from regularly refreshing their copies of the root zone file without disrupting the operation of the Internet, and has no other lever to compel cooperation. At the same time, however, the root server operators cannot designate a new A Root without splitting the root zone file, because ICANN and the U.S. government control a substantial minority of the root servers and these root servers will point to the "official root" no matter what the other root server operators do.[78]

Verisign's Discontent with Industry Regulation

Finally, Verisign, the successor to Network Solutions and the dominant gTLD registry and registrar, has grown increasingly restive under ICANN's regime. In 1999, Verisign consented to contract with ICANN and acknowledge its authority. In the contract, Verisign secured for itself a guarantee that ICANN could not impose new regulations on Verisign unless ICANN could document that the new regulations resulted from a documentable "consensus" within the Internet community. Verisign also understood that ICANN would not act as a general regulator of its business practices.[79]

Verisign has discovered, however, that its commercial rivals and others ill-disposed to it can use ICANN's process to, at the very least, delay introduction of new registry services. For example, in 2002, Verisign sought to introduce a new service at the registry level called the "Wait List Service," which allowed parties to register for names already registered, in the hopes that registration would expire. Because ICANN had to approve the new service, Verisign had to endure a referral to the Domain Name Supporting Organization (DNSO),[80] a public comment, a task force report, a vote on the task force report by the DNSO, and then a Board decision.[81]

This engendered more than a mere delay of several months. The DNSO, populated with Verisign's commercial rivals and customers (as the relevant stakeholder community), initially recommended either rejection or strict price controls and other conditions. Although the Board ultimately decided to approve the service, it chose to impose limited conditions of its own. Furthermore, had the Board wished to deny permission, the DNSO report provided ample evidence of "consensus" as defined in the ICANN-Verisign agreement to warrant ICANN's denying Verisign's request to implement the service.

Verisign has, so far, limited its complaints to lobbying the Department of Commerce to keep ICANN on a tight leash[82] and angry protest to ICANN that it lacks authority to act as a regulator.[83] If pressed too far, however, Verisign could use the same threat of splitting the root as the ccTLD registries.

ICANN's Need for Bigger Guns: Growing Closer to Governments

In response to this growing discontent, ICANN has drawn increasingly closer to sovereign governments, which have the power to compel actors that reside within their borders. Facilitating this effort have been calls by Congress for tighter supervision of ICANN by the Department of Commerce to restrain ICANN's arbitrary exercise of its existing authority.[84] As governments become increasingly involved in ICANN and DNS, ICANN comes more and more to resemble either a U.S. government agency (if supervised by the Department of Commerce) or a multinational treaty organization (if managed by ICANN's Government Advisory Committee [GAC]).[85]

Governments have the trump card that they can act unilaterally if they wish, threatening to put residents of their country in jail for refusing to follow their rules. For example, the government of South Africa has acted unilaterally to assume control of its ccTLD, .za, through the expedient of making it a crime to operate the .za ccTLD except in the manner prescribed by the South African Government.[86] China has asserted rights in any system of domain names using Chinese characters, and has acted unilaterally to redirect Internet traffic away from Web sites it does not want its citizens to see to "approved" Web sites by requiring Internet service providers in China to use what amounts to the Chinese government's own DNS.[87]

As a result, despite the express purpose of establishing ICANN to insulate the DNS from government control, ICANN has always acted with solicitude toward requests from the Government Advisory Committee, and ICANN has increasingly become a way for governments to impose their will on DNS management. One of the first acts of the GAC was to publish a statement on the proper relationship between managers of country codes and the sovereign states associated with those codes. The policy invokes traditional language used by sovereign states when regulating public resources, describing ccTLD registries as trustees responsible to the community they serve. This policy has become a basis for ICANN's policy on ccTLD delegation.[88] When the GAC requested that ICANN prevent the registration of two- and three-letter country codes in the new .info top-level domain and generally act to protect country names in new TLDs, ICANN complied immediately, circumventing the normal name policy formulation process to give the GAC what it wanted.[89] When the GAC replied with criticism to the ICANN proposal for evolution and reform, ICANN's president and its chairman fairly gushed with gratitude for the GAC's valuable insights and promised to address its concerns.[90]

As a result of this solicitude toward governments, ICANN cannot give the RIRs and ccTLDs what they want—freedom from regulation. From the point of view of world governments, ICANN has two purposes: to remove the DNS from exclusive U.S. control and to provide a mechanism for regulating the DNS. This is incompatible with insulating critical elements of the DNS from potential regulation.

Relations with the U.S. Government

Further complicating matters, members of Congress have increasingly called on the Department of Commerce to take a more active role in managing ICANN. Although having no direct authority over ICANN, Congress can exercise its power over the Department of Commerce and, through the Department of Commerce, over the DNS. The Department of Commerce must maintain positive relations with relevant members of Congress with authority over the department's budget. In addition, if pushed, Congress can direct the Department of Commerce to take action to implement U.S. policy over the DNS.[91]

This pressure has the paradoxical effect of driving ICANN further into the arms of world governments. As they did in 1998, the parties in support of ICANN see world governments as a counterweight to dominance by the U.S. government. The Department of Commerce, which has a broad e-commerce agenda and must negotiate with the same international parties not merely on DNS but on other matters, tends to take a more internationalist view than Congress.

As a result, ICANN finds itself pulled apart by contradictory demands of its key stakeholders. The private parties with DNS assets have grown increasingly disenchanted with the ICANN "privatization" and insist on written guarantees of independence. World governments insist on a right to greater influence over ICANN policy. The U.S. Congress demands increased direct supervision by the Department of Commerce.

Governments Ascendant: The 2002 Reorganization

In this tug-of-war, ICANN and the Department of Commerce have sought to foster stronger ties between ICANN and world governments. ICANN's initial reform plan would have abandoned the pretense that it represents a privatization of DNS management by seating five government representatives on the Board. In exchange, governments would have provided ICANN with funding.[92] Although the GAC rejected this suggestion, it called for a greater role in managing ICANN.[93]

The Department of Commerce has also supported this approach, despite the opposition of Congress. In September 2002, the Department of Commerce again renewed ICANN's contract to manage the DNS. In doing so, however, it expressed its disappointment with ICANN's failure to date to reach an agreement with the ccTLDs, root server operators, or RIRs. Its solution, however, was to commit the Department of Commerce to work through the GAC to facilitate "stable agreements" between the ccTLD registries and ICANN and the RIRs and ICANN.[94] The Department of Commerce also charged ICANN to develop "an effective advisory role" for governments and pledged that the department would "work within the GAC to ensure that it serves as an effective voice for governmental input into ICANN."

As a result, the new bylaws privilege the GAC in ways that ensure its position as a dominant voice in ICANN policy formation. The GAC has sent a permanent nonvoting liaison to the Board. It may also send nonvoting liaisons to any other committee or policy organ in ICANN. The GAC has a representative on the nominating committee that will select the majority of ICANN's directors. The Board must notify the GAC. The GAC may also initiate policy by requesting that the Board take direct action, thus circumventing the other policy organs of ICANN. The ICANN Board will presumptively follow the

GAC's recommendations, and explain in detail to the GAC where it cannot. If the ICANN Board feels it cannot act in accordance with the GAC's recommendations, the Board has a further obligation to attempt to resolve the differences. Finally, ICANN explicitly states that its own action cannot preempt action by individual GAC member states.[95]

Theoretically, this still leaves ICANN as the ultimate arbiter of DNS policy independent of governments. But the veneer of private decisionmaking is wearing increasingly thin. The new structure provides the GAC with an independent route to developing policy within ICANN without input from any other set of stakeholders while having input into every other ICANN policy formation process.

The Coming Crisis: Increased Instability or Full-Fledged Government Regulation

The situation continues to be inherently unstable. ICANN cannot compromise on the essential demand of the ccTLDs, the RIRs, and the root server operators that ICANN insulate them from potential regulatory control without antagonizing the governments it has courted for support. It cannot divorce itself from Department of Commerce's oversight without antagonizing Congress, and it cannot unilaterally impose its will on Verisign in accordance with the expressed consensus of its relevant policy development organs without chancing that Verisign will find the risk of instability preferable to an intrusive regulatory regime.[96]

Sadly, ICANN's past behavior indicates its willingness to put the stability of the Internet naming system at risk to achieve its political ends. So far, ICANN and the DNS asset managers have avoided a catastrophic confrontation. The difficulty with brinkmanship, however, is that it is possible for the parties to misjudge either the effects of their actions or the willingness of other parties to take unilateral action. Although none of the parties desire to split the root, that could happen if the tension between the DNS asset managers and ICANN continues to increase.

If ICANN avoids a catastrophic confrontation, it appears most likely to evolve into an even more explicitly regulatory organization coming to resemble more and more a traditional government agency or multinational treaty organization. Such an approach, however, seems unlikely to serve the dynamic development of the Internet. Indeed, as ICANN has marched toward realization of its regulatory destiny, it has ballooned enormously. ICANN's 1999 operating budget was $1.5 million. The projected budget for 2002–03 is more than $6 million. Staff has grown from 15 in 2000 to 27 projected in 2003.[97] This is supported by increasing contributions from the domain name registries and registrars (and, if ICANN succeeds, the RIRs), who in turn pass this on to name (and number) registrants. In essence, ICANN is increasingly supported by user fees and taxes, just as any regulatory agency is. Unfortunately, because ICANN has no constraints, it can continue to increase the fees it charges registries without restraint.[98]

More important, however, ICANN is simply a bad regulator. Its members, chosen to satisfy criteria of "representativeness" from various technical and political interests and to reflect geographic diversity, lack any relevant experience in the public policy issues they seek to master. As a result, ICANN has behaved in an inconsistent and arbitrary manner, without any of the constraints generally associated with administrative agencies or multinational treaty organizations.[99]

This is reflected in ICANN's achievements to date. ICANN has selected new gTLDs in a process strongly reminiscent of the Federal Communications Commission's long-discredited "comparative hearing" method, and ICANN's negotiation of further regulatory constraints imposed lengthy delays on the introduction of new TLDs.[100] To introduce retail competition, ICANN developed a scheme similar to the FCC's "unbundled network element" policy (under which competing telecommunications carriers have access to the networks of their rivals).[101] In other words, ICANN recapitulates the FCC but does it badly.

Finally, the rhetoric of privatization that supported ICANN's formation correctly observed that traditional governance processes take far too long and allow governments to pursue parochial interests at the expense of technological development. Unlike a nation-based telecommunications resource, such as spectrum management, in which individual countries can experiment with different management schemes without impacting neighboring countries, management of the DNS of necessity impacts the global Internet.

A Possible Solution: Reducing ICANN to a Ministerial Function

Even at this stage, it remains possible to privatize the DNS in the sense of removing intrusive regulatory oversight and insulating it from government control. This approach is politically least likely because it faces the opposition not merely of world governments but of special interests that desire an organization capable of regulating the global Internet (even if they dislike the way ICANN is structured). Nevertheless, genuine privatization is a preferable outcome to a destabilizing event caused by the sudden withdrawal of a DNS asset manager and the resulting "split" in the root, or to the transformation of ICANN into a regulatory agency supported by the coercive power of sovereign states.

In 1997, the U.S. government could have privatized the DNS by simply allowing the existing government contracts to lapse—possibly establishing a mechanism for routine addition of new top-level domains first. While Network Solutions would have had a commanding lead with .com, .org, and .net, other competitors could have entered the market without regard to any cumbersome "official" process. Now, the process is more difficult. ICANN has succeeded in introducing two intrusive regulatory schemes into the DNS. These rules cannot be simply eliminated without creating considerable political uproar from the politically powerful stakeholders that managed to create the rules in the first place and from those whose economic well-being now depends on the existence of those rules.

First, because ICANN declined to create true competition to .com by allowing the introduction of enough generic TLDs to create an unconcentrated market, it created a more intrusive mechanism. It created an artificial split between the retail market and the wholesale market, maintained the wholesale monopoly, and allowed regulated competition in the retail market. ICANN required Verisign to develop an open platform permitting ICANN-certified "registrars" to sell domain names in Verisign's TLDs to the public. Verisign, as the "registry," receives six dollars per name registered by any "registrar." Although Verisign is permitted to act as both a registry and a registrar,[102] other gTLD registries are not. As ICANN has approved new gTLDs, it has fixed the wholesale price for the new registries by contract and perpetuated the registry/registrar split.[103]

The second mechanism is the Uniform Dispute Resolution Process (UDRP). All gTLD registrants agree to abide by an arbitration process developed by ICANN when a claimant believes it has a right to a domain name held by another.[104] Technically, the UDRP is supposed to allow trademark holders to challenge names registered or used in "bad faith" and in which the registrant has no "legitimate interest."[105] In practice, however, some UDRP arbitrators have awarded names to challengers that do not hold trademarks or have found "bad faith" and no legitimate interest under questionable circumstances. Given the popularity of the UDRP with politically powerful organizations dedicated to promoting trademark and intellectual property interests, eliminating the UDRP is effectively impossible.

ICANN is not necessary, however, to maintaining these two schemes. The contracts between the registries and registrars remain binding. Contracts requiring registrants to submit to the UDRP remain binding. It does not require any ongoing supervision by ICANN to maintain the contractual regime.

The one issue that requires coordination is the issue that created the initial rupture within the Internet community that led to the formation of ICANN in the first place—the introduction of new gTLDs. There is some debate in the technical community on how many new TLDs could be added without destabilizing the Internet (it is argued by some that, at some point, the volume of information the root servers must process to resolve names becomes sufficiently large that it creates congestion). All technical experts agree, however, that the current DNS could support hundreds of top-level domains.[106] The current scarcity of gTLDs is entirely artificial. It results from the opposition from trademark interests who fear an increase in policing costs, registries that benefit from the lack of alternatives, and ICANN, which derives much of its regulatory power from the existing scarcity.

Fortunately, the problem of allocation is a straightforward one and has been well developed in other contexts. A mechanism under which some limited number—but large enough to ensure genuine competition—of TLDs becomes available on a regular basis will introduce genuine competition and thus replace the need for regulation with a genuinely market-based regime. To the extent consumer protection is warranted, national governments retain their traditional powers to act against the registries within their borders.

In an ideal world, ICANN would be reduced to a purely administrative body responsible for entering changes to the root zone file requested by the already designated holders of the relevant databases. On a regular basis, say, every year, this "ICANN-lite" would announce a filing window for some number of new TLDs, say, 50. If, at the end of the window, it had received more applications than available TLDs, it could resolve the matter by auction. Conflicting applications for the same string, such as multiple applications for ".web" or ".kids," could also be resolved by auction. The proceeds of the auction and modest administrative fees would adequately fund the reduced operations.

The holders of the DNS resources would then be free to act on their own. ICANN-lite would exercise no authority over the management and operation of the name space or IP address space. Sufficient incentives to cooperate—notably the fear of splitting the root and the desire of all DNS asset managers to maintain a globally accessible Internet—exist outside of any coercive contracts. With competition at a registry level to prevent exploitation of monopoly power, and consumer protection available at a national level to prevent other forms of market abuse, the need for an expensive, bureaucratic, and intrusive regulatory regime vanishes entirely, to the benefit of the Internet and the public generally.

Conclusion

The defenders of ICANN justified its creation and continued existence on two grounds: first, that ICANN represented a privatization of the DNS out of the hands of the U.S. government and an insulation from government control; second, that it would contribute to the stability of the Internet by replacing the voluntary coordination of the pieces of the DNS under uncertain authority with contracts clearly delineating responsibilities, expectations, and lines of authority.

None of these justifications has borne the slightest resemblance to reality. ICANN represented a step away from privatization to a regulated regime. It has unsettled expectations by disrupting the long-standing relationships that predated it and thereby destabilized the previously stable DNS regime. It has increasingly become a mechanism for government regulation of the DNS. Along the way, ICANN has introduced a bloated bureaucracy and an intrusive regulatory regime into the heart of DNS management.

As a result, ICANN has come to decisional crossroads. It can continue in its present course of seeking to impose its will on the RIRs, ccTLDs, root server operators, and Verisign. That path appears likely to ultimately cause a rupture within the root itself when ICANN and one of the parties operating a critical Internet resource decide to risk splitting the root rather than submit to onerous demands. Alternatively, ICANN can drop the pretense of being a private entity and embrace its role as a quasi-government agency or quasi-multinational treaty organization. That path, however, means embracing a regulatory regime with potentially far-reaching consequences to the Internet as a whole.

There still remains, however, the road not taken in 1997: the road of genuine privatization. Although more difficult to achieve now than before ICANN introduced significant regulation into the DNS, it remains a viable alternative. Embracing this alternative while eliminating ICANN would preserve the DNS and the Internet in its dynamic and stable state.

ICANN serves as a cautionary tale. Its founders hoped to inoculate the DNS from regulation by creating a structure outside of a formal government regime and capable of just enough regulation to satisfy powerful political interests present at the birth. This intention seemed preferable from the other alternative, a genuinely unregulated free market. But even a "little bit of regulation" has proved impossible to contain.

In retrospect, it seems rather naive to believe that governments wanting to leverage the centralized DNS databases for regulatory purposes could be neatly "cabined" in an advisory committee or that industry participants would not seek to game the system for their own advantage. Nor did making the industry regulator a nongovernmental nonprofit magically eliminate the problems inherent in industry regulation, as ICANN's founders had hoped. As others propose new systems for global regulation of the Internet in the interest of "stability," they would do well to question whether the Internet would be better served by voluntary cooperation in a free market—despite the "instability" and messiness the free market brings.

13. Does Cyberspace Need Antitrust?

Eric P. Crampton and Donald J. Boudreaux

Introduction

Somewhere in Canada, a shopper sat at home and ordered the latest bestseller from http://www.bn.com. While Canadian antitrust authorities pondered whether the Chapters chain of booksellers constituted a monopoly, our Internet shopper gave the lie to claims of monopolization. Early Internet enthusiasts claimed that "the Internet interprets censorship as damage and routes around it," meaning that the distributed nature of the Web makes the policing of it rather difficult. DARPANET, the precursor to the Internet, was designed to withstand a nuclear strike against any of its nodes by routing information around the damage. Economists specializing in industrial organization theory could as easily quip that the Internet interprets local monopolies as arbitrage opportunities for careful shoppers, allowing them to route around the higher prices.

While our Canadian shopper waited for her new book to arrive, the European Commission deliberated whether MCI and WorldCom should be allowed to merge. Though neither company had a substantial presence in Europe, the Commission was able to ensure that MCI divested its Internet backbone infrastructure before the companies could consummate their merger. The Commission noted that the proposed merger "between two U.S. telecommunications companies would have worldwide effects. The Internet is global in nature; Internet access and service providers, Internet content providers, end-customers, all demand universal connectivity to the World Wide Web. ... The impact of this merger between these two U.S. companies affected not only U.S. consumers but also inter alia European Union consumers."[1]

The two examples highlight the double-edged nature of e-commerce and Internet applications for antitrust. While the Internet massively increases the size of the relevant market for a host of transactions, subverting would-be monopolists and encouraging

363

worldwide competition, it also increases the jurisdictional scope of national antitrust authorities. Many countries and the European Commission use an economic effects rule to determine jurisdiction. Since a Web site may engage in purely electronic transactions without knowing where its customers are physically located, it may be subject to the jurisdiction of dozens of antitrust authorities around the world.

Jurisdiction and extraterritoriality issues are not a new problem in antitrust enforcement. The 1945 *Alcoa* decision extended the Sherman Act's reach beyond America's borders to apply to commercial activity affecting American commerce, regardless of its physical location. Thus, for example, if prices in the United States are affected by commerce occurring only in foreign jurisdictions, U.S. antitrust law applies.

For much of the 20th century, antitrust effectively remained an American institution as few jurisdictions outside America had substantive competition laws; extraterritoriality problems were mostly found in the enforcement of the Sherman Act beyond the borders of the United States. Today, however, more than 90 countries have antitrust statutes and more are drafting competition codes;[2] together, more than 86 percent of world trade takes place in jurisdictions with antitrust statutes.[3] In this chapter, we discuss the workings of international antitrust enforcement, how the Internet affects and is affected by antitrust legislation, and the challenges that Internet suppliers and consumers face in the global antitrust environment.

International Antitrust

Although antitrust was not invented in the United States,[4] during most of the 20th century it effectively remained an American institution. For the first half of the century, the Sherman Act applied only within American borders,[5] but the 1945 *Alcoa* ruling extended its reach to foreign conduct affecting American commerce.[6] Until the early 1990s, "international antitrust" largely referred to the problems associated with extraterritorial enforcement of American antitrust law against overseas corporate activity.

Alcoa defined the American stance on the jurisdictional limits of antitrust. In that case, Canadian and European aluminum companies colluded to restrict aluminum production, limiting the amount of aluminum ingot that they would export to the United States. Judge

Learned Hand's Second Circuit Court ruled that the foreign cartel was subject to action under the Sherman Act because its activities both intended and subsequently resulted in substantial negative effects on American commerce. This "effects test" became enshrined in American antitrust law over the latter half of the century.[7] While some rulings attempted to inject comity considerations into the effects test,[8] the Supreme Court's ruling in *Hartford Fire*[9] strongly limited the application of comity to those cases in which foreign law conflicts with American law to such an extent that the foreign company cannot comply with the statutes of both countries. *Alcoa's* effects test remains the determinant of jurisdiction.

Extraterritorial enforcement of the Sherman Act has not gone without complaint from the foreign jurisdictions affected. Several countries have put in place blocking legislation to impede American antitrust enforcement. In addition, "claw-back" legislation allows foreign defendants in American antitrust cases to seek damages in their home countries' courts from the plaintiff in the American antitrust action.[10] However, these types of problems in extraterritorial enforcement are not the main concern of this chapter; they are now the boilerplate of international business and antitrust textbooks.[11]

Of more recent concern is the worldwide proliferation of antitrust statutes. Assistant Attorney General Charles James quipped in a recent address that "antitrust has been one of the United States' most successful exports."[12] While countries with McDonald's restaurants still outnumber those with antitrust statutes, James was not hyperbolizing. As recently as 1973, only 27 countries had adopted competition codes.[13] As of the end of 1996 that number had grown to 70, 61 percent of which had instituted their codes in the 1990s.[14] The most recent figures put the number at more than 90, with 20 more countries in the process of drafting codes.[15] Because many of these countries' codes also employ an economic effects test to determine jurisdiction, any given transaction may be subject to scrutiny by dozens of antitrust authorities.

The proliferation of antitrust authorities presents far more difficult problems than those posed by an extraterritorially activist Federal Trade Commission. Multiple agencies now can and do claim jurisdiction over a variety of corporate activities, most notably over mergers. More than 60 countries now require or provide for prenotification merger filings.[16] Consequently, large merging companies sometimes now need to file such notifications with more than a dozen jurisdictions. The compliance costs for merging companies can be burdensome, especially in cases in which the relevant antitrust authorities provide contradictory rulings.[17]

To minimize friction in the application of antitrust laws, the United States has pursued bilateral agreements with Australia, Brazil, Canada, Germany, Israel, Japan, Mexico, and, most notably, the European Community.[18] At minimum, these agreements provide for notification and consultation on cases in which the interests of both parties are involved. Agreements with several jurisdictions, including the EC, also include positive comity provisions allowing each jurisdiction to request that the other enforce its own laws to remedy activity taking place within its borders.[19]

By most accounts, cooperation between antitrust authorities is strong and growing.[20] However, no amount of interagency cooperation can prevent conflict when the antitrust agencies of different jurisdictions have irreconcilable differences regarding the purpose of antitrust legislation. Two merger cases involving the United States and the EC serve here as examples: Boeing/McDonnell Douglas and GE/Honeywell.

In the Boeing/McDonnell Douglas case, the FTC determined that the merger posed no anticompetitive threats, while the EC objected to exclusive supply contracts despite efficiency-enhancing characteristics of those contracts.[21] Daniel Gifford and Thomas Sullivan argue that the EC ruling may constitute an attempt on the part of the EC to raise Boeing's costs to provide an advantage to Airbus, the well-connected and well-subsidized European consortium airplane manufacturer.[22] Following EC threats of enforcement action, Boeing abandoned its exclusive supply contracts.

Similarly, in GE/Honeywell, strong cooperation between the Department of Justice and the EC preceded divergent rulings. Because the merging parties waived confidentiality rights, Justice and the EC shared all information provided by GE and Honeywell. Consequently, communication and cooperation between the two agencies was "tremendous."[23] Nevertheless, Justice approved the merger while the EC disallowed it. While both agencies agreed that the merged company would offer improved products and lower prices, Justice deemed the resulting efficiencies to justify the merger while the EC worried that those efficiencies would harm the merged company's competitors.[24] Assistant Attorney General James contrasts EC competition law with American law by noting that the purpose of American antitrust laws "is not to protect business from the working of the market; it is to protect the public from the failure of the market."[25] Although we disagree with his assessment of American antitrust law,[26] the contrast is accurate. Goals other than efficiency underlie much of European competition law.[27]

Leaving political considerations to one side for the moment, antitrust policy is based on economic theory. And economists in different parts of the world do not fully agree with one another. Karl Aiginger, an economist from Austria, and his coauthors find that American economists specializing in industrial organization are more likely than their European counterparts, for example, to view the behavior of oligopolists as conforming to Bertrand or Cournot predictions rather than pure collusion—that is, to restrict output and raise price not by as much as would a pure monopolist but, rather, in a noncollusive way that reflects each oligopolist's strategic guess about how the other oligopolists in its industry will behave.[28] Consequently, American economists are more likely to be skeptical of antitrust action in oligopolistic markets. European industrial organization economists disagree systematically with Americans on a wide range of questions of importance to antitrust policy.[29] Theories long since discarded in the United States remain quite in vogue elsewhere. While American economists and antitrust authorities now tend to be skeptical of predatory pricing arguments, their European counterparts worry greatly about the use of predatory pricing.[30] Fundamentally divergent approaches to antitrust policy can quickly arise from these differences.

In addition, public choice considerations—viewing government officials as being just as self-interested as people in the private sector—lend skepticism to public interest theories of antitrust regulation. Although recent cases like *Boeing* point to protectionism as a driving force behind antitrust enforcement actions, the phenomenon is not at all new. Antitrust legislation might be seen as a substitute (by ensuring that domestic firms are subject to vigorous competition) for open international markets,[31] but the empirical record does not bear up that analysis. Instead, antitrust seems to serve as a substitute for tariffs. Shughart, Silverman, and Tollison find that foreign competition correlates *positively* with antitrust agency funding in the

United States.[32] In addition, Palim finds that countries adopting competition codes do not see them as substitutes for international competition.[33] The recent proliferation of antitrust statutes occurred during a wave of globalization and lower tariffs. This suggests that antitrust statutes might serve as an additional method of protecting domestic firms from foreign competition when other methods of protectionism are waning.[34]

E-Competition: Antitrust and the Internet

The only difference between economics and e-conomics is a hyphen. Economic principles hold as strongly in a wired world as they do in the world of bricks-and-mortar. Mythologies have developed around the economics of the Internet, some of which see the Internet as demanding more activist antitrust policy, others of which argue that the Internet obviates the need for antitrust. We find the arguments for strengthened antitrust enforcement do not hold up to serious scrutiny. On balance, economic arguments favor reduced antitrust activity as a consequence of the Internet. However, antitrust is a political institution and matters politic seem likely to favor increased activism.

Cartels Are Restrained in a Global Digital Marketplace

Traditional antitrust concerns surrounding cartels, price signaling, and other violations of antitrust law can emerge as easily in e-commerce as in traditional business. However, the Internet can mitigate some of these problems. Because individual consumers shopping from home can now quickly access a global marketplace, cartels and price-fixers must become global in scope to be truly effective; local cartels cannot extract rents from Internet-savvy consumers that are larger in magnitude than shipping costs from outside the boundaries of collusion. And as shipping costs fall, the scope for less-than-global cartelization shrinks—for all a consumer need do to escape a local cartel's attempt to charge monopoly prices is to order the desired merchandise or service from outside of the local cartel's geographic area.

Digital Dominance Is Checked by Low Marginal Costs

Economists Richard McKenzie and Dwight Lee raise interesting caveats for antitrust analysis in the digital world.[35] They point out that market dominance cannot be exploited in digital markets in the same way as in the market for physical products. A dominant firm in ordinary markets can increase prices by restricting output; because of their inability to exploit similar economies of scale, competitors cannot simply increase their production to make up the difference. In digital markets marked by infinitesimal marginal costs of production, competitors can quickly and easily increase output to match the reduction in the dominant firm's output. Should Microsoft attempt to exploit its dominant position in the provision of office software, Corel could quickly reap the benefits by expanding its output; doing so would cost Corel next to nothing.

Limits of "Network Effects," "Tipping," "Lock-In," and "Leveraging"

Some authorities worry that the Internet may pose a new antitrust concern—the possibility that network effects may lead to the establishment of global monopolies. Four interrelated economic concepts drive these arguments favoring strong antitrust vigilance in Internet markets: network effects, tipping, lock-in, and the leveraging of monopoly power from one market into others.

Markets in which consumer valuation of a product depends on the number of other people also using the product are described as being subject to network effects. A telephone is of little value if no one else has one; similarly, the Microsoft operating system would not be as desirable if it only commanded a small percent of the market. Once the installed client base for a product reaches a certain size, consumers reason that it will become the standard and the market "tips" in favor of the dominant product. At that point, the market becomes "locked in" to the new standard; superior products may exist, but unless consumers can coordinate to switch to the alternative product, the existing standard will remain dominant. The owner of a standard can then "leverage" its existing monopoly to erode competition in other markets.[36]

We have reason to be wary of network effects arguments favoring strong antitrust enforcement activity. Even if a firm's product has achieved total market dominance, its market power remains rather limited. Should the firm seek to exercise market power, it could encourage entry. Given low marginal costs of distribution once the fixed costs of development have been paid, a rival can quickly establish a network by essentially giving away the initial version of its software and recouping its fixed costs through later sales of upgrades.[37]

The "leveraging" argument is equally suspect. Some critics of Microsoft have claimed that Microsoft has leveraged its Windows monopoly into the browser market. By integrating its browser into the Windows software, Microsoft is alleged to have foreclosed the market to competitors. Of course, customers preferring Netscape or other browsers can simply (and frequently at no cost) download alternate browser software. However, the argument suggests that customers are simply too lethargic to search out alternatives to the software already provided with the computer. If we take the leveraging argument seriously, we should also worry that Microsoft is attempting to extend its reach into the market for search engines. Users mistyping an Internet address in Microsoft's Internet Explorer are quickly routed to Microsoft's own search engine to assist them in finding their Web site. However, Google is the search engine of choice on the Internet, not MSN Search. Microsoft provides no links to Google on its desktop, nor does Internet Explorer automatically link to Google, but almost 80 percent of Internet searches are conducted using Google's engines.[38] Microsoft exerts as much "leveraging" to push customers to its MSN Search product as it does to push customers to use its browser. Internet Explorer passes the market test and MSN Search doesn't; "leverage" doesn't enter into the equation.[39]

Even were we to grant for the moment the argument that network effects can lead to locked-in monopolistic markets, the question of remediability quickly comes to the fore. Paul David, the foremost proponent of "lock-in"–based theories of market failure, suggests comprehensive measures delaying adoption of any technological standard to ensure that the right path is set upon before path dependence sets in.[40] However, it is quite unclear that such delays could survive cost-benefit analysis. While the benefits are only probabilistic and depend critically on the delay actually resulting in the adoption of a more efficient standard, the costs of delay are certain—they must consist of the discounted value of the network benefits that would have accrued during the period of delay. And we have no reason to believe the most efficient standard can be chosen outside of a market discovery process.[41]

Precisely because networks and product familiarity are valuable to consumers, a well-working market will supply these valuable aspects. But it is perverse then to conclude that the market has failed because the successful supplier of a network or of an especially high degree of comfortable product familiarity could, if it chose, raise its prices and restrict its output for a time. Of course it could; such ability is an inevitable consequence of success at pleasing consumers in these ways. (If a firm were unable, even in the short run, to raise its price even slightly without losing significant market share, then this fact would mean that consumers attach no or only minuscule value to the network or to product familiarity.)

However, ability to raise prices above costs in the short run (and to increase short-run profits) does not imply that the firm has real monopoly power. If a firm refrains from exploiting consumers today with higher prices because this firm worries that doing so would cause consumers to shift their patronage to other firms tomorrow, then, in our view, this firm is no monopolist. A genuine monopolist behaves monopolistically. A firm that doesn't behave monopolistically, even though it might be able to do so for a time, is a firm that is foolish or altruistic or fearful of rivals' responses.

Government policy need not concern itself with foolish or altruistic firms; the former write the script of their own doom and the latter are agents of philanthropy (for as long as their shareholders' wealth and goodwill last). Nor should government concern itself with firms fearful of rivals' responses, for such firms are competitive, even if no currently existing competitor is on the scene.

A general principle applies here, which is this: the best evidence of monopoly power is the actual exercise of monopoly power—most notably, raising prices and restricting output. Reality provides very few, if any, actual examples of firms achieving sustained monopoly power—as evidenced by harm to consumers (rather than to competitors)—without government-enforced barriers to entry. The ratio of fears of monopolization to actual monopolization is quite high.[42]

Because history supplies so few examples of the successful private achievement of monopoly power, a sound rule is to require evidence of actual price hikes and output restrictions as necessary (although not sufficient) preconditions to launching antitrust actions.[43] Such a rule will eliminate much of the anti-competitive uses of antitrust that mar its history without significantly increasing risks to consumers of suffering exploitation by a monopolist.

This rule is especially appropriate for the Web and other industries that enjoy exposure worldwide. The number of actual and potential competitors is immense, as are competitors' sources of financing. All it takes is one among millions of people familiar with the Web to have a creative idea on how to serve consumers better than the currently dominant firm is serving consumers. The larger the market, the larger the pool of creative talent and entrepreneurship available to keep it competitive and dynamic.

The network features of this market do not necessarily work against the forces of competition. Of course, it is precisely the difficulty of imagining the massive coordination necessary to replace one network with another that makes competition in such markets seem unlikely. But the empirical evidence gathered by Liebowitz and Margolis shows that competition among actual networks is remarkably robust.[44]

Reflection shows that these empirical findings should not be as surprising as they might at first appear. Competition in network economies occurs at the level of the network. Precisely because the gains from becoming the "dominant" network supplier are so large, the competition to become this supplier will be unusually intense. Entrepreneurs and investors have every incentive to search for ways to displace the currently "dominant" firm—and, knowing that, the currently "dominant" firm has every incentive to keep its prices and product quality as attractive as possible to consumers.

Of course markets might fail. No entrepreneur in the world might recognize the potential for profit. Or even if several cash-strapped entrepreneurs *do* recognize the potential, every single investor worldwide might refuse to finance any such ventures. But so, too, might political and legal processes fail to detect the true state of the market. Indeed, politicians, bureaucrats, and judges are much less likely to make sound decisions about such markets than are entrepreneurs and investors. The latter specialize in taking the pulse of, and investing in, specific markets; the former specialize in legal and political endeavors. Moreover, entrepreneurs and investors put their own wealth at stake on the actual outcome of their decisions; government and judicial functionaries have a much less personal stake in whatever antitrust decisions they make.[45]

Who Rules the Web?

In *Alcoa*, Judge Hand found as "settled law" that "any state may impose liabilities, even upon persons not within its allegiance, for conduct outside its borders that has consequences within its borders that the state reprehends, and that these liabilities other states will ordinarily recognize."[46] While the ruling certainly facilitated the prosecution of anti-competitive behavior beyond America's borders, it raises a dangerous precedent. There remain few activities that some state does not reprehend, and all are now a mouse click away from every jurisdiction in the world. The other papers in this volume provide excellent resources on the implications of this for free speech and other important matters.

The consequences of Hand's decision, and the extension of the economic effects rule to jurisdictions encompassing the vast majority of the world's production and trade, will prove damaging to e-commerce and to the Internet. Antitrust remains a highly politicized part of economic policy, and history suggests that antitrust legislation frequently serves to protect domestic firms from foreign competition. As e-commerce increases global competition, pressure for increased antitrust activism against foreign firms seems likely to increase.

The International Competition Policy Advisory Committee warned against this use of antitrust in its 2000 "Final Report." As Committee Co-Chair Rill suggests, "the threat of seriatim balkanization of e-commerce by multiple, inconsistent, and uncoordinated national regulators threatens economic growth and can be used to impair competitive entry and expansion."[47] Guarding against such state activity has become a matter of increasing concern for the FTC. Indeed, the FTC has begun urging individual states to remove protectionist barriers against Internet competition.[48] However, such actions are much more difficult against foreign states. As much as the United States uses antidumping provisions to protect domestic interests ranging from logging to steel, foreign jurisdictions can launch spurious antitrust complaints against American companies threatening their firms through Internet-based competition.

In many cases, foreign antitrust complaints against e-commerce firms will be relatively minor. For many small countries, ability to enforce antitrust remedies against e-commerce firms may be limited to prohibiting those firms from legally dealing with residents of the country. For instance, a small country's antitrust agency will have a difficult time enforcing a remedy calling on a foreign Fortune 500 company to divest portions of its business, but it may be able to shut the firm out of its markets. And, while shutting the firm out may actually be the goal of such actions, the negative consequences will largely fall on the imposing jurisdiction. In such cases, antitrust provides a way of protecting domestic firms from foreign competition without falling afoul of the General Agreement on Tariffs and Trade or the World Trade Organization.

More troubling are cases in which the litigating jurisdiction is capable of enforcing its remedies on firms outside of its borders. Among jurisdictions with the power to extraterritorially enforce rulings, the ruling of the most restrictive jurisdiction is likely to prevail.[49] Traditional protectionist mechanisms have been quite limited by comparison; while countries have been able to impose tariffs on products crossing the border, they have not been able to force actual restructuring of industries abroad. While the EC could impose tariffs on the imports of American aircraft, they could not dictate the structure of the American aircraft manufacturing industry. The economic effects rule in international antitrust provides that ability.

Of course, countries will be somewhat constrained in applying explicitly protectionist extraterritorial remedies. Extraterritorial enforcement hinges on the agreement of the company's home country; absent that cooperation, enforcement action is limited to preventing the offending firm from selling its wares within the jurisdiction. If cases like Boeing/McDonnell Douglas arise too frequently, cooperation between the United States and the EC on antitrust matters will deteriorate considerably and claw-back and blocking statutes will again become the norm in international antitrust. However, not all cases involve such prominent and well-connected firms.

Because e-commerce allows local consumers to route around the rents earned by local monopolies, we can expect firms whose rents are in danger to lobby strenuously for their protection. If antitrust authorities employed a pure efficiency standard and if political considerations were never a part of antitrust analysis, this would pose little threat to the e-commerce firm. Unfortunately, the world is not nearly so benign.

What's to Be Done?

Given antitrust's long history of abuse, along with an even longer history of markets proving to be remarkably adept and creative at protecting consumers from private monopolies, any proposed antitrust treatment of cyberspace should be examined skeptically. What forms of international antitrust might be best able to withstand skeptical examination, given the practical reality that governments will exercise some form of antitrust scrutiny over cyberspace?

Harmonization is one option, but one that we emphatically oppose. Harmonization, by its nature, eliminates jurisdictional competition—which would be especially ironic for antitrust. Even without interest-group pressures that might bias antitrust rules away from protecting consumers and toward protecting politically influential firms, harmonization's success requires that the single standard chosen and applied interjurisdictionally be sound. If it isn't— if those who select the standard err when doing so—the lack of alternative, competing antitrust regimes makes discovering the single standard's weaknesses unlikely.

Multilateral accords among national governments present another possibility for providing global antitrust regulation. One advantage of this approach is that much of the institutional structure is already in place in the form of the WTO. The multilateral trade agreement put into effect by signatory nations through the WTO can be supplemented with a chapter dealing with antitrust issues.

Specifically, we encourage signatory governments to agree to an origin-based policy of regulation. That is, governments should agree that the antitrust policy applied in any particular instance is the policy of that jurisdiction, and only of that jurisdiction, in which the defendant firm has the greatest substantive presence. The location of the firm's headquarters is a good candidate for establishing greatest substantive presence, although alternative criteria—such as country of incorporation—are available. The particular criterion chosen for establishing greatest substantive presence is less important than adopting a policy that will shield international firms from the uncertainty of being subject to myriad agencies enforcing different, often conflicting, antitrust policies. Such an approach will maintain jurisdictional competition among antitrust regimes—a result that antitrust enthusiasts should vigorously applaud.

For Further Reading

Balto, David A. "Emerging Antitrust Issues in Electronic Commerce." Presentation given at The Antitrust Institute conference "Distribution Practices: Antitrust Counseling in the New Millennium." Available at http://www.ftc.gov/speeches/other/ecommerce.htm, 1999.

Federal Trade Commission. "Antitrust Analysis in High-Tech Industries: A 19th Century Discipline Addresses 21st Century Problems." Prepared remarks of Robert Pitofsky, Chairman, Federal Trade Commission, before the American Bar Association Section of Antitrust Law's Antitrust Issues in High-Tech Industries Workshop, February 25–26, 1999, Scottsdale, Arizona.

Kahn, Tina. "The Protection of Trading Interests Act of 1980: Britain's Response to U.S. Extraterritorial Antitrust Enforcement." *Journal of International Law and Business* 2, no. 2 (Autumn 1980).

Notes

Introduction

1. "A Declaration of the Independence of Cyberspace," Available at http://www.eff.org/pub/Publications/John_Perry_Barlow/barlow_0296.declaration.

2. See generally Matthew Newman, "So Many Countries, So Many Laws," *Wall Street Journal*, April 28, 2003, p. R8; "The Internet's New Borders," *The Economist*, August 9, 2001, www.economist.com/opinion/displaystory.cfm?story-ID=730089.

3. Michael Totty, "Taming the Frontier," *Wall Street Journal*, Jan. 27, 2003, p. R10.

4. Zoe Baird, "Governing the Internet: Engaging Government, Business, and Non-profits," *Foreign Affairs*, November/December 2002. Excerpt available at http://www.foreignaffairs.org/20021101facomment9989/zoe-baird/governing-the-internet-engaging-government-business-and-nonprofits.html.

5. For an overview of such new proposed and existing programs and regulations, see Clyde Wayne Crews Jr. and Adam Thierer, "The Digital Dirty Dozen: The Most Destructive High-Tech Legislative Measures of the 107th Congress," *Cato Institute Policy Analysis* no. 423, February 4, 2002, http://www.cato.org/pubs/pas/pa-423es.html; and, Thierer, Crews, and Thomas Pearson, "Birth of the Digital New Deal: An Inventory of High-Tech Pork-Barrel Spending," *Cato Institute Policy Analysis* no. 457, October 28, 2002, http://www.cato.org/pubs/pas/pa-457es.html.

6. Robert D. Atkinson, "The Failure of Cyber-Libertarianism: The Case for a National E-Commerce Strategy," *PPI Policy Report*, June 2001, http://www.ppionline.org/documents/E-com_Strategy.pdf.

7. David Bollier and Tim Watts, *Saving the Information Commons: A New Public Interest Agenda in Digital Media* (Washington: New America Foundation and Public Knowledge, 2002).

8. Joseph E. Stiglitz, Peter R. Orszag, and Jonathan M. Orszag, *The Role of Government in a Digital Age* (Washington: Computer & Communications Industry Association, October 2000), http://www.ccianet.org/digital_age/report.pdf.

9. Declan McCullagh and Nicholas Morehead, "Nader Wants Internet Control," *Wired News*, January 10, 2001, http://www.wired.com/news/politics/0,1283,41106,00.html.

10. Doug Brown, "Central Question: Whose Internet Is It?" *Interactive Week* 7, no. 15, April 17, 2000, p. 98.

11. Jennifer Balderama, "Free Speech—Virtually," *Washington Post*, December 19, 2002, p. E8. http://www.washingtonpost.com/wp-dyn/articles/A9204-2002Dec18.html.

12. Patricia Jacobus, "Building Fences, One By One," *CNET News.com*, April 19, 2001. http://news.com.com/2009-1023-255774-2.html?legacy=cnet.

13. See, for example, Cass Sunstein, *Republic.com*, (Princeton, N.J.: Princeton University Press, 2001).

14. See http://www.ekidsinternet.com.

15. See Crews, "Is the Internet Bad for Democracy?" *Cato TechKnowledge*, No. 18, August 31, 2001. http://www.cato.org/tech/tk/010831-tk.html. See also Thierer and Crews, "Just Don't Do It: The Digital Opportunities Investment Trust (DO IT) Fund," *Cato TechKnowledge*, No. 35, May 6, 2002. http://www.cato.org/tech/tk/020506-tk.html.

16. Steve Fox, "The Incredible Shrinking Internet," *CNET.com*, July 13, 2000. http://www.cnet.com/insider/0-121949-7-2253424.html.

17. Ibid.

18. Ibid.

19. Agence France-Presse, "Internet Users to Reach 655 Million by Year-End," November 19, 2002. http://www.smh.com.au/articles/2002/11/19/1037599406943.html.

20. See "U.S. Judge Says Yahoo Not Bound by French Nazi Ban," *Yahoo! News*, November 7, 2001.

21. See Lawrence Lessig, "Cyberspace Prosecutor," *The Industry Standard*, February 21, 2000, http://www.thestandard.com/article/0.1902.10885.00.html.

22. Lisa M. Bowman, "Whose Laws Rule on the Wild Wild Web," *CNET News.com*, May 29, 2002, http://zdnet.com.com/2100-1106-927370.html.

23. Geoffrey Robertson, "The Internet on Trial," *Wall Street Journal*, July 18, 2002, p. A12.

24. See Jonathan Krim, "Internet Libel Fence Falls," *Washington Post*, December 11, 2002, p. A10; Dugie Standeford, "Dow Jones Loses Bid to Move Internet Defamation Case to U.S.," *Washington Internet Daily*, 3, no. 238, December 11, 2002, p. 1.

25. Pontifical Council for Social Communications, "Ethics in Internet," February 22, 2002. Also see Farhad Manjoo, "What Would Jesus Surf?" *Wired News*, March 1, 2002, LINK.

26. Tom Rahman, "Italian Police Close Down Porn Web Sites with Catholic Imagery," Associated Press, July 9, 2002.

27. *Significant Developments in Global Internet Law in 2002* (Washington: Covington & Burling, February 2003), p. 3, http://www.cov.com/publications/321.pdf.

28. Dugie Standeford, "U.S. Objects to ITU Official's Call for Internet Regulation," *Washington Internet Daily*, February 11, 2003, p. 4.

29. Such a standard has been frequently debated within the European Union to help resolve jurisdictional disputes. See Terry Lane, "EU E-Commerce Directive Will Retain Country-of-Origin Language," November 15, 2001, pp. 2–3.

30. "The Revenge of Geography," *The Economist*, March 15, 2003, p. 19.

Chapter 2

1. See *State v. Maxwell*, 767 N.E.2d 242, 248-50 (Ohio 2002).

2. 15 U.S.C. §1125(d) (2003).

3. 15 U.S.C. §1125(d)(2) (2003).

4. 15 U.S.C. §1125(d)(2). See also http://www.verisign-grs.com/aboutus/.

5. From http://www.offshore-radio.de/fleet/sealand.htm.

6. See http://www.havenco.com/.

7. See HavenCo's Acceptable Use Policy, http://www.havenco.com/legal/aup.html.

8. *Dow Jones & Company, Inc. v. Gutnick* (2002) 194 A.L.R. 433, [2002] H.C.A. 56.

9. Seymour M. Hersh, "Lunch with the Chairman," *The New Yorker*, March 13, 2003 (posted online on March 10, 2003), available at http://www.newyorker.com/fact/content/?030317fa_fact.

10. Adam Daifallah, "Perle Suing over New Yorker Article," *New York Sun*, March 12, 2003, National p. 2.

11. James C. Goodale, "The Right Forum for Richard Perle," *New York Law Journal* 229 (April 4, 2003): 3.

12. *Twentieth Century Fox Film Corp. et al. v. iCraveTV*, Civ. Action No. 00-121 (W.D. Pa. February 8, 2000).

13. See ibid., paragraphs 9–13.

14. Motion Picture Association of America, "iCraveTV Signs Settlement Agreement That Shuts Down Website," February 28, 2000, available at http://www.mpaa.org/Press/iCrave_Settlement.htm.

15. See *Twentieth Century Fox Film Corp. et al. v. iCraveTV*, Civ. Action No. 00-121 (W.D. Pa. February 8, 2000), Exhibit A.

16. *American Library Association v. Pataki*, 969 F.Supp. 160 (SDNY 1997).

17. 969 F.Supp. 160, 167.

18. See *Dow Jones & Company, Inc. v. Gutnick* (2002) 194 A.L.R. 433, [2002] H.C.A. 56.

19. *Yahoo! v. La Ligue contre le Racisme et l'Antisemitisme and L'Union des Etudiants Juifs de France*, 169 F.Supp. 2d 1181, 1194 (N.D. Cal. 2001).

20. Digital Freedom Network, "Public Pledge on Self-Discipline for China Internet Industry," available at http://dfn.org/voices/china/selfdiscipline.htm.

21. John Perry Barlow, "A Declaration of the Independence of Cyberspace," February 8, 1996, available at http://www.eff.org/~barlow/Declaration-Final.html.

22. David R. Johnson and David G. Post, "Law and Borders: The Rise of Law in Cyberspace," *Stanford Law Review* 48 (1996): 1367.

23. *Zeran v. America Online, Inc.*, 129 F.3d 327 (4th Cir. 1997).

24. *Zeran v. Diamond Broadcasting, Inc.*, Nos. 98-6092 and 98-6094, Order and Judgment (10th Cir. January 28, 2000).

25. Austan Goolsbee and Jonathan Zittrain, "Evaluating the Costs and Benefits of Taxing Internet Commerce," *National Tax Journal* 52 (1999): 413.

26. ICANN, "Uniform Domain-Name Dispute-Resolution Policy General Information," available at http://www.icann.org/udrp/.

27. 15 U.S.C. §1125(d) (2003).

28. See, for example, *Sallen v. Corinthians Licenciamentos LTDA and Desportos Licenciamentos LTDA*, No. 01-1197 (1st Cir. December 5, 2001).

29. Interim Court Order, County Court of Paris, France, (November 22, 2000) available at http://www.cdt.org/speech/international/001120yahoofrance.pdf (containing the Opinion of the Consultants Ben Laurie, Fançois Wallon and Vinton Cerf, *La Ligue contre le Racisme et l'Antisemitisme and L'Union des Etudiants Juifs de France v. Yahoo!, Inc. and Yahoo France*).

30. See, for example, Quova's Geopoint, described at http://www.quova.com/services/geopoint.html.

31. Jonathan Zittrain and Benjamin Edelman, "Localized Google Search Result Exclusions," October 2002, available at http://cyber.law.harvard.edu/filtering/google/.

32. Mark Ward, "Experts Question Yahoo! Auction Ruling," BBC News, November 29, 2000, available at http://news.bbc.co.uk/1/hi/sci/tech/1046548.stm.

33. For an insightful expression of this concern, and an exploration of the theories by which a country should choose to enforce another's judgment even if it would never endorse such a judgment when it was rendered locally in the first instance, see Molly S. Van Houweling, "Enforcement of Foreign Judgments, the First Amendment and Internet Speech: Notes for the Next *Yahoo! v. LICRA*," 2003 (on file with the author).

34. See the Internet Services Unit's homepage, available at http://www.isu.net.sa/index.htm.

35. See the Internet Services Unit's explanation of its Content Filtering practices, available at http://www.isu.net.sa/saudi-internet/content-filtering.htm.

36. Jonathan Zittrain and Benjamin Edelman, "Documentation of Internet Filtering in Saudi Arabia," December 2002, available at http://cyber.law.harvard.edu/filtering/saudiarabia/.

37. Jonathan Zittrain and Benjamin Edelman, "Empirical Analysis of Internet Filtering in China," March 2003, available at http://cyber.law.harvard.edu/filtering/china/.

38. Information on the system is available at http://cs1.cs.nyu.edu/waldman/publius.html.

39. See September 17, 2002, Order of Court of Common Pleas of Montgomery County, Pennsylvania, In the Matter of the Application of D. Michael Fisher, Attorney General of the Commonwealth of Pennsylvania for an Order Requiring an Internet Service Provider to Remove or Disable Access to Child Pornography, July 2002, no. Misc 689 (on file with the author).

40. John Perry Barlow, "A Declaration of the Independence of Cyberspace," February 8, 1996, available at http://www.eff.org/~barlow/Declaration-Final.html.

Chapter 3

A version of this paper appeared under the same title in *University of Chicago Law Review* 68, no. 4 (Fall 1998): 1199–1250. For their comments and discussion, I thank Bill Arms, Caroline Arms, Curtis Bradley, Stephen Choi, Richard Craswell, David Currie, Larry Downes, Richard Epstein, Michael Froomkin, Elizabeth Garrett, Andrew Guzman, Larry Kramer, Larry Lessig, Doug Lichtman, Richard Posner, David Post, Cass Sunstein, Tim Wu, and participants at workshops at the University of Chicago and the University of California (Boalt Hall). I also thank Kyle Gehrmann and Greg Jacob for excellent research, and the Arnold and Frieda Shure Research Fund for support.

1. See Communications Decency Act of 1996 (CDA), Pub. L. No. 104–104. 110 Stat. 133, codified at 47 U.S.C.A. §§ 223, 230, 303, 560–61, 609 (1991 & Supp. 1998); *Reno v. ACLU*, 117 S. Ct. 2329, 2346 (1997) (holding that CDA's prohibition on Internet transmission of indecent or offensive messages to minors violates the First Amendment).

2. I shall use the terms "state," "nation," and "jurisdiction" interchangeably to refer to national, as opposed to subnational, legal authority. I shall indicate when the analysis differs for subnational units. Although the term "cyberspace" has a broader meaning, I shall use it here loosely as a synonym for the Internet—the transnational network of computer networks.

3. See James Boyle, "Foucault in Cyberspace: Surveillance, Sovereignty, and Hardwired Censors," *University of Cincinnati Law Review* 66 (1997): 177, 178. ("For a long

time, the Internet's enthusiasts have believed that it would be largely immune from state regulation.") The leading regulation skeptics, and this chapter's primary targets, are David R. Johnson and David Post. See David R. Johnson and David Post, "Law and Borders—The Rise of Law in Cyberspace," *Stanford Law Review* 48 (1996): 1367, 1367. See also David Post and David R. Johnson, "Borders, Spillovers, and Complexity: Rule-Making Processes in Cyberspace (and Elsewhere)," draft presented at the Olin Law & Economics Symposium on International Economic Regulation at Georgetown University Law Center, April 5, 1997 (copy on file with *University of Chicago Law Review*); David Post and David R. Johnson, *The New 'Civic Virtue' of the Internet* (also published in *The Emerging Internet*, February 1998, the Annual Review of the Institute for Information Studies), available online at www.cli.org.paper4.htm (visited September 28, 1998); David G. Post, "Governing Cyberspace," *Wayne Law Review* 43 (1996): 155; David G. Post, "Anarchy, State, and the Internet: An Essay on Law-Making in Cyberspace," *Journal of Online Law* (1995), Article 3, available online at www.wm.edu/law/publications/jol/post.html (visited September 10, 1998). Commentators who have made similar arguments include John T. Delacourt, "The International Impact of Internet Regulation," *Harvard International Law Journal* 38 (1997): 207; John Parry Barlow, *A Cyberspace Independence Declaration*, available online at www.eff.org/barlow (visited September 10, 1998); Dan L. Burk, "Federalism in Cyberspace," *Connecticut Law Review* 28 (1996): 1095; Joel R. Reidenberg, "Governing Networks and Rule-Making in Cyberspace," *Emory Law Journal* 45 (1996): 911.

4. See, for example, *ACLU v. Reno*, 929 F. Supp. 824, 832 (E.D. Pa. 1995), aff'd, 117 S. Ct. 2329, 2348 (1997); *Digital Equipment Corp v. Altavista Technology, Inc.*, 960 F. Supp. 456, 462 (D. Mass. 1997); *American Libraries Associations v. Pataki*, 969 F. Supp. 160, 170 (S.D.N.Y. 1997).

5. See, for example, Thomas E. Weber, "The Internet (A Special Report): Debate: Does Anything Go? Limiting Free Speech on the Net," *Wall Street Journal*, December 8, 1997; Vinton G. Cerf, "Building an Internet Free of Barriers," *New York Times*, July 27, 1997, section 3, p. 12; George Black, "Call for Controls: The Internet Must Regulate Itself," *Financial Times*, April 1, 1998, part 4, p. 12.

6. Johnson and Post, p. 1367 (cited in note 3).

7. See generally Irwin Lebow, *Information Highways and Byways: From the Telegraph to the 21st Century* (New York: IEEE Press, 1995); Dan Lacy, *From Grunts to Gigabytes: Communications and Society* (Urbana, Ill.: University of Illinois Press, 1996).

8. See, for example, *Naxos Resources (U.S.A.) Ltd. v. Southam, Inc.*, 1996 U.S. Dist. LEXIS 21757, *13–15 (C.D. Cal.) (defamation); *Panavision International, LP v. Toeppen*, 938 F. Supp. 616, 619 (C.D. Cal. 1996) (interference with economic advantage); Sally Greenberg, *Threats, Harassment, and Hate Online: Recent Developments, Boston University Public Interest Law Journal* 6 (1997): 673, 673–675, 680–684 (harassment and threats).

9. See, for example, *Thompson v. Handa-Lopez, Inc.*, 998 F. Supp. 738 (W. D. Texas 1998) (contract made online).

10. See, for example, *United States v. Thomas*, 74 F.3d 701, 704–05 (6th Cir.), cert. denied, 117 S. Ct. 74 (1996) (pornography); www.personal.psu.edu/users/j/m/jmf11/aterror.txt (visited September 10, 1998) (bomb-making tips).

11. See, for example, *Zippo Manufacturing Co. v. Zippo Dot Com, Inc.*, 952 F. Supp. 1119, 1121 (W.D. Pa. 1997) (trademark infringement); *Religious Technology Center v. F.A.C.T.-NET, Inc.*, 901 F. Supp. 1519, 1521–22 (D. Colo. 1995) (copyright infringement); "Anatomy of a Cyber Break-in," *Newsweek*, February 27, 1995 (data theft).

12. See, for example, *Maritz, Inc. v. CyberGold, Inc.*, 947 F. Supp. 1328, 1329 (E.D. Mo. 1996) (unfair competition); Robert A. Robertson, "Personal Investing in Cyberspace and the Federal Securities Laws," *Securities Regulation Law Journal* 23 (1996): 347, 397–405 (fraudulent securities).

13. The arguments from this paragraph are drawn from Johnson and Post, pp. 1368–70 (cited in note 3); Post and Johnson, "The New 'Civic Virtue,'" pp. 5–6 (cited in note 3); Reidenberg, pp. 912–16 (cited in note 3).

14. See Johnson and Post, pp. 1374–75 (cited in note 3); Burk, pp. 1110–12 (cited in note 3).

15. Post and Johnson, "Borders, Spillovers, and Complexity," p. 5 (cited in note 3).

16. See Johnson and Post, pp. 1370–72 (cited in note 3); Post and Johnson, "Borders, Spillovers, and Complexity," p. 6 (cited in note 3).

17. See Johnson and Post, pp. 1372–73 (cited in note 3).

18. Ibid., pp. 1374–76.

19. Ibid., p. 1374.

20. See Post, paragraphs 39–40 (cited in note 3).

21. See Johnson and Post, p. 1376 (cited in note 3); Burk, pp. 1123–34 (cited in note 3).

22. See Post and Johnson, "Borders, Spillovers, and Complexity," p. 38 (cited in note 3); Post and Johnson, "The New 'Civic Virtue,' " pp. 5–6 (cited in note 3); Burk, pp. 1123–34 (cited in note 3).

23. See Johnson and Post, pp. 1370, 1379, and note 33 (cited in note 3).

24. The skeptics' views about territorialism and choice of law are remarkably similar to Story's and Beale's. See, for example, Joseph Story, *Commentaries on the Conflict of Laws*, 2d. ed. (New York: Little, Brown, 1841), p. 7; Joseph Henry Beale, *A Treatise on the Conflict of Laws or Private International Law* 118 (Cambridge, Mass.: Harvard University Press, 1916).

25. The claim that the territorialist premises of the traditional approach to choice of law were flawed does not necessarily mean that the traditional choice-of-law rules that were based on these premises cannot in some circumstances be justified on independent grounds. See Alfred Hill, "The Judicial Function in Choice of Law," *Columbia Law Review* 85 (1985): pp. 1585, 1619–36.

26. The classic criticisms of the traditional view are Brainerd Currie, *Selected Essays on the Conflict of Laws* (Durham, N.C.: Duke University Press, 1963), and Walter Wheeler Cook, *The Logical and Legal Bases of the Conflict of Laws* (Cambridge, Mass.: Harvard University Press, 1949).

27. This is one reason why so many of the transformative mid-century constitutional choice-of-law decisions involved public regulations rather than private law. See, for example, *Clay v. Sun Insurance Office, Ltd.*, 377 U.S. 179, 182–83 (1964) (insurance); *Watson v. Employers Liability Assurance Corp.*, 348 U.S. 66, 72–73 (1954) (insurance); *United States v. Aluminum Co. of America*, 148 F.2d 416, 444 (2d Cir. 1945) (antitrust); *Pacific Employers Insurance Co. v. Industrial Accident Commission of California*, 306 U.S. 493, 497 (1939) (workmen's compensation); *Alaska Packers Association v. Industrial Accident Commission of California*, 294 U.S. 532, 538 (1935) (workmen's compensation); *Bradford Electric Light Co. v. Clapper*, 286 U.S. 145, 150–51 (1932) (workmen's compensation); *Home Insurance Co. v. Dick*, 281 U.S. 397, 405–08 (1930) (insurance).

28. See, for example, Cook, *The Logical and Legal Bases*, pp. 311–22, 354–70, 433–37 (cited in note 26); Walter Wheeler Cook, "The Jurisdiction of Sovereign States and

the Conflict of Laws," *Columbia Law Review* 31 (1931): 368, 372–80; Ernest G. Lorenzen, *Selected Articles on the Conflict of Laws* (New Haven, Conn.: Yale University Press, 1947), pp. 305–21.

29. See Cook, *The Logical and Legal Bases,* pp. 35–36 (cited in note 26); Hessel E. Yntema, "The Hornbook Method and the Conflict of Laws," *Yale Law Journal* 37 (1928): 468, 478.

30. See Leon E. Trakman, *The Law Merchant: The Evolution of Commercial Law* (Fred B. Rothman, 1983), pp. 39–44; Bradford R. Clark, "Federal Common Law: A Structural Reinterpretation," *University of Pennsylvania Law Review* 144 (1996): 1245, 1280–81.

31. See Friedrich K. Juenger, "American Conflicts Scholarship and the New Law Merchant," *Vanderbilt Journal of Transnational Law* 28 (1995): 487, 491.

32. The main approaches used by the several states today are the traditional vested rights approach, interest analysis, the Second Restatement, comparative impairment, and the better law approach. See Lea Brilmayer, *Conflict of Laws: Cases and Materials,* 4th ed. (New York: Little, Brown, 1995), pp. 203–314. Even states that purport to use the same methodology—for example, interest analysis or the Second Restatement— often do so in name only, with important differences in practice.

33. In the United States, the horizontal nonuniformity fostered by different choice-of-law regimes in different states was exacerbated by the rule that federal courts sitting in diversity apply state choice-of-law rules. See *Klaxon Co. v. Stentor Electric Manufacturing Co., Inc.,* 313 U.S. 487, 496 (1941).

34. *Phillips Petroleum Co. v. Shutts,* 472 US 797, 818 (1985), quoting *Allstate Insurance Co. v. Hague,* 449 U.S. 302, 312–13 (1981).

35. For example, in the case in which this modern standard was formulated, the Supreme Court held that Minnesota could apply its plaintiff-favoring insurance law to an accident in Wisconsin among Wisconsin residents based on the fact that the decedent worked in Minnesota, the insurance company did business there, and the beneficiary moved there from Wisconsin after the accident. See *Hague,* 449 U.S. 315–20. On the weaknesses and uncertainties of the *Hague* test, see Brilmayer, *Conflict of Laws,* pp. 140–43 (cited in note 32).

36. The Permanent Court of International Justice famously established a very weak effects test for extraterritorial jurisdiction and suggested a default rule that favored extraterritorial jurisdiction. See *The Case of the S.S. "Lotus,"* 1927 Permanent Court of International Justice (ser. A) No. 10 at 18–25. Section 403 of the Restatement (Third) of the Foreign Relations Law (American Law Institute 1987), recognized the effects test as a basis for extraterritorial jurisdiction, but added the caveat that a state may not exercise such jurisdiction when it would be "unreasonable" to do so. This reason-ableness requirement has little basis in state practice and does not reflect customary international law. See William S. Dodge, "Extraterritoriality and Conflict-of-Laws Theory: An Argument for Judicial Unilateralism," *Harvard International Law Journal* 39 (1998): 101, 139–40 n. 241–42.

37. See, for example, *Blackmer v. United States,* 284 U.S. 421, 436 (1932); *United States v. Reeh,* 780 F.2d 1541, 1543 n. 2 (11th Cir. 1986); Restatement (Third) of the Foreign Relations Law § 402(2). International law also permits a nation to regulate extraterritorial conduct that threatens local security [Restatement (Third) of the Foreign Relations Law § 402(3)], and might permit a nation to regulate certain extraterritorial acts against its citizens (ibid. at comment g).

38. See *Shutts,* 472 U.S. 823; *Hague,* 449 U.S. 307; Restatement (Third) of the Foreign Relations Law § 403(3).

39. Some courts will not enforce choice-of-law agreements in which the "chosen state has no substantial relationship to the parties or the transaction and there is no other reasonable basis for the parties' choice." Restatement (Second) of Conflict of Laws § 187(2)(a) (1971). This restriction has less force in transnational contexts in which there are often good reasons for parties to choose a neutral law unrelated to the parties. (ibid. § 187 comment f).

40. See, for example, *Moses v. Business Card Express, Inc.*, 929 F.2d 1131, 1138 (6th Cir. 1991).

41. See, for example, Hague Convention on the Law Applicable to Succession to the Estates of Deceased Persons, Art. 5, 28 International Legal Materials 146, 150 (1989) (providing that an individual may designate either the law of habitual residence or the law of nationality to govern succession); Hague Convention on the Law Applicable to Trusts and on Their Recognition, Art. 6, 23 International Legal Materials 1389 (1984) ("A trust shall be governed by the law chosen by the settlor."); *McDermott Inc. v. Lewis*, 531 A.2d 206, 215 (Del. 1987) (holding that law of place of incorporation governs internal corporate affairs); William Grantham, Comment, "The Arbitrability of International Intellectual Property Disputes," *Berkeley Journal of International Law* 14 (1996): 173, 190–95 (describing how parties' choice of law governs intellectual property disputes).

42. See Michael J. Trebilcock, *The Limits of Freedom of Contract*, 58–77, 145–63 (Cambridge, Mass.: Harvard University Press, 1993).

43. See, for example, *Vimar Seguros y Reaseguros, SA v. M/V Sky Reefer*, 515 U.S. 528, 540–41 (1995) (noting that transnational parties cannot reduce their liability under the Carriage of Goods at Sea Act by contracting around its provisions); *Mitsubishi Motors Corp. v. Soler Chrysler-Plymouth, Inc.*, 473 U.S. 614, 637 n. 19 (1985) (noting that transnational parties cannot contract around the Sherman Act). Private parties can, of course, circumvent mandatory laws to the extent that they can shift the location or effects of their activities beyond the mandatory law's enforceable scope. For further discussion, see note 166.

44. See, for example, United Nations Convention on Contracts for the International Sale of Goods (CISG), UN Doc A/CONF.97/18, reprinted at 19 International Legal Materials 671 (1980). A related solution is to develop uniform laws like the Uniform Commercial Code, which minimize choice-of-law difficulties by ensuring that every jurisdiction's local law is (in theory) the same.

45. See, for example, Convention on the Law Applicable to Contractual Obligations (Rome Convention), June 19, 1980 (80/934/EEC) 1980 OJ (L266/1), p 1.

46. See, for example, ibid., Arts. 3(3), 5(2), 6(1), and 7(1)–(2) (acknowledging various mandatory law restrictions on choice-of-law governing contracts).

47. I say "usually" because sometimes there will be parallel litigation of the same matter in two nations, each of which attempts to apply its own law. See, for example, *Laker Airways Ltd. v. Sabena*, 731 F.2d 909, 917–20 (D.C. Cir. 1984).

48. See Andreas F. Lowenfeld, *International Litigation and the Quest for Reasonableness: Essays in Private International Law* 5 (New York: Clarendon, 1996).

49. In my discussion here and throughout the chapter, I shall follow the skeptics in assuming that the spillovers produced by unilateral regulation of transnational activity are negative spillovers. This will not always be true, but it will usually be true in situations in which one state regulates extraterritorial conduct that the territorial government would regulate differently.

50. 509 U.S. 764 (1993).

51. Ibid., p. 796.

52. See "McDonnell Douglas-Boeing Link Gets Europe Approval," *New York Times*, July 31, 1997, p. D4.

53. See *Hague*, 449 U.S. 306, 319–20.

54. See *In re Grand Jury Proceedings United States v. Bank of Nova Scotia*, 691 F.2d 1384, 1391 (11th Cir. 1982).

55. See *Alaska Packers*, 294 U.S. 539–44.

56. See *Babcock v. Jackson*, 12 N.Y.2d 473, 240 N.Y.S.2d 743, 191 N.E.2d 279, 284–85 (1963).

57. See *Barclays Bank PLC v. Franchise Tax Board*, 512 U.S. 298, 310–15 (1994).

58. This is the goal, for example, of such different approaches as the Restatement of the Foreign Relations Law's interest-balancing approach, see Restatement (Third) of the Foreign Relations Law § 403; William Baxter's comparative impairment approach, see William F. Baxter, "Choice of Law and the Federal System," *Stanford Law Review* 16 (1963): 1, 4–20; Larry Kramer's multistate canons of construction, see Larry Kramer, "Rethinking Choice of Law," *Columbia Law Review* 90 (1990): 277, 319–38; and Lea Brilmayer's strategy to maximize state policy objectives, see Brilmayer, pp. 169–218 (cited in note 32).

59. See David W. Leebron, *Lying Down with Procrustes: An Analysis of Harmonization Claims*, in Jagdish N. Bhagwati and Robert E. Hudec, eds., *Fair Trade and Harmonization* 1 (Cambridge, Mass.: MIT Press, 1996), pp. 41, 43–50.

60. For more general discussions of this point, see Joel R. Reidenberg, "Lex Informatica: The Formulation of Information Policy Rules through Technology," *Texas Law Review* 76 (1998): 553; Lawrence Lessig, "Reading the Constitution in Cyberspace," *Emory Law Journal* 45 (1996): 869, 895–99; M. Ethan Katsh, "Software Worlds and the First Amendment: Virtual Doorkeepers in Cyberspace," *University of Chicago Legal Forum* (1996): 335, 339–47; Post, Article 3, paragraphs 20–21 (cited in note 3).

61. Of course, computer hardware—keyboards, monitors, modems, disk drives, processors, and the like—also affects how individuals experience cyberspace. Many software instructions that are interpreted by a computer could be instantiated in hardware rather than software. For the most part, however, hardware is less significant than software in creating and shaping one's experience of cyberspace. See Katsh, pp. 339–43 (cited in note 60).

62. www.dell.com/dell/legal/disclwww.htm (visited April 1, 1998).

63. International Institute for the Unification of Private Law (UNIDROIT), *Principles of International Commercial Contracts* (Rome, Italy: UNIDROIT, 1994); ICC, *Uniform Customs and Practice for Documentary Credits*, ICC Pub. No. 500, 1993.

64. Such a regime will invariably be underspecified and will require supplementation by some default law regime.

65. "Virtual Magistrate" is the name of the decisionmaker in a relatively new online project "for resolving disputes that arise on worldwide computer networks about online messages, postings, and files. . . ." *The Virtual Magistrate Project Concept Paper*, available online at vmag.vcilp. org/docs/vmpaper.html (visited April 1, 1998).

66. See Reidenberg, pp. 558–68 (cited in note 60).

67. See Jack Goldsmith and Lawrence Lessig, *Grounding the Virtual Magistrate*, available online at www.mantle.sbs.umass.edu/vmag/groundvm.htm.

68. See, for example, Johnson and Post, pp. 1387–91 (cited in note 3); I. Trotter Hardy, "The Proper Legal Regime for 'Cyberspace,'" *University of Pittsburgh Law Review* 55 (1994): 993, 1028–33.

NOTES TO PAGES 43–46

69. See generally Eric A. Posner, "The Regulation of Groups: The Influence of Legal and Nonlegal Sanctions on Collective Action," *University of Chicago Law Review* 63 (1996): 133, 165–97.

70. See Goldsmith and Lessig, *Grounding the Virtual Magistrate*, pp. 3–4 (cited in note 67); Johnson and Post, pp. 1395–1400, and notes 102–03 (cited in note 3).

71. The skeptics challenge the normative basis for nations to apply mandatory laws to regulate the private legal regimes of cyberspace.

72. See *Buchanan v. Rucker*, 9 East 192, 103 Eng. Rep. 546, 547 (KB 1808) ("Can the Island of Tobago pass a law to bind the rights of the whole world?").

73. I set aside for present purposes two other relatively rare methods of extraterritorial enforcement: military invasion—see, for example, *United States v. Noriega*, 746 F. Supp. 1506 (S.D. Fla. 1990)—and secondary boycotts—see, for example, Cuban Liberty and Democratic Solidarity (Libertad) Act of 1996 (Helms-Burton Act), Pub. L. No. 104-114, 110 Stat. 785, codified at 22 U.S.C.A. §§ 6021–91 (1994 and Supp. 1998) (sanctioning nations that engage in certain transactions with Cuba).

74. I explain below why local regulation of service or content providers that produces multijurisdictional spillover effects is legitimate and fair; my goal for now is to show that the scope of national regulation of cyberspace is much narrower than the skeptics claim.

75. See U.S. Const., Art. IV, § 1; Roger C. Crampton et al., *Conflict of Laws: Cases-Comments-Questions*, 5th ed. (Belmont, Calif.: West Group, 1993), pp. 735–37.

76. See *Asahi Metal Industry Co. v. Superior Court*, 480 U.S. 102, 108–09 (1987). This is the test for specific jurisdiction; such jurisdiction is limited to cases in which the cause of action arises out of or relates to the defendant's contacts with the forum. A court may also assert general personal jurisdiction over a defendant for a cause of action that accrued anywhere. General jurisdiction is normally limited to the defendant's domicile and anywhere else where it may have "continuous and systematic . . . contacts." *Helicopteros Nacionales de Columbia v. Hall*, 466 U.S. 408, 414–16 (1984). Courts are unanimous that a Web page accessible in a jurisdiction does not by itself establish general jurisdiction there. See, for example, *Weber v. Jolly Hotels*, 977 F. Supp. 327, 333–34 (D. N.J. 1997).

77. For broader treatments, see Henry H. Perritt, Jr., "Jurisdiction in Cyberspace," *Villanova Law Review* 41 (1996): 1, 13–25; Burk, pp. 1107–23 (cited in note 3).

78. See, for example, *Cybersell, Inc. v. Cybersell, Inc.*, 130 F.3d 414, 419–20 (9th Cir. 1997); *Weber*, 977 F. Supp. 334; *Panavision International, LP v. Toeppen*, 938 F. Supp. 616, 622 (C.D. Cal. 1996). For more comprehensive analyses of the many Internet personal jurisdiction cases, see Howard B. Stravitz, "Personal Jurisdiction in Cyberspace: Something More Is Required on the Electronic Stream of Commerce," *Santa Clara Law Review* 49 (1998): 925; Christopher W. Meyer, Note, "World Wide Web Advertising: Personal Jurisdiction around the Whole Wide World?" *Washington & Lee Law Review* 54 (1997): 1269.

79. See Burk, pp. 1117–20 (cited in note 3).

80. I should emphasize the term "enforceable" here, because many commentators talk as if there are (or should be) customary international law limits on exorbitant assertions of personal jurisdiction. See, for example, Restatement (Third) of the Foreign Relations Law § 421. This talk does not appear to be supported by state practice followed from a sense of legal obligation, the usual requirements for a rule of customary international law. The Brussels and Lugano Conventions are treaties that specify the legal bases for personal jurisdiction among members of the European Union.

See Convention on Jurisdiction and the Enforcement of Judgments in Civil and Commercial Matters, September 27, 1968, 1990 OJ (C 189) 2 (consolidated); Convention on Jurisdiction and the Enforcement of Judgments in Civil and Commercial Matters, September 16, 1988, 1988 OJ (L 319) 9. These rare treaties on the subject prove the point that there is no effective or established customary international law that regulates personal jurisdiction, for the Brussels-Lugano regime permits exorbitant assertions of personal jurisdiction against defendants from non-European countries. See Friedrich Juenger, "Judicial Jurisdiction in the United States and in the European Communities: A Comparison," *Michigan Law Review* 82 (1984): 1195, 1211.

81. The U.S. Constitution's Full Faith and Credit obligation does not extend to judgments of foreign nations. See U.S. Const., Art. IV, § 1 (requiring states to give full faith and credit to acts, records, and proceedings "of every other *State*") (emphasis added). The enforceability of these judgments is generally regulated by state law and is weaker than the obligation imposed by the Full Faith and Credit Clause. See Gary B. Born, *International Civil Litigation in United States Courts: Commentary & Materials*, 3d ed. (The Hague, Netherlands: Kluwer Law International, 1996), pp. 938–62. In Europe, the Brussels and Lugano Conventions, which regulate the enforcement of foreign judgments among European Union members, are again an exception to the general rule.

82. See Born, *International Civil Litigation*, pp. 942–43 (cited in note 81) (discussing examples from Japan, Germany, and England).

83. See, for example, *Bachchan v. India Abroad Publications, Inc.*, 154 Misc. 2d 228, 585 N.Y.S.2d 661, 664–65 (N.Y. Sup. Ct. 1992) (declining to enforce English money judgment for libel against a newspaper whose activities would have been protected by the First Amendment in the United States). See generally Born, pp. 942–43 (cited in note 81).

84. See U.S. Const., Art. IV, § 2, cl. 2; 18 U.S.C. § 3182 (1994).

85. See *Innes v. Tobin*, 240 U.S. 127, 131 (1916); *Hyatt v. People*, 188 U.S. 691, 711–12 (1903); *Gee v. Kansas*, 912 F.2d 414, 418 (10th Cir. 1990). This jurisdictional limitation does not apply, of course, when a person in one state commits a federal crime in another. See *United States v. Thomas*, 74 F.3d 701, 709–10 (6th Cir. 1996).

86. For an overview, see I. A. Shearer, *Extradition in International Law* (Manchester, U.K.: Manchester University Press, 1971).

87. See John T. Soma, Thomas F. Muther Jr., and Heidi M. L. Brissette, "Transnational Extradition for Computer Crimes: Are New Treaties and Laws Needed?" *Harvard Journal on Legislation* 34 (1997): 317, 323–26.

88. See, for example, Johnson and Post, p. 1374 (cited in note 3).

89. This component of the skeptics' argument is in tension with their concerns about the threat of multiple regulation. If, as they claim, cyberspace users can easily relocate the source of their transmissions to evade legal enforcement, and if, as they further claim, the physical location of parties transacting in cyberspace is "*indeterminate* both *ex ante* and *ex post*"—see Post and Johnson, "Borders, Spillovers, and Complexity," p. 3 (cited in note 3)—then cyberspace users have little to fear from multiple national regulation.

90. See Post, Article 3, paragraph 40 (cited in note 3).

91. Telnet allows a computer user to log into a remote computer over the Internet. Once connected to the foreign computer, the user can perform any Internet function, such as sending e-mail or "telnetting" to yet other servers, as though she were logged on to a terminal at the foreign computer's location. An anonymous remailer is a

service that allows the sender of an e-mail to remain anonymous by sending the message through an intermediary that strips the message of the identifying character-istics of the original sender. The receiver of the e-mail can respond to the e-mail by sending an e-mail to the intermediary, which then forwards it to the sender.

92. See generally Stephen D. Krasner, "Global Communications and National Power: Life on the Pareto Frontier," *World Policy Journal* (1991): 336, 343–46.

93. Ibid.

94. Consider two of many examples. Pending legislation in the United States Congress would impose criminal penalties on persons in the United States who gamble on the Internet. See Internet Gambling Prohibition Act of 1998, S. Amend. 3266 to S. 2260, 105th Cong., 2d Sess., July 22, 1998; Internet Gambling Prohibition Act of 1998, H.R. 4427, 105th Cong., 2d Sess., August 6, 1998. Chinese law punishes in-state Internet users who access or transmit a broader array of prohibited informa-tion. See Computer Information Network and Internet Security, Protection and Man-agement Regulations (approved by the State Council on December 11, 1997, and promulgated by the Ministry of Public Security on December 30, 1997), available online at www.gilc.org/speech/china/net-regs-1297.html (visited September 11, 1998).

95. For example, a new German law imposes liability on Internet service providers if they knowingly offer a venue for content illegal in Germany and fail to use techni-cally possible and reasonable means to block it. See "Germany to Enforce Child-Friendly Internet," *Chicago Tribune*, July 5, 1997, p. 4. Australia is about to implement a similar law. See *Electronic Frontiers Australia, Internet Regulation in Australia*, avail-able online at www.efa.org.au/Issues/Censor/cens1.html (visited September 10, 1998). In the United States, pending federal Internet gambling legislation would authorize the federal government to order service providers, at risk of penalty, to discontinue the availability of illegal gambling sites. See Internet Gambling Prohibi-tion Act of 1998, S. Amend. 3266 to S. 2260 (cited in note 94). Legislation is also pending that would require senders of unsolicited commercial e-mail to identify themselves in a way that would enable Internet service providers to filter such messages. See Jeri Clausing, "Compressed Data; House E-Mail Effort Raises Censor-ship Issues," *New York Times*, August 10, 1998, p. D3. And some states have held Internet service providers liable for facilitating the transmission of illegal extraterrito-rial content into the regulating jurisdiction. See, for example, *Stratton Oakmont, Inc. v. Prodigy Services Co.*, 1995 WL 323710, *4–5 (N.Y. Sup. Ct.).

96. Compare Matt Beer, "The Wagers of the Web; Lawsuit Could Unravel On-Line Gaming Industry," *San Francisco Examiner*, August 17, 1998, p. B1 (describing lawsuit by Internet bettor against credit card companies that financed on-line gambling).

97. As Lessig notes:

> A regulation need not be absolutely effective to be sufficiently effective. It need not raise the cost of the prohibited activity to infinity in order to reduce the level of that activity quite substantially. If regulation increases the cost of access to this kind of information, it will reduce access to this information, even if it doesn't reduce it to zero. . . . If government regulation had to show that it was perfect before it was justified, then indeed there would be little regulation of cyberspace, or of real space either. But regulation, whether for the good or the bad, has a lower burden to meet.

Lawrence Lessig, "The Zones of Cyberspace," *Stanford Law Review* 48 (1996): 1403, 1405.

98. See Nathaniel Nash, "Holding CompuServe Responsible," *New York Times,* January 15, 1996, p. D4.

99. Ibid.

100. See, for example, Johnson and Post, p. 1373, and note 20 (cited in note 3).

101. See Edmund L. Andrews, "Germany's Efforts to Police Web Are Upsetting Business," *New York Times,* June 6, 1997, p. A1.

102. Ibid; "Germany Brings Criminal Charges against CompuServe Manager," *Eurowatch,* May 2, 1997. The CompuServe executive was later convicted, even though at trial's end the prosecution sought acquittal because it agreed with the defense that, at the time of the indictment, CompuServe lacked the technological means to block the illegal material. *Battle of the Somm* (May 29, 1998), available online at www.wired.com/news/ news/politics/story/12607.html (visited September 10, 1998).

103. Jordan Bonfante, "The Internet Trials: Germany Makes an Early Attempt at Taming the Wide, Wild Web. But Many are Crying Foul—or Folly," *Time* (intl. ed.) July 14, 1997, p. 30 (emphasis added).

104. See ACLU White Paper, *Fahrenheit 451.2: Is Cyberspace Burning? How Rating and Blocking Proposals May Torch Free Speech on the Internet* (1997), available online at www.aclu.org/issues/cyber/burning.html (visited April 1, 1998) (warning of censorship threats posed by rating and filtering proposals that flourished in wake of *Reno*); Lawrence Lessig, "Tyranny in the Infrastructure," *Wired,* July 1997, available online at www.wired.com/wired/5.07/cyber_rights.html (visited April 1, 1998) (same).

105. See Lessig, "Tyranny in the Infrastructure," *Wired* (cited in note 104); Boyle, pp. 191–96 (cited in note 3).

106. In addition to the discussion below, see Jonathan Weinberg, "Rating the Net," *Hastings Communications and Entertainment Law Journal* 19 (1997): 453; Paul Resnick, "Filtering Information on the Internet," *Scientific American,* March 1997, pp. 62–64; Reidenberg, pp. 556–68 (cited in note 60).

107. For example, Sexroulette.com includes the following conditions upon entry to its pages:

> WARNING: You are about to enter an ADULT ONLY area. You must agree to the following terms before proceeding: . . . If you are under the age of eighteen years . . . you are not authorized to download any materials from XPICS and any and all such downloading shall constitute intentional infringement of XPICS's rights in such materials.
>
> All materials, messages, and other communications contained at XPICS are intended for distribution exclusively to consenting adults in locations where such materials, messages and other communications do not violate any community standards or any federal, state or local law or regulation of the United States or any other country. No materials from any parts of XPICS designated as "XXX" are authorized to or otherwise may be downloaded to persons located in the following areas: Alabama, Florida, except Ft. Lauderdale, Miami, and St. Petersburg, Georgia, except Atlanta, Kansas, except Kansas City, Kentucky, Minnesota, Missouri, Mississippi, North Carolina, Ohio, except Cleveland and Cincinnati, Pennsylvania, except Philadelphia and Pittsburgh, South Carolina, Tennessee, except for Nashville, Utah, Afghanistan, Kuwait, Iran, Iraq, Japan, Jordan, Libya,

Pakistan, The Republic of China, Singapore, Saudi Arabia, Syria, The United Arab Emirates, or any other place in which to do so would constitute a violation of any law, regulation, rule or custom. Any and all unauthorized downloading of materials from XPICS shall constitute intentional infringement of XPICS's rights in such materials.

... If you agree with the above, you may ENTER. If you don't agree, you must EXIT.

members.sexroulette.com (visited April 1, 1998).

108. See, for example, The Adult Check System, www.adultcheck.com (visited September 10, 1998).

109. In many of the well-known cyberspace regulation cases, the defendants knew that they were sending content into the regulating jurisdiction because they had conditioned the users' request for the content on the presentation of information (including geographical identification) by fax or mail. See, for example, *Thomas*, 74 F.3d 705; *Playboy Enterprises, Inc. v. Chuckleberry Publishing, Inc.*, 939 F. Supp. 1032, 1035 (S.D.N.Y. 1996); *State v. Granite Gate Resorts, Inc.*, 1996 WL 767431, *4 (Minn. Dist. Ct.), *aff'd*, 568 N.W.2d 715 (Minn. App. 1997).

110. See generally *Introduction to Client Digital ID's* [SM], available online at www.verisign.com/repository/brwidint.htm (visited April 1, 1998); A. Michael Froomkin, "The Essential Role of Trusted Third Parties in Electronic Commerce," *Oregon Law Review* 75 (1996): 49, 55–60.

111. First-generation software filters blocked access to individually compiled lists of prohibited Internet addresses. See Weinberg, p. 457 (cited in note 106). More recently, a much more sophisticated industrywide standard for labeling, rating, and filtering Internet information has emerged. This standard, known as PICS, establishes content-neutral labeling formats and distribution methods. The PICS format does not specify a labeling vocabulary or what should be done with the labels. Instead, the PICS format allows both content providers and independent entities to label content along several dimensions. Selection software then decides what to do with these labels—whether to block them, restrict access, highlight them, organize them in certain ways, or whatever else the software is designed for.

112. See Timothy S. Wu, Note, "Cyberspace Sovereignty?—The Internet and the International System," *Harvard Journal of Law and Technology* 10 (1997): pp. 647, 649–56; Delacourt, pp. 208–19 (cited in note 3); Paul Resnick, *PICS, Censorship, & Intellectual Freedom FAQ*, version 1.14, available online at www.si.umich.edu/~presnick/pics/intfree/faq.htm (visited April 1, 1998).

113. See Wu, Note, p. 651 (cited in note 112) ("As of July 1996, at least thirty-three states were completely unconnected.").

114. Ibid, pp. 652–54 (China, Singapore); Madanmohan Rao, *Persian Gulf Net Censorship: Governments Force Server Blockades* (October 3, 1997), available online at media info.elpress.com/ephome/ news/newshtm/webnews/glob1003.htm (visited April 1, 1998) (United Arab Emirates).

115. See text accompanying notes 98–103.

116. See Christopher Stern, "V-Chip on Fast Track as FCC OK's Tech Spex," *Variety*, March 16–22, 1998, p. 27; Brooks Boliek, "Television Sharpens Bite: V-Chip Wins FCC Approval," *Hollywood Reporter*, March 13, 1998, p. 15.

117. See Clausing (cited in note 5).

118. Many predict that Congress will more broadly require filtering or digital identification technology to be built into the architecture of cyberspace. See Boyle,

pp. 193, 202–04 (cited in note 3); Lawrence Lessig, "What Things Regulate Speech: CDA 2.0 vs. Filtering," *Jurimetrics Journal* 38 (1998): 629. Even in the absence of direct governmental mandates, the threat of such regulation has already spurred the development and adoption of an array of private de facto Internet discrimination standards that facilitate extensive private regulation of the Internet.

119. See J. M. Balkin, "Media Filters, the V-Chip, and the Foundations of Broadcast Regulation," *Duke Law Journal* 45 (1996): 1131, 1141–44 (describing the filtering of information in print and broadcast media).

120. Ibid., p. 1143.

121. See Robert H. Reid, *Architects of the Web: 1000 Days that Built the Future of Business* (Hoboken, N.J.: Wiley, 1997), pp. xxiii–xxiv.

122. Some civil libertarians favor information filtering technologies because they allow individuals—rather than the government—to decide what information is appropriate for their own (or their children's) consumption. See, for example, Brief of Feminists for Free Expression as Amicus Curiae in support of Appellees, *Reno v. ACLU*, 117 S. Ct. 2329 (1997), available at 1997 WL 74382, *15–16.

123. Resnick, p. 3 (cited in note 112).

124. See Johnson and Post, pp. 1373–74 and note 20 (cited in note 3); notes 116–118 and accompanying text.

125. See, for example, Weinberg, pp. 459–70 (cited in note 106); Johnson and Post, pp. 1373–74 (cited in note 3); Electronic Privacy Information Center, *Faulty Filters: How Content Filters Block Access to Kid-Friendly Information on the Internet*, available online at www2.epic.org/reports/filter_report.htm (visited April 1, 1998).

126. See, for example, Johnson and Post, pp. 1372–74 (cited in note 3).

127. See note 97 and accompanying text.

128. See, for example, Johnson and Post, pp. 1375–76 (cited in note 3).

129. See notes 107-110 and accompanying text.

130. In December 1996, the World Intellectual Property Organization (WIPO) reached agreement on a treaty that significantly extended international copyright protection for digital property. See WIPO Copyright Treaty, adopted December 20, 1996, WIPO Pub. No. 226(E) 1997; Seth Schiesel, "Global Agreement Reached to Widen Law on Copyright," *New York Times*, December 21, 1996, p. 1. Within a year, the European Commission issued a draft directive to bring European law into line with these international obligations. See "Draft EC Directive Provides Strong Online Copyright Protection, Outlaws Devices Facilitating Infringement," *BNA Electronic Commerce and Law Report*, March 13, 1998, available online at www.bna.com/e-law/main.htm (visited April 1, 1998). The United States is in the process of enacting similar legislation. See WIPO Copyright Treaties Implementation Act, H.R. 2281, 105th Cong., 1st Sess., July 29, 1997; Digital Millenium Copyright Act of 1998, S. 2037, 105th Cong., 2d Sess., May 6, 1998.

131. The digital protection treaty signed in Geneva operates as a protocol to the Berne Convention for the Protection of Literary and Artistic Works, a treaty regime that began in 1886. See *Berne Convention for the Protection of Literary and Artistic Works* (Geneva, Switzerland: WIPO, 1970).

132. See Clifford Krauss, "8 Countries Join in an Effort to Catch Computer Criminals," *New York Times*, December 11, 1997, p. A12.

133. See Anne-Marie Slaughter, "The Real New World Order," *Foreign Affairs*, September/October 1997, pp. 183, 189–92.

134. For example, in February 1997, the United Nations Commission on International Trade Law (UNCITRAL) began to draft model international digital signature legislation. See *Report of the Working Group on Electronic Commerce*, Thirty-First Session, New York, February 12–28, 1997. See also UNCITRAL Working Group on Electronic Commerce, *Planning of Future Work on Electronic Commerce: Digital Signatures, Certification Authorities, and Related Legal Issues* A/CN.9/WG.IV/WP. 71, December 31, 1996. Similarly, in November 1997, the International Chamber of Commerce issued the General Usage for International Digitally Ensured Commerce (GUIDEC), a set of guidelines for ensuring trustworthy digital transactions over the Internet, available online at www.iccwbo.org/guidec2/htm (visited April 5, 1998). And the Organisation for Economic Co-operation and Development (OECD) recently adopted principles to guide countries in formulating their own policies and legislation relating to the use of cryptography. See *OECD Cryptography Policy: The Guidelines and the Issues*, Unclassified OECD/GD(97)204 (1997), available online at www.oecd.org/dsti/sti/it/secur/prod/GD97-204.htm (visited April 2, 1998).

135. See Leebron (cited in note 59).

136. See, for example, Krasner, pp. 337–60 (cited in note 92); Andrew T. Guzman, "Is International Antitrust Possible?" *New York University Law Review* 73 (1998).

137. See text accompanying notes 58–59.

138. Perritt, p. 3 (cited in note 77).

139. Post and Johnson, "Borders, Spillovers, and Complexity," pp. 2–3 (cited in note 3).

140. Many European conflict systems demonstrate that it is both possible and useful to design choice-of-law rules that are context-sensitive and not beholden to any grand choice-of-law theory. See, for example, Swiss Private International Law Statute of December 18, 1987, translated in Andreas Bucher and Pierre-Yves Tschanz, *International Arbitration in Switzerland* (Basle, Switzerland: Helbing & Lichtenhahn, 1988), p. 225.

141. See *London Film Productions v. Intercontinental Communications, Inc.*, 580 F. Supp. 47, 48–49 (S.D.N.Y. 1984) (involving a British corporation suing an American corporation for copyright infringement in Chile, Venezuela, Peru, Equador, Costa Rica, and Panama); Eugene F. Scoles and Peter Hay, *Conflict of Laws*, 2d ed. (St. Paul, Minn.: West, 1992), p. 631 (describing choice-of-law rules for multistate libel).

142. See generally Larry Kramer, "Choice of Law in Complex Litigation," *New York University Law Review* 71 (1996): 547, 551–65.

143. See, for example, *Rutherford v. Goodyear Tire and Rubber Co.*, 943 F. Supp. 789, 790–91 (W.D. Ky. 1996), *aff'd*, 142 F.3d 436 (6th Cir. 1998).

144. For an excellent analysis of how traditional choice-of-law rules might apply to copyright violations in cyberspace, see Jane C. Ginsburg, "Copyright without Borders?: Choice of Forum and Choice of Law for Copyright Infringement in Cyberspace," *Cardozo Arts and Entertainment Law Journal* 15 (1997): 153, 168–74.

145. See Kramer, p. 583 (cited in note 142).

146. This is known as "depecage." See Brilmayer, p. 366 (cited in note 32).

147. See Peter S. Smedresman and Andreas F. Lowenfeld, "Eurodollars, Multinational Banks, and National Laws," *New York University Law Review* 64 (1989): 733, 734–37 (discussing the bank deposit problem); Andreas F. Lowenfeld, "In Search of the Intangible: A Comment on *Shaffer v. Heitner*," *New York University Law Review* 53 (1978): 102, 115–17, 122–24 (exploring situs of debt problem largely in context of personal jurisdiction).

148. See Larry Kramer, "Vestiges of Beale: Extraterritorial Application of American Law," *Supreme Court Review* (1991): 179, 190 note 36. A similar problem is presented by multistate contracts. When contractual negotiations and signings take place in two states, the place of the contract might be either state, depending on what contact the forum's choice-of-law rule deems dispositive for this purpose.

149. See Lowenfeld, p. 5 (cited in note 48).

150. See Dodge, pp. 108–10 (cited in note 36).

151. The same analysis applies in the international context for the extraterritorial application of other regulatory laws like RICO and the antitrust and securities laws. The question in these cases is whether Congress intended for federal law to apply to conduct abroad. If so, these laws apply. If not, the court dismisses the case without considering the application of foreign law.

152. See Johnson and Post, pp. 1372–73 (cited in note 3).

153. Ibid.

154. See Britta Gordon, *Gaming on the Internet: The Odds Are on the House, But How Long Will It Last?* 5, available online at www.cyberlaw.law.ttu.edu/cyberspc/jour9.htm (visited April 1, 1998).

155. There is currently legislation pending in Congress that would extensively regulate Internet gambling by, among other things, penalizing online bettors and authorizing governmental officials to order Internet service providers to shut down offending online cites. See note 94.

156. See text following note 23.

157. See text accompanying notes 98–103.

158. See notes 34–37 and accompanying text.

159. See *Hartford Fire Insurance Co.*, 509 U.S. 795–99.

160. In late 1996, CompuServe had 335,000 German subscribers and employed more than 250 workers there. "CompuServe May Curb German Operations," *New York Times*, November 19, 1996, p. D6.

161. There might of course be substantive objections akin to the First Amendment found either in German law or in international human rights law. As I mentioned at the outset, such substantive limitations on cyberspace regulation are not my concern here.

162. See Johnson and Post, pp. 1378–91 (cited in note 3).

163. I glean this formulation from *Phillips Petroleum Co. v. Shutts*, 472 U.S. 797, 807 (1985); *Allstate Insurance Co. v. Hague*, 449 U.S. 302, 312–13 (1981) (plurality opinion); *Clay v. Sun Insurance Office, Ltd.*, 377 U.S. 179, 182 (1964); *Watson v. Employers Liability Assurance Corp*, 348 US 66, 72–73 (1954); and *Home Insurance Co. v. Dick*, 281 US 397, 410 (1930). Like all formulations of constitutional limitations on choice of law, this one is open to debate because the Court's analysis in these decisions is maddeningly vague, and because the Court has mixed due process and full faith and credit concerns. See note 34 and accompanying text. But at the very least, the formulation in the text is close enough to the constitutional requirement of notice to consider the application of this test to cyberspace.

164. See text accompanying notes 77–83.

165. What is foreseeable will also be informed, in a circular fashion, by what the law requires. If the law permits one jurisdiction to hold a content provider in another jurisdiction strictly liable for the mere act of placing information on a Web page, then this result is foreseeable. The pertinent question is what level of foreseeability the law *should* require, and this analysis is informed by the factors listed in the text.

NOTES TO PAGES 67–68

166. There are of course some private legal orders that are relatively immune from this requirement, either because the costs of defecting from the private order are greater than the costs of continued participation—see Lisa Bernstein, "Opting Out of the Legal System: Extralegal Contractual Relations in the Diamond Industry," *Journal of Legal Studies* 21 (1992): 115; Posner, pp. 165–97 (cited in note 69)—or, relatedly, because the members of the order structure their affairs to circumvent mandatory laws. See Frank H. Easterbrook and Daniel R. Fischel, *The Economic Structure of Corporate Law* 3 (Cambridge, Mass.: Harvard University Press, 1991) (corporate context). Even these prominent examples of mandatory law circumvention, however, are not clear-cut. For example, Bernstein's paradigmatic examples of private legal orders are sometimes subject to mandatory law interventions. See Bernstein, *Journal of Legal Studies* 21 (1992): 125 and note 24, 129 and note 35 (noting that arbitration awards can be vacated for procedural irregularity and that the group's actions must conform with antitrust regulations). Similarly, a corporation's ability to circumvent mandatory law restrictions is dependent in large part on the settled but by no means inevitable choice-of-law rule that the law of the place of incorporation governs internal corporate affairs. Mandatory corporate laws would be harder to avoid if nations and states instead applied local corporate law on the basis of the local effects of corporate transactions. See, for example, *Western Airlines, Inc. v. Sobieski*, 191 Cal. App. 2d 399, 12 Cal. Rptr. 719, 727–29 (1961) (applying California cumulative voting rule to Delaware corporation doing significant business in California). Because for a variety of reasons it frequently will be difficult for cyberspace communities to completely circumvent mandatory law restrictions, I will set aside this possibility in the analysis.

167. Two excellent introductions to international commercial arbitration are Gary B. Born, *International Commercial Arbitration in the United States: Commentary and Materials* (The Hague, Netherlands: Kluwer Law International, 1994), and Alan Redfern and Martin Hunter, *Law and Practice of International Commercial Arbitration*, 2d ed. (London, U.K.: Sweet & Maxwell, 1991).

168. The most prominent international arbitration rules are those promulgated by the International Chamber of Commerce, the American Arbitration Association, the London Court of International Arbitration, and the UNCITRAL. These rules are generally similar but contain important differences. See Born, *International Commercial Arbitration*, pp. 10–16, 50–96 (cited in note 167).

169. In the United States, this law is the Federal Arbitration Act, Pub. L. No. 282, 61 Stat. 669 (1947), codified at 9 U.S.C. §§ 1 et seq. (1994).

170. The Convention is reproduced at 9 U.S.C. § 201 (1994). For general commentary, see Born, *International Commercial Arbitration*, pp. 18–20 (cited in note 167); A. Jan van den Berg, *The New York Arbitration Convention of 1958: Towards a Uniform Judicial Interpretation* (The Hague, Netherlands: Kluwer International Law, 1981).

171. The exceptions, which are narrowly construed, can be grouped in four categories. First, the Convention has certain jurisdiction prerequisites. For example, it does not apply to oral arbitration agreements, to domestic arbitrations, or to noncommercial arbitrations. New York Convention on the Recognition and Enforcement of Foreign Arbitral Awards, Arts. I, II, June 10, 1958, 330 UNTS 38. Second, the obligation to enforce arbitration agreements and awards does not extend to matters that, under national law, are nonarbitrable or violate a strong public policy. Ibid., Arts. II(1), V(2). I discuss this exception further below. See note 175. Third, the duty to enforce arbitral awards does not extend to awards rendered without minimal due process

protections (such as notice). Ibid., Art. V(1)(b). And fourth, the duty to enforce arbitral awards does not extend to ultra vires awards. Ibid., Art. V(1)(c).

172. It is possible, however, that an agreement in cyberspace constitutes an agreement in writing. For an overview of various responses to this problem, see Michael E. Schneider and Christopher Kuner, "Dispute Resolution in International Electronic Commerce," *Journal of International Arbitration* 14 (1997): 5, 13–15; Jasna Arsíc, "International Commercial Arbitration on the Internet: Has the Future Come Too Early?" *Journal of International Arbitration* 14 (1997): 209, 215–17.

173. See, for example, 9 U.S.C. § 4 (1994) (authorizing federal court to order arbitration "within the district in which the petition for an order directing such arbitration is filed"); 9 U.S.C. § 10(b) (1994) (providing for limited judicial review by "the United States district court for the district wherein an award was made").

174. Under the current international arbitration legal regime, national arbitration laws govern many issues of judicial assistance other than enforcement of the agreement and award. These issues include, for example, certain aspects of discovery, the selection of arbitrators when the parties have not done so, and provisional relief. National court jurisdiction over these issues is almost always determined by the fact that the arbitration takes place within the jurisdiction. Because the locus of an arbitration in cyberspace is difficult to identify, many jurisdictions might assert the power of judicial review and assistance. One answer to this problem is coordination of the judicial assistance function. Such enforceable coordination could be accomplished most effectively by international treaty. Indeed, the New York Convention's judicial enforcement provisions could be modified to cover judicial assistance. Another (less effective) possibility is to make national arbitration laws uniform, so that it doesn't matter which court provides judicial assistance. This is the basic strategy of the UNCITRAL model arbitration law. See generally Born, *International Commercial Arbitration*, pp. 37–38 (cited in note 167). For an overview of other solutions to these difficulties, see Arsíc, pp. 217–20 (cited in note 172).

175. The Supreme Court, for example, has ruled that antitrust, RICO, and securities claims are arbitrable. *Shearson/American Express, Inc. v. McMahon*, 482 U.S. 220, 242 (1987) (holding RICO claims to be arbitrable); *Mitsubishi Motors Corp. v. Soler Chrysler-Plymouth, Inc.*, 473 U.S. 614, 632–40 (1985) (holding Sherman Act claims to be arbitrable); *Scherk v. Alberto-Culver Co.*, 417 U.S. 506, 518–20 (1974) (holding claims under the Securities and Exchange Act of 1934 to be arbitrable). See generally Born, *International Commercial Arbitration*, pp. 322–66 (cited in note 167). These decisions are not required by the New York Convention. To the contrary, the New York Convention and national arbitration laws permit an exception to national courts' obligation to enforce arbitration agreements and awards when the arbitration involves a nonarbitrable subject. See New York Convention, Arts. II(1), V(2) (cited in note 171). But this exception has been construed in an increasingly narrow fashion, as nations increasingly delegate the task of enforcing mandatory laws to private arbitrators.

176. See Born, *International Commercial Arbitration*, pp. 147–52 (cited in note 167).

177. I have tried to avoid analysis of the merits of particular regulatory regimes in this article, but it is perhaps worth noting that this adhesion contracts concern has relatively little force in the cyberspace context where users have an array of options for the large majority of functions and services.

Chapter 4

Thanks to Tom Bell, Paul Berman, Jeff Dunoff, Jack Goldsmith, Dan Hunter, David Johnson, Larry Lessig, Neil Netanel, Dawn C. Nunziato, and Eugene Volokh for their comments on earlier drafts, and to Shannon Burke for research assistance. A version of this paper is to appear in the *Berkeley Technology Law Journal* (forthcoming, 2003).

1. Jack L. Goldsmith, "Against Cyberanarchy," *University of Chicago Law Review* 65 (1998): 1199.

2. Ibid., pp. 1204–05.

3. Ibid., p. 1205.

4. Ibid.

5. Ibid.

6. Ibid.

7. Ibid.

8. Ibid.

9. Ibid.

10. Ibid., pp. 1239–40 (emphasis added); see also Jack L. Goldsmith, "The Abiding Significance of Territorial Sovereignty," *Indiana Journal of Global Legal Studies* 5 (1998): 475, 479 [hereinafter "The Abiding Significance"] ("Internet activities are functionally identical to these non-Internet activities. People in one jurisdiction do something—upload pornography, facilitate gambling, offer a fraudulent security, send spam, etc.—that is costly to stop at another jurisdiction's border and that produces effects within that jurisdiction deemed illegal there."); Allan R. Stein, "The Unexceptional Problem of Jurisdiction in Cyberspace," *International Law* 32 (1998): 1167, 1180 ("The Internet is a medium. It connects people in different places. The injuries inflicted over the Internet are inflicted by people on people. In this sense, the Internet is no different from the myriad of ways that people from one place injure people in other places . . .").

11. Goldsmith, "Against Cyberanarchy," p. 1234.

12. Ibid.; see also Stein, p. 1191 ("Jurisdiction in cyberspace is not unproblematic. My point is that it is not *uniquely* problematic.") (emphasis added).

13. Goldsmith, "Against Cyberanarchy," p. 1234.

14. Ibid., p. 1201.

15. Ibid., pp. 1200–01.

16. Ibid., p. 1199.

17. Ibid., p. 1200–01.

18. Ibid., p. 1200.

19. Ibid.

20. Ibid., p. 1205.

21. Ibid., p. 1206.

22. Ibid., p. 1208 (emphasis added).

23. Ibid., p. 1206 (emphasis added).

24. Ibid., p. 1208.

25. Ibid., p. 1206 (noting that these "significant changes in the world" led to an "unprecedented increase in multijurisdictional activity" and "put pressure on the rigid territorialist conception.").

26. Ibid., p. 1207; see also Stein, p. 1169 ("As people and transactions became more mobile, jurisdictional rules based solely on the current location of the defendant were strained. Courts increasingly had a need to assert authority over persons not currently within their borders, and improvements in communications and transportation rendered travel to a distant judicial forum less onerous than it once had been.").

27. Goldsmith, "Against Cyberanarchy," p. 1208.

28. Ibid. (emphasis added).

29. Ibid., p. 1240; see ibid., p. 1239 ("a nation's right to control events within its territory and to protect its citizens permits it to regulate the local effects of extraterritorial acts"); ibid., p. 1209 (noting the "clear command of "customary international law" that "permits a nation to apply its law to extraterritorial behavior" when such behavior has "substantial local effects."); see also Goldsmith, "The Abiding Significance," p. 479 ("The effects criterion tells us that it is legitimate for a nation to apply its regulation to an extraterritorial act with harmful local effects"); Neil Weinstock Netanel, "Cyberspace Self-Governance: A Skeptical View from Liberal Democratic Theory," *California Law Review* 88 (March 2000): 395, 491 (idea that a sovereign "cannot properly legislate or otherwise prescribe law" that applies to extraterritorial conduct is "fundamentally incorrect as a matter of positive international law"); ibid., p. 490 n. 395 (2000) (sovereign "has a *right* to prohibit . . . speech if [speakers] can be said to have communicated their speech within [sovereign's] territory or, . . . if [the] speech is deemed to occur entirely [elsewhere] but nevertheless has substantial effect within [the sovereign's territory]") (emphasis added) (citing Vol. 1 Sir Robert Jennings and Sir Arthur Watts, *Oppenheim's International Law* 9th Ed. 460, 472–76 (Addison-Wesley Longman, Inc., 1992) (stating that customary international law allows a state to assert jurisdiction over offenses having their culmination in the state even if not begun there and, more controversially, over conduct taking place abroad that has substantial effects within the state); Goldsmith, "Against Cyberanarchy," p. 1239 ("a nation's right to control events within its territory and to protect its citizens permits it to regulate the local effects of extraterritorial acts"); ibid., p. 1209 ("The 'clear' command of "customary international law" that "permits a nation to apply its law to extraterritorial behavior" when such behavior has "substantial local effects"); Restatement (Third) of Foreign Relations, § 402(1)(c) (concluding that unless "unreasonable," a state has jurisdiction to prescribe law with respect to "conduct outside its territory that has or is intended to have substantial effect within its territory").

30. Goldsmith, "Against Cyberanarchy," p. 1208.

31. Ibid.

32. Ibid., p. 1230.

33. Ibid.

34. Ibid., p. 1240.

35. Ibid.

36. Ibid., p. 1239.

37. Ibid., p. 1212.

38. Ibid., p. 1239.

39. Ibid., p. 1212.

40. Ibid.

41. Ibid., p. 1208.

42. Ibid., p. 1239.

43. See notes 25–27, supra.

44. See H. Hong and E. Hong, eds. *Søren Kierkegaard's Journals and Papers,* Vol. 1 (Bloomington, Ind.: Indiana University Press, 1967), p. 450.

45. Goldsmith, "Against Cyberanarchy," p. 1240 (emphasis added).

46. Confronted with the assertion "that in all the vast countries of America, there is but one language," Thomas Jefferson pondered the question: "what constitutes identity, or difference, in two things, in the common acceptation of sameness?" This is, he wrote:

> ... a question of definition, in which every one is free to use his own ...
> All languages may be called the same, as being all made up of the same
> primitive sounds, expressed by the letters of the different alphabets. But,
> in this sense, all things on earth are the same, as consisting of matter....
> [and] it may be learnedly proved, that our trees and plants of every kind
> are descended from those of Europe, because, like them, they have no
> locomotion, they draw nourishment from the earth, they clothe themselves
> with leaves in spring of which they divest themselves in autumn for the
> sleep of winter, etc. Our animals too must be descended from those of
> Europe, because our wolves eat lambs, our deer are gregarious, our ants
> hoard, etc.

Thomas Jefferson to John Adams, May 27, 1813.

47. Goldsmith, "Against Cyberanarchy," p. 1240 (emphasis added).

48. Ibid., p. 1234 (emphasis added).

49. See Per Bak, *How Nature Works* (New York: Springer-Verlag, 1996), especially Chapter 3 ("The Sandpile Paradigm") and Chapter 4 ("Real Sandpiles and Landscape Formation") for an extensive discussion of the complex ways in which avalanches propagate through sandpiles; Stuart Kauffman, *At Home in the Universe* (New York: Oxford University Press, 1995), pp. 235–43.

50. The chaotic dynamics of coupled pendulums are discussed in Bak, pp. 39–48; David Tritton, "Chaos in the Swing of a Pendulum," in *Exploring Chaos: A Guide to the New Science of Disorder*, ed. N. Hall (New York: Norton, 1991) pp. 22–33; James Gleick, *Chaos: Making A New Science* (New York: Penguin Putnam, 1987), pp. 39–44. A more technical treatment can be found in D. D'Humieres, M. R. Beasley, B. A. Huberman, and A. Libchaber, "Chaotic States and Routes to Chaos in the Forced Pendulum," *Physics Revue* A26 (1982): 3483–96.

51. See Stein, p. 1191 ("The Internet geometrically multiplies the number of transactions that implicate more than one state. *But it is a problem of quantity, not quality.*") (emphasis added); Goldsmith, "Against Cyberanarchy," pp. 1237–38 (discussing the "dramatic increase in the number and speed of transactions" in cyberspace in the context of "a nation's incentives to regulate" and the efficacy of regulation).

52. The repudiation of "hermetic territorialism" was a kind of "phase transition" in the law—one orderly arrangement of the interlocking parts of a complex system gives way, rather suddenly, to an entirely different arrangement. Think of the transformation of liquid water into solid ice. As the temperature falls, the individual components of the system—the hydrogen and oxygen atoms and the bonds between them—slowly change, releasing small quanta of energy, while retaining the orderly arrangement that defines the "liquid" state. But at the freezing point, the system abandons gradualism, changing abruptly into a different kind of orderly arrangement of its atoms, an entirely different configuration. We don't know, I would submit, very much at all about phase transitions in the law—how small changes in the many interlocking doctrines, judicial decisions, statutory provisions that underlie any particular legal domain can lead to a systemic reconfiguration of those interlocking parts.

53. *Religious Technology Center v. Netcom Online Services, Inc.*, 907 F. Supp. 1361 (N. D. Cal. 1995).

54. 17 U.S.C. § 106 (2002).

55. *Religious Technology Center*, 907 F. Supp. 1374 (noting that there was "no question" that Netcom neither knew nor "should have known of Erlich's infringing activities" before receipt of notification from the Plaintiffs).

56. Ibid., p. 1368.

57. Ibid.

58. Ibid., p. 1373.

59. Ibid., p. 1370; see also p. 1371 ("knowledge is not an element of direct infringement").

60. Ibid., p. 1367.

61. Ibid., p. 1368.

62. Ibid., p. 1369, citing *MAI Systems Corp. v. Peak Computer, Inc.*, 991 F.2d 511 (9th Cir. 1993).

63. *Religious Technology Center*, 907 F. Supp. 1368.

64. Ibid.

65. Ibid., p. 1370.

66. Ibid., p. 1372.

67. Ibid., p. 1368.

68. Ibid., p. 1370 (emphasis added).

69. Ibid., p. 1369.

70. Ibid.

71. Ibid. (emphasis added).

72. Ibid., p. 1372.

73. Ibid. (emphasis added).

74. Ibid., p. 1373.

75. Ibid. A different judge—a less creative, or a less courageous judge, perhaps—would have taken the time-honored route of obfuscation, twisting the "fuzzball factors" of the fair use doctrine; see Frank E. Easterbrook, "Cyberspace and the Law of the Horse," *University of Chicago Legal Forum* (1996): 207, 208, to fit the facts at hand; see also *Religious Technology Center*, 907 F. Supp. 1378–1381 (holding that Netcom's copying was not a "fair use" as a matter of law).

76. Goldsmith, "Against Cyberanarchy," p. 1239

77. Ibid, p. 1212 (emphasis added).

78. Ibid., p. 1234.

79. Ibid., p. 1239.

80. See Restatement (Third) Foreign Relations Law of the United States, § 402 cmt.d, (the "effects principle is not controversial with respect to acts such as shooting or even sending libelous publications across a boundary").

81. *Religious Technology Center*, 907 F. Supp. 1369.

82. Ibid., p. 1372.

83. Ibid., p. 1373.

84. Ibid., p. 1372.

85. Ibid.

86. Ibid., p. 1369.

87. Ibid.

88. Preamble, Declaration of Independence (U.S. 1776).

89. See Stein, p. 1176 ("Unlike the law of sovereigns, the scope of . . . *private ordering* is limited to persons who have consented to the particular rules in question") (emphasis added); Goldsmith, "Against Cyberanarchy," p. 1216 (concluding that because there are many cyberspace activities "for which *ex ante* consent to a governing legal regime is either infeasible or unenforceable," these activities "are not amenable to *private* ordering") (second emphasis added); ibid., p. 1215 (because "it remains an open question how to generate consent across cyberspace networks"); ibid., p. 1216

("*private* legal ordering" can resolve "many, but not all, of the challenges posed by multijurisdictional cyberspace activity") (emphasis added); ibid., p. 1216 ("Consent-based legal orders are limited by a variety of national mandatory law restrictions."); see also, Netanel, p. 406 (acknowledging the argument that application of foreign law to Digitalbook.com's Web site "violates the liberal democratic principle of government by consent of the governed," but concluding that because consent "makes up only one side of the liberal democracy equation," where "foreign resident conduct has substantial effect within the legislating country and runs strongly against that country's fundamental public policy, the prescriptive outcome of the legislating country's democratic process should prevail").

90. Goldsmith, "Against Cyberanarchy," p. 1241 (emphasis added). That's an odd, though telling, formulation; I would have thought that the need to demonstrate consent "begins" with the "self-evident truth" that governments "derive their just power from the consent of the governed."

91. Ibid., p. 1212 (emphasis added).

92. Ibid., p. 1208 (emphasis added).

93. "Against Cyberanarchy" has been called, among other things, a "trenchant" and "withering" critique of the regulation skeptics' claims (Netanel, p. 402), and a "decisive response to the widespread view that cyberspace is not regulable" [Cass Sunstein, Republic.com (Princeton, N.J.: Princeton University Press, 2001), p. 204.] As of this writing (March 2002) it has been cited, according to a Lexis search (Lawrev database), nearly 100 times. It has also become a staple of cyberspace law courses; for just a small sample of the courses for which Goldsmith's article is required reading, see, for example, the reading list for "Seminar on Law and Technology" course, Fall 1999 semester, Indiana University School of Law-Indianapolis (http://www.slis.lib.indiana.edu/courses/crews/l563fa99.htm); reading list for "Cyber Law Seminar" course, Spring 1999 semester, Harvard Law School (http://cyber.law.harvard.edu/columbia/cgi/syllabus.cgi); reading list for "Electronic Commerce Law" course, Spring 2001 semester, University of Melbourne Law School (http://graduate.unimelblaw.com.au/gradlaw.nsf/docs/4H33EB355); reading list for "Cyberlaw" course, Spring 2000 semester, Catholic University of America–Columbus School of Law (http://law.cua.edu/faculty/fischer/cyberlawsyl.htm); reading list for "Cyberlaw" course, Fall 2000 semester, University of California–Berkeley School of Law (http://www.law.berkeley.edu/institutes/bclt/courses/fall00/cyberlaw/cybersyllabus.html); reading list for "The Internet and the State" course, Fall 2000 semester, University of Miami School of Law (http://www.law.miami.edu/~froomkin/inet00/syllabus2.htm); reading list for "Cyber Law: Legal Issues in a Digital Business Age" course, Fall 2001 semester, Arts at the University of Waterloo (http://www.arts.uwaterloo.ca/ACCT/courses/acc415/).

94. Among the "Facts ... submitted to a candid world" in the Declaration of Independence to substantiate "repeated injuries and usurpations" to which the King of England had subjected the American colonists was that the King had "combined with others to subject us to a jurisdiction foreign to our constitution, and unacknowledged by our laws; giving his Assent to their Acts of pretended Legislation[.]"

Chapter 5

The author would like to thank the Social Sciences and Humanities Research Council of Canada Initiative on the New Economy program, the Uniform Law Conference of

Canada and Industry Canada for their financial support in sponsoring this paper; Teresa David and William Karam for their research assistance; Vaso Maric, Rene Geist, Harvey Goldschmid, Ted Killheffer, Denis Rice, as well as the participants at the Consumer Measures Committee/Uniform Law Conference of Canada April 2001 Workshop on Consumer Protection and Jurisdiction in Electronic Commerce, the Telecommunications Policy Research Council 2001 Conference, and the Georgetown University Advanced E-Commerce Institute, for their comments on earlier versions of this paper; and to the editors of the *Berkeley Technology Law Journal* for their excellent work in bringing the paper upon which this is based to publication. Any errors or omissions remain the sole responsibility of the author.

1. Digital Equip. Corp. v. Altavista Tech., Inc., 960 F. Supp. 456, 462 (D. Mass. 1997).

2. *Yahoo!, Inc. v. LICRA*, C-00-21275 JF, 2001 U.S. Dist. LEXIS 18378, at *6, 7 (N.D. Cal. November 7, 2001) (citing the French court's decision in *UEJF et LICRA v. Yahoo! Inc. et Yahoo France*).

3. See, for example, Louis Trager, "Unhappy Holidays at Toys 'R' Us," *ZDNet Interactive Week*, January 12, 2000, http://www.zdnet.com/filters/printerfriendly/-0,6061,2421416-35,00.html.

4. See, for example, Cornell Law School Legal Information Institute, "Products Liability Law: An Overview," http://www.law.cornell.edu/topics/products_liability.html (last visited Nov. 26, 2001).

5. See, for example, *UEJF et LICRA v. Yahoo! Inc. et Yahoo France*, T.G.I. Paris, May 22, 2000, N° RG: 00/05308; see also *Braintech, Inc. v. Kostiuk*, [1999] 171 D.L.R. (4th) 46, 63-64 (B.C.C.A.).

6. The U.S. Federal Trade Commission has noted:

> Shifting to a pure country-of-origin approach to address challenges inherent in the current system risks undermining consumer protection, and ultimately consumer confidence in e-commerce. The same would be true under a "prescribed-by-seller" approach to the extent it would allow contractual choice-of-law and choice-of-forum provisions dictated by the seller to override the core protections afforded to consumers in their home country or their right to sue in a local court.

U.S. Federal Trade Commission, Bureau of Consumer Protection, Consumer Protection in the Global Electronic Marketplace: Looking Ahead (Staff Report), available at http://www.ftc.gov/bcp/icpw/lookingahead/electronicmkpl.pdf, September 2001.

7. See *Yahoo!France*; see also "Yahoo! Ordered to Bar French from Nazi Sites," *Reuters*, November 20, 2000, available at http://www.zdnet.co.uk/news/2000/-46/ns-19192.html.

8. In Canada, see *Irwin Toy Ltd. v. Doe* [2000] O.J. No. 3318 (Ont.). In the United States see *J. Erik Hvide v. "John Does 1-8,"* No. 99-22831-CA01 (Fla. Cir. Ct. Jun. 14, 2001). See also *John Doe, also known as Aquacool_2000 v. Yahoo! Inc.*, No. 00-20677 (Cal. Super. Ct. filed May 11, 2000); see generally C. S. Kaplan, "Judge Says Online Critic Has No Right to Hide," *New York Times Cyber Law Journal* (June 9, 2000) (on file with the author).

9. 326 U.S. 310, 316 (1945).

10. Ibid. (quoting *Milliken v. Meyer*, 311 U.S. 457, 463 [1940]).

11. World-Wide Volkswagen Corp. v. Woodson, 444 U.S. 286, 291 (1980).

12. Ibid. p. 297.

13. *Hanson v. Denckla*, 357 U.S. 235, 253 (1958).

14. See *Calder v. Jones*, 465 U.S. 783, 789 (1984) (upholding jurisdiction in which conduct was allegedly calculated to cause injuries in the forum state and the cause of action arose from this conduct).

15. *Burger King v. Rudzewicz*, 471 U.S. 462, 475 (1985).

16. Ibid., pp. 476–77.

17. *Zippo Mfg. Co. v. Zippo Dot Com, Inc.*, 952 F. Supp. 1119, 1122-23 (W.D. Pa. 1997).

18. Ibid., p. 1124.

19. Ibid., p. 1127.

20. *Inset Systems, Inc. v. Instruction Set, Inc.*, 937 F. Supp. 161 (D. Conn. 1996).

21. Internet domain names, which have become a ubiquitous part of commercial advertising, enable users to access Web sites simply by typing in a name such as "www.inset.com" in their web browser. The "www" portion of the address identifies that the site is part of the World Wide Web; the "inset" portion is usually the name of a company or other identifying words; and "com" identifies the type of institution, in this case a company. Domain names, the subject of several other litigated cases, are administered in the United States by a government-appointed agency, Network Solutions Inc. (NSI), and are distributed on a first-come, first-served basis. See Cynthia Rowden and Jeannette Lee, "Trademarks and the Internet: An Overview," November 4, 1998, available at http://www.bereskinparr.com/art-pdf/TM&InternetOverview.pdf.

22. *Inset*, 937 F. Supp. 163.

23. World-Wide Volkswagen Corp. v. Woodson, 444 U.S. 286, 291-92 (1980).

24. *Inset*, 937 F. Supp. 160.

25. Ibid., p. 165.

26. Ibid.

27. Ibid.

28. Ibid.

29. Ibid.

30. Ibid., pp. 162–63.

31. See, for example, *Heroes, Inc. v. Heroes Found.*, 958 F. Supp. 1, 5 (D.D.C. 1996) (citing *Inset* with approval in finding that a Web site sustained contact with the District of Columbia); *Panavision Int'l, L.P. v. Toeppen*, 938 F. Supp. 616 (C.D. Cal. 1996) (finding that use of a trademark-infringing domain name in Illinois was an act expressly directed at California).

32. *Bensusan Rest. Corp. v. King*, 937 F. Supp. 295 (S.D.N.Y. 1996), *aff'd* 126 F.3d. 25 (2d Cir. 1997).

33. Ibid., p. 297.

34. Ibid., p. 298.

35. Ibid., pp. 297–98.

36. Ibid., p. 297.

37. Ibid., p. 299.

38. Ibid.

39. Ibid.

40. Ibid.

41. Ibid.

42. *Bensusan Rest. Corp. v. King*, 126 F.3d 25, 29 (2d Cir. 1997).

43. See, for example, *Hearst Corp. v. Goldberger*, No. 96 Civ. 3620 PKL AJP, 1997 WL 97097, at *15 (S.D.N.Y. Feb. 26, 1997). The *Goldberger* court relied heavily upon the *Bensusan* analysis in refusing to assert personal jurisdiction in a trademark infringement matter involving the domain name "Esqwire.com." Ibid. The *Goldberger* court

carefully reviewed Internet case law to that point, noted its disagreement with decisions such as *Inset*, *Maritz*, and *Panavision*, and cautioned that:

> Where, as here, defendant has not contracted to sell or actually sold any goods or services to New Yorkers, a finding of personal jurisdiction in New York based on an Internet website would mean that there would be nationwide (indeed, worldwide) personal jurisdiction over anyone and everyone who establishes an Internet website. Such nationwide jurisdiction is not consistent with traditional personal jurisdiction case law nor acceptable to the court as a matter of policy.

Ibid. p. *13.

44. Michael Geist, "The Reality of Bytes: Regulating Economic Activity in the Age of the Internet," *Washington Law Review* 73 (1998): 521, 538.

45. 952 F. Supp. 1119, 1126 (W.D. Pa. 1997).

46. Ibid., p. 1121.

47. Ibid.

48. Ibid.

49. Ibid.

50. Ibid.

51. Ibid.

52. Ibid.

53. One case omitted from the discussion but relied upon by the *Zippo* court was *CompuServe Inc. v. Patterson*, 89 F.3d 1257 (6th Cir. 1996). Although the *Zippo* court refers to the decision as an Internet case, in fact, the activity in question did not involve the use of the Internet. Rather, Patterson used CompuServe's proprietary network to distribute certain shareware programs. Accordingly, Patterson's contacts with Ohio, CompuServe's headquarters and the location of the litigation, were confined to an offline contractual agreement and the posting of shareware on a CompuServe server that was available to users of its proprietary network (not Internet users at large).

54. *Zippo*, 952 F. Supp. 1127.

55. Ibid., p. 1124 (internal citations omitted).

56. See, for example, *American Eyewear, Inc. v. Peeper's Sunglasses and Accessories, Inc.*, 106 F. Supp. 2d 895 (N.D. Tex. 2000); *America Online, Inc. v. Huang*, 106 F. Supp. 2d 848 (E.D. Va. 2000); *Citigroup v. City Holding Co.*, 97 F. Supp. 2d 549 (S.D.N.Y. 2000); *Standard Knitting, Ltd. v. Outside Design, Inc.*, No. 00-2288, 2000 WL 804434 (E.D. Pa. Jun. 23, 2000); *Decker v. Circus Circus Hotel*, 49 F. Supp. 2d 748 (D. N.J. 1999); *Hasbro, Inc. v. Clue Computing, Inc.*, 66 F. Supp. 2d 117 (D. Mass. 1999); *Blumenthal v. Drudge*, 992 F. Supp. 44 (D.D.C. 1998); *Mallinkrodt Med., Inc. v. Sonus Pharm., Inc.*, 989 F. Supp. 265 (D.D.C. 1998); *Resuscitation Techs., Inc. v. Cont. Health Care Corp.*, No. IP 96-1457-C-M/S, 1997 WL 148567 (S.D. Ind. Mar. 24, 1997); *Smith v. Hobby Lobby Stores, Inc.*, 968 F. Supp. 1356 (W.D. Ark. 1997); *TELCO Communications v. An Apple A Day*, 977 F. Supp. 404 (E.D. Va. 1997); *Conseco, Inc. v. Hickerson*, 698 N.E.2d 816 (Ind. App. 1998); *State by Humphrey v. Granite Gate Resorts, Inc.*, (Minn. App. 1997).

57. 130 F.3d. 414 (9th Cir. 1997).

58. Interestingly, the principals behind Cybersell Arizona were Laurence Canter and Martha Siegel, attorneys who are infamous among Web users as the first Internet "spammers" or junk e-mailers. Ibid., p. 415.

59. Ibid., p. 419.

60. Ibid., p. 418.

61. Ibid.

62. Ibid.

63. Ibid., p. 420.

64. *Stomp, Inc. v. Neato LLC*, 61 F. Supp. 2d 1074 (C.D. Cal. 1999). The court also recognized that:

> Such a broad exercise of personal jurisdiction over defendants who engage in commerce over the Internet might have devastating effects on local merchants and small businesses that seek to expand through the Internet. These small businesses make up the backbone of the American economy and should not have to bear the burden of defending suits in distant fora when they intend only to sell to local consumers their wares from the convenience of their own homes. This concern must be balanced against the ability of a distant consumer to press its cause against a defendant who uses the Internet to do business within the forum while remaining outside the boundaries of the jurisdiction.

Ibid., pp. 1080–81.

65. Ibid.

66. In addition to the cases discussed *infra*, see also *Panavision Int'l., L.P. v. Toeppen*, 141 F.3d 1316, 1320 (9th Cir. 1998); *CompuServe v. Patterson*, 89 F.3d 1257 (6th Cir. 1996); *Neogen Corp. v. Neo Gen Screening, Inc.*, 109 F. Supp. 2d 724, 729 (W.D. Mich. 2000); *Search Force v. Data Force Intern.*, 112 F. Supp. 2d 771, 777 (S.D. Ind. 2000); *Uncle Sam's Safari Outfitters, Inc. v. Uncle Sam's Navy Outfitters—Manhattan, Inc.*, 96 F. Supp. 2d 919, 923 (E.D. Mo. 2000); *Bochan v. La Fontaine*, 68 F. Supp. 2d 692, 701-02 (E.D. Va. 1999); *Rothschild Berry Farm v. Serendipity Group LLC*, 84 F. Supp. 2d 904, 908 (S.D. Ohio 1999).

67. 465 U.S. 783 (1984).

68. Ibid., p. 789.

69. Ibid., p. 784.

70. Ibid., p. 789.

71. Ibid., pp. 789–90.

72. 751 A.2d 538 (N.J. 2000).

73. Ibid., pp. 543–48.

74. Ibid.

75. Ibid., 543.

76. Ibid., p. 556.

77. 89 F. Supp. 2d 1154 (C.D. Cal. 2000).

78. Ibid., p. 1157.

79. Ibid.

80. Ibid., p. 1158.

81. Ibid.

82. Ibid., p. 1160.

83. Ibid.

84. Ibid.

85. Ibid.

86. Ibid., p. 1159.

87. No. Civ. A. 399-CV-2339-L, 2000 WL 1030619 (N.D. Tex. July 25, 2000).

88. Ibid., p. *2.

89. Ibid., p. *1.

90. Ibid., p. *4.

91. Ibid., p. *4.

92. Ibid.

93. CCB-01-3096 (D. Maryland, 2002).

94. Civil App. No. 01-1812, 2002 WL 1309000 (4th Cir. June 14, 2002).

95. Ibid.

96. See *Braintech, Inc. v. Kostiuk* [1999] 171 D.L.R. (4th) 46, 61 (B.C.C.A.); see also *Barrett v. Catacombs Press*, 44 F. Supp. 2d 717, 728 (E.D. Pa. 1999).

97. *People Solutions, Inc. v. People Solutions, Inc.*, No. Civ. A. 399-CV-2339-L, 2000 WL 1030619, at *4 (N.D. Tex. Jul. 25, 2000).

98. Ibid.

99. The Canadian government's e-commerce policy is stated as follows:

On September 22, 1998, the Prime Minister announced Canada's Electronic Commerce Strategy, outlining initiatives designed to establish Canada as a world leader in the adoption and use of electronic commerce. Working in close collaboration with the private sector, the federal government has concentrated on creating the most favorable environment possible in areas which are critical to the rapid development of e-commerce.

Industry Canada, "Electronic Commerce in Canada: Canadian Strategy," available at http://www.ecom.ic.gc.ca/english/60.html (last modified February 14, 2001).

The U.S. government shares a similar e-commerce policy:

Commerce on the Internet could total tens of billions of dollars by the turn of the century. For this potential to be realized fully, governments must adopt a non-regulatory, market-oriented approach to electronic commerce, one that facilitates the emergence of a transparent and predictable legal environment to support global business and commerce. Official decision makers must respect the unique nature of the medium and recognize that widespread competition and increased consumer choice should be the defining features of the new digital marketplace.

White House, "A Framework for Global Electronic Commerce," July 1, 1997, available at http://www.ta.doc.gov/digeconomy/framework.htm.

100. John Gedid noted the following at an international conference on Internet jurisdiction:

The *Zippo* opinion is comprehensive, thorough and persuasive. . . . The court's review of precedents is sweeping and thorough, and its logic is compelling. The *Zippo* court fully understood and explained difficult precedents, so that they could be understood in terms of the *International Shoe* criteria. While there are some who would question the approach on the theories that it does not go far enough or that it goes too far, nevertheless, it is an attempt at stating a more comprehensive and coherent approach to Internet jurisdiction cases. The result was that the *Zippo* opinion is probably the most persuasive and influential opinion that has been published on the subject of cyberspace jurisdiction.

John L. Gedid, "Minimum Contacts Analysis in Cyberspace—Sale of Goods and Services," July 1997, http://ilpf.org/events/jurisdiction/presentations/gedid_addl.htm.

See generally Charles H. Fleischer, "Will the Internet Abrogate Territorial Limits on Personal Jurisdiction?," *Tort and Insurance Law Journal* 33 (1997): 107; Michael J. Sikora III, "Beam Me into Your Jurisdiction: Establishing Personal Jurisdiction Via Electronic Contacts in Light of the Sixth Circuit's Decision in *CompuServe, Inc. v. Patterson*," *Capital University Law Review* 27 (1998): 163, 184–85.

101. Jerry Kang, "Information Privacy in Cyberspace Transactions," *Stanford Law Review* 50 (1998): 1193, 1226–29.

102. Ibid.

103. *Zippo Mfg. Co. v. Zippo Dot Com, Inc.*, 952 F. Supp. 1119, 1126 (W.D. Pa. 1997).

104. See, for example, *Barrett v. Catacombs Press*, 64 F. Supp. 2d 440 (E.D. Pa. 1999).

105. David Legard, "Average Cost to Build E-Commerce Site: $1 Million," *The Standard*, May 31, 1999 (on file with the author).

106. 139 F. Supp. 2d 696 (D. Md. 2001).

107. Ibid., p. 700.

108. Ibid.

109. Ibid.

110. 2001 WL 1862870 (E.D.Mo. October 25, 2001).

111. Ibid.

112. Organisation for Economic Co-operation and Development, "Recommendation of the OECD Council Concerning Guidelines for Consumer Protection in the Context of Electronic Commerce," p. 5, available at http://www.oecd.org/dsti/sti/it/consumer/prod/CPGuidelines_final.pdf (last visited November 26, 2001).

113. See American Bar Association, "Achieving Legal and Business Order in Cyberspace: A Report on Global Jurisdiction Issues Created By the Internet" (on file with the author). In the interests of full disclosure, it should be noted that the author was chair of the Sale of Services Working Group, one of nine working groups tasked with developing Internet jurisdiction recommendations. http://www.abanet.org/buslaw/cyber/initiatives/draft.rtf.

114. Ibid., p. 30.

115. Currently in beta, Google offers searchers the ability to configure their Google searching to translate automatically any results that appear in a foreign language. See Google, http://www.google.com/machine_translation.html (last visited November 26, 2001).

116. *Graves v. Pikulski*, 115 F. Supp. 2d 931 (S.D. Ill. 2000); *Kilgallen v. Network Solutions*, 99 F. Supp. 2d 125 (D. Mass. 2000); *Rudder v. Microsoft Corp.*, [1999] 2 C.P.R. (4th) 474 (Ont.).

117. *Kilgallen*, 99 F. Supp. 129.

118. Ibid., p. 126.

119. Ibid.

120. Ibid.

121. Ibid., p. 129.

122. No. CV 99-7654 HLH, 2000 WL 525390 (C.D. Cal. March 27, 2000).

123. Ibid.

124. Ibid., p. *3.

125. Ibid.

126. Ibid.

127. Ibid.

128. Ibid.

129. Ibid.

130. Ibid. (emphasis added)

131. 126 F. Supp. 2d 238 (S.D.N.Y. 2000).

132. Ibid., p. 252.

133. Ibid., pp. 242–43.

134. Ibid.

135. 150 F. Supp. 2d 585 (S.D.N.Y. 2001).

136. 306 F.3d 17 (2d. Cir., 2002).

137. Ibid., p. 595.

138. Ibid.

139. Furthermore, unlike the user of Netscape Navigator or other clickwrap or shrink-wrap licensees, the individual obtaining SmartDownload is not made aware that he is entering into a contract. SmartDownload is available from Netscape's Web site free of charge. Before downloading the software, the user need not view any license agreement terms or even any reference to a license agreement and need not do anything to manifest assent to such a license agreement other than actually taking possession of the product. From the user's vantage point, SmartDownload could be analogized to a free neighborhood newspaper, readily obtained from a sidewalk box or supermarket counter without any exchange with a seller or vendor. It is there for the taking. The only hint that a contract is being formed is one small box of text referring to the license agreement, text that appears below the screen used for downloading and that a user need not even see before obtaining the product: "Please review and agree to the terms before downloading and using the software for the Netscape Smart Download software license agreement." Couched in the mild request, "Please review," this agreement reads as a mere invitation, not as a condition. The language does not dictate that a user must agree to the license terms before downloading and using the software. While clearer language appears in the License Agreement itself, the language of the invitation does not require the reading of those terms or provide adequate notice either that a contract is being created or that the terms of the License Agreement will bind the user. Ibid., pp. 595–96.

140. *Mendoza v. AOL* (Cal. Super. Ct.) (unreported, on file with the author).

141. Ibid.

142. Ibid.

143. For another example in which a Massachusetts state court refused to enforce the AOL forum selection clause in a class action suit over AOL system software see *Williams v. AOL*, No. 00-0962 (Mass. Super. Ct. Feb 2001) (on file with the author).

144. For example, the *Wall Street Journal* reports that Bermuda has become a haven for dot-com operations seeking to avoid tax and other regulatory measures in North America. Michael Allen, "As Dot-Coms Go Bust in the U.S., Bermuda Hosts a Little Boomlet," *Wall Street Journal*, January 8, 2001, p. A4.

145. See generally David R. Johnson and David G. Post, "Law and Borders: The Rise of Law in Cyberspace," *Stanford Law Review* 48 (1996): 1367.

146. *American Libraries Ass'n v. Pataki*, 969 F. Supp. 160 (S.D.N.Y. 1997).

147. Ibid., p. 170.

148. Bob Tedeschi, "E-Commerce: Borders Returning to the Internet," *New York Times*, April 2, 2001 (on file with the author).

149. In addition to the discussion below, see Jack L. Goldsmith and Alan O. Sykes, "The Internet and the Dormant Commerce Clause, *Yale Law Journal* 110 (2001): 785, 810–12.

150. See, Information Technology Association of America, "E-Commerce Taxation and the Limitations of Geolocation Tools," http://www.itaa.org/taxfinance/docs/geolocationpaper.pdf (last visited October 22, 2002).

151. As Lessig points out, "A regulation need not be absolutely effective to be sufficiently effective." The same applies to bordering technologies; whether used for

targeted marketing or to ensure legal compliance, it need not be perfect. Larry Lessig, "The Zones of Cyberspace," *Stanford Law Review* 48 (1996): 1405.

152. B. Tedeschi, http://www.nytimes.com/2001/04/02/technology/02ECOM-MERCE.html (last visited October 8, 2002).

153. "Nevada Governor Signs Internet Gambling Bill," *Associated Press* June 14, 2001, http://library.northernlight.com/EE20010614910000041.html?cb=200&dx=2006&sc=0#doc> (last visited September 22, 2002).

154. Nevada Assembly Bill 466 (71st Assembly) http://www.leg.state.nv.us/71st/bills/AB/AB466_EN.html (last visited July 30, 2001).

155. Anick Jesdanun, "The Potential and Peril of National Internet Boundaries," *San Francisco Examiner*, March 4, 2001, http://interactiveprivacy.com/showstory.asp?ID=234 (last visited October 8, 2002).

156. See Akamai, http://www.akamai.com/en/html/services/edgescape.html (last visited October 8, 2002).

157. See Quova, http://www.quova.com (last visited October 8, 2002).

158. Stephanie Olsen, "Tracking Web Users into European Territory," *CNET News.com*, April 3, 2001, http://news.com.com/2100-1023-255213.html (last visited October 8, 2002).

159. Patricia Jacobus, "CinemaNow Appeases Studios By Locating Web Surfers," *CNET News.com*, February 26, 2001, http://news.com.com/2100-1023-253169.html (last visited October 8, 2002).

160. See, Showtime Online, http://www.showtimeonline.com (last visited October 12, 2002).

161. Declan McCullagh, "Google Excluding Controversial Sites," *CNET News.com*, October 23, 2002, http://news.com.com/2100-1023-963132.html (last visited October 30, 2002).

162. Except where as required by law. See, for example, Anick Jesdanun, "The Potential and Peril of National Internet Boundaries," *San Francisco Examiner*, March 4, 2001, available at http://www.examiner.com/business/-default.jsp?story=b.net.0107.

163. See, for example, Martin H. Redish, "Of New Wine and Old Bottles: Personal Jurisdiction, The Internet, and the Nature of Constitutional Evolution," *Jurimetrics Journal* 38 (1998): 575. Redish notes:

> The most effective defense of an Internet exception to the purposeful availment requirement is not that state interest should play an important role only in Internet cases, but rather that the technological development of the Internet effectively renders the concept of purposeful availment both conceptually incoherent and practically irrelevant. An individual or entity may so easily and quickly reach the entire world with its messages that it is simply not helpful to inquire whether, in taking such action, that individual or entity has consciously and carefully made the decision either to affiliate with the forum state or seek to acquire its benefits.

Ibid., pp. 605–06.

164. *People v. World Interactive Gaming*, 714 N.Y.S.2d 844 (Sup. Ct. 1999).

165. Ibid.

166. No. 00 Civ. 4647 (DLC), 2001 WL 417118 (S.D.N.Y. Apr. 23, 2001).

167. Ibid., p. *4.

168. Thomas Heath, "Capitals Owner Puts Pittsburgh Fans on Ice," *Washington Post*, April 14, 2001 (on file with the author).

169. In March 2001, the Electronic Commerce and Information, Consumer Protection Amendment and Manitoba Evidence Amendment Act (S.M. 200, c. E55. 77) and the Internet Agreements Regulations (Man. Reg. 176/2000) took effect within the province. Designed to foster an online environment where consumer confidence will flourish, the new laws apply exclusively to the online retail sale of goods or services or the retail lease-to-own of goods between buyers and sellers. Under the new rules, binding e-commerce transactions require the seller to provide certain obligatory information to the buyer under threat of a purchaser contract cancellation remedy.

170. Compare Joel R. Reidenberg, "The Yahoo! Case and the International Democratization of the Internet," Fordham Law and Economics Working Paper no. 11, 2001 (arguing that online bordering facilitates democracy by allowing democratically elected governments to implement policy choices that affect their citizens both offline and online), available at http://papers.ssrn.com/paper.taf?ABSTRACT_ID=267148 (last visited November 26, 2001).

Chapter 6

Portions of this chapter first appeared as "Federalism in Cyberspace," *Connecticut Law Review* 28 (1996): 1095. Copyright 2002 by Dan L. Burk.

1. Jack L. Goldsmith and Alan O. Sykes, "The Internet and the Dormant Commerce Clause," *Yale Law Journal* 110 (2001): 785; Allan R. Stein, "The Unexceptional Problem of Jurisdiction in Cyberspace," *International Lawyer* 32 (1998): 1167; see also Joseph H. Sommer, "Against Cyberlaw," *Berkeley Technology Law Journal* 15 (2000): 1145.

2. See Stein.

3. See *New State Ice Co. v. Liebmann*, 285 U.S. 262, 311 (1932) (Brandeis, J., dissenting) (describing the states as the laboratories of democracy).

4. See, for example, Richard Epstein, "Exit Rights Under Federalism," *Law and Contemporary Problems* 55 (1992): 147.

5. See Mancur Olson, *The Logic of Collective Action: Public Goods and the Theory of Groups* (Cambridge, Mass.: Harvard University Press, 1965); James M. Buchanan and Gordon Tullock, *The Calculus of Consent: Logical Foundations of Constitutional Democracy* (Ann Arbor, Mich.: University of Michigan Press, 1962).

6. See Gordon Tullock, "The Welfare Costs of Tariffs, Monopolies and Theft," *Western Economic Journal* 5 (1967): 224, 232.

7. See Richard A. Posner, *Economic Analysis of Law*, 4th ed. (New York: Aspen Law and Business, 1992), p. 638.

8. See Epstein, p. 1454 ("How do the people compel the holders of governmental monopoly power to act as though they could only obtain a competitive return for their services? Federalism facilitates a solution by allowing easy exit, as well as by allowing voice." [citation omitted]).

9. See Albert Hirschman, *Exit, Voice, and Loyalty: Responses to Decline in Firms, Organizations, and States* (Cambridge, Mass.: Harvard University Press, 1970).

10. See Albert Breton, "The Existence and Stability of Interjurisdictional Competition" in *Competition among States and Local Governments: Efficiency and Equity in American Federalism*, ed. Daphne A. Kenyon and John Kincaid (Washington: Urban Institute Press, 1991), p. 40.

11. Charles Tiebout, "A Pure Theory of Local Expenditures," *Journal of Political Economy* 64 (1954): 416.

12. For a review of the literature, see Lucian A. Bebchuck, "Federalism and the Corporation: The Desirable Limits on State Competition in Corporate Law," *Harvard Law Review* 105 (1992): 1435.

13. See William L. Carey, "Federalism and Corporate Law: Reflections upon Delaware," *Yale Law Journal* 83 (1974): 663.

14. See Daniel Fischel, "The 'Race to the Bottom' Revisited: Reflections on Recent Developments in Delaware's Corporation Law," *Northwestern Law Review* 76 (1982): 913; Peter Dodd and Richard Leftwich, "The Market for Corporate Charters"; "Unhealthy Competition Versus Federal Regulation," *Journal of Business* 53 (1980): 259.

15. See Epstein, p. 152.

16. See Roberta Romano, "Law as a Product: Some Pieces of the Incorporation Puzzle," *Journal of Law, Economics and Organization* 1 (1985): 225.

17. See Joseph Stiglitz, "The Theory of Local Public Goods" in *Local Provision of Public Services: The Tiebout Model after Twenty-Five Years*, ed. George R. Zodrow (New York: Academic Press, 1983), p. 19.

18. See Posner, p. 638.

19. See Joel P. Trachtman, "International Regulatory Competition, Externalization, and Jurisdiction," *Harvard International Law Journal* 34 (1993): 47, 73.

20. See George J. Stigler, "A Theory of Oligopoly," *Journal of Political Economy* 72 (1977): 44.

21. The "Prisoner's Dilemma" model serves as a standard example of a noncooperative game in which the rational self-interest of the players leads to a suboptimal outcome for each player. David M. Kreps, *Game Theory and Economic Modeling* (New York: Oxford University Press, 1990), pp. 37–39. However, the outcome is dependent on the assumption that the players cannot communicate with one another to collude and that the game is a single round event. See John E. Chubb, "How Relevant Is Competition to Government Policymaking" in *Competition among States and Local Governments: Efficiency and Equity in American Federalism*, ed. Daphne A. Kenyon and John Kincaid (Washington: Urban Institute Press, 1991), pp. 57, 58. In at least some instances, however, this dynamic may change if the game continues through multiple rounds. See Robert Axelrod, *The Evolution of Cooperation* (New York: Basic Books, 1984).

22. See Lester Telser, "A Theory of Self-Enforcing Agreements," *Journal of Business* 53 (1980): 27.

23. See Breton, pp. 48–49.

24. See Epstein, p. 1455 ("National regulation prevents unhealthy types of competition among jurisdictions. . . .")

25. Ibid.

26. Preston Gralla, *How the Internet Works*, 6th ed. (Indianapolis, Ind.: Que, 2002), p. 13–15.

27. Ibid., p. 41.

28. Ibid., pp. 13–15.

29. Ibid., pp. 17–19.

30. Ibid., pp. 29–30.

31. See J. H. Saltzer et al., "End-to-End Arguments in System Design" in *Innovations in Internetworking*, ed. Craig Partridge (Norwood, Mass.: Artech House, 1988), pp. 195–206; Mark A. Lemley and Lawrence Lessig, "The End of End-to-End: Preserving the Architecture of the Internet in the Broadband Era," *UCLA Law Review* 48 (2001): 925.

32. See Gralla, pp. 41–43.

33. Ibid., pp. 26–27.

34. See Dan L. Burk, "Virtual Exit in the Global Information Economy," *Chicago-Kent Law Review* 73 (1998): 943.

35. Ibid., p. 978.

36. See Dan L. Burk, "Jurisdiction in a World without Borders," *Virginia Journal of Law and Technology* 1 (1997): 3.

37. See *Hanson v. Denckla*, 357 U.S. 235, 250 (1958) ("As technological progress has increased the flow of commerce between the states, the need for jurisdiction over nonresidents has undergone a similar increase."); *Burger King v. Rudzewicz*, 471 U.S. 462, 476 (1985) ("It is an inescapable fact of modern commercial life that a substantial amount of business is transacted solely by mail and wire communications across state lines, thus obviating the need for physical presence within a state in which business is conducted.")

38. *Pennoyer v. Neff.*

39. See *Burnham v. Superior Court*, 495 U.S. 604 (1990).

40. See *Hess v. Pawloski*, 274 U.S. 352 (1927).

41. See *Hutchinson v. Chase & Gilbert*, 45 F.2d 139 (2d Cir. 1930).

42. See, for example, *Shaffer v. Heitner*, 433 U.S. 186 (1977).

43. See *Harris v. Balk*, 198 U.S. 215 (1905).

44. 326 U.S. 310 (1945).

45. Ibid., p. 158.

46. Ibid.

47. See *Helicopteros Nacionales de Columbia, S.A. v. Hall*, 466 U.S. 408 n. 9 (1984).

48. See *International Shoe*, 326 U.S. 318.

49. See 326 U.S. 318.

50. Ibid., *Burger King v. Rudzewicz*, 471 U.S. 462, 473 (1985).

51. *World-Wide Volkswagen*, 444 U.S. 297.

52. Ibid.

53. See, for example, *America Online, Inc. v. Superior Court*, 108 Cal. Rptr. 2d 699 (Cal. App. 2001) (holding unenforceable as against public policy a mass-market forum selection clause). But see also *Koch v. America Online, Inc.*, 139 F. Supp. 2d 690 (D. Md. 2000) (granting ISPs motion to dismiss for improper venue where plaintiff failed to show that forum selection clause was unreasonable).

54. 465 U.S. 783 (1984).

55. See, for example, *Core-Vent Corp. v. Nobel Industries AB*, 11 F.3d 1482, 1486-87 (9th Cir. 1993).

56. Several courts across the United States have previously recognized this in other contexts. See, for example, *Far West Capital, Inc. v. Towne*, 46 F.3d 1071, 1079 (10th Cir. 1995); *Southmark Corp. v. Life Investors, Inc.*, 851 F.2d 763, 772 (5th Cir. 1988) (rejecting broad "effects test" for personal jurisdiction); *Wallace v. Herron*, 778 F.2d 391, 394 (7th Cir. 1985) (same).

57. 465 U.S. 789.

58. Ibid., p. 790 (citing *New York Times Co. v. Sullivan*, 376 U.S. 254 (1964)).

59. Ibid., p. 790.

60. *Burger King*, 471 U.S. 477.

61. Ibid. In addition, where jurisdiction over foreign nationals is at issue, the Supreme Court has indicated that potential interference with the procedural and substantive policies of other nations, as well as the impact on the foreign relations

policies of the United States, may constitute additional fairness factors for consideration. *Asahi Metal v. Superior Court*, 480 U.S. 102, 115 (1987). A full consideration of the these additional factors goes beyond the scope of this paper, but in practice will often be required due to the scope of the Internet.

62. *La Ligue contre le Racisme et L'Antisémitisme v. La Société Yahoo! Inc.*, T.G.I. [App. Ct] Paris, November 20, 2000.

63. Ibid. But see *Yahoo! Inc. v. La Ligue contre le Racisme et L'Antisémitisme*, 169 F. Supp. 2d 1181 (N.D. Cal. 2001) (holding the order of the French court unenforceable in declaratory judgment action).

64. See Goldsmith and Sykes, p. 811.

65. Ibid.

66. See A. Michael Froomkin, "Flood Control on the Information Ocean: Living with Anonymity, Digital Cash, and Distributed Databases," *Journal of Law and Commerce* 15 (1996): 395, 402.

67. David E. Sorkin, "Technical and Legal Approaches to Unsolicited Electronic Mail," *University of San Francisco Law Review* 35 (2001): 325.

68. See A. Michael Froomkin, "The Internet as a Source of Regulatory Arbitrage," *Borders in Cyberspace: Information Policy and the Global Information Infrastructure*, ed. Brian Kahin and Charles Nesson (Cambridge, Mass.: MIT Press 1997), p. 129.

69. *Playboy Enterprises, Inc. v. Chuckleberry*, 939 F. Supp. 1032 (S.D.N.Y. 1996).

70. See Brilmayer, p. 92, note 70 ("The reasonable anticipation standard] begs the question because the only difference between that and forseeability is the legal conclusion whether the defendant is subject to jurisdiction.")

71. Ibid., pp. 91–92.

72. See *United States v. Caroll Towing*, 159 F.2d 169 (2d Cir. 1949) (stating the inequality as "B < PL," where B denotes the cost of taking precautions, P denotes the probability of harm, and L denotes the cost of the harm); see also Posner, pp. 163–66 (expanding the Learned Hand analysis).

73. Posner, p. 164.

74. Ibid., p. 185 ("[One] meaning of unforseeability in the law of torts is that high costs of information prevented a party from taking precautions against the particular accident that occurred; put differently, B in the Hand Formula was prohibitive once information about risk is recognized to be a cost of avoiding risk.")

75. Ibid., pp. 644–45.

76. See Brilmayer, p. 85.

77. Cf. John Leubsdorf, "The Standard for Preliminary Injuctions," *Harvard Law Review* 91 (1978): 525, 540–42 (discussing the standard for preliminary relief in terms of comparative costs of error). Judge Posner has transformed Professor Leubsdorf's insight into a symbolic notation: $P(H_p) > (1 - P)H_d$, where P is the probability that the plaintiff will prevail at trial, (1 - P) is concomitantly the probability that defendants will prevail, H_p is the irreparable harm that plaintiffs will suffer if preliminary relief is erroneously denied, and H_d is the irreparable harm that defendants will suffer if preliminary relief is erroneously granted. See *American Supply Hospital Corp. v. Hospital Products*, 780 F.2d 589, 593; see also Posner, pp. 553–54. Although I would hesitate to attempt to reduce the due process fairness factors to symbolic notation, the principle is much the same.

78. See, for example, *Hanson v. Denckla*, 357 U.S. 235, 251 (1958) ("These [due process] restrictions are more than a guarantee of immunity from inconvenient or distant litigation. They are a consequence of the territorial limitations on the power

of the respective States."); *World-Wide Volkswagen*, 444 U.S. 293 ("The sovereignty of each state, in turn, implied a limitation on the sovereignty of all of its sister States— a limitation express or implicit in both the original scheme of the Constitution and the Fourteenth Amendment.")

79. See Bruce Kobayashi and Larry Ribstein, "State Regulation of Electronic Commerce," *Emory Law Journal* 51 (2002).

80. See Brilmayer, p. 95 ("The State's incentive is always to expand jurisdiction to the detriment of out-of-state enterprises and the out-of-state consumers to whom the costs are passed.").

81. Ibid., p. 96.

82. Ibid.

83. 40 U.S.P.Q.2d (BNA) 1826 (S.D. Cal. 1996).

84. Ibid., p. 1828.

85. See, for example, *Inset Systems, Inc. v. Instruction Set, Inc.*, 937 F. Supp. 161 (D. Conn. 1996); *Maritz v. Cybergold*, 40 U.S.P.Q. 2d (BNA) 1729 (E.D. Mo. 1996).

86. *Zippo Mfg. Co. v. Zippo Dot Com, Inc.*, 952 F. Supp. 1119 (W.D. Penn. 1997).

87. See, for example, *Pavlovich v. Superior Court*, 29 Cal. 4th 262; 58 P.3d 2 (2002).

88. *Quill v. North Dakota*, 112 S.Ct. 1904, 1913 (1992) ("Under the Articles of Confederation, State taxes and duties hindered and suppressed intestate commerce; the Framers intended the Commerce Clause as a cure for these structural ills.").

89. *Philadelphia v. New Jersey*, 437 U.S. 617 (1978).

90. See *Pike v. Bruce Church, Inc.*, 397 U.S. 137, 142 (1970).

91. *West Lynn Creamery, Inc. v. Healy*, 114 S.Ct. 2205, 2211 (1994).

92. *Baldwin v. G.A.F. Seelig, Inc.*, 294 U.S. 511, 527 (1935) (What is ultimate is the principle that one state in its dealings with another may not put itself in a position of economic isolation.").

93. *Pike v. Bruce Church, Inc.*, 397 U.S. 137 (1970).

94. *Bibb v. Navajo Freight Lines, Inc.*, 359 U.S. 520, 529 (1959).

95. *Dean Milk Co. v. City of Madison*, 340 U.S. 349, 354 (1951); *Hunt v. Washington State Apple Advertising Comm'n.*, 432 U.S. 333, 350 (1977).

96. *Milk Control Board of Pennsylvania v. Eisenberg*, 306 U.S. 669 (1939).

97. *Mintz v. Baldwin*, 289 U.S. 346 (1933).

98. See *H.P. Hood & Sons, Inc., v. DuMond*, 336 U.S. 525, 533 (1949) ("This distinction between the power of the state to shelter its people from menaces to their health or safety and from fraud, and its lack of power to retard, burden or constrict the flow of such commerce for their economic advantage is one deeply rooted in both our history and our law.").

99. *Southern Pacific Co. v. Arizona*, 325 U.S. 761, 1525 (1945).

100. Cf. Epstein, p. 160 (discussing multistate coordination problems).

101. Ibid.

102. See also Lloyd Cohen, "Holdouts and Free Riders," *Journal of Legal Studies* 20 (1991): 351 (discussing the problem of hold-outs generally).

103. See *American Library Ass'n v. Pataki*, 969 F. Supp. 160 (S.D.N.Y. 1997).

104. 457 U.S. 624 (1982).

105. 457 U.S. 627.

106. Ibid., pp. 642–43.

107. The Illinois statute was held by a majority to be unconstitutional under a dormant commerce balancing analysis rather than under an extraterritoriality analysis.

108. 491 U.S. 324 (1989).
109. Ibid., pp. 336–37.
110. Ibid., pp. 336.
111. Ibid., p. 337.
112. 517 U.S. 559 (1996).
113. . Ibid., p. 22.
114. Ibid. The Court declined to specifically opine on whether states could attempt to force violators to alter their extraterritorial *unlawful* conduct.
115. Cf. Posner, pp. 638–39 (discussing the role of the commerce power in deterring states from taxing nonresident consumers or excluding nonresident producers).
116. 112 S.Ct. 1904 (1992).
117. Ibid., p. 1911.
118. Ibid., p. 1916.
119. See *Quill*, 112 S.Ct. 1913.
120. Ibid., pp. 1913–14.
121. See Patrick McGeehan, "Cyber-Swindles Taking Root," *USA Today*, January 31, 1996, p. 1A.
122. See ibid.; see also Jared Silverman, "Cyberspace Offerings Raise Complex Compliance Issues," *New Jersey Law Journal*, December 25, 1995, p. 10 (analysis of on-line securities regulation by former New Jersey regulator).
123. See Ted Sherman, "Scam Artists Logging onto Computer Network; Old Frauds Keep Pace with Technology," *Times-Picayune*, January 22, 1995, p. A3 (quoting Jared Silverman).
124. See Dan L. Burk, "The Trouble with Trespass," *Journal of. Small and Emerging Business Law* (2000); Niva Elkin-Koren, "Let the Crawlers Crawl: On Virtual Gatekeepers and the Right to Exclude Indexing," *University of Dayton Law Review* 26 (2001): 179; Maureen O'Rourke, "Shaping Competition on the Internet: Who Owns Product and Pricing Information?" *Vanderbilt Law Review* 53 (2000): 1965.
125. See, for example, *eBay v. Bidder's Edge*, ____ F. Supp. ____ (N.D. Cal. 2000); *Verio v. Register.com*, ____ F. Supp. ____ (2001).
126. Cf. Epstein, p. 160 ("Knowing that [inconsistent state demands] may await them, some entrepreneurs will avoid making the kinds of investments that will expose them to this sort of risk. . . .").
127. See Goldsmith and Sykes, p. 812.
128. See 18 Pa.C.S. § 7330 (2000).
129. See, for example, September 17, 2002, Order of Court of Common Pleas of Montgomery County, Pennsylvania, In the Matter of the Application of D. Michael Fisher, Attorney General of the Commonwealth of Pennsylvania for an Order Requiring an Internet Service Provider to Remove or Disable Access to Child Pornography (No. Misc. 689, July 2002).
130. See Laura Gurak, *Cyberliteracy: Navigating the Internet with Awareness* (New Haven, Conn.: Yale University Press, 2001), pp. 29–37 (discussing Internet characteristics of speed and reach).
131. Thomas Kuhn, *The Structure of Scientific Revolutions*, 2d ed. (Chicago: University of Chicago Press 1970).
132. See Froomkin, cited in note 66.

Chapter 7

This chapter builds upon a previously published article by the authors, "State Regulation of Electronic Commerce," *Emory Law Journal* 51 (2002): 1. The authors acknowledge helpful comments on earlier versions of this chapter from Michael Greve, Eugene Volokh, Harold Lewis, and two anonymous referees, as well as from participants in the American Enterprise Institute Roundtable Series on Competitive Federalism (January 30, 2001) and the Federalist Society Faculty Division Conference (January 4, 2001). The authors also acknowledge financial support from the Law and Economics Center at George Mason University and from the American Enterprise Institute's Federalism Project.

1. See FTC, Final Report of the FTC Advisory Committee on Online Access and Security (hereafter FTC Report), available at http://www.ftc.gov/acoas/papers/finalreport.htm (May 15, 2000); Privacy Online: Fair Information Practices in the Electronic Marketplace: A Report to Congress (May 22, 2000), available at http://www.ftc.gov/reports/privacy2000/privacy2000.pdf.

2. See Children's Online Privacy Protection Act of 1998, Pub. L. No. 105-277, 112 Stat. 2681-728 (codified as amended at 15 U.S.C. § 6501) (establishing regime of notice, disclosure, parental consent for collection of personal information on children); Gramm-Leach-Bliley Act (Financial Services Modernization Act of 1999), Pub. L. No. 106-102, 113 Stat. 1338 (codified as amended at 15 U.S.C. § 6805) (regulating disclosure of information by financial institutions); Health Insurance Portability and Accountability Act of 1996, Pub. L. No. 104-191, 110 Stat. 1936 (hereafter HIPAA) (regulating online health information). Congress has considered additional regulation. See, for example, Hearing on Privacy Legislation before the Senate Commerce Committee, 2000 WL 23833311, October 3, 2000.

3. See Uniform Computer Information Transactions Act, Final Act with Comments, available at http://www.ucitaonline.com (September 29, 2000).

4. See FTC Workshop, "Warranty Protection for High-Tech Services," Matter no. P994413 (October 26–27, 2000), available at http://www.ftc.gov/bcp/workshops/warranty/index.html.

5. See Fred H. Cate, *Privacy in Perspective* (Washington: AEI Press, 2001), p. 40.

6. See Robert W. Hahn and Anne Layne-Farrar, "The Benefits and Costs of Online Privacy Legislation," pp. 13–25, AEI-Brookings Joint Center Working Paper no. 01-14, 2001, available at http://papers.ssrn.com/ paper.taf?abstract_id = 292649; Robert W. Hahn, "An Assessment of the Costs of Proposed Online Privacy Legislation," available at http://www.actonline.org/pubs/hahnstudy.pdf (May 7, 2000).

7. See, for example, "Voter/Consumer Research," p. Q14, available at http://www.actonline.org/pubs/polls/toplines.pdf (last visited January 27, 2002) (showing 62 percent polled agreed that new laws should be federal in nature). See also Jay P. Kesan and Andres Gallo, "Neither Bottom-Up nor Top-Down: A Tacit Public-Private Cooperative Solution for Internet Regulation," University of Illinois Law and Economics Research Paper no. 00-31, 2001, available at http://papers.ssrn.com/paper.taf?abstract_id = 289668 (analyzing the nature of appropriate government regulation of the Internet without discussing which government should regulate or assuming that any regulation should be at the federal level).

8. For other discussions of how protection of information can increase incentives to disclose, see, for example, Frank H. Easterbrook, "Insider Trading, Secret Agents, Evidentiary Privilege, and the Production of Information," *Supreme Court Review* 1981 (1982): 309 (discussing contractual prohibition against disclosure of information); Edmund W. Kitch, "The Law and Economics of Rights in Valuable Information," *Journal of Legal Studies* 9 (1980): 683 (same); Richard S. Murphy, "Property Rights in

Personal Information: An Economic Defense of Privacy," *Georgetown Law Journal* 84 (1996): 2381 (discussing privacy laws and the disclosure of information).

9. See, for example, Julie E. Cohen, "Examined Lives: Informational Privacy and the Subject as Object," *Stanford Law Review* 52 (2000): 1373; Jessica Litman, "Information Privacy/Information Property," *Stanford Law Review* 52 (2000): 1283; Joel R. Reidenberg, "Resolving Conflicting International Data Privcy Rules in Cyberspace, *Stanford Law Review* 52 (2000): 1315; Joel R. Reidenberg, "Restoring Americans' Privacy in Electronic Commerce," *Berkeley Technology Law Journal* 14 (1999): 771; Joel R. Reidenberg, "Setting Standards for Fair Information Practice in the U.S. Private Sector," *Iowa Law Review* 80 (1995): 497, 516–18; Pamela Samuelson, "Privacy as Intellectual Property?" *Stanford Law Review* 52 (2000): 1125; Paul M. Schwartz, "Privacy and Democracy in Cyberspace," *Vanderbilt Law Review* 52 (1999): 1609; Christopher D. Hunter, "Recoding the Architecture of Cyberspace Privacy: Why Self-Regulation and Technology Are Not Enough," available at http://www.asc.upenn.edu/usr/chunter/p3p.html (February 2000).

10. See, for example, Cohen; Reidenberg, "Resolving International Data Privacy;" Schwartz.

11. See HIPAA, 15 C.F.R. pt. 160.

12. To be sure, there are overlaps between categories, as where medical information is used for commercial purposes without revealing intimate secrets. See Part I.B.1.

13. Such restrictions in effect allow the parties to opt out of the "first sale" doctrine in copyright law under 17 U.S.C. § 109 (1994), which limits the ability of the copyright holder to place post-sale restrictions on the resale or disposal of the copyrighted work by the buyer. See Larry E. Ribstein and Bruce H. Kobayashi, "State Regulation of Electronic Commerce," *Emory Law Journal* 51 (2002): note 17.

14. See, for example, Richard A. Posner, *Overcoming Law* (Cambridge, Mass.: Harvard University Press, 1995), pp. 533–34; George J. Stigler, "An Introduction to Privacy in Economics and Politics," *Journal of Legal Studies* 9 (1980): 623, 628–33.

15. See Murphy, p. 2405 (citing Equifax Survey showing that 78 percent agreed that "because computers can make use of more personal details about people, companies can provide more individualized services than before").

16. See Paul H. Rubin and Thomas M. Lenard, *Privacy and the Commercial Use of Personal Information* (Boston: Kluwer, 2002) pp. 23–24.

17. See Rubin and Lenard, pp. 64–69; Solveig Singleton, "Privacy versus the First Amendment: A Skeptical Approach," *Fordham Intellectual Property, Media and Entertainment Law Journal* 11 (2000): 97, 145–46; Solveig Singleton, *Privacy as Censorship: A Skeptical View of Proposals to Regulate Privacy in the Private Sector,* CATO Institute Policy Analysis no. 295, available at http://www.cato.org/pubs/pas/pa-295es.html (January 22, 1998).

18. See Richard A. Posner, *The Economics of Justice* (Cambridge, Mass.: Harvard University Press, 1981), pp. 233–34.

19. 114 F. Supp. 2d 896 (N.D. Cal. 2000), *aff'd in part, rev'd in part and remanded,* 239 F.3d 1004 (9th Cir. 2001).

20. *Napster,* 239 F.3d 1027 (citing *Sony Corp. v. Universal City Studios,* 464 U.S. 417, 442-43 (1984)).

21. See, for example, A&M Records v. Napster, 2001 WL 227083 (N.D. Cal 2001) (entering modified preliminary injunction).

22. See *A&M Records v. Napster,* 284 F.3d. 1091, 1096 (2001) *affirming* modified preliminary injunction and order to shut down.

23. See Nick Wingfield, "Napster Files for Chapter 11," *Wall Street Journal*, June 4, 2002, p. B6. A federal bankruptcy court subsequently blocked the sale of Napster's assets to media giant Bertelsmann AG. See Frank Ahrens, "Judge Blocks Napster's Sale to Bertelsmann," *Washington Post*, September 4, 2002, p. E1. Napster is currently negotiating a second sale. See "Health and Technology: Napster Nears Sale of Assets, Avoids Chapter 7 Closure," *Wall Street Journal*, September 30, 2002, p. B6.

24. For a discussion of the use of GUID technologies, see Jonathan Weinberg, "Hardware-Based ID, Rights Management, and Trusted Systems," *Stanford Law Review* 52 (2000): 1251, 1261–63. Unique identifiers attached to individual copies of copyrighted works are also being considered to battle P2P piracy. For example, each copy of the rock band Bon Jovi's recent release "Bounce" has a unique serial number that fans can use to register for the Bon Jovi fan club. Registration requires that the fan submit personal information. In return, the registered member is offered "exclusives" that are intended to make purchase of a legitimate CD relatively more attractive to a fan who otherwise would have downloaded MP3 files through a P2P network. In addition, the personal data collected will be used in the future to market the band directly to registered members. See Jennifer Ordonez and Charles Goldsmith, "Music Industry Hopes Exclusives Can Blow Pirates Out of the Water," *Wall Street Journal*, September 16, 2002, p. B8.

25. Other methods of tracking use of copyrighted materials also raise privacy concerns. The Recording Industry Association of America attempted to have a federal court enforce a prelitigation subpoena under Section 512(h) of the Digital Millenium Copyright Act to force Verizon to disclose the identity of a subscriber suspected of making copyrighted music available for downloading to Kazaa users. See Declan McCullagh, "Music Body Presses Anti-Piracy Case," available at http://news.cnet.com (August 21, 2002). Verizon opposed enforcement of the subponea citing privacy concerns and potential legal liability. Ibid. Privacy groups also object to enforcement of the RIAA's subpoena. "Verizon, RIAA in Copyright Showdown," available at http://news.cnet.com (October 4, 2002); Brief of Amicus in Support of Verizon's Opposition of RIAA's Motion to Enforce, *RIAA v. Verizon*, Civ. No. 1:02MS00323, available at http://www.eff.org/Cases/RIAA_v_Verizon/20020830_eff_amicus.rtf.

Resistance to the use of low-cost disclosures has caused copyright owners to explore ways in which to address P2P copyright violations without having to obtain the identity of the person committing the copyright violation. The RIAA is supporting proposed federal legislation that would limit the liability of copyright holders that disable or otherwise interfere with (e.g., through the use of a directed denial of service attack) the unauthorized distribution of copyrighted works over P2P networks. See P2P Piracy Prevention Act, 107 Cong., 2d sess., HR 5211, July 25, 2002. Critics of this self-help approach have suggested that this approach may compromise security and result in disruption of legitimate networks. Limits on liability can result in inadequate incentives on the part of copyright holders to avoid errors. For example, the widespread use of bots to identify short phrases and titles consistent with titles of copyrighted works can result in large numbers of erroneous identifications of copyright violations and will result in large type I error costs when these sites or accounts are erroneously disabled. Such costs could easily surpass the privacy costs contemplated in the Verizon case discussed above. See, for example, Declan McCullagh, "P2P Hacking Bill May Be Amended," available at http://news.net.com.

26. See Rubin.

27. See Murphy. Also see, generally, Harold Demsetz, "Toward a Theory of Property Rights," *American Economic Review* 57, Papers and Proceedings (1967): 347 (showing that technological changes that alter the relative value of certain resources have resulted in the creation of new property rights).

28. Because such information would be produced without property rights protection, the benefits of legal protection are unlikely to outweigh the increased costs of monopoly and expression. See, for example, William M. Landes and Richard A. Posner, "An Economic Analysis of Copyright Law," *Journal of Legal Studies* 18 (1989): 325, 347–49 (noting that strengthening intellectual property protection can reduce welfare by increasing the cost of producing subsequent works). Where consumer marketing information is used to produce valuable databases and other works, federal statutory intellectual property rights can cover subsequent uses of these materials under some circumstances but not the facts themselves or obvious compilations. See Ribstein and Kobayashi, "State Regulation of Electronic Commerce," note 32.

29. See Richard A. Posner, "Privacy," in *The New Palgrave Dictionary of Economics and the Law,* ed. P. Newman (New York: Stockton Press, 1998).

30. See, for example, Murphy; Jerry Kang, "Information Privacy in Cyberspace Transactions," *Stanford Law Review* 50 (1998): 1193.

31. See Restatement (Second) of Torts § 652A-C (1976) (providing that the right of privacy is invaded by unreasonable intrusion upon the seclusion of another, appropriation of the other's name or likeness, the unreasonable publicity given to the other's private life, or the publicity that unreasonably places the other in a false light before the public).

32. See Robert Gellman, "Does Privacy Law Work?" in *Technology and Privacy: The New Landscape,* eds. Phillip E. Agre and Marc Rotenberg (Cambridge, Mass.: MIT Press, 1997); Murphy, pp. 2389–92; Schwartz, p. 1634.

33. See Murphy.

34. See Litman.

35. See Murphy, p. 2410; see also Richard A. Posner, *Economic Analysis of Law,* 5th ed. (New York: Aspen Law and Business, 1998), pp. 271–72 (noting identity of economic analyses of tort and contract law).

36. See Ronald Coase, "The Problem of Social Cost," *Journal of Law and Economics* 3 (1960): 1, 16–17; Harold Demsetz, "When Does the Rule of Liability Matter?" *Journal of Legal Studies* 1 (1972): 13, 16–18; see also Lemley, p. 1554 (noting that allocating strong rights to consumers is inefficient because high transactions costs will prevent the value increasing transfer of such rights).

37. Frank H. Easterbrook and Daniel R. Fischel, "Contractual Freedom in Corporate Law," *Columbia Law Review* 89 (1989): 1416, 1433; Charles J. Goetz and Robert E. Scott, "The Mitigation Principle: Toward a General Theory of Contractual Obligation," *Virginia Law Review* 69 (1983): 967, 971. But see Ian Ayres and Robert Gertner, "Filling Gaps in Incomplete Contracts: An Economic Theory of Default Rules," *Yale Law Journal* 99 (1989): 87 (arguing that penalty defaults can be efficient).

38. 793 P.2d 479 (Cal. 1990).

39. Ibid., pp. 492–93.

40. See Anthony T. Kronman, "Mistake, Disclosure, and the Law of Contracts," *Journal of Legal Studies* 7 (1978): 1; see also sources cited in Ribstein and Kobayashi, note 44.

41. Disclosure of medical information is now regulated by HIPAA which contains strict requirements for disclosure of all potential uses of medical information, including research purposes requiring treatment of the individual).

42. 652 N.E.2d 1351 (Ill. App. 1 Dist. 1995).

43. Ibid., p. 1356.

44. Ibid. The court also held that plaintiffs failed sufficiently to allege damages from defendants' practices and affirmed dismissal of the tort intrusion claim for failure to show intrusion. Ibid., p. 1357.

45. 1999 WL 494114, at *5 (Mass. Super. June 29, 1999).

46. The court subsequently certified a class of Massachusetts CVS customers that received a mailing. See *Weld v. CVS Pharmacy, Inc.*, 1999 WL 1565175 (Mass. Super. 1999). However, the court also noted that the misappropriation claim was probably preempted by the privacy statute cited above. Ibid., pp. *6–7.

47. See Posner, *Economic Analysis of Law*, pp. 112–13.

48. See *ProCD, Inc. v. Zeidenberg*, 86 F.3d 1447, 1449-50 (7th Cir. 1996). For economic analyses of selling information that is shared by multiple users, see Yannis Bakos, "Shared Information Goods," *Journal of Law and Economics* 42 (1999): 117; Stanley M. Besen and Sheila N. Kirby, "Private Copying, Appropriability, and Optimal Copying Royalties," *Journal of Law and Economics* 32 (1989): 255; Stanley J. Liebowitz, "Copying and Indirect Appropriability: Photocopying of Journals," *Journal of Political Economy* 93 (1985): 945.

49. For an economic analysis of self-help, see Kenneth W. Dam, "Self Help in the Digital Jungle," *Journal of Legal Studies* 28 (1999): 393. Michael J. Meurer, "Price Discrimination, Personal Use and Piracy: Copyright Protection of Digital Works," *Buffalo Law Review* 45 (1997): 845, 876–77, arguing that facilitating price discrimination is not necessary given superior substitutes such as digital self-help. Some have questioned the legality of broad self-help rights. See Julie Cohen, "Copyright and the Jurisprudence of Self-Help," *Berkeley Technology Law Journal* 13 (1998): 1089, 1129.

50. See Robert W. Gomulkiewicz, "The License Is the Product: Comments on the Promise of Article 2B for Software and Information Licensing," *Berkeley Technology Law Journal* 13 (1998): 891, 898; Raymond T. Nimmer, "Breaking Barriers: The Relation Between Contract and Intellectual Property Law," *Berkeley Technology Law Journal* 13 (1998): 827, 835, available at http://www.2bguide.com/docs/rncontract-new.html (last visited November. 6, 1999).

51. As to the conclusion that copyright law does not protect databases like the one involved in *ProCD*, see *Feist Publ'ns, Inc. v. Rural Tel. Serv. Co.*, 499 U.S. 340, 353 (1991) (rejecting the "sweat-of-the-brow" theory of copyright). See generally Jane C. Ginsburg, "Copyright, Common Law, and Sui Generis Protection of Databases in the United States and Abroad," *University of Cincinnati Law Review* 66 (1997): 151.

52. See Michelle M. Burtis and Bruce H. Kobayashi, "Intellectual Property and Antitrust Limitations on Contract," in *Dynamic Competition and Public Policy*, ed. J. Ellig (Cambridge, U.K.: Cambridge University Press, 2001).

53. U.S. Const. Art. I, § 8, cl. 8. See Douglas G. Lichtman, "The Economics of Innovation: Protecting Unpatentable Goods," *Minnesota Law Review* 81 (1997): 693, 694–95; John S. Wiley Jr., "Bonito Boats: Uninformed but Mandatory Innovation Policy," *Supreme Court Review* 1989 (1990): 283, 299–301.

54. See David Friedman, "In Defense of Private Orderings: Comments on Julie Cohen's 'Copyright and the Jurisprudence of Self-Help,'" *Berkeley Technology Law Journal* 13 (1998): 1151, 1158.

55. See, for example, Schwartz. The FTC Report, citing survey reports, notes that consumer "apprehension likely translates into lost online sales due to lack of confidence in how personal data will be handled. See FTC Report, p. 2. See also Murphy

(citing results of Equifax surveys showing large increases in percentage of those responding who were "concerned" about their privacy). However, there is substantial reason to question the accuracy of many of the surveys of consumer concerns about privacy. See generally Jim Harper and Solveig Singleton, "With a Grain of Salt: What Consumer Privacy Surveys Don't Tell Us," Competitive Enterprise Institute, June 1, 2001, available at www.cei.org/gencon/ 025,02061.cfm (last visited March 20, 2002).

56. See George A. Akerlof, "The Market for 'Lemons': Quality Uncertainty and the Market Mechanism," *Quarterly Journal of Economics* 84 (1970): 488.

57. See generally Benjamin Klein and Keith B. Leffler, "The Role of Market Forces in Assuring Contractual Performance," *Journal of Political Economy* 89 (August 1981): 615; Benjamin Klein et al., "Vertical Integration, Appropriable Rents, and the Competitive Contracting Process," *Journal of Law and Economics* 21 (1978): 297. As to the nature and size of reputation penalties, see Jonathan M. Karpoff and John R. Lott Jr., "The Reputational Penalties Firms Bear from Committing Criminal Fraud," *Journal of Law and Economics* 36 (1993): 757, 796–97; Mark L. Mitchell, "The Impact of External Parties on Brand-Name Capital: The 1982 Tylenol Poisonings and Subsequent Cases," *Economic Inquiry* 27 (1989): 601, 610–12; Mark L. Mitchell and Michael T. Maloney, "Crisis in the Cockpit? The Role of Market Forces in Promoting Air Travel Safety," *Journal of Law and Economics* 32 (1989): 329, 330–33.

58. See, for example, http://www.anonymizer.com (making available free software that allows anonymous surfing); http://www.adsubtract.com (offering a cookie customizer that allows users to manage cookies); http://www.junkbuster.com; see also David P. Hamilton, "Freedom Software Lets You Get Some Privacy While Surfing the Website," *Wall Street Journal*, August 10, 2000, p. B1 (discussing software that lets users hide behind alternate identities).

59. See Nick Wingfield, "DoubleClick Moves to Appoint Panel for Privacy Issues," *Wall Street Journal*, May 17, 2000, p. B2.

60. See Alan Schwartz and Louis L. Wilde, "Intervening in Markets on the Basis of Imperfect Information: A Legal and Economic Analysis," *University of Pennsylvania Law Review* 127 (1979): 630, 636; see also Jeffrey R. Brown and Austan Goolsbee, "Does the Internet Make Markets More Competitive? Evidence from the Life Insurance Industry," NBER Working Paper no. W7996, available at http://papers.ssrn.com/paper.taf?abstract_id = 248602 (Nov. 2000) (showing evidence that Internet comparison shopping for life insurance has caused general price decreases across demographic groups).

61. For commentary critical of enforcement of analogous "shrinkwrap" contracts formed when consumers use software sold with licenses in plastic wrapping, see Mark A. Lemley, "Beyond Preemption: The Law and Policy of Intellectual Property Licensing," *California Law Review* 87 (1999): 111, 120, note 20; Lemley.

62. See *ProCD, Inc. v. Zeidenberg*, 86 F.3d 1447, 1453 (7th Cir. 1996) (noting that "competition among vendors, not judicial revision of a package's contents, is how consumers are protected in a market economy"); Declan McCullagh, "Why Internet Privacy Is Over-rated," April 29, 1999, available at http://www.speakout.com (noting that consumers are not at the mercy of Amazon because they can always go to Barnes & Noble).

63. See generally Friedman, pp. 1157–58.

64. See infra note 86 and accompanying text (discussing P3P protocol).

65. See Cohen; A. Michael Froomkin, "The Death of Privacy?" *Stanford Law Review* 52 (2000): 1461, 1504–05 (arguing that consumers are "myopic").

66. See David G. Post, "What Larry Doesn't Get: Code, Law, and Liberty in Cyberspace," *Stanford Law Review* 52 (2000): 1439, 1446–47; Weinberg, p. 1275. The net effect of price discrimination is ambiguous because some consumers will be better off and total welfare can increase. Weinberg, pp. 1275–76;

67. See Murphy, p. 2405 (citing Equifax survey reporting that 42 percent polled refused to provide information to a business because of privacy concerns).

68. A recent anecdote tends to confirm this. *Wired* magazine offered its readers a free device called "CueCat," a barcode reader for connecting subscribers with advertisers' Web sites. *Wired*'s publisher wrote that "many [readers] aren't crazy about the idea." "Rants & Raves," *Wired*, January 2001, p. 43. All three letters to the editor that the magazine reprinted on the subject complained that advertisers could use the device to obtain information about readers. For example, one said: "Are we too dumb to notice that the point of the Cat is to track our shopping behavior? I'm not giving up that info for nothing." Ibid. *Wired* readers, though more sophisticated than average, may be the marginal consumers for whom Web sites are designed.

69. Because the Web site operator needs incentives to create additional value through the collection and aggregation of consumers' data, it would be inefficient to let the consumer extract all or most of this additional value. See supra note 45 and accompanying text.

70. See Cohen, pp. 1380–91.

71. See Reidenberg, "Resolving Conflicting International Data Privacy," pp. 1346–47. More generally, it is claimed that this information may construct a particular type of social truth that excludes other perspectives. See Cohen, p. 1380.

72. See Schwartz, p. 1611.

73. This is analogous to the ambiguity regarding the failure of the Dvorak keyboard.

74. This problem would seem to be exacerbated by proposals to increase the level of P3P protection by enabling functions preferred only by the most privacy-sensitive users, such as the ability to ask detailed questions of the Web site operator. See Hunter (noting critique of P3P by privacy advocates that users cannot ask questions about such matters as the type of business, where it is incorporated, whether it is a subsidiary of another company, and contact persons).

75. See Cohen, p. 1398.

76. Even for simple disclosure, the costs may not be trivial and the benefits may be low. See Cate, pp. 33–34 (discussing notice requirements contained in HIPAA and Gramm-Leach-Bliley) and 52–55 (discussing compliance costs of these regulations). Cate notes that recently enacted federal laws require notice in cases where the collection of information is obvious and no other use of the information is intended. See also Hahn, p. 6, note 11; Hahn and Layne-Farrar, pp. 40–41. A recent article indicates the number of alternatives regulators and firms must face regarding these issues as well as those discussed in the following subsection. See Christina L. Kunz et al., "Click-Through Agreements: Strategies for Avoiding Disputes on Validity of Assent," *Business Law* 57 (2001): 401 (listing 15 strategies vendors should use in such agreements to minimize legal problems, covering such issues as viewing terms before assent, assent before access to Web site, ease of viewing terms, format and content of disclosures, consistency of Web site disclosures with other information, clarity of choice consumers make in assenting to terms, words of assent or rejection, clarity of the method of signifying assent, consequences of assent, notice of such consequences, consumers' opportunity to correct errors, vendors' maintenance of records of assent

process, users' ability to retain records of assent, and accuracy of vendors' records reflecting assent).

77. See Rubin.

78. See *ProCD, Inc. v. Zeidenberg*, 86 F.3d 1447, 1451 (7th Cir. 1996); J. Howard Beales III, "Economic Analysis and the Regulation of Pharmaceutical Advertising," *Seton Hall Law Review* 24 (1994): 1370, 1381; J. Howard Beales III et al., "The Efficient Regulation of Consumer Information," *Journal of Law and Economics* 24 (1981): 491, 533–34.

79. One set of minimum standards is embodied in so-called "Fair Information Practices." See, for example, Schwartz, pp. 1670–72. An emerging standard of such practices is the "Guidelines on the Protection of Privacy and Transborder Flows of Personal Data," available at http://www.oecd.org/dsti/sti/it/secur/prod/PRIV-EN. HTM (last updated January 5, 1999), as developed at the 1980 Organisation for Economic Co-operation and Development. See Ribstein and Kobayashi, "State Regulation of Electronic Commerce," note 94 (listing general principles).

80. These organizations may not accurately be characterized as "self-regulatory," but rather as providing "regulation" based on contract or, like private ordering generally, as operating in the shadow of the law. See Mark A. Lemley, "Private Property: A Comment on Professor Samuelson's Contrbution," *Stanford Law Review* 52 (2000): 1545, 1554 (describing self-regulation as "illusory").

81. See David R. Johnson and David Post, "Law and Borders—The Rise of Law in Cyberspace," *Stanford Law Review* 48 (1996): 1367, 1383, 1390–91.

82. Ibid., p. 1392.

83. Ibid., p. 1389–90.

84. See http://www.truste.org. TRUSTe licensees must abide by TRUSTe's policies concerning collection and use of consumer information, subject to TRUSTe's monitoring and auditing of licensees and resolution, reporting, and possible referral to the FTC of consumer complaints. Other private organizations sponsoring consumer privacy efforts include those established by the Better Business Bureau (bbbonline) and the American Institute of Certified Public Accountants. See Kesan and Gallo, pp. 119–20 (analyzing the role of such third-party organizations and interaction with government regulation, focusing on bbbonline).

85. See Gillian K. Hadfield, "Privatizing Commercial Law: Lessons from the Middle and the Digital Ages," Stanford Law School, John M. Olin Program in Law and Economics, Working Paper no. 195, March 2000, p. 39, available at http://www. law.stanford.edu/olin/workingpapers/WP195HADFIELD.pdf.

86. See Lawrence Lessig, *Code and Other Laws of Cyberspace* (New York: Basic Books, 1999), p. 160 (endorsing P3P as giving individuals a kind of automated property right in their information).

87. See "Developments in the Law—The Law of Cyberspace," *Harvard Law Review* 112 (1999): 1574, 1646–47.

88. See Johnson and Post, pp. 1391–94.

89. For general discussions of the economics of interest group organization, see Robert E. McCormick and Robert D. Tollison, *Politicians, Legislation and the Economy* (Boston: M. Nijhoff, 1981); Mancur Olson, *The Logic of Collective Action* (Cambridge, Mass.: Harvard University Press, 1971); Robert D. Tollison, "Public Choice and Legislation," *Virginia Law Review* 74 (1998): 339, 361–62.

90. As noted below, large global companies also might seek federal regulation to establish a level playing field with nonglobal companies that do not have to comply with more stringent non-U.S. regulation.

91. See Richard A. Epstein, "Exit Rights under Federalism," *Law and Contemporary Problems* (1992): 147.

92. Charles M. Tiebout, "A Pure Theory of Local Expenditures," *Journal of Political Economy* 64 (1956): 416, 419; see also the following chapters from *Competition among Institutions*, ed. L. Berken (New York: St. Martin's Press, 1995): Bruno S. Frey and Reiner Eichenberger, "Competition among Jurisdictions: The Idea of FOCJ," p. 209; Luder Gerken, "Institutional Competition: An Orientative Framework," p. 1; Wolfgang Kerber and Viktor Vanberg, "Competition among Institutions: Evolution within Constraints," p. 33.

93. See Bernard S. Black, "Is Corporate Law Trivial? A Political and Economic Analysis," *Northwestern University Law Review* 84 (1990): 542, 544.

94. See Saul Levmore, "Variety and Uniformity in the Treatment of the Good-Faith Purchaser," *Journal of Legal Studies* 21 (1987): 43, 44.

95. Thus, merchants rather than customers "shop" for the applicable law but do so with their customers' demands in view.

96. For a discussion of this issue, see Larry E. Ribstein and Bruce H. Kobayashi, "An Economic Analysis of Uniform State Laws," *Journal of Legal Studies* 25 (1996): 131, 134. See also Cate, pp. 53–54 (discussing overbroad application of recent federal approaches to privacy). Although it is theoretically possible for a federal or other centralized body to produce laws tailored toward specific industries and particular types of data, the centralized lawmaker is unlikely to have enough information to produce regulation appropriately tailored to specific contexts.

97. Indeed, Web site regulation is only one aspect of regulation of an industry, and this choice will reflect measuring the costs and benefits of one state's package of laws and regulations against that of another state.

98. See Jack L. Goldsmith and Alan O. Sykes, "The Internet and the Dormant Commerce Clause," *Yale Law Journal* 110 (2001): 785, 821 (discussing benefits of state experimentation); Jack Knight, "A Pragmatist Approach to the Proper Scope of Government," *Journal of Institutional and Theoretical Economics* 157 (2001): 28, 35 (noting the advantage of federalism in permitting experimentation with institutional forms); Martti Vihanto, "Competition between Local Governments as a Discovery Procedure," *Journal of Institutional and Theoretical Economics* 148 (1992): 411, 430–33.

99. This is an example of how the network externalities argument, even if it is valid, can work against as well as for regulation.

100. See Armen A. Alchian, "Uncertainty, Evolution, and Economic Theory," *Journal of Political Economy* 58 (1950): 211. (observing that a study of the "adaptive mechanism" of the market may be more fruitful than that of individual "motivation and foresight").

101. There is also evidence of such evolution with respect to the demand for statutory forms. See Bruce H. Kobayashi and Larry E. Ribstein, "Evolution and Spontaneous Uniformity: Evidence from the Evolution of the Limited Liability Company," *Economic Inquiry* 34 (1996): 464, 470–71.

102. See Johnson and Post, p. 1379.

103. For general discussions, see Committee on Cyberspace Law, "Achieving Legal and Business Order in Cyberspace: A Report on Global Jurisdiction Issues Created by the Internet," *Business Law* 55 (2000): 1801 (hereafter *Order in Cyberspace*); Jeremy Gilman, "Personal Jurisdiction and the Internet: Traditional Jurisprudence for a New Medium," *Business Law* 56 (2000): 395 (summarizing recent case law).

104. See Jack L. Goldsmith, "Against Cyberanarchy," *University of Chicago Law Review* 65 (1998): 1199, 1235, 1237.

105. Restatement (Second) of Conflict of Laws § 188(2) (1971).

106. Ibid., § 6.

107. U.C.C. § 1-105 (1995).

108. See Restatement, § 152 and comment c (stating that law of place of invasion applies unless some other state has more significant relationship under § 6); ibid. §§ 145 comment f, 153 (noting importance of plaintiff's domicile in multistate cases).

109. For an argument that default choice-of-law rules should call for application of a buyer's state because sellers would be in the best position to contract around this default, see Erin A. O'Hara and Larry E. Ribstein, "From Politics to Efficiency in Choice of Law," *University of Chicago Law Review* 67 (2000): 1151, 1201.

110. 449 U.S. 302 (1981).

111. Ibid., p. 318, note 24. Justice Stevens, concurring, said that the parties' expectations are significant under the Full Faith and Credit Clause, ibid., p. 324, note 11, and suggested that the Due Process Clause would raise fairness concerns if the parties had made their expectations explicit by providing for application of a particular law, ibid., pp. 328–29.

112. For analysis and criticism of one author's argument against the constitutionality of enforcing choice-of-law clauses under the Full Faith and Credit Clause, see text accompanying note 198.

113. See Larry E. Ribstein, "Choosing Law by Contract," *Journal of Corporate Law* 18 (1993): 245, 287–94.

114. See Posner, *Economic Analysis of Law*, pp. 699–700; Daniel R. Fishel, "From MITE to CTS: State Anti-Takeover Statutes, the Williams Act, the Commerce Clause, and Insider Trading," *Supreme Court Review* 1987 (1988): 47, 48, 54–56; Saul Levmore, "Interstate Exploitation and Judicial Intervention," *Virginia Law Review* 69 (1983): 563; compare *Hatch v. Superior Ct.*, 94 Cal. Rptr. 2d 453, 470-72 (2000) (holding California statute did not violate Commerce Clause because statute did not punish conduct outside of California).

115. See Dan L. Burk, "Federalism in Cyberspace," *Connecticut Law Review* 28 (1996): 1095 (arguing the Due Process Clause of the Fourteeth Amendment and Dormant Commerce Clause significantly curtail the ability of states to regulate the Internet). For cases invalidating statutes prohibiting distribution of obscene material to minors on the Internet, see *ACLU v. Johnson*, 194 F.3d 1149, 1160-61 (10th Cir. 1999); *American Ass'n v. Pataki*, 969 F. Supp. 160, 169 (S.D.N.Y. 1997) (reasoning that the Internet "must be marked off as a national preserve to protect users from inconsistent legislation that, taken to its most extreme, could paralyze development of the Internet altogether"). But see *Hatch*, 94 Cal. Rptr. 2d at 470-72 (holding that California statute did not violate the Commerce Clause because the statute did not punish conduct outside of California).

116. See Goldsmith and Sykes, pp. 804–05.

117. See generally *World-Wide Volkswagen Corp. v. Woodson*, 444 U.S. 286 (1980); *Int'l Shoe Co. v. Washington*, 326 U.S. 310 (1945). In *Burnham v. Superior Court of California*, 495 U.S. 604 (1990), the Court held that jurisdiction over an individual defendant in a divorce suit could be predicated on service of process on the defendant while he was in the forum to visit his children even in the absence of other contacts with the forum. Justice Scalia, announcing the Court's judgment, wrote for four

justices. Justice Brennan's concurrence argued that presence should create only a presumption of jurisdiction. Ibid., p. 629.

118. See *Asahi Metal Indus. Co. v. Super. Ct.*, 480 U.S. 102 (1987). Although five justices refused to endorse the standard summarized in the text, only one (Stevens) remains on the Court, while three of the four justices who supported the more restrictive standard cited in the text remain on the Court. See also Richard A. Epstein, "Consent, Not Power, as the Basis of Jurisdiction," *University of Chicago Legal Forum* 2001 (2001): 1 (advocating requiring extensive contact with the state as the basis of the exercise of personal jurisdiction). Note that a court may assert general jurisdiction over a defendant that has extensive local contacts such as maintaining a principal place of business, even if the contacts did not arise out of or relate to the particular transaction at issue. See *Helicopteros Nacionales De Columbia v. Hall*, 466 U.S. 408 (1984). Merely selling through a Web site into a forum is clearly insufficient for this purpose. See *Digital Equip. Corp. v. Altavista Tech., Inc.*, 960 F. Supp. 456, 465-66 (D. Mass. 1997); see also *Coastal Video Communications Corp. v. Staywell Corp.*, 59 F. Supp. 2d 562, 565-68 (E.D. Va. 1999) (holding no specific jurisdiction in Virginia for declaratory judgment action by the out-of-state plaintiff based on the accessibility of the defendant's interactive Web site in Virginia, although general jurisdiction might be supported by proof the Web site was accessed by many residents in the forum, indicating continuous and systematic contacts).

119. See Full Faith and Credit Clause, U.S. Const., Art. IV, § 1. For recognition of this principle, see *Shaffer v. Heitner*, 433 U.S. 186, 210 n. 36 (1977).

120. See *Inset Sys., Inc. v. Instruction Set, Inc.*, 937 F. Supp. 161, 164-65 (D. Conn. 1996); *Maritz, Inc. v. Cybergold, Inc.*, 947 F. Supp. 1328, 1331 (E.D. Mo. 1996) (basing jurisdiction on the defendant's decision to transmit advertising information to all Internet users). The Virginia Internet Privacy Act pushes this approach to its outermost reach, providing for jurisdiction in Virginia based on using a computer network located in Virginia, which might include simply routing of e-mail or other Internet transmissions through Virginia. See Va. Code Ann. § 8.01-328.1(B) (Michie 2000). This is probably unconstitutional under the more restrictive approaches to jurisdiction discussed in the text below.

121. See *Bensusan Restaurant Corp. v. King*, 937 F. Supp. 295, 299 (S.D.N.Y. 1996), *aff'd*, 126 F.3d 25, 29 (2d Cir. 1997) ("The mere fact that a person can gain information on the allegedly infringing product is not the equivalent of a person advertising, promoting, selling or otherwise making an effort to target its product in New York."); Goldsmith, pp. 1218–19, 1221.

122. See *Cybersell, Inc. v. Cybersell, Inc.*, 130 F.3d 414, 418-20 (9th Cir. 1997) (holding that the court should look to the level of interactivity and analyze contacts in the jurisdiction; in this case, the site invited visitors to submit their names to get more information; passive Web site operation is not enough); *Zippo Mfg. Co. v. Zippo Dot Com, Inc.*, 952 F. Supp. 1119, 1124 (W.D. Pa. 1997) (holding that for an interactive Web site the court must determine the degree and nature of the information exchange through the site).

123. See *Park Inns Intern, Inc. v. Pacific Plaza Hotels, Inc.*, 5 F. Supp. 2d 762, 764 (D. Ariz. 1998) (finding Web site could take hotel reservations); *Stomp, Inc. v. NeatO, LLC*, 61 F. Supp. 2d 1074, 1077 (C.D. Cal. 1999) (finding Web site permitted a small number of online sales); *Online Partners.Com, Inc. v. Atlanticnet Media Corp.*, 2000 WL 101242, p. *6 (N.D. Cal. 2000) (finding Web site permitted online subscriptions); *Citigroup Inc. v. City Holding Co.*, 97 F. Supp. 2d 549, 564-66 (S.D.N.Y. 2000) (finding

Web site permitted customers to apply for loans online, print out applications for fax submission, click on a "hyper link" to "chat" online with a representative of defendants, and e-mail defendants, with home loan questions with a quick response from an online representative).

124. 199 F.3d 1343 (D.C. Cir. 2000).

125. Ibid., pp. 1349–50.

126. Note, "Civil Procedure—D.C. Circuit Rejects Sliding Scale Approach to Finding Personal Jurisdiction Based on Internet Contacts," *Harvard Law Review* 113 (2000): 2128, 2133.

127. See *Robbins v. Yutopian Enterprises*, 202 F. Supp. 2d 426 (D. Md. 2002) (denying jurisdiction in Maryland despite 46 transactions there and maintenance of an active Web site); *Nam Tai Electronics, Inc. v. Titzer*, 113 Cal. Rptr. 2d 769, 776 (2001) (although the defendant in the libel case registered aliases and posted almost 250 messages on a California-maintained Web site, there is no jurisdiction in California in the absence of evidence that messages "were directed at Californians or disproportionately likely to be read by residents of this state" or that plaintiff's "relationships with residents of California were of particular importance to its business and likely to be impacted negatively by the messages posted on the Web sites"); *Roche v. Worldwide Media, Inc.*, 90 F. Supp. 2d 714, 717-18 (E.D. Va. 2000) (though the Web site solicited customer e-mail addresses and credit card numbers, there was no evidence that products were sold in Virginia or that any advertising or other promotional activity was directed specifically to Virginia); *Rannoch, Inc. v. Rannoch Corp.*, 52 F. Supp. 2d 681, 685 (E.D. Va. 1999) (denying jurisdiction in infringement case, where Web sites included section for ads that could be placed online, but there were no sales online, stating that there was no evidence that the defendant had any dealings with any Virginia resident, placed any classified ads on its Web site for products or persons in Virginia, did any business in Virginia, or conducted any advertising or other promotional activity specifically directed to Virginia); compare *Uncle Sam's Safari Outfitters, Inc. v. Uncle Sam's Army Navy Outfitters-Manhattan, Inc.*, 96 F. Supp. 2d 919, 923 (E.D. Mo. 2000) (holding that disclaimer resale of merchandise in Missouri is unavailing because it was posted after the commencement of the suit).

128. See "Order in Cyberspace," pp. 1821, 1881. For example, a Web site might announce exclusion, or an operator might post a notice excluding residents of certain countries. Ibid., p. 1892.

129. Ibid., pp. 1879, 1893–94.

130. See Goldsmith, pp. 1218–19, 1226–27.

131. For a general discussion of uniformity in this area, see Bruce H. Kobayashi and Larry E. Ribstein, "Uniformity, Choice of Law and Software Sales," *George Mason Law Review* 8 (1999): 261, 299–301.

132. See Edward J. Janger, "Predicting When the Uniform Law Process Will Fail: Article 9, Capture, and the Race to the Bottom," *Iowa Law Review* 83 (1998): 569, 577–81, 592.

133. Larry T. Garvin, "The Changed (and Changing?) Uniform Commercial Code," *Florida State University Law Review* 26 (1999): 285, 359–60 (also noting the potential impact on drafters of focused interest group criticism of proposed laws); Janger, pp. 576, 582–83; Ribstein and Kobayashi, "An Economic Analysis of Uniform State Laws," p. 142.

134. See Larry E. Ribstein and Bruce H. Kobayashi, "Uniform Laws, Model Laws and Limited Liability Companies," *University of Colorado Law Review* 66 (1995): 947,

975–79 (discussing the dissolution provisions of the Uniform Limited Liability Company Act).

135. See Janger, pp. 585–86.

136. Some argue that states have incentives to adopt uniform laws that restrain their own ability to export costs to avoid costs imposed on them by other states. See Larry Kramer, "Rethinking Choice of Law," *Columbia Law Review* 90 (1990): 277, 314 (noting states' incentives to act reciprocally in deciding choice-of-law issues). However, legislators in many situations may lack incentives to act reciprocally. See Ribstein and Kobayashi, "An Economic Analysis of Uniform State Laws," p. 140.

137. See Garvin, p. 354, note 403 (noting the empirical deficiency in the drafting process); Janger, pp. 585–86 (noting the possibility of interest group capture of uniform lawmakers on issues requiring technical expertise); Edward L. Rubin, "Thinking Like a Lawyer, Acting Like a Lobbyist: Some Notes on the Process of Revising UCC Articles 3 and 4," *Loyola of Los Angeles Law Review* 26 (1993): 743, 770–73.

138. The competition among groups suggests that UCITA could yield vague compromises. See Alan Schwartz and Robert E. Scott, "Political Economy of Private Legislatures," *University of Pennsylvania Law Review* (1995): 595, 599.

139. See Kobayashi and Ribstein, pp. 280–82.

140. See generally ibid.

141. Ibid., p. 150.

142. Ibid., pp. 146–48 (discussing NCCUSL's ability to cause the adoption of its proposals).

143. For general overview of the law and policy on enforcing contractual choice, see Larry E. Ribstein, "From Efficiency to Politics in Contractual Choice of Law," *Georgia Law Review* 37 (2003) (forthcoming article).

144. Thus, the problem is not simply that the rules are unclear. Rather, even clear rules that always apply the forum rule and that the consumer can obtain jurisdiction anywhere over the merchant would present the same problems. See O'Hara and Ribstein, pp. 1187–90.

145. See *Lieschke v. RealNetworks, Inc.*, 2000 WL 198424, p. *1 (N.D. Ill. February 11, 2000), *additional opinion*, 2000 WL 631341 (N.D. Ill. May 8, 2000), discussed below in text accompanying note .

146. See 2000 Va. S. 767 (2000).

147. See Restatement, § 187(2).

148. See Ribstein, "Choosing Law by Contract," pp. 284–85; Symeon C. Symeonides, "Choice of Law in the American Courts in 1997," *American Journal of Comparative Law* 46 (1998): 233, 273. Thus, the U.S. rule in this context resembles the apparently more liberal rule in the leading U.K. case of *Vita Food Products Inc. v. Unus Shipping Co.*, [1939] A.C. 277 (P.C. 1939) (enforcing a provision applying English law to a transaction whose only connection with England was the choice-of-law clause).

149. For discussions of these statutes, see Ribstein, "From Efficiency to Politics," (forthcoming article); Larry E. Ribstein, "Delaware, Lawyers and Choice of Law," *Delaware Journal of Corporate Law* 19 (1994): 999, 1003–06.

150. U.C.C. § 1-105(1) (1995).

151. For an example of this decisionmaking process in an electronic commerce case, see note 190.

152. Revision of Uniform Commercial Code, Draft for Approval (UCC Draft), § 1-301, available at http://www.law.upenn.edu/bll/ulc/ucc1/Ucc161401.htm (last visited February 2, 2002).

153. Ibid., § 1-301(b)(1).

154. Ibid., § 1-301(e).

155. Ibid., § 1-301(d)(2).

156. See *Burger King Corp. v. Rudzewicz*, 471 U.S. 462, 466-67 (1985); *Nat'l Equip. Rental, LTD. v. Szukhent*, 375 U.S. 311, 316 (1964).

157. See *Carnival Cruise Lines, Inc. v. Shute*, 499 U.S. 585, 596-97 (1991); *M/S Bremen v. Zapata Off-Shore Co.*, 407 U.S. 1, 19-20 (1972).

158. See *Carnival Cruise Lines*, 499 U.S. 593–95 (enforcing choice-of-forum clause on passenger ticket).

159. 9 U.S.C. § 2 (1994).

160. See, for example, *Circuit City Stores, Inc. v. Adams*, 532 U.S. 105 (2001); *Gilmer v. Interstate/Johnson Lane Corp.*, 500 U.S. 20, 35 (1991) (employment discrimination); *Rodriguez de Quijas v. Shearson/American Express, Inc.*, 490 U.S. 477, 485-86 (1989) (securities law claim); see also *Equal Employment Opportunity Commission v. Waffle House, Inc.*, 122 S. Ct. 754, 761 (2002) (acknowledging that "employment contracts, except for those covering workers engaged in transportation, are covered by the [Federal Arbitration] Act" but holding that an arbitration agreement between an employer and an employee does not bar the EEOC from pursuing victim-specific judicial relief).

161. See Bruce H. Kobayashi and Larry E. Ribstein, "Contract and Jurisdictional Freedom," in *The Fall and Rise of Freedom of Contract*, ed. F. H. Buckley (Durham, N.C.: Duke University Press, 1999), pp. 325, 329.

162. Whether or not the parties have contractually selected the forum, courts have the alternative of dismissing on *forum non conveniens* grounds or, in federal court, transferring the case to the jurisdiction whose law is chosen. See "Forum Non Conveniens as a Substitute for the Internal Affairs Rule," *Columbia Law Review* 58 (1958): 234, 234–355, 247.

163. See Goldsmith, pp. 1246–49 (arguing for solving many problems through international arbitration operating through contract, national arbitration law, and international enforcement treaty).

164. See Kobayashi and Ribstein, "Contract and Jurisdictional Freedom," p. 330.

165. See Gary M. Anderson et al., "On the Incentives of Judges to Enforce Legislative Wealth Transfers," *Journal of Law and Economics* 32 (1989): 215, 219; W. Mark Crain and Robert D. Tollison, "Constitutional Change in an Interest Group Perspective," *Journal of Legal Studies* 8 (1979): 165, 171; W. Mark Crain and Robert D. Tollison, "The Executive Branch in the Interest-Group Theory of Government," *Journal of Legal Studies* 8 (1979): 555, 562; William M. Landes and Richard A. Posner, "The Independent Judiciary in an Interest Group Perspective," *Journal of Law and Economics* 18 (1975): 875, 879.

166. See Keith N. Hylton and Christopher R. Drahozal, "The Economics of Litigation and Arbitration: An Application to Franchise Contracts," Boston University School of Law, Law and Economics Working Paper no. 01–03, 2001, p. 25, available at http://papers.ssrn.com/paper.taf? abstract_id = 266545.

167. See Johnson and Post, p. 1399, note 102.

168. But see *Klocek v. Gateway 2000, Inc.*, 104 F. Supp. 2d 1332, 1341 (D. Kan. 2000) (holding against enforceability in this context because plaintiff did not accept the relevant terms).

169. 105 F.3d 1147 (7th Cir. 1997).

170. Ibid., p. 1149.

171. *Westendorf v. Gateway 2000, Inc.*, 41 U.C.C. Rep. Serv. 2d (CBC) 1110, 1114 (Del. Ch. March 16, 2000).

172. 676 N.Y.S.2d 569 (1998).

173. Ibid., pp. 570, 572.

174. Ibid., pp. 573–74.

175. Ibid., p. 575.

176. 2000 WL 198424 (N.D. Ill. February 11, 2000), *additional opinion, In re RealNetworks, Inc.* Privacy Litigation, 2000 WL 631341 (N.D. Ill. May 8, 2000).

177. See *Lieschke*, 2000 WL 198424.

178. *In re RealNetworks*, 2000 WL 631341, p. *1.

179. See *Hill v. Gateway 2000, Inc.*, 105 F.3d p. 1149.

180. *In re RealNetworks*, 2000 WL 631341, p. *5. Citing the presumption of arbitrability under the Federal Arbitration Act, the court held that plaintiffs' noncontract arguments were those "arising under" the agreement pursuant to the arbitration clause, and rejected their arguments that they should not be required to arbitrate because of the high cost of arbitrating individual claims. *Lieschke*, 2000 WL 198424, p. *2–3.

181. In re RealNetworks, 2000 WL 631341, p. *5–7.

182. *Decker v. Circus Circus Hotel*, 49 F. Supp. 2d 743, 750 (D.N.J. 1999).

183. *CompuServe, Inc. v. Patterson*, 89 F.3d 1257, 1263 (6th Cir. 1996). However, one court refused to enforce contractual choice of California law in a case involving a Texas plaintiff's participation in Internet computer games run by a defendant whose principal place of business and server were located in California. *Thompson v. Handa-Lopez, Inc.*, 998 F. Supp. 738, 741 (W.D. Tex. 1998). The court held that the choice of law clause was not a forum selection clause because, although the contract provided for final and binding arbitration in California, it did not require filing a suit in California. Ibid., p. 745. The court added that Texas had a strong interest in protecting its citizens from breach of contract, fraud, and violations of the Texas Deceptive Trade Practices Act that outweighed the defendant's burden of defending in Texas. Ibid.

184. See Samuelson, p. 1152.

185. Uniform Computer Information Transactions Act § 109(a) (Draft for Approval at NCCUSL Meeting, July 23–30, 1999), available at http://www.2bguide.com/drafts.html (last visited January 25, 2002). The parties in their agreement may choose the applicable law. However, the choice is not enforceable in a consumer contract to the extent that it would vary a rule that may not be varied by agreement under the law of the jurisdiction whose law would apply under subsections (b) and (c) in the absence of the agreement. The default rule under § 109(b) applies the law of the state in which the licensor is located in cases involving electronic delivery. Pursuant to § 109(d), a party is located for purposes of this section at its place of business if it has one place of business, at its chief executive office if it has more than one place of business, or at its place of incorporation or primary registration if it does not have a physical place of business. Otherwise, a party is located at its primary residence. For a discussion of choice of law under UCITA, see Kobayashi and Ribstein, "Uniformity, Choice of Law, and Software Sales," pp. 299–301.

186. See text accompanying note 147.

187. See UCITA, § 109, official comment 2(a).

188. Ibid. § 109(d).

189. Ibid. § 110, official comment 3.

190. 150 F. Supp. 2d 585 (S.D.N.Y. 2001).

191. Ibid., p. 588. The court applied California law on the issue of contract formation because Netscape's principal offices were in California, the product was designed in California, and the product was distributed from a Web site maintained in Netscape's California offices, citing California's interest in arbitration regarding products created locally by California-based corporations and in whether such a corporation has created a product that violates federal law. Ibid., p. 591.

192. Ibid., p. 588.

193. Ibid., p. 596.

194. Ibid., p.595. Enforceability of a forum selection clause in the clickware context also has been questioned because of the manner in which the user was required to indicate assent. See *Williams v. America Online, Inc.*, 2001 WL 135825 (Mass. Super. Ct. 2001) (denying motion to dismiss where user was required twice to override agreement to the terms of service, including a provision for exclusive jurisdiction in Virginia, to avoid harm allegedly caused by installation of the product); see also *Kunz et al.*, (discussing cases involving validity of procedures for clickware agreements).

195. See "Order in Cyberspace," pp. 1822, 1893. The Committee notes, however, that in light of the many contracting options on the Web site and the fact that many Internet sellers are small firms, U.S. courts are likely to defer to choice of law and forum contracts that are not unconscionable. Ibid., pp. 1829, 1832, 1894.

196. *Specht*, 150 F. Supp. 2d 593.

197. See Keith Perine, "States To Weigh in on Privacy," Industrial Standard, available at http://www.thestandard.com/article/display10,1551,21620,00.html (January 25, 2001) (discussing actions by state attorneys general and their opposition to federal regulation).

198. Richard K. Greenstein, "Is the Proposed U.C.C. Choice of Law Provision Unconstitutional?" *Temple Law Review* 73 (2000): 1159, 1166–70.

199. Some cases have recognized First Amendment limitations on regulating Internet privacy. See *U.S. West, Inc. v. FCC*, 182 F.3d 1224, 1239 (10th Cir. 1999) (FCC regulation restricting telephone companies' use of customers' personally identified data unless the customers opted into such use violated the First Amendment because the regulation was more restrictive than necessary); *United Reporting Publ'g Corp. v. Cal. Highway Patrol*, 146 F.3d 1133, 1140 (9th Cir. 1998), *rev'd sub nom. Los Angeles Police Dep't v. United Reporting Publ'g Corp.*, 528 U.S. 32, 40 (1999) (invalidating statute authorizing release of arrestees' addresses for "scholarly, journalistic, political, or governmental" but not commercial purposes because it was "directed at preventing solicitation practices"). These limitations have been strongly defended. See generally Eugene Volokh, "Freedom of Speech and Information Privacy: The Troubling Implications of a Right to Stop People from Speaking about You," *Stanford Law Review* 52 (2000): 1049. However, as Professor Volokh recognizes, *contractual* restrictions on consumer marketing information should survive the First Amendment, including statutory restrictions that the parties can contract around. Ibid., p. 1062. State mandatory rules can be viewed as default rules to the extent that the parties can avoid them by choice-of-law clauses. By this reasoning, enforcement of such clauses may be essential if facially mandatory restrictions on use of consumer marketing information are to withstand First Amendment attack.

200. See Kobayashi and Ribstein, "Contract and Jurisdictional Freedom," pp. 332–46. For further evidence supporting our hypothesis that firms use jurisdictional choice to avoid oppressive laws, see Hylton and Drahozal, p. 13, note 30.

201. See Goldsmith and Sykes, p. 810 (discussing technology that allows Web site operators to identify the geographical origin of a user's Internet Protocol address so that they can tailor content to and comply with different jurisdictions' regulations). Goldsmith and Sykes note that this technology is more accurate for national origin (99 percent) than for state origin (80–90 percent), and that buyers who reside in a regulating state can access a computer with an address in a nonregulating state. Ibid., p. 811 (noting that users can frustrate geographical origin technology through America Online's proxy server, Internet anonymizers, and remote telnet and dial up connections). However, this technology is developing and likely to improve, which would make jurisdictional choice more effective.

202. See generally Albert O. Hirschmann, *Exit, Voice, and Loyalty: Responses to Decline in Firms, Organizations, and States* (Cambridge, Mass.: Harvard University Press, 1970) (discussing the trade-off between exit and voice).

203. See Kobayashi and Ribstein, "Contract and Jurisdictional Freedom," p. 344.

204. For evidence of the importance of exit as a potential constraint on state regulation, see Epstein, pp. 162–65 (discussing the use of exit taxes to deter the withdrawal of automobile insurance companies from New Jersey and Massachusetts). See also Beatrice E. Garcia, "Aetna Takes Off Gloves on Car Insurance," *Wall Street Journal*, June 7, 1990, p. A4 (reporting Aetna's challenge of laws in Pennsylvania and Massachusetts that control its exits from these states). For other examples of regulation-induced exit, see "California Smashup," *Wall Street Journal*, November 15, 1988, p. A22 (discussing exit of 40 insurers from California due to Proposition 103 rate rollback); "Squaring Off Question: Should Washington's Insurance Commissioner Post Become a Gubernatorial Appointment?" *Wall Street Journal*, August 16, 2000, p. NW4 (noting exit of health insurance companies from Washington State due to state policies); and Stephen Kreider Yoger, "Political Operator: Insurance Regulator in California Woos Voters, Bashes Firms," *Wall Street Journal*, August 10, 1992, p. A1 (discussing withdrawal of Ohio Casualty Corporation from California Market because of excess regulation and poor underwriting results).

205. See text accompanying notes 227–229 (discussing lawyers' interests in promoting state competition regarding electronic commerce law). It follows from this analysis that courts are wrong not to weigh states' "interest" in the enforcement of contracts that choose their laws against any interest regulating states may have in the enforcement of their laws. For an example of this analytical error, see note 191.

206. Enforcement of contractual choice of law therefore could result from interest group pressure, and not necessarily by relying on judges and lawyers who are immune from those pressures, as Paul Stephan suggests. See Paul B. Stephan III, "Regulatory Cooperation and Competition—The Search for Virtue," University of Virginia Working Paper no. 99–12, June 1999, available at http://papers.ssrn.com/paper.taf?abstract_id=169213.

207. This tension between pro-regulatory and pro-local business interests may explain Iowa's waffling regarding enforcement of contractual choice of UCITA. See note 223.

208. See, for example, Maureen O'Rourke, "Progressing toward a Uniform Commercial Code for Electronic Commerce or Racing toward Nonuniformity," *Berkeley Technology Law Journal* 14 (1999): 635, 656.

209. See Goldsmith, p. 1215; Johnson and Post, pp. 1395–1400 and notes 102–03.

210. See Ted J. Janger, "The Public Choice of Choice of Law in Software Transactions: Jurisdictional Competition and the Dim Prospects for Uniformity, *Brooklyn*

Journal of International Law 26 (2000): 187, 190–93; William J. Woodward Jr., "Contractual Choice of Law: Legislative Choice in an Era of Party Autonomy," *Southern Methodist University Law Review* 54 (2001): 697, 739; William J. Woodward Jr., "'Sale' of Law and Forum and the Widening Gulf Between 'Consumer' and 'Nonconsumer' Contracts in the UCC," *Washington University Law Quarterly* 75 (1997): 243, 244.

211. See Woodward, "Party Autonomy," p. 741.

212. See Woodward, "'Sale' of Law and Forum," p. 257, note 59 (conjuring a "vision" of consumers with shopping carts "ambling down" grocery store aisles).

213. See William Cary, "Federalism and Corporate Law: Reflections upon Delaware," *Yale Law Journal* 83 (1974): 663, 666–72.

214. See Ralph K. Winter Jr., "State Law, Shareholder Protection, and the Theory of the Corporation," *Journal of Legal Studies* 6 (1977): 251, 256.

215. See *Brower v. Gateway 2000, Inc.* 676 N.Y.S.2d 569, 574 (A.D. 1998).

216. See text accompanying note 60; see also Stephan, pp. 40–41.

217. See Mark R. Patterson, "On the Impossibility of Information Intermediaries," Fordham Law and Economics Research Paper no. 13 (July 2001), at http://papers.ssrn.com/abstract=276968; see also Woodward, "Party Autonomy," p. 762 (noting that "there are no consumer groups or other services that give parties to form contracts meaningful information through which they can easily compare the terms of the form contracts").

218. One author notes that Gateway continued selling its computers with arbitration clauses without apparent damage to its reputation even after these clauses were subject to the widely publicized litigation discussed above. See Woodward, "Party Autonomy," p. 762 , note 287. Woodward produces no facts about the effects or noneffects on Gateway's sales, and does not explain why a noneffect, if that was the case, would simply show that consumers were not concerned about the term.

219. See text accompanying note 214.

220. See Patterson. Patterson's article draws its title from Sanford J. Grossman and Joseph E. Stiglitz, "On the Impossibility of Informationally Efficient Markets," *American Economic Review* 70 (1980): 393, 404 (arguing that capital markets cannot be strong-form efficient and still offer incentives to produce information that create the condition of efficiency).

221. See note 197 and accompanying text.

222. Janger, p. 196 (noting that "jurisdictions that have many licensees and few licensors, or a strong tradition of consumer protection, will be unlikely to adopt the location of licensor rule").

223. See Iowa Code § 554D.104 (2000). Iowa is, however, reconsidering its resistance to contractual choice of UCITA. The legislature swiftly repealed the "bomb shelter" provision effective July 1, 2001, explicitly stating that it was considering whether to adopt UCITA. See 2000 Iowa Acts (78 G.A.) ch. 1189, § 32 (approved May 15, 2000). The following year it delayed the repeal to 2002. See Iowa Legis., H.F. 569, § 1 (approved April 16, 2001).

224. See Roberta Romano, "Law as Product: Some Pieces of the Incorporation Puzzle," *Journal of Law, Economics and Organization* 1 (1985): 225.

225. See Douglas J. Cumming and Jeffrey G. MacIntosh, "The Role of Interjurisdictional Competition in Shaping Canadian Corporate Law," *International Review of Law and Economics* 20 (2000): 141, 159–60; Susan Rose-Ackerman, "Risk Taking and Reelection: Does Federalism Promote Innovation?" *Journal of Legal Studies* 9 (1980): 593, 594 (observing that legislators may be unable to capture benefits from engaging

in the competition because other jurisdictions easily can free-ride on their efforts by copying successful legislation); Henri I. T. Tjiong, "Breaking the Spell of Regulatory Competition: Reframing the Problem of Regulatory Exit," Max-Planck Project Group Preprint no. 2000/13, August 2000, at http://papers.ssrn.com/paper.taf?abstract_id = 267744 (arguing that there is no political "feedback mechanism" to translate firm mobility into optimal regulation).

226. See Rose-Ackerman, p. 605.

227. For fuller discussions of lawyers' ability and incentives to lobby for efficient laws, see generally Jonathan R. Macey and Geoffrey P. Miller, "Toward an Interest-Group Theory of Delaware Corporate Law," *Texas Law Review* 65 (1987): 469 (discussing lawyers' role in corporate context); Ribstein, "Delaware Lawyers and Choice of Law," pp. 1007–12; Larry E. Ribstein, "Lawyer Licensing and State Law Efficiency," available at http://hal-law.usc.edu/cleo/papers/alea/Ribstein.pdf (April 9, 2001). A Michigan law firm apparently was active in promoting the new Michigan cybercourt law, discussed in note 232, including by establishing a Web site providing information about the proposed and eventually enacted legislation. See http://www.michigancybercourt.net.

228. See Carol R. Goforth, "The Rise of the Limited Liability Company: Evidence of a Race between the States, But Heading Where?" *Syracuse Law Review* 45 (1995): 1193, 1220–62.

229. See Larry E. Ribstein, "Statutory Forms for Closely Held Firms: Theories and Evidence from LLCs," *Washington University Law Quarterly* 73 (1995): 369, 396–98.

230. For a discussion and application of this theory, see Ronald J. Gilson, "The Legal Infrastructure of High Technology Industrial Districts: Silicon Valley, Route 128, and Covenants Not to Compete," *New York University Law Review* 74 (1999): 575, 588.

231. Ibid., p. 579 (discussing the role of the state's law on enforcement of noncompetition agreement and its effect on local diffusion of knowledge among skilled workers).

232. See Va. Code Ann. §§ 59.1-501.1 (2001). Virginia has offered other inducements to Internet firms, including through a long-arm jurisdiction law designed to benefit local Internet service providers such as AOL. See note 140. See also text accompanying note 146 (discussing Virginia proposal to permit Web site domestication). Maryland's subsequent version of UCITA, which became effective first, modifies UCITA, most importantly by partially excluding consumers from some provisions as to warranty modification. See Md. Code Ann., commercial law, § 406(i), (j) (2000). Another example of active state competition for high-tech business is the new Michigan "cybercourt" law, which provides for streamlined electronic procedures for handling certain types of cases. See Mich. Comp. Laws §§ 8001-8029. The law "is meant to attract 'new economy' businesses to Michigan." Anita Ramasastry, "Michigan's Cybercourt: Worthy Experiment or Virtual Daydream?" February 6, 2002, available at http://writ.news.findlaw.com/commentary/20020206_ramasastry.html.

233. Among other things, the overall effects of "legal infrastructure" may be complex, because the same features that increase states' payoffs from becoming centers of electronic commerce also induce firms to remain in established centers and inhibit other states from entering the market. See Ribstein, "Delaware Lawyers and Choice of Law," pp. 1010–11. This "lock-in" may or may not be an example of the "network externalities" phenomenon discussed in the next subsection.

234. See UCITA § 209, discussed in Kobayashi and Ribstein, "Uniformity, Choice of Law and Software Sales," pp. 265–66.

235. For general discussions of network externalities and lock-in, see Joseph Farrell and Garth Saloner, "Standardization, Compatibility, and Innovation," *Rand Journal of Economics* 16 (1985): 70, 71–72 (characterizing the problem as one of excess inertia); Michael L. Katz and Carl Shapiro, "Network Externalities, Competition, and Compatibility," *American Economic Review* (1985): 424; Michael L. Katz and Carl Shapiro, "Systems Competition and Network Effects," *Journal of Economic Perspectives* (Spring 1994): 93; Michael L. Katz and Carl Shapiro, "Technology Adoption in the Presence of Network Externalities," *Journal of Political Economy* 94 (1986): 822.

236. See Marcel Kahan and Michael Klausner, "Path Dependence in Corporate Contracting: Increasing Returns, Herd Behavior, and Cognitive Biases," *Washington University Law Quarterly* 74 (1996): 347, 359–65; Marcel Kahan and Michael Klausner, "Standardization and Innovation in Corporate Contracting (Or 'The Economics of Boilerplate')," *Virginia Law Review* 83 (1997): 713, 762; Michael Klausner, "Corporations, Corporate Law, and Networks of Contracts," *Virginia Law Review* 81 (1995): 757, 790, 809; Tara J. Wortman, Note, "Unlocking Lock-In: Limited Liability Companies and the Key to Underutilization of Close Corporation Statutes," *New York University Law Review* 70 (1995): 1362, 1374–80.

237. See Klausner, pp. 842–47.

238. For criticisms of the theory as applied to products and services, see S. J. Liebowitz and Stephen E. Margolis, "The Fable of the Keys," *Journal of Law and Economics* 33 (1990): 1 (arguing that network externalities do not demonstrate whether the QWERTY keyboard was superior to the Dvorak keyboard, or the VHS videotape format was inferior to Betamax); see also Stan J. Liebowitz and Stephen E. Margolis, *Winners, Losers and Microsoft: Competition and Antitrust in High Technology* (Oakland, Calif.: Independent Institute, 1999), pp. 135–36 (showing evidence that Microsoft's victory in software markets is due to the superiority of their products rather than network externalities); S. J. Liebowitz and Stephen E. Margolis, "Network Externality: An Uncommon Tragedy," *Journal of Economic Perspectives* 133 (1994): 133. For criticisms of the application to contracts and statutes, see Clayton P. Gillette, "Lock-In Effects in Law and Norms," *Boston University Law Review* 78 (1998): 813, 826; Mark A. Lemley and David McGowan, "Legal Implications of Network Economic Effects," *California Law Review* 86 (1998): 479, 562–86.

239. See Larry E. Ribstein and Bruce H. Kobayashi, "Choice of Form and Network Externalities," *William and Mary Law Review* 43 (2001): 79, 81–83.

240. Those advocating federal law questionably assume that this will produce a better solution than the decentralized state solution. Analogously, commentators have questioned whether antitrust regulations should be used to alter market outcomes that resulted in choice of a dominant standard. See Liebowitz and Margolis, "Winners, Losers and Microsoft," pp. 266-67. In both cases, government intervention involves substitution of a federally imposed outcome for a more decentralized one—either by suppressing potential competition or by inducing competition against a dominant standard. In both cases, the federal standard may increase costs and reduce efficiency as compared to the market equilibrium.

241. For a list of recent examples, see Ribstein and Kobayashi, "State Regulation of Electronic Commerce," note 269.

242. 15 U.S.C. § 6801.

243. See *BNA E-Commerce & Law Report* 5 (April 5, 2000): 334, 336; see also HIPAA, 15 C.F.R. pts. 160, 160.202, 203(b) (allowing states to enforce "more stringent" privacy laws).

244. For a recent example of the complexities of the preemption issue, see *Geier v. American Honda Motor Co., Inc.*, 529 U.S. 861 (2000) (holding that although tort action for defective design for failure to equip a car with driver's side airbag was not precluded by express preemption provision of National Traffic and Motor Vehicle Safety Act, it was preempted under general preemption principles because it conflicted with the federal standard requiring driver's side airbags in some but not all 1987 cars).

245. See Jonathan R. Macey, "Federal Deference to Local Regulators and the Economic Theory of Regulation: Toward a Public-Choice Explanation of Federalism," *Virginia Law Review* 76 (1990): 265 (arguing that federal legislators have incentives to refrain from legislating in an area of law if they would lose more support than they would gain from acting, as where federal regulation would dissipate a substantial state capital investment in regulation).

246. See Reidenberg, "Resolving Conflicting International Data Privacy," p. 1357.

247. See generally William A. Niskanen, "Bureaucrats and Politicians," *Journal of Law and Economics* 18 (1975): 617, 635 (discussing overspending by government bureaus). This problem may be exacerbated by statutes in which multiple agencies have oversight and enforcement responsibility. See Gramm-Leach-Bliley Act, 15 U.S.C. § 6805 (delegating rulemaking and enforcement authority to the FTC, Treasury Department, Comptroller of the Currency, Federal Reserve, Federal Deposit Insurance Corporation, the National Credit Union Association, and the Securities and Exchange Commission).

248. See FTC Press Release, "FTC Announces Settlement with Bankrupt Web site Toysmart.com regarding Alleged Privacy Policy Violations," July 21, 2000, available at http://www.ftc.gov/opa/2000/07/toysmart2.htm (announcing settlement of charges that Toysmart.com violated Section 5 of the FTC act when it violated its own privacy policy never to share customer information with third parties). But see Steven Hetcher, "The FTC as Internet Privacy Norm Entrepreneur," *Vanderbilt Law Review* 53 (2000): 2041, 2046 (arguing that the FTC has attempted to guide self-regulatory efforts through regulation).

249. See *Supnick v. Amazon.com, Inc.*, 2000 WL 1603820, *2 (W.D. Wash. May 18, 2000) (certifying class action based on 18 U.S.C. §§ 2510-2522, relating to interception of electronic communications, and ibid. § 2701, relating to unlawful access to stored communications); Stephen F. Ambrose Jr. and Joseph W. Gelb, "Consumer Privacy Regulation and Litigation," *Business Law* 56 (2001): 1157, 1175–77 (2001) (discussing privacy suits against Intuit and Amazon under various federal and state laws relating to consumer marketing and other information).

250. See David A. Skeel Jr., "Rethinking the Line Between Corporate Law and Corporate Bankruptcy," *Texas Law Review* 72 (1994): 471, 490 (arguing that federal law has "vestigialized" state law).

251. See COPPA, 215 U.S.C. § 6501 (1998). Some have suggested that the provisions of COPPA be expanded to apply to all collection of information. For a discussion of this issue, see Cate, p. 63.

252. FTC, Children's Online Privacy Protection Rule, Final Rule, 16 C.F.R. pt. 312, November 3, 1999.

253. See FTC, "How to Comply with Children's Online Privacy Protection Rule," available at http://www.ftc.gov. Individually identifiable information includes names, e-mail or home addresses, telephone numbers, and any other information (e.g., interests or hobbies collected through cookies) when tied to individually identifiable information. The FTC rule requires those covered by the Act to post prominent links

to a notice describing what information will be collected and how it will be used; requires parental consent, including some method by which parents can review and request deletion of information collected; and prohibits conditioning use of the Web site on providing more information than is reasonably necessary. See 16 C.F.R. pt. 312. The parental consent requirement depends on how the Web site will use the information collected. The most stringent requirements are imposed when a site wishes to collect and disclose information to third parties, in which event the Web site must obtain parental consent by telephone contact, presentation of valid credit card information, e-mail with a digital signature, or a printed copy of the parents' consent.

254. 16 C.F.R. pt. 312 (noting that failure to collect such information may be used as evidence of evasion of COPPA by the site).

255. See 15 U.S.C. § 6501 (1998).

256. Ibid., § 6803(a) (1998).

257. See Cate, pp. 33, 53.

258. 12 C.F.R. §§ 40.3(o), 216.3(o), 332.3(o), 573.3(o) (2001).

259. See FTC, Privacy of Consumer Financial Information, Final Rule, 16 C.F.R. pt. 313, May 24, 2000.

260. See HIPAA, 15 C.F.R. pt. 160.

261. See Cate, p. 54.

262. Ibid. See also text accompanying notes 38–40 (discussing deterrent effect of disclosure in context of medical research).

263. Pub. L. No. 106-29, 114 Stat. 464 (2000) (codified at 15 U.S.C. §§ 7001-7031).

264. Ibid., § 101(c)(1).

265. See Jane K. Winn, "Electronic Commerce Law: 2001 Developments," *Business Law* 57 (2001): 541, 542 (noting that "if E-SIGN largely succeeded in closing one can of worms—namely, the mostly unwarranted degree of concern over the validity of electronic records and signatures—it opened several more that may prove just as difficult to resolve").

266. See Albert Breton and Pierre Salmon, "External Effects of Domestic Regulations: Comparing Internal and International Barriers to Trade," *International Review of Law and Economics* 21 (2001): 135, 138–43.

267. U.S. Const., Art I, § 8; Art. IV, § 1. For a leading proposal favoring a federal choice-of-law statute, see Michael H. Gottesman, "Draining the Dismal Swamp: The Case for Federal Choice of Law Statutes," *Georgia Law Journal* 80 (1991): 1.

268. See O'Hara and Ribstein, pp. 1224–25.

269. See 28 U.S.C. § 1738 (2001).

270. Ibid., § 1738c.

271. See Macey, p. 270.

272. See generally Reidenberg, "Resolving International Data Privacy."

273. These are based on the OECD standards discussed in note 79. Currently, U.S. privacy policies have not been harmonized to conform to the strict European Union fair information practices. Under a March 2000 privacy accord reached by the EU and the United States, U.S. firms are immune from legal actions by EU governments if they meet safe harbor guidelines developed by the U.S. Department of Commerce in consultation with the EU. See Paul Greenberg, "U.S. and EU Reach Data Privacy Accord," March 15, 2000 available at http://www.ecommercetimes.com/perl/story/2738.html. The Safe Harbor guidelines include elements such as notice, choice, access,

security, and enforcement. See http//www.export.gov/safeharbor. U.S. firms wishing to make use of the safe-harbor must self-certify annually to the U.S. Department of Commerce in writing that they agree to adhere to the safe-harbor requirements, and must state the requirements in their published privacy policies. Compliance with the safe-harbor guidelines by U.S. firms is strictly voluntary, and firms may withdraw their certifications at any time. However, violations of the voluntarily agreed-to safe-harbor guidelines can be considered to be a deceptive practice, subjecting the firm to FTC enforcement under Section 5 of the FTC act. Ibid.

274. 18 Pa. C.S.A. § 7330(a).

275. See In the Matter of the Application of D. Michael Fisher, Order Requiring Internet Service Provider to Remove or Disable Access to Child Pornography, September 12, 2002. According to the Pennsylvania Attorney General, since the law went into effect on April 22, 2002, Internet service providers have blocked access to more than 200 child pornography Web sites. See "Judge to WorldCom: Block Kid Porn," September 18, 2002, available at http://www.wired.com/news/politics/0,1283,55248,00.html.

276. See Letter of Craig Silliman, September 23, 2002, available at http://politechbot.com/docs/worldcom.pa.reply.092402.pdf.

277. Significantly, the suit did not involve Yahoo!'s French subsidiary, www.yahoo.fr. Both of these Web sites, and Yahoo!'s other country-specific Web sites, can be accessed from computers anywhere in the world.

278. See §R645-1 of the French Criminal Code (prohibiting exhibition of Nazi propaganda and artifacts for sale).

279. High Court of Paris, May 22, 2000, Interim Court Order No. 00/05308, 00/05309.

280. Yahoo Auction Guidelines, http://user.auctions.yaho.com/html/guidelines.html (visited October 19, 2002).

281. The facts concerning the English suit are drawn from *Dow Jones & Co., Inc. v. Harrods, Limited*, 2002 WL 31307163 (S.D.N.Y., Oct. 15, 2002).

282. In a similar action, the Australian High Court upheld a lower court ruling that allowed Joseph Gutnick, an Austrialian businessman, to sue Dow Jones in Australia over a story that appeared in the U.S. publication *Barron's* and was subsequently distributed over the Internet. The Australian High Court rejected Dow Jones's attempts to move the case to New Jersey and to apply U.S. defamation law. See "Australia to Hear Web Libel Suit in Landmark Case," *Wall Street Journal*, December 11, 2002, p. A3.

283. For an article recognizing a distinction between these contacts, although not emphasizing the contractual element, see Christoph Engel, "Organizing Co-Existence in Cyberspace: Content Regulation and Privacy Compared," Max-Planck Project Group Preprint no. 2002/12, 2002, available at http://papers.ssrn.com/paper.taf?abstract_id = 325360 (arguing that international cooperation works better with privacy than with content regulation because there are fewer actors to control in the former context).

284. Such a contract may be enforced "to the extent only that it allows the consumer to bring proceedings in another court." See Hague Conference on Private International Law, "Preliminary Draft Convention on Jurisdiction and Foreign Judgments in Civil and Commercial Matters," Art. 4, para. 7(3)(b), available at http://www.hcch.net/e/conventions/draft36e.html (adopted by the Special Commission on October 30, 1999).

437

285. See generally *Hilton v. Guyot*, 159 U.S. 113, 163-64 (1895) (stating that comity "is neither a matter of absolute obligation, on the one hand, nor of mere courtesy and good will, upon the other").

286. See Michael Whincop, "The Recognition Scene: Game Theoretic Issues in the Recognition of Foreign Judgments," *Melbourne University Law Review* 23 (1999): 416, 422.

287. See David Pringle, "Some Worry French Ruling on Yahoo! Work to Deter Investments in Europe," *Wall Street Journal*, November 22, 2000, p. B2.

288. *Yahoo!, Inc. v. La Ligue contra le Racism et L'Antisemitisme*, 145 F. Supp.2d 1168 (N.D. Cal. 2001).

289. 169 F.Supp.2d 1181(N.D. Cal. 2001).

290. The district court's decision has been appealed. In addition, a French Holocaust survivors group, angered by Yahoo's! actions, filed charges in a French criminal court against former Yahoo! CEO Timothy Koogle. Koogle was charged with "justifying a crime against humanity" and with the "exhibition of a uniform, insignia, or emblem of a person guilty of crimes against humanity." Koogle was tried in absentia. The second charge was dropped prior to trial, and he was acquitted of the first charge. See "French Court Acquits former Yahoo! Boss in Nazi Memorabilia Case," *Agence France Presse*, February 11, 2003. Koogle was singled out because there is no criminal corporate liability under French law. Although Koogle theoretically faced a five-year prison term and a fine of 46,000 Euros on the first charge, and a fine of 1,500 Euros on the second, the French prosecutor had called for no punishment to be levied in case of conviction. In the event of a conviction, France would have had to ask the United States to extradite Koogle. Such a request would not be granted under U.S. State Department rules, which require Koogle to have violated a similar U.S. law. See "French Prosecution Argues for No Sentence for Former Yahoo! Boss on Trial," *Agence France Presse*, January 7, 2003.

291. See *Dow Jones*.

292. The possibility of retaliation was played out in the *Laker* case, described in note 293.

293. For an earlier counterpart to *Dow Jones*, see *Laker Airways Limited v. Sabena, Belgian World Airlines*, 731 F.2d 909 (2d Cir. 1984) (affirming a preliminary injunction permitting prosecution of a U.S. antitrust claim as against English proceedings seeking to block the U.S. action). The standoff between U.S. antitrust action and English anti-suit action courts finally ended when the English high court backed down. *British Airways Board v. Laker Airways, Ltd.*, [1985] A.C. 58. (H.L. (E.)).

294. An example is recent litigation against the owners of the peer-to-peer file sharing program KaZaa. A U.S. Federal Court in California held that then owner Sharman Networks, Ltd., based on the Pacific Island of Vanuatu, could be sued in California. See *Metro-Goldwin-Mayer Studios, Inc., v. Grokster, Ltd.*, 2003 WL 186657 (C.D. Cal 2003). However, any judgment would be ineffective against operations like KaZaa's that are based offshore. In addition KaZaa is not illegal everywhere. A Dutch appeals court ruled that KaZaa is not liable under Dutch law for copyright infringement committed by its users. See Brian Grow, "Netherlands Court Ruling Offers a Haven to File Sharing Services," *Wall Street Journal*, December 18, 2002.

295. See Macey, pp. 289–90.

Chapter 8

This paper is based, in part, on an amicus brief written by the author with Ann Brick of the ACLU of Northern California in *Yahoo!, Inc. v. La Ligue contre le Racisme et l'Antisemitisme*, Case No. 01-17424 (9th Cir.).

1. The Internet is a decentralized, self-maintained networking system that links computers and computer networks around the world; the World Wide Web is a publishing forum consisting of millions of individual Web sites that may contain text, images, illustrations, video, and animation. While recognizing that they are distinct entities, this paper refers to the Web and the Internet collectively as the "Internet" for the sake of simplicity.

2. See, for example, *Reno v. ACLU*, 521 U.S. 844 (1997), *aff'g*, 929 F. Supp. 824 (E.D. Pa. 1996) (*Reno I*); *Cyberspace Communications, Inc. v. Engler*, 238 F.3d 420 (6th Cir. 2000); *ACLU v. Johnson*, 194 F.3d 1149 (10th Cir. 1999), *aff'g*, 4 F. Supp. 2d 1024 (D.N.M. 1998); *PSINet, Inc. v. Chapman*, 167 F. Supp. 878 (W.D. Va. 2001); *ACLU v. Napolitano*, Civ. 00-505 TUC ACM (D. Ariz. February 21, 2002); *American Bookseller's Foundation for Free Expression v. Dean*, No. 1:01-C-46 (D. Vt. April 18, 2002); and *American Libraries Ass'n. v. Pataki*, 969 F. Supp. 160 (S.D.N.Y. 1997).

3. *Ashcroft v. ACLU*, 122 S.Ct. 1700 (2002).

4. *Reno I* at 851, 852 (quoting 929 F. Supp. at 842).

5. Ibid. at 883.

6. *ACLU v. Reno*, 31 F. Supp. 2d 473, 476 (E.D. Pa. 1999), *aff'd*, 217 F.3d 162 (3d Cir. 2000) (*Reno II*), *rev'd and remanded* on other grounds, *Ashcroft*.

7. *Blumenthal v. Drudge*, 992 F. Supp. 44, 48 n.7 (D.D.C. 1998) (citation omitted).

8. *Reno I*, pp. 849, 854 (quoting 929 F. Supp. 844).

9. *Ashcroft*, p. 1703.

10. *Reno I*, p. 851.

11. *Reno II*, p. 169 (quoting *Doe v. Roe*, 955 P.2d 951, 956 (Ariz. 1998)).

12. *Pataki*, p. 169.

13. *Reno II*, p. 168.

14. Art. R645-1 provides: "The act, other than for the purposes of a film, show or exhibition incorporating an historical theme, of wearing or exhibiting in public a uniform, insignia or emblem recalling uniforms, insignia or emblems worn or exhibited either by the members of an organisation declared to be criminal under Article 9 of the statutes of the International Military Tribunal annexed to the London Agreement of 8 August 1945 or by a person declared to be guilty by a French or international court of one or more crimes against humanity . . . shall be liable to a fine provided for in respect of Class 5 offenses."

15. *La Ligue contre le Racisme et l'Antisemitisme v. Yahoo! Inc.*, No. RG: 00/05308 (November 20, 2000).

16. Ibid., p. 4 (emphasis added).

17. Ibid.

18. Sebastian Mallaby, "Taming the Wild Web," *Washington Post*, March 12, 2001, p. A17.

19. Pontifical Council for Social Communications, "Ethics in Internet," February 22, 2002, www.vatican.va/roman_curia/pont.../rc_pc_pccs_doc_20020228_ethics-internet_en.htm.

20. Ibid., sec. II.

21. Ibid., secs. III–IV.

22. See, for example, "Sins of the Fathers," *Newsweek,* March 4, 2002, pp. 42–52.

23. Sebastian Mallaby, "Taming the Wild Web," *Washington Post,* April 2, 2001, p. A19. Mallaby apparently liked the title "Taming the Wild Web" so much that he used it for two different columns in the space of three weeks.

24. Mallaby, "Taming the Wild Web," March 12, 2001.

25. Ibid.

26. Ibid.

27. Sebastian Mallaby, "The Tangled Web of E-Commerce," *Washington Post,* April 30, 2001, p. A17.

28. Ibid.

29. Jack Goldsmith, "Yahoo! Brought to Earth," FT.com, November 26, 2000, http://news.ft.com/ft.../ftc?pagename = View&c = Article&cid = FT3W85A41GC&liv%20e = tru.

30. Ibid.

31. Ibid. See also Jack Goldsmith, "Against Cyberanarchy," *University of Chicago Law Review* 65 (1998): 1199–1250; and Jack L. Goldsmith and Alan O. Sykes, "The Internet and the Dormant Commerce Clause," *Yale Law Journal* 110 (2001): 785–834.

32. Reporters without Borders, *Enemies of the Internet* 5 (2001) www.rsf.org/enemis.php3. Reporters without Borders compiled a report on repressive measures worldwide, ranging from outright bans on the Internet (e.g., North Korea) and government control over the network (e.g., China and Saudi Arabia), to laws restricting disfavored content (e.g., France). See also Leonard R. Sussman, *Censor Dot Gov: The Internet and Press Freedom* 2 (2000) www.freedomhouse.org/pfs2000/sussman.html (reporting that countries in all regions restrict domestic and transnational news flows).

33. See People's Republic of China, Ministry of Information Industry Regulation, Managing Internet Information-Release Services, November 7, 2000, www.mii.gov.ch/mii/index.html (in Chinese); see also "China Regulations on Managing Internet Information-Release Services," *China Online,* November 13, 2000, www.chinaonline.com/issues/internet_policy/NewsArchive/Secure/2000/November/C0011064.asp. Other restrictions target a variety of disfavored groups, particularly supporters of the Falun Gong spiritual movement. See "China Press Internet Security Law," *China Online,* December 29, 2000, www.chinaonline.com/issues/internet_policy/NewsArChive/Secure/2000/December/C00122805.asp.

34. See "You Don't Say: China Forbids Publication of Seven Types of Content," *China Online,* August 13, 2001.

35. Sussman, pp. 2–3.

36. See Complete Archives of *Dacankao Daily News,* www.bignews.org (visited April 12, 2002). Chinese government agents shut down Xinwenming, a China-based pro-democracy Web site, www.hrichina.org/Xinwenming/index.htm (last visited February 27, 2001).

37. U.S. Department of State, *Country Reports on Human Rights Practices, Singapore 2001* (2002).

38. Ibid.; see also "Singapore Net Law Dismays Opposition" *BBC News,* August 14, 2001, http://news.bbc.co.uk/hi/english/world/asia-pacific/newsid_1490000/1490425.stm; and John Aglionby, "Singapore Plans Purge of Net Politics," *The Guardian,* July 27, 2001, www.guardianunlimited.co.uk/internetnews/story/0,7369,528129,00.html.

39. Saudi Arabia, Council of Ministers Resolution, Saudi Internet Regulations, February 12, 2001, www.al-bab.com/media/docs/saudi.htm; see also Brian Whitaker, "Losing the Saudi Cyberwar," *The Guardian*, February 26, 2001, www. guardianunlimited.co.uk/elsewhere/journalist/story/ 0,7792,443261,00.html.

40. Ibid.

41. Human Rights Watch, *World Report 1999: Freedom of Expression on the Internet*, www.hrw.org/hrw/worldreport99/special/internet.html.

42. See "Adieu Pikachu," *ABC News.com*, March 26, 2001, www.abcnews.go.com/ sections/world/DailyNews/pokemon010326.html.

43. See Syrian Constitution, Art. XXXXII; and Reporters without Borders, p. 101.

44. Ibid., pp. 101–2.

45. Australia, Broadcasting Services Act, 1992 (amended 1999), part 15, § 216B, sched. 5, part 3, div. 1.

46. See, for example, Australian Office of Film and Literature Classification, *Guidelines for the Classification of Films and Videotapes*, September 18, 2000.

47. Australia, Broadcasting Services Act, part 15, § 216B, sched. 5, part 4.

48. Italian Constitution, Art. XXI, § 6.

49. Ibid., Art. XXI, § 4; see also Art. XIII, § 3.

50. *In the Matter of Moshe D.*, Italy. Cass., closed session, November 17–December 27, 2000, Judgment No. 4741.

51. Ibid.

52. Ibid.

53. Ibid.

54. Sweden, Lag (1998:112) om ansvar för elektroniska anslagstavlor [Act (1998:112) on Responsibility for Electronic Bulletin Boards], Art. V, § 1 (1998), http://dsv.su.se/ jpalme/society/Swedish-bbs-act.html.

55. Ibid.

56. See Drew Cullen, "It's Bloody Hard to Run a Forum (in Sweden)," *Register* (United Kingdom), March 8, 2002, www.theregister.co.uk/content/6/24352.html.

57. *Pataki*, p. 175 (citation omitted).

58. Ibid., p. 174.

59. White House, *A Framework for Global Electronic Commerce*, July 1997, p. 18, http://216.239.51.100/search?q = cache:QbYQn4KDbVcC:iitf.doc.gov/eleccomm/ ecomm.htm + +%22a + framework + for + global + electronic + commerce%22&hl = en&ie = UTF8.

60. U.S. Department of Commerce, *Digital Economy 2000*, December 2000, p. 22, http://www.esa.doc.gov/de2000.pdf.

61. *Wilson v. Marchington*, 127 F.3d 805, 808 (9th Cir. 1997), *cert. denied*, 523 U.S. 1074 (1998).

62. *Ackermann v. Levine*, 788 F.2d 830, 837 (2d Cir. 1986); *Laker Airways Ltd. v. Sabena, Belgian World Airlines*, 731 F.2d 909, 929, 931, 937, 943 (D.C. Cir. 1984); and *Yuen v. U.S. Stock Transfer Co.*, 966 F. Supp. 944, 948 (C.D. Cal. 1997). See *Hilton v. Guyot*, 159 U.S. 113 (1895) (outlining fundamental principles of comity).

63. *Ackermann*, p. 841; see Hilton, p. 164, 193; and *Somportex Ltd. v. Philadelphia Chewing Gum Corp.*, 453 F.2d 435, 443 (3d Cir. 1971), *cert. denied*, 405 U.S. 1017 (1972).

64. See, for example, *Matusevitch v. Telnikoff*, 877 F. Supp. 1 (D. D.C. 1995), *aff'd on other grounds*, 159 F.3d 636 (D.C. Cir. 1998) (Table); and *Bachchan v. India Abroad Publ'ns. Inc.*, 585 N.Y.S.2d 661 (N.Y. Sup. Ct. 1992).

65. *National Socialist Party of America v. Village of Skokie*, 432 U.S. 43 (1977) (per curiam).

66. *Whitney v. California*, 274 U.S. 357, 375 (1927) (Brandeis and Holmes, J.J., concurring).

67. *United States v. Playboy Entertainment Group, Inc.*, 529 U.S. 803, 826 (2000).

68. Ibid., p. 818.

69. See, for example, *New York Times Co. v. Sullivan*, 376 U.S. 254 (1964).

70. *Telnikoff v. Matusevitch*, 702 A.2d 230, 238–39, (Md. 1997). See also *Bachchan* at 665 (protections of free speech "would be seriously jeopardized by the entry of foreign libel judgments granted pursuant to standards deemed appropriate in England but considered antithetical to the protections afforded the press by the U.S. Constitution").

71. *Ellis v. Time, Inc.*, 1997 WL 863267, 26 *Media Law Reporter* 1225 (D.D.C. 1997).

72. Ibid. at 1235. See also *DeRoburt v. Gannett Co.*, 83 F.R.D. 574, 580 (D. Haw. 1979) ("the public policy of the United States requires the application of the First Amendment to libel cases brought in the courts of this country").

73. 47 U.S.C. § 230(c)(1).

74. Ibid., §§ 230(b)(1), (b)(2).

75. *Zeran v. America Online, Inc.*, 129 F.3d 327, 330 (4th Cir. 1997), *cert. denied*, 524 U.S. 937 (1998).

76. Ibid. p. 327 (AOL not liable for postings to bulletin board by third party); accord *Ben Ezra, Weinstein, & Co. v. America Online, Inc.*, 206 F.3d 980, 984–85 (10th Cir. 2000) (AOL not liable for incorrect information available through its Quotes & Portfolios service), *cert. denied*, 121 S. Ct. 69 (2001); *Blumenthal* at 50 (AOL not liable for defamatory material appearing in publication made available to subscribers to its service); *PatentWizard, Inc. v. Kinko's, Inc.*, 163 F. Supp. 2d 1069 (D.S.D. 2001) (Kinko's not liable for allegedly defamatory statements transmitted by renter of its computer); *Does v. Franco Prods.*, 2000 WL 816779 (N.D. Ill. June 22, 2000) (GTE and PSINet not liable in their capacities as Web site hosts for material originating with others); *Schneider v. Amazon.com, Inc.*, 108 Wash. App. 454, 31 P.3d 37 (2001) (Amazon not liable in tort for unflattering review of plaintiff's book posted on its Web site); *Kathleen R. v. City of Livermore*, 87 Cal. App. 4th 684, 104 Cal. Rptr. 2d 772, 776, 781 (2001) (public library not liable for providing unrestricted Internet access); *Doe v. America Online, Inc.*, 783 So. 2d 1010 (Fla. 2001) (AOL not liable for third party's sale of child pornography depicting plaintiff's son); *Doe v. Oliver*, 755 A.2d 1000, 1003 (Conn. Super. Ct. 2000) (AOL not liable for e-mail sent by one of its subscribers using AOL's e-mail service).

77. *Godfrey v. Demon Internet, Ltd.*, 3 ILR (P&F) 98 (Q.B. 1999).

78. Ibid.

79. *Yahoo!, Inc. v. La Ligue contre le Racisme et l'Antisemitisme*, 169 F. Supp. 2d 1181, 1192 (N.D. Cal. 2001).

80. Ibid.

81. Ibid. at 1194.

82. Ibid.

83. Brief for Appellants, *Yahoo!, Inc. v. La Ligue contre le Racisme et l'Antisemitisme*, Case No. 01-17424 (9th Cir., filed March 22, 2002), p. 19.

84. Article 23 of the Press Law of 1881, as amended, prohibits making "an apology of . . . war crimes, crimes against humanity or crimes or misdemeanours of collaboration with the enemy" using "any means of audio-visual communication."

85. Tribunal Correctionnel de Paris, *L'Amicale des Deportes d'Auschwitz v. Yahoo!*, www.foruminternet.org/telechargement/documents/tgi-par20020226.pdf (February 26, 2002).

86. Ibid.

87. Ibid.

88. Council of Europe, Draft of the First Additional Protocol of the Convention on Cybercrime Concerning the Criminalisation of Acts of a Racist or Xenophobic Nature Committed through Computer Systems, March 26, 2002, www.coe.int/T/E/ Legal%5Faffairs/Legal%5Fco%2Doperation/Combating%5Feconomic%5Fcrime/ Cybercrime/Racism_on_internet/PC-RX(2002)15E.pdf.

89. Ibid., paragraph 31.

90. *West Virginia State Bd. of Educ. v. Barnette*, 319 U.S. 624, 641 (1943).

91. John Larkin, "Behind the Tyrant's Mask," *Far Eastern Economic Review*, May 2, 2002, www.feer.com/articles/2002/0205_02/p012region.html.

92. Lech Walesa, foreword to *War of the Black Heavens: The Battles of Western Broadcasting in the Cold War* by Michael Nelson (Syracuse, N.Y.: Syracuse University Press, 1997), p. xi.

93. Ibid., p. 24.

94. Goldsmith, "Yahoo! Brought to Earth."

Chapter 9

1. See, for example, United Nations Universal Declaration of Human Rights, Article 19; European Convention for the Protection of Human Rights and Fundamental Freedoms, Article 10.

2. High Court of Australia 56, December 10, 2002, available online at http:// www.austlii.edu.au/au/cases/cth/high_ct/2002/56.html.

3. The site for the litigation is, of course, important to plaintiffs not only for the convenience of the forum but to obtain the benefit of laws under which recovery is dramatically easier than in the United States. Australia's defamation laws, like those of the United Kingdom, are far more plaintiff-friendly than those of the United States.

4. Ibid., paragraph 26.

5. Ibid., paragraph 44.

6. Ibid., paragraph 54.

7. T.G.I. Paris, November 20, 2000, 6 ILR (P&F) 434. An English translation of the case also is available at www.cdt.org/speech/international/001120yahoofrance.pdf.

8. Those with an interest in the broader issues underlying this case may wish to see Joel R. Reidenberg, "Yahoo! and Democracy on the Internet," *Jurimetrics* (American Bar Association, Section on Science and Technology) (Spring 2002).

9. The message, translated from French, stated as follows: "Lastly, if in the context of a search made on www.yahoo.fr based on a tree structure, key words, the results of this search were to lead to sites, pages or chats the title and/or the content of which constitute a breach of French law, in particular due to the fact that Yahoo! France cannot control the content of these sites and external sources (including the content referenced on other Yahoo! sites and services around the world), you should cease your consultation of the site concerned on penalty of incurring the sanctions applicable under French law or of having to respond to lawsuits brought against you."

10. In particular, the panel focused on "Internet protocol addresses," the unique identifiers used by each computer that accesses the Internet. IP addresses often—

but do not always—reflect the geographic origin of the computer that is attempting to access a Web site. By blocking access to IP addresses assumed to be of French origin and taking a few other measures, the panel found that some 90 percent of French nationals could, in fact, be blocked from accessing content that violates French law. (IP addresses are not a perfect mechanism for blocking access because a sophisticated user can configure a computer to utilize an IP address from a different geographic area.)

11. For a discussion of the case, see Steve Kettmann, "German Hate Law: No Denying It," http://www.wired.com/news/politics/0,1283,40669,00.html, and Weisman, "Germany Bans Foreign Web sites for Nazi Content," www.newsfactor.com/perl/story/6063.html. German law contains several provisions that address speech offenses. A section on "incitement of the people" criminalizes incitement to violence by appeals to racial or ethnic hatred. A section on "incitement to racial hatred" criminalizes the display of "documents which incite racial hatred" or depict violence against humanity in a positive light. A section on "slander on confessions, religious groups and association of world views," criminalizes slandering the views of religious groups in an attempt to breach the peace. Another provision includes a prohibition against the *Auschwitlfüge*, the denial of the Holocaust, and denigrating the memory of the dead.

12. The Web site that is the subject of the prosecution may be accessed at http://www.adelaideinstitute.org/.

13. A translation from German of the arrest warrant issued against Mr. Toben published on a revisionist Web site may be accessed at http://www.ihr.org/other/990409warrant.html.

14. See Cass., closed session, December 27, 2000, n. 4741, V (English translation available at http://www.cdt.org/speech/international/001227italiandecision.pdf). The names of the complainant or the Web sites involved in the attempted prosecution are not published in the court's decision.

15. See "Italian Police Shutter Sacrilegious Web Sites," *International Herald Tribune,* July 10, 2002, p. 6, available at http://www.iht.com/.

16. See "U.S. Citizen Becomes First Journalist Tried under Zimbabwe's New Press Law," *News Media Update* (Reporters Committee for Freedom of the Press), July 1, 2002. Some 10 domestic journalists have been prosecuted under the law as well, and a Zimbabwe journalist stands as a codefendant with Mr. Meldrum in the current prosecution in Harare.

17. See Geoffrey Robertson, "Mugabe Versus the Internet," *The Guardian,* June 17, 2002, available at http://www.guardian.co.uk/Archive/Article/0,4273,4435071,00.html.

18. Ibid., p. 2.

19. See "American Reporter in Zimbabwe Acquitted But Ordered Deported," *Media Law Letter* (Media Law Resource Center), July 2002, p. 55.

20. The E-Commerce Directive pertains too much more than simply jurisdiction, and many of the other issues resolved by that directive are of interest to U.S. and European Internet publishers. Four other major provisions of that directive deal with the following issues:

> *Online Service Provider Liability* (Article 12). Where a service provider is a mere conduit for materials posted by someone else and does not initiate the transmission, select the recipient, or modify the information, the service provider will not be liable. This limitation on liability covers service providers that (1) transmit information provided by a user or (2) provide access to a communications network.

Caching (Article 13). Where a service provider conducts automatic, intermediate and temporary storage of information for the sole purpose of making the transmission of such information more efficient, the provider is not liable if it (1) does not modify the information; (2) complies with conditions on accessing the information; (3) complies with industry standards for updating the information; (4) does not interfere with technology used to obtain data on information use; and (5) removes information or makes it inaccessible after obtaining notice that the information has been removed from its initial location on the network, that access to it has been disabled, or that a competent authority has ordered that the information be removed or access to it restricted.

Hosting (Article 14). Where a service provider stores information at the request of a user, the service provider would not be liable if it does not have "actual knowledge" of illegal activity or, in the case of a claim for damages, is not aware of facts or circumstances from which illegal activity is apparent. To qualify for this limitation on liability, the provider, upon obtaining such knowledge, must promptly remove the illegal materials or block access to them.

No monitoring (Article 15). Member States are prohibited from imposing on service providers that operate as a mere conduit, or engage in caching or storage, any general obligation to monitor information transmitted or stored. Member States likewise cannot impose a general obligation on service providers to "actively seek" facts or circumstances indicating illegal activity.

21. E-Commerce Directive, recital 22.

22. For a description of this proposal, see Media Law Resource Center, "Response to the European Commission's Consultation on a Preliminary Draft Proposal for a Council Regulation on the Law Applicable to Non-Contractual Obligations," available online at http://www.europa.eu.int/comm/justice_home/unit/civil/consultation/contributions/mlrc_en.pdf.

23. http://curia.eu.int/common/recdoc/convention/en/c-textes/brux-idx.htm.

24. http://ananse.irv.uit.no/trade_law/doc/ED.Applicable.Law.Contracts.1980.html.

25. On November 3, 1998, the Consumer Affairs Council of Ministers adopted a resolution on consumer protection in the Information society. The resolution is available online at http://europa.eu.int/comm/dg24/library/legislation/ap/ap01_en.html.

26. See "Consultation for a Preliminary Draft Proposal for a Council Regulation on the Law Applicable to Non-Contractual Obligations," available online at http://www.europa.eu.int/comm/dg24/library/legislation/ap/ap01_en.html.

27. For a synthesis of the comments that were filed, and links to the comments of each party, please see http://www.europa.eu.int/comm/justice_home/unit/civil/consultation/contributions_en.htm.

28. See, for example, *International Shoe Co. v. Washington,* 326 U.S. 310 (1945); *World-Wide Volkswagen Corporation v. Woodson,* 444 U.S. 286 (1980).

29. The same section of the Restatement provides that a U.S. court may not enforce a foreign judgment where the foreign court was without jurisdiction to adjudicate under the principles of § 421. However, jurisdiction in this analysis means jurisdiction in accordance with the law of the foreign country. See § 421(b) and Comment c. The argument outlined in the text does not assert that the foreign court was without

jurisdiction but that the jurisdiction it in fact exercised failed to comport with due process of law.

30. Note that the enforceability of foreign judgments is determined on the basis of state law. See 13 A.L.R. Fed. 208 (1972). States provide for such enforcement under the Uniform Foreign Money-Judgments Act. Federal cases have often relied on principles of comity as the rationale for enforcement. See, for example, *Hilton v. Guyot*, 159 U.S. 113 (1895).

31. See, for example, Maryland's Uniform Foreign-Money Judgments Recognition Act of 1962 and the Uniform Enforcement of Foreign Judgments Act of 1964, at Md. Code Ann., Cts. & Jud. Proc. § 10–703.

32. See, for example, *Tahan v. Hodgson*, 662 F.2d 862 (D.C. Cir. 1981) (enforcing Israeli default judgment though process served upon defendant while in Jerusalem was in Hebrew).

33. 877 F. Supp. 1 (D.D.C. 1995) (answering question certified from the D.C. Circuit Court of Appeals), 1998 U.S. App. LEXIS 556 (D.C. Cir. May 5, 1998), conforming to judgment of Maryland Court of Appeals, 702 A.2d 230 (Md. 1997).

34. The court noted that the judgment did not require the plaintiff to prove falsehood; that the judge had instructed the jury to disregard context in contravention of *Moldea v. New York Times Co.*, 22 F.3d 310 (D.C. Cir. 1994); and that the judgment did not rest upon a finding of actual malice, in contravention of *New York Times v. Sullivan*. See *Matusevich v. Telnikoff*, 877 F. Supp. 1.

35. Ibid., p. 4.

36. 169 F. Supp. 2d 1181 (N.D. Cal. 2001).

37. Case No. C00-21275 JF, Complaint at 10, available at http://www.cdt.org/speech/international001221yahoocomplaint.pdf.

38. *Yahoo! Inc. v. La Ligue Contre Le Racisme et L'Antisemitisme*, Case No. 00-21275 JF (N.D. Cal. June 7, 2001), available at http://www.cdt.org/jurisdiction/010607yahoo.pdf.

39. 1994 WL 419847 (S.D.N.Y. May 4, 1994).

40. Ibid.

41. 154 Misc. 2d 228 (N.Y. Sup. Ct. 1992).

42. Ibid., p. 235; see also *Ellis v. Time, Inc.*, 1997 WL 863267 (D.D.C. November 18, 1997).

43. 719 F. Supp. 670 (N.D. Ill. 1989).

44. 83 F.R.D. 574 (D. Haw. 1979).

45. Ibid.

46. Ibid., p. 580.

47. See T. Leatherbury, "Modified ALI Proposal on International Judgments Still Troubling to First Amendment Advocates," *MLRC Media Law Letter*, January 2003, p. 5.

48. International Covenant for Civil and Political Rights, December 16, 1966, 999 U.N.T.S. 171.

49. European Convention for the Protection of Human Rights, Art. 10.

50. See, for example, *The Sunday Times v. United Kingdom*, 14 Eur. H.R. Rep. 229, para. 45 (1992).

51. *Matusevich v. Telnikoff*, 877 F.Supp. 4 (quoting *Gatley on Libel and Slander*, ed. M. A. Philip Lewis [London: Sweet and Maxwell, 1981]).

52. Ibid., (quoting Colin Duncan and Brian Neill, *Duncan and Neill on Defamation* (London: Butterworths, 1983), p. 51; see also Julie A. Scott-Bayfield, *Defamation Law and Practice* (London: Sweet and Maxwell, 1996).

53. *Ellis*, 1997 WL 863267 at *12.

54. See Restatement (Third) of the Foreign Relations Law of the United States § 402 and comment a.

55. United Nations Declaration on the Inadmissibility of Intervention in the Domestic Affairs of States and the Protection of their Independence and Sovereignty, A/RES/2131 (January 14, 1996).

56. Restatement (Third) of the Foreign Relations Law of the United States § 421 and comment a.

57. The Conference on Private International Law, established in 1893, meets two or three times each year at the Hague to negotiate and draft multilateral treaties, or conventions, in the field of private international law.

58. See generally Proposed Hague Convention on Jurisdiction and Foreign Judgments in Civil and Commercial Matters, available online at http://www.hcch.net/e/workprog/jdgm.html (hereinafter "Proposed Convention").

59. See Khoi D. Nguyen, Note, "Invisibly Radiated: Federalism Principles and the Proposed Hague Convention on Jurisdiction and Foreign Judgments," *Hastings Constitutional Law Quarterly* 28 (2000): 145, 149.

60. Anandashankar Mazumdar, "Jurisdiction Diplomatic Conference Draws Out Problems Implicated by Proposed Jurisdiction Treaty," Bureau of National Affairs, June 27, 2001, http://lists.essential.org/pipermail/hague-jur-commercial-law/2001-June/00133.html.

61. Shelley Souza, "Outside The Box: A Fundamentalist Internet?" Optionetics.com, June 22, 2001, http://biz.yahoo.com/opt/010622/pomdnrwgzaguhj8a_h_fba.html.

62. Proposed Convention, Art. 10.

63. Although it is possible to restrict one's Internet audience, it is difficult and expensive to limit access to Web pages to people located in particular states.

64. Proposed Convention, Art. 23(a).

65. Ibid., Art. 25.

66. Ibid.

67. Ibid.

68. Ibid., Art. 28.

69. See "Tied up in Knots," *The Economist*, June 9, 2001 ("Different interest groups within each country would like the convention to be modified in different ways.").

70. Boris Grondahl, "Your Court or Mine?," *Industry Standard Magazine*, June 25, 2001.

71. Kingshuk Nag, "And Now a Net Dispute Redressal System," *The Times of India*, June 25, 2001, available online at http://www.timesofindia.com.

72. Souza.

73. Billy Tauzin, Statement on Impediments to Digital Trade, Hearings before the 107th Congress House Subcommittee on Commerce, Trade, and Consumer Protection, May 22, 2001.

74. See, for example, Grondahl; Lisa M. Bowman, "Global Treaty—Threat to the Net?" *Interactive Week*, June 22, 2001.

75. TACD Resolution on the Proposed Hague Convention on Jurisdiction and Foreign Judgments in Civil and Commercial Matters, Doc. No. Ecom-22-01, May 2001.

76. Ibid.

77. See Grondahl.

78. See "Tied up In Knots."

79. In preparation for the Diplomatic Session, several informal meetings were held, four special commissions convened, expert meetings on intellectual property and e-commerce occurred in Geneva and Ottawa, and a preliminary draft convention was drawn up in October 1999.

80. French Court Imposes Speech Restrictions beyond Its Borders, November 20, 2000, Center for Democracy and Technology, http://www.cdt.org/jursidiction.

81. James Love, "Hague Diplomatic Conference Ends, Badly for Now," Notes on Information Policy issues from CPT, June 20, 2001, http://legalminds.lp.findlaw.com/list/info-policy-notes/msg00124.html.

82. Dan Gilmore, "Hague Convention Could Be Big Risk to Corporate Rights," *San Jose Mercury News*, May 31, 2001, p. D6.

83. Ibid.

84. Ibid.

85. See Tauzin.

86. See Mazumdar.

87. Ibid.

88. In preparation for part two, the Commission on General Affairs and Policy will meet early in 2002. The conference members decided that intense consultations should begin immediately to prepare for the meeting, evaluating whether the conditions necessary for negotiations to successfully conclude have been met.

89. See Grondahl.

90. See Kevin M. Clermont, "Jurisdictional Salvation and the Hague Treaty," *Cornell Law Review* 85 (1999): 89, 130.

Chapter 10

I am indebted to Kate Crawford for helpful comments and research assistance.

1. Janet E. Moran and Jeffrey Kummer, *U.S. and International Taxation of the Internet*, 712 Practising Law Institute, Patents, Copyrights, Trademarks, and Literary Property Course Handbook Series 405 (2002).

2. See, for example, Robert J. Cline and Thomas S. Neubig, "Masters of Complexity and Bearers of Great Burden: The Sales Tax System and Compliance Costs for Multistate Retailers," Ernst & Young, September 1999 (estimating compliance costs from 14 percent of taxes collected for large retailers to 87 percent for small retailers).

3. See, for example, Andrew Wagner and Wade Anderson, "Origin-Based Taxation of Internet Commerce," *State Tax Notes*, July 19, 1999, p.187; Terry Ryan and Eric Miethke, "The Seller-State Option: Solving the Electronic Commerce Dilemma," *State Tax Notes*, October 5, 1998, p. 881.

4. See Michael S. Greve, "E-Taxes: Between Cartel and Competition," AEI Federalist Outlook no. 8, September 2001, available at http://www.aei.org/publications/pubID.13124/pub_detail.asp; Aaron Lukas, "Tax Bytes: A Primer on the Taxation of Electronic Commerce," Cato Institute Trade Policy Analysis no. 9, December 17, 1999, 37–38; Jessica Melugin, "Internet Sales Taxation: Beyond the Moratorium," Competitive Enterprise Institute Policy Brief, March 28, 2000; and Adam D. Thierer, "E-Commerce: A Taxing Issue," March 23, 2000, http://www.heritage.org/Press/Commentary/ED032300a.cfm. For a thoughtful proposal for international origin-based e-commerce taxation see Shane Ham and Robert D. Atkinson, *A Third Way Framework for Global E-Commerce*, Progressive Policy Institute, March 2001.

5. See, for example, Andrew Wagner and Wade Anderson, "Proposal of an Origin-Based Tax Solution for the Possible Taxation of Digitized Products Sold Over the Internet," November 8, 1999, Testimony submitted to the Advisory Commission on Electronic Commerce, http://www.ecommercecommission.org/proposal.htm; Michael S. Greve, Testimony submitted to the U.S. Senate Committee on Finance on Internet Sales Taxation, August 1, 2001, http://www.senate.gov/%7Efinance/080101mgtest.pdf.

6. Perhaps the most sophisticated defense of a (limited) destination-based sales tax regime is Daniel Shaviro, *Federalism in Taxation: The Case for Greater Uniformity* (Washington: American Enterprise Institute, 1993).

7. Early in the e-commerce debate, proposals surfaced to nationalize sales taxes and to distribute the proceeds to the states. Those proposals, mercifully, have died a well-deserved death. Any form of joint state-federal taxation would eventually transform the states from autonomous actors into supplicants and administrators of federal largesse. That result cannot be in anyone's interest.

8. The origin principle is an efficient solution—in fact, the only efficient solution—for all contexts where contractual regimes promise to work best. In those contexts (such as the sale of goods and services), origin-based regulation will operate as a quasi-contractual default rule for cases in which the parties have failed to specify the choice of law. See Wolfgang Kerber, "Rechtseinheitlichkeit und Rechsvielfalt aus Oekonomischer Sicht," in *Systembildung und Systemluecken in Kerngebieten der Harmonisierung: Europaeisches Schuldvertrags- und Gesellschaftsrecht,* ed. Stefan Grundmann, (Tübingen: Mohr, 1999), p. 67. Questions involving harm to strangers—such as libel—pose more vexing jurisdictional questions, which are beyond the scope of this article.

9. OECD, Committee on Fiscal Affairs, "Electronic Commerce: Taxation Framework Conditions," Report presented to Ministers at the OECD Ministerial Conference, "A Borderless World: Realising the Potential of Electronic Commerce," Ottawa, 1998, p. 4, http://www.oecd.org/pdf/m000015000/m00015517.pdf.

10. Ibid., p. 5.

11. Organisation for Economic Co-operation and Development (OECD), "Taxation and Electronic Commerce: Implementing the Ottawa Taxation Framework Conditions," 2001, p. 26.

12. Ibid,. p. 20.

13. OECD, 2001, pp. 30, 37.

14. David Hardesty, "EU Withdraws Proposal for VAT on Digital Sales," Ecommercetax.com, http://www.ecommercetax.com/doc/o2o4o1.htm.

15. OECD, 2001, p. 6.

16. Ibid., pp. 32–33.

17. Ibid., pp. 20–21.

18. Ibid., p. 36.

19. Ibid., p. 37.

20. For a concise summary and discussion see Nigel Kempton and Taylor Wessing, "EU Tax Plan Will Affect Non-EU Suppliers," *World eBusiness Law Report* (September 12, 2002).

21. Moran and Kummer.

22. Many states tax certain kinds of services, such as utilities, hotels and restaurants, and amusement centers. But there is no *general* sales tax on services, and state attempts to introduce such a tax (for example, by Florida) have met with ferocious political

opposition. See, for example, Jon Nordheimer, "Florida Politicians Demoralized after Repeal of Services Tax," *New York Times*, December 12, 1987, p. A12. Services of the kind that are now often provided over the Internet are usually untaxed.

23. The e-tax debate is little more than a rehash of a similarly inconclusive scholarly and legislative debate that raged over mail-order sales during the 1980s. See, for example, Paul J. Hartmann, "Collection of the Use Tax on Out-of-State Mail-Order Sales," *Vanderbilt Law Review* 39 (1986): 993.

24. *Quill v. North Dakota*, 504 U.S. 298 (1992).

25. John C. Blase and John W. Westmoreland, "*Quill* Has Been Plucked! MTC States Are Slowly Eroding the Substantial Nexus Standard," *North Dakota Law Review* 73 (1997): 685.

26. Internet Tax Freedom Act, P.L. 105-277, 112 Stat. 2681-719 (1998) (codified at 47 U.S.C. para. 151). The act is mislabeled because it does not "free" Internet commerce from any tax that applies to comparable sales.

27. Christopher Swope, "States Approve Sales-Tax Pact," *Governing*, January 2003, p. 44.

28. Brian Krebs, "State Coalition Approves Internet Sales Tax Plan," *Washington Post*, TechNews, November 12, 2002.

29. Brian Krebs and Jonathan Krim, "Big Stores to Charge Sales Taxes Online: Retailers Agree to Collect for States," *Washington Post*, February 7, 2003.

30. Jon W. Abolins, Chief Tax Counsel and Vice President, TAXWARE International, Inc., Testimony to the House Judiciary Subcommittee on Commercial and Administrative Law, July 18, 2001 http://commdocs.house.gov/committees/judiciary/hju73964.000/hju73964_0f.htm, p. 65.

31. See, for example, Kendall L. Houghton and Walter Hellerstein, "State Taxation of Electronic Commerce: Perspectives on Proposals for Change and Their Constitutionality," *Brigham Young University Law Review* (2000): 9, 29–30 (describing unsuccessful simplification efforts).

32. See Shaviro.

33. See Janice C. Griffith, "State and Local Revenue Enhancement and Tax Policies in a Digital Age: E-Commerce Taxation, Business Tax Incentives, and Litigation Generated Revenues," *Urban Lawyer* 34 (2002): 429, 432–438 (arguing that even current, limited "streamlining" proposals pose a serious threat to local tax autonomy).

34. Penelope Lemov, "The Untaxables," *Governing Magazine*, July 2002.

35. See, for example, Houghton and Hellerstein; OECD, 2001, pp. 11, 18.

36. A small sample of McLure's stream of articles on the subjects includes the following: "Taxation of Electronic Commerce: Economic Objectives, Technological Constraints, and Tax Laws," *Tax Law Review* 52 (1997): 269; "Achieving Neutrality Between Electronic and Nonelectronic Commerce," *State Tax Notes* (July 19, 1999): 193, 197; "Radical Reform of the State Sales and Use Tax: Achieving Simplicity, Economic Neutrality, and Fairness," *Harvard Journal of Law and Technology* 13 (2000): 567; and "Rethinking State and Local Reliance on the Retail Sales Tax: Should We Fix the Sales Tax or Discard It?" *Brigham Young University Law Review* (2000): 77. When the idea of origin-based taxation received passing consideration by a congressionally appointed study commission, McLure mobilized 116 academics to urge strict adherence to destination-based taxation: "Appeal for Fair Taxation of Internet Commerce," available at http://www.law.wayne.edu/mcintyre/text/appeal%20with%20names%20jan%207.pdf.

37. Charles E. McLure, Jr., "Taxation of Electronic Commerce," p. 277, note 9 (1997) (responding to Walter Hellerstein, "Transaction Taxes and Electronic Commerce: Designing State Taxes That Work in an Interstate Environment," *National Tax Journal* 50 (1997): 593, 603 note 24; McLure, "Taxation of Electronic Commerce," p. 411 ("I plead guilty as charged, because I do not see any other way to achieve a satisfactory resolution to the problem of taxing electronic commerce.").

38. McLure, "Achieving Neutrality," p. 197.

39. McLure, "Taxation of Electronic Commerce," p. 400–01.

40. McLure, "Achieving Neutrality," p. 194 note 5.

41. McLure, to his credit, has acknowledged the point: "Taxation of Electronic Commerce," pp. 372–73. Local sales taxation operates on the point of sale (not the destination), not only intrastate but even when the parties are from different states. If I, as a Virginia resident, buy a lacrosse stick for my son on a business trip to North Carolina, I will be charged the North Carolina sales tax. If my son purchases the next stick from the same company, which has no store in Virginia, over the Internet or by phone or mail order, he (or more likely I) will not pay North Carolina tax. We will instead owe the Virginia use tax—technically speaking, since neither of us has ever paid or been asked to pay that tax. Under the existing and under the proposed, "simplified" system, it matters whether the stick came to me or I came to the stick. An origin-based system would harmonize the tax treatment.

42. See, for example, Houghton and Hellerstein, p. 54 (noting the "apparent elegance and simplicity" of origin-based taxation; rejecting the general proposal as flawed but potentially useful for taxing the sale of digital products to consumers).

43. The exception to this uncharitable characterization is aforementioned locational neutrality argument. As noted, however, the argument has played only a marginal role in the political debate. The argument has force only at a very theoretical level and, at that level, pushes toward a wholly centralized tax regime—a position that the governmental advocates of destination-based taxation neither wish to convey to the public nor, for the most part, actually hold. (Governments want to maximize their revenue authority under an intergovernmental tax cartel; they do not wish to *surrender* it.) Even as a purely theoretical matter, moreover, the argument is less than fully persuasive. The deadweight losses attendant to tax competition—relative to a neutral regime—look monstrously inefficient on a blackboard at MIT. In the real world, those losses may easily pale in comparison to the risks attendant to taxation by a central authority that is subject to no competitive discipline.

44. See, for example, Houghton and Hellerstein, p. 54.

45. In "Taxation of Electronic Commerce," p. 381, McLure comes close to conceding the point:

> To the extent that public services are provided primarily to households and are complementary to private consumption, it is appropriate to levy a tax on consumption . . . as a quasi-benefit tax; *to the extent they are provided primarily to business and are complementary to production, a production-based tax (such as an origin-based VAT) would be more appropriate.* While there is no easy answer to this question, *I believe* that consumption-based taxes levied under the destination principle are more appropriate. *If this is true,* tax should be applied to all sales to consumers in a given state . . . (emphases added).

46. The source of the term and the theory of a "political residuum" is James M. Buchanan, "Federalism and Fiscal Equity," *American Economic Review* 40 (1950): 583.

451

47. For a cogent exposition see Douglas Laycock, "Equal Citizens of Equal and Territorial States: The Constitutional Foundations of Choice of Law,"*Columbia Law Review* 92 (1992): 249.

48. See, for example, *Saenz v. Roe*, 526 U.S. 489, 501–11 (1999) (Stevens, J.).

49. *Quill* explicitly overruled the holding of *National Bellas Hess, Inc. v. Dept. of Revenue of State of Illinois*, 386 U.S. 753 (1967), where the Supreme Court determined that the Due Process Clause provided a constitutional barrier, insurmountable by congressional legislation, to the imposition of tax obligations on sellers without a nexus to the taxing jurisdiction.

50. For a terrific exposition of the notion of "sovereignty" underlying these paragraphs see Jeremy Rabkin, *Why Sovereignty Matters* (Washington: American Enterprise Institute, 1998).

51. The United Nations proposal for an international tax organization can be found at http://www.un.org/esa/ffd/a55-1000.pdf. For a sharp critique see Dan Mitchell, "United Nations Seeks Global Tax Authority," *Prosperitas*, August 2001, http://www.freedomandprosperity.org/Papers/un-report/un-report.shtml. For examples of academic support, see Jack M. Mintz, "The Role of Allocation in a Globalized Corporate Income Tax," Working Paper no. 98-134, International Monetary Fund, 1998, p. 36; and Vito Tanzi, *Taxation in an Integrating World* (Washington: Brookings Institutition, 1995), p. 140. For a similar suggestion in the context of e-commerce transaction taxes see also and predictably McLure, "Taxation of Electronic Commerce," p. 393 (international tax cooperation "must include the possibility of sanctions against nations that provide a hospitable setting for those who desire to operate in a sheltered environment in order to avoid taxes on their sales and income.")

52. Stephen Weatherill and Paul Beaumont, 3rd ed. *EU Law*, 788–90 (London: Penguin Books, 1999).

53. See Bruce H. Kobayashi and Larry E. Ribstein, "A Recipe for Cookies: State Regulation of Consumer Marketing Information," *Emory Law Journal* 51 (2002): 1.

54. Ryan and Miethke p. 883 note 11.

55. The Mobile Telecommunications Sourcing Act, P.L. 106-252, 114 Stat. 626, 628–629 (2000), codified at 4 U.S.C. para. 119(a)(2)(C), 120(b)(1) (providing for taxation of mobile telecommunications services at customer's address, regardless of the actual origin or destination of a call).

56. The expectation that such average reciprocity would *not* prevail is a central reason for the existing, destination-based sales and use tax system. In the 1930s, when that system came into being, "consumer" states feared that "producer" states would reap all the advantages from an origin-based system, thus leaving stranded the states that were most in need of revenues (Ryan and Miethke, p. 888). That concern, however, is misplaced in a modern economy where few goods are sold at their place of production.

57. Compare *Goldberg v. Sweet*, 488 U.S. 252 (1989) (sustaining state excise tax on interstate telecommunications on, inter alia, reciprocity grounds).

58. The proposal may seem constitutionally problematic, since the participating states would in some sense "discriminate" among their sister states. (They would in effect abolish their domestic use tax for goods from some states but not all states.) The Supreme Court has held that reciprocity agreements among states—unlike true state compacts of the SSTP variety, which would require the transfer of state authority to a permanent interstate body—do not require congressional consent under the Compact Clause of Article I, Section 10 of the Constitution. (The correct reason for

this doctrine, although not the reason articulated by the Supreme Court, is that reciprocity agreements eliminate obstacles to interstate commerce, whereas compacts impede or restrict it. See Michael S. Greve, "Compacts, Cartels, and Congressional Consent", *Missouri Law Review*_____ (2003):_____. See also *General Express Ways, Inc. v. Iowa Reciprocity Bd.*, 163 N.W. 2d 413, 420 (Iowa 1968) (so holding). The question of whether *selective* reciprocity agreements pass constitutional muster is more difficult. The Supreme Court has struck down one such agreement under the Commerce Clause: *Sporhase v. Nebraska*, 458 U.S. 941 (1982). For reasons beyond the scope of this article, I am inclined to think that *Sporhase* is both wrong and distinguishable. In any event, it is undisputed that Congress may permit states to conclude such agreements: *Northeast Bancorp v. Board of Governors of the Federal Reserve System*, 472 U.S. 159 (1985).

Chapter 11

1. Samuel D. Warren and Louis D. Brandeis, "The Right to Privacy," *Harvard Law Review* 4 (1890): 193.

2. 277 U.S. 438 (1928).

3. Ibid., pp. 478–79 (Brandeis, J., concurring).

4. 389 U.S. 347 (1967).

5. Ibid., p. 351.

6. Ibid., p. 361 (Harlan, J., concurring).

7. *Terry v. Ohio*, 392 U.S. 1, 9 (1968); *Smith v. Maryland*, 442 U.S. 735, 740 (1979).

8. *Whalen v. Roe*, 429 U.S. 589 (1977).

9. *Restatement (Second) of Torts* § 652B.

10. Ibid., § 652D.

11. Ibid., § 652E.

12. *Time, Inc. v. Hill*, 385 U.S. 374, 387–88 (1967).

13. *Cantrell v. Forest City Publishing Company*, 419 U.S. 245 (1974).

14. 5 U.S.C. §§ 552a(e)(1)–(5) (1988).

15. Ibid., § 552a(t)(2).

16. Ibid., § 552(a)(b)(1)–(12).

17. 15 U.S.C. §§ 1681–1681t, 1681b(a), 1681a(d) (1994).

18. Department of Defense Appropriations Act, 1997, H.R. 3610, 104th Cong., 2d sess. §§ 2401–2422 (September 30, 1996) (codified at 15 U.S.C. §§ 1681–1681t (Supp. 1997)).

19. William Safire, "Nosy Parker Lives," *New York Times*, September 23, 1999, p. A29.

20. Federal Trade Commission, "Individual Reference Services: A Report to Congress," 1997, http://www.ftc.gov/bcp/privacy/wkshp97/irsdoc1.htm.

21. See http://www.networkadvertising.org/.

22. Federal Trade Commission, "Online Profiling: A Report to Congress," 2000, http://www.ftc.gov/os/2000/06/onlineprofilingreportjune2000.pdf; Federal Trade Commission, "Online Profiling: A Report to Congress—Part 2: Recommendations," 2000, http://www.ftc.gov/os/2000/07/onlineprofiling.pdf; Network Advertising Initiative, "Self-Regulatory Principles for Online Preference Marketing by Network Advertisers," http://www.ftc.gov/os/2000/07/NAI percent207-10 percent20Final. pdf, accessed on October 30, 2002.

23. Federal Trade Commission, "Privacy Online: A Report to Congress," 1998, pp. 23, 27–28, http://www.ftc.gov/reports/privacy3/priv-23a.pdf.

24. The Children's Online Privacy Protection Act of 1998, Pub. L. No. 105-277, 112 Stat. 2681 (1998).

25. Federal Trade Commission, "Privacy Online: Fair Information Practices in the Electronic Marketplace—A Report to Congress," 2000, p. 11, http://www.ftc.gov/reports/privacy2000/privacy2000.pdf.

26. Ibid., p. 4.

27. 15 U.S.C. § 45(a)(1).

28. *GeoCities*, Docket No. C-3849, February 12, 1999, http://www.ftc.gov/os/1999/9902/9823015d&o.htm.

29. S. 2201, 107th Cong., 2d sess. (2002), http://frwebgate.access.gpo.gov/cgi-bin/getdoc.cgi?dbname = 107_cong_bills&docIbid = f:s2201rs.txt.pdf.

30. Darrell M. West, "Assessing E-Government: The Internet, Democracy, and Service Delivery by State and Federal Governments," 2000, http://www.brown.edu/Departments/Taubman_Center/polreports/ egovtreport00.html, Security, Privacy, and Disability Access.

31. Gramm-Leach-Bliley Financial Services Modernization Act, 106 Pub. L. No. 102, 113 Stat. 1338 (1999).

32. Standards for Privacy of Individually Identifiable Health Information, 65 Fed. Reg. 82,462 (2000) (HHS, final rule) (to be codified at 45 C.F.R. pt. 160, §§ 164.502, 164.506), http://www.hhs.gov/ocr/hipaa/finalreg.html.

33. Standards for Privacy of Individually Identifiable Health Information, 67 Fed. Reg. 43,181 (2002) (HHS, final rule) (to be codified at 45 C.F.R. pt. 160, §§ 164.502, 164.506), http://www.hhs.gov/ocr/hipaa/privrulepd.pdf. The unofficial text of the final rule as amended may be found at http://www.hhs.gov/ocr/combinedregtext.pdf.

34. Texas Health & Safety Code § 181.001.

35. Pub. L. No. 103-322, 108 Stat. 2099-2102 (1994) (codified at 18 U.S.C. § 2721 (1997)).

36. Department of Transportation and Related Agencies Appropriations Act, 2000, § 350, 106, Pub. L. No. 69, 113 Stat. 986 (1999).

37. Bill 204, Family Privacy Protection Act of 2002 (codified at S.C. Code §§ 30-2-10 to 30-2-30).

38. Directive 95/46/EC of the European Parliament and of the Council on the Protection of IndivIbiduals with Regard to the Processing of Personal Data and on the Free Movement of Such Data (Eur. O.J. 95/L281), http://europa.eu.int/smartapi/cgi/sga_doc?smartapi!celexapi!prod!CELEXnumdoc&lg = EN&numdoc = 31995L0046&model = guichett.

39. Ibid., Art. 2(b).

40. Ibid., Art 2(a).

41. Ibid., Art. 3(2).

42. Ibid., Art. 7.

43. Ibid., Art. 8.

44. Ibid., Art. 11(1).

45. Ibid., Art. 22.

46. Ibid., Art. 26(1).

47. Phyllis Schlafly, Testimony, Hearing on Financial Privacy and Consumer Protection before the Committee on Banking, Housing, and Urban Affairs, U.S. Senate,

September 19, 2002, available online at http://banking.senate.gov/02_09hrg/091902/schlafly.htm.

48. IBM Multi-National Consumer Privacy Survey, 1999, p. 22.

49. Federal Trade Commission, "Workshop on the Information Marketplace: Merging and Exchanging Consumer Data," March 31, 2001 (comments of Ted Wham), http://www.ftc.gov/bcp/workshops/infomktplace/transcript.htm.

50. "Briefs," *Circulation Management*, May 1999 (referring to the U.S. Postal Service's Household Diary Study, 1997).

51. Brief for Petitioner and Interveners, pp. 15–16, *U.S. West, Inc. v. Federal Communications Commission*, 182 F.3d 1224 (10th Cir. 1999), *cert. denied* 528 U.S. 1188 (2000).

52. Star Systems, "Financial Privacy: Beyond Title V of Gramm-Leach-Bliley," 2002, p. 9, www.star=systems.com/privacy.pdf.

53. IBM Multi-National Consumer Privacy Survey, p. 22.

54. Board of Governors of the Federal Reserve System, Report to the Congress Concerning the Availability of Consumer Identifying Information and Financial Fraud, 1997, p. 2, http://www.federalreserve.gov/boarddocs/RptCongress/privacy.pdf.

55. Bill Pryor, "Protecting Privacy: Some First Principles," Remarks at the American Council of Life Insurers Privacy Symposium, July 11, 2000, p. 4.

56. Robert E. Nolan Company, Inc., *Common Components of Confidentiality Legislation—Cost and Impact Analysis*, 1999; Fitch IBCA, *HIPAA: Wake-Up Call for Health Care Providers*, 2000; Barbara Kirchheimer, "Report Predicts Huge HIPAA Price Tag," *Modern Healthcare*, October 2, 2000, p. 48.

57. Brief for Petitioner and Interveners, pp. 15–16.

58. Ernst & Young LLP, *Customer Benefits from Current Information Sharing by Financial Services Companies*, 2000, p. 16, http://www.privacyalliance.org/resources/glassman.pdf.

59. Robert W. Hahn, "An Assessment of the Costs of Proposed Online Privacy Legislation," 2001, http://www.activate.org/pubs/HahnStudy.pdf.

60. Michael A. Turner and Lawrence G. Buc, "The Impact of Data Restrictions on Fund-Raising for Charitable and Nonprofit Institutions," *Direct Marketing Association*, 2002, pp. 2–3.

61. Michael E. Staten and Fred H. Cate, "The Impact of Opt-In Privacy Rules on Retail Credit Markets: A Case Study of MBNA," _____ *Duke Law Journal* _____ (forthcoming 2003).

62. Edward M. Gramlich, Testimony on Financial Privacy before the Subcommittee on Financial Institutions and Consumer Credit of the Committee on Banking and Financial Services, U.S. House of Representatives, July 21, 1999.

63. Helena Gail Rubinstein, "If I Am Only for Myself, What Am I? A Communitarian Look at the Privacy Stalemate," *American Journal of Law and Medicine* 25 (1999): 203.

64. *U.S. West*, 182 F.3d 1239.

65. Timothy J. Muris, "Protecting Consumers' Privacy: 2002 and Beyond," Privacy 2001 Conference, October 4, 2001, http://www.ftc.gov/speeches/muris/privisp1002.htm.

66. Robert E. Litan, "Balancing Costs and Benefits of New Privacy Mandates," AEI-Brookings Joint Center for Regulatory Studies Working Paper 99-3, 1999, p. 11, http://aei.brookings.org/admin/pdffiles/phpi4.pdf.

67. "Final Report of the Federal Trade Commission Advisory Committee on Online Access and Security," 2000, p. 15, reprinted as an appendix to "Privacy Online," http://www.ftc.gov/acoas/papers/finalreport.htm.

68. Ibid., p. 4.

69. "Privacy Online" (Commissioner Swindle, dissenting).

70. David Aaron, Testimony, Hearing on the EU Data Protection Directive: Implications for the U.S. Privacy Debate before the Subcommittee on Commerce, Trade, and Consumer Protection of the Energy and Commerce Committee, U.S. House of Representatives, 107th Cong., March 8, 2001, http://frwebgate.access.gpo.gov/cgi-bin/getdoc.cgi?dbname = 107_house_hearings&docid = f:71497.pdf.

71. *Feist Publications, Inc. v. Rural Telephone Services Company*, 499 U.S. 340, 344–45, 349 (1991) (quoting *Harper & Row*, 471 U.S. 556).

72. Ibid., p. 349 (quoting *Harper & Row Publishers, Inc. v. Nation Enterprises*, 471 U.S. 539, 589 (1985) (Brennan, J., dissenting)) (citations omitted).

73. *Philadelphia Newspapers, Inc. v. Hepps*, 475 U.S. 767, 777 (1986).

74. *New York Times Company v. United States*, 403 U.S. 713 (1971).

75. *Landmark Communications, Inc. v. Virginia*, 435 U.S. 829 (1978).

76. *Smith v. Daily Mail Publishing Company*, 443 U.S. 97 (1979).

77. *Florida Star v. B.J.F.*, 491 U.S. 524 (1989); *Cox Broadcasting Corp. v. Cohn*, 420 U.S. 469 (1975).

78. *Martin v. Struthers*, 319 U.S. 141 (1943).

79. *Lamont v. Postmaster General*, 381 U.S. 301 (1965).

80. *Denver Area Educational Telecommunications Consortium, Inc. v. Federal Communications Commission*, 518 U.S. 727 (1996).

81. *U.S. West, Inc. v. Federal Communications Commission*, 182 F.3d 1224, 1239 (10th Cir. 1999), *cert. denied* 528 U.S. 1188 (2000).

82. *Bartnicki v. Vopper*, 532 U.S. 514, 526 note 21 (2001) (quoting *Time, Inc. v. Hill*, 385 U.S. 374, 388 (1967) (quoting *Thornhill v. Alabama*, 310 U.S. 88, 102 (1940)).

83. "ASPs Warn: EU Data Protection Laws Fail to Keep Pace with Technology," *Business Wire*, March 6, 2001.

84. Hearing on the EU Data Protection Directive (statement of Jonathan Winer).

85. Consumers International, "Privacy@net: An International Comparative Study of Consumer Privacy on the Internet," 2001, p. 6, http://consumersint.eval.poptel.org.uk/document_store/Doc30.pdf.

86. Letter from the Dutch Minister of Justice to the Dutch Parliament on the review of the data protection directive, October 23, 2002.

87. Data Protection Directive (95/46/EC) Proposal for Amendment Made by Austria, Finland, Sweden, and the United Kingdom, Explanatory Note, para. 3, http://www.privacyinternational.org/intl_orgs/ec/dpd-proposed-amend-9-02.pdf.

88. Ibid., para. 4.

89. Ibid., para. 8.

Chapter 12

The author would like to thank Andrew Jay Schwartzman, President/CEO, Media Access Project; Professor Alan Feld, Boston University School of Law; Professor Milton Mueller, Syracuse University School of Informatin Studies; and Professor Lawrence Lessig, Stanford School of Law, for their invaluable help, criticism, and insight in preparing this chapter.

1. Presidential Directives on Electronic Commerce, Directive 5, cited in Department of Commerce: Relationship with the Internet Corporation for Assigned Names and Numbers, U.S. General Accounting Office, 2000, p.7 (hereafter "GAO 2000").

2. GAO 2000, p. 7.

3. The most exhaustive and informative studies can be found in Milton L. Mueller, *Ruling the Root: Internet Governance and the Taming of Cyberspace* (Cambridge, Mass.: MIT Press, 2002) (exhaustively tracing evolution of DNS management in framework of property rights regime) and A. Michael Froomkin, "Wrong Turn in Cyberspace: Using ICANN to Route around the APA and the Constitution," *Duke Law Journal* 50 (2000): 17 (analyzing the formation of ICANN in the context of the Non-Delegation Doctrine, the Administrative Procedure Act, and other relevant U.S. laws). Jonathan Weinberg, "ICANN and the Problem of Legitimacy," *Duke Law Journal* 50 (2000): 187 provides an excellent analysis from the perspective of one of the members of the U.S. government interagency working group that addressed the "DNS question" in 1997–98. For a "pro-ICANN" version of the evolution of ICANN, see Joe Sims and Cynthia Baurely, "A Response to Professor Froomkin: Why ICANN Does Not Violate the APA or the Constitution," *Journal of Small and Emerging Business Law* 6 (2002): 65. But see A. Michael Froomkin, "Form and Substance in Cyberspace," *Journal of Small and Emerging Business Law* 6 (2002): 109 (responding to *Sims and Baurely* and disagreeing with several key statements and conclusions).

4. Tamar Frankel, "The Managing Lawmaker in Cyberspace: A Power Model," *Brooklyn Journal of International Law* 27 (2002): 859, 878.

5. The root zone file, a database critical to matching domain names with the numeric addresses actually used by machines, is explained in more detail in the section describing "the root."

6. A "generic" top-level domain is not associated with a geographic region, unlike a "country code" or ccTLD (see note 7). Who may register in a "generic" TLD may still be restricted. For example, only organizations chartered by the United Nations may register in ".int." These restricted gTLDs are referred to as "sponsored" TLDs, with the sponsor responsible for policing the registration. See "ICANN: New TLD Program," available at http://www.icann.org/tlds (last viewed November 26, 2002).

7. The root server operators are an essential link in the DNS chain. They mirror the root zone file, distributing the load of DNS queries from one central computer— the "A Root" with the authoritative copy of the root zone file—to 12 other computers. These 12 field queries from individual networks looking to resolve unknown names. See Internet Management: Limited Progress on Privatization Project Makes Outcome Uncertain, General Accounting Office, 2002, pp. 19–20 (hereafter "GAO 2002").

8. Initially, the developers of the DNS intended to have only gTLDs. This led to complaints from Internet developers outside the United States. As a result, John Postel, the primary decisionmaker in the development of DNS pre-ICANN, decided to delegate country code TLDs. After some discussion within the DNS community, and desiring to avoid the thorny question of what constituted a country, the Internet Assigned Numbers Authority (IANA) (the formal vehicle through which Postel worked) decided to award every country or independent economy listed on the International Standards Organization list of two-letter country codes (the ISO-3166-1 list) a top-level registry corresponding to its two-letter country code. Nearly all of these delegations were made prior to the formation of ICANN. Before 1994, they were made through the informal process of John Postel selecting a "responsible person" in the Internet community of the relevant country. Subsequently, delegations were made by a more formal process (but over which Postel still exercised personal authority) in accordance with an Internet policy document called RFC 1591. See Mueller, *Ruling the Root*, pp. 88–89, 125–27.

9. The RIRs hold blocks of IP address space. They allocate these to large telecommunications carriers that provide Internet traffic transport. These "Tier 1" providers then allocate smaller blocks of address space to regional or "Tier 2" providers, and so on down the chain to individual network administrators. See Daniel Karrenberg, Gerard Ross, Paul Wilson, and Leslie Nobile, "Development of the Regional Internet Registry System," *The Internet Protocol Journal* (December 2001), available at http://www.cisco.com/warp/public/759/ipj_4_4/ipj_4_4_regional.html (last viewed November 26, 2002). The RIRs and other relevant Internet institutions are described in greater detail in the next sections.

10. As discussed below, the "payoff" for these parties is smooth functioning of those parts of the Internet that require some coordination and regular database updates (described below as the "IANA function") and freedom from direct government regulation. Because the relevant parties have become suspicious of ICANN's ability to deliver either of these benefits, they have declined to enter agreements.

11. Stuart Lynn, "President's Report: ICANN—The Case for Reform," February 24, 2002, available at http://www.icann.org/general/lynn_reform_proposal_24feb02.htm (last viewed November 26, 2002).

12. See "New Bylaws Adopted October 31 in Shanghai," available at http://www.icann.org/minutes/minutes_appa_31oct02.htm (last viewed November 26, 2002).

13. "RIR Blueprint for Evolution and Reform of Internet Address Management," October 10, 2002, available at http://www.ripe.net/ripencc/about/regional/nrr_blueprint_20021009.html (last viewed November 26, 2002) (proposing alternative structure for ICANN address policy development centered in RIRs).

14. See David Post, "Nominet Speaks Out on ccTLD Policy Development Process," ICANNWatch, November 19, 2002, available at http://www.icannwatch.org/article.php?sid=1024&mode=thread &order=0 (last visited November 26, 2002) (suggestion by .uk ccTLD registry that ccTLDs must continue to explore alternatives to ICANN).

15. It is unclear who regulates IP address allocations and ccTLD registries. Countries have advanced various claims of sovereignty over "their" names. This argument lacks a valid historical basis since, as described below, the initial system of address allocation was both private and voluntary. Claims to regulate RIRs and root server operators have even shakier foundations than claims for ccTLDs, since there is no association with any sovereign entity.

16. Unless otherwise indicated, the general source for how the DNS works on a technical level is GAO 2002, pp. 17–21, and Froomkin, "Wrong Turn in Cyberspace," pp. 37–49.

17. Frankel, "The Managing Lawmaker in Cyberspace," pp. 871–72.

18. As discussed below, ICANN's regulatory power derives from its ability to make changes to the root zone file. Froomkin, "Wrong Turn in Cyberspace," pp. 47–50.

19. Froomkin, "Wrong Turn in Cyberspace," p. 40. For general information regarding ccTLDs and their current relationships with their governments, see the ccTLD Governance Project, http://www.ccTLDinfo.com.

20. Mueller, *Ruling the Root*, pp. 78–79.

21. The exceptions: the .mil and .gov TLDs, operated by the U.S. military and the U.S. General Services Administration, respectively.

22. In March 2000, Verisign, Inc., acquired Network Solutions. References in this chapter to "Verisign" refer to Verisign, Inc., as the successor to Network Solutions.

23. Froomkin, "Wrong Turn in Cyberspace," pp. 57–59.

24. Froomkin, "Wrong Turn in Cyberspace," pp. 40, 54–56.

25. See generally Karrenberg et al.

26. Froomkin, "Wrong Turn in Cyberspace," p. 38.

27. Mueller, *Ruling the Root*, pp. 87–88.

28. ARIN, "About ARIN," available at http://www.arin.net/about_us/about.html (last viewed November 26, 2002). At the October 2002 ICANN meeting in Shanghai, ICANN blessed the formation by the RIRs of a new RIR for South and Central America, LACNIC. "IANA Report on Recognition of LACNIC," November 7, 2002. Available at http://www.iana.org/reports/lacnic_report_07nov02.htm (last viewed November 26, 2002).

29. The dynamics of the formation of the community around the DNS, notably the IANA, IETF, and ISOC, are chronicled in Mueller, *Ruling the Root*, at 73–140. A shorter description is found in Froomkin, "Wrong Turn in Cyberspace," pp. 51–59.

30. For the centrality of John Postel as trusted figure and the extent to which coordination of DNS was personalized in Postel as the head of the IANA, see Weinberg, "ICANN and Legitimacy," p. 204.

31. Froomkin, "Wrong Turn in Cyberspace," pp. 54–57. See generally, Mueller, *Ruling the Root*.

32. Mueller, *Ruling the Root*, pp. 161–62.

33. Weinberg, "ICANN and Legitimacy," p. 215.

34. Mueller, *Ruling the Root*, pp. 89–99.

35. Ibid., pp. 89–91, 94–96.

36. Ibid., pp. 96–98. The federal agencies funding DNS activities through 1997 acted through the Federal Networking Council (FNC). The FNC acted essentially as a clearinghouse and support mechanism for private policy development rather than as a means of creating federal policy. Ibid., pp. 99–101, 136–37.

37. Ibid., pp. 101–02.

38. Froomkin, "Wrong Turn in Cyberspace," pp. 57–59. As explained below, NSF transferred its contract to the Department of Commerce in 1997 when the Clinton administration began to take an active role in DNS policy.

39. Weinberg, "ICANN and Legitimacy," pp. 200–01; Mueller, *Ruling the Root*, pp. 127–30.

40. Mueller, *Ruling the Root*, pp. 126–140.

41. Ibid., pp. 129–40.

42. Unless otherwise noted, this section relies on Mueller, *Ruling the Root*, pp. 106–70. See also Frankel, "The Managing Lawmaker in Cyberspace," pp. 875–78.

43. See generally "Global Framework on Electronic Commerce," released by the Clinton administration on July 1, 1997, available at http://www.nyls.edu/cmc/papers/whgiifra.htm.

44. See Hobbes' Internet Timeline v5.6: 1995, "NSFNET Reverts Back to a Research Network, Main U.S. Backbone Traffic Now Routed through Interconnected Network Providers," available at http://www.zakon.org/robert/internet/timeline/#1990s (last viewed November 22, 2002).

45. Mueller, *Ruling the Root*, pp. 154–56.

46. Weinberg, "ICANN and Legitimacy," p. 205; Froomkin, "Wrong Turn in Cyberspace," pp. 61–62.

47. Mueller, *Ruling the Root*, p. 156; Weinberg, "ICANN and Legitimacy," p. 205; Froomkin, "Wrong Turn in Cyberspace," pp. 61–63.

48. See generally, Mueller, *Ruling the Root*, pp. 163–84; Frankel, "The Managing Lawmaker in Cyberspace," pp. 875–78, Froomkin, "Wrong Turn in Cyberspace," pp. 62–75; Weinberg, "ICANN and Legitimacy," pp. 200–12.

49. For example, angry protests from Latin American governments and network operators that the initial Board of ICANN did not contain representation from Latin America yielded a pledge of geographic diversity for the future but did not lead to any substantive change of the initial ICANN Board. See, for example, "Comments on Private Sector Proposals," available at http://www.ntia.doc.gov/ntiahome/domainname/proposals/comments/dns10698.htm (complaint regarding lack of Latin American representation).

50. National Telecommunications and Information Administration, "Management of Internet Names and Addresses," 63 Fed. Reg. 31741 (1998) (hereafter "White Paper").

51. The Department of Commerce has renewed this agreement annually after the original expiration. See Amendment 2 to Department of Commerce/ICANN Memorandum of Understanding (September 11, 2000); Amendment 4 (September 28, 2001); and Amendment 5 (September 20, 2002). These extensions have allowed the Department of Commerce to hedge on whether it will ever turn over full authority over the root zone file to ICANN. See GAO 2000, p. 25 (no plans to transfer authority); but see Department of Commerce Statement Regarding Extension of Memorandum of Understanding with ICANN, September 20, 2002 (indicating willingness to transfer authority after successful completion of tasks set forth in Memorandum of Understanding) (hereafter "Department of Commerce Renewal Statement") available at http://www.ntia.doc.gov/ntiahome/domainname/agreements/docstatement_09192002.htm.

52. The one arguable exception to this is the redelegation of the .us ccTLD. The Department of Commerce informed the ICANN of its selection, following which ICANN approved the delegation and forwarded the recommended change in the root to the Department of Commerce for approval and implementation. See Froomkin, "Form and Substance," p. 115. ICANN Statement, Redelegation of .us Country Code Top Level Domain, http://www.icann.org/announcements/announcement_19nov01.htm (last viewed November 26, 2002).

53. ICANN Bylaws, November 6, 1998, Article V, Section 5. Available at http://www.icann.org/general/archive_bylaws/bylaws_06nov98.htm (last viewed December 2, 2002).

54. Ibid., Article VII, Section 3(a).

55. White Paper, 63 Fed. Reg., p. 31743.

56. Ibid., 31746–47.

57. See Jonathan Weinberg, "ICANN, 'Internet Stability,' and New Top Level Domains," presented at the 29th Telecommunications Policy Research Conference, October 28, 2001; available at http://www.arxiv.org/abs/cs.CY/0109099.

58. White Paper, 63 Fed. Reg., p. 31747.

59. ICANN's bylaws required it to abide by the consensus decisions of the relevant "supporting organization," which supposedly distilled the consensus of relevant stakeholders. As demonstrated by Weinberg, this method generally resulted in "consensus" directives of such generality as to provide no constraint on the Board or staff of ICANN in implementing "consensus." Weinberg, "ICANN and Legitimacy," pp. 243–44. Indeed, ICANN's Board ultimately dropped even this vestige of "bottom up" decisionmaking. In March 2002, it determined that it, rather than the supporting

organization, was the ultimate arbiter of consensus and that the Board remained free to reject the "advice" of the relevant supporting organization if the Board felt that another policy would better serve the "Internet community." The bylaws and policies adopted as part of ICANN's reform drop the fiction that the support organizations develop policy and vest all decisionmaking power explicitly in the Board. See generally Tamar Frankel, "Accountability and Oversight of the Internet Corporation for Assigned Names and Numbers: Report to the Markle Foundation," July 12, 2002, available at http://www.markle.org/news/ICANN_fin1_9.pdf; Froomkin, "Form and Substance." Milton Mueller, "Why ICANN Can't," IEEE Spectrum (July 2002).

60. Weinberg, "ICANN and Legitimacy," pp. 235–37; Mueller, "Why ICANN Can't;" Milton Mueller, "Government and Country Names: ICANN's Transformation Into an Intergovernmental Regime," presented at the PTC 2002 Conference, January 2002, pp. 3–6. Available at http://istweb.syr.edu/~mueller/ (last viewed December 3, 2002).

61. Department of Commerce 2002 Renewal Statement (observing continuing failure to conclude contracts with root server operators, RIRs, and most ccTLD registries).

62. Froomkin, "Wrong Turn in Cyberspace," p. 89–93.

63. Ibid., pp. 73–74.

64. See, for example, Jim Wagner, "Some Say ICANN Loses Legitimacy," Internetnews.com, October 30, 2002; "World Wide Alliance of Top Level Domain Names: Communique from Shanghai Meeting," October 29, 2002 (establishing working group to determine alternative to ICANN) available at http://www.cctld.dnso.icann.org/communique/20021029.ccTLDshanghai_communique.html; RIR Blueprint for Evolution and Reform of Internet Address Management, October 2002 (proposing alternate ICANN reorganization plan) (hereafter "RIR Blueprint"). Available at http://www.ripe.net/ripencc/about/regional/nrr_blueprint_20021009.html

65. A record of ICANN's budgets, including the assessed fees, is available at http://www.icann.org/financials.

66. For the complaints of the RIRs, see Regional Internet Registries: The ICANN Reform Process, http://www.ripe.net/ripence/about/regional/icann_reform_20021001.html#4 (correspondence with ICANN setting forth complaints). For the ccTLD grievances, see Notes of ccTLD Meeting at Shanghai, October 27–28, available at http://www.wwtld.org/~shanghai/Shanghai_notes.html; ccTLD Response to the Committee on Evolution and Reform's Blueprint for ICANN Reform, June 25, 2002, available at http://www.wwtld.org/meetings/cctld/Bucharest2002/ccTLD_response_ERC.html

67. See Preliminary Report of ICANN Meeting, Montevideo, September 10, 2001, available at http://www.icann.org/minutes/prelim_report_10sep01.htm#01.92

68. See generally Frankel, "Accountability and Oversight;" Mueller, "Why ICANN Can't."

69. Frankel, "The Managing Lawmaker in Cyberspace," pp. 888–91.

70. ICANN Resolution 1.89, available at http://www.icann.org/minutes/prelim_report_10sep01.htm.

71. See Post.

72. See Milton Mueller, "Competing DNS Roots: Creative Destruction or Just Plain Destruction?" presented at the 29th Telecommunications Policy Research Conference, October 2001, p. 7.

73. See generally Mueller, "Competing DNS Roots." See also Stuart Lynn, "Discussion Draft: A Unique, Authoritative Root for the DNS," ICANN, May 2001; Internet

Architecture Board, "IAB Technical Comment on the Unique DNS Root," RFC 2826, Internet Society, May 2000.

74. See David Post, "ccTLD Update: ICANN Changes Root Entries for .at," ICANN-Watch, October 5, 2002, http://icannwatch.org/article.php?sid=971; David Post, "Zones, Roots, ccTLDs," ICANNWatch, September 23, 2002, http://icannwatch.org/article.php?sid=952; CENTR Comments on the ICANN AXFR Requirements for ccTLDs, June 25, 2002, http://www.centr.org/news/ICANN_AXFR.html.

75. See generally Notes of ccTLD Meeting at Shanghai, October 27–28, http://www.wwtld.org/~shanghai/Shanghai_notes.html; Proposed Resolution on Name Server Updates, September 13, 2002 (resolution introduced by ccTLDs to ICANN Names Council on failure of ICANN to properly administer the root), http://www.dnso.org/clubpublic/council/Arc11/msg00035.html.

76. Karenberg et al.

77. The Department of Commerce insisted in the White Paper that the entity to which it would award the root must have authority over names, IP numbers, and the root server operators. White Paper, 63 Fed. Reg. p. 31744. Accordingly, ICANN included this in its initial draft bylaws and has maintained it ever since.

78. Froomkin, "Form and Substance," pp. 119–21.

79. Froomkin, "Wrong Turn in Cyberspace," pp. 89–92. See also J. Beckwith Burr, David Johnson, and Susan Crawford, "When Consensus Doesn't Matter, and What Does," ICANNWatch, July 15, 2002, http://icannwatch.org/article.php?sid=859.

80. The DNSO is ICANN's policy development body for domain names (as opposed to policy on IP Addresses, the "Address Supporting Organization" or "ASO"). The DNSO consists of representatives of various "constituencies" recognized by ICANN and generally representing the interests present at ICANN's formation: the Business Constituency, the Intellectual Property Constituency, the ISP Constituency, the gTLD Constituency, the Registrar Constituency and the Noncommercial Constituency. As one might imagine, these constituencies have particular policy interests that are played out in policy formation without regard to technical merits. In the case of the Wait List Service, registrars, who ran a competing service, protested that Verisign remained dominant. End users such as the Business and Noncommercial constituencies supported price controls and other safety conditions on the service.

81. This is set forth in the minutes of the ICANN Shanghai Board meeting approving the Wait List Service, http://www.icann.org/minutes/minutes_23aug02.htm#02.100.

82. David McGuire, "Internet Registry Giants Want ICANN Heeled," *Washington Post*, August 1, 2002, (Verisign and major ccTLD registries submit a letter to the Department of Commerce urging it to restrain ICANN), available at http://www.washingtonpost.com/ac2/wp_dyn?pagename=article&node=&contentId=A31870_2002Aug1&notFound=true. A copy of the letter is available at http://www.verisign.org/corporate/policy/news/20020801DENIC.html.

83. Letter of Phillip L. Sbarbaro, Deputy General Counsel, Verisign, Inc., to Joe Sims, Counsel, ICANN, October 16, 2002 (objecting to conditions on WLS service and process). Available at http://www.icann.org/correspondence/sbarbaro_letter_to_sims_16oct02.htm.

84. See GAO 2002, pp. 15–16; Michael Froomkin, "House Members Are Losing Patience with ICANN," ICANNWatch, June 21, 2002, http://www.icannwatch.org/article.php?sid=821 (reprinting a letter from chairs and ranking members of relevant

congressional committee and subcommittee demanding closer supervision of ICANN by the Department of Commerce).

85. See generally Frankel, "The Managing Lawmaker in Cyberspace," pp. 901–02; Mueller, "Government and Country Names," pp. 5–10.

86. Frankel, "The Managing Lawmaker in Cyberspace," p. 890 note 88. Ultimately, South Africa agreed to include the current .za delegee as part of its new .za authority. Leslie Stones, "Selection Panel to Be Named Today for Internet Domain Authority," *Business Day (South Africa)*, November 22, 2002.

87. Bill Dong, "How China Censors the Net By Domain Name Hijacking," http://www.rense.com/general30/sase.htm (Operator of Voice of America Chinese Web site explains how China redirects Internet traffic). IDG News Service, "China Hacks Google's Domain Name," September 10, 2002, http://www.idg.net/ic_946304_4394_1_1681.html. Jonathon Storper, "Bringing the Internet to Others: Domain Names in Chinese, Japanese, and Korean Characters," http://www.hansonbridgett.com/publications/newsletters/TIPS/TIPS010101.html.

88. http://www.iana.org/cctld/cctld.htm. See also Mueller, "Governments and Country Names," pp. 5–7.

89. Mueller, "Governments and Country Names," pp. 7–10.

90. Letter of Stuart Lynn, President, ICANN, to Paul Twomey, Chair, Government Advisory Committee, July 5, 2002, available at http://www.icann.org/correspondence/lynn_to_twomey_05jul02.htm.

91. Recently, for example, Congress passed a law requiring the Department of Commerce to establish a ".kids" second-level domain within the .us ccTLD. See Dot Kids Implementation and Efficiency Act of 2002, Pub. L. No. _____. Congress took this step after ICANN failed to approve creation of a .kids gTLD when it approved new gTLD applications in November 2000. Congress initially proposed requiring a .kids gTLD, but ultimately yielded to requests from the Department of Commerce, ICANN, and other governments to refrain. House Report on Dot Kids Implementation and Efficiency Act of 2002, H.R. Rep. 107–449, 2002, pp. 6–7. This has caused some to consider this a victory for ICANN. This misses the point. While the U.S. Congress refrained from mandating a change to the global DNS in this instance, it indicated that it could, if sufficiently motivated, take unilateral action.

92. See Lynn.

93. GAC Statement on ICANN Reform, June 26, 2002, available at http://www.icann.org/committees/gac/statement_on_reform_26jun02.htm.

94. Department of Commerce 2002 Renewal Statement, http://www.ntia.doc.gov/ntiahome/domainname/agreements/docstatement_09192002.htm.

95. New Bylaws, adopted October 31, Article XI, Section 2.1, http://www.icann.org/minutes/minutes_appa_31oct02.htm#XI_2.1.

96. It is also possible that if ICANN's regulation of the namespace becomes overintrusive in ways that inconvenience significant numbers of users, a critical mass of network operators could voluntarily point to an "alternate root," either triggering disaster or rendering ICANN irrelevant. The likelihood of this, however, appears exceedingly remote.

97. http://www.icann.org/financials.

98. ICANN attempted to charge a $1 per name fee in 1999. Opposition from Congress caused ICANN to withdraw the plan. Frankel, "The Managing Lawmaker in Cyberspace," p. 884. As the current funding strategy demonstrates, however,

ICANN can achieve the same results by billing the registries rather than establishing a direct pass-through to consumers.

99. Frankel, "Accountability and Oversight;" Weinberg, "ICANN and Legitimacy," pp. 231–34 and note 239.

100. See generally Weinberg, "ICANN, 'Internet Stability,' and New Top Level Domains."

101. Compare the registry/registrar split with 47 U.S.C. Sec. 251 (requiring the FCC to develop an unbundled network elements scheme).

102. Froomkin, "Wrong Turn in Cyberspace," pp. 80–82. Mueller, *Ruling the Root*, pp. 188–89. Initially, Verisign was to have divested itself of either the registry or registrar operation. In 2001, however, ICANN and Verisign renegotiated the agreement to allow Verisign to keep its .com and .net registries and registrar operations in exchange for divesting the .org registry and a substantial payment to ICANN. "Amendment 24 to DoC/Verisign Cooperative Agreement," May 25, 2002, available at http://www.ntia.doc.gov/ntiahome/domainname/agreements/amend24_52501.htm.

103. See Weinberg, "ICANN, 'Internet Stability,' and New Top Level Domains." By requiring certification, ICANN perpetuates it regulatory power by requiring registries and registrars to agree to ICANN regulation, and to include in any contract for domain name registration a "flow-down" clause requiring any name registrant to abide by any changes made to the registration agreement.

104. A general discussion of the UDRP, the manner in which it was imposed on the DNS, and its substantive and procedural flaws is beyond the scope of this chapter. For a general discussion, see Elizabeth G. Thornburg, "Fast, Cheap, and Out of Control: Lessons from the ICANN Dispute Resolution Process," *Journal of Small and Emerging Business Law* 6 (2002): 191; A. Michael Froomkin, "ICANN's 'Uniform Dispute Resolution Policy'—Causes and (Partial) Cures," *Brooklyn Journal of International Law* 67 (2002): 605, available at http://www.law.miami.edu/~froomkin/articles/udrp.pdf.

105. See ICANN Uniform Dispute Resolution Policy at http://www.icann.org/dndr/udrp/policy.htm.

106. Mueller, "Why ICANN Can't."

Chapter 13

1. Commission of the European Parliament, "Report from the Commission to the Council and the European Parliament on the Application of the Agreements between the European Communities and the Government of the United States of America and the Government of Canada regarding the Application of Their Competition Laws, 1 January 2000 to 31 December 2000," Brussels, p. 4.

2. Merit E. Janow, "Observations on Two Multilateral Venues: the International Competition Network (ICN) and the WTO," Presented at the Fordham Corporate Law Institute 29th Annual Conference on International Antitrust Law and Policy, October 31 and November 1, 2002, p. 1.

3. Mark R. A. Palim, in "The Worldwide Growth of Competition Law: An Empirical Analysis," *The Antitrust Bulletin* 43, no. 1 (Spring): 105–145, notes that as of the end of 1996, the 70 countries with competition laws comprised 79 percent of world output and 86 percent of world trade. More countries have adopted competition laws since then.

4. Abbot P. Lipsky Jr., "The Global Antitrust Explosion: Safeguarding Trade and Commerce or Runaway Regulation?" *The Fletcher Forum of World Affairs* 26, no. 2 (Summer/Fall): 59–68, p. 59. Lipsky points out that price-fixing grain dealers could be put to death in Periclean Athens, more than two millennia before the Sherman Act.

5. See *American Banana Co. v. United Fruit Co.*, 213 U.S. 347, 356–57 (1909).

6. See *United States v. Aluminum Co. of America* (Alcoa), 148 F.2d 416, 443–44 (2d Cir. 1945).

7. Andrew Udin, "Slaying Goliath: The Extraterritorial Application of U.S. Antitrust Law to OPEC," *American University Law Review* 50 (2001): 1321, provides a good summary of the "effects test" and of the cases that relied on and further strengthened its application. See also Daniel J. Gifford and E. Thomas Sullivan, "Can International Antitrust Be Saved for the Post-Boeing Merger World? A Proposal to Minimize International Conflict and to Rescue Antitrust from Misuse," *The Antitrust Bulletin* (Spring 2000): 55–118.

8. See *Timberlane Lumber Co. v. Bank of America*, 549 F.2d (9th Cir. 1976). The Ninth Circuit proposed certain comity considerations for determination of jurisdiction.

9. See *Hartford Fire Ins. Co. v. California*, 509 U.S. (1993).

10. See Canada's Foreign Extraterritorial Measures Act and the United Kingdom's Protection of Trading Interests Act, for example. See also "The Protection of Trading Interests Act of 1980: Britain's Response to U.S. Extraterritorial Antitrust Enforcement," *Journal of International Law and Business* 2, no. 2 (Autumn 1980).

11. Textbooks discussing extraterritoriality and antitrust include Donald Ball, Wendell H. McCulloch, et al., *International Business: The Challenge of Global Competition* (New York: McGraw-Hill, 2001); and Ralph H. Folsom, John A. Spanogle, and Michael W. Gordon, *International Trade and Investment in a Nutshell* (Belmont, Calif.: West Group, 2000). The interested reader may also wish to consult the Autumn 1980 symposium issue "Transnational Issues in American Antitrust Law" of the *Journal of International Law and Business* for an early overview of the topic. Nicholas Davidson, "U.S. Secondary Sanctions: The U.K. and EU Response," *Stetson Law Review* 27, no. 4 (Spring 1998) discusses the extension of claw-back and blocking provisions to other extraterritorial enforcement actions.

12. Charles A. James, "International Antitrust in the 21st Century: Cooperation and Convergence," Address of the Assistant Attorney General, Antitrust Division, U.S. Department of Justice before the OECD Global Forum on Competition, Paris, France, October 17, 2001, p. 4. Note, however, Gerber, who argues that EC competition law is indigenous rather than a U.S. import (David J. Gerber, *Law and Competition in Twentieth Century Europe: Protecting Prometheus* [New York: Oxford University Press, 1998]).

13. Corwin Edwards, "The Future of Competition Policy: A World View," *California Management Review* 14 (1974): 112–13.

14. Palim, pp. 105–6.

15. James, p. 2.

16. International Competition Policy Advisory Committee to the Attorney General and Assistant Attorney General for Antitrust (ICPAC), "Final Report," 2000, p. 2.

17. Robert D. Paul, "The Increasing Maze of International Pre-Acquisition Notification," *International Company and Commercial Law Review* 11, no. 4 (April 2000).

18. James.

19. Merit E. Janow, "Transatlantic Cooperation on Competition Policy," *Antitrust Goes Global: What Future for Transatlantic Cooperation*, ed. Simon J. Evenett, Alexander Lehmann, et al. (Washington: Brookings Institution, 2000), p. 33.

20. Simon J. Evenett, Alexander Lehmann, et al., eds., "Antitrust Policy in an Evolving Global Marketplace," *Antitrust Goes Global: What Future for Transatlantic Cooperation* (Washington: Brookings Institution, 2000), pp. 18–20; John J. Parisi, "Enforcement Cooperation among Antitrust Authorities," Address before the IBC UK Conferences Sixth Annual London Conference on EC Competition Law, London, May 19, 1999 (updated October 2000); and Janow, "Transatlantic Cooperation on Competition Policy." See also Konrad von Finkenstein's 2002 address at the opening conference of the International Competition Network (ICN) ("International Antitrust Policy and the International Competition Network," Address by Konrad von Finkenstein, Q.C., Commissioner of Competition, Canadian Competition Bureau and Chair, International Competition Network Steering Group, to the Fordham Corporate Law Institute 29th Annual Conference on International Antitrust Law and Policy, New York, October 31, 2002.) The ICN provides a forum in which competition agencies can consult with one another and develop "best practices" recommendations. See also Janow, "Observations on Two Multilateral Venues." For a contrary perspective, see Andrew T. Guzman, "Is International Antitrust Possible?" *New York University Law Review* 73 (November 1998): 1501–48.

21. See Gifford and Sullivan; Joel I. Klein, "Anticipating the Millennium: International Antitrust Enforcement at the End of the Twentieth Century," Address by Joel I. Klein, Assistant Attorney General, Antitrust Division, U.S. Department of Justice, to the Fordham Corporate Law Institute 24th Annual Conference on International Law and Policy, New York, 1997.

22. Gifford and Sullivan, p. 116.

23. James, p. 5.

24. James, pp. 5–6; Lipsky, p. 63.

25. James, p. 6, citing *Spectrum Sports, Inc. v. McQuillan*, 506 U.S. 447, 458 (1993). Note, however, that EC policy may be shifting. As of this writing, the European Court of Justice has overturned two EC merger prohibitions. As a result, Commissioner Monti is moving toward reform of the EC merger control process. Whether this reform proves substantive remains to be determined.

26. For more thorough analysis of American antitrust law, see Robert Bork, *The Antitrust Paradox: A Policy at War with Itself* (New York: Basic Books, 1978).

27. See Gifford and Sullivan for discussion of nonefficiency goals in EC, U.S., and Japanese antitrust law.

28. Karl Aiginger et al., "Do American and European Industrial Organization Economists Differ?" *Review of Industrial Organization* 19, no. 4 (December 2001): 383–404. Oligopolistic markets are those that are dominated by a very small number of firms. In the Bertrand model, even a market with only two firms will result in the competitive outcome as each firm can win the entire market by slightly underpricing the other; the result then is that both firms price at marginal cost. In the Cournot model, each firm takes the other's output as given and optimizes accordingly; output is higher and prices are lower than in the pure monopoly case.

29. Note Aiginger et al.: "Compared to European IO economists, the Americans are less likely to want to restrict research joint ventures (question 6), more optimistic about the positive effects of mergers on profitability (19), less likely to interpret the higher price-cost margins of large firms as a consequence of market power (20), somewhat less likely to expect collusion in markets with only a few firms (21), more likely to believe that market power is a short-run phenomenon (22), more likely to believe that the importance of predation has been widely exaggerated (23), more

likely to believe that consumer protection laws generally reduce economic efficiency (24), more likely to favor reducing the influence of regulatory authorities (7), less likely to believe that the deregulation of telecoms has led to new monopolies (25), more willing to count producers surplus in addition to consumers surplus in regulatory policy (8), less willing to use competition policy to attack tacit collusion (9), less likely to condemn the exchange of information among competitors (10), more likely to believe that international competition has made the regulation of monopolies an outdated policy (26), more likely to believe that effective concentration has been reduced in the last two decades by globalization (27), and less likely to think of the goal of antitrust policy as inducing firms to equate price and marginal or average cost (11)." (p. 391–92). The authors of this chapter lie firmly on the Western side of the Atlantic.

30. Niels, Gunnar, and Adriaan ten Kate, "Predatory Pricing Standards: Is there a Growing International Consensus?" *The Antitrust Bulletin* (Fall 2000): 787–809.

31. See Thomas DiLorenzo, "The Origins of Antitrust: An Interest Group Perspective," *International Review of Law and Economics* (1985): 73–90. In the absence of foreign competition, antitrust statutes can keep dominant domestic firms in check.

32. William F. Shughart, Jon D. Silverman, and Robert D. Tollison, "Antitrust Enforcement and Foreign Competition," *The Causes and Consequences of Antitrust: The Public Choice Perspective*, ed. Fred S. McChesney and William F. Shughart (Chicago: University of Chicago Press, 1995).

33. Palim, pp. 105–145.

34. Evenett, Lehmann, et al., pp. 14–15.

35. Richard B. McKenzie and Dwight R. Lee, "How Digital Economics Revises Antitrust Thinking," *The Antitrust Bulletin* (Summer 2001): 253–98.

36. For discussion of these issues, see Joel I. Klein, "Rethinking Antitrust Policies for the New Economy," Address by Joel I. Klein, "Rethinking Antitrust Policies for the New Economy," Address by Joel I. Klein, Assistant Attorney General, Antitrust Division, U.S. Department of Justice, at the Hass/Berkeley New Economy Forum, May 9, 2000.

37. In addition, as software is a durable good, a firm must compete with its own existing product base—consumers can always choose to continue using older versions of the software. The digital monopolist can never rest on its laurels; it could quickly find itself with a 100 percent share of a market with no sales.

38. Josh McHugh, "Google vs. Evil," *Wired* 11, no. 1 (January 2003).

39. Note also Stan J. Liebowitz and Stephen E. Margolis, *Winners, Losers and Microsoft: Competition and Antitrust in High Technology* (Oakland, Calif: The Independent Institute, 1999).

40. Paul David, "Path Dependence, Its Critics and the Quest for 'Historical Economics,'" in *Market Failure or Success: The New Debate*, eds. Tyler Cowen and Eric P. Crampton (Oakland, Calif.: The Independent Institute, 2002).

41. See Tyler Cowen and Eric P. Crampton, eds., *Market Failure or Success: The New Debate* (Oakland, Calif.: The Independent Institute, 2002a).

42. Donald J. Boudreaux and Burton W. Folsom, "Microsoft and Standard Oil: Radical Lessons for Antitrust Reform," *The Antitrust Bulletin* (Fall 1999).

43. Our recommendation accords with Richard Epstein's principle that complex worlds are best governed by simple rules. See Richard Epstein, *Simple Rules for a Complex World* (Cambridge, Mass.: Harvard University Press, 1995).

44. Liebowitz and Margolis.

45. Donald J. Boudreaux and Eric P. Crampton, "The Economics of False Consciousness," *The Independent Review* (Summer 2003).

46. 148 F.2d at 443.

47. ICPAC, p. 292.

48. The FTC held a public workshop on state impediments to e-commerce in October of 2002. Comments from that workshop are available at http://www.ftc.gov/opp/ecommerce/anticompetitive/index.htm. See also "Prepared Statement of the Federal Trade Commission before the Subcommittee on Commerce, Trade, and Consumer Protection Committee on Energy and Commerce, U.S. House of Representatives," September 26, 2002.

49. See Timothy Muris, "Merger Enforcement in a World of Multiple Arbiters," prepared remarks of the Chairman, Federal Trade Commission, before the Brookings Institution Roundtable on Trade and Investment Policy, Washington, December 21, 2001.

Contributors

Donald J. Boudreaux
Donald J. Boudreaux is chairman of the Department of Economics at George Mason University in Fairfax, Virginia. Previously, he was president of the Foundation for Economic Education; associate professor of legal studies and economics at Clemson University; and assistant professor of economics at George Mason University. In 1996 Professor Boudreaux was a John M. Olin Visiting Fellow in Law and Economics at the Cornell Law School. He has lectured internationally on the role of markets, the nature of law, antitrust, law and economics, and international trade. His writing has appeared in publications such as the *Wall Street Journal*, *Investor's Business Daily*, *Regulation*, *Reason*, the *Washington Times*, *Cato Journal*, and the *Supreme Court Economic Review*.

Dan L. Burk
Dan Burk is the Oppenheimer, Wolff and Donnelly Professor of Law at the University of Minnesota, where he teaches courses in patent law, copyright, and biotechnology law. An internationally prominent authority on issues related to high technology, he is the author of numerous papers on the legal and societal impact of new technologies, including scientific misconduct, the regulation of biotechnology, and the intellectual property implications of global computer networks. Professor Burk has served as policy adviser on matters of technology to a variety of private, governmental, and intergovernmental organizations.

Fred H. Cate
Fred Cate is a distinguished professor at the Indiana University School of Law—Bloomington and director of the University's Center for Applied Cybersecurity Research. He also serves as a senior policy adviser to the Hunton and Williams Center for Information Policy

Leadership, where he leads the Center's Global Data Protection Framework Project. He testifies regularly before Congress on privacy and other information law issues, and is a member of Microsoft's Trustworthy Computing Academic Advisory Board and of the board of editors of *Privacy and Information Law Report*. Professor Cate directed the Electronic Information Privacy and Commerce Study for the Brookings Institution, chaired the International Telecommunication Union's High-Level Experts on Electronic Signatures and Certification Authorities, and was a member of the Federal Trade Commission's Advisory Committee on Online Access and Security. He is the author of many articles and books, including *Privacy in the Information Age, Privacy in Perspective,* and *The Internet and the First Amendment.*

Vinton G. Cerf

Vinton Cerf is senior vice president of Architecture and Technology for WorldCom. In December 1997, President Clinton presented the U.S. National Medal of Technology to Cerf and his partner, Robert E. Kahn, for their role in developing the Internet. Prior to rejoining MCI in 1994, Cerf was vice president of the Corporation for National Research Initiatives. During his tenure with the U.S. Department of Defense's Advanced Research Projects Agency, Cerf played a key role leading the development of Internet and Internet-related data packet and security technologies. Cerf serves as chairman of the board of the Internet Corporation for Assigned Names and Numbers (ICANN) and has served as founding president of the Internet Society. In addition, Cerf is honorary chairman of the IPv6 Forum, dedicated to raising awareness and speeding introduction of the new Internet protocol. Cerf has served as a member of the U.S. Presidential Information Technology Advisory Committee since 1997 and serves on several national, state, and industry committees focused on cybersecurity.

Eric P. Crampton

Eric Crampton is lecturer in economics at the University of Canterbury. Crampton edited *Market Failure or Success?* with Tyler Cowen and has published articles in *The Journal of Private Enterprise, The Independent Review,* and *Foreign Policy.*

470

Clyde Wayne Crews Jr.

Wayne Crews is the director of technology policy at the Cato Institute, where he studies Internet and technology issues, including digital copyright, privacy, content regulation, and antitrust. On broader regulatory reform issues, Crews authors *Ten Thousand Commandments: An Annual Snapshot of the Federal Regulatory State*. Earlier, Crews was a policy director of competition and regulation policy at the Competitive Enterprise Institute and a legislative aide to Sen. Phil Gramm (R-Tex.), working on regulatory and welfare reform issues. He has been an economist and policy analyst at Citizens for a Sound Economy Foundation and a research assistant at the Center for the Study of Public Choice at George Mason University. Crews has published in the *Wall Street Journal*, *Forbes*, the *Washington Times*, *Policy Sciences*, and the *Electricity Journal*, and many other publications. He has appeared on various television and radio networks, including CNN, Fox News, and PBS. Crews is co-editor of *Copy Fights: The Future of Intellectual Property in the Information Age*, co-author of *What's Yours Is Mine: Open Access and the Rise of Infrastructure Socialism*, and a contributor to *The Half-Life of Policy Rationales: How New Technology Affects Old Policy Issues*.

Robert Corn-Revere

Robert Corn-Revere is a partner in the Washington, D.C., office of Davis Wright Tremaine LLP, specializing in First Amendment, Internet, and communications law. He has served as counsel in First Amendment litigation involving the Communications Decency Act, the Child Online Protection Act, Internet content filtering in public libraries, public broadcasting regulations and export controls on encryption software. In 1999, Corn-Revere was listed on a 30th Anniversary Roll of Honor by the American Library Association Office of Intellectual Freedom and Freedom to Read Foundation for his role as lead counsel in *Mainstream Loudoun v. Board of Trustees of the Loudoun County Library*. He successfully argued *United States v. Playboy Entertainment Group, Inc.*, in which the United States Supreme Court struck down Section 505 of the Telecommunications Act of 1996 as a violation of the First Amendment. Corn-Revere also served as lead counsel in *Motion Picture Association v. FCC*, in which the U.S. Court of Appeals for the District of Columbia Circuit vacated

471

video description rules imposed on networks by the Federal Communications Commission. Before joining Davis Wright Tremaine LLP., Corn-Revere served as chief counsel to interim chairman James H. Quello of the FCC. He has written extensively on First Amendment, Internet, and communications-related issues and is a frequent speaker at professional conferences. Corn-Revere is co-author of a three-volume treatise entitled *Modern Communications Law* and is editor and co-author of the book *Rationales and Rationalizations*. He is a member of the editorial advisory board of Pike and Fischer's *Internet Law and Regulation*. He has taught at the Catholic University of America, is chairman of the Media Institute's First Amendment Advisory Council, and is a member of the institute's board of trustees. From 2000–2002, Corn-Revere served on the board of trustees of the Freedom to Read Foundation. He is also an adjunct scholar to the Cato Institute in Washington, D.C.

Christopher Cox

Rep. Christopher Cox (R-Calif.), an eight-term congressman from California's 48th congressional district, serves as chairman of the House Policy Committee and was also recently selected to head the new Homeland Security Committee in the House. He is a member of the Leadership Steering Committee, which makes committee assignments in the House, and also serves on the House Committee on Energy and Commerce Subcommittee on Energy and Air Quality, as well as the Subcommittee on Telecommunications. Prior to winning election to Congress in 1988, Rep. Cox served as senior associate counsel to the president in the White House, a partner with the international law firm Latham and Watkins, a lecturer on business administration at the Harvard Business School, and a clerk for the U.S. Court of Appeals.

Harold Feld

Harold Feld is the associate director of the Media Access Project, a nonprofit public interest law firm which promotes the public's First Amendment right to hear and be heard through electronic media. He has also worked in private practice and for the federal government. Feld focuses on how network architecture and the structure of mass media affect free expression. A participant in the policy debates that culminated in the formation of ICANN and a participant in ICANN's deliberations for several years, Feld served as a member of the ICANN Names Council in 2002–2003.

Michael Geist

Michael Geist is the Canada Research Chair of Internet and E-commerce Law at the University of Ottawa and serves as technology counsel to Osler, Hoskin and Harcourt LLP. Geist has written numerous academic articles and government reports on the Internet and law and is a columnist on technology law issues for the *Toronto Star*, creator and consulting editor of *BNA's Internet Law News*, editor of *Internet and E-commerce Law in Canada*, and founder of the Ontario Research Network for E-commerce. He is on the advisory boards of several leading Internet law publications including *Electronic Commerce and Law Report*, *Journal of Internet Law*, and *Internet Law and Business* as well as the author of the textbook *Internet Law in Canada*, now in its third edition. Geist's work has been recognized with several awards and grants including the 2002 Canadian Association of Law Teachers Scholarly Paper Award and a major research grant from the Social Sciences and Humanities Research Council Initiative on the New Economy for his research on Internet jurisdiction. In 2003, Geist became the first law professor to receive the Ontario Premier's Research Excellence Award, obtained a significant grant from Amazon.com to establish Canada's first technology law public interest litigation clinic at the University of Ottawa, and was named one of Canada's Top 40 Under 40.

Jack L. Goldsmith

Jack Goldsmith is professor of law at the University of Chicago Law School, currently on leave serving as special counsel to the general counsel of the Department of Defense. Before teaching at the University of Chicago, Goldsmith was an associate professor of law at the University of Virginia School of Law and an Associate at Covington and Burling. Goldsmith has published widely in the fields of foreign relations law and public and private international law. His work has appeared in the *Yale Law Review*, the *Supreme Court Review*, the *Stanford Law Review*, the *University of Chicago Law Review*, and the *Harvard Law Review*, among other publications. He is currently working on two books to be published by Oxford University Press: *A Theory of International Law* (with Eric Posner), and *Reining in the Net: How Governments Are Putting Borders in Cyberspace, and Making It a Better Place*.

Michael S. Greve

Michael Greve is the John G. Searle Scholar at the American Enterprise Institute in Washington, D.C., where he directs the AEI Federalism Project and the AEI Liability Project. His research and writing cover American federalism and its legal, political, and economic dimensions. Greve co-founded and, from 1989 to February 2000, directed the Center for Individual Rights, a public interest law firm. CIR served as counsel in many precedent-setting constitutional cases, including *United States v. Morrison* and *Rosenberger v. University of Virginia*. Greve currently serves on the board of directors of the Competitive Enterprise Institute. He has written widely on constitutional and administrative law, federalism, environmental policy, and civil rights. He is editor, with Fred L. Smith, of *Environmental Politics: Public Costs, Private Rewards* and author of *The Demise of Environmentalism in American Law*, and, most recently, of *Real Federalism: Why It Matters, How It Could Happen*.

Bruce H. Kobayashi

Bruce Kobayashi is professor of law at George Mason University. Kobayashi's teaching and research interests are in the application of economics to law. His articles—which examine the law and economics of intellectual property, antitrust law and regulation, litigation and procedure, evidence, uniform laws, and federalism—have appeared in numerous books and journals, including the *Journal of Legal Studies, Journal of Law, Economics and Organization, International Review of Law and Economics, Research in Law and Economics, Research in Transportation Economics, Economic Inquiry, RAND Journal of Economics, Supreme Court Economic Review*, and *Journal of Economic Behavior and Organization*. He has written entries for the *New Palgrave Dictionary of Economics and the Law*, and for the *Encyclopedia of Law and Economics*. Kobayashi has been a lecturer in the Law and Economics Center's Antitrust Institute for Federal Judges and Economics Institute for Law Professors. He also has served as a contributing editor for the *Supreme Court Economic Review*. Kobayashi previously served as a senior economist in the Division of Economic Policy Analysis of the Federal Trade Commission, senior research associate at the United States Sentencing Commission, and economist for the Antitrust Division of the U.S. Department of Justice.

David G. Post

David Post is currently professor of law at Temple University Law School, where he teaches intellectual property law and the law of cyberspace, and is senior fellow at the Tech Center at George Mason University Law School. He is also co-founder and co-editor of ICANN Watch, the Cyberspace Law Institute, and Disputes.org. After graduating from Georgetown Law Center, he clerked with then-judge Ruth Bader Ginsburg on the D.C. Circuit Court of Appeals, spent six years practicing intellectual property and high technology commercial transactions law at the Washington law firm Wilmer, Cutler and Pickering, and clerked a second time for Justice Ginsburg during her first term on the Supreme Court of the United States. Post has published numerous articles on the law of cyberspace in the *Stanford Law Review*, the *Chicago-Kent Law Review*, Esther Dyson's *Release 1.0*, the *Journal of Online Law*, the *University of Chicago Legal Forum*, the *Computer Law Reporter*, and the *Wayne Law Review*, as well as several articles on legal theory in the *Journal of Legal Studies*, the *Georgetown Law Journal*, and the *Vanderbilt Law Review*. He is currently working on a book on Thomas Jefferson and cyberspace law, tentatively entitled *Jefferson's Moose: Notes on the State of Cyberspace*.

Larry E. Ribstein

Larry Ribstein is the Richard and Marie Corman Professor at the University of Illinois College of Law, having also held full-time posts at the law schools of George Mason and Mercer and visiting appointments at Southern Methodist, Washington University, St. Louis University, and University of Texas. He has also served as editor of the *Supreme Court Economic Review*. Professor Ribstein has published six books: *Unincorporated Business Entities, Business Associations, Bromberg and Ribstein on Partnership, Bromberg and Ribstein on LLPs and RUPA, Ribstein and Keating on Limited Liability Companies,* and *The Constitution and the Corporation*. He has written almost 100 articles on corporate and partnership law, constitutional law, legal ethics, bankruptcy, conflict of laws, family law, electronic commerce, and uniform laws.

Adam Thierer

Adam Thierer is director of telecommunications studies at the Cato Institute, where he conducts research on how government regulations are hampering the evolution of communications networks, including telephony, broadcasting, cable, satellite, and the Internet. He also examines the broader economic and constitutional aspects of telecommunications policy. His writing has been published in the *Washington Post, Newsweek, Wall Street Journal, Investor's Business Daily, Journal of Commerce, Forbes,* and *The Economist.* He has made media appearances on NPR, PBS, Fox News Channel, CNN, MSNBC, BBC, Radio Free Europe, and Voice of America. Before joining Cato, Thierer spent nine years at the Heritage Foundation, where he served as the Alex C. Walker Fellow in Economic Policy. In that capacity, he covered telecommunications and Internet policy and also wrote extensively on antitrust, electricity and energy policy, the airline industry, and federalism. Before moving to Washington, Thierer worked at the Adam Smith Institute in London, England, where he examined reform of the British legal system. He is the author or editor of three previous books: *The Delicate Balance: Federalism, Interstate Commerce, and Economic Freedom in the Technological Age, Copy Fights: The Future of Intellectual Property in the Information Age,* and *What's Yours Is Mine: Open Access and the Rise of Infrastructure Socialism.*

Kurt Wimmer

Kurt Wimmer is the managing partner of the London office of Covington and Burling. He concentrates on media and information technology law for video content companies, broadcasters, Internet publishers and software companies. He also has advised journalists and legislators in more than 18 emerging democracies on proposed laws concerning media, access to information, and protection of journalists, and he was named by the Organization for Security and Co-operation in Europe and the United Nations to the Advisory Group on Defamation and Freedom of Information Legislation for Bosnia and Herzegovina. Wimmer is the incoming chair of the First Amendment Advisory Counsel of the Media Institute and a member of the institute's board of trustees; chairman of the board of directors of the International Research Exchanges Board, and co-chair of the International Media Law Committee of the Defense Council Section of the Media Law Resource Center. He received the Joseph A. Sprague Award for his First Amendment work. He is co-editor of the American Bar Association's *Communications Lawyer*.

Jonathan Zittrain
Jonathan Zittrain is the Jack N. and Lillian R. Berkman Assistant Professor for Entrepreneurial Legal Studies at Harvard Law School, and a faculty director of its Berkman Center for Internet and Society. His research includes the technologies and politics of control of Internet architecture and protocols, the influence of private intermediaries upon online behavior, and the empirical measurement of Internet phenomena. He also has a strong interest in creative, useful, and unobtrusive ways to deploy technology in the classroom.

Index

Aaron, David, 327
ABA. *See* American Bar Association (ABA)
Abdullah v. Sheridan Square Press, 253
access
  conditioned, 42–44, 186–187, 318–319
  government denial of, 4–5
  and identity theft, 324–326
  IP address screening for, 133–136, 161, 318, 431*n*, 443*n*–444*n*
Access to Information and Protection of Privacy Bill (Zimbabwe), 246
active Web sites, 93. *See also* passive-*vs.*-active test
  discouragement of, 103
Address Supporting Organization (ASO), 462*n*
adhesion contracts, 188, 190–191
adjudicate, jurisdiction to, 257–258
adjudicator, link between choice of law, forum and, 189
advertising
  and privacy issues, 304–305
  standards, 154
  Web site, targeting of, 163
AEI-Brookings Joint Center on Regulation, 320
Aiginger, Karl, 367
Aimster, 163
Airbus, 366
Akamai, 114
Alabama, 147, 290, 319
Alaska, 40
Alcoa decision, 364–365, 373
ALI. *See* American Law Institute (ALI)
AllAdvantage.com, 326
Allstate Insurance Co v. Hague, 182
alternate root community, 351–352, 359, 362, 463*n*
Amazon.com, 161, 280, 284, 285
American Arbitration Association, 394*n*
American Bar Association (ABA)
  Committee on Cyberspace Law, 183–184, 193

Global Cyberspace Jurisdiction Project, 106–107
American Civil Liberties Union, 264
American Enterprise Institute, *xxxi*, 271
American Express, 165–166
American Information Corp. v. American Infometrics, 106
American Institute of Certified Public Accountants, 422*n*
American Law Institute (ALI), 185, 188, 240
  "International Jurisdiction and Recognition of Judgments," 254–255
  Restatement (Second) of Conflict of Laws, 181, 187–188, 196, 383*n*
American Liberties Ass'n v. Pataki, 112–113
American Library Association, 264
America Online (AOL), *xxii*, 16, 22, 111, 149, 178, 407*n*, 431*n*
A&M Records v. Napster, 163
anonymizer systems, 134, 326
anonymous remailers, 135, 387*n*
Anticybersquatting Consumer Protection Act, 16, 24
antitrust law, *xxxii*, 292, 345–346, 363–375
  economic theory behind, 367–368, 369–372
  extraterritorial enforcement of, 364–367, 373–375
  international, 364–368, 375
  and Internet, 368–372
  proliferation of, 365–366, 368
AOL (America Online), *xxii*, 16, 22, 111, 149, 178, 407*n*, 431*n*
arbitration clause, 189, 190–191, 193, 209
arbitration law, 68–70, 359–360, 394*n*–395*n*
Arizona, 220
A Root, 337, 341, 353, 457*n*
Arts and Technology Group, *xix*
Asahi Metal Indus Co. v. Super. Ct., 425*n*

Cato Institute

Founded in 1977, the Cato Institute is a public policy research foundation dedicated to broadening the parameters of policy debate to allow consideration of more options that are consistent with the traditional American principles of limited government, individual liberty, and peace. To that end, the Institute strives to achieve greater involvement of the intelligent, concerned lay public in questions of policy and the proper role of government.

The Institute is named for *Cato's Letters,* libertarian pamphlets that were widely read in the American Colonies in the early 18th century and played a major role in laying the philosophical foundation for the American Revolution.

Despite the achievement of the nation's Founders, today virtually no aspect of life is free from government encroachment. A pervasive intolerance for individual rights is shown by government's arbitrary intrusions into private economic transactions and its disregard for civil liberties.

To counter that trend, the Cato Institute undertakes an extensive publications program that addresses the complete spectrum of policy issues. Books, monographs, and shorter studies are commissioned to examine federal budget, Social Security, regulation, military spending, international trade, and myriad other issues. Major policy conferences are held throughout the year, from which papers are published thrice yearly in the *Cato Journal.* The Institute also publishes the quarterly magazine *Regulation.*

In order to maintain its independence, the Cato Institute accepts no government funding. Contributions are received from foundations, corporations, and individuals, and other revenue is generated from the sale of publications. The Institute is a nonprofit, tax-exempt, educational foundation under Section 501(c)3 of the Internal Revenue Code.

CATO INSTITUTE
1000 Massachusetts Ave., N.W.
Washington, D.C. 20001
www.cato.org

Cato Institute

Founded in 1977, the Cato Institute is a public policy research foundation dedicated to broadening the parameters of policy debate to allow consideration of more options that are consistent with the traditional American principles of limited government, individual liberty, and peace. To that end, the Institute strives to achieve greater involvement of the intelligent, concerned lay public in questions of policy and the proper role of government.

The Institute is named for *Cato's Letters*, libertarian pamphlets that were widely read in the American Colonies in the early 18th century and played a major role in laying the philosophical foundation for the American Revolution.

Despite the achievement of the nation's Founders, today virtually no aspect of life is free from government encroachment. A pervasive intolerance for individual rights is shown by government's arbitrary intrusions into private economic transactions and its disregard for civil liberties.

To counter that trend, the Cato Institute undertakes an extensive publications program that addresses the complete spectrum of policy issues. Books, monographs, and shorter studies are commissioned to examine federal budget, Social Security, regulation, military spending, international trade, and myriad other issues. Major policy conferences are held throughout the year, from which papers are published thrice yearly in the *Cato Journal*. The Institute also publishes the quarterly magazine *Regulation*.

In order to maintain its independence, the Cato Institute accepts no government funding. Contributions are received from foundations, corporations, and individuals, and other revenue is generated from the sale of publications. The Institute is a nonprofit, tax-exempt, educational foundation under Section 501(c)3 of the Internal Revenue Code.

CATO INSTITUTE
1000 Massachusetts Ave., N.W.
Washington, D.C. 20001
www.cato.org